Globalization and Progressive Economic Policy

Economists and other social scientists widely hold that a new stage has been reached in the relationship between capitalism and the nation-state. *Globalization* is the umbrella term – indeed the ubiquitous buzzword – conveying the sense that a fundamental transformation is occurring in the contemporary world economy. Governments and opposition political parties throughout the world rewrite their economic programs to take account of the perceived new realities. In particular, policy makers and other analysts have increasingly become committed to the "neo-liberal" model of open economies, minimal government interventions, and free markets –including free global capital movements and 'flexible' labor markets – as the only effective policy approach in the new global economy.

Globalization and Progressive Economic Policy challenges mainstream thinking about the nature of globalization. Its authors are not hostile to markets per se. But they are persuaded that capitalist market processes, left to operate freely, are prone to generate injustice, insecurity, instability, and inefficiency. Taking full account of the new realities of globalization, the papers in this volume explore an unusually wide range of subjects, including trade integration, multinational corporations, global labor markets and migration, international capital flows, macroeconomic and environmental policy, and the central roles of the International Monetary Fund and World Bank. The papers also advance alternatives to neo-liberal orthodoxy, developing policy measures that counter the destructive features of markets and promote equality as well as efficiency. The approach in this volume is particularly illuminating for understanding the Asian financial collapse of 1997-98 and similar recent crises. The volume also includes comments on each paper by a wide range of distinguished economists, producing a lively, fruitful and often controversial set of interchanges.

Dean Baker is Senior Economist at the Economic Policy Institute in Washington, D.C. His recent work includes *Getting Prices Right: the Battle over the Consumer Price Index* (1997), and *Defusing the Baby Boomer Timebomb: Projections of Income in the 21ˢᵗ Century* (1998). He is the co-author, with Mark Weisbrot, of *Social Security: the Phony Crisis* (1999).

Gerald Epstein is Professor of Economics and Co-Director of the Political Economy Research Institute (PERI) at the University of Massachusetts-Amherst. He is co-editor of *Macroeconomic Policy After the Conservative Era: Studies in Investment, Saving, and Finance* (1995) and two other books. Epstein has published numerous book chapters and journal articles in the areas of domestic and international monetary policy, international capital mobility and macroeconomic theory.

Robert Pollin is Professor of Economics and Co-Director of the Political Economy Research Institute (PERI) at the University of Massachusetts-Amherst. He was previously Professor of Economics at the University of California-Riverside. He is editor of *The Macroeconomics of Saving, Finance, and Investment* (1997), co-author of *The Living Wage: Building a Fair Economy* (1998) and co-editor of two other books. Pollin has published widely in professional journals, book chapters in edited collections, and in more popular forums in the areas of macroeconomics, finance, employment and political economy.

Globalization and Progressive Economic Policy

edited by

Dean Baker
Economic Policy Institute

Gerald Epstein
University of Massachusetts-Amherst

Robert Pollin
University of Massachusetts-Amherst

CAMBRIDGE
UNIVERSITY PRESS

Published in association with
The Political Economy Research Institute
University of Massachusetts-Amherst

PUBLISHED BY THE PRESS SYNDICATE OF THE UNIVERSITY OF CAMBRIDGE
The Pitt Building, Trumpington Street, Cambridge, United Kingdom

CAMBRIDGE UNIVERSITY PRESS
The Edinburgh Building, Cambridge CB2 2RU, UK   http://www.cup.cam.ac.uk
40 West 20th Street, New York, NY 10011–4211, USA   http://www.cup.org
10 Stamford Road, Oakleigh, Melbourne 3166, Australia
Ruiz de Alarcón 13, 28014 Madrid, Spain

First published 1998
Reprinted 1999

Printed in the United Kingdom at the University Press, Cambridge

Typeset in Times

A catalogue record for this book is available from the British Library

Library of Congress Cataloguing in Publication data applied for

ISBN 0 521 64360 0 hardback
ISBN 0 521 64376 7 paperback

Contents

Figures

Tables

List of tables

Contributors

DEAN BAKER, Economic Policy Institute, 1600 L Street NW, Washington, D.C. 20036.

TAMIM BAYOUMI, International Monetary Fund, Washington, D.C. 20431.

AMIT BHADURI, Centre for Economic Studies and Planning, School of Social Sciences, Jawaharlal Nehru University, New Delhi 110 067, India.

ROBERT BLECKER, Department of Economics, American University, 4400 Massachusetts Avenue NW, Washington, D.C. 20016.

C.P. CHANDRASEKHAR, Centre for Economic Studies and Planning, School of Social Sciences, Jawaharlal Nehru University, New Delhi 110 067, India.

HA-JOON CHANG, Faculty of Economics and Politics, University of Cambridge, Sidgwick Avenue, Cambridge CB3 9DD, U.K.

JAMES CROTTY, Department of Economics, University of Massachusetts-Amherst, Amherst, Mass. 01003.

JANE D'ARISTA, Boston University School of Law, Boston, Mass. 02215.

GREGORY DEFREITAS, Department of Economics, Hofstra University, 1000 Fulton Avenue, Hemstead, N.Y. 11549.

J. BRADFORD DELONG, Department of Economics, University of California-Berkeley, Berkeley, Calif. 94720.

PETER DORMAN, James Madison College, Michigan State University, 313 South Case Hall, East Lansing, Mich. 48824-1205.

GARY DYMSKI, Department of Economics, University of California-Riverside, Riverside, Calif. 92521-0427.

ROBERT EISNER, Department of Economics, Northwestern University, 2003 Sheridan Road, Evanston, Ill. 60208-2400.

GERALD EPSTEIN, Department of Economics, University of Massachusetts-Amherst, Amherst, Mass. 01003.

DAVID FELIX, Department of Economics, Washington University, St. Louis, Mo. 63130.

ANDREW GLYN, Corpus Christi College, Oxford University, Oxford OX1 HJF, U.K.

EBAN GOODSTEIN, Department of Economics, Lewis and Clark College, Portland, Ore. 97219.

ILENE GRABEl, Graduate School of International Studies, University of Denver, 2201 S. Gaylord Street, Denver, Colo. 80208.

KEITH GRIFFIN, Department of Economics, University of California-Riverside, Riverside, Calif. 92521-0427.

LAURENCE HARRIS, Department of Economics, School of Oriental and African Studies, University of London, Thornhaugh Street, Russell Square, London WC1H 0XG, U.K.

DORENE ISENBERG, Department of Economics, Drew University, Madison, N.J. 07940.

PATRICIA KELLY, Department of Economics, Quinnipiac College, 275 Mt. Carmel Ave., Hamden, Conn. 06518.

TIMOTHY KOECHLIN, Department of Economics, Skidmore College, Saratoga Springs, N.Y. 12866.

MEHRENE LARUDEE, Department of Economics, University of Kansas, 213 Summerfield Hall, Lawrence, Kan. 66045

THEA LEE, Economic Research Department, AFL-CIO, 815 16th Street NW, Washington, D.C. 20006.

ARTHUR MACEWAN, Department of Economics, University of Massachusetts-Boston, Boston, Mass. 02125-3393.

JONATHAN MICHIE, Clore Management Centre, Department of Management, Birkbeck College, University of London, Malet Street, London WC1E 7HX, U.K.

SULE OZLER, College of Administrative Sciences and Economics, Koc University, Cayir Cad. No. 5, Istinye, 80860 Istanbul, Turkey.

PRABHAT PATNAIK, Centre for Economic Studies and Planning, School of Social Sciences, Jawaharlal Nehru University, New Delhi 110 067, India.

UTE PIEPER, Department of Economics, Graduate Faculty, New School for Social Research, 65 Fifth Avenue, New York, N.Y. 10003.

ROBERT POLLIN, Department of Economics, University of Massachusetts-Amherst, Amherst, Mass. 01003.

SAMIR RADWAN, Development and Technical Cooperation Department, International Labour Office, 4 Route des Morillon, CH-1211, Geneva, 22, Switzerland.

JAIME ROS, Department of Economics, University of Notre Dame, Notre Dame, Ind. 46556.

MARC SCHABERG, Department of Economics, University of California-Riverside, Riverside, Calif. 92521-0427.

JIM STANFORD, Canadian Auto Workers, Suite 1306-2000, Barrington Street, Halifax, Nova Scotia, Canada, B3J 3K1.

BOB SUTCLIFFE, Department of Economics, University of the Basque Country, Bilbao, Spain.

LANCE TAYLOR, Department of Economics, Graduate Faculty, New School for Social Research, 65 Fifth Avenue, New York, N.Y. 10003.

Editors' acknowledgments

"Globalization" is the term on everyone's lips — but that doesn't make it any easier to bring together 40 odd economists from around the world to think seriously about the subject. Thanks to the support of the Economic Policy Institute and its leadership of Jeff Faux, Larry Mishel, and Eileen Appelbaum, we were able to do this, not just once, but twice — invading the EPI Washington offices in October 1995 and June 1996. Of course, large academic conferences with an international cast of characters face a high probability of descending into a chaotic jumble. We were fortunate that Stephanie Scott-Steptoe of the EPI staff made sure this didn't happen.

This volume has 37 contributors, so there is no chance that it could be mistaken for anything but a broad collective enterprise. In fact, though, the breadth of contributors extends beyond those whose words appear in these pages. Several additional people participated in one or both of the two conferences, injecting fresh perspectives and constructive controversy. These include Robin Broad, John Cavanagh, Stanley Fischer, Jeffrey Frankel, Stephanie Griffith-Jones, Caren Grown, Will Milberg, Barbara Stallings, and Kimberly Stanton. We especially want to acknowledge the contributions of the late David Gordon, who was his usual spirited and insightful self at the October 1995 conference despite a serious illness, and who died tragically before he was able to keep to his plan to return the following June.

John Haslam of Cambridge University Press has given us excellent support in moving this project from a nearly foot-high stack of papers to the infinitely more coherent and manageable volume you are now holding. Our crack team of copyeditor Patrick Watson, graphics designer Kim Arbogast, and indexer James Connell have sustained unbeatable professional standards and good humor amid a ridiculously tight deadline that they calmly predicted they could meet, and then, sure enough, did meet. And on top of that, the book they produced looks superb. We are also happy that production of this volume has been supported in part by the Political Economy Research Institute (PERI) at the University of Massachusetts-Amherst. This is the first project supported by PERI, of which Jerry and Bob are founding co-directors, and we look forward to many more in the future.

Finally, we wish to make some individual acknowledgments.

Dean: I owe a great debt to my co-editors, who carried a disproportionate weight on this book so that I had time to fight other battles. I also thank Helene, Walnut, and Fulton for their patience and understanding.

Jerry: I want to thank my son, Eli Epstein-Deutsch, for his penetrating comments and questions about economics and globalization. I hope this book has at least a few of the answers. If not, I'm sure I'll hear about it. I also want to thank Francine Deutsch for helping me learn about globalization first-hand by insisting that I go on a lot of exotic vacations.

Bob: I owe a special debt to my UC-Riverside colleague Keith Griffin, who generously shared his deep knowledge of the global economy at many stages of this project, and whose acts of friendship allowed us to complete this volume on schedule. I am also grateful to his secretary, Paula Hackbarth, for her assistance. As always, my parents, Abe and Irene Pollin, have given me enthusiastic and generous support, for which I am deeply grateful. My cousin Howard Goldstein lent us his home for an economists' dinner party, and was thoughtful enough to even insist that he enjoyed it. Emma and Hannah Pollin keep asking me really hard questions, and while I can't hope to answer all of them myself, perhaps the 36 other authors in this book will help get us a little further than usual. Sigrid Miller Pollin, among many other things, created the beautiful and unforgettable workplace where most of my ideas for this book were hatched.

1

Introduction

Dean Baker, Gerald Epstein, and Robert Pollin

The evolution of capitalist economies has always been intimately bound up with nation-states and national economic policies. Economists have correspondingly placed the nation-state and national policy questions at the center of their analyses. Adam Smith, for one, could not have been more clear that his primary concern was to understand the nature and causes of the wealth of *nations*, not merely the wealth of individuals, households, or regions. In large measure, Smith's famous book was criticizing the position of the mercantilists on the causes of national wealth and, in particular, their view that export-promoting economic policies could make a nation wealthier by making its trading partners poorer.

In his model of comparative advantage, David Ricardo was also focused on the economic interactions between nations, demonstrating in the model – contrary to the mercantilists – how all countries, not merely those most aggressive at exporting, would benefit from foreign trade. But for Ricardo, this did not mean that the economic significance of national boundaries would diminish over time. In fact, what is not well known about Ricardo's famous exposition of trade between Portugal and England, with Portugal the more productive economy, is his conclusion that the benefits of foreign trade rested entirely on an assumption of capital immobility between nations. He wrote that:

> It would undoubtedly be advantageous to the capitalists of England, and to the consumers in both countries, that under such circumstances, the wine and the cloth should both be made in Portugal, and therefore that the capital and labour of England employed in making cloth, should be removed to Portugal for that purpose.... Experience, however, shews, that the fancied or real insecurity of capital, when not under the immediate control of its owner, together with the natural disinclination which every man has to quit the country of his birth and connexions, and intrust himself with all his habits fixed, to a strange government and new laws, check the emigration of capital. These feelings, which I should be sorry to see weakened, induce most men of property to be satisfied with the low rate of profits in their own country, rather than seek a more advantageous employment for their wealth in foreign nations (Ricardo 1951, 136–7).

We are grateful for the constructive and illuminating comments of Colin Day, Keith Griffin, Michael Howard, two anonymous referees, and seminar participants at the Program in Social Theory and Comparative History at the University of California–Los Angeles and the Harvey Goldberg Center for the Study of Contemporary History at the University of Wisconsin-Madison.

Karl Marx also considered at length the relationship between economic development and the nation-state. However, he was far less persuaded than Ricardo about the disinclination of capitalists to leave the "country of their birth and connexions" when profit opportunities beckoned abroad. He therefore held a very different view about the extent to which the advance of capitalist relations would be constrained by national boundaries. As Marx wrote with Engels in the *Communist Manifesto*:

> The need for a constantly expanding market for its products chases the bourgeoisie over the whole surface of the globe. It must nestle everywhere, settle everywhere, establish connections everywhere....The cheap prices of its commodities are the heavy artillery with which it batters down all Chinese walls....It compels all nations, on pain of extinction, to adopt the bourgeois mode of production; it compels them to introduce what it calls civilization into their midst....In one word, it creates a world after its own image (Tucker 1972, 338–9).

In various permutations, such questions about the relationship between economic development and national boundaries have carried through to the present. In the mainstream literature, this is most evident through the thought process in which economies are first examined as closed national systems, then reexamined under the assumption of openness to trade with other nations. At a less abstract level, the economics of imperialism – the domination of one national economy by another – has long played a central role in the Marxian tradition, and it has also been examined by many non-Marxists such as Joseph Schumpeter.

Over the past 15 years, a widespread perception has emerged that a new stage has been reached in the relationship between capitalism and the nation-state. *Globalization* is the umbrella term – indeed the ubiquitous buzzword – conveying the sense that a fundamental transformation is occurring in the contemporary world economy. Governments and opposition political parties around the world rewrite their economic programs to take account of the perceived new realities engendered by globalization. Books, articles, and editorial pronouncements all pour forth, both in the economics literature and in the press, about its supposed benign or malign effects. And now, in your hands, is yet another contribution to the understanding of globalization.

What is driving these new perceptions, including ours, about the nature and causes of globalization? It is widely believed, first of all, that the extent of economic interactions between people in different countries is simply growing, at an ever-accelerating rate: that there is increasingly more trade, more foreign exchange transactions, more foreign investment, and more people migrating. But in addition to the increase in international economic interactions, it is also widely held that something more fundamental is occurring: that the quantitative increase in interactions is producing a qualitative change in the way that nation-states operate within any given country's economy. In particular, most discussions of globalization hold that the power of nation-states to influence economic activity is eroding as economies become more integrated, while the power of private businesses and market forces is correspondingly rising.

Are these perceptions accurate? Has economic integration between nations reached an unprecedented level? Is the power of nation-states eroding as integration proceeds? Is such a development inevitable? Does globalization correspondingly mean more autonomy to market forces throughout the world? Would such a development advance or retard the goal of broadly shared well being?

These are not easy matters to resolve, which at least partially explains why an already enormous literature has developed offering a wide variety of answers to these and related questions. This volume represents our own attempt at addressing the central questions at hand. It is the product of a multiyear research project coordinated under the auspices of the Economic Policy Institute in Washington, D.C. The project involved participants from throughout the world, and included two conferences, in October 1995 and June 1996, organized around the papers and discussants' comments presented in this volume.

The contributors to this volume offer a range of perspectives. But it should be quickly clear to readers that this volume does not offer an eclectic collection of views from across the spectrum. As with the Economic Policy Institute itself, the authors of the papers in this book are clearly on the left side of the economics profession. What does this mean? We are not hostile to markets per se, as few can deny the ability of markets to create effective material incentives within a competitive environment, and thereby to impose discipline on economic activity. But, more than most economists, we are also persuaded that capitalist market processes, left to operate freely, are also prone to generate injustice, insecurity, instability, and inefficiency.

Broad theoretical approaches follow fairly readily from such "preanalytic visions." Contemporary neo-classical economics is predisposed toward the idea that free market processes will tend to yield outcomes that are both efficient and equitable. The authors of this volume's papers do not believe that such a predisposition is a viable basis for understanding the operations of capitalist economies, in either this contemporary epoch of globalized capitalism or in previous epochs. We do not offer a unified theoretical alternative to neo-classical economics in these papers. But it will be clear that the authors are informed in various ways by the perspectives of Keynes, Marx, Kalecki, Polanyi, and other contributors to what Keynes himself once termed the "underground" tradition in economic thought. It is of course impossible in a few phrases to capture how this analytic tradition departs significantly from the mainstream. But, at a minimum, four central concepts do stand out:

(1) Capitalist economies typically operate at well below their level of physical and human capacity, so that policies to increase aggregate demand can yield substantial gains in economic opportunities;

(2) Pervasive uncertainty affects the investment decisions of firms and wealth holders in capitalist economies. Financial markets exist in large measure to mitigate the problems investors face due to uncertainty. And while financial markets do successfully spread risks, they also encourage a short-term bias and unproductive speculation among investors.

(3) Greater income and wealth inequality produces not only less equity and social solidarity, but can also engender less efficiency. Intelligently applied egalitarian government policies can therefore increase an economy's production possibilities.

(4) Wide disparities in political power flow from corresponding differences in income and wealth. These differences in political power influence economic policy formation in ways that reinforce existing disparities, and they diminish opportunities for the successful application of policies to improve economic performance through raising aggregate demand and increasing equality.

How can such theoretical perspectives be turned into concrete policy approaches within the contemporary global economy? We take pains in this volume to explore policy measures to counter the destructive features of markets and to promote equality as well as efficiency in ways that markets alone are unlikely to accomplish. Such initiatives constitute what we are terming here "progressive" economic policies. We focus on the role of nation-states to advance progressive economic policies, but not because we are enamored of the ability of states to increase economic well being. The simple fact is that states, in particular nation-states, represent the single most important alternative to market forces in determining economic outcomes. At the same time, just because we recognize the serious failings of markets and the need for public interventions, we do not assume that governments will necessarily be capable of carrying out the tasks to which they are assigned. If policy interventions are successful, it would be because the policies were designed in recognition of government's limited capacities and because policy makers faced significant standards of accountability. We thus explore policy measures that utilize state power efficiently and democratically to maximize the benign effects of both markets and public interventions and minimize their destructiveness. And if globalization has indeed changed the relationship between markets and nation-states to a significant degree, then it clearly becomes necessary to rethink the ways through which nation-states can intervene effectively in behalf of egalitarian policy initiatives. In a world of increasing global integration, one obvious issue for consideration is how to most effectively pursue international coordination in behalf of progressive economic policy.

The range of views presented here is hardly uniform. In addition to differences among the authors of papers, a still wider range of perspectives is represented by our distinguished group of discussants. As the reader will see, the discussants make invaluable contributions by sharpening the debate and, in particular, forcing those taking dissenting views to be as clear as possible on the precise nature of their dissent. This has produced an unusually lively and fruitful set of interchanges, which is especially appropriate given that the nature, causes, and consequences of globalization remain open questions.

Table 1 *Merchandise exports as a percentage of GDP*

	1820	1870	1913	1929	1950	1973	1992
World	1.0	5.0	8.7	9.0	7.0	11.2	13.5
Western Europe	——	10.0	16.3	13.3	9.4	20.9	29.7
Eastern Europe	——	2.1	3.5	4.9	3.6	7.1	0.5
U.S.	2.0	2.5	3.7	3.6	3.0	5.0	8.2
Asia	——	1.3	2.6	2.8	2.3	4.4	7.2
Latin America	——	9.0	9.5	9.7	6.2	4.6	6.2
Selected Africa:							
Egypt	——	14.0	32.0	——	29.0	10.0	3.0
Ghana	——	2.6	25.2	——	25.5	16.5	6.0
South Africa	——	——	49.2	——	22.7	20.4	18.7

Source: Angus Maddison, *Monitoring the World Economy, 1820–1992,* OECD 1995.

Contours of contemporary globalization

What is globalization? Let us return to the working premise suggested above that it entails an accelerating rate and/or a higher level of economic interaction between people of different countries, leading to a qualitative shift in the relationship between nation-states and national economies. To give greater specificity to this concept, it will be useful here to review some basic evidence on changes in the global patterns of economic activity. We will consider the movements of trade, foreign direct investment, portfolio investment, and people. Not surprisingly, many of the same patterns are discussed in the various papers in the volume. But it is nevertheless beneficial to provide an immediate lay-of-the-land before proceeding further.

Trade

Table 1 shows the ratio of merchandise exports to gross domestic product between 1820 and 1992. To begin with, we see that, at 13.5 percent, the ratio of merchandise trade to GDP is at a historic high as of 1992. This represents a steady increase from the 1973 figure of 11.2 percent and the 1950 figure of 7.0 percent. Note, however, that the 1950 figure represented a fall from the earlier 20th century figures of 8.7 percent (1913) and 9.0 percent (1929). So in part, the rise since 1950 represents a catching up from the level of the early 20th century. We can also see here that rising levels of trade integration are concentrated in three regions, West Europe, Asia, and the United States. For Latin America and the selected African countries for which we have data, the level of trade integration was actually well below that of the 1870–1929 period. The 40 years of Communist governments make Eastern Europe a unique case. It is still notable that the most recent figures for exports relative to GDP are quite low in historical terms.

Table 2 *Rate of change in merchandise exports/GDP*
(average annual rate of change, in percentages)

	1820–70	1870–1913	1913–29	1929–50	1950–73	1973–92
World	+8.0	+1.7	+0.2	-1.1	+1.7	+1.1
Western Europe	——	+1.5	-1.1	-1.1	+5.3	+2.2
Eastern Europe	——	+1.5	+8.8	-1.3	+4.3	-4.8
U.S.	+0.5	+1.2	-0.2	-0.8	+2.9	+3.4
Asia	——	+2.3	+0.5	-0.8	+4.0	+3.3
Latin America	——	+0.1	+0.1	-1.8	-1.1	+1.8
Selected Africa:						
Egypt	——	+3.0	——	——	-2.8	-3.7
Ghana	——	+20.2	——	+0.1	-1.5	-3.3
South Africa	——	——	——	——	-0.4	-0.4

Source: Angus Maddison, *Monitoring the World Economy, 1820–1992*, OECD 1995.

We get a somewhat different view of changing trade patterns in Table 2, where we consider the rate of change between periods in the merchandise trade/GDP ratio. For the world as a whole, we see that trade expands most rapidly in the 19th century. For the 20th century, the most rapid period of trade growth was between 1950 and 1973, at an average annual rate of 1.7 percent. The growth of trade then slows between 1973 and 1992 to an average annual rate of 1.1 percent. This worldwide pattern of trade growth in the 20th century, in which the peak period of growth is 1950–73, is reflected in the experiences of most of the countries reported in Table 2. The one significant exception is the United States, in which trade growth accelerates between 1973 and 1992 to 3.4 percent, somewhat above the 2.9 percent figure for 1950–73.

Overall, considering these figures on levels and growth rates of trade, the argument on trade integration having reached a qualitatively new phase would have to be made in terms of a threshold point having been reached by 1992, not in terms of an acceleration in the rate of trade integration. Moreover, even in terms of levels of trade, the figures presented in Tables 1 and 2 overstate the growth of exports relative to GDP, since these figures measure both exports and GDP in constant rather than current prices. This is a concern because, as Andrew Glyn explains in his contribution to this volume, the prices of exports systematically rise more slowly than do prices for output as a whole, reflecting the more rapid rise of labor productivity in export sectors. As Glyn shows, current price measures of exports/GDP show a much less substantial increase than what we observe in Table 1 with constant prices for both exports and GDP, and would show even lower growth rates of the export/GDP ratio than what we see in Table 2. In any case, the overall perception from these figures is that, in recent decades, the growth of trade has not been increasing substantially relative to GDP.

However, these figures for overall trading patterns are not themselves sufficiently detailed to document a crucial qualitative change that has occurred in the current

Table 3 *Manufacturing exports as a percentage of total exports*

3A: 1970–94 period

	1970	1980	1990	1994
World	60.9	64.2	71.1	74.7
Industrialized countries	72.0	70.2	78.0	79.2
Eastern Europe	59.1	50.2	43.9	53.0
Developing countries	18.5	17.7	54.3	66.1
Asia	22.4	23.5	65.5	73.4
Latin America	10.6	14.7	30.8	48.7
Africa	7.0	4.0	15.1	17.8

3B: 1913–53 period

	1913	1928	1937	1953
U.S. and Canada	25.8	38.5	44.7	60.7
United Kingdom	70.0	74.8	72.0	73.7
Northwest Europe	52.0	65.0	63.1	57.3
Asia, excluding				
China and N. Korea	21.2	30.9	28.1	25.3
Latin America	3.2	2.1	1.7	2.3
Africa	3.7	2.5	3.7	8.5

Sources: For 1970–90, *World Employment Report 1995,* ILO, p. 33; for 1994, *U.N. Handbook of International Trade and Development Statistics 1995,* Tables A.1 and A.13; for 1913–55, P. Lamartine Yates, *Forty Years of Foreign Trade,* New York: Macmillan, 1959, p. 55.

epoch of globalization. This qualitative change in trading patterns has occurred in the area of manufacturing trade, the figures for which are shown in Tables 3 and 4. Beginning with Table 3A, giving data for 1970–94, we see that, for the world as a whole, manufactures rose significantly as a share of total exports, from 60.9 percent in 1970 to 74.7 percent in 1994. Considering this pattern in more detail, we see that manufacturing exports of the developed countries rose over this period, but only modestly, from 72 percent to 79.2 percent. The dramatic change has taken place in the share of manufacturing exports from developing countries, from 18.5 percent to 66.1 percent; in fact, this rapid increase in manufacturing exports from developing countries really only began after 1980. Not surprisingly, by far the largest absolute advances came from Asia, which saw its proportion of manufacturing exports explode, from 23.5 percent to 73.4 percent between only 1980 and 1994. However, Latin America and Africa have also experienced dramatic increases in their share of manufacturing exports.

We can also see in Table 3B that the contemporary rise in the proportion of manufacturing exports from less-developed regions is historically unprecedented. In Asia, the proportion of manufacturing exports from 1913 to 1953 was roughly comparable to that for the 1970s, i.e., before the dramatic increase in the region's

Table 4 *Shares of world manufacturing exports by region and industry, 1980–95 (in percentages of world exports)*

Export area	Textiles		Chemicals		Machinery and transport		Metals		Other	
	1980	1995	1980	1995	1980	1995	1980	1995	1980	1995
Developed economies	61.7	42.0	87.2	79.3	86.1	76.4	78.9	63.1	68.8	70.0
Transitional economies	4.3	4.2	5.0	4.2	8.2	1.6	6.2	13.5	14.0	3.2
Developing economies	34.0	53.8	7.8	16.4	5.8	22.0	14.9	23.4	17.2	26.8
Developing, by region:										
Latin America	2.3	3.0	2.0	2.6	1.0	2.9	5.0	7.6	1.5	2.9
Africa	1.5	1.9	0.9	1.1	0.1	0.2	3.8	2.7	1.5	2.9
Asia	30.1	48.9	4.8	12.6	4.6	18.9	6.0	13.1	10.0	22.3

Source: U.N. World Economic and Social Survey, 1997, p. 248, Table A.17.

manufacturing exports. For Latin America and Asia, the proportion of manufacturing exports was generally well below that for even 1970. For the industrialized economies, the rise in the proportion of manufacturing exports is substantial since 1913, but only negligible for the U.K. and Northwest Europe.

Thus, considering trade figures alone, the most important evidence for a qualitative change having taken place in the contemporary era of globalization is that countries are increasingly trading each other's manufactured goods. In particular, the manufactured goods of the developing countries represent an increasing share of total trade. From the standpoint of the advanced countries, this evidence supports the view that their manufacturing sectors face rising competition from low-wage countries. This conclusion becomes even more clear in Table 4, where we present data on manufacturing exports by region and industry between 1980 and 1995. What this table shows strikingly is that the rise of manufacturing capacity in developing economies is not concentrated in low-technology industries, such as textiles. Rather, developing economies are gaining increasing shares of export markets across all manufacturing industries, with the most rapid area of increase being in machinery and transportation equipment, an area requiring substantial technical capabilities.

Foreign direct investment

Table 5A, to begin with, shows foreign direct investment patterns from 1913 to 1995. We see here a somewhat ambiguous pattern. To begin with, it is clear that foreign direct investment has clearly grown relative to the 1960s. This is true according to all three measures shown – FDI as a share of output; FDI inflows as a percentage of gross capital formation; and sales of foreign affiliates relative to exports. But it also appears that the level of foreign direct investment is not significantly higher than that for the late 19th century and early 20th century. Table 5A shows that the ratio of world FDI/output was 9.0 in 1913, not much below the 10.1 percent for 1995. Looking also at the pattern of the foreign asset/exports ratio in Table 5B, we see that the figures for 1885–1913 are at least comparable to, if not higher than, those for 1995. Overall then, the

Table 5 *Foreign direct investment*

5A: Foreign direct investment relative to output, capital formation, and exports

	1913	1960	1975	1985	1991	1995
World FDI stock as percent of world output	9.0	4.4	4.5	5.4	7.2	10.1
World FDI inflows as percent of world gross fixed capital formation	——	1.1	1.4	1.8	2.9	5.2
World sales of foreign affiliates as percent of world exports	——	8.4	9.7	9.9	12.2	——

5B: World overseas assets as percentage of world exports

	1885	1900	1913	1938	1995
	2.2	2.3	1.9	1.6	1.6–2.1*

Sources: Table 5A: for 1913–91, Richard Kozul-Wright, 1995, p. 158; for 1995, UNCTAD, *World Investment Report, 1997,* Tables B.5 and B.6.
Table 5B: for overseas foreign investment, 1855–1938, Fishlow 1985; for 1995, *BIS Annual Report,* June 1996, Table VVV.1, p. 140; for world exports, 1855–1913, W.A. Lewis 1995, A. Maddison 1995, p. 238; for FDI stock 1995, UNCTAD, *World Investment Report 1996,* Table A.3.

* The 1.6–2.1 range of figures for 1995 results from the lower figure excluding and the higher figure including net foreign direct investment. The earlier numbers partially include FDI. So, to be fully compatible, some FDI should be incorporated into the 1995 figure.

crucial change with FDI has been the substantial growth since the early 1980s, even though this growth only brings us to a level roughly equal to that for the pre-World War I period.

Capital flows
Here again, the picture is ambiguous. To clarify things, it is crucial to distinguish between gross capital flows and net flows, i.e., net financial resource transfers between countries.

The picture in terms of gross flows is dramatic. There has been a great expansion of international lending and an explosion of secondary market trading in stock, bond, foreign exchange, and derivative markets since the demise of Bretton Woods and the emergence of deregulated domestic financial markets. We see these trends in Table 6. To begin with, Table 6A shows the total amount of funds raised on international financial markets relative to world exports from 1950 to 1996. For 1950, this figure was only 0.5 percent. It rises to 1.8 percent by 1970, still prior to the collapse of Bretton Woods. But post-Bretton Woods the ratio rises rapidly in the mid-1970s through the mid-1980s. By 1985, the ratio is 13.5 percent – a sixfold

Table 6   *The growth of financial market transactions*

6A: Funds raised on international financial markets as percentage of world exports

1950	1960	1970	1975	1980	1985	1990	1996
0.5	1.0	1.8	4.6	5.8	13.5	10.5	20.0

6B: Cross-border transactions in bonds and equities as percentage of GDP

	1980	1985	1990	1995
U.S.	9.0	35.1	89.0	135.5
Japan	7.7	63.0	120.0	65.7
Germany	7.5	33.4	57.3	168.3
France	——	21.4	53.6	178.2
Italy	1.1	4.0	26.6	250.9
Canada	9.6	26.7	64.4	192.0

Sources: Table 6A: *OECD International Capital Market Statistics;* A. Maddison, *Monitoring the World Economy 1820–1992; IMF World Economic Outlook, October 1996;* for 1996, exports from *World Trade Organization Annual Report 1997,* Table A.3; for funds raised on capital markets, *OECD Financial Market Trends, February 1998,* Table 1. Table 6B: BIS, *66th Annual Report,* p. 98, and *67th Annual Report,* p. 119.

Note on Table 6A: the 1996 figure for "funds raised on international financial markets" includes only "committed facilities," i.e., it excludes "uncommitted facilities," which maintains consistency with the figures for 1950–90.

increase over 1970. By 1996, the figure is up to 20.0 percent, showing a continuing dramatic rise.[1]

Table 6B shows a more detailed breakdown of foreign transactions since 1980 in bonds and equities as a percentage of GDP for six countries of the OECD (Organization for Economic Development and Cooperation), including here both secondary trading as well as primary issues. In all six cases, the jump in cross-border flows from 1980 has been spectacular – e.g., for the United States, the ratio of cross-border transactions/GDP rose from 9.0 percent to 135.5 percent. The largest jump was that of Italy, where the ratio rises from 1.1 percent to 250.9 percent between 1980 and 1995. The small exception to the pattern of huge expansion is Japan, where we see a rapid increase in cross-border flows through 1990 but a very sharp decline by 1995 back to the level of 1985.

There are no reliable time-series figures for foreign exchange trading prior to the late 1980s. However, we do have figures since 1989 from the Bank of International

---

1   But even this 20.0 percent figure for 1996 is a conservative estimate, in that, for purposes of comparability across the full period, we exclude the category "uncommitted facilities," as reported by the OECD for this year. Had we included these "uncommitted" as well as the "committed facilities" in our total for funds raised, the ratio of funds raised/exports for 1996 would be 30.0 percent.

Table 7 *Current account surpluses or deficits as percentage of GDP: weighted average for 12 countries* (in absolute values)*

1895–99	3.3
1910–14	3.8
1925–29	2.5
1935–39	1.4
1950–54	1.8
1970–74	1.4
1980–84	2.0
1985–89	2.3
1990–96	2.7

Source: For 1895–1989: A.M. Taylor, "International Capital Mobility in History: The Saving/Investment Relationship," NBER Working Paper No. 5743, 1996; for 1990–96, *IMF International Capital Markets 1997*, p. 235.

* Countries in sample are Argentina, Australia, Canada, Denmark, France, Germany, Japan, Norway, Sweden, the U.K., and the U.S.

Settlements, showing that overall trading began exceeding an average of $1 trillion per day by 1995. The total figure for foreign exchange trading in 1995 was about 50 times the total volume of world trade for that year – i.e., $50 in foreign exchange transactions occurred for every dollar of trade in goods and services.

Especially given such indicators of enormous growth in world financial markets, it is remarkable that the picture is dramatically different when we consider net resource transfers through capital markets, as we can observe in Table 7. This shows the ratio of current account to GDP, as a weighted average for 12 countries. Considered over a 125-year period from 1870 to 1995, we see that this ratio is substantially higher in the period before the 1930s depression. And while there has been a fairly steady rise in this ratio since the 1960s, by 1990–96 the figure, at 2.7 percent, is either below or roughly the same as those for any five-year interval between 1870 and 1929.

Migration

There have been significant changes in migration patterns, though here again the picture is not entirely straightforward. Consider first the data in Table 8, which show migration patterns for the U.S. and Canada and for Europe since the late 19th century. For the U.S. and Canada, the rate of migration has been positive since the mid-1980s, but still at a rate of increase well below that of the 1870–1910 period. For Europe, we see that the new outflow of migrants ends in 1950–60. By the 1970s, a pattern of positive, if negligible, immigration begins and continues through the most recent years.

Table 9 provides more detail on the distribution of migrants throughout the world since 1965. The first two columns show the percentage of foreign-born residents in

Table 8   *Net migration rates for United States/Canada and Europe (immigration [+]; emigration [-])*

	1870–1910	1950–60	1960–70	1970–80	1980–85
U.S. and Canada	+5.4	+2.7	+2.3	+4.0	+2.8
Europe	-2.6	-0.8	——	+0.5	+0.1

Sources: For 1870–1910: A.M. Taylor and J.G. Williamson, "Convergence in the Age of Mass Migration," NBER Working Paper No. 4711, p. 26, Table 1; for 1950–85, OECD, *The Changing Course of International Migration,* 1993, p. 38.

Table 9   *World distribution of immigrants*

	Foreign born as percent of total population		Growth of foreign born as percent of total population growth
	1965	1990	1965–90
Industrialized countries	3.0	4.5	+ 11.4
U.S. and Canada	6.0	8.6	+ 17.5
Europe	3.3	5.0	+ 18.3
Oceania	14.4	17.8	+ 24.3
Developing countries	1.9	1.6	+ 1.2
Persian Gulf states	12.4	36.5	——
North Africa and W. Asia	4.1	6.0	+ 7.9
Latin America	2.4	1.6	+ 0.6
Sub-Saharan Africa	2.8	2.8	+ 2.8
Southern Asia	2.8	1.8	+ 0.4
Eastern and S.E. Asia	1.9	1.2	- 0.1

Sources: For 1870–1910: Taylor and Williamson, "Convergence in the Age of Mass Migration," NBER Working Paper No. 4711, 1994, p. 26; for 1965–90, "Trends in Total Migration Stock, Revision 3," United Nations, Department of Economic and Social Information and Policy Analysis, Population Division, 1995.

various regions in 1965 and 1990. The number of foreigners living in the industrialized countries increased between these two periods, from 3.0 percent to 4.5 percent. These ratios are higher for the U.S. and Canada and Oceania, though the rates at which the proportion of foreign-born residents has risen in these areas is also relatively modest. However, the last column of Table 9, showing the rate of increase in foreign-born residents relative to total population growth, provides a different perspective. Here we see that migrants account for a substantial share of the increase in population between 1965 and 1990 – 11.4 percent overall for the industrialized countries and even higher for the U.S. and Canada, Europe, and Oceania. What these figures are capturing is positive rates of migration combined with relatively low rates of population growth, so that the growth in the foreign-born population appears high in these regions. This pattern of rapid immigration growth becomes even more clear when we examine the percentage of immigrants among new labor market entrants, discussed below in the summary of Gregory DeFreitas's contribution to this volume.

For low- and middle-income countries, we see that the share of foreign-born residents actually declines from 1965 to 1990. The great exception, of course, are the Gulf states. Immigration has also been fairly high in North Africa.

In short, there appear to be two big changes in migration patterns. First, among the industrialized countries, we can see the basis for the impression that immigration rates are rising, even while, in absolute terms, the rate at which foreign-born residents are increasing is unexceptional. Second, the oil-rich countries, along with the industrialized countries, have clearly become a second pole of attraction for the world's migrants.

Price convergence

Thus far, we have been considering measures of globalization that focus on quantity flows internationally – flows of goods, money, and people. But there is another standard way of measuring international integration, i.e., through price convergence. Indeed, for many economists globalization should be properly measured by the extent to which different national markets are being combined into one big market. We can observe this according to how much markets are converging toward a single world price for any given product.

Yet again, the evidence is mixed on the extent to which price setting across countries is coming to approximate the law of one price. To consider some evidence first on commodity prices, an extremely interesting study by Froot, Kim, and Rogoff (1995) examined annual commodity price data from England and Holland over a span of seven centuries. Their dataset incorporated transaction prices on eight commodities – barley, butter, cheese, eggs, oats, peas, silver, and wheat – as well as pound/shilling nominal exchange rates. They found that the volatility and persistence of deviations from the law of one price have been remarkably stable over the full period they measure. Moreover, moving forward into more contemporary times, they find no increase in the rate of price convergence in the current period (1973–91) relative to 1900–91 or relative to the 19th century.

In terms of financial integration, the standard measure of price convergence is the extent to which interest rate parity exists across national markets – i.e., whether similar assets generate equal expected rates of return regardless of where, or in what currency, the assets are issued. Unfortunately, there is no single appropriate measure of interest rate parity. The least-stringent test is whether identical offshore short-term assets issued in different currencies have the same returns when exchange rate risk is held constant. The asset markets in most industrialized countries pass this test, and have done so consistently since the early 1980s. The most stringent test on parity of short-term bonds asks whether real interest parity holds when bonds are issued in different countries and currencies. Here, expected real interest rate

Table 10 *Convergence rates of real wages and productivity across 15 OECD countries,* 1870–1987 (average annual rate at which convergence occurs)*

	Real wage convergence	GDP/work hour convergence
1870–1913	0.35	0.36
1913–50	-0.07	-0.37
1950–87	0.79	3.14

Source: A.M. Taylor and J.G. Williamson 1994, p. 27.

* The countries included in the sample are Australia, Belgium, Canada, Denmark, France, Germany, Great Britain, Ireland, Italy, the Netherlands, Norway, Portugal, Spain, Sweden, and the United States.

differentials must just exactly offset expected changes in inflation-adjusted exchange rates. Most countries' assets fail this test most of the time, and there has been no general movement toward greater market convergence according to this measure (Herring and Litan 1995, Chapter 2). Most analysts argue that this lack of movement toward convergence is due to the difficulties investors face in rationally forecasting returns, exchange rate changes, and changes in government policies in an uncertain world. Finally, parity tests on long-term financial assets and real assets, such as foreign direct investment, almost always fail to show evidence toward convergence, probably for similar reasons to those for short-term bonds (Epstein 1996).

These interest parity tests are even less likely to hold outside of the mature industrial countries. Capital controls are still on the books around the globe; in many parts of the world, domestic capital markets themselves are highly segmented (Blecker 1997; Chin and Dooley 1995). Finally, Zevin points out that financial market integration, as measured by the law of one price, while lower in the 1950s and 1960s than it is now, was relatively high in the late 19th century (Zevin 1992). In short, as measured by interest parity relations, international financial markets are more integrated now than in the 1950s and 1960s, but they are still integrated in an only limited sense in the highly industrial markets and even less so in the less-developed countries of Asia and elsewhere.

Measuring the extent of wage convergence over time is also difficult, especially if we want to measure wages relative to productivity growth levels. In Table 10, we present evidence developed by Taylor and Williamson (1994). It shows that wages across 15 OECD countries were converging at an average annual rate of 0.35 percent in 1870–1913, but that this process of convergence ended between 1913 and 1950. The rate of convergence then accelerates to 0.79 percent per year in the period 1950–87. However, the rate of productivity convergence over these same periods is far more rapid. Productivity convergence was 0.36 percent per year from 1870 to 1913. This convergence process is then essentially reversed in the 1913–50 period, but then accelerates tremendously to 3.14 percent during 1950–87. In other words, there is a dramatic difference in the two periods of convergence. In 1870–1913, wage convergence essentially matched the rate of productivity convergence. Over 1950–87, wages converged at only 25 percent of the rate of productivity. This suggests that institutional forces in labor markets played a far stronger role in the most recent period in setting relative wage norms than in the earlier historical period.

This, of course, is a very partial look at the rate of price, interest rate, and wage convergence. However, from this it is clear that this convergence toward uniform markets obeying the law of one price is not taking place to a significant extent.

Considering the quantity and price data we have presented, it will be useful now to summarize the basic patterns in terms of what globalization means in the current period.

There certainly has been an acceleration in the rates of integration according to a range of measures. In terms of trade, no dramatic changes have occurred in either the overall level of trade relative to GDP or the overall growth of trade. On the other hand, the growth in the proportion of manufacturing exports, especially coming from developing economies, has been rising sharply in the contemporary period of globalization. This will increasingly create more direct forms of competition between producers of manufactured goods throughout the world, especially as developing economies continue to successfully appropriate a wide range of manufacturing technologies. Foreign direct investment has also grown since the 1960s, though here clearly to a level not significantly greater than the turn of the century. Net financial flows – i.e., real financial resource transfers – have also not grown substantially. But, more importantly with respect to financial flows, gross flows have risen spectacularly since the demise of Bretton Woods. Finally, there has been an increase in the rate of migration to the industrialized economies, and that rate appears to be accelerating relative to the growth of the population and domestic labor forces in these regions.

To consider these patterns overall, there have been two quite dramatic changes. The first is the rise in the proportion of manufacturing exports among the less-developed economies. The second is the explosion of short-term capital movements. Otherwise, what we observe is a steady rise in the rates of global integration relative to the 1960s, but for the most part to levels of integration comparable to the early 20th century. How significant are these changes overall?

To help address that question, these patterns should be placed in a broader historical context. The first contextual issue to consider is that, in the current period, global integration is occurring in a very different world than that of the early 1900s. The most important difference is that the role of government has changed dramatically since the end of World War II. Considering first the OECD economies, Table 11 shows total government expenditures as a share of GDP for six representative countries between 1880 and 1996. This ratio rises from 10.0 percent in 1880 to 11.7 percent in 1913 to 45.7 percent in 1992, before falling slightly as of 1996 to 45.1 percent. These differences over time would be even greater if we considered only nonmilitary expenditures.

With respect to most of the developing economies, it is only since the end of World

Table 11 *Total government expenditures as a percentage of GDP*

	1880	1913	1938	1950	1973	1992	1996
France	11.2	8.9	23.2	27.6	38.8	51.0	54.7
Germany	10.0	17.7	42.4	30.4	42.0	46.1	49.7
Japan	9.0	14.2	30.3	19.8	22.9	33.5	36.6
Netherlands	na	8.2	21.7	26.8	45.5	54.1	50.9
United Kingdom	9.9	13.3	28.8	34.2	41.5	51.2	42.3
U.S.	na	8.0	19.8	21.4	31.1	38.5	36.7
Average	10.0	11.7	27.7	26.7	37.0	45.7	45.1

Source: A. Maddison, *Monitoring the World Economy,* Tables 3–5, p. 65; for 1996, IMF, *International Financial Statistics,* March 1998.

War II that formally independent governments existed at all. There were a few exceptions, but for the most part the ruling governments in the less-advanced countries were the colonial authorities. These countries had thus already considerable experience with "globalization" in the form of the spread of European and U.S. empires.

In short, among both the advanced and developing countries, government has played an increasingly important role, especially over the post-World War II period, in seeking to increase economic welfare within domestic economies. This continues to be true at present, even though, since the 1980s, countries throughout the OECD have made substantial cuts in the extent of their welfare states, and many developing economies, following programs of austerity and "structural adjustment" originating at the International Monetary Fund and World Bank, have reduced the extent of government ownership of assets and regulation of markets.

But is such a central role for government compatible with a more integrated global environment? This certainly has been a major concern among commentators on globalization, and it is a question we will address at length in this volume. Whatever the answer, the question clearly must be posed in a very different way in the current context relative to how one might have addressed it in 1900.

This concern over how globalization might be affecting economic performance becomes more pointed still when we also consider the patterns of globalization alongside the other major shift in the world economy since the 1970s, i.e., the declining rate of output growth for most of the world. Indeed, it is now clear that we can divide the post-World War II epoch into two distinct periods, a Golden and a Leaden Age of output growth. Golden Age growth coincides roughly with the years of low globalization, i.e., from 1950 to 1973, while the Leaden Age is roughly coincident with the rise of globalization beginning in the mid-1970s. As we see in Table 12, world per capita economic growth from 1973 to 1992, at 1.2 percent, is less than half that over 1950–73 and is slightly below that for 1870–1913 as well.

The most recent figures available, for 1991–96, do show an increase in the world's average annual growth rate, to 1.9 percent. However, this increase is unlikely to represent a transition out of the Leaden Age. These most recent figures are for five

Table 12 *Average annual rate of growth of per capita GDP*

	1870–1913	1950–73	1973–92	1991–96
World	1.3	2.9	1.2	1.9
Western Europe	1.3	3.9	1.8	1.1
U.S., Canada, Australia	1.8	2.4	1.4	1.7
Southern Europe	1.1	4.9	1.7	na
Eastern Europe	1.0	3.5	-1.1	-6.5
Latin America	1.5	2.5	0.5	1.3
Asia	0.6	3.8	3.2	7.5
Africa	0.4	2.0	-0.1	-0.6

Source: A. Maddison, *Monitoring the World Economy*, Table 3.1, p. 60 for first three columns; for last column, 1991–96, *U.N. World Economic and Social Survey 1997*, p. 233, for all regions except U.S., Canada, and Australia, which come from IMF *International Financial Statistics*, March 1998.

years only, and, even still, the higher growth performance is still to a level far below that of the Golden Age of 1950–73.[2] Moreover, as is clear from Table 12, virtually all of the growth in 1991–96 was due to the phenomenal 7.5 percent average annual growth experienced in Asia over these years. With Asia continuing to experience a severe economic crisis as we write in April 1998, it certainly appears implausible to expect that Asia will return in the foreseeable future to anything approaching its growth performance of the early 1990s.

These long-term growth figures raise a crucial question. The Golden Age of capitalism was associated with the rise of big government in the immediate post-World War II years, including the emergence of independent governments in the developing economies. But big government presupposes *national* economies that national governments can effectively influence. Has globalization eroded the capacity of national governments to guide national economies? And if so, is such a diminution in the capacity of government associated with the downward trajectory of world economic growth?

Parables of globalization

This of course is a major question upon which we hope this volume sheds some light. But how one begins to think about this question depends on how one views the process by which we have arrived at this historical juncture. It will be useful to consider two distinct *parables* – short, simple stories from which a moral lesson may be drawn – of how we got from here to there.

2   The cause of the overlap between the 1973–92 and 1991–96 periods reported in Table 12 is that the two sets of figures are taken from different data sources, as the citation at the bottom of the table states.

Neo-classical parable

As we have seen, the world economy was highly integrated in the early 20th century, with the West European imperialist powers – in particular Britain – serving as the system's central geographical and financial hubs. The British strongly supported free trade, and this provided a major impetus to integration, especially, of course, within Britain's own vast sphere of influence. But progress toward the spread of free trade and greater integration was dramatically ruptured by World War I, the Great Depression, and World War II. In this parable, the tensions created by European imperialism and British free trade policies were not themselves responsible for the era of war and depression. Indeed, the actual causes of these calamities were many and varied, but in general had little to do with the level of global integration. Indeed, if anything in this parable, global integration and free trade offered a rational counterbalance to the extreme nationalist ideologies that brought the collapse of economic growth and reasonable political discourse in this era.[3]

However, the prevailing political sentiments that emerged out of World War II drew a different, and erroneous, lesson from the experiences since 1914. Throughout the world, governments believed that economic welfare would best be promoted through limiting free trade and capital mobility and generally using the power of government to strongly regulate and guide economic activity. The formation of Communist states after World War II represented an extreme case of governments mistakenly suppressing free market forces in the effort to promote economic welfare. In short, the worldwide reaction to the calamities of the first half of the 20th century disrupted progress toward global integration. We are now witnessing a return to the essentially benign process of integration that had been spreading steadily up until World War I. This renewed process of integration has been strongly supported by advances in communication and transportation technologies. But in the neo-classical parable, the fundamental force behind globalization is the worldwide recognition – from the former Communist countries to the formerly heavily regulated capitalist economies in the West and South – that free market capitalism is the most effective framework for delivering widespread economic well being.

Heterodox parable[4]

The heterodox parable begins with a far less benign view of how markets and capitalism operate, and is therefore far less sanguine about the prospects of markets becoming freer and more integrated and for governments to increasingly use their power to enforce free trade and the prerogatives of capital. The heterodox parable also views the economic history of the 20th century far differently. In this view, the

3   One recent reference reflecting this perspective is K. Ohmae (1994). This view is also expressed forcefully in Joseph Schumpeter's *Imperialism and Social Classes* (1951), in which violent conflict is explained as a failure of a market-dominated political ethos of rational acquisitiveness to gain hegemony over vestigial nationalist sentiments associated with feudalism.

4   Two representative references here would be Hobsbawm (1994) and Glyn, Hughes, Lipietz, and Singh (1991).

process of integration at the early part of the century did yield benefits, as feudal structures disintegrated and modern technologies spread. Marx himself emphatically anticipated such benefits, as in the passage from the *Communist Manifesto* quoted above. But the spread of capitalist productive relations also produced its own set of profound social tensions, as Marx himself also obviously anticipated. The most destructive conflicts were due to the struggle among the imperialist European nation-states to integrate the global economy on terms most favorable to themselves. This was the underlying cause, if not the proximate detonator, of World War I.

In various permutations, the postwar systems of welfare state capitalism, social democracy, and even Communism were based on the view – forcefully articulated by Polanyi in *The Great Transformation* – that competitive market processes had to be embedded in social structures of solidarity to ameliorate the social tensions created by acquisitiveness and inequality. The inherent macroeconomic instability of free market capitalism described by Keynes also required extensive regulations, both within domestic economies and internationally.

The early post-World War II period – characterized by big governments and Keynesian macro management in the North and import substitution policies in the South – coincided with the Golden Age of growth, the most prosperous era in the history of capitalism. Of course, it remains an open question as to how such government policies may have contributed to the Golden Age. But it is at least clear that big government and strong regulations were *not incompatible* with successful growth under capitalism. In the heterodox parable, big government was fundamental to the Golden Age, through promoting stability and reducing inequality within domestic economies, and through regulating international trade and capital mobility with relative success.

But as we have seen, the Golden Age yielded to the Leaden Age. Big government policies increasingly came into question as a result. In the advanced capitalist economies, the stagflation of the 1970s undermined the authority of mainstream Keynesianism and provided the initial opening for the revival of free market economics in the form of Monetarism and New Classical doctrines. In the Third World, the debt crisis of the 1980s provided the opening for a widespread abandonment of government-led development policies such as the import substitution model, even though it was never evident that big government policies themselves were primarily to blame for the excessive debt buildups and subsequent crises. And of course the collapse of the Soviet system eliminated this challenge to capitalist hegemony, even though the governments professing to Communism had long since abandoned any serious claim to a democratic, egalitarian alternative to free market capitalism. But huge new areas of the world were now newly opened to globalized capitalism, as the successors to the Communist governments embraced free market tenets with the fervor of converts.

It remains, of course, to leaven these simple stories with substance. Let us now take a tour through the various papers contributed to this volume, so that we can identify the main substantive findings as well as the most important issues of continuing debate.

Globalization in the neo-liberal regime

We have tried to make clear that the contemporary process of globalization can only be understood within the specific context in which it is occurring. The driving force behind globalization in the contemporary world is the ideology and policy formulations associated with free market capitalism. As we will see, though, such developments only rarely entail actual dismantling of state power, but rather a shift in the role of the state in favor of the interests of large-scale capitalist enterprises and especially finance capital.

The role of laissez faire ideology and policy throughout the world is examined in Ute Pieper and Lance Taylor's paper, "The revival of the liberal creed: the IMF, the World Bank, and inequality in a globalized economy." Pieper and Taylor describe the modern form of laissez faire policy – what they also term "The Liberal Creed" and "The Washington Consensus" – as these policies are disseminated through the International Monetary Fund (IMF) and World Bank, the sister institutions created out of the famous Bretton Woods conference of 1944.

Pieper and Taylor build from the work of Polanyi, who, in *The Great Transformation*, sought to explain how the "liberal creed" contributed to the catastrophes of war and depression associated with the first half of the 20th century. Polanyi's central argument – which in fact can be traced back to Adam Smith himself – is, again, that markets do indeed promote efficiency and change, but that they achieve this through undermining social coherence and solidarity. Markets must therefore be embedded within social institutions that mitigate their negative consequences.

But Pieper and Taylor argue that the global spread of free market policies has been accompanied by the decline of countervailing institutions of social solidarity; indeed, a main feature of the introduction of market-friendly policies has been to weaken local institutions of social solidarity. They argue as well that the IMF and World Bank have been the chief purveyors of the liberal creed throughout the world, and they analyze numerous case studies of IMF stabilization programs and World Bank structural adjustment policies throughout the world. They show how bad economic theory deriving from straightforward neo-classical models combined with superficial understanding of local economies by the Washington-based IMF/World Bank economists have produced enormously harmful macroeconomic policies throughout the developing world.

Complementary to the Pieper/Taylor study is the paper, "India: *dirigisme*, structural adjustment, and the radical alternative," by Prabhat Patnaik and C.P. Chandrasekhar. This is a careful analysis of the historical background as well as the proximate causes and consequences to date resulting from the implementation of an IMF/World Bank structural adjustment program in India in 1991.

Patnaik and Chandrasekhar document the shift in approach by the Bretton Woods institutions from the initial post-World War II period to the present. Beginning in the late 1970s, the IMF was no longer satisfied to operate as it had previously, i.e., accepting and operating within existing domestic economic arrangements. It assumed the posture of a "gendarme" of international rentier interests, with the specific aim of opening the financial systems of developing countries to international capital markets. The World Bank also redefined its mission in this period. In particular, it became actively involved in infiltrating local policy-making institutions, with the aim of establishing a policy-making elite more in concert with the Bank's approach. Patnaik and Chandrasekhar emphasize that such efforts proved highly successful in India, in part because India had a strong "liberalization lobby" domestically, including broad sections of both domestic capital and the Indian middle class.

The most obvious effect of structural adjustment policies they find has been the increase in rural poverty, as local producers of agricultural goods find themselves unable to compete with foreign exporters. In terms of the macro picture, India also experienced a decline in per capita income growth through the mid-1990s, a sharp decline in public and private investment ratios, and a failure of foreign direct investment to increase by more than a negligible amount. At the same time, short-term portfolio investments rose dramatically. But this increase of international portfolio investments has not contributed to growth or stabilization; rather, it has retarded growth because it increased instability in the economy, particularly through rapid interest rate fluctuations.

Patnaik and Chandrasekhar sketch an alternative policy approach that they argue would promote growth with equality. The main components of their approach are public investment to develop domestic industries, including export industries; capital flow controls with a nonconvertible currency to reduce the influence of short-term portfolio investments; and egalitarian land reforms, supplemented by public investment in agricultural infrastructure such as irrigation programs.

Foreign direct investment in the neo-liberal regime

We have seen that the current wave of globalization is most directly characterized by the expansion of global financial markets. But foreign direct investment and the globalization of production are also expanding rapidly. As the papers in this section of the volume show, the implications of this growth are equally important for understanding the broad transformations in the contemporary world.

In "Globalization, transnational corporations, and economic development" Ha-Joon Chang reports, for example, that since the early 1980s foreign direct investment has been growing four times faster than international trade; that there has been a large increase in foreign direct investment flows to developing countries, with a shift in the composition of the investments in developing countries from primarily extractive industries to manufacturing and services; and that transnational corporations now manage about 75 percent of world trade in manufacturing goods.

Chang argues that figures such as these are often used to support the myth that transnationals are in the business of scouring the globe for havens of low wages, low taxes, and lax regulations. But Chang shows that a serious examination of the evidence on transnationals is not consistent with this notion of stateless, footloose, and overwhelmingly powerful economic entities. For one thing, while the flows of foreign direct investment to low-wage developing countries have been increasing, the bulk of foreign direct investment is still concentrated in the industrialized economies. Moreover, over 70 percent of the foreign investment that is going to developing countries is targeted at only 10 countries, and China alone received over 25 percent of the developing economies' foreign direct investment between 1990 and 1994.

The case of China underscores the weakness in the view that transnationals are primarily seeking low-cost, low-regulation havens. In fact, China has placed quite restrictive regulations on transnationals, and it has also used its bargaining power to direct transnational investment into particular sectors and regions of its economy. What then makes particular countries attractive to transnationals? Chang cites evidence that rapid rates of economic growth, valuable domestic resources such as a trained workforce and reliable infrastructure, as well as political stability are key factors. Chang thus concludes that domestic policies to promote economic growth – including in particular domestic industrial policies – are a more effective way of attracting foreign direct investment than the types of liberalization policies promulgated by the World Bank.

In "Multinational corporations in the neo-liberal regime," James Crotty, Gerald Epstein, and Patricia Kelly also focus on the role of transnational corporations and foreign direct investment in the global economy. Their central argument is that, within the neo-liberal policy framework that dominates the process of globalization at present, it becomes increasingly difficult for host countries to capture broadly shared economic benefits.

For Crotty, Epstein, and Kelly, three factors are crucial for determining the impact of foreign direct investment on host countries: the state of aggregate demand; the nature of the domestic and international regulations governing investment; and the nature of similar sets of regulations concerned with competition. They hold that benefits can flow from foreign direct investment when aggregate demand in the host country is robust and the domestic economy is effectively regulated. But foreign direct investment can correspondingly become quite destructive of egalitarian policy aims, in particular when it flows to countries with high rates of unemployment and deregulated markets.

Crotty, Epstein, and Kelly focus on two mechanisms through which the domestic economic environment in host countries determines the costs and benefits of foreign direct investment: first, how the domestic environment influences relative bargaining power; and second, whether domestic governments can adequately solve the coordination problems needed to capture the benefits of foreign direct investment. If host countries are not capable of establishing some significant bargaining strength and do not solve the policy coordination problems associated with regulating transnational firms, they can fall into "prisoner dilemma"-type situations in which transnationals are able to bargain down wage rates, taxes, and regulations to suboptimal levels, even, ironically, from the viewpoint of transnationals in some cases.

An important paradox results when host countries seek foreign direct investment from a weak bargaining position. As Chang argues, transnational firms are attracted to countries with robust domestic markets, a well-trained workforce, and well-functioning infrastructure. But countries that have embraced the neo-liberal agenda have increasing difficulties in creating such an economic environment. Austerity policies undermine demand, while reducing taxes and the size of the public sector means less support for education, training, and physical infrastructure.

Globalization of finance

As we have already noted, global integration over the past 25 years has proceeded most rapidly – indeed spectacularly – in the realm of finance. We explore various implications of the process of financial integration in this section of the volume.

In "Implications of globalization for macroeconomic theory and policy," Amit Bhaduri develops an innovative analytic framework to capture the basic features of the contemporary globalization process. Bhaduri's paper begins with a compact yet illuminating overview of "globalization: then and now," comparing the current period with the era of the gold standard in terms of trade patterns, foreign direct investment, and international finance. In utilizing this historical framework to focus on current concerns, Bhaduri finds that, while international capital mobility is very high, trade flows do not adjust easily to exchange rate fluctuations because a substantial proportion of the trade account is dominated by intrafirm trading. Bhaduri then develops a simple model in which the capital account adjusts very quickly to capital inflows, and the propensity to import adjusts along with fluctuations in the capital account. Thus, the influx of short-term capital raises the value of a country's currency and its propensity to import. This then produces a decline in domestic production, so that the capital inflows have become "de-industrializing."

Bhaduri draws three implications from this model. First, short-term macroeconomic policy in developing countries should not be oriented toward raising interest rates to attract capital. Second, financial restructuring should rather be focused on measures to facilitate the flow of funds from portfolio investments to productive investments in plant and equipment. And third, because international capital mobility has weakened the ability of domestic policy makers to construct such channels between short-term capital markets and long-term productive investments, measures should be taken to circumscribe the short-term capital markets. Bhaduri proposes two such measures: a "Tobin tax" on foreign exchange transactions to reduce their flow, and a discriminatory domestic tax structure that raises rates on interest income relative to that on income from profit from productive investment.

In "Asia and the crisis of financial globalization" David Felix argues that there has been a fundamental and, in his view, profoundly mistaken transformation in orthodox assumptions and policy concerning the international movements of capital. The Bretton Woods accords were initially developed around the assumption that unregulated international capital mobility was incompatible with free trade, full employment, and rapid economic growth. However, the new orthodoxy promoted by the IMF, the U.S. Treasury Department, and most international financiers and economists claims that unfettered capital mobility is a virtual prerequisite for the success of a global free-trading system. Felix contends that policy measures guided by this mistaken conception are, among other things, largely responsible for the current Asian financial crisis.

Felix argues that the "new" orthodoxy, which harkens back to pre-Keynesian notions of the 1920s, is justified by neither theoretical rigor nor empirical evidence. The new orthodoxy is based on two related ideas. The first is that international capital markets price assets accurately according to underlying fundamentals. The second is that international capital flows transfer savings from areas with low marginal productivity investments to areas with higher productivity investments. In doing so, free capital mobility promotes investment and economic growth worldwide.

With regard to the first point, Felix explains that there are numerous new-Keynesian models of noise trading which show that, in markets where traders ignore fundamentals, it is rational for even fundamentalists to jump on the speculative bandwagon and drive prices away from their underlying "correct" price. Felix then elucidates a more traditional Keynesian view which argues that no unique fundamentals exist in any case, since the correct asset price depends on the distribution of income, political power, and a host of unknowable endogenous factors. This perspective is consistent with new models of exchange rate crises which show that, even in the face of neo-classical "rationality," international capital markets have multiple equilibria; thus, if speculators attack, they can move the economy from a sustainable point to an inferior position. On the empirical side, a growing body of evidence suggests that international capital markets badly misprice assets, including, importantly, the exchange rate.

In terms of the second point, Felix shows that relatively little in the way of net flows of investment occurs from one country to another. Rather, most international capital transactions are between financial customers who are hedging or speculating rather than investing in real plant and equipment. Felix argues that real interest rates rise as a result of the expansion of speculative financial markets. The rise in real interest rates, in turn, dampens real investment and economic growth while serving to concentrate wealth and political power within a growing worldwide rentier class.

How would Felix address these problems? In his view, the solution is certainly not to promote more deregulation and free capital mobility, as the IMF is insisting in Asia and elsewhere. But Felix also rejects an alternative proposed by some on both the right and left, i.e., abolish the IMF. In his view, a lender of last resort like the IMF is a necessary evil because of the inherent instability of financial markets. But Felix says the IMF must be transformed. Among other things, it must approve more controls on international capital movements, as it did in its initial decades of operation.

Like Bhaduri, Felix supports an international Tobin tax on international financial transactions. This tax would have the effect of taxing shorter-term investments at higher rates than longer-term investments. He argues that such a tax would lower real interest rates, give governments more macroeconomic autonomy, and reduce the tendencies now inherent in world capital markets toward instability and crises.

Various contributors to this volume hold that creating a robust macroeconomic environment is crucial for absorbing external capital flows in a productive way. But how might financial globalization be affecting the capacity of domestic policy makers to create such a desirable macroeconomic environment? This is the question Marc Schaberg addresses in "Globalization and financial systems: policies for the new environment."

Focusing on the evolution of monetary policy within the process of global financial integration, Schaberg argues that a convergence is occurring in the operating procedures of central banks. He observes that, increasingly, central banks are relying on indirect methods of market intervention, such as open market operations, relative to direct measures, such as quantity controls or interest rate ceilings. In addition, Schaberg shows that this reliance on indirect policy tools is part of a broader movement toward deregulated, capital-market-based financial systems in the Anglo-American tradition, as opposed to the more administratively controlled bank-based systems such as those that developed in Germany, France, and most East Asian economies, including Japan.

Drawing on a wide literature, Schaberg argues that the capital-market-based systems have engendered greater financial instability and shorter time horizons for investors. Indeed, the single most important cause of the 1997–98 Asian financial crisis was that these economies had opened their financial markets to short-term foreign investors without having an adequate financial regulatory system that could channel capital inflows toward productive uses.

Recognizing this worldwide pattern toward the Anglo-American model, Schaberg still holds that governments can implement effective policies for reducing the problems of short-termism and financial instability. First, central banks should regain greater authority in directly influencing the lending practices of all financial intermediaries. Specifically, he proposes that all financial institutions – not merely the traditional banks – become subject to reserve requirements. He also suggests that central banks impose differential asset reserve requirements for all intermediaries as a way of encouraging the allocation of credit to more productive and socially useful investment projects. Finally, Schaberg proposes the implementation of a securities transaction excise tax for countries with active capital markets, which would raise transaction costs and thus discourage speculative financial trading.

As Gary Dymski and Dorene Isenberg show in "Housing finance in the age of globalization: from social housing to life-cycle risk," the provisioning of housing finance provides a striking example how politics and ideology, rather than purely market pressures emanating from globalization, can be the driving forces for change in national financial systems.

Dymski and Isenberg study the evolution through the post-World War II period in housing finance patterns in the U.S., U.K., France, and Germany. They show that there have been some significant common changes in housing finance in these four cases. But they argue that these changes have not resulted from market forces per se, especially since mortgage and other housing finance markets remain as relatively untraded financial assets. What has rather happened is that thinking has shifted in all the countries with respect to the consideration of housing as a social good.

In all the countries, market-based innovations have occurred in housing finance, including privatization and deregulation of the housing market and securitization of mortgage instruments. However, Dymski and Isenberg find, perhaps surprisingly, that governments have not reduced the extent of their overall subsidy to housing. Indeed, paradoxically, continued government subsidies for housing have been essential to the securitization of mortgage instruments. But the character of the government subsidy has shifted: from directly providing credit to consumers to subsidizing the private financing of mortgages.

According to Dymski and Isenberg, a major reason given for this shift in the nature of subsidies has been to increase the efficiency of the housing finance market. But Dymski and Isenberg argue that such thinking follows from a misguided understanding of the nature of efficiency in housing. They demonstrate this point by defining an important distinction between "financial efficiency" – referring to the net risks and benefits to financial intermediaries – and "life-cycle efficiency," which refers to the net benefits and risks facing households. The shift in policies in the four countries studied has indeed increased "financial efficiency," but it has worsened "life-cycle" efficiency by raising the risks of borrowing for most households. The net effect of financial innovation has therefore been to reduce access to housing finance for a significant share of the population, in particular less-affluent households.

Global labor markets and the environment

What is the effect of free trade policies on working people in the North and South? Labor-friendly economists have had a hard time grappling with this question. Part of the difficulty stems from the theoretical premises underlying this question. In an orthodox Heckscher-Ohlin model (devoid of market failures and increasing returns), the effects of trade integration between a Northern (high-wage) and Southern (low-wage) country are straightforward. Wages in the North will fall while those in the South will rise as markets in the two countries integrate. But the Heckscher-Ohlin model also finds that the overall impact for both countries is a gain in efficiency, so that even if Northern workers lose in wages, they can be compensated through the overall gain in national income resulting from increased efficiency. This is the logic behind orthodox economists' enthusiasm for free trade agreements such as the North American Free Trade Agreement (NAFTA).

The papers by Jim Stanford and Mehrene Larudee challenge many of the basic premises of this approach. In "Openness and equity: regulating labor market outcomes in a globalized economy," Stanford advances a thoroughgoing critique of the neo-classical advocacy of free trade in general and of NAFTA in particular. At a most basic level, Stanford criticizes the key neo-classical assumption that free labor markets will produce full employment at wages equal to the marginal product of workers. As embedded within the theory of comparative advantage, this theory then implies that changes in labor costs cannot affect the competitiveness of a country; they can only affect the *sectors* in which a country will have a comparative advantage.

Stanford draws on heterodox theories to explain why labor markets do not clear as a rule within a free-market setting. Demand deficiency is the traditional Keynesian explanation for involuntary unemployment. When an economy is demand constrained, trade integration will create unemployment when a country's labor costs are above those of its foreign competitors.

But economies face several constraints in addition to that for demand, so it does not necessarily follow that free trade will harm labor. In the spirit of agnosticism, Stanford proceeds from the idea that the effects of free trade on growth and income distribution can be decided only empirically in any given situation. He considers the case of Canada through a computable general equilibrium model that simulates the effects of NAFTA and the U.S–Canada Free Trade Agreement. Stanford finds that free trade agreements have directly driven down income for Canadian workers, but that the size of this effect is small. But Stanford also argues that the indirect effects of these agreements have been large, in particular through influencing the constraints on macroeconomic policy. Furthermore, Stanford contends that the free trade agreements have shifted the Canadian macroeconomy from being "wage led" to being "profit led." A "wage-led" macroeconomy implies that an exogenous increase in wages produces higher output, but wage increases in a "profit-led" economy will reduce output.

Stanford concludes by stressing that, even given its free trade agreements, Canadian policy makers can still positively influence output, employment, and income distribution, but that policy interventions need to be carefully designed in recognition of the new constraints imposed by trade openness. As one example, Stanford finds that policies to promote public and private productive investment will have broad positive effects on Canada's macroeconomic performance. This policy result is thus consistent with arguments in several other papers in the volume, including those by Patnaik and Chandrasekhar, Harris and Michie, and Pollin.

Mehrene Larudee's paper, "Integration and income distribution under the North American Free Trade Agreement," is a companion to that by Stanford in that she analyzes the effects of NAFTA on Mexico. If the Heckscher-Ohlin theory is correct, low-wage workers in Mexico should benefit from NAFTA. But Larudee concludes that Mexican workers have not yet benefited and that, simply through considering the full implications of Heckscher-Ohlin theory itself, we should not be so optimistic that they will benefit in the future.

Larudee recognizes that Mexico's financial crisis and deep recession following the December 1994 peso devaluation is the major reason why wages in Mexico have fallen dramatically since NAFTA took effect. The implementation of NAFTA in January 1995 was at least partially to blame for the crisis, even though the proximate cause of the crisis was financial speculation rather than anything emanating directly from the dynamics of freer trade per se. Still, the impact of Mexico's recession should dissipate after a few years, while the benefits of free trade within the Heckscher-Ohlin model are expected to fully emerge within a long-run growth framework. But Larudee argues that Mexican workers will not likely benefit from NAFTA even within such a long-run framework.

Larudee develops this perspective by showing that several key assumptions of the Heckscher-Ohlin model are likely to be violated within NAFTA. Most importantly, the model requires that the trading countries produce using the same set of technologies in their tradable sectors, and Larudee argues that this does not hold between Canada, the U.S., and Mexico. As a result, as trade opens up, domestic producers and transnationals in Mexico will adopt new labor-saving technologies, reducing demand for Mexican workers; maize farmers in Mexico will be especially hurt through such technological changes. In short, even though labor productivity in Mexico should rise due to technological changes associated with NAFTA, Larudee argues that the demand for labor will fall by a greater extent, meaning that Mexican wages will fall in turn. Larudee shows that the solution to this problem is to incorporate into NAFTA a stipulation that labor incomes will rise with productivity, and she suggests various specific proposals for accomplishing this.

In "Malthus redux? Globalization and the environment," Eban Goodstein examines the impact of globalized trade and investment on the environment, with a particular focus on how these issues play out in the United States. He argues that there are two principal channels through which globalization of trade and investment can negatively affect the environment. The first is when Northern countries protect their environment through exporting environmentally damaging production processes, i.e., seen from the other side, satisfying their demand for "dirty products" by importing them from the South. In addition, globalization may increase pressures for a leveling down of environmental standards to the extent that firms choose to locate where environmental regulations are most lax.

Goodstein shows that Northern consumption of timber, minerals, livestock, and agricultural products often come at the expense of the environment of Southern countries. Moreover, the share of dirty production processes located in the South has been rising since the early 1970s. At the same time, Northern imports of dirty products from the South have not been increasing, nor are Northern firms relocating their production sites to a significant degree to "pollution havens" in either the North or South.

Goodstein builds from these observations by studying the relationship in the U.S. between levels of environmental regulation in an industry and that industry's relative trade performance. Goodstein considers this question over two time periods, 1973–78 and 1979–85. He finds that, during the initial period, export performance did suffer when industries faced stricter environmental standards. However, this result is reversed in the second period. Indeed, over 1979–85, Goodstein finds that industries with more stringent regulations performed better in trade.

Goodstein concludes that neither trade nor globalization more generally necessarily entails a lowering of environmental standards. Globalization can even be seen as supportive of environmentalism to the extent that it creates broader markets for innovative clean technologies.

Migration

Concern over migration has created intense controversy and social tension in the United States and Western Europe, as large sectors of the population, and perhaps majorities, fear that rising immigration threatens living standards for native workers. Such conflicts are reflected in the perspectives of economists. As Bob Sutcliffe writes in his contribution, "Freedom to move in the age of globalization," "If we knew the views of an economist on nine subjects we could probably predict with great accuracy his or her opinion on almost any tenth. Almost – because the exception would be immigration."

Sutcliffe's paper frames the issue boldly with his argument that, as a matter of principle, international borders should be open. He acknowledges that this is a utopian perspective in the current environment. However, Sutcliffe argues that a clear policy approach flows from his principled position – first, that borders should be open to the maximum extent and, second, that the rights of immigrants in host countries should be broadened. Sutcliffe argues that the absence of principled perspectives in Western Europe has been a major factor poisoning attitudes toward migrants there.

Gregory DeFreitas' contribution focuses on the practical constraints on immigration in the United States and, in particular, the impact of the rise of immigration on U.S. labor markets and the public sector. He shows that, considering the post-World War II period as a whole, immigration has significantly increased in the United States over the 1980s and 1990s. What has been the effect of this increased immigration on wages and employment in the United States? DeFreitas surveys over a decade's worth of econometric research on this topic, including some of his own contributions. He finds that, even with the increased immigration rates in the 1980s and 1990s, current levels of immigration have had little or no net impact on natives' wages or employment opportunities. What explains this finding? DeFreitas contends that, first, immigration does not just expand the supply of labor, it also increases demand, through immigrants' expenditures and the multiplier effects of these on the economy. Immigrants also average higher self-employment rates, creating their own business demand for related business services and materials. In addition, many of the most recent immigrants are more complements than substitutes for native workers, since they take the harshest, low-status jobs that even low-wage natives tend to spurn. DeFreitas reports that comparable findings on immigration impacts have emerged from research on Western Europe.

Though DeFreitas does not find any consistent evidence that immigration has had sizable negative effects on U.S. wages or employment, he emphasizes that these results would not necessarily hold if the rate of immigration increased significantly above current levels. He therefore argues that immigration must necessarily be restricted, and that priorities be established on humanitarian, not economic, criteria.

"Notes on international migration suggested by the Indian experience," by Prabhat Patnaik and C.P. Chandrasekhar, focuses on the effects of emigration of less-skilled workers in developing economies. The authors find that, in this setting, emigration produces unequivocally beneficial effects for the sending country. To begin with, work opportunities increase both for the migrants and for those who stay behind. Migrants earn higher wages at their new location, while those who stay behind gain from the reduction in the local supply of labor.

In addition, the migrant workers' remittances often play a significant role in increasing welfare in developing economies. For example, Patnaik and Chandrasekhar argue that the widely celebrated achievements in Kerala, India in terms of social indices are due to the inflow of remittances to the region. Along with both Sutcliffe and DeFreitas, Patnaik and Chandrasekhar recognize that it is not practical for progressives in the advanced economies to support open borders. However, the authors stress that the severity of this practical constraint operates only as long as existing economic policy priorities prevail. For example, the movement of macroeconomic policies in the West toward sustainable full employment could serve to reduce the barriers to accepting more immigrants.

Macroeconomic policies

Does globalization place constraints on countries pursuing full employment policies or other egalitarian macroeconomic initiatives? This question is the focus of the four papers in this section of the volume.

The concept of NAIRU – the non-accelerating-inflation rate of unemployment – has had a formidable impact on macroeconomic theory and policy since it was first developed by Edmund Phelps and Milton Friedman in the late 1960s. In particular, the NAIRU concept has been important in establishing firm limits on the capacity of expansionary demand policies to alleviate unemployment and slow growth. In "The NAIRU: Is it a real constraint?" Dean Baker suggests that the NAIRU may be seriously misspecified, in that the relationship between unemployment and inflation may be asymmetrical depending on whether the economy is above or below its NAIRU. Baker develops this point from research done by Robert Eisner on the U.S. economy. In a series of econometric tests, Eisner found that, when the economy is above its NAIRU, the relationship between unemployment and inflation is as theory predicts: higher unemployment reduces inflationary pressures. But Eisner then finds that inflation does not necessarily accelerate when the economy is below its NAIRU. This could be due to the rise in productivity that typically occurs when unemployment is low, since firms will be trying to make full use of previously idle labor. Other factors may also contribute to this result.

Baker's paper examines whether Eisner's results are sustained when his approach is tested in the context of 11 other OECD economies. However, Baker's results produced little support for the idea that an asymmetric NAIRU relationship holds in these other economies. As Baker explains, this may be due in part to difficulties in obtaining adequate data on all the 11 OECD countries in question. More generally, though, Baker shows that the European OECD economies have had actual unemployment rates significantly above their estimated NAIRU rates. This makes it difficult to construct an adequate test for the symmetry of the NAIRU relationship. But the fact of unemployment rates persistently above NAIRU rates also means that, whether or not an asymmetric NAIRU relationship exists in these countries, there is still considerable room in the OECD for expansionary demand policies to reduce unemployment without generating accelerating inflation.

This conclusion by Baker invites the question as to why expansionary policies are not pursued in the OECD. Andrew Glyn addresses this issue in "Internal and external constraints on egalitarian policies." The "internal" influences are those that would operate regardless of any trend toward globalization. Within a European context, Glyn identifies these as: (1) a sluggish investment response to an initial government-induced demand expansion; (2) the rise of workers' bargaining power that would accompany the decline in employment, which in turn could squeeze profitability; (3) the rise of government debt that would accompany a deficit-financed expansion; (4) the opposition of financial markets to any program that could increase inflationary pressures; and (5) a broad rise in taxes that would follow from an expansionary program that sought to minimize the problems associated with budget deficits.

Glyn emphasizes that the problem of conflicting claims at full employment – the issue that Michal Kalecki had so powerfully illuminated in the early stages of the Keynesian revolution – is dominant. This is because the inability to moderate conflicting claims over an expanding national income is what will both produce the inflationary pressures that will cause financial market retribution and lead to sluggish investment response to an expansionary stimulus. The problem of conflicting claims will therefore also make the financing of an expansion, either through deficits or taxes, much more difficult.

Glyn then argues that there are "external" forces associated with global integration that increase the constraints on expansionary policy. The most fundamental problem is that international financial integration "has increased the speed at which, the drama with which, and the costs imposed when financial markets bring retribution on governments whose policies are not deemed credible." But even given this increased power of financial markets, the problem would not arise in the first place, according to Glyn, if distributional conflict within the domestic economies could be ameliorated.

South Africa is one country where the government does have the credibility and goodwill to pursue full employment policies. But as Laurence Harris and Jonathan Michie make clear in "The effects of globalization on policy formation in South Africa," the African National Congress (ANC) government has not departed dramatically from the policies of its predecessor governments. This despite the fact that, as of January 1997, poverty was pervasive and unemployment was still between 30 and 40 percent.

Harris and Michie consider to what extent external pressures – the forces of globalization – are responsible for the cautious policy initiatives of the ANC government. They argue that, for South Africa specifically and the world in general, globalization is occurring primarily within various regional blocs. It is therefore most useful to examine policy alternatives in terms of a "fractured globalization" process rather than a general framework of global integration.

South Africa is most closely tied to two regional blocs, one with the European Union and the other within Southern Africa. According to Harris and Michie, South African policy should be designed in ways that will most effectively integrate the country into these two regional blocs. However, this process need not bind South Africa to a strategy of seeking export competitiveness through lowering real wages. Rather, the authors argue that integration can be compatible with domestic objectives of accelerated growth with full employment and rising mass living standards. This is because, if growth is based on high value-added, high-productivity tradable products, competitive labor costs can be achieved with high real wages.

Harris and Michie contend that global financial markets, especially as these operate within South Africa's regional bloc, would not necessarily react negatively to such a public-sector-led growth program, since the markets are not concerned with the details of job creation policies. A program financed either by taxation or deficits with higher real interest rates need not have any significant impact on financial markets. A program financed to a significant degree by monetary expansion would push the nominal exchange rate lower. But Harris and Michie argue that South Africa may be able to afford this cost if the expansion leads to job creation and a crowding-in of private sector activity. Such a crowding-in would also ameliorate domestic supply constraints on growth.

Robert Pollin's article, "Can domestic expansionary policy succeed in a globally integrated environment?" considers more generally some of the questions raised by both Glyn and Harris and Michie. Pollin initially addresses the widely held view that the international constraints on expansionary policy mean that expansions cannot take place unless supportive international policies exist. International cooperation would undoubtedly create a far more supportive environment for such policies. However, creating a viable framework of international cooperation is a difficult and, in any case, long-term project. Thus, within the short to medium run, successful expansionary programs will have to be achieved primarily through domestic policy initiatives.

Pollin examines various techniques for implementing a short-term but sustainable expansionary program. That first entails addressing the problems associated with inflation. Pollin then considers the role of the output composition of expansion. An expansion can be led by private consumption, private investment, public consumption, or public investment. The relative weights given to these potential growth nodes is important, since the ability to minimize various constraints will depend on which sectors expand more rapidly.

Pollin then addresses an array of primarily financial questions. One is the relative merits of different sources of finance – a balanced-budget multiplier, deficit spending, or monetary expansion. He argues that each financing approach offers a different set of opportunities and constraints; the impact of a given expansionary impulse should thus vary considerably depending on the relative mix of these financing options. He then considers the implications of any expansionary strategy on a country's balance of payments and exchange rate. He argues that any type of expansion is likely to create balance-of-payments problems as well as pressures on the currency. He therefore proposes that countries pursuing expansionary policy be prepared to implement short-term safeguards, such as capital controls, that can be used to cushion the impact of most such situations. He finally considers how to construct domestic financial regulations that can create "circuit breakers" against the effects of speculative attacks against one's currency. The immediate aim of such policies would be to reduce the need for capital controls and similar initiatives. However, Pollin argues that financial regulations could also be used to channel credit toward activities that promote the broader employment and egalitarian growth agenda.

As should be clear by now, an enormous array of important issues are raised by the contributors to this volume. We believe that the volume advances understanding of globalization to a substantial extent. Among other contributions, the reader wending his or her way through the papers and comments should be able to identify important areas both where a broad consensus has been reached as well as areas of continued sharp controversy.

We are first of all in agreement that globalization is real. The extent of integration is certainly unprecedented for the post-World War II period of big government capitalism. No matter what else, this means that the increase in integration at least raises questions about the effective design and even the very viability of nationally based economic policies.

We also agree that considering globalization per se – independently of the institutionally and historically specific circumstances in which it is taking place – is not illuminating. We are most interested in the effects of globalization on employment, growth, income distribution, environmental sustainability, and democracy. What therefore is crucial about globalization is not any specific measure of integration or how advances in communications and transportation technologies have accelerated the pace of integration. What is rather central is that, throughout most of the world, integration is taking place within a neo-liberal policy framework of marketization, deregulation, and macroeconomic austerity.

Our contributors did not identify a sole reason for the ascendancy of this policy environment. However, there was broad agreement that the globalization of financial markets along with the creation of powerful rentier interests on the global stage have had major and for the most part detrimental impacts on economies in both the North and the South. Any progressive policy to deal with the problems created by globalization must address international financial capital mobility. The Asian economic crisis, which is ongoing as we write, has only brought greater urgency to this concern.

We also agreed that institutional reforms at the international and regional levels may greatly facilitate the creation and implementation of progressive policies. Nevertheless, implementing an egalitarian growth agenda must begin within a domestic policy framework, even as the constraints of globalization are fully recognized and addressed. If domestic governments are not willing and able to undertake progressive policies at home, they are likely to be thrown out of office before they have the chance to do so in the international arena. Waiting for international coordination to solve the problems created by globalization is like waiting for Godot.

What kinds of domestic policies can be most effective? Views differed on this question, but there was wide agreement that aggregate demand management policies can still be quite effective for a broad range of economies in raising average living standards and reducing unemployment. There was also broad accord on the viability of public investment as a growth node for aggregate demand expansion, as a means of overcoming a range of supply constraints as demand expands, and as a tool, more generally, for advancing a domestic policy agenda within a framework of global integration.

What are the major areas of continued controversy? First, disagreements remain with regard to the overall importance of international versus domestic factors in determining the high levels of unemployment, increasing inequality, and stagnation that characterize most of the world's economies. Second, and relatedly, there are differences in the assessment of the importance of multinational corporations in generating inequality, stagnation, and unemployment. Third, the desirability of trade protection, international labor and environmental standards, and controls on multinational corporations is still controversial. Fourth, differences remain concerning the desirability of adopting more outward-oriented versus inward-oriented development policies. Finally, we were not of one mind regarding the desirability of an open borders policy with regard to immigration.

Yet even where disagreements remain, we believe that the project has made substantial progress in clarifying the key issues and sources of controversy. We hope that you, the reader, will find the ring of truth in this highly favorable self-evaluation, and that this volume will serve as a useful instrument toward your own understanding of the new realities created by the contemporary global economy.

Part I

The IMF, the World Bank, and neo-liberalism

2

The revival of the liberal creed: the IMF, the World Bank, and inequality in a globalized economy

Ute Pieper and Lance Taylor

Half the people and two-thirds of the countries in the world lack full control over their own economic policy. Expatriate "experts" managed by industrial country nationals and based in Washington, D.C. regulate these countries' macroeconomics, investment projects, and social spending. The principles guiding these instructions from afar are even known as a "Washington consensus" (after Williamson 1989).

The foreigners who fly in with policy packages for developing and post-socialist countries staff two international agencies – the World Bank and the International Monetary Fund (IMF). Arguably, many actions that the IMF and the World Bank "recommend" to governments are intellectually ill founded and counterproductive in practice. However, their suggestions are heeded for several reasons. The two institutions are backed by the United States and other economic powers such as England and (less enthusiastically) Japan.

Their emissaries arrive in local capitals with substantial hard currency credit lines in hand – a strong incentive for the authorities to take their proposals to heart. Finally, the proposals are based on the "neo-liberal" or "market-friendly" brand of policy analysis that has become intellectually predominant over the past dozen years. In some cases – notably Mexico's since 1982 – local policy makers have been even more enthusiastic about neo-liberalism than are their friends from Washington.

Such "globalization" of economic policy is not entirely new. Argentina's transformation of its central bank in the 1990s into a "currency board" replicates ancient monetary customs of the British colonies, and the Princeton "money doctor" E.W. Kemmerer's missions of the 1920s closely resembled those of the IMF today. Beyond Kemmerer, dramatic shifts in economic and social policy during the 1980s go far toward re-creating the environment prior to the Great Depression; advocates of "neo-liberalism" say little unfamiliar from debates now many decades past.

Progressive critiques also exist. The great social scientist Karl Polanyi provided

Comments on previous versions by Gerry Helleiner, Inge Kaul, Arthur MacEwan, Stanley Please, Paul Streeten, anonymous referees, colleagues at the New School for Social Research, and participants at the Economic Policy Institute conference, "Globalization and Progressive Economic Policy," are all gratefully acknowledged. The Office of Development Studies of the United Nations Development Program and the Center for Economic Policy Analysis at the New School helped support our research.

one in *The Great Transformation*, ironically published in 1944, the year in which the World Bank and the IMF were founded: "Nowhere has liberal philosophy failed so conspicuously as in its understanding of the problem of change. Fired by an emotional faith in spontaneity, the common-sense attitude toward change was discarded in favor of a mystical readiness to accept the social consequences of economic improvement, whatever they might be" (Polanyi 1944, 33). In the 1920s "economic liberalism made a supreme bid to restore the self-regulation of the system by eliminating all interventionist policies which interfered with the freedom of markets" (p. 231).

The catastrophic sequels to this "bid" in the 1930s and 1940s exemplify Polanyi's grand theme that a fully liberalized market system is socially and politically impossible. "Self-regulating" markets cannot endure, particularly in the key areas of labor, finance, and international trade. Attempts at full deregulation give rise to unstable, speculative behavior or else to such concentrations of income and wealth that there is a social reaction leading to reimposition of the state's latent powers of market control. In Polanyi's phrase, there is a "double movement," first toward deregulation and then (as financial instabilities and social tensions mount) toward its reversal.

Polanyi's theories speak to the present debate on globalization under which national capacities to reconcile market and social contradictions are increasingly impaired by external economic and financial constraints. From the disaster of World War II emerged an international consensus for "economic collaboration of governments and the liberty to organize national life at will" (p. 254). The will to establish global coordination led to the formation of the World Bank and the IMF. Paradoxically, for developing countries these institutions today represent the intellectual backbone and political force behind the dismantling of the truly utopian ideas of the 1940s.

Globalization and the institutions

The charters of the World Bank and the IMF were written at a New Hampshire ski resort, which is why they are dubbed the "Bretton Woods institutions," or BWIs. Their histories after 1944 help show how they attained economic suzerainty over the Second and Third Worlds, why they adopted the policies they support, and why the policies often fail in practice.

The goal of the Bretton Woods conference was a well-ordered international economic system. There was general agreement that governments should play a central role in regulating both national and international economic systems; the theoretical basis had been provided in the 1930s in the intellectual revolution led by John Maynard Keynes.

This attitude was to reverse over the next decades. One reason was the apparent inability of social democratic/Keynesian policies in the industrialized countries to deliver sustained output growth and high employment after the post-World War II

"Golden Age" that ended around 1970. Thereafter, first transnational corporations (TNCs) and then international financial markets extended their domains, leading to increased pressures on poor economies to liberalize the current and capital accounts of their balances of payments, respectively.

The international economic environment also changed dramatically. Many small, poor countries (especially in sub-Saharan Africa) were hit hard by the oil shocks and a long-term downtrend in the primary commodity terms of trade beginning in the late 1970s. At first, middle-income countries benefited from recycled oil rents, which they borrowed at low or negative real interest rates in the 1970s. But they were soon adversely affected by the world interest rate hikes after 1979 (engineered for anti-inflationary purposes by central bankers in the industrialized countries and sustained by global capital market liberalization that encouraged financial investors to seek aggressively the higher bidders for their funds) and the debt crisis in 1982.

The outcome for both sets of countries was massive macroeconomic adjustment. In the wake of the debt crisis, for example, erstwhile borrowers were forced to switch from trade deficits of several percent of gross domestic product to surpluses of the same magnitude as "fresh money" ceased to come in while interest obligations mounted. An external shock approaching 10 percent of GDP is difficult to handle for any economy; inflationary, contractionary repercussions were observed worldwide.

Occam's razor notwithstanding, mainstream economists attributed these problems not to macroeconomics but to past policy "errors," including the pursuit of import-substituting industrialization (ISI), which was said to have distorted the price system so badly as to make the economy unmanageable. The increasing difficulties and final collapse of the Soviet system also meant that ideological backing for ISI, and "planning" more generally, along with political support for non-free market policies, faded away.

As the residual intellectual claimant, neo-liberalism took the center of the policy stage. It was directed there by the rich shareholders of the BWIs on the basis of their own new economic predilections along with the objective interests of both their TNCs, as they integrated their operations worldwide, and of their financial centers, as they invested in "emerging" markets. The staffs of the World Bank and the IMF helped create the new policy line and have been adjusting it gradually. Whether they would be willing to accept major changes, however, is a question postponed to the final sections of this paper.

The roles of the institutions

Basically because the United States chose not to foot the bills, the IMF as it emerged from Bretton Woods has always been too cash strapped to advance money for the long periods that many countries require for "soft landings" from big current account deficits. To make sure that borrowers could be constrained, "conditionality" attached to IMF loans became standard practice. Policy limitations and "performance targets" tied to credit lines advanced under "standby agreements" were universal by the 1960s. The fiscal and monetary details have scarcely changed since they were worked out by then-IMF Research Director Jacques Polak in 1957. Costs and benefits of Polak's "financial programming" techniques are assessed below.

In contrast to the IMF, the World Bank has changed its orientation several times. It was created to finance large public infrastructure projects, first in Europe and later in developing countries. In the 1970s, when Robert McNamara became its president, the Bank responded to Washington's spirit of the times by discovering that "trickle-down" from its investment projects was not benefiting the poor. Poverty alleviation became the Bank's conceptual focus and in effect a moral goal. Its loans were redirected toward investments that were supposed to help targeted poverty groups.

In the 1980s, this vision was superseded by an emphasis on "market-friendly" economic reform. Thinking among Bank staff began to focus on stimulating economic growth precisely to enhance trickle-down, because more directed antipoverty policies did not seem to be having much impact. The means toward the growth stimulation end took the form of neo-liberalism, in response to the ideological sea change represented by British Prime Minister Margaret Thatcher and U.S. Presidents Ronald Reagan and George Bush. The World Bank moved alongside the IMF into the business of providing balance-of-payments support to countries afflicted by the debt crisis and falling export prices, adding newly invented "structural adjustment loans" to its project credits.

These policy gyrations informed the Bank's contributions to the debate about economic development and growth. McNamara launched an eclectic research program. With Washington's ideological shift of the 1980s, however, its main thrust switched toward papers "demonstrating" that government interventions in the market slow economic growth and similar neo-liberal assertions.

This bias provoked reaction. For example, prodded by the Japanese delegation, which circulated a paper stating that the Anglo-American influence on its thinking was too strong, the World Bank reviewed the interventionist development strategies that Japan and its neighboring economies historically pursued. Contrary to Japan's apparent intentions, the resulting *East Asian Miracle* report (World Bank 1993) presents an interpretation of the role of the East Asian state that differs significantly from that of many scholars.

Although, as demonstrated by Wade (1995), the arguments are stretched, the gist is that East Asian governments "got the fundamentals right" by economywide, functional interventions such as providing ample public education and keeping the real exchange rate stable. Their selective actions such as aiding specific enterprises or undertaking sectoral interventions were allegedly counterproductive. In fact, Wade, Amsden (1989), and many others argue that both functional and selective policies played essential roles in supporting the region's rapid economic growth.

In a sense, the Bank's 1993 stand is more realistic than the extreme antistate rhetoric that it emitted in the 1980s. But the halfway position is still disquieting. Rewriting history is tempting for any bureaucracy, and the Bank's ability to affect the policy climate in developing countries makes the practice more than usually harmful. As Amsden (1994) observes, "What makes the Bank so powerful is that it has no real rival. The Bank has become a virtual monopoly, if not in its lending then in its research work." Disguising a multimillion-dollar ideological marketing operation as research has not been a heartening trend over the past dozen years for the World Bank.

The Washington consensus

This history shows that the Washington consensus is a phenomenon of a particular time and place. It amalgamates longstanding IMF macroeconomic stabilization policies, the World Bank's adoption of the market deregulation and supply side economics ideas in vogue in Washington early in the Reagan period, and London's zeal for privatizing public enterprises, which crossed the Atlantic a few years later.

As the *East Asian Miracle* episode illustrates, the consensus has evolved over time, often away from originally extreme positions. The essentials, however, have not changed. Synthesized in the 1980s to attack problems in poor countries that are longstanding and largely stem from their insertion in the international economic order, Washington's remedies have not been able to overcome these difficulties as they persist years later. To see why, we have to examine the strategy's details.

The first one is that there is an explicit division of labor in market-friendly packages. They try to assure economic "reform" with payoffs in the form of faster output growth and rising real incomes by first "stabilizing" the macroeconomy and then "adjusting" the market so that it can perform more efficiently. This sequencing reflects concerns of the BWIs dating from long before the Washington package was assembled.

The IMF contribution

Stabilization has always been the domain of the IMF. Unchanged over 40 years, its central policy prescription aims at reducing the trade deficit (especially the volume of imports) by cutting aggregate demand. Inflation may also be a target, but it is often less amenable to policy control. The most important components of IMF programs are fiscal and monetary austerity and exchange rate adjustment.

Fiscal and monetary austerity causes lower GDP growth, perhaps slower inflation, and almost always a reduction in imports. Typical policies include cuts in public spending, high interest rates, and credit restraints (especially for the public sector). "Financial programming" based on the country's balance-of-payments, fiscal, and monetary accounts is used to set "performance criteria" for indicators such as the permissible growth of the money supply and the proportion of the fiscal deficit to GDP. Polak's macroeconomic model presupposes that reducing the fiscal deficit automatically leads to a lower trade deficit with no effects on output. Such projections frequently turn out to be false.

The second component, exchange rate adjustment, raises complex issues.

The nominal exchange rate is a key "macro" price because it affects the economy through many channels. In developing countries, three are especially important. A trade deficit can be attacked by devaluing (or weakening) the local currency, which is supposed to make production for export more profitable and imports more expensive. Complications are that exports may not respond rapidly, and that devaluation drives up internal prices of traded goods, cutting purchasing power and aggregate demand. These inflationary, contractionary side effects are rarely mentioned in IMF country documents, but in practice can be politically disruptive enough to derail a program.

The impact of exchange rate adjustments on the price structure is the second channel. One implication is that lowering internal prices of internationally traded products by strengthening the exchange rate can help control inflation. Using a fixed exchange rate as a "nominal anchor" for inflation has been a key component of IMF-backed stabilization packages (especially in Latin America and Eastern Europe) since the 1970s.

A typical outcome in the case of Argentina is analyzed by Chisari, Fanelli, and Frenkel (1996). After stabilization in the early 1990s, the consumer price index (dominated by nontraded goods) increased by more than the nominal wage, which in turn increased by more than the wholesale price index (dominated by traded goods in an economy in which the current account of the balance of payments had been heavily liberalized). Hence, workers' real purchasing power declined at the same time as real labor costs for producers of traded goods went up. Both distributional conflict a la Polanyi and inadequate incentives are built directly into such a relative price regime. In Argentina the package has not (yet) collapsed, in part because Brazil, the country's main trading partner, saw its currency, the real, become even more overvalued than the peso in the wake of its 1994 inflation stabilization.

When controls on external trade and capital movements are relaxed (more details below), the exchange rate becomes an asset price to which foreign investors pay close attention when deciding whether to direct funds toward the economy concerned – this is the third channel. Rate movements either way can have violent repercussions in the thin capital markets of most poor economies, with potential adverse (or favorable) feedbacks into domestic interest rates and financial markets. In the case of real exchange appreciation, likely deterioration of the trade account means that steps have to be taken to secure capital inflows. One obvious move is to raise real internal interest rates, with consequent ill effects of investment demand and capital accumulation.

On the whole, IMF packages in small, poor countries tend to emphasize devaluation – the aim is to improve the trade balance through the mechanisms discussed above. Devaluation may also be undertaken to "reassure" investors when they begin to pull money out of the country. This maneuver is tricky, because it reduces the foreign currency value of the national assets that investors already hold but makes future acquisitions cost less. Sometimes it is effective – as in India in 1991 – and at other times a disaster – Mexico in 1994–95. The difference between the two cases may be that Wall Street suffered billions of dollars of capital losses because it had already invested heavily in Mexico before its economic authorities devalued.

Use of the exchange rate to fight inflation can also be a two-edged sword. Combined with its role as an asset price, the adverse trade and production effects of the exchange rate pegged as a nominal anchor can upset stabilization efforts. Especially when capital movements in and out of the economy have been decontrolled, a worsening trade balance under an appreciating (but nominally pegged) exchange rate can provoke capital flight leading to an unavoidable "maxi" devaluation and associated price jumps and output losses. From Latin America's Southern Cone in the late 1970s to Mexico in late 1994 and Argentina (again) in 1996, the IMF and the World Bank have repeatedly supported combinations of exchange rate appreciation and capital market liberalization that were doomed to fail. Was it because the financial communities of their main shareholders were pushing them in that direction?

Despite such anti-inflationary misadventures, the basic aim of most IMF packages is still to reduce trade and fiscal deficits to "sustainable" levels of a few percent of GDP. Such efforts may well make sense – an economy with large financial deficits on its external, government, or private sector accounts is skating on thin ice. In practice, however, the IMF moves fast and imposes several contractionary policies at once. The impact is often to slice imports by generating a recession – this familiar outcome is the reason why the IMF is accused of policy "overkill." Historically, the IMF's chief target has been to cut the trade gap, and its policy package hits that mark. Whether it reduces inflation (sometimes) or leads to renewed, equitable economic growth (rarely) are altogether different questions.

World Bank adjustments
The World Bank's specialty is "adjustment" aimed at raising GDP growth. Since around 1980, when it decided to fight poverty with market friendliness, the Bank's main thrust has been to improve the allocative efficiency of the price system. The basic idea is that removing price "distortions" will produce visible output gains, e.g., cutting "artificially high" real wages will induce companies to hire more workers, who will in turn make more goods. Such a negative correlation between wages and output is often not observed. Much more common is a positive correlation, with both variables going down. Like devaluation, wage cuts can reduce effective demand and lead to more income concentration; the political reactions can easily sink an adjustment program.

Attempts to improve resource allocation in Bank-sponsored adjustment packages include the following policy moves:

Foreign trade should be liberalized, beginning with replacement of import quotas by tariffs, and subsequent reduction of the tariffs and export subsidies. By driving internal relative prices toward world levels, these maneuvers are supposed to underwrite exports via cost reductions and efficiency gains, but there are few such cases on record (Helleiner 1995).

Simultaneously, or a bit later, barriers to external capital flows such as controls on foreign exchange transactions and profit remittances should be cut back to make it easier for external suppliers of funds to invest in the local economy. The fact that foreign money (some of it "hot") can move out as fast as it moves in has not been stressed by the BWIs until very recently.

A third target is deregulation or "derepression" of the home financial market. The aim is to equalize rates of return to different financial assets. The view in the 1980s was that raising interest rates that had been held down or "repressed" as a subsidy to borrowers would stimulate saving. Such a response proved impossible to detect empirically, and is no longer emphasized. Rather, the current Washington view is that positive real interest rates lead to better resource allocation along standard neo-classical lines.

There was also little discussion in the 1980s about the need for prudential money and capital market regulation in the form of careful audits by the authorities of the risk and performance of portfolios combined with sanctions on financial institutions in trouble. This omission is surprising, because liberalization packages that the agencies have supported have led to speculative booms and crashes all over the Second and Third Worlds (the Mexican crisis of 1994 and its Asian sequels in 1997 are only the most recent examples).

As Akyuz (1994) points out, simultaneously decontrolling two inherently volatile market systems – for external capital movements and internal financial instruments – is an explosive policy mix. The powder may be especially dry in the emerging stock markets that have been expanded by public enterprise privatization campaigns and an influx of portfolio investment from rich countries. The 1995 IMF report on *International Capital Markets* suggests that the BWIs are beginning to grasp this problem, but their learning curves even after the 1994 Mexican crisis have not been steep.

Fourth, there should be deregulation of labor markets and business decision making.

Fifth, taxes should be rationalized. In conditions such as those in sub-Saharan Africa, they may need to be raised to provide a financial base for badly needed civil service reforms. Despite Washington's rhetoric (but in practice in programs that the BWIs support), growth in such "success cases" as Ghana and Uganda has been driven by states, not private sectors, and has been accompanied by visible increases in the size of the government.

Sixth, privatization of public enterprises began to preoccupy the Bank in the late 1980s, as doctrines put into practice by British Conservative governments drifted westward. This effort is based on the idea that privately owned enterprises are intrinsically more efficient than firms owned by the state – a proposition that careful reviews of the evidence by scholars such as Chang and Singh (1993) fail to endorse. In practice, selling off state-owned firms often amounts to a fiscal stopgap to close budget deficits opened by rapid tax reductions. As noted above, the new shares in the hands of the public have served to launch not necessarily stable stock markets all around the world. The Bank enthusiastically supported this process.

Finally, by reducing state intervention and adding "transparency" to the economy, liberalization and privatization are supposed to reduce unproductive resource diversion due to corruption and seeking for "rents" or the returns garnered from a state-assured market position, e.g., the possession of an import quota. But as Boratav, Turel, and Yeldan (1996) observe, "...in most Third World countries the bourgeoisie itself is a creation of the state. This historical phenomenon has created cultural, sociological, and economic traits which do not disappear with changes in the policy model." They deduce that liberalization is not likely to do away with rents arising from advantageous positions of specific business groups, because "...the very process of rent-seeking emanates from the bourgeoisie, [and] not the state per se."

In countries undergoing adjustment, instead of disappearing under market-friendly policies, corruption has surged over recent years, spawned by export incentives, speculative urban finance, privatization and stock exchange operations, and fiscal incentives – the popular soap opera starring the family of former Mexican President Carlos Salinas is just the best-known example. Such social developments are beyond the ken of the Washington model, which cannot absorb the fact that rents and corruption often rise instead of declining when old forms of market regulation are suppressed. In most countries, these sins have not been absolved by notable accelerations of economic growth.

Country experiences with structural adjustment programs

What are the effects of market-friendly interventions, combined with macroeconomic shocks? Numerous scholars have jumped into this contested terrain, with conclusions that vary widely. One reason for the disagreement is that the methodologies they have utilized are not compatible. Broadly speaking, three assessment techniques are in regular use:

First, historically based, individual country analyses try to put the impacts of both macroeconomic shocks and policy initiatives into the context of the economy at hand. Examples range from simple "before and after" comparisons of purported policy effects to "thick descriptions" like the country papers collected in Taylor (1988, 1993, 1996), which serve as the basis for much of the following discussion.

Second, cross-country econometric studies try to make "adjusting versus nonadjusting" comparisons of the impacts of policies and shocks, sometimes attempting to use control groups or other statistical ploys. In assessing structural adjustment, econometric analysis tends not to be very robust (different authors extract contradictory results from similar or even identical data sets), largely because time series are short and economic data from developing countries are far from precise (for examples, see Taylor and Pieper 1996).

Finally, "counterfactual" explorations of the implications of pursuing alternative economic strategies can be pursued. These ask questions about how the economy "would have" behaved if historically observed policies or macro perturbations were replaced by something different. The problem is that any counterfactual result depends on a specific model of the economy at hand. Alternative causal schemes giving diametrically opposite results can be easily imposed on any given model's macroeconomic accounting framework; e.g., devaluation can raise or lower the level of output depending on whether it is assumed to be broadly supply or demand determined. Without a careful, essentially historical analysis of how a subject country functions macroeconomically, the counterfactual methodology is unconvincing. This defect has not prevented it from being generously applied to the case of sub-Saharan Africa, for which counterfactual defenses of Washington-style policies that don't seem to be working very well abound.

In using historical case studies to inquire about modes of structural change, one can pose two sorts of questions:

(1) Have "successful" developing economies relied on market-friendly economic policies?

(2) Where the Washington blend has been applied, has it generated economic "success?" Why or why not?

Answers to such queries are never clear cut in economics, because policy outcomes are strongly affected by historical contingencies and sociopolitical dislocations. Still, one can learn by applying these questions to country experiences. We begin with one to which both sets are relevant.

Chile

Chile is often cited as the No. 1 success case for liberal policy, on the basis of its rapid, export-led growth since the mid-1980s. However, its output surge was not solely due to orthodox stabilization attempts and market-friendly economic reforms that national policy makers as "owners" designed in close collaboration with the World Bank and IMF. Targeted industrial policies and ample access to foreign exchange at critical moments played their parts.

The first point to observe is that the country paid a high social price through a prolonged transition toward sustained growth under a very tough military government – General Pinochet took over in 1973. Despite their use of the best BWI medicines and generous official financial support, the general's economic teams did not contain inflation or curtail output losses for a dozen years, until exports took off.

Thus, even if Chile is taken as a testimonial for market friendliness, its history suggests that Washington's remedies do not work very fast. When it came, moreover, rapid export growth owed as much to state intervention as to market forces. Exports were led by copper mining, in which the government undertook massive public (not private) investment, and forestry products, fishmeal, and fruits. In all three latter commodity groups, industrial promotion policies over several decades in the form of production subsidies, enterprise reform, and technological upgrading laid the base for ultimate export success. Trade liberalization, a centerpiece of reform efforts, did not play much of a role in stimulating exports, although real wage reductions via currency devaluation early in the boom period certainly did.

Other historical factors were also favorable. Chile was hit less hard than its neighbors by the debt crisis. The state had good access to foreign exchange through its control of copper exports and was treated generously by the BWIs. In the crucial mid-1980s, for example, external finance permitted the economy to run trade deficits between 5 percent and 10 percent of GDP, and the export terms of trade rose by almost 40 percent later in the decade.

Despite (or perhaps because of) this good fortune, however, the economic authorities botched several opportunities to stop inflation. Price stability did not precede adjustment (and in fact rested on the latter), contrary to the preferred Washington chronology. It was ultimately based on wage repression to the benefit of cost reductions and the profits of commodity exporters. Earlier programs relying on austerity and external and internal market liberalization failed to brake the price spiral and instead provoked an output collapse in the mid-1970s and an import surge and an orgy of stock market speculation around 1980.

The speculation was abetted by "groups" of enterprises that formed when the government sold off firms nationalized by the previous Allende regime to its political allies at rock bottom prices, in one of the first privatization waves in the developing world. The stock market expanded in tandem, and group managers proceeded to borrow from banks under their control to bid up the prices of their own companies' shares – a now-classic example of insider manipulation that adequate financial regulation could have ruled out. The BWIs did not push for any such action, but did provide loans to help pick up the pieces of the financial system after it crashed.

The resulting bailout was a classic of its kind. The central bank issued interest-bearing liabilities to the tune of 35 percent of GDP to buy up assets of troubled financial institutions, over 40 percent of which were nonperforming. The World Bank then acquired a "big bond" of around 40 percent of GDP from the treasury, with the proceeds being used to service its new liabilities. The treasury in turn refinanced much of its big new obligation abroad, but in the final analysis Chilean taxpayers have to service the debt. Even after a decade of rapid growth, the payment flow amounts to a couple of percent of GDP.

Looking backward, Chileans in the upper income strata now say that their rapid output growth justified the dozen years they spent engaged in such maneuvers. But had they been able to look forward in 1973 with foreknowledge of the difficulties that reform would create, it is not so clear that they would have chosen the market-friendly path. Even after a decade of robust GDP expansion, real income levels for most households are not far above their levels of 1970, as an initially unequal income distribution became strikingly worse.

The summary answers to the questions posed above are that Chile's "success" was not wholly due to Washington policies, which in some ways prolonged and worsened the transition. (The economy suffered 15 percent output reductions in 1974 and 1982, in direct response to failed orthodox price stabilization attempts.) Chile did emerge from its travails as a vibrantly capitalist primary product exporter, combining strong public and private sector partnership in an environment of free market rhetoric – which does not fully describe the economy at hand.

Mexico

Since the debt crisis erupted in 1982, Mexico has been a laboratory for economic policy moves. Most of the experiments were orthodox and designed in collaboration with the BWIs, but there were heterodox elements as well. All were subject to historical contingency, with the main success being a heterodox anti-inflation program that took advantage of favorable initial conditions created by a previously orthodox phase. The great failure, of course, was the financial crisis of 1994, although it is fair to add other drawbacks, such as increased income concentration and stagnant economic growth.

The roots of the disaster of 1994 trace back to well before the debt crisis. In 1982 Mexico was faced with the problems unleashed by loan pushing on the part of commercial banks and the country's too-ready acceptance of foreign credits to undertake expansionary policies aimed at putting into concrete the jump in national wealth that the massive oil discoveries in the mid-1970s had brought about. At least during the 1970s growth was rapid, but more disquieting developments included real exchange appreciation under inflation rates that rose to 100% per year, capital flight, and a massive accumulation of external debt. Obscured by these fireworks, there were other questions pending – were the benefits of the ISI strategy that had been pursued for decades finally running out, and should the economy be opened to foreign trade and financial flows to some degree?

After the debt crisis broke in August 1982, Mexico was forced to transform an external current account deficit of about 5 percent of GDP to a 3 percent surplus to compensate for the loss of "fresh money" in the form of new loans the commercial banks had cut off. The economic team achieved the current account adjustment using the IMF's time-tested tools. They induced a recession by devaluing the peso and cutting the fiscal deficit and monetary emission. Such actions usually have stagflationary consequences, as they certainly did in Mexico – GDP growth averaged out at zero between 1982 and 1988, but by 1987 prices were rising 160 percent per year.

During the 1987–88 presidential transition, stagflation was attacked in two ways. One succeeded by breaking away from the Bretton Woods line. Despite IMF opposition, in 1987–88 an "Economic Solidarity Pact" aimed at stabilizing prices combined a wage freeze, a pegged nominal exchange rate, trade liberalization, and more austerity. This heterodox package did brake inflation, but at some cost. Real wages were reduced once again, and the $10 billion in foreign reserves built up after 1982 was spent on supporting the fixed exchange rate and bringing in imports. The output growth rate, however, did not improve.

The authorities tried to stimulate growth by resorting to extreme market friendliness, answering in the affirmative the questions posed above about the desirability of abolishing mercantilism and pursuing openness in foreign trade and finance. They privatized state-owned industries, further liberalized foreign trade by dismantling export subsidies and an import quota system that had been built up over decades, and removed restrictions on inflows of direct and portfolio investment. The push to sign the North American Free Trade Agreement was the capstone of all these efforts.

Revenues from privatization helped secure the strong fiscal position prior austerity had put in place. However, as of mid-decade, there had been neither striking improvements in efficiency on the part of the firms concerned, nor had newly vigorous entrepreneurs emerged at their helms. As in other countries such as Turkey and Russia, where a bureaucracy in charge of distributing rents was not replaced by new forms of market regulation under a newly "liberal" regime, large-scale corruption (at least to judge by the anecdotes) had markedly increased without creating any spillover into higher productivity or economic growth.

The macroeconomic outcomes of freeing external trade and financial flows were even less favorable, on at least seven counts:

First, foreign capital came in, letting the trade balance shift from a small surplus in 1988 to a deficit of about $20 billion in 1993; the current account deficit was around 6 percent of GDP in 1993 and 9 percent in 1994. Output growth rose to 4.4 percent in 1990, but tailed off thereafter. In the 1970s by contrast, Mexico combined external deficits of 5–6 percent of GDP with 6–7 percent GDP growth.

Second, the capital inflows were partly enticed by a Mexico/U.S. interest rate spread exceeding 10 percent (and an internal Mexican real interest rate of about 5 percent). Perhaps an even stronger incentive took the form of capital gains on the stock market, or *bolsa*. The share price index rose from around 250 in 1988–89 to over 2,500 early in 1994, but it then fluctuated erratically as unnerving political events and interest rate reductions of a few hundred basis points around midyear made Mexico a less attractive place to invest. Lustig and Ros (1993) suggest that the financial actors who determined movements of funds across the border were bulls (mainly foreign), bears (mainly Mexican), and "sheep" who followed in between to generate a teeter-totter market with multiple equilibria – a boom in the early 1990s, an unstable intermediate balance in 1994, and then a crash.

Third, while it lasted the external capital inflow had to enter the economy via the widening trade deficit already noted – there was no other channel. The deficit was engineered partly by a steadily appreciating real exchange rate and partly by trade liberalization. Measured pesos-to-dollars in Latin style, the real exchange rate in terms of both consumer and producer prices fell by about 45 percent between the mid-1980s and 1994, with most of the drop prior to 1991. One reason for depreciating the nominal rate more slowly than price growth was to restrain inflation, but Mexican authorities were also pushed toward a powerful peso by the outward-shifting supply curve in the foreign exchange market. Of course, in the midst of radical trade liberalization, allowing the peso to strengthen so markedly was a perilous policy to pursue.

Fourth, in contrast to external financial investment, real capital formation within Mexico did not rise much above 20 percent of GDP, despite increases in the early 1990s from the extremely depressed levels of the previous decade. From the side of demand, low domestic absorption was the basic cause of slow growth. Private investment was not robust for several reasons: real interest rates were high; profit margins of companies in the traded goods sector were held down in real terms by the strong peso; and public investment that historically had "crowded in" private projects was cut back as part of the liberalization/austerity program. For both consumption and investment spending, the import content shot up.

Fifth, the macroeconomic "story" is that investment fell back from historical levels, but private saving dropped even more – from roughly 15 percent to 5 percent of GDP in the 1990s, despite high interest rates. The resulting incremental increase in the private sector's financial deficit (or investment minus saving) was immediately reflected into a bigger "twin" trade deficit supported by the strong peso/high interest rate/trade liberalization policy mix already discussed. As in Chile before its financial crash early in the 1980s and Argentina and Brazil in the 1990s, somehow the allegedly beneficial effects of public sector thrift did not transmit themselves to private firms and households. Their thriftless saving shortfall had to be covered by the inflow of foreign funds.

Sixth, while the game lasted, foreign money did keep pouring in, blind to de-valuation risk. The foundation for this house of cards was an ever-increasing stock of external debt. It began to crumble when prices on the *bolsa* stopped rising after the first few months of 1994 while American interest rates continued to increase. The collapse came with Mexico's devaluation the Tuesday before Christmas.

Finally, one can argue that "mistakes" in policy such as reduced interest rates in anticipation of the September 1994 presidential election worsened the situation by deterring capital inflows. But the more important point is that the balance of international financial power strongly influenced the endgame. When inflows slowed, the Mexican authorities issued a new instrument – peso-denominated *tesobonos* that were indexed to the dollar/peso exchange rate. Asset-holders switched en masse from nonindexed government debt to the *tesobonos*, apparently on the belief that they could be cashed in for dollars freely. After the crisis hit in December, the U.S. Treasury/IMF bailout loans were made conditional on *tesobono* convertibility. An alternative (permitted under Article 6 of the IMF charter) would have been for Mexico to redeem *tesobonos* in pesos and impose controls to deter dollar flight. But that option was denied by Washington. The result was that *tesobono* holders on Wall Street were bailed out, while Mexico incurred tens of billions of dollars of additional debt to pay them off. The widely circulated assertion that *tesobonos* were *dollar*-denominated was a followup public relations move by the U.S. financial community to cover its players who had guessed wrong in increasing their Mexican exposure.

Such a public relations "spin" cloaks but does not erase the basic contradiction: by the early 1990s, Mexico had come as close as practical politics permits toward adopting a fully orthodox package of fiscal, monetary, and external adjustments. The fiscal account was in surplus, there was adequate monetary control (the central bank was just acting as a traditional lender of last resort in partially sterilizing speculative capital outflows throughout 1994), and barriers to external transactions had been removed. Yet the foreign account was heavily in deficit because private savings had collapsed and hot money was flowing in.

All that an orthodox stabilizer could try to do to overcome such problems would be to increase the fiscal surplus (cutting back aggregate demand still more, and thereby private incentives for capital formation and capacity growth), raise interest rates (drawing in more short-term external capital but amplifying macroeconomic pressures toward further recession, a stronger exchange rate, and a greater trade deficit), or depreciate the currency (dealing a capital loss to foreign investors and daring them to pull out – as they did in December). In effect, an "adjustment" or "structural" problem of excessively high import demand derailed the entire stabilization-cum-liberalization attempt.

Most Mexicans would be better off now had their government kept policy autonomy by not jumping into liberalization and used it to spur investment and support wages and jobs for people in the population's bottom 80 percent who lost real income steadily after 1982. A few simple but important lessons can be drawn from Mexico's experience.

One is that there is no instant policy to promote productive efficiency of firms, e.g., the failure of privatization and liberalization to bear fruit in Mexico. Indeed, as illustrated by South Korea's experience discussed below, all successful industrializations in the past were based on directed state intervention, a degree of mercantilist semiwithdrawal from the world system of relative prices, and some system of collaboration among the state, capital, and labor.

As already noted, rapid liberalization of either the current or capital side of the external accounts can provoke destabilizing reactions, e.g., the savings collapse in Mexico as the bourgeoisie opted for imported consumer goods, and the capital withdrawal when Wall Street saw its ever-increasing capital gains on the *bolsa* come to an inevitable halt. As will be seen, Korea also suffered from similar effects of liberalization in 1997.

All standard economic policy tools have complicated effects, e.g., devaluation can be inflationary and contractionary in the short run but necessary to sustain exports over the long haul. Moreover, the strength and direction of such effects is often extremely difficult to predict on the basis of historical experience.

Finally, large segments of the population can be left behind in attempted economic transitions, provoking political backlash. The roots of rebellion in Chiapas and elsewhere in Mexico are very deep, but recent events are not unrelated to the distributional changes provoked by the liberal policy stance of the 1980s. As of late 1997, orthodox hopes were pinned on an easing of social tensions to be induced by sustained export-led income growth spurred by the massive devaluation of 1994. It remains to be seen whether this expectation will amount to anything besides whistling past a graveyard.

Turkey

Through the late 1980s, Turkey was touted as an orthodox miracle. Now, in the wake of a financial crisis beginning in late 1993, it has become a prime example of the BWIs' neglect of the potentially destabilizing effects of the changes in the income distribution implicit in their programs. The miracle's reversal in less than a decade marked the rapid progress of a "double movement."

Exports shot up in the early 1980s after a fairly standard IMF-brokered stabilization that was supported by ample capital inflows responding to geopolitical factors. Moreover, the new economic team "owned" the package since its chief, Turgut Ozal, had spent years working around the BWIs. He cut real wages, peasants' incomes via adverse shifts in controlled agricultural prices, and government spending. The outcome was a sharp drop in domestic demand.

At the time, the saving grace was that Turkey had built up an industrial base over decades of statist, inward-oriented policies. With depressed internal markets, producers started to look for sales abroad. By happenstance, demand for the medium-tech manufactured goods that Turkey could supply soared in the region, thanks to the 1979 oil shock and then the Iran–Iraq war. Aided by currency depreciation and ample, targeted, and illiberal subsidies (up to one-third of the value of foreign sales), exports boomed and helped output to grow rapidly through the mid-1980s.

For several reasons, the miracle unraveled soon after. In the new economic environment, the provision of state support to enterprises was taken out of the hands of a relatively impartial bureaucracy and relocated in (by then) Prime Minister Ozal's office. Payoffs and "rents" were passed out politically, angering elements of the entrepreneurial class omitted from the largesse. As discussed earlier, corruption flourished in the newly market-friendly environment, contrary to all orthodox expectations.

More ominously, workers and peasants reacted against their income losses and forced massive wage increases and pro-agriculture price shifts in the late 1980s. Inflation took off, and the distributional framework for the miracle collapsed. The authorities responded by opening the economy to external financial inflows, many of them "hot," which paid for import-led demand and domestic speculative booms in 1992–93 (reminiscent of Chile's double booms 13 years before and concurrent events in Mexico).

The foreign money started to move out late in 1993, underscoring the foolhardiness of jointly liberalizing external and internal financial markets. Interest rates shot up to 15–20 percent in real terms per month, bankrupting financial houses and banks. A contractionary stabilization with the usual regressive consequences and large-scale financial bailouts followed in April. Probably the economy will not grow again for several years, in the dying gasp of the program of the 1980s. Despite favorable external circumstances and its incorporation of (sometimes) shrewd market interventions, in the final analysis a reform package actively supported by the BWIs disastrously failed.

Post-socialist Eastern Europe
Orthodox policy played a substantial role in worsening the macroeconomic disorder that now rules in Eastern Europe and the former Soviet Union, although it was underway well before Communism's political collapse. The local versions of Structural Adjustment Programs (SAPs), moreover, may long postpone the renewal of industrial growth (Amsden, Kochanowicz, and Taylor 1994).

During the late 1980s, the breakdown of socialist planning was associated with rising inflation rates and declining output levels in economies all across the region. These trends took a distinct turn for the worse when Western advisors helped local authorities apply Washington-style "global shock" stabilization and liberalization packages during the transition years of 1990–93.

The protracted or aborted BWI programs in Chile, Mexico, Turkey, and elsewhere were well known at the time. Nonetheless, the architects of reform promised that instantly liberalizing prices in global shocks would lead to rapid adjustment to a full-employment, inflation-free macroeconomic equilibria while the invisible hand would painlessly reshape preexisting industry along Western lines. As Kornai (1993) observes, no "...forecast of...serious recession [can] be found in the early theoretical writings to outline the program for the transition...."

In fact, many countries' real incomes and outputs fell between 20 percent and 40 percent of GDP over a couple of years, while price increases accelerated to triple-digit annual rates. Although inflations slowed into double digits and incomes stabilized outside the former USSR in 1992–93, output levels continued to decline or scarcely grew (the somewhat positive 1993–95 GDP growth rates in Poland and the Czech Republic are unique exceptions). Real incomes have yet to recover, poverty has risen sharply, and income distributions are becoming increasingly unequal.

The key problem with global shocks was their macroeconomics. Socialist economies had historically utilized administrative methods such as rations and queues instead of the price system to limit demand to available supply. A longstanding state preference for rapid capital accumulation and acquisition of goods by the military led to a "shortage economy" due to "soft budget constraints" for favored sectors, in a metaphor proposed by Kornai (1981). Consumers found their available supplies and budgets limited, leading to "repressed inflation" in the economic sphere.

When administrative restrictions in all markets were suddenly lifted in shock programs incorporating near-total price liberalization, demand surged above supply. Some new restraining mechanism had to appear. With inflation no longer held in check by controls, price jumps were the only possible outcome, e.g., the triple-digit inflation in Poland in 1990 and the many-fold price jumps in Russia in January 1992.

Mechanisms such as the "inflation tax" and "forced saving" kicked in to make demand plummet – when prices jump up, households and enterprises simply have less real purchasing power to spend (Taylor 1991). As a consequence, inflationary pressure abated. However, there was no natural mechanism to assure that real incomes would stop falling just at the level required to support demand at the full capacity level. Under macro policies aimed at wage restraint (certainly the case under post-socialism) and with increasingly structural inflation, demand continued its trajectory downward.

Inflation-induced real wealth and income losses were an essential aspect of this transition. Orthodox theory was blind to their inevitability because (as noted previously) it postulates inverse and not direct linkages between real wages and output. However, other factors were important as well. Traditional linkages among producers fell apart. This breakdown of previously planned commodity transactions reduced potential supply by squeezing intermediate inputs, forcing still more inflation to drive demand downward. On the demand side, high interest rates and other austerity measures led to a collapse of capital formation in economies that historically had been investment led.

Against this backdrop, prospects for sustained recovery are not bright. High interest burdens and low wages have deindustrialized large sectors of manufacturing. Wage cuts are not key to profitability in the mid-tech industries that grew under socialism – machinery and engineering products, chemicals, iron and steel, and even cotton spinning and weaving. Outdated technology and poor product quality, not excessive costs, make these branches suffer in international competition.

Aggressively marketed by the World Bank, the logic of shock therapy was to restructure worthy state-owned firms through privatization, not the credit subsidies and directed supports that have been used by all successful capitalist industrializing countries this century. Few foreigners have been willing to invest in Eastern Europe and the former USSR. The authorities have turned to domestic "voucher" privatization schemes instead. In the absence of injections of technology, skills, managerial know-how, and capital for restructuring, such cosmetic ownership changes will not reanimate potentially viable firms, as the collapse of the widely praised Czech voucher scheme in 1997 underlines. Technically advanced productive capacity will wither as Eastern Europe resumes its traditional role in the international division of labor – a poor cousin supplying labor and cheap, labor-intensive exports to the rest of the continent.

Finally, stagflation coupled with unregulated privatization attempts have worsened "financial fragility," in the phrase of Minsky (1986). Investment is flat, in most countries there is still little economic growth, and income distributions have grown more regressive. Under such circumstances, new wealth holders are tempted to look for big financial gains, since there is scant money to be made from simply producing commodities.

The speculative adventures of Chile, Mexico, and Turkey discussed above and similar episodes elsewhere (in Argentina, the Philippines, etc.) reflect such forces. In Eastern Europe, they have led thus far only to Ponzi games and pyramid schemes like the Caritas bubble in Rumania in late 1993 (multibillion dollar losses in an economy with at best a $40 billion GDP) and Russia's MMM affair a year later (in which millions of shareholders lost their wealth). As in the rest of the world, the designers of SAPs have been blind to such risks and have only recently begun to push for regulation of internal and external financial markets. If a Chile- or Mexico-scale financial crisis erupts in Russia, the implications for global political stability could be grave.

Sub-Saharan Africa

A few words should be added about the plight of sub-Saharan Africa, where only a handful of more than 40 economies have positive per capita income growth. The region has been under intensive BWI care now for more than a decade, with minimal returns even though many countries are receiving capital inflows on the order of 10 percent of GDP (not a large sum in absolute terms for a nation with, say, 5 million people at a per capita income of $300).

No one has a clear solution for Africa's weak economic performance. "Surplus extraction" from export agriculture to benefit urban-based industrialization was an important element of the region's development strategies after World War II (Jamal 1993). Although there were substantial internal resource transfers, several factors supervened to make the strategy unsuccessful.

Externally, trends in the export terms of trade for the food, beverage, fiber, and mineral exports it produces were consistently unfavorable. Internally, lack of investment in infrastructure and technological improvement hampered agricultural output growth, while industrial strategies did not bear fruit. More recently, there have been continuing adverse shifts in the terms of trade, escalating interest obligations on its external debt, and donor proliferation. As described by Killick (1993) "...the volume of work in servicing...negotiations [with donors] is colossal. The potential opportunity costs are hence large, especially since the brunt of the work is often borne by the same small group of key economics officials who would be best qualified to advise the government on economic policy if only they had the time."

Beyond excessive cross-conditionality and imposition of negotiation burdens, the Washington approach to policy creates other problems. First, if neo-liberal policies take an extended period of time to work in places like Chile and fall apart in Mexico and Turkey, what is their promise for Africa? At the moment, African "success" cases like Ghana are basically being held afloat for demonstration purposes by continuing aid inflows. They finance intermediate imports to support selected investment projects and keep production going. Needless to say, these incoming loans are piling up substantial interest obligations for the future; in other words, a repayments crisis for official debt is beginning to loom, while private investment flows remain at levels of a few percent of GDP. World Bank initiatives in 1995–96 to roll over or "forgive" the bulk of this debt are more than welcome.

Second, until recently when it cut back on loans for additional production of tropical beverage crops, the Bank pushed all African countries to expand their primary product exports, even though an enhanced global supply of such commodities is bound to drive down their prices. Failing to recognize this "fallacy of composition" – a staple of elementary economics courses – is another example of how the BWIs can be slow learners. An easy thing for them to do would be to put resources into schemes via which collaborating national commodity producers could regulate and restrain supply to stabilize primary commodity prices at "reasonable" levels, although their liberal principles may preclude it.

Finally, as we will see in discussing South Korea, concerted state intervention in that economy was an essential part of its development strategy. Such an approach might well be inappropriate in Africa, for a variety of reasons. However, the degree of Bretton Woods control in the region is so great that no nation would be permitted to attempt the Korean model, even if a democratically chosen national leadership wanted to try it.

South Korea
One conclusion from these vignettes is that when SAPs put an economy on a path of sustained output growth (as they finally did in Chile), they do so thanks to contingent events and a dose of nonorthodoxy. By creating conflicts (at least latently and sometimes actively) and financial speculation as opposed to real investment, they run a strong risk of failing, as in Mexico and Turkey, while the Eastern European experience demonstrates that rapid market liberalization can lead to medium-term stagflation as opposed to growth. In all cases, high interest rates to lure in foreign capital and a strong exchange rate to facilitate a trade deficit to accommodate the capital inflows make the prospects for investment-led expansion that much worse, and financial fragility is an ever-present danger.

Morals for alternative approaches to policy can be drawn from these observations. Before turning to them, however, it makes sense to address our first question above – have successful developing economies generally adopted the Washington model? In one important case – that of South Korea – the answer is clearly no (Amsden 1989; Chang 1993).

Korea's development strategy was consistent over several decades, emphasizing capital formation and technology acquisition to build production capacity. It did incorporate such orthodox recommendations as prudent fiscal policy and a stable, not overly strong real exchange rate. However (contrary to the interpretation in the World Bank's *East Asian Miracle* report) these "functional" policies were aggressively combined with "selective" actions to protect the domestic market, hold down consumption, and target credits via a nationalized banking system toward production sectors deemed "priority" at any time.

The state also intervened to support investment demand to mobilize the saving that its tight fiscal policies and consumption restraint created. Inflation was kept in check by targeted wage and price controls. Finally, distributional equity was maintained by devices such as farm subsidies supported by tariff barriers and consistent passthroughs (at rates greater than zero but well less than 100 percent) of productivity gains into real wage increases.

Industrial strategy was pursued on several fronts. A theme continually developed in official documents was that "the market mechanism cannot be entirely trusted to increase competitive advantage by industries," so that branches likely to enjoy high productivity growth or income-elastic demand were to be promoted as "promising strategic industries" (Chang 1993). They were given custom-designed financial, technical, and administrative support.

Corrective feedback to the selection process was provided by ongoing, broad reporting of activities of "priority" firms to the government. The economic bureaucracy thus had access to detailed business information, which proved essential for effective industrial policy. It used its acquired knowledge to weed out inefficient production operations in successive waves of rationalizations, mergers, and liquidations. Individual conglomerate firms (the famous *chaebols*) were clearly subject to discipline, even though as a group they had privileged access to state resources. Noise and static in dealings between the state and producers were reduced by the fact that large, centralized organizations were engaged on both sides of the dialog.

Second, intense effort was devoted to acquiring technology (a huge public investment in education was economically mobilized exactly in this fashion). Direct foreign investment was strictly regulated while foreign technologies were banned in sectors in which domestic counterparts were available. Firms were pushed into reverse engineering, along with licensing and purchase of technologies not available at home – all under bureaucratic guidance.

Third, there was a constant emphasis on attaining economies of scale. This goal was reflected in many small-firm mergers initiated by the government, e.g., in the chemical, automobile, fertilizer, and other sectors. Entry and capacity expansion were regulated to curtail "excessive competition" in the form of big swings in investment and price wars in industries with decreasing costs.

Fourth, within the generally expansionary macroeconomic environment, credit allocation was aggressively practiced (aided by tight foreign exchange restrictions). "Policy loans" with subsidized interest rates and/or priority rationing accounted for over half of the loans granted by the state-controlled banking system in the 1960s and 1970s.

These features of Korean industrial planning suggest several conclusions relevant elsewhere. One is that there can be a bargaining solution among the state and enterprises to restrain rent seeking, with rapid output growth and the government's power to punish recalcitrants in the background. Rents were certainly created for the *chaebols* by their privileged position, yet they became production powerhouses and not leeches thriving on public largesse.

The economic bureaucracy was an essential Korean player. In contrast to BWI staff members flying in, in Polanyi's fashion it was "embedded" in the society (Evans 1995). It could act autonomously for the public good as it saw fit, without completely being taken over by patronage and rent seeking. Planners often sacrificed short-term allocative efficiency ("getting prices right" along Washingtonian lines) to attain long-term productive efficiency or rapid productivity growth.

Finally, the institutional basis for the Korean miracle was invented over a relatively short time. *Chaebols*, trading companies, the planning bureaucracy, and the macroeconomic policy mix all emerged in the early 1960s in a creative burst. Obviously, such institutions cannot be transferred without modification to other national contexts, but partial functional equivalents could prove relevant elsewhere.

The Korean crisis of 1997

Given its successful production system, why then was South Korea hit by a huge external shock in late 1997? The answers will be hotly debated for years, but Chang (1997) argues that they may well center around a badly designed attempt at liberalization. His analysis goes as follows:

Korea's "fundamentals" in 1997 were far sounder than Mexico's three years before. The won was overly strong, but even so the current account deficit was only about 3 percent of GDP. Furthermore, most foreign loans were financing investments in export sectors rather than speculative asset positions and imports of consumer goods, as was the case in Mexico. The Korean budget was largely in balance, and gross public debt amounted to only 3 percent of GDP. There was little significant inflationary pressure. The main substantive change from the past was government emphasis on "deregulation," undertaken in part from intellectual conviction but also in response to international (especially American) pressure.

In one key area, the government abandoned its traditional role of coordinating investments in large-scale industries to avoid "excess competition." It allowed excess capacity to emerge in sectors such as automobiles, shipbuilding, steel, petrochemicals, and semiconductors, which eventually led to a fall in export prices and a runup of nonperforming loans.

Second, in the name of financial liberalization, the government failed to monitor foreign borrowing activities, especially by inexperienced merchant banks. This resulted in a rapid buildup of $150 billion of external debt, with 60 percent of the obligations having less than one year to maturity and over 25 percent maturing in 90 days. The major similarity with the Mexican crisis lies here – the private sector acted in destabilizing fashion while the government had its fiscal house in order.

Third, the authorities were sold on the ideas that inflation control was the most important objective of macro policy and that the exchange rate should be the principal anchor. The predictable real appreciation damaged export performance.

Finally, the government committed "mistakes" and suffered a run of bad luck as its economic troubles worsened. It dithered over the fate of the third-largest car manufacturer, Kia, unnecessarily undermining confidence. As the crisis grew, it wasted $10 billion (more than one-third of foreign reserves) trying to defend an indefensible exchange rate, exacerbating the foreign exchange shortage. External events also came into play. Southeast Asia's doldrums reduced demand for Korean exports and dealt a blow to financial companies that had been speculating in that region's capital markets. The entrance of new Taiwanese semiconductor manufacturers drove down the prices of memory chips, which accounted for nearly 20 percent of Korean exports when their prices were high. But the main problem was a failure of oversight by a government priding itself on deregulation.

The IMF package the Koreans were forced to accept at year end came with the usual fetters. Its contractionary bias made the credit crunch that firms were already facing even worse, leading to a chain of bankruptcies and possibly driving the economy toward depression. In the previous crises, such as the one from external bank debt in 1982, the Koreans had actually expanded credit. The IMF's 5 percent inflation target was already too strict, given that the economy had to deal with a big rise in import prices due to devaluation; with the excess liquidity released by financial sector bailouts and further depreciation likely, 5 percent inflation looked unattainable. Consequently, in a common problem with IMF packages, nominally set fiscal targets would become tighter in real terms than had originally been foreseen.

More worrying than the contractionary bias of the program was the IMF's insistence on financial liberalization. Bad debt abounded, and it needed to be cleaned up along Chile's early 1980s lines before the banks could be granted more freedom. The IMF also wanted a quick opening of financial markets to foreign participation, potentially exposing the economy to high volatility and the enterprise sector to politically risky external takeovers. Washington's Christmas Eve bailout package protected (among others) U.S. banks that had been lending to Korea at the cost of an increased debt burden for the nation, but that's a familiar story.

Together with a sharp expected increase in unemployment over 1998, these developments were leading to widespread talk of national humiliation and foreign trusteeship. One possible outcome is that the IMF program will be met by massive social resistance. As this chapter was being written, Korea's economic and political future was in jeopardy, largely because of a misguided attempt to restructure its economic system along neo-liberal lines. The problem that its newly elected government faced was how to circumvent the IMF and reinvigorate the coordinating and regulatory mechanisms of previous regimes without their negative features such as corruption, nepotism, and growing bureaucratic rigidity. Meanwhile, it had to keep the private sector's tendencies toward cut-throat competition and destabilizing financial behavior under control. In a globalized economy, more than just their own country's fate may ride on how successful the Korean authorities turn out to be.

Policy outcomes and the distribution matrix

The example of Korea shows that the state can effectively intervene in the economy – at least until it abandons its previous principles. The examples discussed earlier suggest that an attempt by the authorities just to stabilize, liberalize, and privatize so that all economic decisions will be taken by the market can backfire for reasons not just confined to the sphere of economics. The more unfavorable consequences include the following:

Contractionary, possibly inflationary impacts of stabilization efforts, which can hold down output growth rates for extended periods of time – overkill, so to speak.

Badly unbalanced relative price structures, especially in the wake of exchange-rate-anchored attempts at stabilizing inflation coupled with external liberalization: high domestic interest rates, overvalued exchange rates, reductions in the purchasing power of the real wage combined with labor cost increases in the traded goods sector.

Financial instability, often centered around stock markets that have been created to accompany public enterprise privatization. This fragility is exacerbated by violent movements of external capital in and out of the local economy via a liberalized capital account.

Visibly increased corruption, even though liberalizations are supposed to abolish rents arising from state intervention and associated rent seeking.

Rising unemployment and regressive income redistribution and deeper poverty, which in some cases have provoked political reactions strong enough to derail BWI adjustment packages completely.

All of these are problems that market friendliness is supposed to overcome. In their presence, what sorts of political coalitions are likely to back economic reform? In Chile, Mexico, Turkey, Eastern Europe, and elsewhere, a Washington-style policy mix has been supported by the Bretton Woods institutions and other foreign actors, industrialists in a position to gain from liberalization and an export push (by no means comprising the total of national firms), financial speculators, households in the top 10–20 percent of the income distribution who can afford an ample array of new consumer goods in a liberalized trade regime, and a local economic technocracy that put the new policy packages in place.

The losers included people in the bottom 80 percent of the distribution, some important industrialists, and old political elites. When all the problems just mentioned began to rear their heads, the reform coalition came under pressure. Observed political outcomes have differed according to circumstance, and surely will change over time. It is safe to say that the political economy of all reforming countries remains highly uncertain, especially when mounting social tensions are brought into the discussion.

Reforming the institutions

What can the foregoing institutional and country descriptions tell us about prospects for reforming the BWIs? As has been observed, there have been recent improvements in the policy stance: recognition of the importance of at least functional public interventions and the need to provide supporting revenues; growing but still inadequate realization that controls on external capital movements and prudential regulation can help contain financial fragility; abandonment of the doctrine that raising the local interest rate will stimulate saving and thereby growth; initiatives to roll over or forgive the bulk of official debt owed by the poorest economies. Whether there will be further steps toward policies truly supporting economic development will depend on political and ideological conjunctures.

The major shareholders of the World Bank and IMF are the nations making up the G-7 (or more to the point, the G-3 or the G-1, comprising the United States only). Their management of the institutions demonstrates that they are committed to the principle of conditionality; hence it will remain. This is one "given" that has to be accepted in considering ways to improve the performance of the BWIs. History also strongly suggests that the agencies will not be granted large increments in their resources relative to the size of the world economy. As will be noted, however, it would make sense to extend their financial base selectively in certain directions.

Perhaps less securely given is the present trend toward globalization of financial markets, which among other developments underwrites the huge capital flows that have gone to Turkey, Mexico, economies in Asia, and elsewhere. Along "double movement" lines, a serious question arises as to whether private capital markets can be counted on to supply finance to developing countries reliably in the long run. Kindleberger (1985) pointed out that there have historically been 20- to 40-year cycles in lending from rich nations to poor colonies or countries. In this century, there were flows of bond finance to Latin America in the 1920s and the bank loans of the 1970s that led to the debt crisis. Now fresh money takes the forms of direct foreign investment and portfolio allocations by mutual funds. In all previous cases, there was a wave of "loan pushing" followed by "revulsion," as the market turned soft.

Of course, this past pattern need not recur – whether Mexico 1994 and Asia 1997 are precursors of greater financial turmoil or just aberrations remains to be seen. But there is at least some chance that developing and post-socialist economies will face a wave of revulsion over the next few years. If it occurs, then the Bretton Woods institutions will be virtually the only sources that they can tap for credit in hard currency. Specifically, the Bank could enhance its role as an intermediary between developing country borrowers and global capital markets. The IMF could dust off its long-underutilized machinery for creating special drawing rights (SDRs) to the benefit of debtor countries, a proposal frequently mooted but never addressed seriously over the past 25 years. More radically, one could think of means for "disciplining" economies with chronic trade surpluses, even though such notions were dropped from serious policy discussion even longer ago.

Another not-so-given may be the ideological underpinnings of the Washington consensus – a piece of patchwork with straining seams in the best of cases. The IMF will presumably hew to its demand-limitation package, which does improve a country's external position once it gets into trouble. But after the IMF applies its performance criteria and conditionalities, will it and the Bank relax their insistence on neo-liberal verities that often don't seem to apply? Can the two institutions be pushed in new directions?

Such changes are more plausible for the World Bank. Its governance runs from the top – the president has great reserved powers and, if he or she does not wield them, then activist vice presidents can. The IMF is more hermetic and staff driven, and its policy focus far narrower. Even so, when it has had more resources on hand, conditionality has been correspondingly less draconian.

Beyond the institutions, forecasting politico-ideological trends is an even less exact science than economics, but perhaps some leeway will emerge. The background is that over five decades, the rich countries have pushed consistently for increased integration of poor countries into the world economy, for reasons discussed above. In the earlier decades there was more tolerance for planning and "developmentalist" states like those in Japan and South Korea, but neo-liberalism is the recent trend. Conceivably, the range of acceptable policy behaviors could swing back to include more *dirigisme*, especially if market-friendly packages continue their unexpected delivery of slow per capita income growth (true believers, both inside and outside the BWIs, really thought that the outcomes would be different). If the ideological (and, to a degree, the rich country interest) constraints are relaxed, there are obvious modifications to the Washington package that could be implemented; many have been suggested by developing country economists (for example, in the papers collected in UNCTAD 1994a):

First, there could be much less conditionality – less nitpicking by the IMF and a full-scale withdrawal by the World Bank from micromanagement of investment projects and price formation via its policy matrixes. Certainly in Latin America and Asia and increasingly in Africa, country economic teams are better qualified technically than the lower rung Ph.D.s from American and European universities to whom the BWIs entrust their missions. Local economists can run through financial programming and the Bank's standard macroeconomic model (known as the "revised minimum standard model" or RMSM) as well as or better than the people from Washington can; they also know how to do investment project analysis. They should be given a chance to apply their knowledge of their own economies to the fullest extent.

Indeed, it might make sense to institute "reverse conditionality" in which countries would propose economic programs to the BWIs, instead of the other way around. Disagreements between BWI staff assessments and those of the country concerned could be resolved directly, or conceivably via mediation or arbitration by management or third parties (teams of independent economists with experience in developing countries have been proposed for the latter function). The scope of macro conditionality could also be restricted, for example, just to a balance-of-payments target, while the country could pursue its own agenda regarding inflation, income distribution, and growth.

Second, BWI resources could be extended and redeployed toward their original intent of supporting countries in difficulty with the external account. Specifically, efforts could be devoted to providing long-term and cheap (in terms both of the interest rate and degree of conditionality) finance to countries exporting raw materials and widely traded agricultural products, in Africa and elsewhere. A tax or voluntary contribution along the lines of the "Okita plan" for recycling Japanese trade surpluses (Okita et al. 1986) could usefully be deployed to such ends.

Given their downward international price trends since the 1970s, trade specialization in primary products appears to be a dead-end street for countries lacking the endowments necessary to produce a diversified and widely demanded primary product mix (as do Malaysia, Chile, and Brazil). But that does not mean the street is easy to back out of. Financial and technical opportunities for export diversification should be provided, if only because rich countries forced their trade specializations on many poor countries in the past, and they benefit from their continuing enslavement to low commodity prices. The Third and Second Worlds would also benefit greatly if steps were taken to restructure the commercial debt overhang from the 1970s, once and for all. With regard to debt from official sources (mostly owed by very poor countries), the recent writedown proposals originating from the World Bank are a development full of hope.

Third, over the past couple of decades the BWIs deserve credit for making countries aware of the dangers of fiscal imprudence and the benefits to be gained from alleviating balance-of-payments restrictions by aggressively pushing exports (ideally not of primary products). They have pointed out that growth may be retarded if prices such as the agricultural terms of trade and real exchange and interest rates are extremely distorted. At the micro level, they have aided enterprise reform.

All these are positive steps, but they have to be offset against the institutions' errors as cataloged above. Spokespersons from the World Bank and IMF claim that they have "learned" from their mistakes. Within their hierarchical, structured bureaucracies, many staff members do push for changes in the institutions' neo-liberal policy stance, at times putting their own careers at risk. However, there is a fundamental contradiction in the way that the BWIs respond to their errors. They don't pay the costs.

A staff member flying business class back to Washington in a chastened frame of mind represents one sort of personal response to a market liberalization attempt which collapsed; a local health worker trying to help malnourished infants recover from the effects of a drastically lower national income is quite another. In the between-World Wars "calculation debate" about the merits of central planning, von Mises (1935), a patron saint of neo-liberals, criticized socialism on the grounds that "as if" planners could never improve upon capitalism because they would just "play" a market game without being disciplined for their mistakes. The same doubts apply to Washington-based bureaucrats "playing" at running national economies with their attention focused on career advancement in the institutions back in the United States.

With regard to research and the intellectual debate more generally, creation of alternative centers of thought about developing and post-socialist economies is essential to break the Washington near-monopoly. Relatively isolated university and United Nations researchers cannot match the Bretton Woods' big battalions, not to mention their access to centers of power and the media. A well-managed United Nations-wide research effort could help redress the balance. Given the diversified and underfunded nature of the U.N., however, such an initiative would have to be paid for and aggressively pushed from the top. Since the days of Dag Hammarskjold, secretaries-general (and their bosses in G-3 governments) have been unwilling to undertake such a task.

Finally, there is a lot to be said for decentralization. BWI staff are grossly over-paid in comparison to their counterparts in developing countries and earn more than Ivy League professors. When on missions they interact with each other more than with the economists of the country they happen to be visiting, and they communicate virtually only among themselves in the office.

Why not use the BWIs' huge salary base to send one or two thousand professionals from each institution to work at the country level, earning generous local wages while undertaking relevant research and participating on equal terms in national policy debates? The benefits from intellectual stimulation and cross-fertilization of ideas could be enormous in comparison to bureaucratic self-absorption in Washington, D.C.

Comment by Arthur MacEwan on
"The revival of the liberal creed: the IMF, the World Bank, and inequality in a globalized economy"

Considering the logic of World Bank and IMF policy makers, one wonders how long it will be until they require that countries receiving their largess abolish laws against slavery. Clearly such social interference with the market reduces efficiency. Consider, for example, the lack of investment in training in many poor countries. If employers could own their workers and thus be sure of attaining the full returns from their training expenditures, surely they would invest more in training programs.

A similar logic, after all, has guided neo-liberal thinking about the environment and land use. In the case of the environment, dumping hazardous waste in poor countries is justified by the low economic value of life and by the claim that a clean environment is a luxury good. With land, from Mexico to Papua New Guinea, Bretton Woods thinking demands that systems of communal land holding give way to private individual plots; this commodification of nature is then supposed to generate economic efficiency and growth.

Argument by *reductio ad absurdum* is seldom fair, but it does help here to make a point. If the generators of ideology at the World Bank and the IMF will not recognize that their advice on the environment, land, and the general role of markets must be viewed in the context of larger social values and social arrangements, perhaps the specter of slavery will at least make them squirm in their seats – if not revise their policy prescriptions.

One of the many merits of the paper by Ute Pieper and Lance Taylor is that it raises this issue of the relation between markets and other aspects of social relations. Using Polanyi's critique, Pieper and Taylor point out not only that market outcomes often conflict with other valuable social institutions. In addition, they emphasize that markets function effectively – even in the narrow terms of output expansion – only when they are "embedded" in society.

Efforts of the Bank and the IMF are designed to make the world safe for markets. They seek to spread and create *market systems*. As Polanyi observed:

> Ultimately...the control of an economic system by the market is of overwhelming consequence to the whole organization of society: it means no less than the running of society as an adjunct to the market. Instead of economy being embedded in social relations, social relations are embedded in the economic system (Polanyi 1944, 57).

Pieper and Taylor do an especially good job of demonstrating the impact of these efforts to make society an "adjunct to the market."

The world's experience with poverty and income distribution in recent decades provides the context for Pieper and Taylor's examination of neo-liberalism and the

role of the Bretton Woods Institutions. On the grandest level, the worldwide distribution of income among countries has become more and more unequal, and within
many countries the trend has been decidedly toward greater inequality. This experience leaves one with little confidence that the Bretton Woods institutions are moving the world in positive directions.

Things have not worsened everywhere; indeed, by an absolute poverty measure,
the proportion of the world's people that is poor has probably fallen over the last
two decades, though the absolute number in poverty has increased. Yet as a broad
generalization the greatest deterioration has taken place in regions where neo-liberalism has been most powerful, especially Latin America, while the more positive
developments have characterized regions where neo-liberalism has had less impact,
especially East Asia.

The thrust of Pieper and Taylor's analysis is that if we continue to leave the
question of equitable development to self-regulating markets, the problems of inequality and poverty that became so severely apparent in recent years are likely to
worsen as we turn to the new millennium. Although recent research tends to support
the existence of the general pattern of Kuznets' inverted "U" in the relation between
income level and inequality, it is clear that there is nothing automatic in this relationship, nothing indicating that the "natural" operation of markets will ultimately
yield greater equality. When he originally hypothesized the relationship, Kuznets
saw the equality that came at later stages of development as having been largely a
political phenomenon rather than a market phenomenon:

> ...in democratic societies the growing political power of the urban lower-income
> groups led to a variety of protective and supporting legislation, much of it aimed to
> counteract the worst effects of rapid industrialization and urbanization and to sup-
> port the claims of the broad masses for more adequate shares of the growing income
> of the country (Kuznets 1955, 17).

Pieper and Taylor's examination of several case studies is particularly valuable in
revealing the vacuity of the Bretton Woods policy prescription, and it is here where
they develop the foundation for concluding that markets do not work even by narrow growth criteria when they are not well embedded in society – when they are, so
to speak, dropped on a society from outside and above. Their very useful review of
experiences in Chile, Mexico, Turkey, post-socialist Eastern Europe, sub-Saharan
Africa, and South Korea is the real meat of the Pieper-Taylor argument. They leave
one wondering how officials and staff at the Bretton Woods institutions can continue to cling to their time-worn nostrums about the benefits of market reforms. All
of this does a very effective job of debunking the myths of neo-liberalism.

I do, however, have one substantial misgiving about the Pieper-Taylor argument.
Their discussion of "Reforming the Institutions" strikes me as problematic. Implicit
in their argument is the idea that the Bank and the IMF have adopted their policy
line as "errors." The Bretton Woods approach is, Pieper and Taylor say, "intellectually ill founded." They acknowledge that the force of these incorrect ideas derives
from the backing that the Bank and IMF receive from the world's most powerful

governments, from their control of resources, and from their support by powerful segments of the ruling classes in poor countries. Yet they give little attention to the way that the Bretton Woods policies, however much they are based on a flimsy intellectual foundation, effectively serve very powerful private economic interests. In fact, the only way we can explain the durability of the discredited Bretton Woods ideas about market reforms is to recognize that, however ineffective they are in achieving their ostensible goals, they do a good job of serving those powerful interests.

Policy lines at the Bank and, to a lesser degree, at the IMF have varied over time, but there has been one consistent element giving a common content to those various lines. Pieper and Taylor acknowledge this common content: "...over five decades the rich countries have pushed consistently for increased integration of poor countries into the world economy...." They do not, however, come to grips with the full implications of this consistency.

Pieper and Taylor take as "given" in their discussion of reforms that the governments of the rich countries – particularly the U.S. government – will continue to insist upon conditionality. The arguments for accepting conditionality as a given, however, also would force us to accept "increased integration of the poor countries into the world economy" as a given. These two givens taken together must imply that this "increased integration" would take place under terms set by the U.S. government and the Bretton Woods Institutions that it dominates. The whole force of the Pieper-Taylor argument is that such a policy pattern is inimical to development, inimical to having markets embedded in the societies where they operate.

It follows that any reform of the Bretton Woods institutions has to begin with *changing the givens*. In the face of the powerful interests that lie behind these givens, perhaps "reform" is too mild a word. Certainly, however we dub the necessary changes, they will require far more force than an intellectual critique of the prevailing ideology. We all know that the conflict here goes well beyond the realm of ideas.

Nonetheless, intellectual critiques are quite useful. The especially useful work embodied in the Pieper-Taylor paper along with parallel studies gives us the basis for some fairly clear conclusions:

The neo-liberal regime that is being imposed on the world economy by the Bretton Woods institutions, the U.S. government, and other powerful public and private actors is doing a great deal of damage.

It is a regime that harms people in all sorts of ways in the name of economic growth, but it does not even do very well at providing economic growth.

The reign of neo-liberalism has not come about as some inevitable historical process, but has been actively constructed by the powerful actors that gain from its establishment.

Alternatives exist, and the alternatives tend to work better on both narrow criteria of economic growth or on broader social criteria.

In the same way that neo-liberalism has been constructed, it is possible to construct various alternatives, and thus the task for people seeking progressive economic options may not be easy, but it is doable.

3

India: *dirigisme,* structural adjustment, and the radical alternative

Prabhat Patnaik and C.P. Chandrasekhar

Post-independence India was one of the classic cases of *dirigiste* – i.e., state-directed – economic development. Not only was the state highly interventionist, but the economy came to acquire a sizable public sector, especially in areas of infrastructure and basic industries. The "mixed" economy that thus came into being, together with the fact that the polity was characterized by multiparty parliamentary democracy with a largely free press and significant freedom of expression, invested the Indian experiment with a novelty and uniqueness, which attracted worldwide attention and gave rise to a vast theoretical literature. Not only did a rich literature on development planning take shape within India, starting with the celebrated plan models of Professor P.C. Mahalanobis, who was a pioneer theoretician of Indian planning (Mahalanobis 1985; Chakravarty 1987, 1993; Byres 1998), but the class nature of the Indian state, the class character of Indian planning, etc., became matters of intense debate, especially in Marxist and radical circles, both within the country as well as internationally (Lange 1970; Bettelheim 1968; Kalecki 1972; Kurian 1975; Mitra 1977).

India's transition in 1991 to a program of "structural adjustment," which entails a regime of "liberal imports," a progressive removal of administrative controls, including a move to "free markets" in foodgrains and a whittling down of food subsidies, a strictly limited role for public investment, the privatization of publicly owned assets over a wide field, an invitation to multinational corporations (MNCs) to undertake investment in infrastructure under a guaranteed rate of return, and financial liberalization that would do away with all priority sector lending and subsidized credit, is an event therefore of great historical significance.

Underlying this transition is a changed international conjuncture on the one hand and an accentuation of the contradictions of the *dirigiste* regime on the other. "Structural adjustment" of course was not inevitable in 1991. The crisis facilitating its introduction did not represent any "collapse" of the earlier economic regime. It was speculation induced and admitted alternative responses in the short run that could have been the prelude to an alternative strategy (Patnaik and Chandrasekhar 1995). But the changed conjuncture did prepare the soil for "structural adjustment." Let us first discuss the changed international conjuncture underlying the role of the Bretton Woods institutions, which has been vital.

The role of the IMF and the World Bank

Traditionally, there have been significant differences between the International Monetary Fund (IMF) and the World Bank. But these have narrowed over time, and the reasons for this narrowing constitute an important element of contemporary political economy.

The Bank has always been opposed to any attempts on the part of the Third World countries to break away through conscious design (which necessarily means conscious state intervention) from the pattern of international division of labor inherited from the days of colonialism and semi-colonialism. If such a break is to be achieved, then it must be achieved, according to its perception, entirely through the mediation of market forces, which means in particular through the predilections of foreign direct investment. The Bank has remained absolutely faithful to this position of opposing state-sponsored industrialization, despite the fact that historical evidence marshaled earlier by Gerschenkron and subsequently by many others shows overwhelmingly that successful industrialization by late industrializers has invariably depended upon active state intervention.[1] What has changed in the case of the Bank over time is, first, the specific argument used by it for opposing state-sponsored industrialization; secondly, the precise tactics it has brought to bear in order to undermine state-sponsored industrialization in Third World countries; and thirdly, the precise package of programs around this basic objective. These changes reflected the changing nature of world capitalism.

In the late fifties and the early sixties the Bank used a macro argument to push its line: substantial unutilized capacity in the industrial sector existed because of a scarcity of foreign exchange; a combination of import liberalization and exchange rate devaluation therefore would set up a virtuous circle of "more imports – more capacity utilization – more exports – still more imports" and so on, which would unshackle the economy from the clutches of *dirigisme* (which was predicated inter alia upon a recognition of demand constraints both in the external and in the internal markets). This was the argument on the basis of which the World Bank pushed the Indian government into adopting an import-liberalization-cum-devaluation package in 1966, with disastrous consequences.[2]

In the Robert McNamara years the emphasis shifted to poverty. But the concern for poverty did not express itself in terms of any argument in favor of an egalitarian alteration in asset or land distribution; it expressed itself in the argument that the domestic intersectoral terms of trade were more unfavorable for agriculture vis-a-vis industry than the terms of trade prevailing in the world market, so that removing trade restrictions and thereby preventing state-sponsored industrialization would benefit the agricultural sector, which is the repository of mass poverty. This argu-

1 An important recent addition to this literature is Amsden (1989).
2 The actual estimates on the basis of which the policy package was recommended were made by the U.S. Agency for International Development (AID), with which the Bank worked in close collaboration. For a discussion as well as a critique of this position, see Raj (1976), reprinted in Nayyar (1994a).

ment was backed up by another one, namely, since the inequality in urban income distribution was larger than that in rural income distribution, a shift in income distribution from the urban to the rural sector, which means in effect from industry to agriculture, would have the effect of lowering overall income inequalities.[3] This argument amounted yet again to an attack on state-sponsored industrialization; the vacuousness of this argument lay inter alia in the fact that the bottom 60 percent of the agriculture-dependent population in a country like India consists of people, namely landless laborers and poor peasants, supplementing their incomes through wage labor and who are net buyers of foodgrains in the market. Since the mechanism for a terms-of-trade shift in favor of agriculture would be an increase in agricultural prices, this increase would be relative to their money incomes as well. In other words, the rural poor would actually be harmed by a rise in food prices, which is espoused by the Bank in the name of poverty reduction.[4]

More recently the Bank has shifted to the well-known micro theoretic "marketist" argument that focuses on the allegedly interrelated phenomena of "inward orientation," "price-distortion," and "inefficiency." Much has been written on the vacuousness of this critique: "outward orientation" as manifested for example in successful export performance has been accompanied by highly state-interventionist neo-mercantilist policies rather than any attempt to "get prices right" in the conventional sense; the alleged "inefficiency" of *dirigiste* industrialization is established through exercises (Ahluwalia 1985) involving dubious concepts such as "total factor productivity" (which is predicated upon the perennial absence of any demand constraint);[5] there is complete silence on the role of the domestic investment effort in explaining growth performance, notwithstanding the overwhelming evidence that exists on its importance (Patnaik and Chandrasekhar 1996), and so on. We shall not dilate on this critique here; the point to note is that the policy package following from this critique is exactly the same as before, namely, to roll back state-sponsored industrialization.

Where the World Bank did change was in two respects: the first relates to its tactics. In the beginning, up until the end of the fifties in the case of India, the Bank studiously avoided giving any loans for government programs. In the early sixties it modified its stance to give loans for social infrastructure projects, but not for any public sector industrial undertakings. It is only when the policy of boycott of public sector undertakings appeared to be counterproductive from its point of view that it

3   These arguments were not manufactured by the Bank. They were doing the rounds at the time, for instance, in Little, Scitovsky, and Scott (1970), and were merely appropriated by the Bank. For a review and critique of this position, see Bagchi (1971).

4   This was an important conclusion of Mitra (1977). It follows that "price reforms" too have a class bias. Even if one believed that price reforms entailing a shift in the terms of trade in favor of agriculture should be carried out under egalitarian land ownership, to support such price reforms when land ownership remains highly concentrated (and hence to support that part of structural adjustment that insists on such price reforms) is a non sequitur. In the regime of structural adjustment, in fact, the tendency has been toward reverse land reforms, i.e., removing ceiling legislation in order to entice agribusiness.

5   See Balakrishnan and Pushpangadan (1994) for a critique of Ahluwalia (1985) on empirical grounds.

started financing investment in such undertakings but with its own conditionalities, such as global tendering, specifying technological details and the scale of plants, etc. This shift from "boycotting" to "infiltrating" the public sector enabled it to exercise great leverage, to induct MNCs directly into the public sector as collaborators, to undermine domestic technological self-reliance and indigenous technological capabilities, to dictate pricing policies and acquire an indirect say on the government budget, and to set up "networks" with bureaucrats and managerial personnel of the public sector. [6] Together with this began the process of World Bank employees shifting to key government positions, especially in the Ministry of Finance, even as they were drawing pensions from the Bank, or even as they kept open the option of moving back to the Bank. They provided a powerful lobby working in concert toward "liberalization-cum-structural adjustment."

The other respect in which the Bank did change was in its new insistence upon a range of financial sector reforms whose overall objective again was to detach the domestic financial institutions and the financial markets from their integration into the domestic development effort (through, for example, low long-term interest rates, subsidized credit, and the allocation of a minimum share of credit disbursements for "priority sectors" such as agriculture, etc.) and to integrate them more closely instead with global financial markets. Together with this went the Bank's demand for privatization not only of the financial domain, where the public institutions held sway, but of public sector assets including natural resources. The economic, as opposed to the ideological, argument for privatization was again utterly dubious: as a means of closing the fiscal deficit it was no different from money created directly for the government's use; as a means of reducing the government's interest burden it could work only under the palpably impossible condition that the rate of return sacrificed on the sold government assets was lower than the interest rate on public debt (which is impossible because the market would never buy assets at such low rates of return, and in practice of course has insisted on obtaining public assets only at virtually throw-away prices); and as a means of introducing "entrepreneurship" it was of no use because the buyers were either "fly-by-night-operators" or, if reputable MNCs, had more complex objectives.

This widening of the Bank's package, from simply rolling back state-sponsored industrialization through a removal of trade restrictions, government controls, and the preeminence of the public sector, to an integration of the domestic economy with the operations of global finance, reflected a fundamental change that was taking place within world capitalism itself, namely a tendency toward greatly increased fluidity of finance across national boundaries, a tendency in short toward a globalization of finance, which is very different from, though often confused with, globalization of production facilities.

6   Several case studies for particular industries illustrate this process. Reference may be made to Biswajit Dhar's "Growth and Technological Change in the Indian Fertiliser Industry," unpublished Ph.D. thesis of Jawaharlal Nehru University, which contains a detailed discussion of how the Bank's insistence upon having fertilizer plants of 1,350 tons per day of ammonia, even in the absence of any evidence of economies of scale, effectively undermined the position of the public sector unit FPDIL, which could set up plants up to 900 TPD capacity.

This very tendency also explains the shift that was taking place in the position of the IMF as well (Chandrasekhar 1995). Earlier the IMF was exclusively concerned with "stabilization." The Polak model, for example, which provided the basis for the IMF's policy prescriptions, concentrated on a few macro-level identities and made no attempts at modeling "structural adjustment." Its assumptions were questionable (e.g., the absence of any recognition of a demand constraint, the attribution of external payments problems exclusively to the government sector's deficit, and the general monetarist bias), but it provided the toolkit for a highly conservative financial institution whose sole concern, especially vis-a-vis Third World countries, was to recover its loans by imposing fiscal discipline upon the latter (the fact that it practiced systematic discrimination between the First and the Third World countries, as distinct from its asymmetric ability to "discipline" surplus and deficit countries, is by now well established) (Sen 1986). This was the conservatism of a narrow-minded financier, not that of an ideologue of development frowning overtly upon any attempt to alter forcibly the colonial pattern of international division of labor. The latter role was left by and large to the World Bank.

A major change took place between the two oil shocks. While the recycling of resources to the Third World, such as it was, was organized in the wake of the first oil shock by the IMF itself, the tremendous growth that took place in the role of the banks in the interim meant that, by the time of the second oil shock, it was the banks that were doing whatever recycling was to be done; the IMF was called upon only to provide "security cover" to the banks. This was the beginning of a process: from being a leading financier the IMF had been reduced to the status of a "gendarme" of international rentier interests. As a gendarme, then, it had to insist that the countries, which were caught under its "conditionalities" and thereby became possible candidates for receiving funds from international rentiers, adopted a host of measures that were to the liking of the rentiers, such as privatization of public assets, "opening up" of financial markets, removal of exchange restrictions, convertibility of the currency on the current and capital accounts, and so on, all of which amounted to an espousal of the kind of "structural adjustment" that the World Bank had also come around to.

To sum up, while the conservatism of the Bretton Woods institutions has continued unabated, there have been major changes in the precise texture of this conservatism, reflecting changes that have been occurring in world capitalism. Not only have the IMF and World Bank come closer together in terms of outlook, breaking down their earlier separateness, but this coming together has itself been promoted to a significant extent by the vastly enhanced role of globalized finance. One might even add that this ascendancy of globalized finance has been responsible, inter alia, for keeping down willy-nilly what Lenin would have called "inter-imperialist rivalry": certainly as far as the Third World is concerned, the governments of the advanced capitalist countries present a remarkably common front and give more or less unanimous support to the structural adjustment measures being imposed by the Bretton Woods institutions. [7]

7 Patnaik (1995b) argues that the situation today resembles the Kautskyite notion of "joint exploitation of the world by internationally united finance capital." But a revival of the role of the nation-state appears inevitable not only in the Third World where "free markets" have

Contradictions of the *dirigiste* regime

This phenomenon of financial globalization was bound to affect the domestic economy, sucking domestic wealth holders into its vortex and in the process undermining the viability of the *dirigiste* alternative. For any state intervention to be even remotely effective, it is essential that there be some "control area" within the domain of the state over which it can ensure a degree of correspondence between the intentions behind its policy actions and their outcomes. If finance can flow in or flow out in response to pressures emanating from abroad, if the domestic wealth holders' behavior, in other words, defies the very concept of a "control area" under the domain of the nation-state, then the possibility of state intervention gets eroded. It is not surprising that virtually all forms of interventionism, not only traditional socialism, but even Keynesianism, welfarism, conventional social democracy, Third World nationalism, and its necessary accompaniment, the *dirigiste* developmental model, have all run into rough weather in recent years. The reason for this is not some sudden realization on the part of "everybody" of the alleged superiority of the market, but the profound change in the context that has taken place in recent years through the phenomenon of financial globalization. [8]

It would be a gross mistake, however, to hold this changed context alone responsible for the eventual transcendence of the *dirigiste* regime. The regime had serious internal contradictions that contributed to an erosion of its social stability as well as of its economic viability, and propelled it toward a situation where, *given its social base,* it could not summon the will for any alternative viable responses to the changed context that we have underscored. In other words, it is the interplay between the changed international context and the accentuating domestic contradictions within the earlier regime that gave rise to the "totality" of circumstances that permitted the enactment of the event of historical significance referred to at the beginning of this essay, and for which the speculation-engendered crisis of 1990–91 provided the immediate occasion. In the present section we shall discuss these internal contradictions.

The economic policy regime erected in the 1950s had its roots in the freedom struggle itself. The economy had been dominated by metropolitan capital and metropolitan commodities in the pre-independence period. Freedom meant freedom from this domination, and this could not be ensured without giving the state in independent India a major role in building up infrastructure, expanding and strengthening the productive base of the economy, setting up new financial institutions, and regulating and coordinating economic activity. This was necessary for building capitalism itself, though some no doubt entertained the fond hope that all this would add

palpably adverse economic effects, but also in the advanced countries where the social crisis, manifested inter alia in the high levels of unemployment, makes such a revival imminent. If progressive opinion does not advance a program to tackle unemployment, then the right may take advantage of the situation for championing its own disturbing version of the revival of the nation-state.

8   We argue below that this does not mean that all prospects of progressive economic policies being pursued in particular countries (it will have to be necessarily in particular countries to start with) have disappeared.

up to a transition to socialism. State capitalism and state intervention, in other words, were essential instruments for the development of a relatively autonomous Indian capitalism, displacing metropolitan capital from the preeminent position it had occupied in the colonial economy. It is this displacement that drew the ire of international agencies like the IMF and World Bank (more explicitly as we have seen of the latter). The manner of their intervention has been alluded to earlier; let us move on now to the internal contradictions.

Three mutually reinforcing and interrelated contradictions need to be noted (Rai 1992). First, the state within the old economic policy regime had to simultaneously fulfill two different roles that were incompatible in the long run. On the one hand it had to maintain growing expenditures, in particular investment expenditure, in order to keep the domestic market expanding. The absence of any radical land redistribution had meant that the domestic market, especially for industrial goods, had remained narrowly based socially; it had also meant that the growth of agricultural output, though far greater than in the colonial period, remained well below potential, and even such growth as occurred was largely confined, taking the country as a whole, to a narrow stratum of landlords-turned-capitalists and sections of rich peasants who had improved their economic status. Under these circumstances, a continuous growth in state spending was essential for the growth of the market; it was the key element in whatever overall dynamics the system displayed. At the same time, however, the state exchequer was the medium through which large-scale transfers were made to the capitalist and proto-capitalist groups; the state, in other words, was an instrument for the "primary accumulation of capital."

It was not of course the only instrument; direct means such as the eviction of tenants, private encroachment on common resources, and private encroachment on state-owned resources such as forests, from whose use the poor were simultaneously excluded, all played their role. But the state exchequer remained the preeminent mechanism for "primary accumulation"; through the nonpayment of taxes (to which the state generally turned a blind eye), through a variety of subsidies and transfers, and through lucrative state contracts, private fortunes were built up at the expense of the state exchequer.

The contradiction between these two different roles of the state manifested itself, despite increasing resort to indirect taxation and administered price hikes, through a growth in the government's revenue deficit. A result of course was that the fiscal deficit also went up; this however reflected not a stepup in public investment but a decline in public savings. In the 1950s and the 1960s the revenue account of the central government at least was in surplus, but in the 1970s even this went into a deficit, and this deficit climbed steadily from Rs.20,370 million (rupees) in 1980–81 to Rs.105,140 million in 1988–89, Rs.119,140 million in 1989–90, and Rs.185,610 million in 1990–91.

The implications of this growing fiscal crisis were obvious: the government had either to cut back the tempo of its investment or to maintain this tempo through increased recourse to borrowing. If the borrowing is from abroad, then the building up of pressure for a change in the policy regime is obvious. If the borrowing is domestic, then (for any given profile of government expenditure and in the absence of any spontaneous increase in private thriftiness) it has an expansionary effect on demand in the economy, which, unless the system happened to be demand constrained to start with, stimulates inflation.[9] Increased recourse to borrowing, in other words, raises, *ceteris paribus*, the inflationary impact of a given tempo of public investment, an impact that would be all the greater if, *because of inflationary expectations,* private wealth holders also decide to shift, in particular years, from holding (direct and indirect) claims upon the government to holding commodities and physical assets. Since rampant inflation cannot be allowed in a system of parliamentary democracy with virtually nonexistent indexation for the vast bulk of the workers, the state would sooner or later have to cut back its expenditure, especially investment expenditure, which would slow down the economy and eventually arouse capitalists' demands for an alternative policy regime. In short, the regime gets progressively engulfed in a crisis. In its efforts to combine political legitimacy with economic dynamism, it increasingly comes a cropper.

The second contradiction lay in the inability of the state to impose a minimum measure of "discipline" and "respect for law" among the capitalists, without which no capitalist system anywhere can be tenable. Disregard for the laws of the land, especially tax laws, was an important component of the primary accumulation of capital. The same disregard, the same absence of a collective discipline that a capitalist class imposes upon itself in any established capitalist country, also meant that a successful transition could not be made from a Nehruvian interventionist regime to an alternative viable capitalist regime with state intervention, but of a different kind. After all, the state is strongly interventionist even in a country like Japan, but it is interventionism based on close collaboration between the state and capital that simultaneously promotes rigorous discipline among the capitalists. To be sure, the extent and nature of state intervention in Japan is itself a result of specific features of the Japanese civil society as it has developed historically and that cannot simply be emulated elsewhere. But the point here is merely a descriptive one, the analysis of which has to be located in the specific nature of the Indian society and polity – a task outside the scope of this paper. The description, however, is important; it provides a proximate explanation of why the retreat from Nehruvian *dirigisme*, instead of leading to an alternative viable capitalist regime carving out a space for itself in the international economy, through an alternative mode of state intervention, has resulted in a situation where the economy is left to the caprices of international capital.

9   It may be thought that since larger government borrowing would push up interest rates, it would have a demand-reducing effect through *this* channel, which would weaken our argument about its stimulating inflation. Such, however, is not the case for two reasons: first, the demand-reducing effect through this channel can never eliminate the stimulus to inflation altogether, for the increase in interest rates itself would not occur unless there is a net expansion of demand. Secondly, and more pertinently, government borrowing in India was at a fixed (and low) interest rate and largely from a captive market, where state-owned banks (and other financial institutions) were obliged to hold a certain minimum ratio of their liabilities in the form of government securities. Increased recourse to borrowing by the government therefore put no pressure on interest rates, since whatever debt was not picked up by banks devolved on the central bank, automatically creating reserve money.

The third contradiction had its roots in the cultural ambience of an ex-colonial society like India. The market for industrial goods was from its very inception, as we have seen, a narrowly based one socially. Capitalism in its metropolitan centers, however, is characterized by continuous product innovation, the phenomenon of newer and ever newer goods being thrown onto the market, resulting in alterations of lifestyles. In an ex-colonial economy like India, the comparatively narrow social segment to whose hands additional purchasing power accrues in a large measure and whose growing consumption therefore provides the main source of the growth in demand for industrial consumer goods is also anxious to emulate the lifestyles prevailing in the metropolitan center. It is not satisfied with having more and more of the same goods that are domestically produced, nor is it content merely with expending its additional purchasing power upon such new goods as the domestic economy, on its own, is capable of innovating. Its demand is for the new goods that are being produced and consumed in the metropolitan centers and which, given the constraints upon the innovative capacity of the domestic economy, are incapable of being locally produced purely on the basis of indigenous resources and indigenous technology.

An imbalance therefore inevitably arises in such economies between what the economy is capable of locally producing purely on its own steam, and what the relatively affluent sections of society who account for much of the growth of potential demand for consumer goods would like to consume. This imbalance may be kept in check by import controls, though such controls inevitably give rise to clandestine imports, through smuggling, which are sold in local "black markets." But even leaving aside such clandestine imports, the more the imbalance between what is produced and what is sought to be consumed is kept in check through controls, the more it grows because of further innovations in the metropolitan economies.

The result is a powerful buildup of pressure among the more affluent groups in society for a dismantling of controls. The fact that this would result in substantial sections of domestic producers going under, i.e., in a deindustrialization in the domestic economy, together with an accentuation of the already precarious balance-of-payments situation, does not come in the way of such pressures being built up. The inculcation of a desire to emulate the fashionable lifestyles prevailing in the metropolitan countries among segments of the underdeveloped economy acts as a powerful instrument in the hands of metropolitan capital in its efforts to pry open the market of such an economy and to wrest back the space that it had yielded as a result of granting political independence. This contradiction between the extant production pattern and the desired consumption pattern of the affluent sections of the population, which contributes to a dismantling of the *dirigiste* economic regime, has been manifest in India too.

The net result of the working out of all these contradictions has been evident in the Indian economy for quite some time. The growth in the index of manufacturing industrial production, which is a barometer of the expansion in the possibilities of productive accumulation, is quite revealing (Table 1).

After 15 years of rapid industrial expansion in the 1950s and the early 1960s, there was a dramatic decline in the rate of manufacturing growth during the next 15

Table 1   *Growth of manufacturing production (annual average compound rates)*

1951–65	7.8%
1965–70	3.3
1970–71 to 1980–81	4.0
1980–81 to 1984–85	5.7
1984–85 to 1989–90	8.8

Notes and sources: The figures up to 1970 have 1960 as base, the figures for the 1970s have 1970 as base, and the figures for the 1980s have 1980–81 as base. These figures are taken from various issues of *Economic Survey*, GOI, and *Report on Currency and Finance*, RBI.

years. Even though the growth rate picked up somewhat in the early 1980s, it was still nowhere near the rates witnessed in the first 15 years of planning. It is only after the mid-1980s that a pronounced boom occurred once again in the manufacturing sector of the Indian industries.

The fact that the 15 years after the mid-1960s, which were characterized by a relative stagnation in manufacturing output, also witnessed a decline in the rate of growth of public investment compared to the earlier period is well known. This decline meant, as discussed earlier, that in promoting "primary accumulation of capital," the state could not adequately fulfill its other role, namely, as an expander of the market: a number of industries that catered to mass consumption or to the investment requirements of the state vanished. And the slower expansion of public investment also meant a slower growth in the productive potential of the industrial sector on account of the resulting infrastructural constraints. [10]

Given the sluggish growth of the home market, breaking into export markets could have provided a new stimulus to industrial expansion and a new basis for capital accumulation in productive channels. But export markets were dominated by metropolitan capital. To permit Indian capital a share of this export market as a junior partner, metropolitan capital demanded a price, namely, a share of the Indian market. On the other hand, breaking into export markets on its own required, besides the backing of the Indian state, a massive effort on the part of Indian capital, which it was incapable of making owing inter alia to its unwillingness to accept a certain minimum "discipline," such as that which underlay the international successes of Japanese capitalism. The export prospects of Indian capital consequently remained bleak.

In this context, a schism developed within the ranks of the Indian capitalists. A section was willing to make compromises with metropolitan capital on the terms that the latter demanded: it was all for allowing metropolitan capital to capture a share of the Indian market even at the expense of the entrenched capitalists, not to mention the public sector, in the hope of being able to better its own prospects as a

10   A number of papers on industrial stagnation in India after the mid-sixties are collected in Nayyar (1994a).

junior partner, both in the domestic as well as in the international market. It was thus in favor of import liberalization, a full retreat from Nehruvian *dirigisme*, and acceptance of the kind of regime that metropolitan capital generally, and the World Bank and IMF as its chief spokespersons, had been demanding. The more powerful and the more entrenched monopoly houses, however, were more circumspect. They would not mind import liberalization in areas other than their own, including in areas dominated by the public sector; they would not mind collaborating with foreign capital to add to their empires and hence a degree of relaxation of controls to further facilitate such collaboration; but they would not like encroachments by metropolitan capital upon their own empires. Their attitude toward Fund–Bank-style liberalization, therefore, was more ambiguous.

Support for Fund-Bank–style liberalization was growing not just among a section of capital. A whole new category of an altogether different kind of businessperson was coming up, who was more in the nature of an upstart, international racketeer, fixer, middleman, often of "nonresident Indian" origin or having nonresident Indian associations, often linked to smuggling and the arms trade; these new businesspeople in any case did not have much of a production base, and their parasitic intermediary status as well as the international value of their operations naturally inclined them toward an "open economy." On the other side, among the affluent groups of consumers, the desire for an "open economy" where they could have access to a variety of goods available abroad but not at home, had also grown strong. And finally, one should not exclude a section of the top bureaucracy itself, which had close links with the Fund and Bank, either as ex-employees who might return any time to Washington D.C., or as someone engaged in dollar projects of various kinds, or as hopeful aspirants for a lucrative berth in Washington D.C.; the weight of this section in the top bureaucracy had been growing rapidly, and its inclination naturally was in the direction of the Fund-Bank policy regime (Kurien 1994). Thus, quite apart from the growing leverage exercised by the international agencies in their capacity as "donors," the internal contradictions of the Nehruvian *dirigiste* policy regime generated increasing support within the powerful and affluent sections of society for changing this regime in the manner desired by these agencies.

The boom after the mid-1980s

It is against this background of two-decade-long sluggish industrial growth on the one hand and growing pressures for a retreat from interventionism and the adoption of Fund-Bank–style "liberalization" package on the other that the economic policies of the latter half of the eighties, which marked in several ways a new departure, have to be located. Briefly, three new features characterized these policies. First, there was a significant increase in the magnitude of the government's deficit as a proportion of gross domestic product at current market prices. The gross fiscal deficit of the central and state governments averaged 9.5 percent of GDP during 1985–86 to 1989–90 and touched 10.1 percent in 1990–91. However, this was not due to any increase in the share of public investment, but largely to a decline in the share of public savings, reflected in the burgeoning revenue deficit (which rose from an average of 2.8 percent of GDP during 1985–86 to 1989–90 to 4.5 percent in 1990–91), with the current expenditure of the state growing at a rate far outstripping the growth in tax as well as nontax revenues, despite hikes in indirect taxation and in administered prices (RBI 1995). Partly this was because of the government's refusal to garner larger direct tax revenues. Partly this was because of the growing expenditure on interest payments (the sins of past deficits catching up with the government), and on subsidies, especially on fertilizers (caused primarily by wrong technological choices involving the setting up of plants with very high capital costs). And partly this was because of general profligacy that characterized the then-government to an unprecedented extent.

The second feature was the liberalization of imports of capital goods and components required for a number of commodities catering to luxury consumption, especially of electronics and automobiles. This was justified in the name of "marching to the 21st century." And important government officials unashamedly put forward the argument that, since even the small segment of the population that demanded such goods amounted in absolute terms to a fairly large number, the country could go forward on the basis of such an industrialization strategy whose benefits would "eventually trickle down" to the poorer sections of the population as well.

The import liberalization of the late 1980s was not tied to a larger export effort; its main immediate thrust was toward producing more goods – luxury goods – for the domestic market. In 1985–86, the first year that the policy was introduced, there was a dramatic increase in the trade and current account deficits, the latter from 1.24 percent of GDP to 2.26 percent. True, it reached a plateau thereafter (1.99, 1.89 and 2.66 percent in the three subsequent years), and thus many have argued that it would be unfair to blame the Rajiv Gandhi government for import profligacy. But this argument misses two important points: first, there was a significant reduction in India's oil import bill, owing to the development of the Bombay High oilfield, between 1984–85 and 1988–89. But for the import profligacy, the trade deficit should have declined significantly in absolute terms, since mineral oil and related products accounted for nearly a third of India's import bill on the former date. Secondly, the remittance inflows during this period had flattened out and "soft loans" were becoming more and more difficult to come by. The need was to conserve foreign exchange, and the maintenance of a high, even though steady, absolute level of the trade deficit was a mark of profligacy. And over two-fifths of the increase in import value between 1984–85 and 1988–89 (barring what are virtually reexported) was on account of machinery and transport equipment, which went to a significant extent into the production of a variety of goods for the "elite."

The third new feature was a systematic resort to commercial borrowing abroad, including from the NRIs. As the trade and current account deficits went up in the latter half of the 1980s, commercial borrowings were increasingly resorted to, which in turn contributed with a lag to keeping up the current account deficit itself (owing to interest payments) and necessitated further borrowing. Debt has a habit of escalating rapidly, feeding upon itself; as fresh debt is contracted to pay off old debt, the terms at the margin become stiffer, the maturity period shorter, and, hence, the rate of escalation of debt even steeper. And this is precisely what happened. The debt in dollar terms nearly quadrupled during the 1980s, from $20,582 million in 1980 to $81,994 million in 1990; debt to banks and private individuals increased more than 10 times, from $1,997 million to $22,387 million. India's debt service payments absorbed 31.2 percent of its exports in 1990 (World Bank 1994).

If the large fiscal deficits of the late 1980s had not been accompanied by large current account deficits on the balance of payments, the inflationary overhang would have grown faster and there would have been much higher inflation in the 1980s than actually occurred. On the other hand, if the current account deficit had been as large as it was owing to import liberalization but the fiscal deficits had actually been smaller, then imported goods would have out-competed domestic goods to a greater extent (since the home market would have been narrower with a smaller fiscal deficit), and there would have been a larger "deindustrialization" and hence a smaller rate of industrial growth.

The odd thing about industrial growth, however, was that, notwithstanding its impressive rate, it had limited impact upon industrial employment. Between the end of March 1985 and the end of March 1990, employment in the (organized) private sector went up by a mere 2,730,000, or 3.7 percent in five years, while in the private manufacturing subsector it actually declined by 16,000. Even in the public manufacturing sector it went up between these two dates by a mere 109,000, or 5.8 percent. Thus, the acceleration of industrial growth appears to have had no impact on industrial employment.

The industrial boom of this period, however, even as it tried to paper over the basic contradictions of the regime, and that too apparently successfully, left the economy on a powder keg. The enormous external debt, a growing portion of it being in the form of short-term borrowing, made the economy acutely vulnerable to currency speculations and "confidence crises" of international investors, a vulnerability that was an entirely new phenomenon for the Indian economy. The liquidity build up in the domestic economy that inevitably followed made it acutely vulnerable to sudden inflationary upsurges. And these are precisely what happened in 1991: an inflationary episode on account largely of speculative stock holding, and a balance of payments crisis on account of Non-Resident Indians taking funds out.

An assessment of the impact of structural adjustment

(1) The first notable consequence of structural adjustment has been a slowdown in the average rate of economic growth relative to the preceding five years (Table 2).

It may be argued that Fund-Bank–style reforms are inevitably associated with deflation in the short run, and it is only after a while that the economy is expected to pick up on the basis of stimuli other than those that prevailed under the *dirigiste* regime. In short, a transitional period of stagnation is expected (though not strictly

Table 2 *Average annual growth rates (1980–81 prices)*

	GDP	Agriculture	Industry	Services
Average VII Plan (1985–90)	6.0%	3.4%	7.5%	7.4%
1990/91–1996/97	5.2	2.5	6.0	6.8

Source: Calculated from the *Economic Survey 1996–97*, GOI.

on the basis of the IMF's theory, which does not take into account any demand constraints), and should not cause undue worry, provided growth subsequently picks up on a new basis. In the case of India, too, there are two distinct phases in the post-reform period, a phase of deflation, during which the goal for the economy was stabilization, and a subsequent phase of recovery, starting from 1993–94.

It is now clear, however, that this recovery was a result of transient phenomena, the stepping up of the fiscal deficit in 1993–94 and, even after the fiscal deficit had been lowered in the subsequent years, the satisfaction of pent-up demand for a variety of hitherto-unavailable luxury consumer goods. Since the rate of growth of the demand for such goods, as opposed to the once-for-all splurge that the satisfaction of pent-up demand entails, is much lower, the stimulus that such demand imparts to industrial production evaporates quickly. This is exactly what has happened.

Industrial performance has been dismal in 1997–98 (Table 3). As a result, compared to an average annual growth rate of 8.4 percent in the index of industrial production (which is distinct from real value-added in industry) during the period 1985–86 to 1990–91, the rate for the seven years 1990–91 to 1997–98 (on the assumption that the growth rate observed in the first half of 1997–98 holds for the year as a whole) comes to 5.9 percent.

This slowing down clearly is a secular phenomenon, not just a short-term consequence of "stabilization." It is an expression of the loss of expansionary stimulus that a "liberalized" economy entails, through the decline of public investment, through higher interest rates, and through the shrinkage of demand owing to import liberalization.

A slowdown is also evident in the agricultural sector, where the growth rate in the production of foodgrains in particular has declined sharply. For a long time now the Indian economy has experienced a secular growth rate of foodgrain production of around 2.5 percent per annum, a little higher than the population growth rate. Even during the 12-year period 1978–79 to 1990–91 (both of which were good agricultural years), the rate of growth of foodgrain production was 2.4 percent, which was above the population growth rate. However, over the period 1990–91 to 1996–97 (again both good agricultural years), the growth rate of foodgrain production dropped to 1.4 percent, distinctly lower than the population growth rate.

We are therefore witnessing the emergence of a serious food crisis. The fact that despite this reduction in output growth rate there has been no actual food shortage till now is of little consolation. It merely shows that purchasing power among the work-

Table 3 *Industrial growth rate*
(percentages)

1991/2	0.6%
1992/3	2.3
1993/4	6.0
1994/5	9.4
1995/6	11.8
1996/7	7.1
1997/8 (April–Sep.)	4.7

Source: Calculated from the *Economic
Survey 1996–97*, GOI.

ers, especially the rural workers, has increased even more slowly in real terms (i.e., when deflated by an index of the administered prices of foodgrains). The reason for this lies partly in the steep escalation in administered prices of food, which occurred in the aftermath of "structural adjustment" as a part of the so-called fiscal correction (for which subsidies had to be kept down), and partly in the shift of emphasis toward export agriculture and away from food crops. Foodgrain production being more employment intensive than the exportable commodities that substitute for it in terms of land use, such as prawn fisheries, sunflower, orchards, etc., a shift of acreage from the former to the latter that occurs as a sequel to "liberalization" has the effect of restricting employment growth. In fact, this latter process explains inter alia both the decline in foodgrain output growth and the decline in employment growth.

There is, however, an additional factor behind the drop in foodgrain output growth: real public investment in agriculture has drastically declined over a long period. Gross capital formation (at 1980–81 prices) under the aegis of the government in the agricultural sector was Rs.17,960 million in 1980–81; it remained way below that level throughout the 1990s, reaching Rs.11,540 million in 1990–91 and only Rs.13,100 million in 1995–96. The deceleration had occurred during the 1980s itself, but the 1990s have done nothing to boost public investment. During the 1990s there has no doubt been a step up in real private gross capital formation in this sector, from Rs.34,400 million in 1990–91 to Rs.49,910 million in 1995–96. But even if the veracity of these figures is accepted, much of the increase in private investment has been in the nontraditional sectors of export agriculture rather than in foodgrains production. It is noteworthy that the growth rate between 1990–91 and 1996–97 shows a sharp decline not only for the coarse grains from which much land has shifted toward export crops like sunflower, but even for rice (1.52 percent compared to 3.35 percent for 1980–81 to 1995–96). This is symptomatic of a decline in investment in traditional food crops.

(2) There has been an overall stagnation of the investment ratio (Table 4), of which this decline is a part.

It is doubtful in view of the absolute decline in capital goods production in 1997–98 if the ratio of 1995–96 has been maintained in subsequent years. But even these figures represent overestimates. The method of estimating capital formation is to

Table 4 *Gross domestic capital formation as percentage of GDP*

1990/1	23.2
1991/2	22.1
1992/3	22.5
1993/4	21.6
1994/5	22.4
1995/6	24.6

Source: *Economic Survey 1996–97*, p. 3.

take some goods that are supposed to be used for capital formation and then see how much of such goods are used in a particular period; or, if some goods are used both for consumption and investment, to divide them in a fixed ratio between these two uses. This necessarily means that, in a period of growing consumerism involving durable goods and luxury construction, such as in the post-liberalization period, the tendency invariably is for an overestimation of investment. It goes without saying that, if the actual investment ratio, far from increasing, has been either stagnant or declining, then the acceleration in growth rate promised by the reforms would not materialize. And with such figures for investment ratio, emulating East or Southeast Asian econo-mies' growth performance (prior to their currency crisis) is clearly out of the question.

This sluggish investment performance is not surprising. The proposition under-lying "neo-liberal" policies that if only more surplus value is handed over to the capitalists they would automatically invest more, is a myth (based on the belief that there can never be a demand constraint under capitalism). In fact, capitalists invest in response to specific stimuli, and in the *dirigiste* regime the main stimulus came, directly or indirectly (via contributing to the growth of agricultural incomes), from public investment (and expenditure in general). This had a "crowding-in" rather than a "crowding-out" effect on private investment. A "liberalized" economy, how-ever, entails a loss of this stimulus, compounded by other factors such as high inter-est rates and loss of domestic markets through liberal imports, which is not offset by any corresponding new stimulus. Exports can constitute such a new stimulus, pro-vided they consist of manufactured goods rather than primary commodities (since larger primary commodity exports, as we have seen, may merely mean diversion of production from home use rather than larger production); but, no matter how rap-idly exports grow (within the bounds of plausibility), they can scarcely be of much importance as an investment stimulus for an economy of India's size. The "rolling back" of state capitalism, therefore, far from increasing the investment ratio, causes its stagnation and even decline.

(3) The usual justification for "rolling back" state capitalism is that the fiscal deficit must be cut, since it is a source of "instability" in the economy. Not only is this argument questionable, but, what is more, liberalization-cum-structural adjust-ment intensifies the fiscal crisis.

A distinction should be drawn here. In an economy that is liberalized, and hence open to speculative capital flows, it may well be the case that speculators look at the size of the fiscal deficit, which thus becomes a determinant of their "state of confidence" (so that denouncing fiscal deficits becomes a self-fulfilling prophecy in a liberalized economy), but this is different from saying that the fiscal deficit per se is destabilizing. The latter is untenable for several reasons.

First, the size of the fiscal deficit, which shows the net demand arising from the government, does not have anything to do directly with "instability" in the sense of either generalized inflationary pressures or an unmanageable trade deficit, since the latter depend upon ex ante excess aggregate demand. Secondly, while borrowing to meet current expenditures does require scrutiny (though it is not always reprehensible, e.g., in a recession), since it is indicative of "living beyond one's means," there is nothing necessarily wrong with borrowing to meet investment requirements. If the focus was on a reduction of the revenue deficit, then it might make sense, but by emphasizing the fiscal deficit as distinct from the revenue deficit, the IMF and the World Bank deliberately try to negate the role of the government as an investor, i.e., to denigrate the public sector, for which there is no justification. Thirdly, a reduction in the revenue deficit, or in the fiscal deficit, can be brought about in a number of different ways, the obvious one being an increase in direct tax revenue. Indeed in any Third World economy where glaring poverty coexists with offensive opulence, increased revenue from direct taxes is urgently called for anyway as a means of reducing inequalities. But the Fund and Bank invariably underplay this avenue of deficit reduction and emphasize cuts in investment and welfare expenditures.

Not only is the theory underlying such cuts invalid, but the fiscal deficit that is invoked to legitimize such cuts gets aggravated because of structural adjustment. Since inviting foreign direct investment becomes an overriding objective of economic policy, the rates at which it is taxed get reduced in competition with other countries. This, for reasons of symmetry, means that direct tax rates on the rich as a whole are lowered, though spurious concepts like the so-called Laffer curve (which purport to show that reduced rates bring in larger revenues) are invoked in justification of it. Since customs duties are cut as part of "import liberalization," and excise duties, again for reasons of symmetry, cannot be raised as a consequence, indirect tax revenues too suffer; and this is aggravated by the sluggishness in output growth rate that structural adjustment engenders. While tax revenues cannot be raised for lowering budget deficits, the increased interest rates, resulting in a larger interest burden on the government, which are another legacy of structural adjustment, add to the expenditure side. Thus structural adjustment, which supposedly aims to restrict the fiscal profligacy of the state, itself works to further aggravate the fiscal situation through lower taxes on the rich and higher interest rates. Not surprisingly then, fiscal adjustment leaves the size of the revenue deficit unchanged, and it impinges heavily on public investment and welfare expenditures.

The Indian experience fully bears this out (Table 5). Structural adjustment has entailed a very specific fiscal regime, which has increased transfers from the state to

Table 5 *Some fiscal magnitudes as ratios of GDP*

	Revenue Deficit	Fiscal Deficit	Interest Payments	Subsidies
1988/89	2.7	7.8	4.0	2.2
1989/90	2.6	7.8	4.3	2.6
1990/91	3.5	8.3	4.5	2.5
1991/92	2.6	5.9	4.8	2.2
1992/93	2.6	5.7	4.9	1.9
1993/94	4.0	7.4	5.0	1.7
1994/95	3.3	6.1	5.1	1.5
1995/96	2.7	5.5	5.1	1.3

Source: *Economic and Political Weekly,* Budget Number, May 1997.

Table 6 *Head-count ratio measure of rural poverty (percentages)*

July 1989–June 1990	34.30%
July 1990–June 1991	36.43
July 1991–Dec. 1991	37.42
Jan. 1992–Dec. 1992	43.47
July 1993–June 1994	38.74

Source: Sen (1996), who uses a World Bank document authored by Ozler, Datt, and Ravallion (1996).

rentiers in the form of interest payments, and has concurrently enforced larger fiscal burdens on the people and cuts in public investment (so that MNCs have to be wooed to step in).

(4) The fourth significant consequence of "structural adjustment" has been a rise in rural poverty. Using the norm set out by the Planning Commission, the headcount ratio measure of poverty for rural India moved as shown in Table 6.

The veracity of these figures may be questioned on the grounds that they are based (except for 1993–94) on consumer expenditure data derived from "thin samples" (the previous "large sample" data are for 1987–88, which was a drought year, and too far back for assessing the impact of structural adjustment). But the results are fairly robust in the sense that other researchers have come to identical conclusions, other poverty measures reveal exactly the same picture, and other social indicators show parallel movements (see Sen and Patnaik 1997).

One element underlying the rise in rural poverty was the sharp increase in the cost of living of the working class in general and of agricultural workers in particular (Table 7).

This acceleration of inflation in a period of slack demand was essentially due to

Table 7 *Increases in the cost-of-living indices (percentages)*

	Agricultural Laborers	Industrial Workers
1985/86–1990/91	47.1%	53.5%
1990/91–1995/96	71.6	62.2

Source: Calculated from various issues of the *Economic Survey.*

hikes in administered prices, which were ordered by the government in order to curtail its subsidy bill, and thereby the fiscal deficit. The commodity whose price was most severely affected in this manner was foodgrains. There were steep hikes in the central issue prices of rice and wheat in December 1991, January 1993, and February 1994. As a consequence of these hikes, by February 1994 the issue price of the common variety of rice had increased by 86 percent compared to the immediate prestructural adjustment level; wheat had increased by 72 percent. It is hardly surprising that the cost of living of the workers, both in urban and rural areas, went up so sharply, and that the cost of living of agricultural laborers, for whom food is an even more important item in the consumption basket than for industrial workers, went up more steeply than for the latter. [11]

There was a second element underlying the rise in rural poverty. The level of rural poverty is linked in India not only to the level of food prices relative to wages, but even more pronouncedly to the magnitude of employment opportunities (for which the ratio of rural nonagricultural to agricultural employment is a good proxy, since agriculture is the repository of unused labor reserves). There has been an accentuation of unemployment, notably in rural India, in the nineties, owing to the shift of acreage from food to nonfood crops, import liberalization that has led to a demand switch away from domestic producers, and, above all, cuts in public development expenditure. The central government's total development expenditure as a proportion of GDP at market prices declined from 12.54 percent in 1985–86 to 8.08 percent in 1995–96 (RE) and 7.74 percent in 1996–97 (BE). Since government expenditure has a crucial employment-generating effect, especially in rural areas, this reduction has been employment contracting (Sen and Patnaik 1997).

Accompanying this increase in poverty there has been a cut in the ratio of social sector expenditure to GDP (Table 8).

(5) The effect of structural adjustment is evident not just in the fact of stagnation or growing poverty and unemployment or the growing desperation in wooing MNCs to overcome infrastructural shortages. It is evident above all in the increased

11 There was a reduction in the inflation rate in 1997–98 because the pace of administered price hikes was somewhat moderated after the mid-nineties: there was, for example, a long pause in raising the administered price of foodgrains after February 1994. The parliamentary elections of 1995 and left opposition within the United Front government that came to power in 1995 to increases in the administered prices of essential commodities may explain this moderation.

Table 8 *Social sector expenditure of union and state governments (percent of GDP)*

	Education & culture	Health, water supply, and sanitation
1989/90	3.36%	1.26%
1990/91	3.25	1.23
1991/92	3.12	1.19
1992/93	3.04	1.17
1993/94	3.04	1.19
1994/95*	3.00	1.17
1995/96**	2.84	1.12

Source: *Alternative Economic Survey 1996–97.*

* Revised estimate.
** Budget estimate.

vulnerability to speculation of the Indian economy. Notwithstanding all the hype about foreign direct investment (FDI) inflows into the economy, the actual inflows under this category have been minuscule – not more than $2 billion per year on average. Most of this has also come into activities catering to the domestic market, which displace domestic producers and constitute implicit deindustrialization (owing to the high import content of FDI production), rather than into activities, such as export-oriented production, that genuinely add to domestic output and employment.

What has come in larger measure, however, is speculative finance capital in the form of "hot money," on the basis of which India's exchange reserves (on October 24, 1997) of $26.3 billion have been built up. Even though the Indian currency is not fully convertible, there is sufficient scope for such speculative capital to destabilize the economy in a manner reminiscent of what has happened in the East and Southeast Asian countries.

This of course underscores what was mentioned earlier, namely, that there is a tendency not so much toward globalization of production as toward globalization of finance. The Fund-Bank structural adjustment package, though advocated on the grounds that its adoption would draw FDI in large quantities, has evolved through time to cater in practice largely to the requirements of international rentier interests. Even when the adoption of this package succeeds in attracting large amounts of hot money, it cannot generate growth in the economy; and of course when hot money flies out, growth suffers through enforced deflation for the sake of creating creditors' confidence. In other words, this package, if conscientiously adopted, binds the economy to stagnation in years of comfortable foreign exchange and retrogression in years of foreign exchange crunch, giving rise to a combination of net retrogression and "denationalization" of the nation's assets and natural resources.

As hot money was feeding India's foreign exchange reserves, there was pressure from the Fund and Bank for liberalizing consumption goods imports on the strength of these reserves. If the Indian government had listened to this advice, it would have ushered in simultaneously a combination of: industrial retrogression owing to liberal imports of consumer goods, a decline in reserves (for financing a consumption splurge by the affluent), and, of course, extreme vulnerability in the event of a capital outflow. It would in effect have undertaken large-scale short-term borrowing for financing the deindustrialization of its own economy. But the compulsions of parliamentary elections together with strong domestic opposition prevented the perpetration of this folly, just as they prevented the realization of full convertibility of the currency.

(6) Finally, many had believed that a "retreat of the state" and the exposure of the economy to the discipline of the market would cut out arbitrariness of decision making and the corruption that is inevitably associated with it. It would streamline the functioning of the economy by making it a "rule-governed system," though admittedly the rules of the market. What has happened instead in the Indian economy during this period of structural adjustment is an increase in the level of corruption, cronyism, and arbitrariness to unprecedented levels. The privatization exercise, as in other countries such as Bangladesh, has been an utter scandal. Precious natural resources, hitherto kept inside the public sector, are handed over for a pittance (and alleged "kickbacks") to private firms with dubious objectives. The case of the Enron deal, where massive contracts were signed without an open tender and at inflated capital costs, with guaranteed rates of return, has already attracted international attention. In short, the "discipline of the market" has proved to be a chimera.

But, as Lenin (1977, 675) pointed out long ago, finance capital is associated with swindles, bribery, and corruption, or what European "professors" of his time condescendingly called "the American ethics."

The alternative

What comes through clearly from the Indian experience with structural adjustment is the dominant role of the process of globalization of finance. We have suggested earlier that the very design of the current package of structural adjustment bears the imprint of this process; and the sequel to the introduction of this package shows that the real mobility witnessed is that of finance rather than that of capital-in-production. But then, if globalization of finance restricts the possibility of intervention within a "national" (or for that matter any supranational but restricted) space by undermining the concept of a "control area," the question naturally arises: can there be any sort of an alternative to the current set of policies? To say that an alternative presupposes *international* coordination, and can no longer be based on a national, or any kind of a spatially restricted, response, a proposition that some radicals argue, amounts de facto to conceding that a feasible alternative to the current set of policies does not exist.

It is our contention, however, that a feasible alternative, not just a desirable one, exists, which is sui generis, in the sense of being different from the neo-mercantilist strategy espoused by the East Asian economies prior to their financial liberalization (Southeast Asian economies were more "liberal," including in the sphere of finance, all along). Such a neo-mercantilist (and in that sense nationalist) strategy is predicated upon a particular international and internal conjuncture that cannot be made to order. To talk of replicating such a strategy therefore is unhistorical. And it is not even necessarily desirable, since neo-mercantilist strategies have been associated with politically authoritarian structures. What we have to discuss therefore is the feasibility of a sui generis strategy.

There is a fallacy in our view in believing that an undermining of the "control area" of the nation-state is tantamount to an impossibility of intervention. What such undermining does is impose an important additional constraint upon the nation-state; the nation-state cannot certainly intervene in the *old* way. It can now intervene with some degree of success only if it takes this constraint into account.

Specifically, for economies like India, this means that the volatility of financial flows has to be kept under check through a combination of: (1) direct regulations; (2) an overall sound balance of payments (in relative terms, which is not synonymous with neo-mercantilism); and, above all, (3) a development strategy that ensures economic advance with social stability.

(1) The main form of direct regulation that we have in mind is a mix of capital flow controls with a nonconvertible currency. This is precisely the kind of regulation that allowed the East Asian countries to pursue meaningful state intervention. In India's case, external pressures against such regulation would no doubt be strong; but the size of the country as well as the fact that it can produce most of the commodities required by the masses (mineral oil is the only exception) gives India great leverage. It can, if it so chooses, show sufficient resilience to stand up to pressures. After all, to date the country has not moved toward import liberalization in consumer goods or full convertibility of the currency despite external pressures.

The real problem, however, is of a different kind: globalization of finance is such a strong process that direct regulations may prove ineffective in stemming illicit flows. But to believe that the existence of regulations makes *no* difference to the behavior of economic agents is fallacious. And the effectiveness of regulations depends upon the character, and hence the social basis, of the state (a proposition that must not be confused with the view that an authoritarian state regulates more effectively; indeed, we argue the contrary). The alternative we have in mind is not confined to merely having regulations by the existing state, but encompasses, as we shall see, a change in the character of the state.

(2) Regulations have to be backed by a sound balance-of-payments position through a sound trade performance. A part of the key to such a sound trade performance lies in the imposition of intelligently devised import controls; at the same time, however, sound export performance is essential. While the importance of boosting exports is stressed by neo-classical economists, they never distinguish between primary commodity and manufacturing exports. In agriculture, if public investment in irrigation, rural infrastructure, and extension services cannot be augmented, either because the system is already agricultural-supply constrained (Kalecki 1972),

and hence up against the inflationary barrier, or because the state is being made to withdraw from its investing role, then an increase in exports necessarily means a lower profile of domestic availability, which has the effect of both impoverishing the domestic working masses and contracting the home market for manufactured goods. Even if private investment occurs in export crops, the diversion of land area from other crops has the effect of reducing the domestic availability of the latter.

Manufacturing exports, however, as Kaldor (1978) argued long ago, are in an altogether different category. To the extent that investment decisions here are induced by larger capacity utilization, larger exports provide both the inducement as well as the material wherewithal (from the supply side) for larger investment, so that they do not impinge on domestic availability. Manufacturing exports, in other words, can provide the basis for a self-sustaining growth process in a way that agricultural exports (except under special circumstances) cannot. The history of colonial India provides ample evidence for this proposition: the last half-century of colonial rule saw both a stagnant per capita agricultural output and a rise in the proportion of exports out of it, resulting in a sharp decline in the per capita availability of foodgrains, from about 200 kg. per year at the turn of the century to about 150 kg. at independence.

An alternative development strategy, therefore, must specifically aim at increasing the exports of manufactured goods. And this requires not "getting prices right" in some neo-classical sense, but above all high rates of investment that increase the flexibility of the economy's response to the changing international environment. The correlation between high investment ratios and high export growth rates in cross-country data relating to a host of underdeveloped countries is strong (Patnaik and Chandrasekhar 1996). The direction of causation is always seen to lie from exports to investment; but a mutuality of causation is much more plausible, in which case it is not exports that need be the initial intervention variable but the investment ratio itself.

(3) This brings us to the main issue, namely, the alternative development trajectory. Any meaningful development strategy for India must aim to bring about an *immediate* improvement in the living conditions of the working masses, especially in the rural sector, i.e., the modus operandi of the development strategy itself must be such an improvement in their living standards. This is not merely an ethical proposition, but a practical necessity, both for the preservation of meaningful democratic structures as well as for arousing the kind of enthusiasm and participation among the masses on the basis of which alone the structures of a more accountable state, a state capable of imposing discipline upon the rich and the capitalists, can be built. Such an immediate improvement must have as its cornerstone an accelerated agricultural growth based on egalitarian land reforms. The East Asian example has shown the importance of land reforms even for a neo-mercantilist strategy of economic nationalism; indeed, it is important for *any* national economic program. The Chinese example has shown the vigor of an industrialization drive based on an expansion of mass markets deriving from accelerated agricultural growth. In their specific context, this growth has been achieved through a breakup of communes,

though on the basis of the groundwork, e.g., the destruction of landlordism and the erection of water-management systems, prepared earlier. In India at the present conjuncture, accelerated and dispersed, i.e., not regionally concentrated, agricultural growth requires the institution of land reforms.

Together with land reforms there have to be a number of complementary measures such as irrigation and water management, rural infrastructure, literacy, sanitation and drinking water facilities, etc. All these would require considerable investment, but investment that is best undertaken under the aegis of elected local-level bodies. The requirement therefore is also for a devolution of resources and decentralization of planning. But the resources themselves have got to be raised, and there is no escape from heavier doses of direct taxation, of property primarily but of incomes as well (including a check on tax evasion through punitive action).

The conflict between the strategy just advocated and "marketism" becomes apparent here. It is often argued by "marketists" that they are all for rural development. But if tax concessions have to be doled out to entice capital to stay in the country, if food prices have to be raised for the surplus food producers (who happen to be the rural rich) while food subsidies are cut, if all talk of land reforms is eschewed, if financial reforms do away with any system of earmarking of credit, and if even infrastructural development like power becomes the responsibility of the private sector, especially foreign capital, with profitability being the main consideration, then there is no scope left for an improvement in the conditions of the rural poor, or for rural development generally. [12]

Concluding observations: the primacy of politics

The early euphoria generated by the "marketist" economic reforms has vanished. The promised economic bonanza has failed to materialize, while the hope that the "withdrawal of the state" would be followed by a less corrupt, less arbitrary, more rule-governed order has been belied. At the same time there are very strong and unmistakable pressures from below for a betterment in living conditions, pressures that sometimes find outlets in the refracted form of "lower caste" demands, and are often contained through so-called "populist" measures.

The only way these pressures can be met is if the basic classes, namely, the workers, both organized and unorganized, and the bulk of the peasantry, make the

---

12   The argument that simply liberalizing the economy and thereby giving price incentives to the farmers would cause a notable increase in agricultural output together with agricultural exports is an untenable one for reasons we have already discussed, namely, that growth in agriculture is not a matter of prices alone, but requires substantial government investment in irrigation, extension, etc., to which private investment then responds.

Moreover, even if it is accepted for argument's sake that higher prices would stimulate higher agricultural growth, since this growth under the extant agrarian structure would be under the aegis of the rich farmers, its effect on employment would be minimal: the elasticity of employment with respect to output in the new Green Revolution areas is very low and for the country as a whole has sharply declined (Bhalla 1987).

alternative program into their own. True, this appropriation of an alternative program would take time, but the conditions for it are ripening.[13]

We shall end with two comments. An essential component of any alternative program over and above the mere nitty-gritty of an economic strategy must be a strengthening of democratic institutions and structures. Only then would its appropriation by the basic classes be a productive and more durable one. In other words, what is essential is not a new bout of social engineering, but a genuine process of social transformation that expands the direct political intervention capacity of the basic classes. Much has been written on the state-versus-market dichotomy, and much of it is facile. What is more, this debate is a red herring that sidetracks the real debate: greater or lesser democracy for the broad masses of the people.

The second comment relates directly to the theme of this volume. The fact that globalization of finance has made the pursuit of progressive economic policies more difficult is obviously undeniable. But, in focusing upon this phenomenon exclusively, we run the risk of missing the dialectics between the external and the internal, of completely ignoring the possibility of domestic mobilization, of ignoring the effect of this mobilization upon the ability to tackle the external constraints, in short of ignoring the "totality" of the situation that defines the scope for praxis. Into the constitution of this "totality" what enters is not only the changes occurring at the level of world capitalism, but also the level of political mobilization of the masses domestically.

13 It is not an accident that in 1995 as well as in 1998 governments that pursued economic policies in conformity with the dictates of the IMF and World Bank were voted out of office.

Comment by Keith Griffin on "India: *dirigisme,* structural adjustment, and the radical alternative"

Prabhat Patnaik and C.P. Chandrasekhar have written an uncompromising criticism of what they call "structural adjustment" in India. The changes occurring in India, however, are broader than the phrase "structural adjustment" implies and are more akin to systemic change of the type that has been occurring simultaneously in the centrally planned economies of China, Vietnam, Eastern and Central Europe, and the former Soviet Union. The economic reforms in India can be understood in this wider global context, and useful comparisons can be made between the transition in India and that in the centrally planned economies.

Between 1947, when India achieved its independence from British rule, and 1991, when the process of economic reform began, India pursued a development strategy that was state led, inward looking, and nationalist in spirit. Emphasis was placed on industrialization, state enterprises occupied the "commanding heights," international trade was tightly regulated, inward and outward movements of capital were insignificant and tightly controlled, and private sector capital formation was regulated by investment licenses. There was an elaborate planning apparatus, although it was highly bureaucratic and not very effective. This system did produce some positive results. Growth was faster than during the colonial period, although usually slower than the average of developing countries as a whole. National self-sufficiency was achieved, and even today, after six years of economic reform, the ratio of exports to total product in India is about half that of China.

I. Patnaik and Chandrasekhar go to considerable length to demonstrate that the old strategy was not about to "collapse" before the reforms were introduced in 1991. No one really disputes this. The authors claim there was "a silent coup." This conspiracy theory, however, is not very plausible. India's mediocre economic performance had long been recognized, namely, the slow rate of growth of per capita income; the persistent high levels of poverty; the neglect of agriculture; the low efficiency in both public and private industrial enterprises; and the rent seeking, corruption, and inequality created by the pervasive system of administrative controls.

Moreover, the rest of Asia was doing much better. China enjoyed faster growth and a lower incidence of poverty. Pakistan had a higher standard of living than India and a faster rate of growth. The same was true of Indonesia, Thailand, Malaysia, South Korea, and Taiwan. India was being left behind. Most people agreed that it was time to change. The alternative wasn't collapse but continued mediocrity.

II. The reforms actually introduced were orthodox, although the speed with which they have been introduced has been slow. Patnaik and Chandrasekhar are highly critical of the reforms and tend to blame the outside world for imposing them on India.

Indeed, the World Bank and the IMF, and their collaborators in the Indian civil service, are the villains of the piece. This is rather curious, since the influence of the Bank and Fund in India has been much less than in, say, Latin America and sub-Saharan Africa.

The development strategy pursued cut India off from private foreign capital in all forms. Aid inflows also were low in relation to gross national product. Self-reliance and semi-autarky reduced the policy leverage of the Bank and Fund, insulated India from outside economic and political influences, and strengthened the position of the national authorities. Indeed the Bank and Fund were minor players in India and, furthermore, they have largely become irrelevant on the global stage. Net lending by the Bank now is very low, and even the gross lending by the Bank is of small and declining significance compared to private international flows of capital. As for the Fund its resources are so small relative to potential needs that it no longer can play a central role in managing monetary disturbances at the global level. The small role played by the IMF in responding to the 1995 financial crisis in Mexico is a case in point. Our authors have attacked straw men.

The reforms in India, I suggest, reflect not tutoring and arm twisting by the Bank and Fund but the lessons of bitter experience in India itself plus the positive examples of more successful countries in other parts of Asia and elsewhere. At a time when world trade was growing much faster than world GDP, India closed its economy and missed a chance to participate in the boom. Modest but unspectacular growth of the manufacturing sector did occur, but the infant industries fostered by planning failed to grow up, and the cost of protection and administrative controls was high, both in terms of a reduced level of output and average incomes and in terms of greater inequality and poverty.

Industrial policy favored the urban rich and harmed the poor, especially the rural poor. State-sponsored industrialization had a pronounced class bias and operated contrary to the interests of the majority of the population. This gradually became widely acknowledged within India, and the Bank and Fund deserve neither credit nor blame for the decision to seek an alternative development strategy.

III. One of the themes that runs through the paper is the importance of public sector investment. I fully agree with the emphasis the authors place on this. First, if the objective is to increase efficiency by changing the composition of output, it is not enough to create a set of prices that reflects marginal social costs and benefits; one must also promote a high rate of capital formation. The reason for this is that the structure of production changes not by sliding along a given production-possibilities curve but by pushing out the production frontier in the desired (i.e., socially profitable) direction by channeling investment into socially profitable activities.

Second, if the objective is to increase the overall rate of growth, public sector investment – in power, transport infrastructure, ports, irrigation, telecommunications, etc. – is necessary in order to encourage a high level of private investment. That is, as the authors say, public investment "crowds-in" private investment and in the medium run is complementary to it. The implication of this view is that the economic reforms should be judged by their effects on long-run rates of investment rather than on whether they "get prices right."

IV. Patnaik and Chandrasekhar sketch an alternative reform package that they believe is superior to the orthodox reforms introduced so far. Their package contains three central elements, namely, (1) capital flow controls with a nonconvertible currency; (2) the imposition of intelligently devised import controls combined with unspecified measures to increase exports of manufactured goods; and (3) egalitarian land reforms supplemented by complementary measures such as irrigation.

Apart from the third element, i.e., land redistribution, the reforms advocated sound similar to the old development strategy. Their reform package is backward looking, perhaps even nostalgic. This is a pity because the core of their analysis, emphasizing capital accumulation, contains an implicit alternative reform program that is very different from the reforms actually implemented as well as those they recommend.

An alternative approach would take as its point of departure an equitable distribution of natural, human, and physical capital. It could be argued, in fact, that this is what characterizes the successful economies in other parts of Asia; getting prices right was of lesser importance, although not unimportant.

China, Vietnam, Taiwan, and South Korea introduced land reforms, created egalitarian systems of ownership and control over natural capital within the agricultural sector, and, unlike India, eliminated the large class of landless agricultural laborers. The rural reforms not only raised incomes of working people in the countryside; they also raised the "reservation price" of labor in the cities and thereby established a fairly high floor to wages in the manufacturing sector.

Moreover, the average skills of the labor force are lower in India than in several of the more successful Asian countries. Secondary education in India lags way behind China, Taiwan, and South Korea, and even Vietnam is catching up rapidly. The education of girls and the education of those who live in rural areas has been seriously neglected in India. Instead, India has concentrated resources on tertiary education for the benefit of the elite. The result is an inequitable distribution of human capital that has contributed both to relatively slow growth and, above all, to income inequality.

Lastly, physical capital also has been distributed unequally. Unlike Taiwan and China, and now Vietnam, which industrialized the countryside and provided space for the emergence of small, labor-intensive manufacturing and service enterprises, India adopted a strategy of industrialization that gave priority to large state enterprises in the public sector and large oligopolistic enterprises in the private sector. The result has been a concentration of capital among a small minority of the population and the creation of large classes of people who are essentially asset-less.

A progressive strategy of "structural adjustment" in India should begin not by rejecting the spirit of the price reforms that have been introduced but the class bias of the reforms. The choice is not between the market mechanism and government intervention, as Patnaik and Chandrasekhar appear to think, but between policies that combine equity and rapid capital accumulation, on the one side, or persistent inequality and inefficiency, on the other. The post-1991 reforms have taken a few tentative steps to reduce inefficiency; they have done little to reduce inequality.

Part II

Foreign direct investment,
globalization, and neo-liberalism

4

Globalization, transnational corporations, and economic development: can the developing countries pursue strategic industrial policy in a globalizing world economy?

Ha-joon Chang

Introduction

During the last quarter of this century, we have witnessed a sea change in the prevailing view on the role of the state. The earlier interventionist orthodoxy that ruled the "Golden Age of Capitalism" (1950–73) has been subjected to some severe, and in some areas fatal, criticisms, and currently the neo-liberal vision, which draws its inspirations from the old liberal world order of the 1870–1913 period, dominates. On the domestic front, the current orthodoxy seeks to restore entrepreneurial dynamism and social discipline by rolling back the boundaries of the state through budget cuts, privatization, and deregulation. At the international level, it seeks to accelerate global integration and convergence (a trend that orthodox economists believe started around 1870 but was reversed after the First World War) by reducing restrictions on the international flows of trade, direct and portfolio investments, and technology.[1]

Yet even when considering the shift in the overall intellectual and policy atmosphere, the debate on developing country governments' policies regarding trans-

---

1   It is interesting to note that most neo-liberal authors hardly mention the issue of international flow of labor, much less the possibility of liberalizing international migration. Cable (1995) is one of the few neo-liberal writers who directly confronts the issue of international labor mobility. For a discussion of this issue from a "progressive" perspective, see Hirst and Thompson (1996, chapter 8).

   For a critical review of neo-liberal economics, see Chang & Rowthorn 1995, introduction.

Parts of this chapter draw heavily from the paper, "Transnational Corporations and Strategic Industrial Policy," presented at the World Institute of Development Economics Research (WIDER) conference, "Transnational Corporations in the Developed, Developing, and Transitional Economies: Changing Strategies and Policy Implications," September 1995, King's College, Cambridge, U.K. The research support from WIDER is duly acknowledged. I benefited greatly from discussions with William Milberg and Richard Kozul-Wright in writing the earlier paper, and from suggestions by the editors of this volume in writing the current chapter.

national corporations (TNCs) has arguably experienced the most dramatic about-turn. (For some recent critical reviews of the literature, see Helleiner 1989 and Lall 1993, introduction). Once regarded by many commentators as agents distorting, if not actually hampering, the development of poorer nations, TNCs are now regarded by many, including even some of their earlier critics, as indispensable agents of development, promoting the integration of developing countries into the emerging network of globalized production and thus enhancing their efficiency and growth (e.g., see Julius 1990, 1994; UNCTC 1992b; Michalet 1994; Brittan 1995). Even some of those who do not agree with this rose-tinted picture of TNCs accept the fact that increasing international economic interdependence, or "globalization," and especially the growth in the importance of TNCs in the process, is now unstoppable. Therefore, they argue, countries should adopt a more accommodating attitude toward TNCs whether they like it or not (e.g., see Stopford 1994).

This chapter critically examines the currently popular view that TNCs are the essential agents of economic development in the globalizing economy, and it discusses whether the rise of TNCs would prevent the pursuit of "strategic" or "selective" industrial policy by developing countries, as it is often alleged. The structure of the paper is as follows. After examining some basic facts about globalization and the rise of the TNCs in that process, we discuss the role of TNCs in economic development, drawing on some recent theoretical literature and on the experiences of certain East Asian countries, especially Korea and Taiwan. We then discuss how much the recent (alleged) rise of TNCs has diminished the ability of developing country governments to conduct strategic industrial policy and examine the policy options open to developing countries on this front. The final section presents our conclusions.

Globalization and the rise of TNCs: myths, facts, and neglected details

Discussions of recent trends in the rise of TNCs are often strewn with impressive facts and figures testifying to the increasing importance of foreign direct investment (FDI) and other activities by TNCs, even when compared to other international economic activities such as international trade.

First, for example, there are many statistics showing that FDI is playing an increasingly important and possibly leading role in the process of globalization (all the following figures are from Stopford 1994, unless indicated otherwise). FDI has been growing four times faster than international trade since 1982. Since the 1970s, the combined output of TNCs has exceeded the volume of international trade. FDI in developing countries has increased dramatically in recent years (for example, from $36.9 billion to $56.3 billion between 1991 and 1993; see Hutton 1995a), suggesting that more and more countries are being drawn into the process of globalization. TNCs manage about 75 percent of world trade in manufactured goods, over a third of which is intra-affiliate trade. They account for 75 percent of all industrial research and development in economies of the OECD (Organization for Economic

Cooperation and Development) (Archibugi and Michie 1995, 130), and they dominate the international trade in technology payments. The examples could go on.

Secondly, it is argued, albeit anecdotally (partially, but not solely, because of an understandable difficulty in collecting the relevant data), that TNCs are becoming more and more "transnational" and thus "stateless." This process, it is argued, occurs not simply because of the sheer increase in the share of TNC activities that are located outside the home countries, but more importantly through the relocation of "core" activities such as R&D, and sometimes even of the corporate headquarters, out of the home countries (this process is described as "complex integration" by UNCTAD, 1993, chapter 5). The emergence of the concept of "world car" or "global car" in the automobile industry or the establishment of R&D centers in the U.S. or Europe by the Japanese and Korean computer TNCs are some of the most frequently cited cases in support of this argument.

Thirdly, the fact that some countries that ostensibly have had "liberal" policies toward FDI (or at least toward some form of active TNC involvement) have performed well is often used as a "proof" that liberal FDI policies benefit the host countries (e.g., see UNCTAD 1995, chapter 5, and Ozawa 1995). The East Asian countries (except Japan, whose illiberal policies toward TNCs are well known) and certain post-reform Latin American countries, especially Mexico (until the 1994–95 crisis), are often cited as examples of countries whose open attitudes toward TNCs led to industrial development and export success. It is argued that open trade and FDI policies have given them the access not only to needed capital but also to advanced technologies, sophisticated managerial practices, and distribution networks in the export markets, thus contributing to their spectacular growth and trade performance.

For many neo-liberal commentators, such facts and figures seem to offer incontrovertible evidence that the world economy is becoming increasingly borderless and globalized, that in this process TNCs are playing an increasingly important (and now arguably leading) role, and that countries with open FDI policies have performed better than those with more restrictive policies. However, such a picture as we shall see below, not only is inaccurate in many respects but, even where it is broadly correct, conceals an important degree of unevenness of the globalization process across regions, countries, and industries. In the rest of this section, we offer an alternative picture to that painted by the supporters of globalization, and try to show how many of their claims are exaggerated and overly generalized. Although some of the facts cited below are well known and are discussed in much further depth and in a much broader context elsewhere (for some recent examples, see Bairoch and Kozul-Wright 1996; Hirst and Thompson 1996; Milberg 1998), it will be useful to state them in summary form here in order to put our later policy discussions into perspective.

First, the bulk of FDI occurs among the developed countries; only a handful of developing countries take part in the transnational investment story (Dicken 1992, chapter 4). For example, in 1989, the Group of Five (G5) economies alone received 75 percent of world FDI (Hirst and Thompson 1992, 366). By comparison, between 1983 and 1989 only 19.7 percent of world FDI went to developing countries (see Table 1). Although this share has increased (to 29.2 percent during 1990–94), it is still

Table 1 *The share of developing countries in world's total foreign direct investment inflows, including and excluding China, 1983–94 (millions of dollars)*

	1983–89 (annual average)	1990	1991	1992	1993	1994*	1990–94 (annual average)
World total	106,827	211,072	162,662	164,399	206,320	231,125	195,116
Developing countries	21,024 (19.7%)	34,687 (16.4%)	40,878 (25.1%)	54,634 (33.2%)	72,642 (35.2%)	82,131 (35.5%)	56,994 (29.2%)
China	2,047 (1.9%)	3,487 (1.6%)	4,366 (2.7%)	11,156 (6.8%)	27,515 (13.3%)	33,800 (14.6%)	16,065 (8.2%)
Developing countries excluding China	18,977 (17.8%)	31,200 (14.8%)	36,512 (22.4%)	43,478 (26.4%)	45,127 (21.9%)	48,331 (20.9%)	40,929 (21.0%)

Note: Figures in parentheses are shares in world total.
Source: Calculated from UNCTAD, *World Investment Report 1995*, Annex Table 1.
* Estimates.

not of the size it is often made out to be. Consider, for example, the recent assertion by Sir Leon Brittan, vice president of the European Commission, that "[o]ver half of world FDI now goes to developing countries" (Brittan 1995, 3). Especially when we exclude the inflows to China, the increase in the share for the developing countries is even smaller (from 17.8 percent to 21.0 percent between 1983–89 and 1990–94).[2] Moreover, even within the developing world, FDI is highly concentrated among a few countries. Between 1981 and 1992, the 10 largest developing countries receiving FDI accounted for 72 percent of the developing country total (UNCTAD 1994, 14, table 1.5).[3] These concentrations of FDI occurred *despite* the liberal FDI policies that many developing countries introduced during this period on the recommendations of neo-liberal economists.

Secondly, while increasing "globalization" of TNCs is occurring, it is happening at a much slower pace and in a more uneven pattern than the proponents of the globalization thesis believe. Most TNCs remain international firms with a strong

2   Some commentators also suspect that a large proportion of FDI into China is in fact domestic investment rerouted through overseas Chinese communities in order to exploit the privileges extended to foreign investors (see e.g., Hutton 1995a).

3   Part of this concentration is obviously due to the fact that many of the largest recipients of FDI are also large economies (in terms of GDP). However, even after adjusting for the size of the economy, the concentration of FDI within the developing world still remains high. During the 1980s (1980–91), the 10 largest developing country recipients of FDI received 16.5 percent of the world's total FDI, even though these countries accounted for only about 7.3 percent of the world's total GDP (for 1980–89). The figures are extracted from Hirst and Thompson (1996), Tables 3.2 and 3.4.

base, in terms of assets and production activities, in their "home" countries, and the alleged recent reduction in the importance of the home countries has been neither marked nor uniform across countries and industries (Hindess and Hirst 1996, 95–7). In addition, at most TNCs, the top decision makers are home country nationals (Kozul-Wright 1995, 160). And when "core" activities are relocated, they are moved primarily to other developed countries, usually in North America, Europe, and Japan (Hirst and Thompson 1992, 368). As a survey by the *Economist* put it, generally speaking, "what [TNCs] have done is to extend their 'home bases' into neighboring countries" (*The Economist,* March 27, 1993, pp. 15–6). Archibugi and Michie (1995) corroborate this statement by showing that the globalization of R&D, which is often regarded as the primary indicator of increasing globalization of TNCs through complex integration, is basically a "regional" phenomenon – specifically, U.S. and Japanese TNCs do not do much R&D outside their home bases (except in Canada in the case of the U.S. firms), while European TNCs do substantial amounts of R&D outside their home bases but mostly in other European economies.[4]

Thirdly, the attempt to support pro-TNC policies by using the examples of East Asian developing countries needs to be critically scrutinized. Many countries in East Asia, while not against hosting TNCs in certain areas, have had rather restrictive policies overall toward FDI. Only Malaysia and Hong Kong had largely (and even then not entirely) liberal attitudes toward TNCs. Singapore heavily relied on TNCs, but deliberately directed FDI toward government-designated priority sectors. Only in these three economies among the seven East Asian developing countries has the contribution of FDI as a source of capital accumulation been exceptionally high by international standards (see Table 2). It should also be noted that, even in the case of these economies, it is general economic conditions and not exceptional FDI-specific incentives that mainly explain the large FDI inflows (World Bank 1985, 130); this phenomenon is observed all over the world, not just in East Asia (Helleiner 1989, 1467). In Korea, Taiwan, and Indonesia, the contribution of FDI to capital accumulation was in fact below the developing country average, with Korea distinguishing itself as having one of the lowest such ratios in the world (if not quite approaching the Japanese level, which is arguably the lowest in the world; see Table 2). In Thailand, which is usually regarded as a model "FDI-driven" economy, the ratio of FDI to gross fixed capital formation was not much above the developing country average, and the ratio has actually slipped below the average in the early 1990s. Thus, the alleged importance of TNCs in East Asian development largely depends on one country's experience, namely Malaysia, if we exclude the very exceptional cases of the two city states of Hong Kong and Singapore.[5]

4   Also note the parallel phenomenon that, despite its allegedly growing importance, intra-industry trade also remains basically a "regional" phenomenon – that is, there is little intra-industry trade between the three regional "blocs" (Rowthorn 1995). Taken together, these two phenomena seem to suggest that there is a minimal efficient scale of the economy, of which all European economies fall short. Of course, this does not imply that size of the economy is the only factor involved in the determination of trade and TNC activities.

5   Some commentators, while agreeing with our assessment of the *past* contribution of FDI to East Asian development, argue that the picture is changing, as shown in the rising importance

Table 2 *Ratio of FDI inflows to gross domestic capital formation for various regions and selected countries (annual average)*

	1971–75	1976–80	1981–85	1986–90	1991–93
All Countries	n.a.	n.a.	2.3%	4.1%	3.8%
Developed	n.a.	n.a.	2.2%	4.6%	3.3%
European Union	n.a.	n.a.	2.6%	5.9%	5.6%
Austria	1.8%	0.9%	1.3%	1.5%	1.5%
France	1.8%	1.9%	2.0%	4.1%	7.7%
Germany	2.1%	0.8%	1.2%	2.0%	1.4%
Netherlands	6.1%	4.5%	6.1%	13.3%	10.6%
Sweden	0.6%	0.5%	1.6%	4.0%	9.5%
UK	7.3%	8.4%	5.6%	14.6%	10.0%
Switzerland	n.a.	n.a.	2.3%	5.3%	3.1%
U.S.	0.9%	2.0%	2.9%	6.9%	3.2%
Canada	3.6%	1.7%	1.0%	5.8%	4.3%
Japan	0.1%	0.1%	0.1%	0.0%	0.1%
Developing	n.a.	n.a.	3.3%	3.2%	5.7%
Africa	n.a.	n.a.	2.3%	3.5%	4.6%
Latin America	n.a.	n.a.	4.1%	4.2%	6.5%
Argentina	0.1%	2.1%	5.0%	11.1%	37.6%
Brazil	4.2%	3.9%	4.3%	1.7%	1.5%
Chile	-7.3%	4.2%	6.7%	20.6%	8.5%
Mexico	3.5%	3.6%	5.0%	7.5%	6.8%
Asia	n.a.	n.a.	3.1%	2.8%	5.5%
Bangladesh	n.a.	n.a.	0.0%	0.1%	0.2%
China	0.0%	0.1%	0.9%	2.1%	10.4%
Hong Kong	5.9%	4.2%	6.9%	12.9%	5.7%
India	0.3%	0.1%	0.1%	0.3%	0.4%
Indonesia	4.6%	2.4%	0.9%	2.1%	4.5%
Korea	1.9%	0.4%	0.5%	1.2%	0.6%
Malaysia	15.2%	11.9%	10.8%	11.7%	24.6%
Pakistan	0.5%	0.9%	1.3%	2.3%	3.4%
Philippines	1.0%	0.9%	0.8%	6.7%	4.6%
Singapore	15.0%	16.6%	17.4%	35.0%	37.4%
Taiwan	1.4%	1.2%	1.5%	3.7%	2.6%
Thailand	3.0%	1.5%	3.0%	6.5%	4.7%
Turkey	n.a.	n.a.	0.8%	2.1%	3.2%
Eastern Europe	n.a.	n.a.	0.0%	0.1%	12.2%

Source: UNCTAD, *World Investment Report 1993*, Annex Table 3 (for the 1971–80 data) and *World Investment Report 1995*, Annex Table 5 (for the rest).

The above discussions show that, while TNCs are increasing in importance, the phenomenon is by no means a truly "global" and even process. Most TNCs are still "national" firms with peripheral operations abroad than truly "stateless" bodies globally rearranging their activities in search of higher profits. Although there are signs that the picture is slowly changing, it is not clear at all how far this process will or can go (see Milberg 1998). Many developing countries and former-Communist countries are still excluded from international FDI flows, and their ability to attract FDI has changed little (with some notable exceptions such as China and Vietnam), despite policy changes they have adopted during the last decade or so at the urging of (their own and foreign) neo-liberal economists.

The alleged importance of TNCs in the developmental process of East Asia also turns out to be highly exaggerated. Many East Asian economies were not particularly reliant on FDI by international standards, and most of their governments have taken "strategic," rather than laissez faire, attitudes toward TNCs to one degree or another and tried to influence the direction and the terms of engagement of incoming FDI. This is the broad empirical background against which we place our discussion.

TNCs and economic development

Those who argue for the liberalization of policies toward TNCs have a strong belief that what is good for TNCs is good for the host country, and that the recent trend in globalization is eliminating whatever minor conflicts of interests may have once existed between the two. So, for example, Julius (1994, 278) argues that "[i]t is no longer appropriate to assume that government and corporate objectives conflict." They regard the restrictive TNC policies that were popular in the 1960s and 1970s in many developing countries as ideologically motivated, and argue that "fortunately" now "[i]nvestment is recognized for what it is: a source of extra capital, a contribution to a healthy external balance, a basis for increased productivity, additional employment, effective competition, rational production, technology transfer, and a source of managerial knowhow" (Brittan 1995, 2).

However, the fact that there are few justifications for the extreme anti-TNC view that was once popular in some developing countries should by no means suggest that TNCs are unambiguously beneficial for economic development. (For some recent literature reviews, see Helleiner 1989; Lall 1993; and Chudnovsky 1993). While some earlier concerns about the "inappropriateness" of the production technology or the product mix of TNCs were often misconceived and exaggerated, the problem itself is real and can be important in certain circumstances. Earlier criticisms of "surplus extraction" through transfer pricing or excessive royalty payments, again,

of FDI within the East Asian region. However, this increase is mainly due to the recent rush of investment out of Japan and the first-tier newly industrializing countries (NICs) to the second-tier NICs and China. A lot of this investment is of a once-and-for-all nature, and therefore it is unlikely to be sustained.

may at times have been out of proportion, but the practices exist and can be significant and damaging. Predatory behavior or manipulation of consumer preference by TNCs may not necessarily be more severe than that carried out by their local equivalents, but these are still practices to be reckoned with. Restrictions imposed by TNC headquarters on the exporting or R&D activities of subsidiaries may not be as widespread or important as once thought, but they nevertheless have to be minimized, especially if the host country government is keen on technological spillovers from the TNCs. The fears about manipulation of the overall national policy regime by TNCs through political influence may have been overplayed in the past, but these fears cannot simply be dismissed as unfounded.

More recently, careful analyses of empirical cases as well as developments in the economics of technology have shown the importance of domestic technological capabilities in sustaining long-term growth, and thus have raised further doubts as to whether inviting TNCs into a country is the best way to promote industrialization (Fransman and King 1984; Fransman 1986; Ul Haq et al. 1996). There is a growing consensus that accepting a "package" of finance, technology, managerial skills, and other capabilities offered by TNCs may not be as good for long-term industrial development as encouraging national firms to construct their own packages using their own managerial skills – with some necessary outsourcing. As Lall (1993) points out, while having more FDI may, on the margin, bring net benefits to the host country, there still is a question of choosing between different strategies regarding the role of FDI in long-term development.

This critique of TNCs does not mean to imply that countries *cannot* develop if they rely extensively on TNCs. Singapore, as one obvious example, has managed to thrive. However, it should be noted that the Singapore government, while welcoming and actively courting TNCs, did not take a laissez faire attitude to TNCs; rather, it deliberately directed FDI into strategic sectors. If Singapore, given its city-state status and unique political economy, looks like too much of an exception (which it is), one can always cite the example of Malaysia, where FDI indeed has played a crucial role in development. However, these cases still do not prove the desirability of a pro-TNC developmental strategy nor the feasibility of its widespread adoption. First of all, given its relative lack of experienced indigenous managers, qualified engineers, and skilled workers – a situation which is at least partly due to its reliance on TNCs – Malaysia is likely to find it difficult to move into the more sophisticated industries that will help it sustain long-term growth (e.g., see Lall 1995). Moreover, as Rowthorn (1996) argues, those who recommend the "Malaysian road" to other developing countries do not realize that an implausibly large amount of additional FDI will have to be generated if the experience is to be replicated on a large scale.[6]

6   Rowthorn (1996) calculates that, if the share of FDI in GDP for the average developing country (excluding the first-tier NICs of Korea, Taiwan, Hong Kong, and Singapore) were to reach the same level as that of Malaysia between 1991 and 1993, namely, 10 percent of GDP, the total world level of FDI, which was already near its historical peak during this period, would have to increase by seven times, reaching a level equivalent to 1.7 times the total manufacturing investment of the OECD countries – a spectacularly unrealistic scenario. Rowthorn, however, does not take account of the fact that the 10 percent figure was exceptional even by

The experiences of the two "star performers" of East Asia, namely, Korea and Taiwan, especially during their earlier days of industrialization, also provide interesting insights into the role of TNCs in economic development. (For more details, refer to Koo 1993 on Korea and Schive 1993 on Taiwan).[7] While these countries have not been hostile to foreign technology or capital per se, they have clearly preferred, if the situation allowed, to use such technology and capital under "national" management, rather than relying on TNCs.[8] This preference was necessarily somewhat more tempered in Taiwan than in Korea, due to the relative absence of large private sector firms in Taiwan, but both their governments have possessed a clear and sophisticated notion of the costs and benefits of inviting in TNCs, and they approved FDI only when they thought there were potential net benefits (the Korean government's 1981 *White Paper on Foreign Investment* provides a fine specimen of such policy vision; see EPB 1981).[9]

The most important policies toward TNCs employed by Korea and Taiwan were the restrictions on entry and ownership. In entry, for example, FDI in industries supplying critical intermediate inputs using sophisticated technology (e.g., petroleum refinery, synthetic fibers) or labor-intensive export industries generating foreign exchange and jobs (e.g., textile, electronics assembly) was encouraged when compared, say, to domestic market-oriented consumer durable goods industries. In Korea as late as the early 1980s, around 50 percent of all industries and around 20 percent of manufacturing industries were still "off-limits" to FDI (EPB 1981, 70–1). Even when entry was allowed, the governments of these countries tried to encourage joint ventures, preferably under local majority ownership, in an attempt to facilitate the transfer of core technologies and managerial skills. Again, in the case of Korea, even in sectors where FDI was allowed, foreign ownership above 50 percent was prohibited except in areas where FDI was deemed to be of "strategic" importance, which covered only

---

Malaysia's own historical standard, and therefore his calculation may exaggerate the situation. However, even if we use the 5 percent benchmark, which is closer to the historical average of Malaysia's ratio of FDI to GDP, the power of his argument is not diminished, as the developing-worldwide replication of the Malaysian strategy will still call for a 3.5-fold increase in world FDI.

7 At the time of final revision to this chapter (December 1997), it was announced that FDI policy is to be greatly liberalized in Korea following the conditionalities of the IMF bailout. However, the details of such changes are as yet not known, and how much change this liberalization will eventually bring to the role of FDI in the Korean economy is not now clear.

8 This tendency was more pronounced in Korea. According to Amsden (1989), only 5 percent of total foreign capital inflow into Korea between 1963 and 1982 (excluding foreign aid, which was important only until the early 1960s) was in the form of FDI (p. 92, table 5).

9 The Korean government's 1981 *White Paper on Foreign Investment* lists various benefits of FDI, such as investment augmentation, employment creation, industrial "upgrading" effect, balance-of-payments contribution, and technology transfer, but it is also clearly aware of its costs from such factors as transfer pricing, restrictions on imports and exports of the subsidiaries, "crowding-out" of domestic investors in the domestic credit market, allocative inefficiencies due to "noncompetitive" market structure, retardation of technological development, "distortion" of industrial structure due to the introduction of "inappropriate" products, and even the exercise of political influences by the TNCs on the formation of policies (EPB 1981, 50–64). It is interesting to note that this list includes more or less all the issues identified by the more recent academic debates that we discussed above.

about 13 percent of all manufacturing industries (EPB 1981, 70).[10] As a result, as of the mid-1980s only 5 percent of TNC subsidiaries in Korea were wholly owned, compared to 50 percent in Mexico and 60 percent in Brazil – countries that are often believed to have had much more "anti-foreign" policy orientations than Korea (Evans 1987, 208). Due to the scarcity of large domestic firms that could become plausible joint venture partners, the Taiwanese government was more flexible on the ownership question, and thus in terms of ownership structure of TNC subsidiaries Taiwan was somewhere in between Korea and Latin America, with 33.5 percent of TNC subsidiaries (excluding the ones owned by overseas Chinese) being wholly owned as of 1985 (Schive 1993, 319).

Policy measures other than the ones concerning entry and ownership were also used to control the activities of TNCs in accordance with national developmental goals. First, there were measures to ensure that the "right" kind of technologies were acquired in the "right" terms. The technology that was to be brought in by the investing TNCs was carefully screened to ensure that it was not overly obsolete and that local subsidiaries were not subject to excessive royalties. Second, there were measures to maximize technology spillovers. Investors who were more willing to transfer technologies were selected over those who were not, unless the willing investors were too far behind in terms of technology. (For an interesting recent example, refer to the case of the Korean fast train project, described in the next section.) Third, local content requirements were strictly imposed in order to maximize technological spillovers from the TNC presence. Targets for localization were set realistically, however, so that the requirements would not seriously hurt the export competitiveness of the host country. It was in fact the case that in some industries they were more strictly applied to the products destined for the domestic market.

In this section, we have argued that the belief by some neo-liberal commentators that what is good for TNCs is also good for the host economy is unwarranted. While some of the earlier criticisms of TNCs may have been misconceived, over-generalized, and exaggerated, there are many important areas where there exists an obvious conflict of interest between the TNCs and the host country. These include the issues of "appropriateness" of technology, transfer pricing, monopolistic practices, restrictions imposed on the subsidiaries, particularly regarding exports and R&D, and even their ability to manipulate the overall national policy regime. Most importantly, recent theoretical developments and empirical studies suggest that long-term productivity enhancement may be better achieved by an industrialization strategy that puts emphasis on building local managerial and technological capabilities and uses TNCs in a selective, strategic manner to accelerate that process. We further illustrated this point with examples of Taiwan and Korea, briefly commenting on

10   These included industries where access to proprietary technology was deemed essential for further development of the industry, and industries where the capital requirement and/or the risks involved in the investment was very large. The ownership ceiling was also relaxed if: (1) the investments were made in the free trade zones; (2) the investments were made by overseas Koreans; or (3) the investments would "diversify" the origins of FDI into the country – namely, investments from countries other than the U.S. and Japan, which had previously dominated the Korean FDI scene. For details, see EPB (1981, 70–1).

their policies on TNC entry, ownership, contractual terms, technological spillovers, and local content requirements. The policies employed in Korea and Taiwan suggest that, while TNCs can and should be used, their role needs to be clearly defined in relation to the overall industrialization strategy and with reference to the specific needs of the particular industries concerned.

Does the rise of transnational corporations make strategic industrial policy by developing countries impossible?

The proponents of the globalization thesis have emphasized the constraints that the high degree of globalization has placed on the policy autonomy of national governments (e.g., Julius 1994; Michalet 1994). While sensible commentators are careful to dismiss the talk of the "demise of the nation state" as too simplistic and premature (e.g., Ostry 1990; Cable 1995), there seems to be a feeling among the majority of the writers on globalization that a serious erosion, if not a total elimination, of national policy autonomy is only a matter of time, if it hasn't already happened. Together with the increased international financial capital flows that restrict the effectiveness of national macroeconomic policy, the role of TNCs in eroding such autonomy is often emphasized (Julius 1994; Michalet 1994).

These commentators argue that, in such an environment, it is not possible any more for developing country governments to employ "strategic" (or "selective") industrial policy.[11] They believe that, whatever the benefits of this policy in the past (which they think were nonexistent or even negative anyway), it is not viable any more, given the increasing importance of TNCs, which can relocate any or all of their activities in search of a better "investment climate." Thus, by "voting with their feet," it is argued, TNCs force the governments to stick close to the industrial policy regimes of their competitors, and indeed to move toward a more liberal policy regime in their competitive bids to attract the FDI that, in their view, is becoming increasingly important for wealth creation.

At one level, it seems difficult to deny such a claim. As firms become less bound by national constraints, it seems only natural that the effectiveness of "strategic" industrial policy at the national level is bound to be reduced. And if this is the case, it also seems only natural that putting restrictions on TNCs when competitor econo-

---

11   Unlike some other terms used in economics, the term "industrial policy," also known as "strategic" or "selective" industrial policy, suffers from a serious definitional ambiguity. While many authors have tried to define it as encompassing all policies that affect industrial performance, we reject such a broad definition, which almost entirely takes away the analytical edge that the term has, and adopt a narrow definition, namely, as a policy that attempts to affect the evolution of specific industries (and even specific firms when they are large enough) through state intervention in order to effect "national" efficiency and growth. See Chang (1994, 58–61) for a more systematic discussion of this problem. Also, it should be noted that, in the context of the present paper, aiming for "national" efficiency and growth does not rule out the use of "foreign" firms, as far as these firms do not seriously undermine national policy autonomy.

mies do not would lead to the exodus of TNCs. However, this kind of reasoning is based on a number of explicit and implicit assumptions that do not have sound empirical justification or are products of unwarranted extrapolation from a limited number of cases. Let us examine them one by one.

First, the argument that TNCs will migrate to the country offering the best deal is based on the assumption that TNCs always have an upper hand in bargaining. (For further discussion of the bargaining issue, see Helleiner 1989). However, the relative bargaining strengths of TNCs and national governments depend on which industry and which country we are talking about and when the bargaining is taking place (relative advantages change over time). While there are some industries for which many countries qualify as investment sites, there are certain other industries for which feasible investments sites are limited for a number of reasons: many mineral-related industries require investments near the depositories; some industries require particular types of skilled labor at reasonable prices, which many countries may not be able to supply; some countries have locational advantages, say, as an entry point into a big market; some countries have exceptionally large and/or fast-growing markets; and so on.

So, it is not just that governments compete for FDI, but also that TNCs compete for attractive host countries. The clearest example of the latter is the recent bargaining between the Chinese government and various automobile TNCs regarding the selection of a partner to produce the "people's car." Lured by the prospect of being the first mover (or at least one of the first movers) in what may soon become one of the biggest passenger car markets in the world, many TNCs (including the German luxury car makers Benz, BMW, and Porsche, which emphasized that its founder, Dr. Porsche, was the original designer of the proverbial "people's car," Volkswagen) were putting forth fiercely competitive bids (*Financial Times*, November 23, 1994).

While few countries can expect to have China's level of bargaining power, they can still extract substantial concessions from TNCs. The recent granting by the Korean government of its fast train project to the Anglo-French joint venture GEC Alsthom, organized around the producer of French TGV (which offered more in terms of technology transfer than the Japanese and German firms that offered superior products) is one such example (*Financial Times*, August 23, 1993). Another instructive example comes from the recent upstaging of GM's talks with the Polish government regarding the takeover and restructuring of the ailing state-owned automobile company FSO by the South Korean automobile maker Daewoo (which, ironically, was a 50–50 joint venture with GM until 1992). Daewoo's offer to inject a large amount of capital ($1.1 billion) in order to transform FSO as its major platform for exports of passenger cars and car parts (engines and gear boxes) to the European Union suddenly gave the Polish government enormous bargaining power. GM upped its offer, but eventually Daewoo clinched the deal (*Financial Times*, various issues between August and October, 1995).[12]

12   It was reported that the granting of the deal for FSO to Daewoo could result in the injection of an extra $1 billion through the establishment of another joint venture to produce vans at FS Lublin, where Daewoo recently entered a separate joint venture to assemble small

These examples show how even governments from countries that do not have the Chinese government's kind of unique bargaining power can play one TNC against another in order to extract greater concessions. Needless to say, many developing countries have few attractive productive assets or locational advantages for which TNCs will compete, and as a result they may not be able to follow the Chinese lead. However, a few will have at least some "bargaining chips." And once TNCs are interested in a country, their political vulnerability as "foreign" firms can make them even more responsive than their domestic equivalents to the demands of the government. It is also worth noting that newly emerging TNCs from East Asia are pursuing an aggressive strategy of expansion in order to challenge the established TNCs from North America and Europe, thus offering valuable additional room for maneuver for host country governments – as was so dramatically illustrated by the Polish automobile industry example cited above.

Second, regarding the freedom of TNCs to seek the best deal, there are certainly some industries with low sunk costs involved in investments and who are therefore "footloose" (e.g., garments, shoes, toys), but many other industries have high sunk costs, not only in terms of dedicated physical equipment (e.g., chemicals, pharmaceuticals) but also in terms of subcontracting networks and other relation-specific activities that firms have taken time to build (e.g., advanced electronics, automobiles). In such industries, TNCs are not entirely footloose, and they cannot pull out at the slightest adverse change in host country policies.

Of course, this does not mean that in such industries governments can do anything they want once TNCs have made the investments, since what the government does now will affect future investment decisions by TNCs. However, as Ostry (1990, 98) suggests, the larger TNCs are able and often willing to accommodate a lot of "restrictive" policy measures, as long as they are stable and the changes predictable. Thus, although we have surprisingly little systematic evidence in this regard, it seems reasonable to say that "[t]he real question to ask of [TNCs] is not why they are always threatening to up and leave a country if things seem to go bad for them there, but why the vast majority of them fail to leave and continue to stay put in their home base and major centres of investment" (Hirst and Thompson 1992, 368).

Third, those who criticize "restrictive" policies toward TNCs assume that FDI decisions are mainly affected by the amount of business freedom granted to them (e.g., Julius 1994, 278–9). However, FDI decisions are much more strongly affected by the overall performance of the economy, especially the prospect for growth. Even the World Bank, which is often associated with liberal policies toward TNCs, argues that "[t]he specific incentives and regulations governing direct investment have less effect on how much investment a country receives than has its general economic and political climate, and its financial and exchange rate policies" (World Bank 1985, 130). In other words, the evidence suggests that growth leads FDI rather than the other way around (see Milberg 1998). If so, it is questionable whether

passenger cars. If that deal were to occur, the total investment from Daewoo could amount to $2.1 billion, which will be just under half the total FDI that has flowed into Poland since its economic reform (*Financial Times*, August 28, 1995).

adopting a more liberal FDI policy will lead to any substantial increase in FDI flows, since there is no evidence that such a policy leads to an improvement in the country's growth performance – which is by far the most effective way to attract FDI.

This argument is also supported by the fact that, as we also have seen above (Table 2), the share of developing countries (not counting China) in the world's total FDI has increased only marginally over the last decade, despite the extensive liberalization of FDI policies. Thus, it may be argued that as far as they do not involve asset appropriation and other measures that threaten basic capitalist property relations, FDI policies seem to be much less important than other factors, such as the growth prospect of the country's domestic market or the country's political stability, in determining investment decisions by TNCs. Such an observation leads us to conclude that the current argument for liberal policies for TNCs in developing countries based on the "globalization" thesis is at best distracting our attention from more important issues, or at worst is being used, if unconsciously, as a stooge in the scare tactic to drive more developing countries onto a neo-liberal "reform" path.

This section discussed how the claims of the impossibility of strategic industrial policy in an era of growing TNC importance have been exaggerated and are based on questionable assumptions. It should be emphasized that, perhaps except for the poorest countries with meager natural resource endowments, small domestic markets, and no locational advantage, potential host countries are not merely passive victims: they have, and often exercise with substantial success, considerable bargaining power in their dealings with TNCs. Claims about the footloose nature of TNCs are also often exaggerated. There are many industries where investments involve a large amount of sunk costs (both in terms of physical capital and production networks) that restrict the mobility of the firms involved. It is also the case that the largest TNCs are able and often willing to live with restrictive policies as long as they are stable and predictable. Overall, the regulatory regime for TNCs is, as far as it is not impossibly restrictive, only a minor consideration in TNCs' choice of investment sites when compared to things like the market growth prospect. Given that promoting growth is the most effective way to attract FDI, having a well-conducted selective industrial policy may, contrary to the conventional wisdom, help the country attract more FDI.

Policy options for developing countries

All the skepticism expressed in the preceding sections regarding the conventional wisdom about the role of TNCs in developing countries is not meant to imply that therefore the rise of TNCs can be comfortably ignored. While the current claims about the end, or at least a serious weakening, of the nation-state are often exaggerated, it is true that the growth in the number and scope of TNCs (and globalization in general) has resulted in restrictions on the scope of strategic industrial policy and other national policies as well (see Panic 1995). Such restrictions result not only from the greater bargaining power that firms will have against national governments due to their ability to shop around for investment sites, but also from the concern by the government that, if it provides TNCs with some help as a part of its industrial policy, the benefits will spill over the national border and thereby reduce the cost effectiveness of the policy (Chang and Rowthorn 1995, 44–5).

Despite such problems, intelligent governments should try, and have tried (as seen in some East Asian countries) to use TNCs in a strategic way in order to acquire necessary capital, technology, marketing networks, and so on. What exactly the "strategic way" means will depend on various factors, such as the country's relative bargaining position, the technological nature of the industry, the role of the particular industry concerned in the bigger scheme of industrial development, and so on, but we illustrate our point with a few examples. (See also Stopford and Strange 1991, chapter 4.)

In those industries where what is needed is a simple injection of capital to create jobs and foreign exchange earning capability, it may be acceptable, or even important, that the country have an open policy toward FDI. "Cash cow" industries like garments, shoes, and toys are examples of such industries. In industries where the capital and technological requirements are high and where the government expects the major return to be the "rent" element – such as oil, mineral, and other natural resource extraction industries – having an open attitude toward FDI may be crucial. However, in such cases, the bargaining skills to extract the largest possible shares of the rent element and, more importantly, the plans to effectively use the rent from such industries for the development of other industries will be crucial to the success of overall industrial policy.

When the industries concerned are ones in which the country hopes to become internationally competitive in the long run but that require a major injection of new technology and capital, TNC participation may be desirable. However, in such industries a tough bargaining position on issues like technology transfer or export and R&D restrictions imposed on the subsidiary will be crucial (as seen in the example of the Chinese car industry and the Korean fast train project cited above). In other industries, where the country is reasonably close to achieving international competitiveness, keeping the TNCs out may be necessary in order to allow local firms the maximum learning opportunities, especially if the domestic market is small. Even in high-tech industries, where the ability to keep up with the technological developments of the most advanced TNCs is (allegedly) becoming crucial, it is possible to devise effective "national" technology policies based on selective interactions with foreign TNCs (see Fransman 1994 for the example of Japan; see Evans 1998 for examples from developing countries).

This list can be further elaborated, but the point here is that an intelligent government pursuing a strategic industrial policy will not have a "uniform" policy toward TNCs across industries, as many neo-liberal economists recommend. Each industry serves different functions in the greater scheme of industrial development, and it would be foolish to have either uniformly restrictive or uniformly liberal policies toward TNCs across different industries. This also means that the same industry may, and indeed should, become more or less open to FDI over time, depending on the changes in the various internal and external conditions that affect it. For example, the government could initially have a liberal FDI policy for a new industry in order to establish it, but subsequently impose tougher restrictions on TNC subsidiaries when it is deemed that the industry has developed enough local technological capability so that, with continued, if diminishing government support, it can operate competitively within the domestic economy and internationally. Alternatively, when there is a major technological change in a certain industry that makes the country's present technological capability inadequate for international competition, the government may relax rules concerning TNC participation in the industry in order to gain access to the new technology.

It is one thing to say that countries should use TNCs in a strategic manner and another to say that they can actually afford to play such a strategic game. The poorest developing countries, for example, will have weak bargaining power vis-a-vis TNCs in most industries, as the industries for which they are attractive investment sites are usually the ones in which TNCs are most mobile. On the other hand, many developing countries have some "bargaining chips," at least in relation to some industries. Some can offer the prospect of a large and/or rapidly growing domestic market, especially in industries where transportation costs are relatively high or where proximity to consumers is important for marketing (for example, China, India, Brazil, and the rapidly growing East Asian countries). Some countries, somewhat paradoxically due to their anticapitalist past, possess workforces that are relatively well educated and well trained for what they cost (for example, Eastern Europe, Vietnam, and China). Some other countries possess the locational (and legal) advantage of having easier access to large markets (for example, Mexico, the Central European countries, and the Southern European countries). Even some very poor economies have mineral and other natural resources to offer.

Needless to say, having such potential bargaining power does not directly translate into the right amount and composition of FDI, unless general economic conditions are right. Achieving the right balance of FDI will require an internally coherent government that is politically willing and administratively capable of actually exercising such bargaining power.[13] However, adopting liberal FDI policies across all sectors and industries will mean giving up one's potential bargaining power in those sectors before even exercising it, and that does not seem particularly wise. Even if many developing countries have relatively little bargaining power vis-a-vis TNCs, and even if such power is diminishing with globalization, they need not give up what little bargaining power they still have, since what national governments do still matters greatly for the determination of the costs and benefits of FDI.

13   Many governments suffer from interdepartmental rivalry in the design and execution of policies toward FDI. Moreover, a large country with a de jure and de facto decentralized power structure (for example, the U.S., China) may see their national bargaining powers weakened due to the competition among the local governments. The author thanks William Milberg for raising this point.

Conclusion

In this paper, we tried to question some myths about globalization and, more specifically, myths about the growing importance of TNCs by presenting some basic but often neglected facts. While the interdependence between different parts of the world may be increasing, and while the role of TNCs in that process is growing, it is still too early to say that we now live in a totally new world in which national policies are at best ineffective and at worst obstacles to the achievement of "world efficiency," as some proponents of the globalization thesis seem to believe.

We also argued that, while some of the early fears about TNCs were clearly unwarranted, there are good reasons to believe that an industrialization strategy based on a laissez faire attitude toward TNCs may not be as successful in the long run as a more selective, strategic approach, as seen in the examples of countries like Korea and Taiwan. Moreover, as we pointed out, despite the recent increases in their importance, TNCs do not have unambiguously superior bargaining power in all industries in relation to all countries. Their bargaining power ranges from almost absolute (e.g., Nike looking for an investment site for shoe production) to close to zero (e.g., automobile TNCs trying to curry the favor of the Chinese government for the people's car), depending on the industry and the country. This observation actually strengthens, and not weakens, the case for strategic industrial policy, because it means that governments should design their policies toward TNCs according to the particular sector concerned, rather than taking a uniform approach across sectors.

Although the constraint imposed by TNCs on national industrial policy may be growing, it is nowhere near the point where a strategic industrial policy is impossible. The current literature tends to regard the process of globalization and the rise of TNCs as an unstoppable process that no one can control and in which nations, especially developing nations, are passive agents that will have to fully embrace the process or perish. However, such a view is misleading, since there is a lot of room for maneuver for national governments, and since such room may even be increasing for some countries in some industries, especially with the recent aggressive expansion of some TNCs from East Asia (also see Milberg 1998 and Evans 1998). It would be a big mistake for a developing country to voluntarily give up all such room for maneuver by adopting a universally liberal FDI policy across all sectors. What is needed is a more differentiated and strategic approach to TNCs, which will allow host countries to intelligently "use" TNCs for their long-term developmental purposes.

Comment by *Tamim Bayoumi* on "Globalization, transnational corporations, and economic development: can the developing countries pursue strategic industrial policy in a globalizing world economy?"

This is an interesting paper about an important topic, namely, the effects of globalization on developing countries. It first highlights some "neglected" details about TNCs and FDI. The rest of the paper is then spent discussing how developing country governments should respond to these new challenges, concluding that they should continue to try and use industrial policies to restrain the forces of globalization, largely by controlling the amount of technological transfer that such investment provides. The exposition is certainly clear but, at the end of the day, I must confess that I remain largely unconvinced by the arguments.

"The facts, ma'am, the facts." The author focuses on several "neglected" details about foreign direct investment. First, most FDI occurs across industrial countries, and is thus not much of a benefit to developing countries. Second, a few favored countries have been receiving the bulk of recent FDI flows. Finally, FDI was not very important in investment and development even in these countries. The overall argument is that FDI's role in development has been overstated.

It is certainly true that most FDI occurs across developed countries, but the issue is considerably more complex than this. The text never mentions the words "greenfield" or "acquisitions," the two categories into which FDI is generally divided because of their different implications for "real" behavior. Greenfield investment occurs when a company comes in and builds a new plant in a country – in other words, its financial investment in a country is supported by physical investment, as measured in the national accounts. If the FDI is used to acquire an existing company, on the other hand, the financial investment is merely used to buy part of the existing capital stock with no immediate increase in physical investment, just as the purchase of a share in a domestic company by you or me does not have any immediate implications for the physical investment being made by that company. Now, most FDI across developed countries involves acquisitions – ownership of capital is swapped around, but with little immediate consequences for "real" activity. By contrast, significantly more FDI in developing countries is greenfield investment, in part because the existing economic and financial infrastructure is so poor. Hence, simply noting that FDI is larger between developed nations than between developed and developing nations says little about its role in growth for the developing world.

That FDI has gone overwhelmingly to a few lucky recipients is well known. It is equally well known that the recipients have generally grown fast, although whether FDI is a symptom or a cause is still unclear. The author attempts to answer this question by looking at FDI as a proportion of investment, which is an intuitively appealing measure of the role of FDI in development. Here again, however, I would advocate caution because of the nature of the data. FDI measures the initial investment made by a company to buy or create a domestic subsidiary. However, once the subsidiary has been obtained, any further borrowing from abroad to expand facilities, etc., will not be defined as FDI; rather, it will migrate to other parts of the balance-of-payments statistics. Hence, the real impact of FDI on local investment is almost impossible to calculate from aggregate data on FDI. In short, I do not think that the "neglected" facts discussed by the author prove the underlying case being made.

I found the discussion of the policies of Korea and Taiwan toward TNCs and technological transfer to be considerably more interesting. It is certainly true that neither of these star performers, particularly when they started on their period of rapid development, was particularly open to foreign investment, and in neither case can TNCs be said to have been central to their subsequent success. An even more obvious example of this argument is Japan, which, as is noted in the text, has an extremely low level of foreign investment even today but whose economic success cannot be questioned. However, Japan, Korea, and Taiwan also had a lot of other characteristics that were beneficial for development, such as high private saving rates, financial systems that were capable of investing these funds into domestic enterprises, relatively honest governments, open trade policies, and highly educated labor forces.

All of this goes to show that FDI is not necessary for successful development, and if this is the point that is being made I fully agree with it. But the argument seems to be extended to say that FDI can be harmful for development if it is not rigorously controlled by the government through industrial policy. This seems to me to be quite a leap of faith. It is certainly true that the countries discussed had controls on FDI. But so did virtually all of developing countries in the 1960s and early 1970s. While Korea, Taiwan, and Japan took off while using active industrial development, I will wager that the three worst performing developing economies in the world over the same period also used industrial policy actively. My basic point is that, if almost everyone is using industrial policies, then saying that successful economies used them successfully provides little information about their effectiveness in general. The successful economies could simply have been lucky in their choices of industries (certainly, the way the Asian nations have overinvested in computer chips over the last decade leaves room for thought about how successful their more recent industrial policies have been), or their other underlying strengths may have propelled them to the head of the pack.

To illustrate the dangers of making general arguments from specific cases, let me point to a country that has successfully used an open door policy to FDI to support growth. The country is Ireland, which has successfully used tax breaks to overseas firms to attract foreign investment, technology, and capital, but with very little active industrial policy. Ireland has grown faster than the rest of the European Union, converging rapidly to the average standard of living. By contrast, Greece, which continued to use industrial policies, has had a much less successful experience. Of course, comparing Ireland and Greece does not prove that an open door policy toward FDI is needed for successful development, any more than looking at Korea, Taiwan, and Japan tells us very much about the overall benefits of industrial policy. What Ireland does illustrate is that aggressive industrial policies with regard to foreign firms are not needed to grow successfully.

The underlying vision of the paper is that industrial policies are implemented by perfect governments that can use them to improve the lives of their citizens. By using selective strategic policies, countries can improve upon the outcome that would have occurred from general rules allowing FDI. Clearly, if policies are operated flawlessly, and the government is really benign, then the argument cannot be faulted. But, by the same logic, central planning should have worked in the Eastern bloc and former Soviet Union. In reality, government rules are open to manipulation by local interests, and industrial policies often spawn unintended consequences. Indeed, countries are much more generally hurt by limiting competition from foreign products and foreign capital than by encouraging it – just look at the contrasting experience of outward-oriented East Asia and inward-oriented Latin America over the 1970s and 1980s. Having said that, it is certainly true that in some countries industrial policies have been pursued successfully during a period of rapid growth. But, until we know a lot more about what sparked rapid development in these countries than we do now, I would be very hesitant to put industrial policies at the top of the list of beneficial factors for these countries, let alone argue that these cases provide an example for others to follow.

5

Multinational corporations in the neo-liberal regime

James Crotty, Gerald Epstein, and Patricia Kelly

Introduction

The left's concern with globalization is, of course, nothing new. Marx wondered whether the process of globalization would crush incipient revolution in his "small corner of the planet." And today, we ponder whether the recent acceleration of globalization will crush all national prospects for egalitarian and sustainable development. Yet, despite a good deal of hand wringing, discussion, and research, we are still quite far from understanding the implications of this much-discussed phenomenon for the lives of people, communities, and nations around the globe.

Here we look at one aspect of globalization: the role of multinational corporations (MNCs) and foreign direct investment (FDI).[1] What has been the effect of MNCs and FDI on wage stagnation, inequality, and unemployment? More generally, what do future trends hold for the long-run impact of MNCs on our standard of living? We identify five views of the likely effect of MNCs on the trajectory of the world economy.

---

1   "Foreign direct investment" refers to an equity investment outside of the parent corporation's home country; it implies some control over economic activity, usually a greater than 10 percent stake. The term "multinational corporations" generally refers to companies that have significant economic operations in more than one country (Caves 1996). We do not use foreign direct investment and multinational corporations interchangeably because, as we briefly discuss below, multinational corporations undertake significant economic activities outside their home countries independently of foreign direct investment, including licensing and outsourcing activities.

The authors would like to thank James Burke and Esra Erdem for excellent research assistance and the Economic Policy Institute for financial help. Thanks to the participants at the previous EPI conferences, and especially to Ilene Grabel, Keith Griffin, Tim Koechlin, Bob Pollin, and Jim Stanford for extremely helpful comments. We also thank participants at seminars given at the University of Denver and University of Massachusetts, and especially Sam Bowles, George DeMartino, Ilene Grabel, Tracy Mott, and Christian Weller. In addition, we received very useful comments from students who participated in Crotty and Epstein's graduate seminar on "Globalization and Inequality" at the University of Massachusetts in spring 1996: Elissa Braunstein, Rob Burns, Stephanie Eckman, Esra Erdem, James Heintz, Mark Howard, Gene Reilley, and Eric Verhoogen. Perhaps our greatest debt is to David Gordon, who, by gently badgering us at the first conference, forced us to rethink many issues and, as a result, greatly helped us to clarify our ideas.

The first is "the race to the bottom" (Bluestone and Harrison 1982; Barnet and Cavanagh 1994; Greider 1997). According to this view, capital will increasingly be able to play workers, communities, and nations off against one another as they demand tax, regulation, and wage concessions while threatening to move. According to this view, increased mobility of MNCs benefits capital while workers and communities lose. A modified version is that the winners in the race to the bottom will include highly educated (or skilled) workers, or workers in particular MNC rent-appropriating professions (e.g., lawyers and investment bankers), along with the capitalists; the losers will be unskilled workers and the unemployed.

The second view, "the climb to the top," is the opposite of the first. It suggests that multinational corporations are attracted less by low wages and taxes than by highly educated workers, good infrastructure, high levels of demand, and agglomeration effects arising from the existence of other companies that have already located in a particular place. According to this view, competition among states for FDI will lead countries in both the North and the South to try to provide well-educated labor and high-quality infrastructure in order to retain and attract foreign investment (Reich 1992). Thus, footloose capital and competition, far from creating a race to the bottom, will induce a climb to the top around the world.

This climb to the top could lead to the outcome represented by the third view: "neo-liberal convergence." This is the widely held mainstream claim that free mobility of multinational corporations, in the context of deregulation and free trade, will produce increased living standards in all countries. This process will, moreover, transfer capital and technology abroad, thereby raising the standards of living of those in the poorer countries at a faster rate than those in the wealthier ones, eventually generating a worldwide convergence in living standards (Sachs and Warner 1995). This may result from the process of competition for capital described above, or simply from the market processes of dissemination of capital and technology throughout the globe.

These same processes could, however, lead to the outcome envisaged in the fourth view, "uneven development." This view has a long and, now, ironic history: it holds that one region of the world will grow at the expense of another region. Of course, for decades, the dominant version of this view was the theory of imperialism: if the South integrated itself with the North, the North would grow at the expense of the South. Now, the fear seems to be the opposite: by having to compete with cheap Southern labor, an integrated world economy will help the South grow, but this time at the expense of the North (Blecker 1997b; Krugman and Venables 1995; Wood 1994, 1995).

The previous four views, though they differ greatly, have at least one thing in common: they hold that FDI and MNCs have a big impact. By contrast, many analysts, both mainstream and heterodox, subscribe to the fifth and final view: "much ado about nothing" (Krugman and Lawrence 1994; Gordon 1988a). As the name implies, according to this view, FDI and MNCs play a rather modest role in generating negative outcomes, such as increases in inequality, unemployment, and wage stagnation. Adherents argue that FDI is still a relatively small percentage of nations' gross domestic products; that most of it is between the rich countries and therefore can generate neither convergence nor a race to the bottom; that, of the FDI that does go to the developing countries, most of it flows to a handful of nations, with 80 percent of developing country FDI going to fewer than 10 countries; and that, while in some countries, like the U.S., there are large FDI outflows, there are also large inflows, so *net* FDI is not very large (UNCTAD 1997).

Which of these views is correct? Of course, we cannot provide a complete answer, nor, we suggest, could anyone else, given the current state of knowledge.[2] In this chapter we develop a framework for thinking about this question and develop a set of hypotheses that only future research can fully evaluate. Our framework does suggest that the race to the bottom outcome is likely in the current context dominated by neo-liberal policies of deregulation and market dominance on a global scale.

More generally, we argue that foreign direct investment is neither inherently good nor bad. Which of the five views best approximates reality will strongly depend on the overall national and international context within which capital mobility occurs. In particular, we focus on three aspects of the overall context that we think are especially important in determining the impact of FDI and MNCs: the state of aggregate demand (AD), the nature of the domestic and international rules of the game and institutions governing investment, and the nature of domestic and international competition. We argue that these three factors have a significant impact on the effects of FDI and MNCs on the economy, and in particular on their effects on wages, inequality, and the level of unemployment.

More concretely, when FDI occurs in a context of high levels of aggregate demand and effective rules of the game, which in turn limit the destructive aspects of competition, then FDI may indeed have a positive impact on nations and communities. On the other hand, when FDI occurs in a context of low levels of aggregate demand and destructive economic and political competition in the absence of effective rules of the game, then FDI can have a significantly negative impact on workers in both home and host countries.

While the mechanisms through which these three factors condition the impacts of FDI and multinational corporations are myriad, we focus on two: the effect of these three factors on the bargaining power of firms relative to workers, nations, and communities; and their contribution to coordination problems that hinder the ability of governments at all levels to make policies that can capture the benefits from FDI. The increased relative bargaining power of capital means that firms' threats to leave can lead to reductions in wages, worsening of working conditions, and low tax rates and revenues for governments. As for coordination problems, this weakened bargaining position and these weakened rules of the game make it more difficult for

2   In fact, there is an enormous amount of recent research on these issues, much more than we can review here. See, for example, the excellent essay by Kozul-Wright (1995) and the excellent book by Greider (1997). Also see the *Journal of Economic Perspectives*, summer 1995, and Federal Reserve Bank of New York, *Economic Policy Review*, January 1995, Vol. 1, No. 1 for recent surveys of this rapidly growing literature.

communities and nations to avoid "prisoner's dilemma" solutions in which countries' wages, tax rates, expenditure choices, and regulatory structures are severely distorted from the point of view of the community as a whole as they try to compete for capital. Indeed, they may become so distorted that they are suboptimal from the point of view of the corporations themselves. As a result, in this context FDI can contribute in a significant way to the problems of unemployment, wage stagnation, and inequality.

This framework leads to the key observation that the same level of FDI can have very different effects in different contexts. For example, consider the contrast between the effects on workers and communities of outward flows of FDI from the United States in the 1960s with the probable effects today. During the 1960s, outward FDI was of roughly the same order of magnitude relative to the size of the economy as in the 1990s. In the high-employment, high-growth era of the 1960s, FDI was more likely to increase exports from domestic companies rather than substitute for them (Epstein 1993). But even when FDI led to domestic plant shutdowns, replacement jobs were much easier to find for workers and communities. As a result, companies had much less bargaining power over workers and communities through threats of shutdown. Companies were therefore much less able to bargain down wages and tax rates. By contrast, in the 1990s, with a shortage of high-paying jobs and critical budget problems, workers and governments are much more subject to the bargaining power of companies as they threaten to move abroad or even from state to state.

Similarly, in Singapore and Malaysia many have benefited from FDI. This has been due to these countries' strong institutional structures and rules of the game vis-a-vis foreign direct investment and the economy more generally. (See Chang in this volume.) Now that these structures are being dismantled, it seems unlikely that they will continue to benefit to the same degree.

We can now state the central claim of this paper. We believe that in the current "neo-liberal" regime, FDI and MNCs make a race to the bottom much more likely than many mainstream economists believe. Our view stems from the claim that within the neo-liberal regime, there are strong *secular* forces that lead to insufficient levels of aggregate demand and therefore chronic unemployment, coercive competition, and destructive domestic and international rules of the game – that is, precisely those factors that undermine the potentially positive effects of FDI. These key components of the neo-liberal regime are well known. (See Pieper and Taylor in this volume.) Some of the most important components include budgetary austerity, financial liberalization, privatization, increased labor market "flexibility," and trade and investment liberalization.

Looking at MNCs and FDI this way helps to resolve several conundrums. First, it helps to explain how the impact of FDI can be much larger than its sheer size would suggest. Threat and spillover effects of FDI create a "magnification effect" beyond what simple quantities of flows or stocks would imply. Second, this framework helps to explain why these problems are created even if FDI flows are primarily between the Northern countries rather than between the North and the South, for it is the mobility and the threat of mobility per se that generates many of the problems, even if that mobility is between similar nations or even between similar states or provinces. For the same reason, workers and communities may be harmed even if a country, for example the U.S., has both large inward as well as large outward flows of FDI, for it is not only *net mobility* of capital but also the problems associated with the possible destructive impact of *gross mobility* of capital in a particular setting. Third, this way of looking at FDI suggests that there may be negative impacts even if countries or locales do not (or indeed especially if they do not) receive any FDI, for at the behest of promoters of neo-liberal ideology and policy, countries and locales may engage in destructive bidding and structural changes to attract FDI, yet not receive much.

This latter point helps to resolve a puzzle that has bothered us for a while: progressives often criticize FDI as a destructive force while at the same time decrying the fact that many poor countries can't seem to attract any. It may be that the only thing worse than engaging in this bidding war and getting FDI is engaging in it and not getting any.

This shift in bargaining power and the destructive competition among nations and locales for capital suggests an important paradox. Studies overwhelmingly indicate that foreign direct investment is attracted by high levels of demand, high-quality infrastructure, and high levels of skills and human capital (Caves 1996). Yet the process of foreign direct investment and capital mobility within the neo-liberal structure undermine those very factors that attract and sustain MNCs. In the neo-liberal regime, countries find it increasingly difficult to offer companies what they need. In the long run, companies may find it increasingly difficult to get the demand, infrastructure, and skills that they want.

More specifically, this analysis has implications for the currently common view, even among critics of massive flows of short-term capital that have wreaked so much havoc on the Mexican and Asian economies, that FDI is a more stable and beneficial type of financial flow and should be encouraged. While there may well be important benefits to be gained from FDI under the right circumstances, the neo-liberal structures that are being implemented and, in some cases, imposed on governments in many parts of the globe (most recently Korea and other parts of Asia) make it much more difficult for workers and communities to reap those benefits. Hence, FDI in that context is unlikely to be a panacea.

We will develop this argument in the rest of the chapter. We do not pretend that in this chapter we have established its truth. Much more theoretical and empirical work remains to be done. We do hope to convince the reader that this way of looking at FDI has the potential to help us understand both the real constraints policy makers face from increased flows of FDI and activities of MNCs, as well as the real options we face for policy reform.

Trends in foreign direct investment

It is difficult to measure worldwide trends in the activities of multinational corporations because the most widely available data, the standard measures of foreign direct investment, have serious problems. Perhaps the most important problem from the perspective of this chapter is that MNCs increasingly engage in international activities in ways that do not involve foreign direct investment. These include licensing, joint ventures, and outsourcing (UNCTAD 1995, 1997; Feenstra and Hanson 1996a, 1996b). We do not yet know how to incorporate these activities into a single measure of the overall activities of MNCs, but there are good reasons to believe that, because of them, standard measures of FDI underestimate the activities of MNCs.

Still, looking only at standard measures, one can see that FDI flows are growing rapidly. Table 1 shows the increase of FDI relative to other measures of international interactions. Clearly, FDI has been growing much more rapidly than trade and other measures of economic activity.

As we argued above, to understand the effects of FDI, it is important to look at both net and gross flows of FDI – inflows plus outflows. As we explain below, under current conditions, gross flows, with their effects on job churning and threats, can have significant impact on wages, income distribution, and the incidence of unemployment. Tables 2 and 3 show how gross FDI flows and stocks relative to the flows of domestic investment and GDP have evolved in recent years in different regions of the world; these tables demonstrate that gross capital mobility has increased dramatically. To be sure, FDI is spread quite unevenly around the globe, with the bulk of it going to the most developed economies. Nonetheless, as these data show, the amount going to the developing world is also growing rapidly (see also Chang in this volume).

Capital mobility, transactions costs, and enforcement

The standard explanation for this explosive growth, favored by mainstream and heterodox economists alike, is that dramatic reductions in transactions and communications costs spurred by the revolution in computer technology have greatly reduced the costs of multinational production. While technological change is undoubtedly important, this explanation fails to come to grips with the fact that, already at the turn of the 20th century, technology was advanced enough to deliver a highly integrated international capital market (Zevin 1992). So the dramatic increase in capital mobility since the 1960s is unlikely to be explained by improvements in technology alone.

What has also changed enormously in the last several decades is the "enforcement structure," the set of domestic and international institutions and rules that secure the property rights and enhance the prerogatives of multinational corporations. These have undergone a revolution in the last 20 years at least as dramatic as

Table 1 *Indicators of growth of international economic activity, 1964–94 (average annual percentage change)*

Period	World export volume	World FDI flows	International bank loans	World real GDP
1964–73	9.2	—	34.0	4.6
1973–80	4.6	14.8	26.7	3.6
1980–85	2.4	4.9	12.0	2.6
1985–94	6.7	14.3	12.0	3.2

Source: United Nations Conference on Trade and Development, *Trade and Development Report, 1997*, Table 24, p. 71.

Table 2 *Ratio of foreign direct investment inflows and outflows to gross fixed capital formation*

	1981–85	1986–90	1991–95	Memo:1995
All economies	4.4	8.8	8.7	10.8
Developed economies	4.9	11.3	9.0	10.7
Western Europe	6.9	14.6	13.6	16.2
Developing economies	4.7	4.4	9.2	12.2
Latin America	4.3	5.1	10.0	16.2
Asia	3.4	4.1	9.2	12.7
Southeast Asia	2.2	5.0	10.7	14.7
Developing economies minus China	5.2	4.8	9.2	10.3

Source: UNCTAD, 1995, 1997 *World Investment Report*, Annex Table B5.

Table 3 *Inward and outward FDI stock as a percentage of GDP*

	1980	1985	1990	1995
All economies	10.5	12.3	16.4	20.0
Developed economies	11.3	13.5	18.1	20.6
Western Europe	12.4	20.1	23.2	29.1
Developing economies	4.8	9.1	10.5	19.9
Latin America	6.8	11.8	12.8	20.1
Asia	4.1	8.1	9.2	20.2
Southeast Asia	4.4	7.6	11.4	22.1
Developing economies minus China	5.3	10.1	11.2	19.9

Source: UNCTAD, 1997 *World Investment Report*, Annex Table B6.

changes in technology and transaction costs (Epstein and Gintis 1992).[3] The North American Free Trade Agreement (NAFTA), while one of the most significant multilateral treaties offering investment protections, is by no means the only such recent agreement. Over the period 1991–96, 95 percent of the 599 changes in countries' regulatory FDI regimes were in the direction of liberalization. "They mostly involved the opening of industries previously closed to FDI, the streamlining or abolition of approval procedures and the provision of incentives," according to the U.N. Conference on Trade and Development (UNCTAD 1997, xviii). The enforcement structure has also been enhanced by bilateral investment treaties (BITs) signed for the protection and promotion of investment. As of January 1, 1997, there were 1,330 such treaties involving 162 countries, a threefold increase in five years. Approximately 180 such treaties were concluded in 1996 alone (UNCTAD 1997). Moreover, the OECD continues efforts to formulate a broader investment agreement, the Multilateral Agreement on Investment (MAI).

This dramatic improvement in the enforcement structure has greatly enhanced firms' exit options. And the promotion by international agencies and others of the idea that FDI is crucial for successful development has contributed to an increase in the desire by countries around the globe to attract and retain FDI. The disintegration of the Soviet Union and the evident discrediting of its economic model, along with decades of attempted sabotage by the U.S. and international organizations of alternative development models, has dramatically enhanced the "TINA" view prevalent among today's governments: There Is No Alternative to integration into the world economy. Hence, there has been a large increase in both developed and developing countries' openness to multinational corporations and increased willingness on the part of developed and developing countries to enter into treaties to protect foreign investment.

It is important to note that the enforcement structure is a political choice. Unlike declines in transactions costs, particular enforcement structures can be more or less efficient. Equally important, the choice of enforcement structure is reversible. Hence, the notion that one cannot reverse the recent trend of increased capital mobility, often stated as one cannot put the "genie back in the bottle," is almost surely incorrect.

How will this new context affect the impact of MNCs and FDI? We will argue that this new enforcement structure, in the context of the other factors we discuss, will not only lead to greater quantities of FDI, but will also likely reduce the quality of FDI from the view point of workers and communities.

---

3   Epstein and Gintis (1992) propose the idea of an "international credit regime." Such a regime consists of both an "enforcement structure" and a "repayment structure" (see also the excellent book by Lipson (1986) and the study of enforcement in the age of Pax Britannica by Kelly (1998)). The "enforcement structure" is the set of institutions and practices, which creditors create internationally and in their home countries, to try to enforce their credit relations. The "repayment structure" is the set of institutions and practices that debtor countries try to establish to attract credit. To simplify the terminology, in this chapter we will refer to the whole international credit regime as the "enforcement structure."

Theories of the effects of FDI and MNCs

Mainstream models

While most mainstream theorists subscribe to the neo-liberal convergence (Sachs and Warner 1995) or "much ado about nothing" schools of thought (Krugman and Lawrence 1994; Slaughter 1995), there are a number of interesting mainstream models that predict uneven development rather than convergence from the joint impact of capital mobility and technological change (Krugman and Venables 1995; Markusen and Venables 1996; Johnson and Stafford 1993; see Stanford in this volume for a review).

A recent influential monograph by Dani Rodrik (1996) is an important addition to the literature, an addition that complements the analysis developed here. Rodrik argues that gross capital mobility and trade, even between countries with similar levels of income, increase the elasticity of demand for labor and thereby can negatively affect the distribution of income. Rodrik's model differs from ours in that it assumes full employment. But his model will have some impacts on labor that are similar to the ones we describe.

In short, there are numerous mainstream models of MNCs, trade, and technological change that allow for the possibility of either uneven development or a race to the bottom. Neo-liberal convergence is only one of a number of possible outcomes and therefore has no theoretical priority even within the mainstream.

Heterodox models

It is important to note that, as in Rodrik's analysis, virtually all the mainstream models assume full employment. In contrast, one advantage of heterodox models is that they do not make the (unrealistic) assumption of full employment. Moreover, they place center stage the distribution of income between capital and labor rather than focus exclusively on the distribution of income between skilled and unskilled labor.

Blecker (1997b) develops a series of heterodox models to investigate the effects of trade and capital mobility on income distribution and growth in the North and South. The distinctive feature of one of Blecker's models is that workers' wages can be affected by *the threat* of moving by MNCs, since the threat can lower the bargaining power and wage share of Northern workers. As we suggest below, the effects of such threats may be the key to understanding why an evidently small share of outward FDI may have a relatively large impact on wages.

An alternative framework

Our alternative framework starts with the point emphasized by Blecker on the importance of bargaining power and threat effects on macroeconomic outcomes. Here, we emphasize three factors that have a strong impact on bargaining power: (1) the level of aggregate demand, (2) the nature of competition, and (3) domestic and international rules of the game. The nature of these three factors in the current neo-liberal regime, we argue, has a directly negative impact on inequality, unemployment, and wage stagnation. But, more relevant to the argument in this chapter, they make it more likely that FDI and MNCs will have a negative impact on these three phenomena.

Our model

Imagine there are two countries and that in each country there are two "communities," at least one of which has an excess supply of labor (i.e., unemployment, measured or disguised). Now assume there are two multinational corporations, one located in each country, so that in each country there is one community without an MNC. Also, to stack the argument against us, assume that there is a substantial fixed cost to moving from one locale to another, but that if the MNC pays that fixed cost, it can close down its operation in one place and move to the other. Similarly, assume that wages and all other costs, including taxes, and productivity levels are initially the same in all four communities. Assume that neither the MNCs nor the communities can collude, that the companies want to maximize expected profits, and that, initially, the communities want to maximize the sum of total wages accruing to them. For simplicity, the workers (working and unemployed) are represented by unions.

Now, let's say that, due to a change in norms or other aspects of the external environment, the two MNCs decide to open their location decisions for bidding and tell all four communities that they are willing to move to the location of the highest bidder. First assume that the only issue on the table is wages. The communities without MNCs located in them will put in a bid low enough to attract the MNCs, that is, low enough to pay for the fixed costs involved in moving, as long as the lower wages are above the opportunity costs of the unemployed workers of taking the jobs (their fallback positions). Whether it is above the fallback position will depend on a host of factors, most notably the level of the fixed cost facing the MNC, the unemployment benefits, and the family structure prevalent in the community (for example, whether unemployed workers are expected to perform child care within the family and are compensated for doing so, etc). The lower the fixed cost, the worse the social safety net, and the lower the opportunity cost within the family of outside employment, the more likely a bid will be put in that is low enough to induce MNC movement.

Given that bid, the workers in the communities where the MNCs are currently located will have to decide whether to lose their jobs or take a pay cut to reduce the differential between their pay and that of the other communities to a level that is less than the fixed cost. If the opportunity costs of employment are the same in all communities, then they will reduce their wage offers to close the gap to a level below the fixed costs. Note that their wages will not be driven all the way down to the offers of the workers in the other communities – they will be driven down to match the other offers only if there are no fixed costs of moving. In either case, the MNCs will not move. There will be no FDI. But *there will be a decline in wages induced by the threat* of moving: this is an example of what we have called the "magnification effect."

In the forgoing analysis, substitute the word "taxes" for "wages" and there will be a decline in tax rates resulting from the threat of moving, despite the fact that there will be no movement of capital whatsoever.

Note that the existence of the other communities not only causes a shift down in the demand curve (actually, the bargained wage curve) for labor. It also increases the elasticity of the curve, making it more difficult to raise wages or taxes (see Rodrik 1996).

Now assume that there is an allotment of new investment that each MNC wants to make and that the cost of the new investment is independent of the locale in which it is placed. Each MNC will initiate a bidding war and, if the four communities are identical, the bidding war will drive down the wages to the opportunity costs of employment in these communities (though one must take into account that some of the communities already have MNCs and therefore their opportunity costs might be different). Assume that the new allotment of investment flows randomly, since the MNCs are indifferent to where it goes and therefore it makes no difference to the outcome whether it goes to one country (net FDI), goes to both countries (no net FDI but gross FDI), or stays in the home country (neither net nor gross FDI). So, in this case there can be declines in wages (or tax rates) even if there is no net investment but there is gross investment. If there are agglomeration effects so that it is more profitable to make the new investment where the old one has already existed, then the wages (or taxes) in the communities where the investment is currently located will not be bid down to the same level as in the other countries, but they will be bid down nonetheless, unless the agglomeration effects are quite large.

Of course, the situation becomes worse for the workers in these two countries if now a third country opens itself up to investment with all the same characteristics as the first two but with lower opportunity costs of employment. Then the FDI will flow away from the first two countries to the newly opened country, say China. But one needn't have this third country to get the changes in wages and taxes pointed to above. Note that if there are risks associated with FDI, and these risks increase with the amount of investment in one locale, then even if the third country does open up, not *all* investment will go there, even absent transaction costs.

Finally, look at the countries that have bid for the FDI but have not received any, because, for example, their productivity levels are too low. They have reduced their tax rates and wage rates. If this, in turn, lowers tax and wage rates already prevailing in these countries, then the existence of this bidding process has altered the distribution of income and reduced the level of public services that the community can afford. In short, bidding can have negative effects even if no investment comes.

Assumptions necessary to drive the results
To deliver these results, first there must be insufficient aggregate demand to provide full employment. Second, there must be a set of practices of multinational corporations that leads them to alter the way that they have done business in the past and put up their location decisions for bidding, while at the same time being willing to lay off workers, close down plants, and move elsewhere to increase profits. Third, there

must be an absence of domestic or international rules of the game that would prevent communities and workers from driving down their own wages and tax rates.

It is these three factors, inadequate aggregate demand, coercive competition, and weak domestic and international rules of the game, that, among others, characterize the neo-liberal regime and lead, we argue, to these negative impacts.

Justifying the basic assumptions: aggregate demand, coercive competition, and rules of the game in the neo-liberal regime

In this section, we will try to justify the claim that the neo-liberal regime has the three key destructive characteristics isolated in the previous section. A basic argument is that the forces operating to raise AD in the new regime are structurally weak, while pressures on firms to lower costs through downsizing or "labor shedding," speedup, and wage cutting are structurally strong. The heightened competition characteristic of the neo-liberal regime in the face of sluggish product market growth is, we argue, likely to generate slow trend growth in the demand for labor. Normal patterns of labor supply growth, therefore, should generate a persistent problem of excess labor supply, resulting in continued high trend levels of unemployment (which will appear in the form of "disguised" unemployment in countries – both Northern and Southern – without an adequate social wage). Secularly high unemployment, along with continued deterioration of the institutions that have sustained workers' economic and political power, should continue to generate slow or stagnant wage growth and rising wage inequality. Within this context, increased mobility of FDI and MNCs will be more likely to have a negative impact on workers and communities than under the old "Golden Age" regime because MNCs will be able to bargain down benefits to workers and communities. Moreover, global labor supply patterns are unlikely to be "normal": a number of countries previously insulated to a substantial degree from the global capitalist marketplace are in a slow, uneven, and incomplete process of integrating themselves within it. Russia, India, China, and Eastern Europe (the "RICE" countries) are most important. Many of these countries have substantial quantities of skilled and educated workers who are low priced by standards of the Organization for Economic Cooperation and Development (OECD) countries. Under the assumption that increased global openness and technical progress make it ever more feasible to locate production, distribution, research and development, and even coordination functions of MNC business in diverse geographical locations, these skilled workers, along with the skilled workers being educated and trained in the East Asian newly industrializing economies (NIEs), will provide lower-cost alternatives for MNCs to many of the higher-wage skilled Northern workers whose jobs and wages were not significantly affected by globalization in the 1980s.

Coercive competition

In our "bargaining" or "conflict" view, the constitution of the bargaining agents, their choices of bargaining strategies, and resultant outcomes are profoundly affected by: (1) the character of interfirm relations or the "competitive regime" (which affects, among other things, the level of economic rents available to be split between the bargainers); (2) the institutional environment within which bargaining takes place; and (3) macroeconomic conditions.

Here we focus on the competitive regime. The idea of the competitive regime and its effect on economic performance is discussed in Crotty (1993). In the "co-respective" competitive regime of the Golden Age in the North, cooperating oligopolistic firms in key Northern industries took advantage of fast market growth and limits on both domestic and international competition to generate substantial, dependable profits and rents. Firms could accumulate capital without excessive concern that national AD would fail to grow, that imports would steal their customers, that financiers would take huge chunks of future profits, or that their new capital would be made prematurely obsolete by the outbreak of fierce cost-cutting battles over market share. High rates of investment and productivity growth followed. Strong unions, government support for the maintenance of a fair share for labor, distributive accords or understandings between capital and labor, and sustained full employment produced a division of substantial oligopoly rents that was satisfactory to the bargainers. The strong real wage growth thus generated in turn helped sustain the rate of growth of AD.

This regime broke down in the 1970s and early 1980s, partly from internal contradictions, but partly under the pressure of the increasingly open national borders associated with the globalization process. It was eventually replaced by a new regime of "anarchic" or "coercive" competition (Crotty 1993). With AD now consistently inadequate to generate rapidly growing markets or full capacity utilization and with barriers to international competition breaking down everywhere, firms entered a more Hobbesian world. In the core industries of the North, firms were forced to reconsider every traditional aspect of the structures and strategies they used in the preceding co-respective regime – geographical location, pricing, financing, product mix, choice of technology, labor relations, and even the organization of the enterprise itself.

Corporate response to these altered circumstances differed substantially across the OECD, though as time goes on the general direction of strategic change is becoming ever more convergent. In the U.S. – the model toward which many countries aspire to converge – the two most important aspects of corporate America's new competitive strategy in the late 1970s and early 1980s were the choice of conflictual rather than cooperative relations with labor (the disavowal of the traditional accords) and a rejection of support for an effective social "contract," one that assured both full employment and the maintenance of an adequate social wage. The corporate attack on labor was multidimensional. It included, among other things, war on unions, political support for stripping workers of their legal rights, the widespread use of replacement workers during strikes for the first time in the post-World War II era, outsourcing, and FDI.

It is crucial to analyze the effects of technical change on Northern labor markets in light of this competitive regime shift and the subsequent move to antiworker corporate strategies. Under severe competitive pressure, companies took advantage of union weakness, a more business-oriented government judicial and regulatory framework, and advances in information processing and computerized machine control to invest in technologies that helped them implement these new strategies. Where neo-classical economists posit exogenous technical change that just happens to be skill biased, we see instead an endogenous process in which corporations under intense competitive pressures chose to develop or adopt technologies that helped them reduce labor costs through downsizing, speedup, and wage cuts. Technical change in the 1980s probably was on balance skill biased, though no more so than in previous decades (Mishel and Bernstein 1994). But its distinctive characteristic was that it was labor saving or labor shedding, and labor disempowering as well.

While we have emphasized the U.S. experience here, there is evidence that as the neo-liberal regime spreads, this process of coercive competition will spread as well. Below we discuss the impact of the recent Asian financial crisis in the South. Here we note that the regime is spreading in the North. For example, in a recent survey of research on comparative industrial relations by Locke, Kochan, and Piore, the authors note that: "In almost every country covered in the study, various government regulations and norms governing recruitment, dismissal/redundancy, lay-offs and the allocation of labor have been relaxed or modified so as to give individual employers greater discretion" (p. 145); "[e]verywhere unions are in decline and management is resurgent" (p. 147); and "in all countries, there was a resurgence in inequalities in income or in employment opportunities" (pp. 151–2). Nonetheless, the authors also stress that workers continue to fare best in those countries with a traditional government commitment to intervention in labor markets and significant union involvement in industry or national bargaining.

Together these processes have two effects relevant for our argument: first, this coercive competition helps to explain why MNCs would alter their strategies toward communities and labor and begin a coercive process of leveling-down bidding as described in the model above. Second, they help explain why inadequate aggregate demand is likely to be an important feature of the neo-liberal regime, a second necessary component of our model. We explain this latter point more fully now.

Global aggregate demand growth
Next we turn to a defense of the assumption that global growth in aggregate demand is likely to be sluggish in the new regime. Quite obviously, AD growth has in fact been relatively slow in the quarter century since the end of the Golden Age. In Europe, for example, real GDP growth since 1973 has been only about half as fast as it had been in the preceding two decades (Glyn 1995b, 43), so that, even with relatively slow measured productivity growth, unemployment rose to double-digit levels. Is growth likely to pick up substantially in the coming years? Consider the components of aggregate demand.

Take consumption spending first. Given our argument about pressures for labor-saving organizational and technical change in the North unless AD growth picks up substantially, high unemployment and stagnant wages will continue to constrain the growth of consumption spending. Investment spending in the North has also grown at a modest pace in the past 20 years, and outside the computer- and software-related industries there may be no forces that will sustain an increase. It is an open question as to how powerful an impetus might emanate from the computer industry itself. As we argued above, this is precisely the industry that facilitates labor shedding and therefore reduces aggregate demand. Assessing the net outcome of these two forces – the labor shedding on the one hand and the spur to new investment on the other – requires further research; but optimists who hail the computer industry as an obvious source of increased labor demand ought to be more cautious in their prognostications. Next we turn to export growth. Export growth has been rapid in the last decade or so, but it seems unlikely it can be sustained in light of the Asian financial problems that, we argue below, are directly related to the neo-liberal model.

As we have seen, consumption, investment, and export demand are all problematic in the neo-liberal regime. To make matters worse, to counter an AD shortfall, they would have to be positive enough to outweigh the enormous deflationary forces emanating from national and international macroeconomic policy that are likely to prevail in the future. First, central banks around the world have adopted the neo-liberal credo that pursuit of low inflation is their primary, perhaps sole, responsibility. Second, the enormous buildup of government debt in the hands of both domestic and foreign rentiers over the past two decades has given them enormous power to punish both fiscal and monetary authorities who adopt expansionary policies that are perceived to be against rentier interests. (See Felix in this volume and the discussion of Asia below.) Since an ever-increasing percent of government debt is in the hands of nonnationals, and since foreign debt holders are quicker to sell it at the onset of inflation, this particular impediment to expansionary policy is likely to strengthen in the future as national financial markets become ever more powerful and globally integrated. Third, both internal and external pressure has mounted in virtually every country to put a stop to the ongoing rise in government deficits and debt-to-GDP ratios brought on by the slow growth and rising unemployment of the past two decades. Fourth, in the absence of internationally coordinated macro policy, it is harder for governments to try to grow at a pace substantially faster than their neighbors and competitors.

In short, inadequate aggregate demand is likely to prevail in the neo-liberal future.

International rules of the game: enforcement and tax competition
In addition to the neo-liberal forces described above that contribute to secular unemployment and coercive competition, changes in the rules and practices governing international enforcement have a significant impact on the relative bargaining power between multinational corporations on the one hand and nations and communities on the other. They also create difficult coordination problems for countries wanting to tax and regulate MNCs for the community's benefit. In this regard, in the period up until the late 1970s many countries, both in the North and the South, imposed numerous conditions and controls on entry and operations of MNCs

(Fatouros 1996, 47). As the data on the increase in bilateral and multilateral investment treaties discussed above show, this is now changing.

Bilateral and international investment agreements, by restricting what governments can do, take a number of policies off the bargaining table and out of the realm of possibility. For example, to the extent that they make performance requirements such as domestic content rules illegal, these agreements reduce the scope for industrial policy. While governments that negotiate such treaties may have no interest in pursuing industrial policy, the treaties, by design, tie the hands of future governments as well.

In sum, these three aspects of the neo-liberal regime, coercive competition, insufficient aggregate demand, and absence of domestic and international rules of the game that would allow countries to control MNCs and avoid bidding wars, are precisely those conditions that our model suggests are likely to contribute to a negative impact of FDI and MNCs on workers' and communities' standards of living.

Evidence on the effects of FDI and MNCs on wages and taxes in the neo-liberal regime

The hypotheses discussed before suggest an entire empirical research program based on the idea that, where the neo-liberal regime is most widespread, one ought to observe a number of negative impacts from FDI and MNCs. For example, threat effects ought to reduce wages and the quality of working conditions; the capital share of income ought to be increasing and, except for those groups of employees who have direct access to MNC rents (lawyers, investment bankers, and the like), the wage share ought to be declining; and there should be an increase in unemployment (real or disguised) associated with an increase in net outflows of FDI and MNCs. In terms of taxation and host bidding, one would expect a decline in taxation of MNCs and an increase of subsidies available to them, as well as a decline in government restrictions facing them, whether or not MNCs actually end up investing in a particular locale. Countries are unlikely to be able to capture many of the benefits from MNC technology transfer unless they have a strong regulatory structure.

There is a great deal of crude evidence consistent with these implications. But a careful consideration of these testable implications requires substantial future research.

The only direct study of threat effects that we are aware of is that of Bronfenbrenner (1996), who reported on a U.S. survey covering 1993 through 1995. It showed that 50 percent of all firms and 65 percent of manufacturing firms that were targets of union organizing campaigns threatened to close down and move if their workers unionized. Though only 12 percent of those firms that ended up unionized subsequently shut down, workers found the threats credible – where threats were made, unions lost a larger percent of elections.

Most of the empirical work directly linking MNCs and FDI to wages has been concerned with their effects on inequality among workers rather than their impacts on labor relative to capital. Still, even in this literature one can get some inkling of the effects on labor versus capital. The most interesting work in this area is that by

Feenstra and Hanson, who study the joint impact of "outsourcing" and technological change. They note that outsourcing, defined as importing of intermediate inputs, has increased substantially within the U.S. manufacturing sector, at an annual rate of 4.6 percent between 1979 and 1990. At the same time, while the production wage share declined substantially during the 1979–90 period (at an annual rate of -1.4 percent), and the nonproduction wage share has only slightly increased, the capital share increased by an average rate of 1 percent a year over the period (Feenstra and Hanson 1997, Table 2). The authors argue that these changes are the result of an imprecisely measured combination of outsourcing and technological change.

There have been a great many studies to determine the employment and wage effects of FDI (see Caves 1996 for a recent survey). For example, Blomstrom, Fors, and Lipsey (1997) find that in the year they studied, 1989, increased sales by U.S. multinational foreign affiliates abroad reduced employment in the U.S. parent multinational, with the impact for employment in MNC investment in less-developed countries being much stronger than for MNC activities in the North. James Burke finds that increased investment abroad by U.S. multinational corporations tends to reduce multinational investment at home for highly indebted U.S. multinationals (Burke 1997).

A number of recent studies have investigated the effects of capital mobility on tax competition and corporate tax rates. For the United States, for example, there has been a dramatic decline in the corporate tax burden in recent years, from an average of 64 percent in the 1970s to 42 percent in the 1990–96 period (Poterba 1997, Table 2). Without further study it is, of course, impossible to tell how much of this may be due to capital mobility, though Tanzi (1995) suggests that capital mobility is an important culprit. Not only might competitive bidding reduce tax rates, but multinational corporate production gives enormous opportunities to reduce tax burdens through such mechanisms as income shifting and transfer pricing (Hines 1996; Grubert and Slemrod 1994; Tanzi 1995).

The "war between the states," as the competition among U.S. states for investment and jobs has come to be called, may well be a microcosm of what could be emerging in the global arena as the neo-liberal regime strengthens. Subsidies and tax breaks to attract investment cost local governments tens of billions of dollars in lost tax revenue; yet as the willingness to offer such concessions becomes universal, they have less and less effect on plant location decisions. The Federal Reserve Bank of Minneapolis has called for a federal law prohibiting state and local tax incentives for particular companies in an attempt to reduce this destructive war (see Federal Reserve Bank of Minneapolis 1994; Holmes 1995).

This competition is spreading more widely to the South as well. In addition to removing barriers to inward capital flows, governments attempt to entice FDI with a variety of investment incentives. However, the empirical literature suggests that investment incentives have not been effective in attracting direct investment flows. Instead, this literature has identified market size as the dominant influence on direct investment inflows (UNCTC 1991, 1992a, 1993). Despite and perhaps due to their pervasiveness, tax holidays do not seem to lure direct investment. Moreover, even if flows arrive they may not benefit the domestic economy, especially if, because of liberalization agreements themselves that lock governments' hands, they cannot regulate the MNCs in the community's interest (UNCTAD 1992a, 1992b, 1994a).

One of the ways in which MNCs could improve growth prospects in the South is by transferring technology and training that would spill over into productivity increases in the domestic economy (UNCTAD 1994a). However, a review of the empirical literature suggests that the spillover effects on wages in developing nations have been low to nonexistent. For example, Chitrakar and Weiss's (1995) analysis of the effects of foreign investment in Nepal indicated that foreign investment had only a small impact on labor income. In addition, Aitken, Harrison, and Lipsey (1995) concluded that foreign direct investment in Mexico and Venezuela had no spillover effect on wages in the domestic sector of those economies.

Although compared to other low- and middle-income nations the East Asian countries demonstrate income equality, Wood (1994) suggests that in recent years their performances on this index have been somewhat mixed. He links these fluctuations to outsourcing to lower-wage countries and slowing of educational expansion. The former is particularly troubling, since it suggests a pernicious leveling-down cycle that now pits middle-income countries against low-income countries as well as high-income countries against low- and middle-income countries.

Domestic structures matter and the spread of neo-liberalism in the South: the Asian financial crisis

All nations, North and South, have had to confront economic pressures emanating from the emerging neo-liberal global regime, but there are enormous differences across countries in the institutions, structures, and social and political priorities that intermediate between firms, workers, and governments on the one hand and MNCs, international rentiers, and international organizations on the other. Since a key point of our analysis is that the context strongly affects the impacts that MNCs have, it should come as no surprise that we believe that these structures have made a significant difference in the way national economies have experienced global economic forces and responded to them. Countries that have been able to insulate themselves from and manage global forces have performed the best. Here the East Asian miracle economies are the most important examples in the South, while Sweden is an example from the North. But now, both models are being undermined by domestic and external forces of neo-liberalism. Their stories suggest how the spread of neo-liberal structures will intensify and broaden the negative practices and institutions we have focused on here.

In this section we briefly discuss the rise and fall of the Asian model from this perspective. In the next section, we study Sweden.

The Asian financial crisis and the rise and fall of the Asian model
Most of the developmental success stories of past decades were in Asia, especially East Asia. Indeed, the outstanding economic performance of Japan, Korea, Taiwan,

China, and others over recent decades has led to widespread recognition of an East Asian "economic miracle" and admiration for what came to be known as the "East Asian model" of economic development (see Amsden 1989; Nembhard 1996). Of course, recognition of the outstanding economic performance of these countries does not imply support for all aspects of their political economy or, in particular, their lack of democracy. Nevertheless, there is no denying that, in countries such as Japan and Korea, enormous economic progress has been made in recent decades, and prosperity has been widely shared.

Though the East Asian model is profoundly anti-neo-liberal, these nations have integrated themselves to varying degrees in international markets (though some, such as Korea and Japan, purposely minimized the role played by foreign MNCs and inward FDI). But they did so, at least until recently, more or less on their own terms and in pursuit of their own economic interests. Though these countries differ in many important ways, development has been guided in every case by some form of state-led industrial policy, utilizing credit allocation, regulated and differential interest rates, government-controlled central banks, regulation of labor markets, high state spending on education and infrastructure, managed trade, and controls over the movement of money capital and inward and outward FDI.

All of the East Asian models have evolved and adapted over time; no specific national political-economic structure or concrete model of state-led development policy can remain effective across decades of growth and change. For a variety of reasons, in the late 1980s and 1990s it became necessary to make significant changes in both state and private sector practices in all of the Asian countries. Over this period, debates arose in every country over how the structures of the "model" should be adapted. Most of the proposals for change involved some degree of deregulation (see Crotty, Epstein, and Kelly 1998).

Of course, the composition and perceived interests of various class strata evolved over time as well. Powerful domestic financial and industrial enterprises and wealthy and politically influential families, having enriched themselves in the process of economic development through state-led industrial policy, came to believe that substantial deregulation, especially of domestic and international financial markets, rather than a revision of reform of state-controls, was in their individual economic interest. The changes they pushed did not constitute a coherent or viable stable model, nor a full neo-liberal package. Indeed, they maintained allegiance to those dimensions of state regulation that continued to suit their interests.

Thus, the issue was not whether change was needed – everyone agreed it was – but what form change should take. However, this internal demand for financial deregulation was strongly reinforced by the forces of global neo-liberalism, which increased in power throughout the 1980s and 1990s. The U.S. and other large Northern countries, important transnational industrial firms and banks, and the international financial institutions (IFIs) came together to pressure Asian nations in the direction of full-blown neo-liberalism.

This brings us to the core of our argument: external neo-liberal forces profoundly influenced, and in some cases may even have determined, the outcomes of these national debates by substantially altering the perceived costs and benefits attached to the various possible new development strategies and structures available. In so doing, they empowered certain domestic class strata and severely weakened others. These forces deflected structural change away from evolution of the East Asian model and toward the neo-liberal path of deregulation, liberalization, and privatization.

The combined influence of this coalition of domestic elites and global forces turned out to be determinate in the period from 1980 through mid-1997. At different times and to different degrees in different countries, governments that had formally regulated domestic financial markets, set interest rates, and carefully monitored the allocation of credit began to cede these functions to the private sector. In like manner, governments that had imposed controls on the movement of money capital across their borders began to loosen them.

The relatively low interest rates in Japan and the U.S. in the early 1990s were an instigating factor in the crisis that followed: investors looking for higher returns now found the Asian markets open and willing. The result was that conditions were constructed that could lead to super-heated Keynes-Minsky speculative boom and bust cycles – super-heated because, if and when the inflow of foreign "hot" money became substantial, it would accelerate speculative fever. And, in the absence of capital controls, the bust phase of the cycle was likely to be exacerbated by a run on the currency by foreign and domestic investors. This is precisely what happened.

In short, ill-conceived deregulation movements and global capital market events turned a number of Asian countries from economic miracles to economic disasters in what seemed to be a matter of weeks. Neo-liberal economists, who had been denying for years that the success of the East Asian miracles had been created by state-led industrial policy, who insisted that it was generated by free markets, now claimed that the crisis was caused by the same powerful but inefficient state industrial policies whose existence they had denied until the crisis broke.

The IMF–U.S. 'rescue'

The International Monetary Fund (IMF)–U.S. "rescue" packages for East Asia were thinly disguised attempts to impose neo-liberal structures on Asian economies and to open them for Western business interests. The rescue package for Korea, for example, was the type likely to create precisely those neo-liberal conditions that we have argued here are so destructive to the effective regulation of globalization in general and FDI in particular: they imposed austerity and the reduction of the state's ability to regulate and control investment and capital mobility.

Take austerity first. Though austerity is standard IMF medicine, in Korea it was applied to a country that did not have the standard symptoms; unlike recipients of IMF aid in Latin America, Korea had low inflation and its budget was in surplus. The IMF insisted on cutbacks in government spending, an increase in (regressive) taxes, and a substantial rise in interest rates, which were already high in real terms

But the U.S.–IMF program demanded far more than austerity; it sought the complete transformation of the Korean "model" and the opening of all Korea's markets to unrestricted access by foreign MNCs, banks, and financial investors. The IMF demanded that the government end its control over central bank policy and give up its influence over the allocation of credit by the private sector – credit allocation would henceforth be regulated solely by considerations of private profit. These steps would destroy the government's remaining ability to direct credit and provide preferential interest rates to targeted firms and industries, a cornerstone of the East Asian model. And experience suggests that independent central banks tend to follow policies designed to minimize inflation at the cost of growth and employment.

The program called for the elimination of managed trade; tariffs and export subsidies were to be drastically reduced or eliminated. Legal impediments to the foreign takeover of Korean firms and banks were to be eliminated by early 1998. Even the prohibition against hostile foreign takeovers was to be ended. This represented such a great victory for Northern multinational banks and nonfinancial corporations (which have been trying for decades to more deeply penetrate Korean markets) and such a potential blow to Korean firms that they could be expected to try to find ways to subvert its intent. Foreign ownership of Korean commercial banks would be especially devastating in a system where large industrial firms have high debt/equity ratios even in normal times, and bank-firm relations are at the core of Korea's success story.

The last IMF dictate we consider is the demand that the government remove all remaining restrictions on cross-border financial flows. Under this regulation, foreigners are able to invest in the Korean financial markets on the same terms as citizens, and all restrictions on foreign investment by Korean nationals are removed. Again, the complete elimination of capital controls over even the shortest-term speculative loans and investments appeared to many observers to be a disastrous policy.

The question arises as to why the Korean government accepted such draconian measures. The answer, in part, is that the major Korean corporations, the *chaebol*, believed that they could use the IMF against the labor unions and the government to win major labor concessions and to eliminate burdensome regulations, including constraints on their ability to borrow abroad. This is an illustration of the key point made earlier: the creation of neo-liberal structures in non-neo-liberal countries is facilitated by the new incentives facing domestic corporations resulting from the emerging neo-liberal international economy.

In sum, the IMF medicine is precisely the type to contribute to the creation of the three negative factors we have emphasized in this chapter: insufficient aggregate demand, coercive competition, and weakened domestic rules of the game.

FDI in the neo-liberal regime: the case of Sweden

We have argued that, while FDI did not have a significant negative effect on working people in the North in the full employment Golden Age regime, it can pose a serious threat to jobs and wages within the structures of the neo-liberal regime. To see how FDI and neo-liberal structures can interact with one another to create an economic and political crisis for workers, consider the case of Sweden, one of the outstanding Northern success stories of the post-World War II era.

MNCs have always been very important in the Swedish economy; they accounted for 69 percent of manufacturing employment in 1970. Yet in the Golden Age FDI was probably helpful to Swedish workers and the Swedish economy. Outward FDI was modest, on average less than 1 percent of GDP per year through the 1970s. Given Sweden's record of sustained full employment, FDI was not a threat to domestic jobs, and, under a centralized bargaining structure that had the allegiance of corporate leaders, FDI did not restrain wages or disrupt the ongoing decline in inequality. To the extent that outward FDI helped facilitate and maintain a high level of Swedish exports (through the maintenance of effective marketing and distribution networks), it helped Swedish firms take advantage of technical change, gain economies of scale, and achieve higher productivity growth rates than would have been possible if production were primarily for the small domestic market. At worst, FDI did not prevent the Swedish economy from posting an outstanding postwar economic performance. Its impressive combination of sustained low unemployment and an egalitarian income distribution was maintained through most of the 1980s.

However, by the early to mid-1980s global instability, world recession, and a falling domestic profit rate began to exacerbate emerging strains in the Swedish corporatist economic system. While unemployment remained extremely low, inflation picked up, creating problems in the crucial export sector. By the mid-1980s Swedish MNCs had become openly antagonistic to the set of traditional relations and mutual obligations connecting business, labor, and the state that had come to be known as the "Swedish model." Lindbeck points to the onset of an "ideological offensive" by capital in the early 1980s designed to replace traditional arrangements with a "more free market oriented position" (1997, 1277). Employers first pulled back from the centralized bargaining system; Sweden's "long-standing solidaristic wage policies followed throughout most of the 1970s gave way somewhat as business pushed hard to decentralize bargaining structures and to lower labor costs" (Locke, Kochan, and Piore 1995, 151). They also pressured the state to deregulate the economy.

The threat of capital flight (moving operations overseas) and capital strike (refusing to invest at home) are two key structural sources of power business can use to pressure labor and the state to bend to its will. The ability of Sweden's MNCs to flee the domestic economy through outward FDI and to substitute foreign for domestic investment gave them leverage over labor (through the threat to jobs and wages) and the government (by making its traditional economic objectives impossible to attain). This leverage was magnified by technical change, which made FDI easier, and by the evolution of the new global regime, which created external pressures to liberalize. Outward FDI was both a major contributor to the deterioration of Sweden's economic performance in the 1980s and, especially, the 1990s, as well as a powerful weapon used by capital to force its neo-liberal political and economic policies on the rest of society.

Sweden's MNCs virtually fled the country in the second half of the 1980s. This created enormous pressure on both labor and the state to accept the MNCs economic and political agenda. Between 1981 and 1992 outward FDI averaged an astounding 13.1 percent of domestic investment, while inward FDI was just 3.2 percent (Glyn 1995b, 44). But the "flow of outward FDI during the 1986–1990 period was almost five times higher than in the 1981–1985 period," so that the "Swedish share of the MNCs production had fallen to below 40 per cent by 1990," down from 61 percent just four years earlier and from 72 percent in 1978 (Blomstrom and Kokko 1994, 5, 34). Outward FDI grew from 1 percent of GDP in the early 1980s to 2 percent by 1985, then skyrocketed to an unprecedented 6 percent (or 28 percent of all investment) by 1989. MNCs were using the high profits of the mid- to late 1980s to finance outward FDI rather than domestic investment.

The problem was not just that this flight of capital cost jobs, income, and exports. Having renounced their commitment to the domestic economy and to the institutions of the Swedish "model," Sweden's MNCs were hollowing out domestic manufacturing, exporting primarily the high value-added, high-skilled parts of the production process to their foreign affiliates while leaving lower-skilled raw material processing and intermediate goods production for their home operations. Blomstrom and Kokko argue that this FDI outflow harmed the economy in numerous ways: the big MNCs now employ a lower share of high-skilled workers than does the rest of Swedish industry; the fruits of Swedish R&D appear in their high-tech foreign operations rather than at home; and there have been serious negative spillover effects on domestic suppliers and subcontractors. Moreover, for the low-tech products left at home, "there is already fierce price competition in global markets" rather than the oligopolistic rents of high-tech markets, so that "continued competitiveness in these industries requires cost reductions and perhaps also falling wages" (Blomstrom and Kokko 1994, 23–4).

Capital flight made it difficult for the state to continue to play its traditional role. Under business pressure, the government began to dismantle important components of its regulatory apparatus. The domestic financial system was deregulated in 1985, forcing domestic interest rate upward toward global levels. Credit rationing had traditionally been one of the state's most important tools of countercyclical macro policy. Thus, the deregulation of domestic financial markets drastically reduced the ability of the state to avoid speculative booms and maintain full employment. Capital controls were weakened, then, in 1989, virtually eliminated. The dismantling of capital flows in turn induced a huge inflow of short-term foreign funds. This helped facilitate a subsequent explosion of credit-financed speculation, creating a cyclical upturn, but overleveraged household and business sectors as well. When this speculative boom eventually went bust, the financial fragility it left behind constrained consumption and investment spending. In the absence of capital controls, funds quickly left the country, putting downward pressure on the krona. The government resisted this pressure through the maintenance of high interest rates right through the recession.

The MNC-led business sector was now in a position to launch an all-out assault on the remaining elements of the traditional structure. Shorn of many of the tools traditionally available for use in resisting recession, and pressured by its MNCs not to do so, the Swedish government turned its back on its half-century commitment to full employment and embraced overly restrictive monetary and fiscal policy (in part to try to converge to EC inflation rates as a prelude to hoped-for membership). The early 1990s saw the deepest recession since the 1930s. Real GDP fell by 5 percent between 1990 and 1993, and unemployment rose to unprecedented heights – from 1.5 percent in 1990 to 9.5 percent in 1994. Yet the government maintained high interest rates and restrictive fiscal policy throughout.

There is no doubt that the Swedish model was destroyed by internal contradictions as well as external pressures: rising capital mobility was hardly the only threat to its reproduction. But it seems reasonable to conclude that the ability to "flee" the country gave Swedish MNCs enormous leverage in their successful campaign to change the structures of domestic industrial relations and the role of the state in the economy. The unprecedented flight of real capital in the 1980s, while to some degree a response to the economic strains that had developed in the late 1970s and early 1980s, clearly helped create the economic crisis that severely damaged the Swedish "model" in the 1990s and gave capital the power to shape the reconstruction of Swedish political economy. Sweden's recent history shows that, within the neo-liberal regime, the greater the importance of MNCs in the economy and the weaker the state's control over cross-border capital flows, the greater the economic and political damage that MNCs can cause through outward FDI.

A framework for policy

We have argued that FDI and MNCs are likely to have a negative impact in terms of wage inequality, wage stagnation, and unemployment where the bargaining power of corporations is significantly increased relative to workers, communities, and nations due to three aspects of the neo-liberal regime: (1) insufficient levels of aggregate demand; (2) institutions and rules of the game that facilitate capital mobility and encourage national and subnational competition for capital; and (3) the promotion of coercive rather than co-respective competition among firms.

What, if anything, can be done to reverse the negative impact that FDI and MNCs will increasingly have as the neo-liberal regime spreads? Are there policies that can restore the relative bargaining power of workers, communities, and nations and can close off the road to the bottom, while reducing international coordination problems to make the climb to the top more likely?

Here we can only propose a framework for thinking about policy in the area of MNCs and FDI, a framework that evolves from the analysis of the problem that we have presented here. Within this framework we give examples that focus on policies and institutions that can address the three central problems we have identified. A distinction must be made among levels of policy implementation as well as between the actors involved. In the first place, we can distinguish among local, national, regional, and international levels of policy implementation. In the second, we can distinguish between state-led policies and worker- or citizen-led actions.

In making the latter distinction, we recognize that a central problem in trying to devise policies to alter the bargaining power between the government and capital is that, in many instances, *capital is the government*. An essential difficulty in devising and implementing any of these policies is the relative lack of power that citizens have in determining government policy.

Insufficient aggregate demand

If our analysis is correct, restoring high levels of aggregate demand and the tight labor markets that follow in their wake would greatly reduce the negative impacts of FDI. Expansionary policies and institutions could be established at the international, regional, or national levels. In this era of large speculative short-term capital flows, policies to reregulate such flows at any or all of these levels will be necessary (see Felix, Schaberg, and Pollin in this volume; Crotty and Epstein 1996).

But even if a national or global Keynesian expansionary policy were initiated, it would have to be supplemented by supply side policies and new capital-labor accords and social contracts to be sustainable (see Glyn and Pollin in this volume). Moreover, with the extremely high levels of surplus labor in the developing world, expansionary Keynesian policy and short-term capital controls would not equalize labor costs around the world, and therefore would not completely eliminate the downward pressures on wages, taxes, and working conditions emanating from global competition.

Institutions, rules of the game, and norms

State-led changes

A second implication of our analysis is that improvements in the norms and rules governing international investment to reduce incentives for a "race to the bottom" is essential if FDI is not to have such negative impacts. There are a number of actions that states and citizens could take to improve domestic and international rules governing FDI.

First, there should be a moratorium on all international agreements promoted by international organizations or Northern countries to liberalize the laws governing controls over FDI, including those taken by the OECD, the World Trade Organization (WTO), and NAFTA (and its proposed extensions). This moratorium should remain in place until an effective set of international rules governing FDI is put into place. An example of such a rule would be an international agreement forbidding unproductive tax competition; this rule could be implemented and enforced by an international organization such as the WTO. Some international organizations are investigating voluntary agreements along these lines (UNCTAD 1995). Such agreements ought to be implemented as well at regional and national levels (Federal Reserve Bank of Minneapolis 1994).

Second, international organizations such as the World Bank and the IMF should stop pressuring developing and transitional countries to open their economies to foreign direct investment as a condition for receiving credit, as they are doing in the case of South Korea. This simply contributes to the wasteful competition we have described.

Citizen-led changes

International labor standards and corporate codes of conduct. More controversial are policies to implement international labor standards. While some standards such as those forbidding slave labor receive widespread support, others, such as enforcing wage and working conditions internationally through the use of social tariffs, are much more controversial (see Michie and Smith 1995; on social tariffs, see Cullenberg and DeMartino 1995). Advocates of such standards argue that they will reduce countries' destructive international bidding over wages and working conditions. Critics argue that standards unfairly penalize the poorest workers of the world to line the pockets of the wealthiest. According to these critics, labor standards are a form of imperialism.

One solution to this controversy is to create a framework within which workers and their representatives from both rich and poor countries can get together and decide what types of standards they want, if any. Currently, most of the debate is waged by economists and policy makers, and few direct representatives of those most affected by the policies in North and South are represented. Efforts in this direction are already ongoing (see, for example, Cavanagh et al. 1996). These groups are also discussing standards for multinational corporate codes of conduct. Initiatives aimed at labeling products to indicate how labor and environmentally friendly their production processes are is another example of "citizen-led international coordination" that ought to be extended.

Reining in coercive competition. The most important national policies for reducing coercive competition would be to reinforce laws and support institutions that make it more difficult for corporations to place excessive burdens of restructuring on workers and communities. We need policies to strengthen unions and rebalance bargaining power, rebuild the social wage or social safety net, and introduce worker and community influence in corporate governance. For example, in the U.S., passing living-wage legislation that would place a higher floor under wages would be an excellent beginning (see Pollin and Luce 1998).

Capital controls. As mentioned above, given the speculative nature of capital markets, some controls on short-term capital flows will also be necessary. Regulatory changes, Tobin taxes, and keeping open the option for stronger controls are also likely to be helpful (see Felix and Schaberg in this volume; Tobin 1978; Crotty and Epstein 1996; Grabel 1996b).

Other measures. If all these measures were taken, additional measures to rein in coercive competition may not be required. However, in the event that they are, policies that limit the rate of increase of imports over a medium-term period may be needed to slow down the pace of structural change and allow companies and communities to adjust. Similarly, controls on the movement of FDI across borders may be needed. Note, however, that changing the overall context within which trade and FDI occur are very likely to go a long way toward solving the problems associated with them, thus reducing the likelihood that direct controls would be required.

Conclusion

We end with the central questions posed for our consideration by this volume: "globalization and progressive economic policy: what are the real constraints and options?" We suggest that increased capital mobility within the neo-liberal regimes is imposing increasingly severe constraints on workers, communities, and states. However, we do not agree with the extreme versions of neo-classical economics or the "globalization thesis" that see these constraints as an inevitable outcome of technological change or as an irreversible juggernaut. On the contrary, our main point is that the effect of FDI depends crucially on the domestic and international context within which it occurs. Different domestic and international structures produce very different outcomes.

Thus, progressive policy options are available. Policies to expand aggregate demand, reduce the destructive effects of competition, and create a more worker- and community-friendly set of domestic and international institutions are being studied and debated in all corners of the globe and are feasible. Thus, pessimism is not the order of the day. Still, we cannot make progress unless we confront and overcome the increasingly powerful constraints imposed by the forces of the neo-liberal regime.

Comment by Tim Koechlin on
"Multinational corporations in the neo-liberal regime"

This very good paper raises a number of important questions and sheds considerable light on most of them. What is the relationship between capital mobility and domestic economic outcomes? Are advances in globalization likely to result in wage erosion, growing economic insecurity, declining corporate tax rates, and stingier welfare states (a "race to the bottom")? Or do advances in openness lead to efficiency and welfare gains ("neo-liberal convergence")? What, in short, should we expect as globalization proceeds, and what, if anything, can we do about it? Crotty et al. make a persuasive argument that, under current conditions, a race to the bottom is a likely outcome. This claim has been made elsewhere, of course, but few others have defended this claim – and articulated the potential hazards of foreign direct investment (FDI) – as carefully and persuasively as Crotty et al.

I like and appreciate this paper for the reasons that I appreciate so much of the authors' previous work: the paper takes on an important set of issues and presents a rich, provocative argument without dodging the hard questions. And further, Crotty et al. present their argument with terrific clarity. This paper enriches considerably the literature on multinational corporations (MNCs), globalization, and progressive economic policy – a literature that is often too simplistic and, as a consequence, not very enlightening – by presenting a useful framework for understanding and addressing this important but ambiguous set of issues. I expect and hope that this paper will compel many readers to think about globalization with greater subtlety.

Crotty et al. argue that the mobility and flexibility of MNCs can help to explain a number of troubling stylized political economic facts, including wage stagnation, growing income inequality, high trend rates of unemployment and underemployment, a declining social wage, and the fiscal crisis of the state (to coin a phrase). Their argument, on the one hand, appears to be quite familiar: advances in the mobility of capital enhance the bargaining power of multinational corporations (MNCs) and, as a consequence, throw workers, communities, and nation-states into a fierce competition for investment and jobs. But their argument goes much further than this. The effects of FDI (and the increasingly viable "exit option" enjoyed by MNCs) "depend on the overall national and international context within which capital mobility occurs." More specifically:

> [W]hen FDI occurs in a context of high levels of aggregate demand and effective rules of the game, which in turn limit the destructive aspects of competition, then FDI may indeed have a positive impact on nations and communities. On the other hand, when FDI occurs in a context of low levels of aggregate demand and destructive economic and political competition in the absence of effective rules of the game, then FDI can have a significantly negative impact on workers in both home and host countries.

The hegemony of neo-liberalism makes this latter scenario – a more or less frantic race to the bottom – increasingly likely precisely because neo-liberalism facilitates and promotes a global political-economic climate characterized by sluggish aggregate demand growth and "rules of the game" that make it more and more difficult for governments and workers to contain the destructive impacts of FDI. Those of us with an interest in progressive economic policy should be concerned, then, for two related reasons: the mobility of productive capital appears to be increasing; and the current "neo-liberal regime" has enhanced the destructive potential of FDI flows.

The argument that globalization threatens the prospects for progressive economic policy – even in its most simplistic form – is compelling and, to one degree or another, surely correct. But it is an argument that is frequently exaggerated, and this is a problem both because exaggerated claims provide a flimsy basis for understanding the determinants of investment, employment, and wages, and because its conclusions tend to be unnecessarily fatalistic. The evidence suggests that productive capital is in fact remarkably immobile, and this calls the premise of the simple globalization model into question. The ratio of outward FDI to domestic investment is very low, and it has grown remarkably slowly over the past few decades (Koechlin 1995). Table 2 in Crotty et al. shows that "gross" FDI flows as a percentage of gross fixed capital formation were no higher for 1991–95 than for 1986–1990. In the aggregate, domestic investment appears to be remarkably unresponsive to foreign profit rates (Koechlin 1992), and a study by Jerry Epstein (1996) finds that affiliates of U.S. MNCs – presumably the most footloose firms of all – do not appear to respond to international profit rate differentials. Most of the output of U.S. foreign affiliates (in poor countries and in rich countries) is sold locally. During the 1980s – a decade characterized by wage stagnation and growing inequality in the U.S. – outward FDI as a share of investment fell while inward FDI boomed.

This evidence surely does not indicate that capital mobility is irrelevant. But it does raise questions about the willingness and ability of MNCs to relocate, especially in response to lower wages, and it indicates that it is a mistake to treat capital mobility and its presumed consequences as self-evident or inevitable facts of life.

Crotty et al., for the most part, avoid this trap. They argue quite correctly that capital is probably more mobile than this body of evidence suggests; that FDI understates the extent to which MNCs shift production (it does not account for outsourcing, for example); and that a viable threat to relocate enhances MNC bargaining power considerably. And, of course, the central argument of this paper is that, in the current climate, any particular level of capital mobility is more destructive than it would be in a world of rapid growth and effective rules of the game. Their argument does not require advances in capital mobility (and so my argument immediately above – that capital is not all that mobile – does not contradict the chapter's central claim). But, it seems to me, this question – how mobile is productive capital? – remains enormously important. Crotty et al.'s brief treatment of this question is quite good but, in my view, too brief to support the conclusion that "gross capital mobility has increased dramatically."

There is plenty of room for debate about the extent and consequences of capital mobility. But it is clear that productive capital is very far from perfectly mobile. Why, with so few obvious barriers to globalization, does investment continue to be so overwhelmingly domestic? This anomaly is explained in part by enforcement costs, which generally increase when capital crosses a border. As we make progress in defining and specifying enforcement costs and their determinants, I suspect that we will have more to say about the pace and pattern of FDI. (Jerry Epstein, by the way, has had as much to say as anyone about enforcement costs and FDI.) The evidence presented in this paper on this matter is terrific and persuasive, e.g., from 1991 to 1996 "95 percent of the 599 changes made in countries' regulatory FDI regimes were in the direction of liberalization." A complete explanation of capital immobility needs to acknowledge that the fixed costs associated with FDI and the various costs associated with being a foreign investor are often quite substantial. The simple model presented in this chapter is quite useful in part because it alludes to the importance of fixed costs. A more complicated model – which is not necessary given Crotty et al.'s project – might attempt to articulate the barriers to mobility more carefully, and speculate about how changes in technology and/or policy might erode or reinforce these barriers.

All of this said, this is an important, impressive paper. Crotty et al. present a rich, historically specific story about the linkages between globalization and a variety of domestic political-economic issues. Its argument that FDI's effects depend on the political-economic context is clear and persuasive, and its conclusion that capital mobility is largely a policy choice is correct and enormously important. I think about globalization differently than I did before reading this paper, and I hope lots of other readers will as well. And the conclusion of the paper is right on the mark: globalization is serious and consequential, but it does not imply that our economic fate is out of our control. In the words of Crotty, Epstein, and Kelly, "progressive policy options are available."

Part III

Globalization of finance

6

Implications of globalization for macroeconomic theory and policy in developing countries

Amit Bhaduri

Globalization: "then" and "now"

The interplay of continuity with change makes historical parallels imperfect. Nevertheless, by highlighting both the similarities and the differences, they may help us understand better complex processes in contemporary history. The process of economic globalization through the expansion of business and commerce, which is proceeding now at a spectacular pace, resembles in many ways a similar process that was underway when the Gold Standard was at its height (approximately 1890–1913). Of the three main economic aspects of globalization usually discussed, namely, expansion in international trade, investment, and finance, at least in the first two aspects globalization "then" under the Gold Standard is comparable with what is going on "now."

Since World War II, international trade has grown rapidly, from a meager 6 percent of world gross domestic product to over 15 percent by the early 1990s; the countries of the OECD (Organization for Economic Cooperation and Development) exported 17 percent of their aggregate GDP in 1992. And yet, these numbers are not unprecedented. In the year 1900, the 16 most industrialized countries exported 18 percent of their GDP, a figure that rose to 21 percent in 1913. Roughly speaking, industrialized countries export one out of every 5 dollars of output they produce today, as they did just before the outbreak of World War I (Maddison 1989).

Although these aggregative pictures of international trade remain comparable, the details are different between "then" and "now" in two interesting respects. First, developing countries were hardly present as exporters of manufactured goods before the First World War. Until 1970, in fact, their share in world manufactured exports remained below 5 percent. Since then, it has increased perceptibly, rising to 22 percent by 1993, and today manufacturing exports account for more than 60 percent of total exports from developing countries. While the conventional view

This paper benefited from comments by various participants in the conference on "Globalization and Progressive Economic Policy," organized by the Economic Policy Institute, Washington, D.C. I would like to record my intellectual debt in particular to Robert Blecker, Jerry Epstein, and Robert Pollin without implicating them in my errors.

that developing countries export only low value-added primary product to import back high value-added manufactured product no longer holds, an important qualification is needed. Only a select group of roughly a dozen developing countries account for the lion's share of manufacturing exports. For the vast majority of developing countries, the picture has changed relatively little.

Second, the mechanism for conducting trade has undergone important changes between "then" and "now." The mechanism that drives trade lies increasingly within the multinational firm, with international trade as its apparent consequence. In 1990, roughly one-third of world trade took place among multinational parent companies and their various foreign affiliates. That figure has since risen to "at least 40 percent of world trade" (EC 1995, 2).

As the relative importance of intrafirm trade grows, so does the scope for "creative transfer pricing" by multinationals to escape from the higher tax rates on corporate profits by particular national governments. Both the desire to "harmonize" national tax rates and to reduce them to their lowest common denominator are concomitant processes that become understandable in this context. Moreover, intrafirm trade among the parent company and its affiliates may be guided by various types of "implicit contracts" that not only avoid higher taxes, but also introduce some "structural rigidities" in the patterns of exports and imports of the national economy. Thus, switching to a cheaper alternative source of supply because of, say, a temporary variation in the exchange rate may be avoided, especially if it gives advantage to a business rival.

That the trade performances of nations are influenced strongly by the underlying pattern of intrafirm trade is suggested also by a variety of evidence. In 1990–91, intrafirm trade accounted for nearly 60 percent of U.S. merchandise trade. The U.S. affiliates of foreign multinationals were responsible for 23 percent of U.S. merchandise exports and 37 percent of imports, even though their share in U.S. GDP was only 6 percent and they employed only 5 percent of the labor force. Some estimates suggest that as much as 88 percent of the U.S. trade deficit was accounted for by the U.S. affiliates of foreign multinationals (Davis 1993, 77, quoted in Hufbauer, Lakdawalla, and Malani 1994). A highly visible case is automobile trade, where already in 1986 Japan ran a trade surplus of $5.6 billion in various automobile components.

Consequently, even if the car-importing countries reduced their trade gap in terms of the final product of automobiles, their total trade deficit might not have decreased correspondingly due to the imported component parts. According to a recent estimate (*The Economist,* December 20, 1997), the highest-ranking exporter in automobile trade in 1997 was Germany. It exported $87 billion-worth and imported $47 billion-worth in intra-industry (not necessarily intrafirm) trade. For the United States, ranking third, exports worth $55 billion were outpaced by $112 billion-worth of imports in intraindustry trade. Another example is Bosch of Germany, which captured 75 percent of the global market for antilock breaking devices that were incorporated in various trade in final products (Jones and Klerskowski 1980). From this point of view, it is not altogether surprising that no clear empirical relation could be found between an importing country's structure of production and its bilateral volume of trade in intermediate products, because the latter might have been shaped significantly by intrafirm and intra-industry trade (Harrigan 1995).

Insofar as international trade is being driven increasingly by intrafirm trade, developing countries that wish to penetrate the international export market find that relying on foreign direct investment (FDI) by multinationals is almost unavoidable. The acute competition among developing countries to attract FDI is partly a result of this need. However, despite this, the overall picture with respect to FDI has not changed dramatically in some important respects between "then" and "now."

Evaluated at historic cost, the accumulated stock of FDI was 8.4 percent of world GDP in 1992, compared to 9 percent just before the outbreak of World War I (Nayyar 1995). Also noticeable is another similarity, namely, the growing relative importance of FDI in recent years in the net resource flows to developing countries. While official flows have remained broadly unchanged since the early 1990s, private capital flows have seen two phases of dramatic upswing. The first was during 1975–81, when private bank lending involving mostly recycled petrodollars dominated. In the current phase FDI dominates, with its share in net resource flow to developing countries rising to 35 percent on average during 1990–96, up from 12 percent during the 1970s. And, as the developing countries compete to attract FDI by offering relative tax and other advantages to foreign investors, the phenomenon of "round-tripping," comparable in some ways to "transfer pricing," is becoming common. By this method, domestic funds are taken out of the country and brought back in again to take advantage of special tax concessions on FDI. In China, for instance, of the $34 billion in FDI received in 1994 (which accounted for 88 percent of FDI flowing to low-income developing countries in that year), 37 percent consisted of these round-tripped funds (World Bank 1997).

There is, however, a marked difference in the sectoral pattern of FDI between "then" and "now." More than half of the FDI in 1913 went to the primary sector, mostly mining and unprocessed raw materials, while manufacturing received less than 10 percent (Dunning 1983). The pattern is almost the reverse now, with almost 40 percent of FDI going to manufacturing and less than 10 percent to the primary sector in 1990. However, in accordance with the geographical pattern of manufacturing exports from developing countries, only a handful of selected developing countries are able to attract FDI to their manufacturing or modern infrastructural services (e.g., telecommunications) sector on any significant scale. For the vast majority of developing countries, not only is FDI flow minimal, but it continues to flow into the primary sector of mining and agricultural raw materials. From their point of view, globalization "now" and "then" is not very different.

Undoubtedly the most striking differences between globalization "then" under the discipline of the fixed exchange rates of the Gold Standard and globalization "now" under today's system of mostly market-determined flexible exchange rates have emerged in the area of international finance. The exploding growth in international private finance is the most dramatic aspect of the ongoing process of globalization without any historical parallel. Within the OECD, it began with the country-by-country abolition of restrictions on international capital movements starting in 1973. In that year, the volume of transactions in the foreign exchange markets around the world averaged around $15 billion per day. As restrictions on international capital movements were removed it began to climb, to $80 billion per day in 1980, to $880 billion in 1992, and to $1,260 billion in 1995 (BIS 1993b, 1996; Eatwell 1996).

Of this staggering sum, only a small fraction – less than 2 percent – is now accounted for by trade in goods and services, compared to 15 percent in 1973. FDI accounts for only a tiny fraction as well. The rest, an overwhelming amount exceeding a trillion dollars per day, surpassing the total gold and foreign exchange reserves of all the central banks put together, consists of transactions by private traders in the markets for foreign exchange in currencies and other financial assets. Moreover, the exchanges are predominantly of a short-term nature, and switch across national borders whenever the mood of the market changes for whatever reason.

This enormous mobility of international financial capital needs to be contrasted against the relative immobility of labor in the present phase of globalization. Approximately 50 million persons migrated from Europe to North America between 1860 and 1913. At about the same time (but starting a little earlier), another 50 million migrated as indentured labor from China and India. Compared to that vast movement of labor in relation to the global population then, international migration is a relatively small trickle now. This marked asymmetry in the mobility of capital and labor, combined with the lightning speed at which short-term financial capital of enormous magnitudes moves across national frontiers at the push of a button, provides an essentially different background to the present phase of globalization. It is also the context in which economic policies now have to be made, in both developing and developed countries.

Implications for macroeconomic theory and policy

The ongoing process of globalization is widening the gap, as never before, between the responsibility for the economic performance of a nation-state and the causes of its economic performance. National governments remain responsible to their electorates for their macroeconomic performance in terms of employment, balance of payments, or growth. And yet, the area of control determining economic performance has shifted increasingly away from the national governments to the multinational corporations and financial institutions, whose loyalty to making profits is certainly stronger than that to their particular countries of origin. This is perhaps the essence of the new political economy that is being shaped by globalization in its present phase.

The most immediate economic consequence of this shift has been to increase the relative importance of the external compared to the internal or home market in almost every nation. This is happening not simply through a rapid expansion of foreign trade and investment, which also took place at a more or less comparable pace in the earlier episode of globalization under the Gold Standard, but also, and more importantly, because national government policies are restraining the internal market from expanding at a fast enough pace. Both the massive volume and the high mobility of international financial capital have encouraged national governments to "play it safe" by avoiding any disturbance of the financial markets that may induce capital flight. Consequently, governments have assumed a restrictive fiscal and monetary stance by aiming at lower budget deficits, keeping interest rates high, and adopting austerity measures for public expenditure even in the face of high unemployment and low growth. It is the logic of this situation that lends acceptability to the "stabilization" and "structural adjustment" programs of the Bretton Woods institutions in developing countries, or to the Maastricht policies in the European Union. At the same time, turning away from the Keynesian policies of demand management in the home or internal market of the national economy are merely the other side of the coin.

With the shift in the center of gravity from the internal to the external market, national economic policies also begin to resemble more closely the economic strategies of multinational corporations. The reason is simple. By and large, individual corporations take the *size* of the market as given, i.e., beyond their control, but they try to capture a bigger *share* of that market. This goal is typically attempted by cutting costs, particularly labor costs in relation to labor productivity, so as to attain a competitive advantage vis-a-vis the rivals. With demand management policies abandoned by governments, the focus of national policies has also shifted away from the size of the market. Since the size of the external market lies largely beyond the control of individual national governments, macroeconomic policy now focuses on capturing a bigger share of the external market by introducing "labor market flexibility" to gain competitive advantage against other nations. The most important fallout for economic policy has been the view, shared by national governments and corporate firms, that wages are merely an element of cost, and not a source of demand or purchasing power. In turn, this view has pushed most national economies away from a path of mass consumption or wage-led expansion of the home market, which was a distinguishing feature of the post-World War II secular boom in OECD countries (cf. Bhaduri and Marglin 1990; Marglin and Bhaduri 1990).

Nevertheless, all countries cannot be successful in capturing a larger share of the external market at the same time; nor can all countries expand their domestic market indirectly by running an export surplus through the "foreign trade multiplier." Therefore, policies aimed at competitive reduction of domestic wage costs might help individual firms, but they lead to a "fallacy of composition" on the global scale. Neglect of demand management in the home market and preoccupation with competitive cost reduction to capture a larger share of the external market, when pursued by all countries, have an in-built tendency toward economic depression.

Competitive devaluation of national currencies and "beggar-thy-neighbor" policies could have been an outcome in such a situation, as was the case during the interwar period. However, this is no longer a viable option. In a regime of market-determined flexible exchange rates, any such interventionist attempt in the market for foreign exchange could provoke overwhelming and unpredictable short-term capital flows with enormous destabilizing potential for the national economy. This has changed fundamentally the very context of macroeconomic policy in the present phase of globalization in a paradoxical way. On the one hand, the external market has gained in relative importance. On the other, short-term external financial flows are now largely exogenous in the sense that they severely constrain national government policies but are not easily influenced by them to suit the economic objectives of national governments.

The central purpose of progressive macroeconomic policies should be to break out of this very awkward situation. And the only way to achieve this goal is to restore the importance of the internal or domestic market in formulating policies – while taking into account the fact that short-term private capital flows will remain largely exogenous in the above sense. From this point of view, it is important to recognize that, even for many developing countries facing various degrees of shortage of foreign exchange, a relatively large *inflow* of short-term external capital need not be an unmixed blessing in a liberalized trade regime. The reason is that, such capital inflows may sustain artificially for some time an import surplus that has a contractionary impact on the size of the domestic market and activity level. At the same time, sustaining an import surplus in this manner builds up external debt and makes the economy more vulnerable to capital flight.

The problem may be analyzed in a starkly schematized form by considering the case of an import-starved, developing economy in which a liberalized import regime is being sustained by exogenous inflow of foreign aid or finance. Assuming saving (S) to be a constant fraction (s) of income (Y), the usual national accounting for the open economy yields:

$$I - S = I - s(Y) = (M - E) = A \qquad (1)$$

where I = investment, M = imports, E = exports, and A = the net inflow of foreign aid or finance.

Consequently, the level of domestic income, determined by the size of the domestic market (or aggregate demand) is given as:

$$Y = (1 / s) (I - A) \qquad (2)$$

As equation (2) shows, a higher net inflow of foreign finance or aid, A, could reduce income through the multiplier mechanism for any given level of investment. The multiplier mechanism driving the contraction of aggregate demand and income in equation (2) does not depend merely on the substitution of domestic by imported goods, which provides only the initial impulse to the Kahn-Keynes multiplier process. This is because as the output of domestic goods decreases through substitution at the initial round of the multiplier, so do profits, wages, and employment in these domestic industries.

This causes, in turn, further decline in demand and output of domestic industries in successive rounds of a convergent geometric series of the multiplier process, as implied by (2). Note that these successive rounds of contraction in demand and domestic output need not involve any *further* substitution of domestic by foreign goods (and therefore does not entail that these domestic goods are less competitive), but they could be driven entirely by the decline in domestic demand (Bhaduri and Skarstein 1996).

While this argument holds strictly in a demand-constrained economy, it can be extended qualitatively even in the case of a supply-constrained economy. For instance, if imports help to relax immediate supply bottlenecks like the shortage of essential maintenance imports, we could visualize potential output from the supply side (Ys) as an increasing function of net capital inflow (A) enlarging the import capacity of the economy. But even in this case, there would be an optimum level of capital inflow, shown by A* in Figure 1 below. In this figure, aggregate demand (Yd) is a decreasing function of A in accordance with equation 2, but aggregate supply (Ys) is an increasing function of A, so that domestic production is maximized at A*. However, beyond A* capital inflow could have its contractionary effect on income.

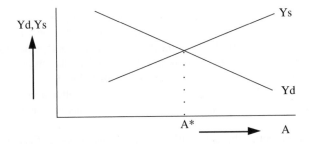

This skeleton model could be embellished in many ways. Its central point, however, is to emphasize how financial liberalization permits firms and domestic financial institutions to contract external debt to make imports exogenous, and not induced by income, in a liberalized trade regime. Thus, as a higher level of exogenous investment has an expansionary impact on aggregate demand and income, a higher level of exogenous imports has a contractionary effect. In a more general case, a higher inflow of short-term external finance may even stimulate both investment and exports, but the contractionary effect would still continue so long as the marginal propensity to import out of external financial inflow exceeds that out of investment and export. More formally, if investment, export, and import are all increasing functions of A, using (1) and (2), we would have:

$$(dY / dA) = (1 / s) [dI / dA) + (dE / dA) - (dM / dA)] \qquad (3)$$

Here, (dY/dA) would be negative so long as the square-bracketed term on the right-hand side of (3) is negative.

Short-term capital inflow in the form of portfolio investment in various financial assets can in some cases exceed the trade (or current account) deficit. In such cases, it may lead to increasing foreign exchange reserves held by the central bank and other financial institutions in the country.

In turn, this accumulation in foreign exchange reserves might lead to an appreciation of the market-determined domestic currency despite trade (or current account) deficits. If the import and export elasticities are large enough to satisfy the so-called Marshall-Lerner condition, an even worse scenario may unfold. On the one hand, the trade deficit widens due to the appreciation (or perceived strength) of the domestic currency, while domestic demand and activity levels contract. On the other, the show is kept going temporarily through a higher inflow of short-term portfolio investment that imposes an increasing burden of external debt and its servicing requirement. This is the recipe for a financial disaster that sooner or later hits the developing country with a liberalized trade and financial regime, where excessive inflow of external short-term finance can ultimately play havoc. Episodes in Mexico in 1994–95 and in Thailand, Malaysia, Indonesia, and South Korea in 1997 suggest that such a scenario is not altogether implausible, although details differ among these countries.

Our preceding analysis was not intended to provide a comprehensive model of an open, developing economy in the contemporary globalized setting. Its purpose was limited to tracing analytically the route through which trade together with foreign exchange and capital market liberalization can precipitate serious problems for a developing country. Four interrelated policy proposals follow from this analysis.

They are connected by the common theme that greater attention needs to be paid to the development of the internal or home market in formulating macroeconomic policies.

First, insofar as short-term capital inflows can have a depressive effect on aggregate demand in the internal market (equations 2 and 3), they need to be countered by macroeconomic policies to stimulate domestic investment. When neither FDI nor private investment by domestic firms can be stimulated easily by policy, the option for increased public investment should not be foreclosed.

Second, and it follows from above, that the "stabilization" and "structural adjustment" programs followed by the Bretton Woods institutions should not degenerate into a euphemism for reducing the role of the public sector. It is fundamentally flawed, both economically and politically, to expect countries to generate a greater export surplus to ride over their balance of payments difficulties in situations where their national income and activity levels are falling. Attention must shift to policies aimed at raising the level of economic activity, not after but during the stabilization program. If a policy of raising public investment, even financed by a higher budget deficit, helps in this respect, it should be adopted. It is when activity levels are rising that the restructuring of public finance through the reduction of external and internal debt should be carried out. In short, *the timing of the current fiscal austerity programs is wrong,* both politically and economically.

Third, public and private investment should be seen as complementary, not competitive. If public investment is consciously restored back to its role of demand management at home, the private sector can mostly benefit through higher capacity utilization. At the same time, high interest rates, often caused by forcing governments in developing countries to borrow in the market or by restricting domestic credit as a critical component of almost all IMF-style stabilization, have a depressive effect both on public and private investment. They "crowd out" both, while attracting at best short-term external portfolio investment. As we have argued, this inflow may accentuate the tendencies toward depression, and may even keep both exchange rate and import surplus artificially high. Thus, the monetary measures currently pursued in stabilization programs are timed poorly as well. In general, more accommodative monetary policies are needed precisely when a country has to overcome its balance of payments difficulties by raising its export surplus. Restrictive monetary policies and higher interest rates only postpone the problem at best by attracting short-term capital. The basic policy must focus on raising export surplus by raising domestic income through expansionary, not contractionary, policies.

Finally, this raises the most awkward dilemma of following expansionary policies in a contemporary, globalized financial market. Expansionary fiscal and monetary policies are constrained severely nowadays by the fear of the massive capital flights they might provoke. Moreover, such fears are greater in a developing country, precisely when it faces serious balance-of-payments difficulties. The current orthodoxy of the Bretton Woods institutions avoids facing this problem by advising developing countries to generate a higher export surplus out of lower national income, which is precipitated typically by conventional stabilization and structural adjustment programs. An alternative must be seriously sought, so that expansionary fiscal and monetary policies are not ruled out in times of balance-of-payments difficulties. It could involve three crucial elements:

Import control. Some degree of import control (at least on a temporary basis) that can be agreed upon between the country concerned and the International Monetary Fund needs to be imposed. The idea that import control is bad in *all* circumstances is merely an article of faith, not a reasoned basis for policy formulation.

Capital control. The issue of capital control, as an integral part of stabilization and structural adjustment programs, requires greater attention both internationally and nationally if we are serious about turning the worst dangers of globalization into opportunities for developing countries. Although some 119 out of the 155 developing countries surveyed in a recent IMF report (IMF 1995a) had some form of capital control in place, the main thrust of the IMF and World Bank official policy has been to press for currency convertibility on the capital account of developing countries. This requires that their currencies be freely convertible for all types of international capital transactions, thereby exposing them even further to the mercy of short-term international capital flows. And, although Article VI of the IMF permits member states to impose capital controls, the IMF has virtually no responsibility in helping developing countries devise and enforce these controls.

Transactions tax. Internationally, the feasibility of a tax on international security and foreign exchange transactions (Tobin tax) that can be agreed upon by IMF member states needs to be put on the agenda. Nationally, regulating the outflow of short-term capital is always far more difficult than regulating its inflow, and developing countries must learn to be prudent when they receive these inflows. The so-called "Chilean model" is a useful pointer in this respect. Currently in Chile, local firms borrowing abroad are required to keep 30 percent of the loan as deposit with the central bank without interest for a year, irrespective of the duration of the loan. This is designed to encourage foreign borrowing with a longer-term perspective, while also raising its cost. A discriminatory national tax structure, which imposes a significantly higher tax rate on income from interest and financial capital gains at the source compared to income from profits on real investment, could provide perhaps another alternative.

"Progressive" economists everywhere must recognize that their main task now is to ensure that, in the process of globalization, the market mechanism does not degenerate into a form of "casino capitalism" in the name of freedom and efficiency. In this, they may take their cue from Keynes:

> The introduction of a substantial Government transfer tax on all transactions (in the Stock Exchange) might prove the most serviceable reform available, with a view to mitigating the predominance of speculation over enterprise... (Keynes 1936, 160).

The context has changed, but not the fundamental problem. The tension between "industry" driven by enterprise and "finance" propelled by speculation is surfacing again, and it poses the greatest challenge to economic policy during the present phase of globalization.

Comment by Robert A. Blecker on
"Implications of globalization for macroeconomic theory and policy in developing countries"

Amit Bhaduri's chapter is really two papers in one: first, a comparison of globalization "then" (in the pre-World War I period) and "now" (in the late 20th century); and second, a Keynesian model of the macroeconomic effects of foreign capital inflows into developing countries in the latter period. The two parts are connected by one overarching theme: the dominance of internationally mobile financial capital in the contemporary process of globalization. It is difficult to cover so much ground in such a short space, and Bhaduri does a good job of surveying such a vast field without yielding to the temptation of oversimplifying or making excessively sweeping generalizations.

In the historical comparisons, Bhaduri is certainly right to emphasize the extraordinary degree of mobility of portfolio capital as the most striking and unique feature of the current global economy. Indeed, the liberalization of financial markets since the 1970s has meant that one of the key theoretical conditions for "perfect capital mobility" – covered interest parity, in which a country's interest rate premium equals the forward discount on its currency – is now empirically fulfilled in most industrialized countries and in a growing group of developing countries (see Frankel 1991, 1993). The recent financial crises in Mexico (1994) and East Asia (1997) have dramatically illustrated the power of financial capital movements to destabilize entire national economies as well as the degree of interlinkage between financial centers across the globe.

Certainly, goods, labor, and "real" capital are not nearly as mobile as financial capital in today's world – a fact attested to by persistent violations of the "law of one price" in international goods markets (i.e., deviations from "purchasing power parity"), as well as by persistent differentials in real wages and (to a lesser extent) rates of return to corporate capital. Nevertheless, while financial markets are by far the most integrated today internationally, it is important not to underestimate the increasing degree of globalization in these other types of markets. Bhaduri argues that the degree to which the world economy is linked by international trade flows and foreign direct investment (FDI) today is only marginally greater than it was in the pre-World War I period, and that labor mobility has significantly diminished. This argument needs to be qualified in two ways.

First, the figures Bhaduri cites showing similar ratios of FDI to GDP today and before World War I may be misleading due to the measurement of the accumulated stocks of FDI at historical cost. As a result of the chronic inflation in the post-World War II period, FDI stocks are underestimated when measured at historical cost, especially when compared to GDP in current prices. In the U.S. case, the conver-

159

sion of official FDI statistics from a historical cost basis to a current cost (or market valuation) basis in the 1980s led to a significant increase in the country's reported net asset position in FDI (see Eisner and Pieper 1990; Blecker 1991). Since there was not a comparable steady inflation in the pre-World War I period, total world FDI as a percentage of GDP at current cost is likely to be significantly higher today than it was before 1914. The increasing importance of FDI is also supported by Bhaduri's own data showing that the share of FDI in total net resource flows into developing countries was higher in the 1990s than in the 1970s.[1]

Second, as Bhaduri acknowledges, the pattern of specialization in North-South trade has changed. Developing country exports consist increasingly of manufactured products that compete with goods produced in the industrialized countries. This increasing specialization of large parts of the South in manufactures has been accompanied – and, to a large extent, induced – by the increasing degree to which FDI in the South has been directed toward manufactures. Especially, the importation of more advanced technology and management can create competitive advantages in unit labor costs in countries where wages are still held down by lower average productivity in the domestic economy due to persistent "dualism."[2] As Bhaduri notes, this process is confined to a relatively small "club" of newly industrializing countries (mostly in East Asia, plus India, Mexico, and a few others) that account for the lion's share of developing country exports of manufactures, but the club is growing as more countries liberalize their trade and foreign investment policies.

Thus, manufacturing production is far more globalized "now" than "then," and shares of exports in GDP do not give a complete picture of the degree of internationalization of production. In the earlier period, manufacturing industries in industrialized countries depended on underdeveloped and colonial areas primarily for raw materials and secondarily for markets; today, manufacturing production itself takes place in a "global factory," managed by large multinational corporations, in which different stages of the manufacture of any given finished product are allocated to diverse countries around the world.

One result of this globalization of production is that it effectively integrates labor markets in different countries, in spite of the greater barriers to international labor mobility that exist today. Industrial workers in any given country have to compete with industrial workers in other countries for jobs, not mainly via migration (although some migration still takes place), but mostly indirectly through the trade in their products as well as the mobility of "footloose" capital in their industries. As emphasized in both the traditional Heckscher-Ohlin trade model as well as some more recent trade models (e.g., Johnson and Stafford 1993; Blecker 1997), such

---

1   One wonders how this observation is consistent with the author's point about the greater mobility of financial capital compared with FDI. Perhaps the resolution lies in the distinction between gross and net capital flows, i.e., a lot of portfolio capital is moving around the world, but it is moving both into and out of developing countries and is not creating large, sustained net inflows of resources – especially after net interest payments are subtracted, as they are in calculating net resource flows.

2   See Brewer (1985) and Milberg (1997) for analyses of how capital mobility makes trade follow absolute rather than comparative advantages.

international competition and capital mobility can have profound effects on income distribution.

Now, I come to the author's theoretical model, which emphasizes the idea that relatively autonomous net inflows of financial capital are the driving force in the balance of payments, and incorporates that idea into a fairly standard open economy Keynesian macro model. The model treats net capital inflows as exogenous and highlights the contractionary nature of the current account deficits that are the other side of the coin (in balance-of-payments accounting) of the net capital inflows into a demand-constrained economy. The model also incorporates a (somewhat ad hoc) aggregate supply function, assumed to be an increasing function of net capital inflows. There is an "optimal" level of capital inflows at which output is maximized, since at higher levels of capital inflows the contractionary demand side effects eventually dominate.

This is an interesting model, which highlights several important features of the global macroeconomy today. Although capital inflows can help to promote growth up to a point, economies that develop excess capacity must eventually reduce their trade deficits or achieve surpluses in order to fully utilize that capacity and sustain their growth. Large capital inflows encourage excessive imports, which can depress domestic production. Moreover, Bhaduri is right on the mark in highlighting the problem that all countries now find themselves pressured to emphasize external markets rather than internal markets as a source of aggregate demand. This in turn implies that wages lose their function as an element of demand, and come to be seen only as an element of costs, in which case countries are tempted to seek competitive wage cuts (or depreciations) in order to take market share (and employment) away from each other.

Unfortunately, the model as presented here is too simple to represent all of the complexity of contemporary macroeconomics that Bhaduri discusses elsewhere in the paper. For one thing, the role of wages is not explicitly modeled. Also, the connections between capital inflows and the finance of domestic expenditures are only briefly addressed. Perhaps most importantly, the model is static and does not incorporate the dynamics of international borrowing and debt accumulation.[3] The problem in many developing countries today is not that *capital inflows* reach an excessive level where they become contractionary, but rather that the *debt positions* created by such inflows over time eventually become unsustainable, causing withdrawals of speculative capital, which in turn precipitate balance-of-payments crises and draconian "adjustment" policies that stifle growth and create massive unemployment.

I fully agree with Bhaduri when he concludes, "The tension between 'industry' driven by enterprise and 'finance' propelled by speculation is surfacing again, and it poses the greatest challenge to economic policy during the present phase of globalization." I can only add that modeling this tension is also the greatest challenge for economic theorists seeking to understand the contemporary process of globalization.

---

3   This is a topic that the same author has covered elsewhere (in Bhaduri 1987), where he analyzes the conditions that can create a permanent debt dependency in a borrowing country.

7

Asia and the crisis of financial globalization

David Felix

Reflecting views then dominant among Anglo-Saxon economists, the Bretton Woods Accords were devised around the basic thesis that free international capital mobility is incompatible with the preservation of reasonably free trade and full employment. The displacement of the Bretton Woods pegged exchange rate regime in the 1970s with floating rates has, however, been paralleled by the displacement of the old orthodoxy by a new one, which holds that free capital mobility is essential for maximizing the global welfare benefits from international trade and investment.[1] Thus, rationalized by economic "science," the U.S., with the International Monetary Fund (IMF) and World Bank as pliant instruments, has been aggressively promoting financial market deregulation and the lifting of capital controls throughout the globe.

This chapter contends, however, that the Bretton Woods incompatibility thesis remains valid. None of the major benefits claimed by the current orthodoxy has been realized. Lifting capital controls has greatly increased the frequency of currency crises and cost-sharing inequities between developed and less-developed economies during crisis management. The general claim that deregulating financial markets produces more economically correct pricing of capital assets and credit allocation has little theoretical standing and has been falsified by experience. The global integration of financial markets has adversely impacted First as well as Third World economies and has retarded the global expansion of output and trade. The policy implication is that curbing the international mobility of financial capital is more than ever a basic requisite for smoothing international economic interchange, and for more stable and equitable First and Third world economies. We elaborate on each contention in turn.

Asymmetric cost sharing during crisis management

The Bretton Woods Accords require member countries with strong balance-of-payment surpluses to assist the adjustment of countries in balance-of-payments distress by appreciating their real exchange rate and/or by adopting expansionary monetary-

---

1   The "new" orthodoxy is largely a resurrection of the economic orthodoxy of the 1920s. The main difference is that, in the 1920s version, free capital mobility needed to be embedded in a fixed exchange rate anchored to gold. The current orthodoxy began by embedding free capital mobility in a floating exchange rate regime (Friedman 1953), but is now divided on the exchange rate issue.

fiscal policies. In practice, the IMF, the designated overseer, has lacked the power to enforce this requirement on surplus economies. It has at times, however, been able to compel Third World deficit economies in crisis to adopt output- and income-depressing adjustment programs, by making adoption a precondition for the receipt of its emergency credits.

During the Bretton Woods era, this asymmetrical imposition of adjustment costs was subordinated to geopolitical priorities. Ex-colonial powers, to protect their co-lonial interests, augmented grants and loans to former colonies in financial distress on easier terms than those of the IMF. More importantly, foreign aid became a major U.S. instrument in the United States' battle with the Soviets for "the hearts and minds" of the Third World. Fending off left-wing political threats to friendly Third World governments by timely allotments of financial aid took precedence over the adoption of IMF-type structural adjustment policies. Stabilization mea-sures such as exchange controls, interest rate ceilings, credit subsidies, and other IMF "no-no's" were tolerated by official lenders.

This changed with the termination of the Bretton Woods pegged exchange rate regime in the early 1970s. Floating exchange rates, the progressive deregulation of domestic financial markets, and lifting of capital controls by the First World coun-tries encouraged an explosive growth of cross-currency financial transactions to hedge against or speculate on exchange rate movements, to exploit international interest rate differentials, and to engage in cross-currency transfers of ownership of financial and physical assets. Viewing the expansion of such private flows to devel-oping countries as a superior substitute for foreign aid, the Group of Seven (G-7) donors, led by the U.S., reoriented official lending away from long-term infrastruc-ture funding toward facilitating private flows.

Private capital flows to the Third World have, however, expanded along an oscillat-ing path, because the frequency of Third World financial crises with dangerous spread potential has called forth frequent emergency injections of official funds from the G-7 to buttress IMF credits.[2] Thus, during 1975–81, rapidly expanding bank lending to Latin America and Asia and the onset of "foreign aid fatigue" raised to 65 percent the private share of net capital flows to the Third World. But in 1982–90 the share fell to 45 percent, reflecting a sharp fall in bank lending and a rise of official "bailout" fi-nancing. Private flows ballooned again in the first half of the 1990s, reaching 81 per-cent in 1996 (World Bank 1997, Figure 1.1).[3] However, the volume and share is once

2   Nearly three-fourths of the 181 members of the IMF suffered one or more periods of banking crises or "significant banking problems" during 1980–95. Banking crises, defined as "cases where there were runs or other substantial portfolio shifts, collapses of financial firms or mas-sive government intervention" afflicted 36 countries. "Significant banking problems" defined as "extensive unsoundness short of a crisis" afflicted another 108 countries (Lindgren et al. 1996, Annex 1). These numbers are being "significantly" augmented by the East Asian crisis.

3   The share data exclude unrecorded private transfers. According to World Bank estimates, such flows have added importantly to the net private flows to Africa, the Middle East, and most of Asia and the Pacific, whereas unrecorded outflows have fully offset immigrant re-mittances and other unrecorded inflows to Latin America and the Caribbean and to East Europe and Central Asia (World Bank 1997, Figure 1.4).

more falling in reaction to the unfolding Asian crisis. In sum, the need for the G-7 and Bretton Woods institutions to man "broom and shovel brigades" to clean up after the inconstant movements of private capital has prevented a smooth phasing down of official capital flows to the Third World. It has also moved the IMF from near marginalization during the Bretton Woods era to center stage.

In response, the IMF has enlarged and reoriented its restructuring programs to assist Washington's effort to force open Third World financial and nonfinancial markets to foreign capital. The programs now give primacy to maintaining foreign debt servicing and reattracting foreign capital over minimizing the recovery costs of less-developed countries (LDCs) in crisis. IMF emergency loans, reinforced by G-7 credits, are tied by the recipients to policy changes that include import liberalization, the repeal of measures privileging local over foreign investors, and a lifting of controls on cross-currency capital movements. In doing so, the IMF has been playing fast and loose with its fiduciary commitments under Article VI of its charter, which requires it to suspend credits to countries using them to facilitate capital flight. Its justification for honoring Article VI in the breach is that abolishing capital controls is essential for regaining access to foreign financial markets.[4]

The worsened recovery costs stem primarily from the macroeconomic approach that the IMF devised for the Bretton Woods era of capital controls, which it continues to rely on in the current era of financial market liberalization. The approach has been to treat the LDC currency crises as domestic excess demand phenomena calling for tighter monetary–fiscal policies. But as the private and government sectors of LDCs become more open and dependent on private foreign borrowing, the likelihood that substantial monetary–fiscal tightening will superimpose a domestic currency crunch on the hard currency squeeze increases. Indeed, as the Mexican and "tequila" crises of 1994–95 and the Asian crises of 1997 graphically illustrate, LDC crises now begin typically with a hard currency squeeze set off by local and foreign portfolio investors dumping the local currency en masse. An abrupt curtailment of rollover lending by foreign banks and bond markets reinforces the squeeze. Exchange depreciation deepens as local banks and firms scramble for hard currency to keep up payments on their foreign liabilities. Reliance on monetary–fiscal tightening to restore "confidence" and an early reaccess to private foreign finance backfires. Local banks, already overloaded with foreign liabilities, find rolling over domestic currency loans too risky, because at the higher interest rates they can no longer distinguish between clients rendered insolvent and those merely rendered illiquid. Downward spiraling of output and employment and upward spiraling of defaults ensue, which transform bank difficulties into a systemic banking crisis. A recent U.S. Federal Reserve study of a large sample of mainly Third World countries found the incidence of banking crises to be strongly correlated with the decontrol of the countries' capital markets (Kaminsky and Reinhart

---

4   The contention is that capital controls upset the financial markets, and are in any event ineffective, since they can be easily circumvented by today's globalized financial markets. However, to reinforce its efforts to promote free capital mobility, the IMF has also been campaigning to replace Article VI with the requirement that members must make their currencies freely convertible for all capital as well as current account transactions (IMF 1995b).

1996). The World Bank estimates the cost of refloating domestic banks in a sample of 14 such crises during 1980–95 to have averaged 10 percent of gross domestic product (World Bank 1997, Box 5.1).

By conditioning their credits on the suppliant's agreeing to decontrol financial and commodity markets and to maintain debt servicing, the IMF-led consortia further unbalance the cost sharing. Tightening of controls to contain capital flight, or import restrictions to channel foreign exchange to priority uses, are ruled out.[5] Socializing private foreign debts by ex post rewriting of contracts to minimize losses to foreign lenders is ruled in.

An early example of the latter was the requirement imposed on Latin American governments early in the 1980s' debt crisis that they guarantee ex post the foreign debt of their private banks and companies. The added fiscal burden intensified inflation and forced additional cutbacks of public investment and social welfare outlays.[6] Socializing private foreign debts is also a component of current bailout negotiations with Thailand, Indonesia, and Korea, though at this writing the IMF-led consortia are meeting more resistance than they did from the indebted Latin American governments.

Especially egregious was the complete bailout of foreign and domestic holders of Mexican *tesobonos* during the Mexican crisis of 1994–95.[7] *Tesobonos* were peso-denominated treasury notes indexed to the dollar/peso exchange rate. Default risk was near zero, since the Mexican government could readily supply the additional pesos as required if the dollar rose. But foreign and domestic *tesobono* holders, fearful of being locked into pesos, were major participants in the flight to dollars that depleted official foreign exchange reserves and produced the peso collapse of December 1994. The Mexican central bank, sanctified by Article VI, could have closed its dollar window to *tesobono* holders until things improved. Fear that Mexico might do that led Washington and the IMF to cobble together $51 billion in short-term credits, contingent on Mexico keeping the dollar window open and tightening instead monetary–fiscal policy to halt the outflow. This left *tesobono* holders "harmless," while the requisite tightening severely deepened Mexico's economic plight. The collapsing exchange rate pushed inflation to near triple digits in 1995. Amidst widespread domestic loan defaults and bankruptcies, GDP fell 7 percent, while the fiscal cost of bailing out its banks is now provisionally estimated at around 13 percent of Mexican GDP.[8]

Confidence that similar IMF-led rescues would be available in future crises reduced downside risk perceptions in the financial markets. Bank lending and portfolio investing in Latin America, Asia, and Eastern Europe again picked up steam in 1996 before abruptly reversing direction in mid-1997. As the Asian crisis unfolds,

5   The IMF defines capital controls quite broadly to include "quantitative controls, taxes, and subsidies applicable to transactions in the capital and financial accounts of the balance of payments" (IMF 1995b, 1).

6   The ex post guarantees added about 25 percent to the region's official foreign debt (Felix 1994, 179–80).

7   In the 1980s debt crisis, the rescued banks took partial hits through selling part or all of their Latin American paper at discounts.

8   It is provisional for two main reasons. The agency that has been buying the overdue loans of the banks – El Fondo Bancario de Proteccion de Ahorro (Fobaproa) – has yet to liquidate

foreign banks are again insisting on government guarantees of rollover loans, while multinational companies and "vulture funds" wait for domestic firms in financial distress to unload assets at bargain prices.

The chronic disconnect between the IMF's pre- and post-crisis assessments of the economies on which it imposes its medicine has become an open scandal. Its 1997 annual report, issued shortly before the Asian crisis, reports that "Directors strongly praised Thailand's remarkable economic performance and the authorities' consistent record of sound macroeconomic policies...welcomed Korea's continued impressive macroeconomic performance [and] praised the authorities for their enviable fiscal record" (Sachs 1997). Until its December 1994 crisis, Mexico was lauded as a free market success and exemplar for other LDCs. Prior to the 1980s debt crises of the Southern Cone countries, which had adopted market liberalizing strategies, IMF spokesmen dismissed concern over mounting current account deficits and private foreign borrowing because, as Walter Robichek, the then-Western Hemisphere director of the IMF, assured a Chilean audience, "private firms can be expected to be careful in assessing the net return from borrowing funds as compared with the net costs, since their survival as an enterprise is at stake" (cited in Diaz Alejandro 1985).

The ex post assessments, by contrast, highlight litanies of policy errors and misdeeds dire enough for investors to lose confidence and rush to exit. Blame is assigned asymmetrically. Invariably the fault lies not with flaws in the structure and behavior of the international financial markets but with those of the stricken economies. To buttress the plausibility of its asymmetrical assessments and remedies, the IMF has not shrunk from deceitful word spinning. In its ex post assessments of the Latin American debt crisis, it was public not private overborrowing that primarily accounted for the oppressive debt accumulation, although the reverse was actually the case in the Southern Cone countries. In post-crisis IMF press releases and documents, the *tesobonos* have become dollar- rather than peso-denominated bonds.

The dire policy errors, however, keep changing. The Southern Cone crises of the 1980s were due to wrong sequencing of correct liberalization measures, although little consensus was reached ex post on the correct sequence (Felix 1994, 188–91). For Mexico and other LDCs enmeshed in the 1980s debt crisis the ex post assessments fingered fiscal deficits and repressed financial markets as the primary causes. Mexico accordingly took the IMF cure, balancing the fiscal budget, privatizing and deregulating its banks, lifting capital controls and most restrictions on foreign direct investment (FDI), and entering the North American Free Trade Agreement (NAFTA). The ex post assessment of its 1994–95 currency crisis uncovered, however, yet another fatal flaw: excessive delays in supplying data on the balance of payments and the state of the Mexican banks had misled portfolio investors to overinvest. A centerpiece of G-7 measures for avoiding future runs has, therefore, been to authorize the IMF to establish a "special data dissemination standard,"

most of these holdings for fear of depressing asset prices. In addition, the government in 1997 embarked on an extensive bailout of private operators of toll roads, which involves taking over their bank debts. The cost of this new bailout may reach $7 billion (Millman 1997).

which offers countries having, or seeking, access to international capital markets, a voluntary means of providing regular, timely, and comprehensive economic data. A key feature of the implementation...will be an electronic bulletin board maintained by the IMF at a World Wide Web site on the Internet (*IMF Survey*, September 9, 1996, 290).

The massive runs on the Asian currencies one year later suggest the bulletin board was merely a way for the G-7 and the IMF to avoid facing reality.

The World Bank now takes a less uncritical view of financial globalization than its sister institution (World Bank 1997), acknowledging that premature integration with the global financial markets can damage LDCs.

> As the Mexican peso crisis has so forcefully demonstrated...there are large potential costs if integration is not carefully managed. There are two reasons for this. First, although international investors are becoming more discerning, market discipline tends to be more stringent when investor confidence is lost – a fact that can lead to large outflows – than during the buildup to a potential problem. Second, and more important, many developing countries lack the preconditions needed to ensure the sound use of private capital and manage risks of large reversals. Financial integration can magnify the effects of underlying distortions and institutional weaknesses in these countries and thereby multiply the cost of policy mistakes (World Bank 1997, 3).

However, the World Bank detects a positive evolutionary process at work. It arrays LDCs along a continuum, the low end consisting of LDCs that are early in the process of building up requisite preconditions for absorbing capital flows effectively, such as "a sound macroeconomic policy framework...a sound domestic banking system with an adequate supervisory and regulatory framework, and a well-functioning market, infrastructure and regulatory framework for capital markets." These LDCs should approach foreign capital cautiously, using capital controls to reinforce monetary–fiscal defenses against sudden surges and withdrawals. But LDCs that have completed the requisite for full financial integration should go for it. Accelerating LDCs along this evolutionary path is the increasing skill of international financial markets in assessing Third World payoffs and risks – "contagion effects of the kind seen after the Mexican crisis are not likely to be long-lasting." Indeed, "aggregate net private capital flows to developing countries are likely to be sustained in the short to medium term because of the continuing decline in creditworthiness risks and other investment risks, the higher expected returns in developing countries, and the fact that these countries are underweighted in the portfolios of institutional investors" (World Bank 1997, 2–5, 78).

To measure the rapidity of movement along the continuum, the report constructs a financial integration index. In 1985–87 only Korea and Malaysia, according to the index, were highly integrated, but by 1992–94 there were 13 LDCs highly integrated and 23 "medium integrated."[9]

9   The index is composed of a country risk rating, a capital flow/GDP ranking, and a flow composition ranking that gives greatest weight to portfolio inflows and bank loans (World Bank 1997, Box 1.1).

The report, however, deduces from the fact that three of the highly integrated – Argentina, Mexico, and Turkey – had nevertheless suffered major financial crises in the first half of the 1990s that still other requirements must be met for stable financial integration. These are: balanced budgets, high savings rates, and export-oriented investment. Such were the requisites that enabled East Asian countries to fend off the "tequila effect" in 1995. Indeed,

> The most dynamic emerging [capital] markets, where progress has been particularly intense during the past five years, include most of high-growth Asia (Korea, Malaysia, and Thailand, with Indonesia and the Philippines not far behind). The East Asian markets stand out for their depth and liquidity, and because of efforts undertaken in the 1990s their infrastructures are now equal to those in Latin America (World Bank 1997, 59).

Unfortunately for the report's evolutionary theory, forecasting skills, and market timing, all five highly integrated dynamic East Asian economies bit the dust as the report was reaching the bookstores.[10]

The failure of both the World Bank and IMF versions of "sound policies" to reconcile financial integration with financial stability intensifies the basic dilemma haunting G-7 policy discussions. Should financial globalization be further encouraged by removing the remaining policy barriers to global capital mobility – the post-Bretton Woods orthodox position – or should it be restrained by strengthening the barriers, which harks back to the Bretton Woods incompatibility thesis?

Theoretical cases for the new and old orthodoxies

The economic case for free capital mobility relies on a strong macro version of the efficient market hypothesis. It holds that capital markets generate asset prices that – given available information – are best estimates of the present values of the future income streams from capital assets. Incomplete information produces "white noise" errors in asset pricing, but these get corrected by excess demand signals. The correction squeezes out "noise traders" who, by speculating on price movements instead of evaluating assets on the basis of fundamentals, can push prices away from equilibrium. That merely activates rational traders who, knowing in which direction equilibrium lies, profit by taking countervailing positions at the expense of the noise traders.

Exogenous supply "shocks," due to technological, demographic, and structural changes, and demand "shocks," primarily due to "policy surprises," alter fundamentals and therefore asset prices. Supply shocks are largely unavoidable, but demand shocks can be minimized if governments provide a nurturing legal framework for private markets and eschew interventionist measures.

---

10 The report appears to have been intended for broad circulation as a didactic sequel to the World Bank's *East Asian Miracle*. It is now unlikely to get the heavy promotion given the earlier book, which is rather too bad, since it contains useful data.

This basic thesis rationalizes the asymmetric cost sharing during currency crises as "tough love" pain, which is rewarded by a sharing of long-run welfare gains from financial globalization. For the *optimum optimorum* to which the process is headed is full global integration of capital markets, with arbitraging flows unifying real interest rates and asset valuation across currencies, and world competition between lenders minimizing the cost of capital, thereby bringing global resource allocation to maximum efficiency.

By contrast, the incompatibility thesis of Bretton Woods takes the darker Keynesian view of financial markets, in which volatility is mainly endogenously generated because bandwagon overbidding for, and herd-like dumping of, financial assets results from rational individual behavior under uncertainty. Interactions in capitalist economies are too complex and changeable for probability distributions of future profit trends to be derivable by statistical inference rather than subjective judgment.[11] The supply-side fundamentals that the efficient market hypothesis takes to be the long-term determinants of asset prices – trends in factor supplies and technological change – get deflected or reinforced by variations in the distribution of political and market power that affect the wage share, income distribution, effective demand, profit and risk assessments, financing conditions, and the level and composition of real investment. Speculating on how other investors collectively react to news about changes in fundamentals, rather than on how the changes might alter equilibrium asset prices per se, is the more rational strategy for professional traders.

This leads, however, to speculative surges that increase the fragility of the banking system. Debt leveraging augments the expected return from speculative position taking, while wide swings of asset prices increase liquidity risk for long-term investors, pushing them toward investments with quicker payoffs. The higher leveraging, faster turnover, and increased price volatility weaken the ability of lenders to collateralize their credit effectively, while competition over market share restrains them from aggressively raising risk premia during bull markets. Conversely, pessimistic news hitting overextended financial markets can spark a selling wave and falling prices that are accelerated by distress selling, settlement defaults, and a drying up of liquidity as banks raise risk premia and cut back credit lines. If the credit crunch extends to production loans, output cutbacks and shrinking aggregate demand add to the defaulting and further weaken bank balance sheets. Systemic financial crises are recurring threats from financial market dynamics.

This Keynesian perspective extended to international capital markets shaped the Bretton Woods Accords, including the IMF's Articles of Agreement. It legitimized a range of "policy surprises," from counterspeculating forays by central banks, to

11 This is Chapter 12 of Keynes' General Theory, elaborated by the late Hyman Minsky and other post-Keynesians. (See Minsky 1975 and the articles in Dymski and Pollin 1994.) The New Keynesian school goes merely halfway. Noise trading generates overshooting, but prices still oscillate around equilibrium asset prices that are primarily determined by the evolution of factor supplies and technology. For post-Keynesians, that long-run path is merely a special case, attainable if trends in aggregate demand and its composition and in technology, finance, and wages happen to converge on a Golden Age outcome, but with market forces as likely to generate less desirable long-run paths (Robinson 1956).

lender of last resort credits from the IMF and central bank consortia, on up to direct capital controls, as useful policy instruments for keeping hot money flows from destabilizing exchange rates, multilateral trade, and employment.

Neither view of capital market dynamics is a logical corollary of a more basic theory about how market economies function. The efficient market hypothesis does not derive from general equilibrium proofs of the existence, stability, and optimality of laissez faire economies, since the proofs merely relate to competitive market economies without modern financial markets. They have been unable to meaningfully incorporate money as a store of value and standard of deferred payment. Similarly, the Keynesian view does not derive from proofs that laissez faire economies are unstable, but is a premise of such proofs. Each is an assertion whose validity depends entirely on how well it fits reality.

In this regard, econometric tests and surveys of trading strategies have been destructive of the empirical validity of the efficient market hypothesis.[12] This has been especially so of foreign exchange trading. Forex traders in First World markets are found to flourish by strategies that systematically violate efficient market rationality but conform to Keynesian rationality. Hard-core believers in the optimality of free markets still try to show in Ptolemaic fashion that by ad hoc respecifications of the information sets negative evidence can be reconciled with the efficient market hypothesis. But that does little to salvage their optimality claim, since efficient markets can generate multiple exchange rate equilibria. By gang attacking a currency in equilibrium, speculators can make a killing by forcing the authorities to move to another equilibrium exchange rate. The requisite is awareness that rising political and economic costs are weakening the will to defend the current exchange rate (Obstfeld 1986). The model, according to a prominent post-mortem analysis of the 1992 Exchange Rate Mechanism (ERM) crisis, fits well the cascading devaluations that collapsed the European Community's exchange rate mechanism (Eichengreen and Wyplosz 1993).

Real vs. financial trends in the global economy

The incongruity between the rapid expansion of global foreign exchange turnover since the demise of Bretton Woods and the global slowdown of the growth of output, productivity, and the volume of trade provides further support for the incompatibility thesis. Table 1 shows that global forex turnover, excluding derivative trading, rose from \$18.3 billion per day in 1977 to \$1.23 trillion ($\$1.23 \times 10^{12}$) per day in 1995. Adding the market value of forex options and related derivatives elevated the daily 1995 turnover to about \$1.3 trillion (Felix 1996A, Table A1). Turnover accelerated after 1980, when the lifting of capital controls, pioneered by the U.S. and Canada, spread to most other countries of the OECD (Organization for Economic Cooperation and Development), facilitating global trading in financial assets, but greatly attenuating the link between commodity trade and forex turnover. Between

12   The test results are summarized in more detail in Felix 1996B and in references cited therein.

Table 1 *Global official reserves, forex trading, and exports, 1977–95*

A. Reserves vs. forex trading volume[a]

	Global official forex reserves (US$ bill.) (1)	Reserves + gold holdings[b] (US$ bill.) (2)	Daily global forex turnover (US$ bill.) (3)	Reserves/daily turnover (days) (1)/(3)	(2)/(3)
1995	1,202.0	1,330.0	1,230.0	1.0	1.1
1992	910.8	1,022.5	820.0	1.1	1.2
1989	722.3	826.8	590.0	1.2	1.4
1986	456.0	552.6	270.0	1.7	2.0
1983	339.7	496.6	119.0[c]	2.8	4.2
1980	386.6	468.9	82.5[c]	4.7	5.7
1977	265.8	296.6	18.3[d]	14.5	16.2

B. Exports vs. reserves and forex trading volume

	Annual world exports (US$ trillion) (4)	Annual global forex volume[e] (US$ trillion) (5)	Forex/ exports(%) (5)/(4)	Reserves/ exports(%) (1)/(4)	Reserves + gold/ exports(%) (2)/(4)
1995	4.80	307.5	6406%	25.0%	27.9%
1992	3.76	205.0	5452	24.2	27.2
1989	2.91	147.5	5068	24.8	28.4
1986	1.99	67.5	3392	20.5	27.8
1983	1.66	29.8	1795	20.5	29.9
1980	1.88	20.6	1096	20.6	24.9
1977	1.31	4.6	351	20.3	22.6

C. Memorandum items

	1961–65	1966–70
1. (Global forex reserves + gold)/exports	43.5%	32.3%
2. (Reserve position with IMF)/exports	3.1	2.8

[a] Net of double reporting of same transactions by intracountry and intercountry counterparties. Excludes trading in options and other derivatives.
[b] Official gold holdings valued at 35 SDRs per ounce.
[c] U.S. volume net only of double reporting of same transactions by domestic counterparties multiplied by 0.17, the average U.S. share of global Forex turnover, 1989–95.
[d] U.S. gross trading volume multiplied by 0.17.
[e] Daily global turnover of column (3) multiplied by 250 trading days.

Sources: BIS 1993a, 1996; N.Y. Federal Reserve Bank 1992; IMF *International Financial Statistics,* various issues.

1977 and 1995 forex turnover rose from 3.5 to 64 times the value of global exports, while official reserves fell from 15 days of daily forex turnover to less than a day.

One consequence has been a dramatic weakening of the power of central banks to counter undesired exchange rate movements. A second has been a reversal of the initial decline in the ratio of official reserves to exports. Proponents of floating exchange rates had predicted that an important benefit from floating would be economizing on foreign exchange reserves, since they would no longer be needed to protect the exchange rate. Table 1 shows, however, that while the global reserve/export ratio declined initially, its subsequent rise has wiped out most of the decline. The need to defend against the volatility of international financial flows evidently motivated the reversal.[13] But the plummeting of the reserve/forex ratio indicates the inadequacy of the defenses.

Tables 2 to 6 record, on the other hand, a persistent worsening of key real growth indicators since the 1960s. Table 2 shows that GDP growth of all the OECD countries slowed substantially and became more volatile after the 1960s. Growth rates improved for almost half the developing countries in the 1970s, while worsening for the rest, mainly reflecting diverging terms-of-trade trends. But in the 1980s they dropped below 1960s levels in all Third World regions except South and Southeast Asia, where merely half the countries had 1980s growth rates below the 1960s (Felix 1996B, Table 5). That exception is now disappearing as a consequence of the Asian crisis.

World, OECD, and G-7 exports of goods and services at constant prices also expanded more slowly after the 1960s. Among the G-7, the sole exception is the U.S., whose export growth in the 1960s was well below the G-7 average. The rising export/GDP ratios of the G-7 and the OECD, shown in Table 4, merely reflect less retardation of trade than output growth, which rather dims the glowing rhetoric about global economic integration.

Table 5 shows that gross fixed investment of the G-7 and the OECD has also expanded at substantially slower rates since the demise of Bretton Woods. This is at odds with the rising G-7 ratio of cross-border transactions in bonds and equities to GDP (Edey and Hviding 1995, Table 4). It's consistent, however, with the finding of Martin Feldstein and associates that the high correlation between domestic saving and investment of the OECD countries during the 1960s has since diminished very little, notwithstanding the explosive expansion of international capital flows (Feldstein 1994). The flows have been transferring ownership but little real resources on balance. Finally, Table 6 shows that the growth of labor, capital, and total factor productivity have all fallen precipitously since the 1960s in the OECD countries.

Nevertheless, most quests for a general explanation of the global growth slowdown have taken as axiomatic that the relation between financial liberalization and allocative efficiency is monotonically positive. The search has instead been for market "distortions," exogenous technology and supply shocks, and factor supply rigidities that in tandem must have more than offset the efficiency gains from liberalizing and

---

13   The World Bank now urges LDCs to set their reserves according "to variations in the capital account, rather than in terms of months of imports, since the level of gross flows is higher following integration" (World Bank 1997, 7).

Table 2 *Annual real GDP growth and coefficients of variation of OECD countries, 1959–94*[a]

I. Individual G-7 Countries

	Canada		France		Germany		Italy		Japan		U.K.		U.S.	
	Gr.	CV	Gr.	CV	Gr.	CV	Gr.	CV	Gr.	CV	Gr.	CV	Gr.	CV
1959–64	4.4	0.4	6.0	0.1	5.7	0.3	5.6	0.3	11.6	0.2	3.7	0.4	3.6	0.4
1965–70	5.1	0.3	5.3	0.2	4.7	0.6	5.5	0.2	10.5	0.3	2.4	0.2	3.6	0.6
1971–76	5.4	0.3	3.6	0.5	2.7	0.9	3.4	1.0	4.5	0.7	2.1	1.3	2.7	0.9
1977–82	2.4	1.1	2.5	0.3	1.7	1.0	3.0	0.7	4.3	0.2	1.1	1.9	1.8	1.4
1983–88	4.4	0.2	2.2	0.5	2.3	0.3	2.7	0.3	4.1	0.3	4.0	0.2	3.9	0.3
1989–94	1.3	1.6	1.7	1.1	3.0	0.7	1.3	1.0	2.5	0.8	1.0	1.9	2.1	0.7
1959–70	4.8	0.4	5.6	0.1	5.2	0.4	5.6	0.3	11.0	0.2	3.0	0.4	3.6	0.5
1971–82	3.9	0.7	3.1	0.5	2.2	1.0	3.2	0.8	4.4	0.5	1.6	1.6	2.3	1.1
1983–94	2.9	0.8	1.9	0.8	2.7	0.6	2.0	0.7	3.3	0.6	2.5	0.8	3.0	0.5

II. Country Groups[b]

	G-7		OECD excluding G-7		All OECD	
	Gr.	CV	Gr.	CV	Gr.	CV
1959–64	5.0	.1	5.3	.1	5.0	.1
1965–70	4.6	.2	5.1	.2	4.6	.2
1971–76	3.3	.7	4.1	.5	3.4	.7
1977–82	2.5	.6	2.3	.3	2.4	.6
1983–88	3.6	.2	2.7	.3	3.4	.2
1989–94	2.1	.4	2.2	.5	2.1	.4
1959–70	4.8	.2	5.2	.1	4.8	.2
1971–82	2.8	.8	3.2	.6	2.9	.7
1983–94	2.8	.4	2.5	.4	2.8	.4

[a] Growth rates are in percent; coefficients of variation are ratios.
[b] Group data are weighted averages, using comparative size of GDP as weights.

Source: OECD, *Economic Outlook,* Annex tables, various issues.

globalizing the financial markets. But this is perverse. Product and labor markets have been liberalizing during the past two decades, and most governments after the 1970s have been privatizing and shrinking their range of economic activities. The effort has been to pin the blame on factors that were strongest when output, trade, and productivity trends were also strongest and have been weakening as those trends weakened, while ruling out a priori the possibility that financial globalization, a major trend that has moved inversely to the real economy trends, might have contributed to the slowdown. To redress the balance, let me cite four ways that this has probably occurred.

Table 3 *Annual growth of exports of goods and services at constant prices (percentages), 1959–94*

I. Individual G-7 Countries[a]

	Canada	France	Germany	Italy	Japan	U.K.	U.S.
A. Six-year average							
1959–64	7.8	9.0	10.1	16.7	15.0	4.1	6.1
1965–70	9.9	10.7	10.8	13.4	17.2	6.0	5.5
1971–76	4.3	7.9	6.4	6.6	11.3	5.6	7.8
1977–82	5.4	4.2	4.6	4.0	7.4	2.1	4.0
1983–88	7.9	3.7	3.4	4.4	4.5	4.2	6.2
1989–94	6.4	5.0	6.0	6.9	4.6	4.1	7.7
B. Twelve-year average							
1959–70	8.8	9.9	10.4	15.1	16.1	5.0	5.8
1971–82	4.8	6.1	5.5	5.3	9.4	3.8	5.9
1983–94	7.2	4.4	4.7	5.7	4.6	4.1	7.0

II. Country Groups[b]

	G-7	OECD	World
A. Six-year averages			
1959–64	7.6	8.6	8.1
1965–70	8.3	8.8	7.9
1971–76	8.1	7.8	8.0
1977–82	4.6	5.0	4.5
1983–88	5.2	5.5	5.9
1989–94	6.5	6.4	5.7
B. Twelve-year averages			
1959–70	7.9	8.7	8.0
1971–82	6.4	6.4	6.2
1983–94	5.9	5.9	5.8

[a] 1959–70 data from IMF, *International Financial Statistics,* deflated by average of U.S. export and import price indices; 1971–94 deflated data from OECD, *Economic Outlook,* Annex Tables.
[b] G-7 and OECD series are weighted averages using relative GDP as weights. World exports 1959–74 are deflated by the average of U.S. import and export price indices; 1975–94 are deflated by the IMF unit export price index.

Sources: OECD, *Economic Outlook,* Annex Tables; IMF *International Financial Statistics,* various issues.

Excessive absorption of resources in asset trading

Charts 1 to 7 show that from 1955 on the shares of GDP generated by finance, insurance, and real estate (FIRE) – activities that service asset trading and the transfer of risk – have been rising almost monotonically in each of the G-7. Until the early 1970s, rising FIRE/GDP was paralleled by rising real growth of goods and nonfinancial services, supporting the orthodox view that financial deepening promotes real growth. Since then real growth of the nonfinancial sectors has slackened

Table 4 *G-7 and OECD ratios of growth rates of export volume to GDP growth, 1959–94*

	Canada	France	Germany	Italy	Japan	U.K.	U.S.	G-7	OECD
I. Six-year average									
1959–64	1.8	1.5	1.8	3.0	1.3	1.1	1.7	1.5	1.7
1965–70	1.9	2.0	2.3	2.4	1.6	2.5	1.5	1.8	1.7
1971–76	0.8	2.2	2.4	1.9	2.5	2.7	2.9	2.4	2.3
1977–82	2.2	1.7	2.7	1.3	1.7	1.9	2.2	1.8	2.1
1983–88	1.8	1.7	1.5	1.6	1.1	1.1	1.6	1.4	1.6
1989–94	4.9	2.9	2.0	5.3	1.8	4.1	3.7	3.1	3.0
II. Twelve-year average									
1959–70	1.8	1.7	2.0	2.7	1.4	1.8	1.6	1.7	1.7
1971–82	1.5	1.9	2.5	1.6	2.1	2.3	2.5	2.1	2.2
1983–94	2.3	2.3	1.7	3.4	1.4	2.7	2.6	2.3	2.3

Source: Tables 2 and 3.

Table 5 *Annual change of gross fixed investment at constant prices (%), 1959–94*

I. Individual G-7 Countries

	Canada	France	Germany	Italy	Japan	U.K.	U.S.
A. Six-year average							
1959–64	5.0	8.7	8.4	5.7	8.4	5.9	4.7
1965–70	4.7	6.0	3.1	3.6	13.7	2.5	3.3
1971–76	6.5	3.3	-0.5	0.3	3.2	0.9	2.8
1977–82	4.1	0.5	1.4	1.4	3.6	-0.9	1.9
1983–88	6.9	1.9	2.6	3.0	6.6	6.9	6.6
1989–94	1.0	0.6	3.8	-0.5	2.8	-0.7	3.3
B.Twelve-year average							
1959–70	4.8	7.3	5.7	4.7	11.0	4.2	4.0
1971–82	5.3	1.9	0.5	0.9	3.4	0.0	2.3
1983–94	3.9	1.2	3.2	1.2	4.7	3.3	4.9

II. Country Groups

	G-7	OECD
A. Six-year average		
1959–64	6.9	6.9
1965–70	5.5	5.4
1971–76	2.5	2.5
1977–82	2.0	1.7
1983–88	5.6	5.4
1989–94	2.3	2.3
B. Twelve-year average		
1959–70	6.2	6.1
1971–82	2.2	2.1
1983–94	3.9	3.8

Source: OECD, *Economic Outlook,* Annex tables, various issues.

Table 6 *Productivity in the business sector (percentage changes at annual rates)*

	Total factor productivity[a]			Labor productivity[b]			Capital productivity		
	1960[c]–73	1973–79	1979–95[d]	1960[c]–73	1973–79	1979–95[d]	1960[c]–73	1973–79	1979–95[d]
United States	2.5	0.2	0.5	2.6	0.4	0.9	2.3	-0.2	-0.2
Japan	5.4	1.1	1.1	8.4	2.8	2.2	-3.3	-3.7	-2.1
Germany[e]	2.6	1.8	0.4	4.5	3.1	0.9	-1.4	-1.0	-0.6
France	3.7	1.6	1.3	5.3	2.9	2.3	0.6	-1.0	-0.6
Italy	4.4	2.0	0.9	6.3	2.9	1.8	0.4	0.3	-0.9
United Kingdom	2.6	0.6	1.5	3.9	1.5	2.0	-0.3	-1.5	0.5
Canada	1.9	0.6	-0.1	2.9	1.5	1.1	0.2	-1.0	-2.4
Total of above countries[f]	**3.3**	**0.8**	**0.8**	**4.5**	**1.6**	**1.4**	**0.3**	**-1.1**	**-0.7**
Australia	2.2	1.1	0.8	3.3	2.4	1.4	0.1	-1.4	-0.2
Austria	3.1	1.0	0.9	5.5	3.0	2.1	-2.0	-3.1	-1.7
Belgium	3.8	1.3	1.2	5.2	2.6	2.1	0.6	-1.9	-1.0
Denmark	2.3	0.9	1.3	3.9	2.4	2.2	-1.4	-2.6	-0.9
Finland	4.0	1.9	2.5	5.0	3.2	3.5	1.4	-1.6	-0.4
Greece	2.5	0.7	-0.3	9.0	3.3	0.6	-8.8	-4.2	-2.0
Ireland	4.6	3.4	2.6	5.1	4.1	3.3	2.3	0.5	-0.2
Netherlands	3.4	1.7	1.1	4.8	2.7	1.6	0.8	-0.1	0.1
Norway[g]	2.0	1.7	-0.1	3.8	3.1	1.5	0.0	0.2	-1.8
Portugal	5.4	-0.2	1.6	7.4	0.5	2.4	-0.7	-2.5	-0.8
Spain	3.2	0.9	1.7	6.0	3.2	2.9	-3.6	-5.0	-1.5
Sweden	2.0	0.0	1.0	3.7	1.4	2.0	-2.2	-3.2	-1.3
Switzerland	2.1	-0.3	-0.2	3.2	0.8	0.3	-1.4	-3.5	-1.6
Total of above smaller countries[f]	**3.0**	**1.0**	**1.1**	**5.1**	**2.5**	**2.0**	**-1.5**	**-2.7**	**-1.0**
Total of above North American countries[f]	2.5	0.2	0.4	2.6	0.5	0.9	2.1	-0.3	-0.4
Total of above European countries[f]	3.3	1.4	1.0	5.1	2.6	1.8	-0.7	-1.4	-0.6
Total of above OECD countries[f]	3.3	0.8	0.8	4.6	1.7	1.5	0.1	-1.3	-0.8

[a] TFP growth is equal to a weighted average of the growth in labor and capital productivity. The sample period averages for capital and labor shares are used as weights.

[b] Output per employed person.

[c] Or earliest year available, i.e., 1961 for Australia, Greece, and Ireland; 1962 for Japan and the United Kingdom; 1964 for Spain; 1965 for France and Sweden; 1966 for Canada and Norway; 1970 for Belgium and the Netherlands; and 1972 for the United States.

[d] Or latest available year, i.e., 1991 for Norway; 1992 for Ireland and Portugal; 1993 for Germany, Austria, Belgium, Finland, Sweden, and Switzerland; and 1991 for Japan, France, the United Kingdom, Australia, Denmark, Greece, the Netherlands, and Spain.

[e] The two first averages concern western Germany. The percentage changes for the period 1979–95 are calculated as the weighted average of western Germany productivity growth between 1979 and 1991 and total Germany productivity growth between 1991 and the latest year available.

[f] Aggregates are calculated on the basis of 1992 GDP for the business sector expressed in 1992 purchasing power parities.

[g] Mainland business sector (i.e., excluding shipping as well as crude petroleum and gas extraction).

Source: OECD, *Economic Outlook,* June 1996, Annex Table 59.

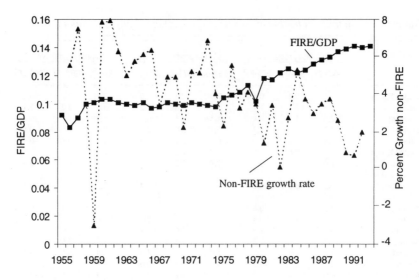

Figure 1 *Canada-FIRE/GDP and non-FIRE real growth rate, 1955–93*

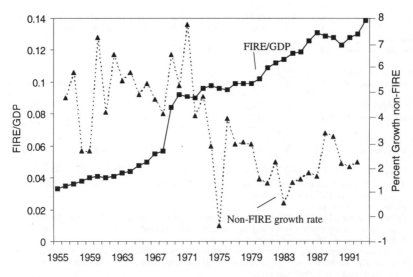

Figure 2 *France-FIRE/GDP and non-FIRE real growth rate, 1955–93*

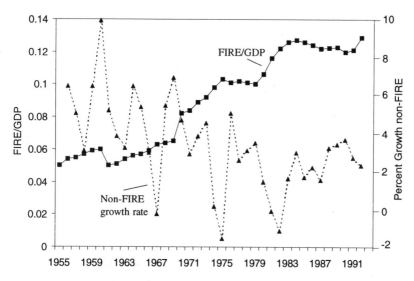

Figure 3 *Germany-FIRE/GDP and non-FIRE real growth rate, 1955–93*

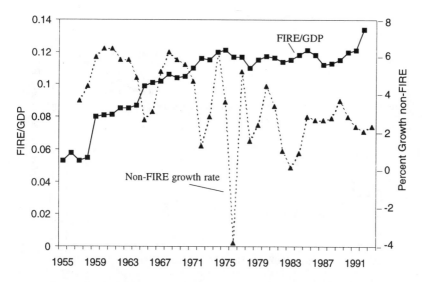

Figure 4 *Italy-FIRE/GDP and non-FIRE real growth rate, 1955–93*

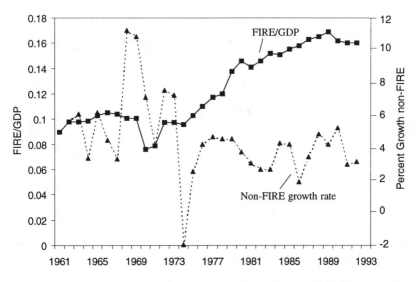

Figure 5 *Japan-FIRE/GDP and non-FIRE real growth rate, 1961–93*

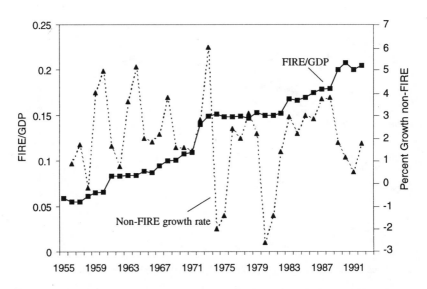

Figure 6 *United Kingdom-FIRE/GDP and non-FIRE real growth rate, 1955–93*

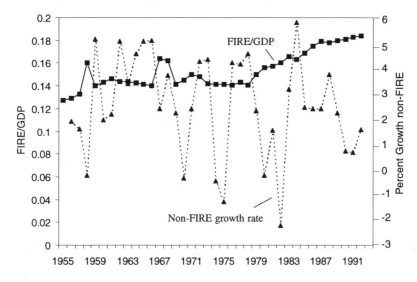

Figure 7 *United States-FIRE/GDP and non-FIRE real growth rate, 1955–93*

even more than has overall GDP growth, implying that the increasing absorption of resources in FIRE activities has become counterproductive.

Other data show a relative rise of resources devoted to finance proper. Finance's share of the OECD's labor force averaged 21 percent higher, and its share of total OECD investment averaged 104 percent higher, in 1980–93 than in 1970–79 (Edey and Hviding 1995, Table 2). Since 1975, finance has been the fastest-growing component of international service trade, rising at 13 percent per annum, while FDI in financial facilities was the leading component of FDI in services during the 1980s (OECD 1994, 38–40).

Financial volatility and investment misallocation

Increasing exchange rate volatility and misalignments have accompanied the rapid expansion of international capital flows. Monthly volatility of the dollar exchange rate with the franc, Deutschmark, yen, and pound averaged 22 percent higher in 1980–84 and 35 percent higher in 1985–89 than in the already volatile 1970s (Blundell-Wignall and Browne 1991, Table 7). During 1980–91 the ratio of the highest to the lowest annual real exchange rate was 2 to 1 for the U.S. dollar, the world's dominant reserve currency, and 1.65 to 1 for the yen and 1.38 for the Deutschemark, the two lesser reserve currencies[14] (Felix 1996B, Table 12).

The distorting effect on investment strategies of the heightened volatility, which encompasses interest rates and other financial prices, helps account for why, despite the rapid spread of innovations in information and production control technology, productivity growth has slackened since the end of Bretton Woods. Higher volatil-

14 The rates are trade weighted.

ity increases liquidity and other risks of investing long term, tilting private investors toward investments with faster payoffs.[15] It has led nonfinancial corporations to raise the investment share devoted to purchases of existing firms and buybacks of their stock and to lower the share devoted to constructing new capacity. The propensity of large corporations in the Bretton Woods era to invest heavily in "greenfield" plants in order to exploit economies of scale in production and protect market share has been replaced by a propensity to invest primarily in improving the utilization rate of existing capacity by reequipping the plants to handle variable production runs more economically, and to outsource cyclically sensitive and labor-intensive phases of production and distribution, while mergers and takeovers have replaced expanding plant size as the preferred means of protecting market share.

This pattern has probably gone furthest in the U.S., where it has generated increasing criticism of corporate "short-termism," that is, an excessive focus on increasing stockholder value through financial maneuvers and downsizing that raise share prices at the expense of other "stakeholders," notably the employees, and of long-term productivity (Twentieth Century Fund 1992; Gordon 1996; Shleifer and Vishny 1990). But under pressure from the globalized financial markets, corporatist practices in Japan and the continental European countries, such as long-term relational banking and sharing commitments with employees and the community, are giving way to short-termism, American style, with its predominant focus on short-term maximizing of shareholder value (*The Economist*, July 13, 1996; Pozen 1996).

Exchange rate volatility as a trade-retarding factor

With heightened exchange rate volatility and misalignment, exporters and importers betting wrong on exchange rate movements can lose big, and when they bet right import-competing firms can lose big. Hedging exchange rate risk has thus motivated much of the increasing forex turnover. Hedging, however, adds to costs, it can only partly transfer risk, and the hedging instruments facilitate speculating on foreign exchange and cross-currency interest rate movements. Multinational corporations (MNCs) and the banks intermediating the hedging have also become speculators, moving between hedging against exchange rate movements and betting on them. Exchange rate volatility has tended, therefore, to be self-generating, promoting more intricate hedging instruments that become new vehicles for speculation. "What's happened in the past 25 years," the head of IBM's global securities and capital markets operations observes, "is that enormous risk has been added to the financial markets. There's liquidity risk, interest-rate risk, exchange-rate risk, port-

---

15 More formally, volatility raises the "hurdle rate," the minimum expected return that will induce investors to invest in projects involving front-end outlays – i.e., fixed costs – and delayed net revenues. Since information about the future time shape of costs and revenues becomes more uncertain the longer the life of the project, delaying the project may reduce risk by allowing more information to be gathered. The hurdle rate of return therefore exceeds the cost of capital by also incorporating a premium for "waiting" in the investment decision. The waiting premium is a ratio of two present values: the present value today of the expected income stream were the project to be delayed, divided by the present value of the expected income stream from starting the project today (Dixit 1992).

folio-composition risk."[16] That the heightened volatility has been partly responsible for the slackened growth of the volume of world trade seems incontrovertible, although empirical studies disagree on how much.

The dominance of the globalized financial markets over macroeconomic policy as a growth-retarding factor

Walter Wriston, the ex-chief executive officer of Citicorp, chortles that the globalized financial markets now hold macroeconomic policy in a tighter grip than under the gold standard. Orthodox economists express this in more muted language, stressing that economic policies must now be "credible" to the global financial markets. The steep rise of real interest rates after the 1970s is a concrete manifestation of this rise to dominance. Table 7 shows that real interest rates on 10-year government bonds of the G-7 in 1983–94, at 4.9 percent, averaged over 12 times the 1971–82 average of 0.4 percent, and almost twice the 2.6 percent average for 1959–70.

Why? Lenders demanding higher inflationary premia is an unsatisfactory explanation. It implies they had suffered from an extended money illusion that allowed real interest rates to fall toward zero in the 1970s when inflation was accelerating, from which they only awakened to demand higher inflationary premia in the 1980s when inflation was decelerating. A more plausible explanation that doesn't denigrate the acuity of financiers is that the decontrol of financial markets in the 1980s unblocked channels for moving loanable funds around the world, which greatly weakened the power of national monetary authorities to influence real interest rates.

In the previous era of capital controls, holders of long bonds, correctly or incorrectly anticipating higher inflation from an easing of credit, could only shift easily to shorter-term bonds and domestic equities. The reactions of holders of long bonds helped the efforts of the monetary authorities to raise output and employment nearer to capacity by lowering the real short-term rate. But with the generalizing of capital market decontrol in the 1980s, quick movements by portfolio investors between domestic and foreign bonds and equities, along with covered and uncovered interest arbitraging across currencies by banks and security houses, now counter government efforts to lower short-term rates. Real short-term rates of the G-7 have also averaged far higher since 1982 than in the 1960s and 1970s, despite higher unemployment and weaker growth rates (see Table 8).

Monetary authorities have been forced to refocus from countercyclical stabilizing to accommodating the appetite of the financial markets for high rates of return. And since financial globalization has rendered manipulation of monetary aggregates as control instruments ineffective, the G-7 authorities have terminated their brief romance with monetarism and reverted to targeting short-term interest rates.[17]

---

16   Kent Price as quoted in "Japanese 'Big Bang' Is Leading to Big Boon for U.S. High-Tech," *Wall Street Journal,* September 16, 1997.

17   OECD economists, using a recursive vector autoregression (VAR) model, have found that, whereas changes in the G-7 monetary aggregates led nominal income changes during the 1970s, the "Granger causality" reversed after the early 1980s, with nominal income changes leading the monetary aggregates (Blundell-Wignall et al. 1990, 9–12 and Tables 2, 3). Using VAR analysis

Table 7 *Annual real interest rates and volatility (coefficients of variation) of G-7 10-year government bonds, 1959–94[a]*

	Canada		France		Germany		Italy		Japan	
	Rate	CV	Rate	CV	Rate	CV	Rate	CV	Rate	CV
I. Six-year average										
1959–64	3.2	0.1	0.0	1.6	3.8	1.0	1.8	2.4	n.a	n.a
1965–70	2.9	0.4	2.3	0.8	4.5	0.7	2.8	1.1	n.a	n.a
1971–76	0.8	2.2	0.5	1.4	2.8	0.4	-2.7	4.3	-3.2	5.7
1977–82	1.8	1.1	0.8	1.8	3.3	0.6	0.1	3.2	2.7	2.0
1983–88	6.4	1.1	5.5	0.8	5.2	0.5	4.3	0.6	3.8	0.6
1989–94	6.1	1.4	5.7	0.6	4.3	1.2	6.3	1.2	3.2	0.5
1995	6.7		6.1		4.7		7.0		3.9	
II. Twelve-year average										
1959–70	3.0	0.7	1.1	1.7	4.2	0.9	2.3	1.9	n.a	n.a
1971–82	1.3	1.8	0.6	1.6	3.1	0.6	-1.3	4.0	-0.3	5.2
1983–94	6.3	1.3	5.6	0.7	4.7	1.1	5.3	1.4	3.5	0.8

	United Kingdom		United States		G-7 Average	
	Rate	CV	Rate	CV	Rate	CV
I. Six-year average						
1959–64	3.2	1.1	2.8	0.5	2.5[1]	1.1[b]
1965–70	3.0	0.9	1.5	0.6	2.8[1]	0.7[b]
1971–76	-1.7	3.9	-0.2	2.3	-0.5	2.9
1977–82	-0.7	3.8	1.4	3.1	1.3	2.3
1983–88	5.5	0.7	6.4	1.4	5.3	0.8
1989–94	2.8	1.1	3.6	0.6	4.6	0.9
1995	5.4		5.0		5.4	
II. Twelve-year average						
1959–70	3.1	1.0	2.1	0.8	2.6[1]	1.2[b]
1971–82	-1.2	4.0	0.6	2.8	0.4	2.9
1983–94	4.2	1.6	5.0	1.8	4.9	1.2

[a] Deflated by respective national CPI.
[b] Excludes Japan.

Source: IMF *International Financial Statistics*.

But that targeting is now governed mainly by the need to pacify financial market expectations. Thus, although the GDP growth rates of the G-7 in 1989–94 had dropped substantially from their 1983–88 average, there was only a slight fall of short- and long-term real interest rates (cf. Tables 2, 7, and 8).

Economists defending the position that globally liberalizing the financial markets has improved economic welfare now avert their eyes from the adverse real economic trends. They instead concentrate narrowly on financial data, and build

"the other Friedman" has shown that the U.S. Federal Reserve's abandonment of monetary targeting in the 1980s was a sensible response to financial market reality (Friedman 1996).

Table 8 *Trends and variability (coefficients of variation) of real short-term interest rates, G–7 countries, 1959–94*

I. Real money market rates[a]

	France		Germany		Italy		Japan	
	Rate	CV	Rate	CV	Rate	CV	Rate	CV
A. Six-year average								
1959–64	-1.1	1.5	1.0	1.4	-0.1	19.6	2.7	1.0
1965–70	2.3	0.3	2.1	0.7	0.6	1.8	1.4	0.7
1971–76	-0.1	25.1	0.4	4.0	-3.0	0.7	-3.2	1.3
1977–82	0.1	36.6	2.6	0.7	-0.8	3.3	1.7	1.2
1983–88	4.4	0.2	3.2	0.3	6.1	0.2	4.0	0.2
1989–94	6.2	0.2	4.3	0.3	6.2	0.2	2.9	0.3
B. Twelve-year average								
1959–70	0.6	3.7	1.5	0.9	0.2	8.0	2.0	1.0
1971–82	0.0	103.0	1.5	1.4	- 1.9	1.4	-0.7	0.3
1983–94	6.2	0.3	3.7	0.3	6.2	0.2	3.5	0.3

II. Treasury bill rates[a]

	Canada		U.K.		U.S.		G–7 average[b]	
	Rate	CV	Rate	CV	Rate	CV	Rate	CV
A. Six-year average								
1959–64	2.3	0.4	1.8	0.8	1.8	0.4	1.2	0.7
1965–70	1.8	0.4	1.9	0.5	1.5	0.4	1.6	0.3
1971–76	-1.3	1.4	-4.9	0.9	-1.0	1.7	-1.9	0.8
1977–82	2.1	1.0	-2.5	1.5	0.6	4.2	0.5	3.5
1983–88	5.0	0.2	5.3	0.2	3.0	0.3	4.6	0.1
1989–94	5.2	0.4	3.1	0.5	1.5	0.7	4.2	0.2
B. Twelve-year average								
1959–70	2.1	0.4	1.9	0.7	1.6	0.4	1.4	0.5
1971–82	0.4	6.4	-3.7	1.2	-0.2	12.7	-0.7	3.0
1983–94	5.1	0.3	4.2	0.5	2.7	0.6	4.4	0.2

[a] Deflated by each country's CPI.
[b] Simple averaging of the table's Treasury bill and money market rates.

Source: IMF *International Financial Statistics.*

their positive welfare case on tautological interpretations. Two recent OECD studies are illustrative. Neither refers to real economic trends in its welfare assessment. One of the studies has found econometrically that about half the increase of real interest rates in the 1980s was due to financial market liberalization, but interprets the increase as simply a measure of the size of the prior allocative "distortion" that liberalization eliminated (Orr et al. 1995). The companion study acknowledges that whether the declining cost of financial transacting and the increased size and diversity of financial services have benefited the real economy "depends on judgments about the value of the financial services being provided, in particular, the extent to which the increased financial activity is viewed as being of economic benefit, rather than representing excessive or unnecessary financial churning." But then, without citing any real economy data, the study concludes that the benefits were indeed substantial. Abolishing interest rate controls and "regulation-driven credit rationing" must have improved allocative efficiency by "opening up opportunities for international portfolio diversification" and by removing a distortion, whose importance is indicated by the substantial increase of the margin between interbank and bank-customer lending rates in the OECD countries after 1980 (Edey and Hviding 1995). To defend the new orthodoxy, premise must now also double as proof.

The sustained increase of real interest rates must indeed have been underpinned by increased financial churning and other non-growth-generating demands for loanable funds. Globally, real investment growth decelerated; and while overall fiscal deficits to GDP of the OECD countries averaged slightly higher in 1983–94 than in the 1970s, primary fiscal deficits declined. That is, the higher overall deficits reflected higher debt service, to which the higher real interest rates contributed recursively (*OECD Economic Outlook,* December 1995, Appendix Tables 30, 31, 32). This leaves debt leveraging by households and businesses unrelated to the creation of new productive capacity as the major source of the accelerating demand for loanable funds. As percentages of household disposable income, both financial assets and liabilities of G-7 households have been rising since 1982, whereas household savings and physical asset holdings have been falling (*OECD Financial Outlook,* December 1995 and June 1996, Annex Tables 58). That is, leveraging by G-7 households has been mainly for consumption and the acquisition of financial assets. Business debt leveraging also appears to have been related mainly to debt financing of mergers and acquisitions, the purchase of privatized government assets, and the acquisition of equity shares for portfolio diversification and speculation.[18]

Policy inferences

The Bretton Woods incompatibility thesis remains valid, though its policy solution is incompatible with today's political environment. Building capital controls into the IMF Articles of Agreement was politically facile, since controls were already in place in most member countries as a result of the financial disorders of the 1930s and the disruptions of World War II.[19] A collective agreement to impose direct controls, absent an uncontrollable systemic breakdown, seems politically infeasible.

But continuation of some of the trends produced by financial globalization is also economically and politically infeasible. Table 9 shows that, on average for the G-7,

18   U.S. outlays on mergers and acquisitions averaged $184 billion per year in 1984–89 compared to an $84 billion annual outlay on new productive facilities (Crotty and Goldstein 1993).

19   However, Article VI of the Articles of Agreement is a watered-down compromise of a tougher British draft proposal, initially favored by Harry D. White and the U.S. mission. Wall Street resistance forced White to pressure Keynes and the Bank of England into accepting a compromise draft that became Article VI (Helleiner 1994).

Table 9 *Real long-term interest rates of the G-7 countries[a] divided by their real GDP growth rates, 1959–94*

	Canada	France	Germany	Italy	Japan	U.K.	U.S.	All G-7
A. Six-year average ratios								
1959–64	0.73	0.00	0.67	0.32	n.a.	0.86	0.78	0.50
1965–70	0.57	0.43	0.96	0.51	n.a.	1.25	0.42	0.61
1971–76	0.15	0.14	1.04	-0.79	-0.71	-0.81	-0.07	-0.15
1977–82	0.75	0.32	1.94	0.03	0.63	-0.64	0.78	0.52
1983–88	1.45	2.50	2.26	1.59	0.93	1.37	1.64	1.47
1989–94	4.69	3.35	1.43	4.85	1.28	2.80	1.71	2.19
1995	3.05	2.77	2.47	2.33	4.33	2.25	2.10	2.76
B. Twelve-year average ratios								
1959–70	0.65	0.21	0.81	0.41	n.a.	1.05	0.60	0.55
1971–82	0.45	0.23	1.49	-0.38	-0.04	-0.72	0.35	0.18
1983–94	3.07	2.92	1.84	3.22	1.10	1.68	1.67	1.83
C. Memorandum: pre-1959 G-7 average ratios								
1881–1913	0.97							
1919–1939	2.40							
1946–1958	0.36							

[a]Annual interest on 10-year government bonds deflated by national CPI.

Sources: 1959–94 data from *OECD Economic Outlook,* Annex tables, various issues, and IMF, *International Financial Statistics,* various issues; pre-1959 data from Michael Bordo, "The Bretton Woods International Monetary System: An Historical Overview," Table 1, in Michael Bordo and Barry Eichengreen eds., *A Retrospective on the Bretton Woods System* (University of Chicago Press, 1993); real GDP per capita growth rates in Bordo's Table 1 multiplied by population growth rates.

real long-term interest rates have been exceeding real GDP growth by an increasing percent since 1982, reaching nearly three times the group's GDP growth rate in 1995. By contrast, real interest rates of the G-7 averaged slightly below GDP growth rates during the gold standard era, which supports Wriston's celebrationist observation.

Table 9, however, also offers a Belshazzar's Feast warning: the interest rate/ growth rate ratio is approaching the interwar period's ratio. With private debt leveraging also raising debt/income ratios, the rentier share of national income has been rising persistently. Yet despite the higher cost of capital indicated by the higher real rates, equity prices have boomed. Add the rising FIRE/GDP ratios and the contrasting diminution of output and productivity growth, and we have the ingredients of an unsustainable pyramid game. Disguised by the increased capitalization and rising share prices of the equity markets, debt is being serviced increasingly by new debt rather than from rising real output. And since the elements reflect mainly private sector behavior, the $64 trillion dollar question is whether capital markets operate with an auto-pilot capable of bringing these trends to a soft landing, or whether the corrections will come via deepening crises.

Faith in the auto-pilot still burns brightly for some academic economists, but not for central bankers. The current Asian crisis is the worst of a succession of crises since 1981 that have evoked collective intervention by the G-7 monetary authorities to contain global repercussions. Cognizant that the interventions, which often involved rescuing large banks under the "too big to fail" doctrine, may sow the seeds of future crises by encouraging more risky bank behavior, the major central banks have been trying collectively to tighten prudential bank supervision by a succession of Basel Accords.[20] The supervised banks, however, have been able to bypass the intent of the restrictions by innovations that reduce transparency and introduce new risks to financial stability, as witness the succession of banking crises. The innovations currently evoking major concern are customized derivatives: options to buy or sell financial assets or the income from such assets at pre-agreed prices. The derivative contracts have involved primarily MNCs and financial firms engaged in cross-currency activities. The intermediating banks, though residual guarantors of the contracts, have treated them as off-balance-sheet items exempt from the equity capital requirements of the 1988 Basel Accords. After the banks fought off attempts to close the loophole by imposing a uniform surcharge on derivative contracts, a new Basel accord was reached in 1996 that allows each bank to apply its own capital-at-risk formula to derivative contracts, with its central bank checking results against its prudential criteria. But in announcing the Federal Reserve's criteria, Chairman Alan Greenspan observed, "We now know that a significant number of balance sheets are obsolete within a day. Thirty years ago it was quite adequate for regulators to look at financial statements on a periodic basis; today they must continuously update regulatory methods" (*Wall Street Journal,* August 8, 1996). Enforcing prudence on derivative dealing may require round-the-clock surveillance!

Concurrently, the dramatic decline of central bank reserves relative to the size of the globalized financial markets shown in Table 1 is enlarging the need to draw on fiscal resources. In the Mexican crisis, drawing on an obscure U.S. Treasury fund established for a quite different purpose was widely condemned in the U.S. Congress and media as an illicit use of taxpayer funds to bail out Wall Street and Mexico. Some of the G-7, resentful that the unusually large IMF credits were engineered without prior consultation, resisted contributing to the bailout. As the cost of bailouts increase, so is resistance to anteing up more fiscal funds.

The effort to overcome this operational crisis by stressing why more bailout funding is essential is exposing the intellectual bankruptcy of the strategy of promoting free capital mobility. Thus, soon after the Mexican crisis, the managing director of the IMF sketched out the road ahead for the IMF and the G-7:

> In today's globalized markets, we must ensure that our ability to react approaches the instant decision making of investors if we want to have the ability to give confidence to markets and our members (Camdessus 1995).

20 Named for the Basel Committee on Banking Supervision, an adjunct of the Bank for International Settlements, located in Basel, Switzerland. The committee is a consortium of 12 major central banks.

Pleading for the U.S. Congress to allot an additional $18 billion to the IMF, Alan Greenspan warned that the Asian crisis may be "a defining characteristic of the new high-tech financial system" and that:

> With the new more sophisticated financial markets punishing errant government-policy behavior far more profoundly than in the past, vicious cycles are evidently emerging more often. Once the web of confidence, which supports the financial system, is breached, it is difficult to restore quickly (Wessel 1998).

Greenspan acknowledged that no one fully understands the workings of the modern global financial system. "At one point, the economic system appears stable, the next it behaves as though a dam had reached a breaking point, and water – confidence – evacuates its reservoir." However he singled out "excessive leverage" and short-term bank loans that "may turn out to be the Achilles' heel of an international financial system that is subject to wide variations in financial confidence" (Wessel 1998). So adios efficient markets; welcome exploding markets!

Bereft of sensible welfare arguments, Washington is now invoking national security. The U.S. secretary of defense's testimony wrapped the national security mantle around the allotment request, a tactic not used in earlier controversies over IMF funding. This reflects the fear that Asian social unrest, forcing a rejection of IMF-dictated policies, poses a greater threat than Latin American unrest did in the crises there.[21]

An opening for the left?

Financial globalization as a welfare-improving strategy may be intellectually bankrupt, but the power of globalized financial markets to block the implementing of more equitable and socially progressive policies remains in force. The bankruptcy provides, however, an opening for the left to promote more favorable preconditions for such policies by exploiting the disarray set off by the Asian crisis to push measures to constrain financial cowboying that can attract allies, even in today's ideological climate.

This requires a more nuanced opposition to more IMF funding. For notwithstanding criticisms shared with the right, the policy goals are far different. For example, ex-Treasury Secretaries George Schultz and William Simon, joined by Walter Wriston, denounce the IMF programs because they "insulate financiers and politicians from the consequences of bad economic and financial practices and encourage investments that would not otherwise have been made." In the Mexico bailout "the government and the lenders were rescued, but not the people...who suffered a

---

21 Populist alliances against the IMF programs incorporating large segments of the wealthy classes are more likely among Asian than Latin American countries for two main reasons. There is less fear of populism among the Asian wealthy, because income and wealth polarization has been much less in Asia than in Latin America. Latin American wealthy, with their propensity for keeping much of their wealth abroad, have not been hurt badly by currency crises, whereas the Asian wealthy have now been caught with their wealth at home or invested in neighboring countries that are also in crisis. Mahon emphasizes these contrasts in relation to the 1980s debt crises (Mahon 1996).

massive decline of their living standards." The request for more funding for the IMF is to "save the pocketbooks of international investors who could face a tide of defaults if these markets are not now shored up" (Schultz et al. 1998). Strong stuff, but then comes the parting of the ways. For Schultz et al. the criticism is preamble to a laissez faire solution. Eliminate the IMF and other official intervention, including lender of last resort, and the encouragement of excessive risk taking will cease, which would stabilize the globalized financial markets while strengthening their disciplinary powers over domestic economic policies.[22] For the left and many moderates that's a sure recipe for a return to the financial chaos of the 1930s.

Since interventions and controls are essential, the objective should be to reprogram rather than eliminate the IMF. Some institutional movement is indicated by the remarks of the IMF's second-in-command at the 1998 Davos Forum that "the IMF recognizes the problem of surges of short-term capital across borders and the need to find ways to deal with that," such as Chile's policy of taxing short-term capital flows (Uchitelle 1998). But that still puts the onus on the victims rather than the originators of the surges. Moreover, a precondition for reprogramming the IMF is for Washington, the godfather of the IMF and G-7, to refocus from promoting to curbing the freedom of capital to move globally. On this no movement is yet evident. At Davos, Clinton administration spokesmen distanced themselves from the suggested new IMF position for fear of adverse political reactions back home (Uchitelle 1998).

Reprogramming the IMF in a welfare-enhancing way would, at the least, require its bailouts to put more of the cost of crisis adjustment on banks that eagerly provide short-term loans but walk away when trouble breaks out. That would induce banks to lend more cautiously in the future and to return to relational banking practices for handling unexpected liquidity problems of their clients.

Bank lending is, however, only one of the channels for the surges. Control over other major channels – cross-currency arbitraging activities of forex trading banks, global portfolio investing of mutual and pension funds, exchange rate speculation by MNCs and hedge funds – requires direct government action. A more "market-friendly" way than exchange controls to reduce these surges would be to tax them at their source. And to minimize evasion through booking in a tax-free haven, an agreement by the major money center countries to levy the tax, set a uniform rate, and allocate the revenue would be needed.

22 For Wriston and Simon, pure laissez faire is for others, not themselves. As its buccaneering CEO, Wriston made Citicorp the largest lender to Latin America in the 1970s, so that when the debt crisis broke out in 1982, its Latino loan exposure was 12 percent of its assets, compared to a 4 percent equity capital base. A default on merely one-third of its Latino loans would have rendered Citicorp insolvent. The bailout saved Citicorp from a preemptive run on its interbank deposits, which could have been fatal.

   During the lending boom, a large share of Citicorp's profits came from its Brazilian loans, where it colluded with Brazilian authorities to perfect "grossing up," an illicit scheme for accumulating fictitious Brazilian tax credits to apply against its U.S. tax liabilities. The IRS in the mid-1970s ruled this illegal, but was overruled by William Simon, then-secretary of the treasury. Shortly after issuing his ruling, Simon left the treasury and joined the board of Citicorp. (For details see Lissakers 1991, Chapter 5, and Kingson 1981.)

This is the essence of the Tobin tax, which has been lurking in the shadows since James Tobin proposed it a quarter-century ago as a way to reduce exchange rate volatility and the power of international financial markets over domestic policy. Instead of capital controls administered by pointy- or round-headed bureaucrats, the tax lets the markets do the selecting. A small tax on all forex turnover would heavily crimp after-tax returns from cross-currency arbitraging and speculation, since these involve brief round trips between currencies, but would lightly impact returns from trade and foreign direct investment, since they involve much longer-term round tripping.[23] The tax would also create requisites for dampening exchange rate volatility,[24] and would generate sizable revenue for domestic use, foreign aid, and/or lender-of-last-resort operations.[25]

Implementation would increase national autonomy over economic policy by partly divorcing interest from exchange rate movements, as well as by augmenting fiscal revenue.[26] But that means the self-interested opposition to the tax proposal from financial markets is reinforced by hostility from conservatives who dislike the tax because it weakens the ability of the globalized financial markets to block countercyclical and reformist policies. That probably explains why the Clinton administration, with its penchant for ingratiating with the powerful, brutally squelched a recent attempt by the U.N. Development Program to circulate a volume of papers by prominent economists assessing the Tobin tax's potential.[27]

The Asian crisis, the weakening support for Washington's bailout strategy, and the specter of the 1930s popping up, however, provide an opening for coalitions – even among groups that otherwise have disparate political agendas – to form around measures to check global financial cowboying and to increase domestic policy autonomy. The left should seize the initiative, since absent such measures its own reform policies remain economically infeasible.

23 The 1992 and 1995 Bank for International Settlements surveys show that over four-fifths of global forex round trips have been for a week or less (Felix 1996A, Table A.5).

24 The debate on whether the tax would reduce volatility has been too narrowly focused on single country liquidity effects. Since the tax would reduce forex turnover, critics have cited examples where the reduction of liquidity from a security transaction tax was followed by increased volatility. The Tobin tax is supposed to be applied globally in order to minimize the evasionary movements that raised volatility in the single country example. Moreover, lowering forex turnover would strengthen the ability of central banks to counterspeculate against unwanted exchange rate movements, and the tax revenue could be drawn on to back up the effort.

25 Professor Ranjit Sau and I, using alternative elasticity and transaction cost assumptions, estimate that a 0.25 percent tax might raise annually between $200 billion and $300 billion globally in 1995 dollars (Felix and Sau 1996).

26 The partial interest–exchange rate divorce is because the tax widens the interest rate difference needed to make cross-currency interest rate arbitraging profitable. For example, a 0.25 percent tax rate would allow country A's interest rate on 30-day paper to diverge from B's by an additional 6 percent before triggering arbitrage flows.

27 The appraisal is published as *The Tobin Tax: Coping With Financial Volatility* (Ul Haq et al. 1996). The suppression by Washington of the attempt to circulate the book widely and promote discussion is described in "Le projet de taxe Tobin, bete noire," *Le Monde Diplomatique,* February 1997.

Comment by Sule Ozler on
"Asia and the crisis of financial globalization"

The author's main contention is that financial globalization has not brought the benefits that were promised by the "current orthodoxy." Taking this one step further, he argues that financial globalization has had growth-retarding effects. As a policy conclusion, the author suggests that money center countries levy a uniform tax to curb financial globalization at its source.

Reading this chapter led me to reflect upon several issues. First, the chapter draws attention to the context in which financial flows take place. I see a sharp break in the post-1973 period from the earlier 1948–73 period in many respects, including ideological, political, and economic ones. In the earlier period, Keynesian aggregate demand management was being implemented internationally as well as nationally; the capital flows provided by the U.S. government in the form of aid is a manifestation of this policy. Even though many developing countries were implementing import substitution policies, the funds were primarily used to purchase capital goods from the U.S. Such policies could of course benefit the U.S. to the extent that it kept its privileged position.

In contrast, the post-1973 period, following the first oil crisis, is a time of capitalist crisis in the core countries and the loss of U.S. hegemony. At this time, "monetarism" – effectively a new version of 19th century liberalism – appeared as a new dominant ideology in reaction to the crisis of declining profit rates. The crucial target for monetarists is government spending; the "invisible hand" of the market need only be set free of Keynesianism to make everyone better off.

Increased liquidity of the eurodollar market, following the first oil shock, gave rise to commercial banks as the major sources of credit at accelerated rates, that is, until the debt crisis of the early 1980s. Current forms of private financial flows are again intimately connected with global changes. Privatization, liberalization of markets, and creation of stock markets are all phenomena of the post-1980 period for many developing countries, and these changes have created opportunities for financial innovations and new forms of lending.

There is nothing inherently good or bad about capital flows to developing countries. The political and institutional context in which financial flows take place is an important determinant of the desirability of increased financial flows. As the author points out, globalization of financial markets has taken place with a shift of power into the hands of private lenders and international financial institutions, in particular the IMF. This process has undermined the ability of economically and politically disadvantaged groups to voice their collective interest. As rather humorously written by a columnist of London's *Financial Times:*

Here is further evidence that, distressing as it may be to be very poor in any circumstances, it is worse under the Tories. This may be set beside the daily accumulation of news items that suggest that since Margaret Thatcher took office in 1979 it has been bliss to be rich, and positive ecstasy to be super rich. A single painting could sum up this view of British society today. It would show a corpulent, sun-tanned power industry boss in a limousine, and a gang of pale, thin, bored, angry young men on the pavement.[1]

Of course, my comment on the painting is that somehow women are invisible. There is significant evidence that women, especially in developing countries that undertake adjustment programs, are among the most adversely affected groups.

The IMF has been getting criticism in the 1990s as a consequence of the devastating social impact of IMF programs in Latin American countries. At this point, even the World Bank in its *Development Reports* emphasizes policies to improve human conditions. This emphasis, of course, is rationalized using the so-called "new" growth theory, which justifies public intervention in the face of market failures.[2] Since the onset of the Asian crisis in 1997 the criticisms have gotten a lot worse, even from the IMF's early supporters. For example, Harvard's Jeffrey Sachs points out that the IMF prescription of tight budgets is the wrong medicine at the wrong time. Others are unhappy that taxpayer money is being used to bail out private lenders and is encouraging them to take on risky investments. Felix raises these two criticisms in his paper as well.

The author argues that globalization of financial markets has led to a global slowdown of the growth of output, productivity, and volume of trade. Statistics on financial transactions are for the world, while statistics on growth are for a number of industrialized countries, including countries of the OECD. First, I am puzzled with this switch to industrialized countries. The chapter, up to this point, is on the sort of issues I describe above. I fail to see the connection and consistency between the point the author makes using these statistics and the primary focus of the paper, which he describes in his introduction as the impact of the removal of capital controls on "the frequency of currency crises and cost-sharing inequities between developed and less-developed economies during crisis management." Second, the trends that are presented use raw numbers, which might be useful to an extent. However, I am not convinced that globalization of financial markets leads to a slowdown of growth and productivity. Moreover, a slowdown of growth in advanced countries and decreased investment opportunities are likely reasons for increased financial flows to the rest of the world.

In the same section the author cites "four ways that this has probably occurred," some of which might be plausible. Nevertheless, unless the plausible links between

1   The *Financial Times*, February 11/12, 1995, section 2, p. 1. I came across this quote in "Assessing Current Development Trends: Reflections on Keith Griffin's 'Global Prospects for Development and Human Society,' " written by Manfred Bienefeld (*Canadian Journal of Development Studies*, Vol. 16, No. 3, 1995).
2   In contrast, the United Nations Development Program Office has a more humanitarian approach based on Amartya Sen's concepts of capabilities and functionings.

globalization of financial markets and growth are theoretically rigorously made, and the alternatives are rigorously tested, the argument will not go beyond one's beliefs.

The author recommends a uniform tax at the source to curb financial globalization. One flaw I see here is that, since it is uniform, the tax would cut flows to all countries. This policy perhaps suggests that there is something inherently wrong with increased finance opportunities. I do not see anything wrong with increased finance availability. National and international conditions, including institutional, political, and economic ones under which countries become indebted, are where the issue lies.

8

Globalization and financial systems: policies for the new environment

Marc Schaberg

Introduction

This chapter examines the process of financial market globalization and its relationship to financial systems and monetary and financial policy. It focuses on the financial systems of Germany, France, Japan, the U.S., and the U.K. These financial systems have been categorized as being either (1) capital market-based, Anglo-Saxon, or exit-dominated systems (U.S. and U.K.) or (2) bank-based or voice-dominated systems (France, Germany, and Japan). Here, following Pollin (1995), these systems will be referred to as either exit-dominated or voice-dominated systems. It has previously been claimed that, as globalization of financial markets proceeds, a convergence will occur toward the exit-dominated model. This chapter highlights findings regarding the convergence of these financial systems along the dimensions of patterns of sources and uses of funds. It then discusses the monetary and financial policy implications of these results, and proposes policy alternatives to reduce the tendency toward speculative finance and increase the amount and stability of productive investment. These are policies designed for stability in light of the observed globalization trend and its implications.

The convergence of voice systems toward the exit model in the area of credit allocation and monetary policy has been substantial in recent years. Countries with voice-dominated systems have made their central banks use increasingly similar instruments of monetary policy in more liberalized and speculative financial environments.

In the past, monetary authorities often conducted monetary policy by directly controlling either the price or the quantity of credit or both. This was done with what are known as direct instruments of monetary policy. These direct instruments include interest rate controls, credit ceilings, and guided lending. *Interest rate controls* involve the government directly regulating interest rates. For instance, deposit rates paid by banks may be capped at a certain level. *Credit ceilings* involve the monetary authority placing a direct limit on the amount of credit available. A credit ceiling is a quantity control on lending that often involves a target level of credit for the economy as a whole and the distribution of this total amount of credit to banks.

Thus, each bank would have a specific quantity of credit it is permitted to supply. Penalties may be levied against banks that exceed their lending limit. *Guided or directed lending* can involve the government directly lending to firms, usually at subsidized rates, or the provision of central bank credit at a discount to banks that make loans to preferred sectors.

Direct instruments of monetary policy began to be dismantled in France and Japan in the early to mid-1980s. This chapter details this dismantling process. Direct credit allocation mechanisms have now been nearly fully dismantled in countries with voice-dominated financial systems, such as France and Japan, where they used to be pervasive. Monetary authorities have adapted to changing financial structures and globalization by dismantling these and other types of direct controls and instead relying on similar indirect monetary policy instruments. Indirect instruments of monetary policy are designed to indirectly affect the price of credit. Three major classes of indirect instruments are open market operations, central bank lending, and reserve requirements.

This chapter argues that the opportunity exists for the use of indirect monetary policy instruments in this era of globalization to achieve some of the allocative goals that were previously addressed by employing direct instruments. It suggests examples of policies that could be part of an integrated package used to work through financial markets to help dampen speculation and promote productive investment. Some indirect instruments, such as reserve requirements on deposits, may be better suited than others to influence the domestic quantity of credit in a globalized environment. An argument here will be that setting reserve requirements on the asset side of financial firms' balance sheets at differential levels for different types of assets, as Pollin (1993) has most recently proposed for the U.S., provides an appropriately designed policy tool for credit allocation in increasingly globalized financial markets. This policy may help promote productive investment by providing a disincentive for financial institutions to lend for the purchase of stocks and other speculative activity.

This chapter also suggests regulatory changes, along the lines of those suggested for the U.S. by D'Arista and Schlesinger (1993), that would bring the new forms of intermediation that have developed outside of the control of monetary authorities under their control. This policy complements the argument for new forms of credit allocation with indirect instruments. As will be shown in the second section, bank lending has fallen as a source of funds for the nonfinancial business sector in France, the U.K., and the U.S. Subjecting nonbank intermediaries to the same regulations as banks, including the asset reserve requirements discussed above, would remove the regulatory advantage that these intermediaries have enjoyed and would allow monetary authorities to have influence over credit flows that have been outside their purview. This influence could be used to help promote productive investment and discourage speculation. In addition to discouraging credit flows used for the purchase of financial assets, financial transactions could be discouraged as well. Taxing financial transactions, as proposed by Baker, Pollin, and Schaberg (1995), could help curb speculation and ease the problem of short-termism.

The organization of the chapter is as follows. The first section discusses the globalization of financial markets and price measures of integration. The second section summarizes empirical evidence on the structural and behavioral differences across financial system types and the convergence of financial systems. It highlights evidence on the trends toward disintermediation, decreased investment, and the increasing purchase of financial assets. The third section explores the implications of this evidence for monetary policy and credit allocation policy. The fourth section details the three specific policy proposals designed to promote investment and reduce financial speculation. The final section concludes the chapter.

Deregulation, liberalization, and the rise of the Euromarkets

A possible understanding of globalization is that it is the process of creating a single global financial market. In order to achieve this homogeneity, differences in national financial markets must be minimized. Differences in financial markets are often due to differences in regulations regarding their operation. Deregulation of national financial markets that seek to harmonize regulations with those of other nations is thus an important aspect of the globalization process. The practices of "regulatory arbitrage" or "regulatory whipsawing" that seek to remove regulations on financial market activity are part of the liberalization of financial markets that has constituted the process of creating a global financial market (Cerny 1994; Herring and Litan 1995). This is a competition in laxity whereby countries remove regulations in order to prevent the perceived threat or actual movement of financial activity abroad. A rethinking of regulations and policy tools is what is needed in order to deal with the real changes that have taken place in financial markets partly as a result of their globalization. It is exactly this type of policy and regulatory response that is explored in this chapter.

The Euromarkets

The creation and growth of the Euromarkets is an important component of the globalization process. These markets are credit and capital markets that are denominated in currencies other than that of the country in which the market is located (e.g., a dollar-denominated bond sold in France or a dollar-denominated loan made in the U.K.). These markets arose in response to earlier attempts to restrict capital flows and regulate financial markets. The Euromarkets have a competitive advantage over domestic markets because Eurocurrency deposits face no reserve requirements, pay no deposit insurance, have no interest rate regulations, and pay low or no taxes. In addition, Eurobonds are virtually unregulated and can be brought to market more quickly and at a lower cost than domestic bonds (Resnick 1989, 36; Sarver 1990). Their presence has both helped to force the liberalization of national markets and provided a significant step in the process of creating a global financial market. The market for loans from these deposits, as well as for Eurobonds, created a source of funds that could be tapped by some classes of borrowers around the globe and served as a pressure point for liberalization. The Euromarkets provided a rupture of the connection between financial markets and national regulation: they were off-shore markets that did not fall within the jurisdiction of any country. In that sense, they marked the creation of a global market outside the context of any national financial system.

Price measures of integration

As financial markets become increasingly globalized, arbitrage should drive the risk-adjusted rate of return on similar financial assets into uniformity. That is, the process of globalization should make it easier for the law of one price to hold for like assets. There are four price measures used to gauge the degree of international financial market integration by examining the behavior of interest rates on assets denominated in different currencies or held across borders: closed interest rate parity, covered interest rate parity, uncovered interest rate parity, and real interest rate parity.

Closed interest rate parity

Closed interest rate parity is achieved when interest rates on comparable financial instruments denominated in the same currency but issued in different countries are the same. Capital controls of various kinds can drive a wedge between the rates of return available on like assets denominated in the same currency but located in different countries. The removal of capital controls in almost all industrialized countries and the increase in cross-border financial flows has allowed arbitrage to force closed interest parity to hold.[1] Offshore and onshore markets of the major industrialized countries for assets denominated in the same currency are nearly fully integrated, if judged by the closed interest rate parity condition.

Covered interest rate parity

The condition for covered interest rate parity is satisfied when the rates of return on like assets denominated in different currencies are equal after allowing for the cost of covering the currency risk with a forward currency contract. The covered interest rate parity condition can be expressed as:

$$i_{mt} - i^*_{mt} = Fd_m \qquad (1)$$

where i_{mt} is the domestic interest rate at time t on an asset with m periods to maturity, i^*_{mt} is the foreign rate, and Fd_m is the foreign discount (premium). For the major industrial economies and a growing number of other countries, covered interest rate parity holds (Herring and Litan 1995).[2]

1   Frankel (1990) discusses the removal of restrictions regarding capital flows in Germany in 1973–74, Japan in 1979–80, and the U.K. in 1979 and the subsequent disappearance of the differential between onshore and offshore rates of return on short-term assets. Blundell-Wignall and Browne (1991) provide time series of these differentials from the mid-1960s to 1990 for a wider group of countries. They show that these differentials disappeared in each of these countries, at different times, between the mid-1970s and the early 1980s.
2   Frankel (1990) found that, as of 1988, out of a group of 23 countries only Greece, Bahrain,

Uncovered interest rate parity

For uncovered interest rate parity to hold, nominal interest rate differentials between assets denominated in two currencies have to equal the expected change in the exchange rate over the period to maturity for these assets. This condition can be expressed as:

$$i_{mt}-i^{*}_{mt} = E[D(S_{mt})] \qquad (2)$$

where $E[D(S_{mt})]$ is the expected change in the exchange rate and the left-hand side the difference between the domestic and foreign rates on assets with m periods to maturity at time t. If covered interest parity holds, then tests for condition (2) have embedded in them the test for the degree to which forward rates are unbiased predictors of future spot exchange rates. This can be seen by combining (1) and (2) to get:

$$Fd_{m} = E[D(S_{mt})] \qquad (3)$$

A large number of studies have found that this condition does not hold: that is, the forward exchange rate premium is not an unbiased predictor of future changes in spot foreign exchange rates.[3] Two explanations of the standard rejection of uncovered interest rate parity in regression tests, McCallum's (1994) and Frankel and Froot's (1990), are consistent with uncovered interest rate parity.[4]

Real interest rate parity

The condition for real interest rate parity can be found by combining (2), the condition for uncovered parity, with the following condition for ex ante purchasing power parity:

$$E[D(S_{mt})]=E(P_{mt})-E(P^{*}_{mt}) \qquad (4)$$

that says the expected change in the nominal exchange rate over m periods is equal to the difference between the domestic expected inflation rate over m periods and the foreign expected inflation rate over the same period of time. Combining uncovered interest parity (2) with ex ante purchasing power parity (4), we get the condition for real interest parity:

Malaysia, and South Africa deviated from covered interest parity to a significant degree. Short-term rate differentials for major industrialized countries were nearly eliminated by 1991 (Frankel 1992). However, covered interest parity did not hold when capital controls were in place. See Frenkel and Levich (1975) and Frankel (1990).

3   See, among others, Froot and Frankel (1989), Fama (1984), and surveys by Levich (1985) and MacDonald (1988).

4   McCallum (1994) argues that uncovered interest parity holds despite the failure of the unbiasedness hypothesis. Froot and Frankel (1989) and Frankel and Froot (1990) use survey data on expectations of exchange rate changes and find that uncovered interest parity holds.

or

$$i_{mt} - E(P_{mt}) = i^*_{mt} - E(P^*_{mt}) \qquad (5)$$

$$E(r_{mt}) = E(r^*_{mt}) \qquad (6)$$

which says that domestic ex ante real interest rates are equal to foreign ex ante real interest rates. Testing this condition is difficult because ex ante interest rates are not observable. Real interest parity has been rejected in the majority of econometric tests.[5] The rejection of real interest rate parity does not mean that financial markets are not integrated. If *financial* markets are integrated in the sense of uncovered interest rate parity being satisfied but *goods* markets are not fully integrated, that is, with purchasing power parity failing to hold, then tests for real interest parity would fail. The failure of real interest rate parity is consistent with both the integration of financial markets and the ability of domestic monetary authorities to have independent effects on interest rates. With flexible exchange rates and distinct economic conditions in different countries, interest differentials across countries should be expected even with "perfect" capital mobility and financial integration.

Changes in financial systems

There is evidence that the voice-dominated systems of France and Japan are converging toward the exit model and that the U.S. and U.K. are becoming even more extreme examples of countries with exit-dominated financial systems. First, there is a trend toward increased purchases of financial assets by the nonfinancial enterprise sectors of France, Japan, the U.S., and the U.K. Second, there is a clear decrease in investment by the nonfinancial enterprise sectors of France, the U.S., and the U.K. and some evidence of such a pattern in Japan. Third, bank loans have fallen as a source of funds in both France and Japan, while there have been periods of recent increases in bank loans to the nonfinancial enterprise sectors of the U.S. and U.K. A brief summary of patterns of sources and uses of funds by the nonfinancial enterprise sectors in the five countries is as follows.

In the mid-1980s French firms began borrowing more in relation to their productive financing needs and using these funds to purchase financial assets. Investment by the French nonfinancial enterprise sector fell from 70.2 percent to 59.5 percent of uses of funds from the period 1975–79 to the 1985–89 period.[6] As investment was falling, purchases of equity shares increased from 1.9 percent to 13.7 percent of total uses.[7] Bank finance fell as a source of financing from 31.3 percent of gross sources in 1975–79 to 16.9 percent over the 1985–89 period.

---

5   See, among others, Cumby and Mishkin (1986) and Modjtahedi (1987).
6   Calculations from *OECD Financial Statistics Part 2*.
7   This evidence is consistent with that presented by the OECD showing that the share of financial investment in total enterprise expenditures rose from 2.6 percent in 1979 to 33.6 percent in 1985 and higher in the later 1980s (OECD 1987, 53).

Investment by the nonfinancial enterprise sector in Japan fell from 70 percent of uses of funds in 1980–84 to 60.1 percent in the period from 1985 to 1989. Over this same period, the purchases of stocks, bonds, and other financial assets increased from 1.0 percent to 10.1 percent of total uses of funds.[8] In Japan, firms and households borrowed more and purchased more financial assets, creating a speculative bubble while fixed investment fell in the latter half of the 1980s (OECD 1989, 101).

The German financial system does not display any similar patterns. Investment has remained stable as a use of funds, and there has not been a significant increase in the purchase of equities by the nonfinancial business sector or a decrease in bank lending to this sector.

In the U.S., investment by this sector fell from 59.6 percent of total uses of funds during the period 1975–79 to 48.2 percent in the period 1985–89. At the same time, equity purchases rose from 4.4 percent to 18.7 percent of total uses, and bank finance increased from 8.3 percent to 10.6 percent of gross sources.[9] U.S. firms were borrowing more but investing less in physical assets while buying more stocks.

The same pattern is found in the data on the sources and uses of funds for the nonfinancial business sector in the U.K. Investment fell from 66.7 percent of uses in the period 1975–79 to 56.7 percent in 1985–89. Over this same period, bank finance increased from 13.4 percent to 27.6 percent of gross sources of funds, and the purchase of equity increased from 8.0 percent to 18.2 percent of uses of funds. As in the U.S., firms in the U.K. were borrowing more but investing less while dramatically increasing their purchase of stocks.

Policy implications of globalization and convergence

One reason differences in financial systems are significant is because the structure of voice-dominated systems allows for a greater degree of central bank control over the supply and allocation of credit as well as a long-term view regarding investment in contrast to the short-term bias of exit-dominated systems (Pollin 1995). One of the implications of the changes in financial structures has been that some of the institutional structures that allowed for this involvement began to be dismantled. Another aspect of convergence has been the movement away from government involvement in direct control over the supply of credit and its allocation in the voice-dominated systems.

This section explores the dismantling of direct credit allocation policies in the voice-dominated financial systems. It also explores how the changes that have taken place in financial systems have affected the structure and effectiveness of monetary policy. One indicator of the effectiveness of monetary policy is the ability of monetary authorities to control certain interest rates.

8   Calculations made from *National Accounts Table for Account 1-Non-Financial Incorporated Enterprises,* published by the Economic Planning Agency of Japan.
9   Data on sources and uses of funds for the U.S. are from *Federal Reserve Board Flow of Funds Accounts,* Table F.102.

Control of interest rates

It is difficult to see how financial market globalization would greatly affect the
ability of monetary authorities to control key short-term interest rates. As long as
banks are forced to hold central bank money, the market for these reserves will be
insulated from the effects of globalization.[10] All of the central banks of the five
countries studied here, with the recent exception of the U.K., have reserve requirements and intervene in the market for reserves to influence their key short-term
rates (Kasman 1992). Therefore, the ability to control these short-term rates remains unaffected by globalization pressures. However, the desire of the central banks
to adjust these rates and the consequences of these adjustments could be impacted
by financial market globalization.[11]

Globalization may not have reduced the ability of monetary authorities to control their key short-term rates, but has it weakened the link between these rates and
other short-term market interest rates? Radecki and Reinhart (1988) investigate how
globalization has affected the link between the federal funds rate and the three-
month Treasury bill rate. In considering the determinants of the spread between
these two rates, they found that foreign short-term rates were significant in explaining the spread. However, they did not find the influence of foreign rates to increase
over time. They also found that a given change in borrowed reserves may have a
larger impact on money market rates than in the past (Radecki and Reinhart 1988,
26). In fact, most recent studies find that monetary policy affects short-term interest
rates (Leeper and Gordon 1992; Christiano and Eichenbaum 1991).

While there is debate as to the strength of the effect, all studies reviewed here
show some influence of short rates on long-term rates.[12] As Akhtar (1995, 121)
points out, there is a dearth of recent studies that address the issue of possible shifts
in monetary policy effects on long rates in recent years, and few use data after
1983.[13] Blundell-Wignall et al. (1985) found a decreasing long-run elasticity of long
rates to short rates from the 1970s to the mid-1980s for the U.S., Japan, Germany,
Italy, Canada, and the U.K. Zevin (1992) finds that nominal government bond yields
have shown the highest degree of correlation among many other interest rates and
asset prices since 1960, while the yield curve is almost completely uncorrelated.
This, along with the empirical literature on the relationship between short-term rates
and long-term rates, is consistent with the view that central banks can't control

10 See Radecki and Reinhart (1988), Goodfriend (1991), and Poole (1991).
11 As will be discussed later in this section, the central banks of Germany, France, and the U.K.
    would lose their ability to independently control short-term rates and monetary policy more
    generally if and when the European Monetary Union is completed.
12 Pollin (1991) shows evidence of an interactive effect whereby short-term rates impact long-
    term rates but long-term rates also influence short-term rates. For evidence of the impact of
    short rates on long rates see Blanchard (1984), Estrella and Hardouvelis (1990), Campbell
    and Shiller (1994), Cohen and Wenninger (1994), Cook and Hahn (1989), Hardouvelis (1994),
    Mankiw (1986), and Radecki and Reinhart (1994). For an excellent review of the empirical
    literature on the relationship between monetary policy and long-term interest rates, see Akhtar
    (1995).
13 This is with the exception of Radecki and Reinhart (1994) and Cohen and Wenninger (1994),
    who use data up to 1993.

long-term interest rates but can significantly impact short-term rates. The evidence as to whether globalization has strengthened or weakened the impact of short-term rates on long-term rates is mixed, but suggests that the relative influence over the movement of long-term rates has shifted toward the growing global bond markets and away from monetary authorities.[14]

Changes in financial structure and the removal of quantity controls and interest regulations have led most monetary authorities to rely on market intervention to influence interest rates as their operating monetary policy strategy. Globalization of financial markets reduces the domestic constraints on funding availability for those borrowers able to tap larger global credit markets. This further reduces the role of quantity constraints and strengthens the role of interest rates as a rationing mechanism. Under a regime of floating exchange rates and free capital flows, monetary policy also operates through changes in the exchange rate. With flexible exchange rates and a high degree of capital mobility, the control of short-term rates bears the cost of exchange rate fluctuations. An expansionary monetary policy in the form of lower short-term rates will lead to capital outflow and currency depreciation. This depreciation can raise net exports. It is through this exchange rate channel that monetary policy is now supposed to function.[15] However, the speculative nature of foreign exchange markets yields the possibility for potentially costly swings in the value of the currency touched off by the expansionary policy. There is also the potential for the currency depreciation to touch off domestic inflation thus limiting the anticipated expansion of exports.[16]

The evidence from aggregate studies of the effect of interest rate changes on output is mixed. There is some evidence that the impact of interest rate changes on output has declined (Kahn 1989; Hirtle and Kelleher 1990). Other studies that include other channels of monetary policy in their examinations, however, have found no decline in the real economy's sensitivity to monetary policy (Mauskopf 1990; Mosser 1992).

Changes in financial systems and the removal of many quantity controls and interest ceilings have made central banks rely more heavily on indirect instruments to affect market interest rates and exchange rates to transmit monetary policy. There is, however, another channel, the lending channel, that could maintain its effectiveness in light of globalization. As will be seen, though, the lending channel is also weakened by globalization.

14 This is consistent with Pollin (1991), who suggests that long-term interest rate trends may create an environment for central bank determined short-term rates to follow.

15 In general, sectoral studies of the incidence of monetary policy in the U.S. have found that it has shifted from the housing sector toward net exports. Bosworth (1989) argues that housing has become less interest elastic while net exports have become increasingly interest sensitive. Kahn (1989) also finds decreased interest sensitivity of housing and increased interest sensitivity of net exports. Housing was also found to be less interest elastic by Friedman (1989). In smaller countries, where net exports comprise a much larger share of output, the net export channel has been important for monetary policy for a longer period of time.

16 Dornbusch and Giovannini (1990) argue that these effects have often been exaggerated. Goodman (1992), however, in looking at the experience in Western Europe since the advent of floating exchange rates, believes that these inflation effects have not been insignificant.

The lending channel

The basic argument for the existence of a lending or credit channel for monetary policy is that monetary policy has supply side effects on *loan supply* in addition to demand side effects caused by interest rate changes and the subsequent impact on components of demand. One of these components is credit demand.[17] That is, monetary policy has an independent effect on the asset side of bank balance sheets.[18] If not all borrowers may substitute away from bank credit, then when tight monetary policy reduces the size of the banking sector's balance sheet it decreases the supply of credit available to those borrowers who are dependent upon banks for their credit needs. These are borrowers who are unable to seek financing from the domestic markets for bonds or commercial paper, the foreign markets, or the Euromarkets.

This effect is likely weaker due to the globalization of financial markets because some borrowers can substitute away from domestic bank loans to other sources of funds. But clearly not all borrowers can do this. That is, the credit market is segmented, and not all borrowers face the same opportunities for credit. Loans and bonds or loans and other sources of credit may be substitutes for some firms, but they are not in general perfect substitutes. It is the larger multinational firms that are more likely to be able to have a broader range of credit substitutes, leaving smaller firms and borrowers trapped in their respective domestic credit structures. There is quite a bit of evidence to support the claim that small firms face significantly stronger liquidity constraints after a tightening of monetary policy.[19] Globalization may be allowing larger firms to evade credit availability constraints during a monetary tightening if they are willing to pay a higher price, but many small- and medium-sized firms are still subject to quantity constraints in credit markets. Thus, the lending channel now operates more through changes in loan supply to smaller firms and on a smaller share of firms seeking credit.

This lending channel has also been weakened by changes in financial systems and globalization pressures that have led to a smaller share of funds being subject to reserve requirements and other types of control by monetary authorities. This weakens the lending channel because policy changes, through either open market operations or changes in reserve requirements, now impact a smaller share of intermediated funds. Evidence that the lending channel has been weakened can be found by examining the sources and uses of funds for the nonfinancial business sectors of the five countries studied here. Bank loans as a source of funds fell in Japan from 37.1 percent of gross sources over the period 1970–74 to 24.3 percent in 1990–94. In France, bank finance fell from 35.4 percent of gross sources to 8.3 percent over the same period.[20] In both France and Japan firms have begun to rely less upon bank loans and more upon retained earnings as sources of funds. With bank loans com-

---

17 For a discussion of the lending channel see Tobin and Brainard (1963) and Bernanke and Blinder (1988).
18 In the framework of Greenwald and Stiglitz (1991), decreasing reserve requirements has the effect of increasing banks' willingness to lend at any given interest rate.
19 See Gertler and Hubbard (1988), Gertler and Gilchrist (1994), and Kashyap, Lamont, and Stein (1994).
20 Economic Planning Agency of Japan and *OECD Financial Statistics Part 2*.

prising a shrinking source of funds for nonfinancial firms, the loan supply effect of monetary policy is weakened.

As the lending channel has been weakened by globalization, the effectiveness of monetary policy has also been influenced by globalization through its impact on the financial structures in which monetary policy is conducted. It is this possibility that we now explore.

Convergence of monetary policy strategies and operating environments

Another dimension along which convergence has occurred is that of the institutional settings and operating strategies of monetary authorities. The instruments and channels of monetary policy in most industrial economies have converged. In a review of monetary operating procedures in the U.S., Japan, Germany, the U.K., Canada, and Switzerland, Kasman (1992) found that their central bank intervention strategies were quite similar. Nearly all of them use interest rate operating targets.[21] Icard (1994, 93) discusses this notion of convergence:

> The globalization of markets is gradually making the way the various national financial systems operate, form expectations, and react the same. This inevitably leads to harmonization of national monetary policy characteristics, due to the growing uniformity of instruments and international coordination.

One of the aspects of the convergence of national financial systems is the increasingly similar ways in which monetary authorities conduct monetary policy. A common occurrence among these countries is the dismantling of direct monetary policy instruments and the movement to an almost singular reliance upon indirect instruments of monetary policy. The institutionally specific systems of direct policy instruments allowed central banks to play a role in directly influencing the quantity and allocation of credit. Changes in the financial structure of these countries conditioned changes in central bank operating strategies. These changes have also diminished the ability of authorities to control the quantity and influence the allocation of credit.

Globalization of financial markets has induced convergence with respect to the instruments and channels of monetary policy in these countries. Previously nationally distinct structures of quantity controls and administered prices have been dismantled and replaced with market-oriented methods for conducting monetary policy.[22] Central banks have witnessed the declining importance of intermediated credit, a growing turnover in financial markets, and the breakdown of the relationship between money and income, and they now use market interest rates both as operating targets and primary vehicles for the transmission of policy. Market operations have

---

21 This move toward indirect instruments of monetary policy is not confined to the major OECD countries discussed here. For a discussion of this phenomenon in developing countries, see Alexander, Balino, and Enoch (1995).

22 For a review of the structure of Japan's earlier monetary control mechanism see Kasman and Rodrigues (1991); and for a discussion of that of France see Loriaux (1991).

replaced quantity controls on lending as the main instrument of policy implementation. This is seen in the removal of the direct instruments that gave central banks considerable control over the supply and allocation of what was the major source of finance, domestic credit.

Dismantling direct controls and credit allocation mechanisms
There has been a movement away from the involvement of the French and Japanese governments in credit allocation and direct measures of control over the credit supply. This retreat can be seen in the decreased reliance upon bank finance by French and Japanese firms discussed earlier in this chapter. Various government credit programs publicly subsidized some of that bank finance. As the French and Japanese governments dismantled their directed credit programs, it is not surprising that bank finance fell as a source of funds. This is evidence of an important dimension of the convergence of voice-dominated financial systems toward the exit model.

In Japan, the system of direct controls that existed in the 1970s as part of a strategy to influence the supply of bank credit has been mostly dismantled, and monetary policy is now transmitted by indirect instruments focused on interest rate changes (Kasman and Rodrigues 1991). In the earlier period, when bank credit was the dominant source of financing, administrative controls on interest rate movements were in place and central bank credit was a major source of bank reserves. Central bank credit was supplied to banks that presented specific demands for credit for particular projects of their industrial customers in a process called window guidance. This put the central bank in the position of monitoring not only the quantity of credit created but also its allocation. As the financial structure of Japan changed and became more globalized, banks were allowed to expand their funding sources both at home and abroad while domestic credit was becoming a much less important source of funds. Bank finance as a share of gross sources of funds for nonfinancial enterprises fell nearly 40 percent from the 1970–74 period to the period 1990–94.[23] Banks were able to expand their sources of funds domestically when they were allowed to issue certificates of deposit in 1979 and money market certificates in 1985 (Calder 1997). Their ability to expand these sources by seeking funds overseas was encouraged by the relaxation of the laws governing foreign exchange transactions. The Foreign Exchange and Foreign Trade Control Law of 1948 and the Foreign Investment Law of 1950 prohibited all foreign exchange transactions unless expressly permitted by the government. These exchange control laws were beginning to be eroded in the 1970s. This erosion accelerated with the Foreign Exchange and Trade Control Law of 1980. It continued with the abolition in 1984 of the "real demand" rule, which required banks to verify that all foreign exchange trades were based on real commercial transactions. The 1985 decision by Japan's Ministry of Finance to allow banks to directly engage each other in yen-dollar trades instead of through the eight regulated Tokyo foreign exchange brokers (Calder 1997) further eroded the exchange control laws. These changes in foreign exchange laws allowed Japanese banks and firms to gain access to funds overseas, particularly the Euromarkets, by the mid-1980s.

23 Calculation based on sources of funds data from Economic Planning Agency of Japan.

Also, banks no longer had to rely on credit from the central bank, and firms no longer had to rely on credit from domestic banks by the mid-1980s in Japan. These factors combined to give the Bank of Japan less direct control over economic activity – it lost its leverage in using window guidance to affect the supply and composition of bank credit. As reliance on central bank credit declined, so did the use of discount window lending as a source of reserves. The practice of window guidance ended in 1982, and the end of the active use of reserve requirements as a policy tool followed soon after (Kasman and Rodrigues 1991). The Bank of Japan moved away from direct instruments that gave it considerable control over the quantity and allocation of credit. It has, instead, increasingly used indirect instruments of monetary policy aimed not at the domestic supply and allocation of credit but at interest rates. The indirect instruments of choice have been open market operations, with the earlier heavy use of discount window lending and reserve requirements having been abandoned.

Similar changes have taken place in France. In earlier periods, the government was more heavily involved in directly controlling the supply and allocation of credit. Three-quarters of all loans to business in France in 1979 came from the state or semipublic financial institutions and their subsidiaries (Loriaux 1997). A system of credit ceilings imposed on private banks called *encadrement du crédit* allowed the government to play an allocative role by granting exceptions to these credit ceilings for preferred loans. This credit ceiling system was a principal tool of French monetary policy; it allowed for specific increases in credit, and it allowed the money supply to be targeted for favored uses. The system of credit ceilings was dismantled in France in early 1987, thus ending this particular credit allocation mechanism (Raymond 1992, 98). The principal focus of monetary control was no longer the quantity of credit given by banks but interest rates on the newly reformed money market. The development of the money market accelerated with the establishment of negotiable bank certificates of deposit in 1984, the establishment of new public short-term instruments, and the expansion of the previously small interbank money market to all firms (Loriaux 1997).

Another way in which the French government influenced the allocation of credit was through subsidizing loans. This practice was diminished during the 1980s as the volume of subsidized credit declined. An example of this decline is the Economic and Social Development Fund. The fund provided industrial credit for investment projects and was a major supplier of industrial credit in the 1950s. It provided financing for 9 percent of industrial capital investment in 1981 and only 0.29 percent by 1992 (Loriaux 1997). Interest rate ceilings were removed, and the administrative control over them was relinquished; the previously dependent central bank became independent, and the system of bank specialization was abolished, allowing all French banks to have the same opportunities with respect to their activities (Bertero 1994). Interest rates have now become the main transmission mechanism for monetary policy in the French economy (Icard 1994, 93; Raymond 1992, 99).

Convergence toward a single European monetary policy: the EMU
If and when the European Monetary Union (EMU) is completed and the European
Central Bank can set monetary policy for Europe, it will mark the complete convergence of the monetary policies of Germany, France, and the U.K. Direct monetary
financing of government deficits will no longer be possible. The completion of the
EMU will also, by law, rule out quantitative credit controls and the regulation of
interest rates. According to the terms of the Maastricht treaty, the third stage of the
European Monetary Union could have begun as early as 1997 if a majority of the
member countries satisfied the convergence criteria established in the treaty.[24]

If these conditions are not met by a majority of European countries by January 1,
1999, then the third stage of the union is scheduled to commence with however
many countries meet the convergence criteria. The first part of stage 3 will lock
participating currencies at existing exchange rates, and the European Currency Unit
will be used in parallel with national currencies at these rates. The second part of
stage 3 replaces these national currencies with a single circulating currency, the
euro. At this point, the European Central Bank (ECB), headquartered in Frankfurt,
Germany, will, together with the national central banks that form the European
System of Central Banks (ESCB), begin to function as *the* central bank for the
union. The ECB will be in charge of the single union monetary policy. It will be an
independent central bank governed by a governing council consisting of the central
bank governors of each participating country. The primary objective of the ECB, as
laid out in the Maastricht treaty, is price stability. Individual countries will no longer
have monetary policy as a tool. There will be no ability to adjust exchange rates.

The completion of the EMU should be viewed as an opportunity to implement
policies designed to work through the financial system to encourage investment and
discourage speculation. The EMU could provide a Europe-wide institutional framework for implementing and overseeing these policies. The fact that agreements as to
how banks would be regulated and by whom have not yet been made (Kregel 1993)
provides an opening for the types of policy alternatives suggested in this chapter. It
is these policies we now examine in detail.

Policies for the new financial environment

Changes have taken place in the financial structures of not only the voice-dominated systems but in the exit-dominated systems like the U.S. and U.K. as well. The
changes in financial structure and monetary policy methods have left monetary authorities with control over a smaller portion of the financial sector and with much
more blunt instruments with which to engage in policy. The direct instruments that,

24   The convergence criteria are: (1) a deficit/GDP ratio of below 5 percent and a debt/GDP ratio
     of below 60 percent, (2) observance of the normal fluctuation margins provided for in the
     Exchange Rate Mechanism (ERM) for at least two years without actively devaluing cur-
     rency, (3) long-term nominal interest rates within 2 percent of the three best-performing
     countries in terms of price stability, and (4) inflation within 1.5 percent of the three best-
     performing countries.

in the past, were used by some central banks to influence the supply and allocation of credit, for the most part, no longer exist. What is needed is a utilization of indirect instruments in more effective ways that allow monetary authorities to more sharply influence both the supply and allocation of credit in the new financial environment as well as curb the tendency toward excessive turnover and speculation in financial markets. In this last section of the chapter, three specific policy proposals are put forward to address these particular problems.

Regain control and strengthen the lending channel
Globalization has led to a higher degree of disintermediation. Domestic bank lending is a less-important source of funds, and this has left monetary authorities with control over a smaller portion of the flow of financing. This reduces the strength of the lending channel and renders problematic policies aimed at increasing the domestic supply of credit, such as lowering reserve requirements. With a smaller share of funds intermediated through the traditional banking sector and subject to reserve requirements, changes in these required reserve ratios will have a smaller effect on loan supply. This smaller loan supply effect also holds for open market operations. The declining share of funds against which reserves must be held leads to a decreased ability of monetary authorities to affect the supply of loans. The decline of domestically intermediated funds and the formation of what D'Arista and Schlesinger (1993), in discussing the U.S. case, call the "parallel banking system" has affected many countries. It has reduced the leverage of monetary authorities as the pool of funds against which reserves must be held has shrunk as a share of total funds. These parallel systems have put pressure on monetary authorities to lower reserve requirements, because institutions that are required to hold reserves are put at a cost disadvantage in comparison with those that are not obligated to hold reserves. The growth of the Euromarkets has provided a significant source of this pressure. What is needed, across countries, is a system, like that proposed for the U.S. by D'Arista and Schlesinger (1993), that subjects all institutions that either make or sell loans or engage in the acceptance of funds from the public to the same requirements as to the holding of reserves with the central bank. The French Bank Law of 1984 has already defined all French financial institutions that engage in deposit taking or the making or selling of loans as credit institutions and placed them under the same regulations (Bertero 1994).

A broad agreement among countries to this policy, as was achieved with respect to capital adequacy requirements in the Basel Accords, and an agreement about the appropriate range for reserve requirements would be beneficial in two ways. First, it would allow monetary authorities to regain control over the flow of funds. Second, it would put an end to the regulatory arbitrage that pits one country's regulations, in this case the level of required reserves, against another's in the attempt to attract or maintain financial firms. The European Commission has already acknowledged the problem of regulatory arbitrage and has sought to reduce it by agreements related to the EMU. The commission's directives concerning competition in banking and financial services state that the prudential regulations applied in individual countries will apply to all institutions operating in those countries (Kregel 1993). This is designed to prevent regulatory competition among European countries. With all of these policies in place, monetary authorities would be able to use reserve requirements in a more active fashion to influence the supply of credit. The lending channel would be strengthened as both open market operations and reserve requirement changes would have a larger impact on credit supply.

If one accepts the proposition that loans and bonds are imperfect substitutes for some classes of borrowers, then it is possible to construct policies aimed at increasing domestic credit availability for those firms that are unable to take advantage of the sources of funds made newly available by globalization. If the market for bonds and the market for bank loans are somewhat segmented, then it is possible to target the market for loans by adjusting reserve requirements on deposits.[25]

The use of reserve requirements as a monetary policy tool in France illustrates this possibility. In France, changing the reserve requirement makes it possible to reduce the link between external and domestic effects of monetary policy (Icard 1994). Lowering reserve requirements allows the French authorities to offset interest rate increases aimed at stabilizing the franc.[26] Lowering reserve requirements increases the willingness of intermediaries to supply credit at any given interest rate. If credit is rationed, changes in the quantity of reserves in the banking system through, for example, open market operations lowers the cost of funds for banks. Banks can respond by lending funds to those who were previously rationed without changing the interest rate. Thus, changes in credit supply are possible without large changes in interest rates. This creates a way for monetary authorities to influence domestic credit conditions without the fear of large bond sales or purchases triggered by interest rate changes that would work through interest rate and exchange rate channels and potentially result in unwanted currency and price fluctuations. The Bundesbank in Germany has also used reserve requirements in this way. In 1980, facing capital outflows to the U.S. and U.K. and the beginning of a recession, the Bundesbank felt it could not lower interest rates for fear of greater capital outflows. Instead, it chose to lower reserve requirements to stimulate domestic liquidity.[27] Germany's use of reserve requirements as an active monetary policy tool is made easier and more effective because its definition of what constitutes a bank is broader than, for example, that of the U.S., and thus a greater share of funds is subject to the Bundesbank's reserve requirements. Reserve requirements could be

---

25 It would also be possible to use differential asset reserve requirements to target credit to these borrowers as discussed below. The point here is that adjusting reserve requirements on domestic deposits will have a somewhat targeted effect on those borrowers that are constrained to obtain bank loans from domestic institutions.

26 Icard (1994, 101) writes: "In October 1991, for instance, the rise in the Banque de France's key rates, intended to stabilize the franc within the ERM band, was combined with a cut in reserve requirements that avoided the need to raise the minimum bank lending rate. A variety of similar, or reverse, steps have been taken successfully in recent years."

27 This policy choice is described in the 1981 Joint Economic Committee of the U.S. Congress report, "Monetary Policy, Selective Credit Policy, and Industrial Policy in France, Britain, West Germany, and Sweden."

lowered on their own, leaving interest rates unchanged, to increase the quantity of domestic lending. The use of reserve requirements to influence the supply of credit is also increasingly appealing because, as banks act to match their assets and liabilities that bear market interest rates, their activity becomes less sensitive to changes in interest rates. The regained ability to use reserve requirements as an active tool will help strengthen the lending channel. This, coupled with the continued ability to affect short-term rates through open market operations and credit supply through the lending channel will leave monetary authorities in a stronger position to influence the quantity of credit available domestically.

Allocate credit using indirect instruments

A stronger lending channel brought about by increased monetary authority control over forms of intermediation that have developed outside of their control will help give them more control over the quantity of credit. However, given changes in financial structures and the tendency toward financial churning and speculation, will increases in credit result in productive investment? Voice-dominated financial systems had institutional structures in place to encourage the channeling of credit toward productive uses. Globalization has changed national financial structures and the ways in which monetary authorities conduct monetary policy, but monetary authorities still have the ability to influence domestic interest rates, particularly on the short end of the yield curve, independently of foreign rates. In this sense, the effectiveness of monetary policy has not been severely reduced by globalization of financial markets. However, declining control over long-term interest rates and growth in the use of credit to fund speculative purchases of already existing assets, as opposed to the productive funding of new assets, puts several points of the effectiveness of monetary policy into question.

The institutional structures and direct instruments that allowed central banks in countries like Japan and France to influence the allocation of credit in favor of productive investment have been largely dismantled. Differential asset reserve requirements like those proposed for the U.S. most recently by Pollin (1993) can be used to regain the ability to influence the allocation of credit in the context of globalization and changing financial structures. This policy, combined with the first proposal to "level the playing field" for all financial firms, would markedly strengthen monetary authorities' ability to allocate credit. This new structure for credit allocation is well suited for the more complex financial structures that have evolved, since it allocates credit via indirect instruments and, coupled with the strengthening of the lending channel, is able to influence the flow of credit through nonbank intermediaries.

The indirect method of credit allocation involves the application of reserve requirements to the asset side of all financial firms' balance sheets at different rates for different types of assets. These differences in asset reserve requirements could be altered to favor the funding of certain types of assets over others. Classes of preferred assets would need to be defined, and a target ratio of preferred assets to total assets would need to be set. Then, in order for the system to be more flexible, the requirements should be implemented, as first proposed by Maisel (1973), as a system of permits that can be auctioned in a market rather than quotas. Institutions that have preferred assets in excess of the specified target could be issued a permit for that excess amount of preferred assets that they could then sell to financial firms whose preferred assets fall below the target. A policy-making process, involving as much democratic participation as possible, would have to be developed that would determine what activities would be selected to qualify as preferred assets.

The effect of this policy would be that financial intermediaries that funded preferred productive investment, such as the purchase of new plant and equipment, would face lower reserve requirements on these assets than those financial firms that funded more nonpreferred assets such as the purchase of stocks, other financial assets, or commercial real estate. These differential asset reserve requirements will be effective because the reserve requirements will raise the cost to intermediaries of funding undesired activity relative to productive investment and will provide an indirect instrument for credit allocation. There is econometric evidence that changes in reserve requirements have an impact upon bank profitability (Kolaris, Mahajan, and Saunders 1988). This, along with other empirical work on the effect of different levels of reserve requirements across different classes of intermediaries (Knight 1977; Rose and Rose 1979), suggests that changes in reserve requirements are capable of influencing lending patterns. There is a concern that, if reserve requirements are set too low, then having differential requirements will have little effect. This is a valid point if an extremely low cap were placed on the level of reserve requirements. However, empirical work has shown that temporary changes in reserve requirements as small as 0.5 percent have effects upon profitability (Kolaris, Mahajan, and Saunders 1988). This same work shows that permanent changes in reserve requirements have a greater profitability effect than temporary changes. A permanent differential reserve requirement that would cost the financial institution as much or more than a 0.5 percent change in a flat reserve requirement should have a large enough effect to impact the institution's behavior. Of course, the differential could be set higher to have larger effects. This policy model provides a simple and flexible system aimed at influencing the allocation of credit to replace the dismantled systems of direct controls, like the *encardement du crédit* in France or strict window guidance in Japan. The system could also replace some of the functions that used to be carried out by narrowly construed intermediaries charged with providing credit to specific types of borrowers or for specific projects. Some of these institutions have disappeared as financial liberalization measures have removed restrictions on the types of activities in which these intermediaries can engage. Instead of providing credit to preferred sources through compartmentalized institutions, differential asset reserve requirements can be used to give preferential treatment to certain types of assets regardless of the institution that holds the assets.

Tax financial transactions
The development of more active capital markets in voice-dominated financial systems and the growing volume of financial transactions present the possibility that the problem of short-term bias that exists in exit-dominated systems will begin to emerge in voice-dominated systems as they converge toward the exit model.

There has been a rapid increase in financial transactions relative to output in both exit-dominated systems like the U.S. and U.K. as well as in voice-dominated systems like Germany, Japan, and France that are experiencing greater turnover in their newly growing capital markets. For example, the value of the volume of financial transactions in stocks and bonds in France rose from 124 billion francs to 3,806 billion francs in 1990. This increase in volume corresponds to an increase in turnover – value transacted divided by value outstanding – from 0.15 in 1980 to 0.878 in 1990, implying a decrease in the average holding period of these assets from nearly seven years to just over one year.[28] This trend is likely to continue in the voice-dominated systems as their capital markets deepen. The growth in financial market churning in voice-dominated systems may begin to erode their longer-term view of investment projects and increase the problem of short-term bias found in exit-dominated systems.

A small tax on financial transactions would both help lower the likelihood of this short-term bias developing in voice-dominated systems as well as reduce the short-termism in exit-dominated systems. A specific type of transactions tax is the "Tobin Tax" (ul Haq, Kaul, and Grunberg 1996). This small tax, proposed by James Tobin, on foreign exchange transactions, is designed to reduce speculation and volatility in the foreign exchange market. The securities transactions tax proposed here is a more general securities tax applied to a broader range of securities transactions, including equity, debt, and derivative transactions.

The purpose of such a tax would be to raise the cost of trading financial assets and thereby reduce speculative activity. The tax should be small enough that it would be negligible when the asset purchased was held for a long period of time but more costly for those who trade frequently. Also, the tax should be relatively simple to administer and to maintain a reasonable balance in establishing rates on different types of assets. A structure that accomplishes these goals is put forward in Baker, Pollin, and Schaberg (1995), and it is this structure I propose here. This securities transaction tax structure would tax equity trades at 0.5 percent of the value of the transaction. This tax represents a smaller share of the anticipated return the longer the investment horizon of the investor. Debt transactions, both public and private, would be taxed at a rate of 0.01 percent per year to maturity. This means that equities are taxed at the equivalence of a 50-year bond. For example, a $100,000 equity transaction would face a tax of 0.5 percent, or $500, and a $100,000 bond transaction, where the bonds had 50 years remaining to maturity, would also be taxed at 0.5 percent, or $500. This sliding rate for debt instruments eliminates any significant discontinuities for firms to exploit with respect to the maturities of their debt issues. Options would be taxed at 0.5 percent of their premiums, and futures contracts would be taxed at 0.02 percent of the contract value.

Many countries have had securities transactions taxes in place at various points in time, but they have been pressured to lower or remove these taxes as they face competition from other countries that do not have these taxes and are thus more

---

28   Author's calculations based on figures from Bertero (1994).

attractive places for financial firms to conduct business.[29] This phenomenon of regulatory competition, like that in the case of reserve requirements and central bank control, calls for an agreement among countries to the implementation of a uniform securities transaction tax. The more countries that agree to the implementation of securities transaction taxes, the less of a problem there will be with tax evasion through movement of operations abroad. While it may be possible for large countries with deep and established financial markets, like the U.S., to tax securities transactions without fear of losing many financial firms, smaller countries face a more serious exit constraint. All countries implementing the tax will see reductions in trading volume depending on the price elasticity of the various securities transactions being taxed. A well-designed securities transactions tax could both raise revenue and decrease turnover and speculation in financial markets.[30]

Revenue from the tax could be used to fund public investment projects that would crowd in private investment. Taxing financial transactions coupled with using differential asset reserve requirements that create disincentives for providing credit for speculative uses can work together to help tilt the playing field toward productive investment and away from speculation.

Conclusion

The argument of this chapter has been that regulatory changes and new policy instruments are needed to increase monetary policy effectiveness and help allocate credit to productive investment while dampening speculative pressures in the new financial environment. Importantly, the new forms of intermediation that have developed need to be brought under the control of monetary authorities. With this regained control over the channeling of credit, monetary authorities should use differential asset reserve requirements, an indirect policy tool suited for the changed financial environment, to allocate credit toward productive investment. A tax on financial transactions implemented together with these differential asset reserve requirements could be used to help curb speculation and promote investment. These three policies should be seen as part of an integrated package that countries could use to intervene through financial markets to promote productive investment and reduce speculation.

29 Baker, Pollin, and Schaberg (1995) describe the pressures to remove these taxes in various countries in order to attract financial firms.
30 Baker, Pollin, and Schaberg (1995) estimate that a securities transactions tax could raise between $35.8 billion and $60.1 billion.

Comment by *Ilene Grabel* on "Globalization and financial systems: policies for the new environment"

Marc Schaberg's paper is an interesting and useful contribution to the prescriptive project to which this volume is devoted. Schaberg's paper addresses two critically important questions: (1) how precisely has globalization transformed the terrain on which monetary policy operates? and (2) how – in this changed environment – can progressive policy makers nevertheless be expected to influence economic outcomes?

Let me begin by reviewing the principal arguments and policies put forth in the chapter. Schaberg maintains that the globalization and liberalization of financial systems in the OECD has caused monetary authorities to rely on indirect as opposed to direct policy instruments. Globalization and liberalization have also brought about a near convergence in the structure of national financial systems, and it is this structural convergence that has given rise to a convergence in the tools utilized by monetary policy makers. Since, according to Schaberg, the instruments of financial control have been transformed by globalization and liberalization, progressives need to look for new means by which the financial system can be put in the service of a progressive policy agenda. Toward this end, Schaberg proposes that monetary authorities increase their control over the lending activities of banks and nonbank institutions; that a system of differential asset reserve requirements be put in place; and that a tax on financial transactions be imposed. I endorse these policies; the imposition of any or all of them would go some distance toward resolving the concerns that motivate Schaberg's paper.

However, a good deal of work remains to be done in order to construct a compelling basis for the claims and the policies that Schaberg advances here. In what follows, I discuss the areas of the chapter that would benefit from further development in future work.

Convergence

Given the centrality of the issue of convergence in the chapter, it is surprising that convergence is treated rather bluntly. In particular, it is important to draw a distinction between three types of convergence – convergence in the structure and regulation of national financial systems, convergence in the tools that monetary authorities utilize, and convergence in economic outcomes. In failing to treat these three types of convergence separately, Schaberg leaves open the issue of whether there is a causal link between the structural convergence of OECD financial systems and observable economic outcomes, on the one hand, and between structural convergence and convergence in the tools of monetary policy making, on the other. In the

215

absence of a nuanced consideration of convergence, the paper does not give sufficient guidance on the question of whether progressives should be devoting their attention to curbing certain types of economic activities or to stemming structural convergence by preserving (or strengthening) the existing institutional and regulatory heterogeneity of OECD financial systems.

Schaberg is sensitive to the importance of the broad milieu in which financial activities occur. Context helps to explain why increased financial market liquidity and trading volatility have had such different effects in the U.S. as compared to France, Japan, and Germany. Schaberg, however, warns that there may be a possibility that the negative outcomes of increased trading activities will spread to non-Anglo-American countries if the present trend of systemic convergence continues. It would be important to address in this regard what specific attributes of the non-Anglo-American financial systems must be preserved in order to prevent this scenario, and whether these specific institutional features are in any way necessarily incompatible with globalized financial markets. Moreover, it is asserted in the paper that globalization itself serves to bring about systemic convergence. The precise mechanism by which globalization forces convergence deserves discussion. It would be appropriate for Schaberg to present here concrete evidence from the non-Anglo-American countries that convergence pressure actually stems from globalization.

On the matter of evidence, Schaberg relies on sources and uses of funds data to support his claim of systemic convergence. But clearly this one type of evidence is not a sufficient basis for demonstrating systemic convergence. Data are not presented for Germany, and this is surprising since Germany is one of Schaberg's sample countries. The data presented for France are from the mid-1980s – it would be useful to present more current data.

In his discussion of systemic convergence, Schaberg (following established precedent) draws a dichotomy between capital-market-based financial systems (which are exit oriented) and bank-based financial systems (which are voice based). He hypothesizes that the financial systems of France and Japan are increasingly becoming both capital market and exit based. But it should be noted that the evolution of financial systems is highly "path dependent," and thus, even though capital markets are becoming more important as a source of finance in Japan and France, their financial systems have nevertheless remained largely voice based (especially in Japan). Capital markets operate quite differently when they are embedded in existing voice-based institutional structures. In noting that the German financial system does not seem to be converging on the dominant capital-market-based model, Schaberg seems to be subverting his own convergence claims. Relatedly, it should be explained why the Euromarket has not forced structural convergence in Germany as it has in France and Japan.

Schaberg also presents evidence that bank loans have recently become more important as a source of finance in the U.S. and U.K. Using Schaberg's convergence criteria, this suggests that the U.S. and U.K. are becoming more bank-oriented financial systems, but clearly this is not the case. What do we make of this evidence, then?

Globalization

The term globalization does too much work in the chapter, especially in terms of accounting for governmental actions. Schaberg correctly notes that governments in OECD countries have recently moved away from involvement in credit allocation policies. But this movement away from credit allocation is presented in a political vacuum. It seems as if Schaberg is claiming that there is a technical incompatibility between globalized finance and national systems of control over credit allocation. This makes the demise of these programs seem to be an inevitable outcome of globalization. This is simply not the case.

Indeed, Schaberg himself acknowledges that it is the *will* of central banks that has changed, and not the technical abilities of central banks to control interest rates. He writes: "the ability to control these short-term rates remains unaffected by globalization pressures. However, the *desire* of the central banks to adjust these rates...could be impacted by financial market globalization" (emphasis added). Does this mean that globalization provides the opportunity for central banks to *invoke* constraints on their operations that are not really there?

This failure of will places on center stage the role of politics, ideological shifts, and changes in governmental spending priorities as critical forces accounting for the demise of credit allocation programs. This point is important in the context of Schaberg's paper not just for rhetorical reasons but for reasons of practical strategy. If the old means of controlling finance cannot work in globalized markets, then we must look as Schaberg does for new ways of controlling finance. But if the problem is that governments will not intervene in finance because they simply will not intervene in markets anymore, then Schaberg's new policies will be as infeasible as the old policies that he argues we cannot resurrect for technical reasons.

Policy

The indirect policy of differential reserve requirements proposed by Schaberg (drawing on Pollin) represents a promising mechanism for funding growth-promoting investment programs. But since OECD governments have largely moved away from identifying such investments as a national priority, this reserve requirement policy is as unlikely to be implemented as are credit controls to be resurrected.

With regard to other proposals for controlling the financial system, Schaberg (as have others) makes a case for the usefulness of imposing a uniform, global securities transaction tax. It is not entirely clear if Schaberg also means to propose a "Tobin tax" on foreign currency transactions. Regardless of which type of tax is being proposed, he suggests that the proceeds of such a tax could be used to finance socially beneficial investments. However, I would suggest that he also consider the proposals of those such as Felix (1993) that such tax revenue be earmarked specifically for developing countries.

Let me close by noting that progressives can do more than propose new constraints on the financial sector such as transaction taxes or lending and credit allocation controls. While these mechanisms should be pursued, progressives should also be making a case for reforms that involve increasing state-mediated financial flows to some groups or some types of socially necessary economic activities (see Grabel 1996a). If some sectors of the economy were recipients of state-mediated finance, then it would not be so important to constrain the activities of participants in market-mediated financial activities.

9

Housing finance in the age of globalization: from social housing to life-cycle risk

Gary Dymski and Dorene Isenberg

> Everyone has the right to a standard of living adequate for the health and well-being of himself and his family, including food, clothing, housing, medical and necessary social services.
>
> – Universal Declaration of Human Rights, Article 25:1

Overview

Innovations have been remaking the U.S. system of housing finance over the past two decades. This revolution of privatization, securitization, risk shifting, and deregulation has not occurred in one country: globally, market-based mechanisms for supplying and financing housing are replacing government mechanisms. Is this revolution an inevitable result of financial integration? Does it mean that governments are withdrawing resources from housing finance and leaving housing to market forces? And will this financial transformation make housing finance systems more efficient? This paper investigates these questions by comparing the transformation in U.S. housing finance with concurrent changes in the United Kingdom, France, and Germany.

Other authors have argued that global financial integration is making housing finance systems more efficient by forcing the reduction of governmental subsidies, less risk bearing by lenders, and a higher relative price of housing credit. We come to very different conclusions here. First, global financial integration itself does not explain the marketization of housing finance in every country. Another aspect of globalization is driving this transformation – governments' global financial deregulation and their global retreat from supplying housing to needy households. National deregulation has affected the character of mortgage financing flows far more than has the actual or threatened movement of funds across borders. And marketization does not mean government withdrawal from housing finance: instead, the public emphasis has shifted from building social housing to supporting the financing of homeownership. Indeed, current efforts to develop sophisticated mortgage-based financial markets depend on continued governmental underwriting and subsidies. Housing prices have not been cleansed of governmental distortions; they only reflect a different pattern of subsidies and guarantees.

The emerging systems are not clearly more efficient than the old ones. Using a broad notion of efficiency, which adds households' shelter-related "life-cycle risks" to the standard roster of financial risks, we conclude that housing finance innovations have not reduced risks but merely shifted them: intermediaries' financial risks have been reduced by parallel increases in households' life-cycle risks.

From "Golden Age" to "Global Age"

In the wake of World War II a new international order prevailed. The decisions at Bretton Woods shaped the new structure of international monetary institutions and financial conduits to meet the needs of this new economic and political order. International financial institutions, trade agreements, conflict resolution processes, and political organizations were created to manage the newly organized world. This international order and the hierarchy of power that supported it also fostered conditions under which governments in Europe and North America were able to broker de facto "social contracts" between their owning and working classes. Under these contracts, owners and managers enjoyed stable profit rates and rising productivity; workers enjoyed increasing real wages and employment security; and governments enjoyed the stable domestic macroeconomic environment that resulted (Bowles et al. 1984). These social contracts underwrote the "golden age of capitalism," which flourished during the 1950s and 1960s (Glyn et al. 1990).

The social contract in each nation encompassed methods of providing adequate housing stock (Feldman and Florida 1990; Harloe 1995). And since housing outlays are large relative to income levels, equally integral was a set of housing finance mechanisms, including government transfers, subsidies, and financial instruments and institutions for accumulating savings or taking on debt. Each nation solved the linked problems of housing supply and finance uniquely: different combinations of government and market roles created diverse patterns of financial and life-cycle risk. These various solutions depended on each nation's historical legacy and on the character of its capital/labor "social contract."

Things have changed dramatically in the past 20 years. The end of Bretton Woods – variable exchange rates, boom-and-bust macroeconomic growth, and persistent current-account imbalances – created the conditions for financial volatility and global capital shifts. Technological advances have further eased capital flows among countries. For many analysts, these changes mean that marketization is now inevitable. In an environment of international financial instability and instantaneous communications, all national economies must compete for financial capital. This means reducing social expenditures, especially those requiring long-term financial commitments.

Financial internationalization versus financial globalization

All analysts would agree that processes of financial globalization have affected the size and distribution of risks within OECD (Organization for Economic Cooperation and Development) financial systems, and hence these systems' social efficiency. But what exactly is this globalization? One definition is suggested by research like that of Fukao and Hanazaki (1987), who find that interest and exchange rates are increasingly being determined in world, not national, markets. Yet empirical evidence does not suggest that widespread capital mobility has completely leveled global differences in financial prices and contractual terms. In recent articles, Mussa and Goldstein (1993) and Herring and Litan (1995) find no evidence of uncovered interest parity, nor financial–price equalization. Nor do they find evidence that domestic saving and investment are independent of each other, as one would expect in a truly globalized capital market since, in that case, saving would flow to the highest bidder anywhere in the world (see Feldstein and Horioka 1980). Technology has created a situation in which innumerable financial contracts *could* be traded electronically around the world, but the prior question is whether all financial contracts must now be written so that they *can* be so traded. And the answer to this question is *no*.

Cerny (1994) argues that globalization consists above all else of organizational changes: the development of both integrated worldwide market structures and of firms with the organizational capacity to center their activities on these markets. We might refine this insight by offering a distinction between internationalized and globalized markets. A financial market is *internationalized* when assets with idiosyncratic risk/return characteristics – that is, whose risks and returns are unique to the regulatory and banking structure of the country of origin – are sold offshore as well as domestically. A financial market can be considered truly *globalized* when it involves the continuous exchange in financial centers around the world of assets whose risk/return characteristics are independent of national regulatory and banking structures. Internationalized markets are integrated to the extent that prices are identical across national borders. Fully integrated markets are globalized markets. Globalization is, in effect, the endpoint of a process of the separation of financial asset characteristics (including prices) from the idiosyncrasies of their countries of origin.

Whether the internationalizing financial markets culminate in a globalized market remains in dispute (Boyer 1996; Wade 1996; Weiss 1997), but the effects of internationalization on governmental activities and expenditures are not. Internationalization has put pressure on governments to extricate themselves from the social and economic spheres – the process of global leveling. This leveling, however, is not complete. Governments have withdrawn from providing social housing, but not mortgage underwriting. The specifics of global leveling depend on historical and structural contexts, as detailed in the sections below.

An efficient markets view versus a social efficiency approach

The international attempt to move governments out of economic decision-making positions derives from an efficient markets view: markets without governmental intervention and in which all information relevant to the product is incorporated into its price are the best. Proponents of this view, such as Diamond and Lea (1992a; 1992b) and Wachter (1990), advocate that countries with the most "open and competitive markets" and with the fewest public subsidies will deliver mortgage finance at the lowest adjusted spreads – that is, most efficiently.

These authors spotlight only certain areas of governmental intervention and focus entirely on return while ignoring risk. But the essential feature of the housing finance transformation is the shifting of risks (as explained below). The risks that should be brought into view are, in the first instance, the *financial risks* – interest rate, liquidity, default, and prepayment risks – generated by the issuance of financial instruments.[1] All of these risks are borne by either the borrower or the lender in any given transaction. In the old U.S. system, except for interest rate risk, these financial risks were borne by lenders. But the innovations associated with financial integration shift more and more risks onto households. It follows in Diamond and Lea's analysis that intermediary risk shedding enhances efficiency; however, their logic fails if we also track the interests of the households who buy the mortgages.

This brings us to our alternative approach to efficiency. Generally, any economic system is efficient insofar as it allows units operating therein to pursue their goals while minimizing their exposure to risks. The efficiency gain or loss in shifting from one set of institutional and market arrangements to another can be determined by examining how this shift affects goal attainment and risk bearing for the units affected thereby. In housing finance, two economic units are relevant: households and financial intermediaries. The former pursue security and material plenty, the latter profits. Both types of units use housing finance contracts to pursue their different goals; but since these contracts create obligations over time that may not be satisfied, they also generate risks.

To encompass the social context of efficiency, we must evaluate households' efficiency position as well as those of intermediaries, and nonfinancial as well as financial risks. Households financing homes are exposed to risks in housing markets just as intermediaries are. And like intermediaries, households are long lived, and their success requires that they adapt to shifting market environments. But unlike intermediaries, the individuals making up households have a life cycle: two dependent phases in which no income is earned, bracketed around a middle phase of income earning. This life cycle is punctuated by occasional geographic relocation and occupational transition. We can describe households' risks in housing markets as follows.

---

1   Any instrument that entitles its holder to fixed (coupon) payments exposes its holder to interest-rate risk because market interest rates (and hence the costs of financing this instrument) may rise or fall over time. Liquidity risk exists for any instrument that cannot be sold on demand at par. Default risk exists when a borrower may be unable to meet the terms of a financing agreement. Prepayment risk arises when the borrower of a debt instrument retains the option of prepaying the principal, thus disturbing the pattern of cash flows anticipated by this instrument's purchaser.

Life-cycle risks of households

(1) Entry risk. Any given individual, when she singly or jointly starts her own household, faces the risk of not finding adequate housing when entering the housing market; in the extreme, entry into the housing market must be deferred.

(2) Tenure risk. Once a given household has acquired an adequate housing unit, it faces the risk of being unable to stay in that unit. This is tenure risk.[2] It has several causes, including earnings instability, increased rental or financing costs, and the demolition or conversion to nonresidential use of one's housing unit.

(3) Reentry risk. Finally, there is the risk that a household vacating a housing unit will be unable to find an adequate replacement unit within its means. This risk depends on two factors – the existence of an available supply of housing at some market price, and income and wealth levels that are adequate to allow a household to purchase rental services.

The main point of introducing life-cycle risks is to capture a neglected efficiency effect of changes in housing systems. From households' perspectives, housing and housing finance markets and policies are efficient if they generate an adequate, affordable housing stock; any market innovation or policy change that reduces life-cycle risk increases "efficiency" in this sense.

Clearly, any system of supplying and financing housing generates different levels of both life-cycle and financial risks. These two categories of risk interact: in particular, enhanced repayment and default risk on an instrument imply enhanced tenure risk. And financial risks, once created through emissions of instruments, must be distributed between financial intermediaries and households; those not borne by intermediaries increase households' tenure risk.

A closer look at institutional change in several countries provides evidence of the complex mix of factors that has globally transformed housing finance. The following sections examine the experience of the U.S., the U.K., France, and Germany.

Housing and mortgage transformation in the United States

U.S. housing policy possesses a dual character. On the one hand, many institutions had been put in place to facilitate households' purchase of homes, the *ne plus ultra* of participation in the American dream. Cheap financing at low rates was available, with the reduced down payments and interest rates due to federal guarantees. Households' life-cycle risks were mitigated through sustained private sector, public, and subsidized building programs, and through robust dedicated circuits of housing finance capital. Risk mitigation was accomplished by a design that imposed substan-

---

2   This terminology purposely suggests the term "tenure status" commonly used in housing economics, which pertains to whether a household owns or rents its homestead. Here we follow the broader definition suggested by Wilson (1979, 11), who argues that tenure status "defines the legal position of households in residential markets with respect to their rights and obligations as participants."

tial financial risks on financial intermediaries and on the government itself. But on the other hand, the right to housing had not been ceded, nor had the principle that households should not bear life-cycle risks. Further, tenure and entry risk were reduced but never eliminated for lower-income households, even in the halcyon days of the U.S. welfare state.

The consequences of the brave new financial world

How has the internationalization of financial markets affected financial and household risks? The emergence of bouts of macroeconomic instability, together with the weakening of the link between macroeconomic performance and generalized household prosperity, clearly imply higher life-cycle risks, even for many relatively prosperous households. And, the balance among governmental provision, household life-cycle risks, and intermediary risk bearing has tilted toward more household risk bearing. This tilt has occurred because government has retreated from the provision of social housing and because intermediaries have shed financial risks.

Housing policy

The restructuring of government's role in the promotion of housing provision has shifted the costs and responsibilities of its provision from the state to the populace. The results have not been uniform: tax codes have been made less progressive, and subsidies for the dependent poor and working poor have been cut while middle- and upper-class subsidies have been spared.[3] Government policies have shifted away from supply side programs that create new social housing for the poor in favor of income-based programs (especially the Section 8 program) that supplement the (demand side) purchasing power of low-income households in the housing market.[4] A deep reduction in the federal social housing budget (Dymski and Isenberg 1996) reflected this retreat. In response, the private market has been slow to build lower-income rental housing, largely due to binding credit market constraints (Dymski and Veitch 1992) on nonprofit builders. The result has been a rapid erosion in the number of lower-cost rental units, even as many lower-income households have been formed and even as the stock of higher-priced units has grown rapidly.[5] In

3   The rise and decline of the American welfare state is documented by Katz (1989); growing inequality in the U.S. is summarized by Goldsmith and Blakely (1992). One of the major middle-class subsidies is the mortgage interest deduction. Recent estimates of federal expenditures for this deduction in 1989 have ranged from $38.8 billion to $109.9 billion (Follain, Ling, and McGill 1993).

4   The shift in emphasis from the supply side to the demand side programs can be seen in the number of housing units aided over time. Starting in 1960 the Department of Housing and Urban Development (HUD) had financed 425,000 public housing units and had no other active programs. By 1980, the number of public housing units financed had risen to almost 1.2 million. Other HUD programs in 1980 reduced mortgage prices for rental and owned housing and provided subsidies for rental units. These aided 377,000, 219,000, and 1,153,000 housing units, respectively. By 1994, public housing provision had stalled at 1.4 million units, while the Section 8 rental subsidy program had almost tripled to more than 3 million housing units (Burchell and Listokin 1995, 599).

5   Masnick (1991) has shown that there were consistent, often deep, declines in the number of

consequence, a gap between the supply and demand of affordable housing has grown steadily. For example, Newman and Schnare (1988) estimate that in 1985 there were 9.3 million households with $8,000 or less in annual income and only 5.3 million housing units affordable for this income class (and 1 million of these units were substandard). Taken together, these shifts have forced lower-income households to bear greater entry and reentry risks – and they have put the very poorest at risk of being squeezed out of the housing market altogether.

Housing finance

The same forces that kicked the U.S. welfare state into reverse triggered massive problems for the savings and loans (thrifts) that supplied most U.S. housing finance. High interest rates and slow income growth generated widespread but undeclared insolvencies among thrifts. Banking acts in 1980 and 1982 attempted to use deregulation to restore the depositories' viability: in exchange for nonbanks entering financial product lines previously reserved for banks and thrifts, banks and thrifts were allowed more freedom in setting prices and in selecting product lines. These changes produced new competitors for the reconstructed battlefield; however, many of these participants still suffered from previous injuries. The problems of the zombie thrifts led to the decade's third banking act in 1989. It attempted to choke off the burgeoning thrift industry insolvency, which had become both profoundly expensive and monumentally ill managed.

As the industry imploded, new methods and sources of housing finance were found. Floating rate mortgages became common. Expanded government underwriting of mortgage sales led to the rapid growth of mortgage securitization, which in turn provided the new sources of credit supply needed to replace lost thrift lending capacity. Increased mortgage securitization, in turn, required increased government (and private) underwriting of mortgage sales and the use of standardized mortgage eligibility criteria in lieu of the earlier system of "relationship" lending.

The result has been a brave new financial world in which financial risks have been shifted onto the households that can least bear them. The adoption of flexible-rate mortgages reduced interest rate risk for institutions but increased tenure risk for households. Institutional shedding of the placement function and use of securitized instruments has raised the implicit risk to government of systemic defaults in a downturn; it has also limited the availability of mortgages to households whose balance sheet ratios and credit and employment histories do not meet standardized criteria. The changes in the housing finance market have produced both an expanded range of financing instruments for the wealthy, often cheaper than before, and stricter admission requirements that the poor often cannot meet. The hollowing out of the income distribution is matched by the housing tenancy gains for the wealthy and the rise in tenancy risks for the poor.

lower-cost ($400 or less in 1989 dollars) rental units in the U.S. between 1974 and 1987. By contrast, expensive rental units ($500 or more) increased by 38% between 1974 and 1980 and by 126% between 1980 and 1987.

Housing finance, housing rights, and risk bearing in three countries

The European countries examined here share some common experiences. Coming out of World War II, they urgently needed to rebuild decimated housing stocks for returning troops and civilians. Over time, households that grew more prosperous moved into owner-occupied units; social housing was left to a lower-income constituency, including an increasing number of immigrants and ethnic minorities. Then, as macroeconomic growth stalled and revenues tightened, social housing was seen as a fiscal drag, and social housing programs became a convenient political target. The political push against social housing, however, has had to face the organized political power of the organizations and localities that had put this housing in place. Indeed, this section will show that while all these countries have moved in the direction of less housing provision, fewer subsidies for lower-income housing, less market segmentation, and less protection of financial customers, their housing finance systems remain distinctly different. Financial globalization per se is not the transformative force behind housing policy decimation and housing finance marketization; the principal impetus is their governments.

Housing policy and finance in the United Kingdom
The United Kingdom's welfare state took shape as a result of the activity of its working-class labor movement. Public housing, a major component of the state's welfare system and the heart of its housing policy, was introduced in 1919, and its role continued to expand into the post-World War II period, when it reached its peak. The annual targets for housing production rose from 300,000 dwellings a year in 1951 to 500,000 by 1970 (Malpass 1986, 6). The policies adopted by the state produced a change in tenure distribution. Prior to World War I, 10 percent were owner-occupiers and 90 percent were private renters. In 1970, 50 percent were owner-occupiers, 20 percent were renters from private landlords, and 30 percent rented from local authorities and new towns (Malpass 1993, 71, Figure 3.1, 72).

The commitment to public housing held until the end of the 1960s; in 1968, for example, net housing production was split evenly between the public and private sectors – 181,467 public and 200,438 private units (Leather and Murie 1986, 43). However, by the end of the 1970s this commitment had succumbed to a stagflationary economy and the rise of neo-liberal ideology as manifested in Margaret Thatcher, Great Britain's new prime minister in 1979. During her legendary term she promoted the rule of the market in place of the socially equalizing policies of the government. In the realm of housing policy and finance Thatcher oversaw institutional deregulation, cuts in social housing production, and the sell-off of social housing into the private sector. Institutional lenders diversified their product lines and mortgages acquired market prices. Public housing production fell and was in short supply. These policy shifts were not tenure or risk neutral. By 1989, tenure distribution was 69 percent owned, 10 percent rented from the private sector, and 22 percent rented from local authorities (Maclennan 1995, 665). Indebtedness had skyrocketed and foreclosures had almost tripled (Whitehead 1993).

Housing finance

An immediate result of marketization was a shift in the types of institutions providing mortgages and in their practices, including the financial instruments they used. Whereas building societies originated approximately 80 percent of mortgages throughout the 1980s, by the end of this decade both banks and centralized lenders (mortgage banks) accounted for a large percentage of originations.[6] Endowment mortgages supplanted self-amortizing mortgages, and securitization along with the use of wholesale funds promoted market-determined capital flows and prices to dominance in the mortgage market.

Endowment mortgages combined the new with the old to produce an even riskier financial position for the borrower. When issued, an endowment mortgage was combined with a life insurance policy, for the mortgage covered only the interest on the loan.[7] The insurance policy payment is "savings" that paid off the principal of the loan when the policy matured. Like the self-amortizing mortgage, the endowment mortgage carried a variable interest rate. Unlike it, however, interest rates were not set by the building society cartel. Now they fluctuated with the market, which had become increasingly volatile in the 1980s. Between April 1988 and February 1990, U.K. interest rates climbed from 9.5 percent to 15.4 percent (Malpass 1993, 91).[8]

The impact of these changes on homebuyers is described in an analysis by the Council of Mortgage Lenders (quoted in Malpass 1993, 91), who find that:

> the steep increase in interest rates meant that repayments which had been just affordable at the point of purchase became very much heavier. The cost of the average first-time buyer loan of £30,000 in 1988 rose by £110 per month by early 1990. In London and the South East first-time buyers in 1988 were generally having to borrow far more than £30,000. The cost of a £50,000 loan would have increased by no less than £308 per month between April 1988 and February 1990.

What was the overall implication of this shift for financial and tenure risk? In a period when domestic capital markets had been opened up to international players, the result was more highly volatile interest rates. By creating an endowment mortgage with a flexible interest rate, financial institutions were highly successful in shielding themselves from interest rate risk; it was all shifted onto the borrower. Additionally, lenders now had an insurance policy to cover the value of the house against which the loan was made. Effectively, the default risk that used to accrue to the lender was shifted from the mortgage originator onto the insurance company.

---

6   By 1982 banks accounted for almost 40 percent of originations, and later in the 1980s centralized lenders originated about 10% (Callen and Lomax 1990, 507–8).

7   Will Hutton notes that the popularity of this mortgage insurance combination was not just based on its floating interest rate. The commission on the insurance policy could be front-loaded, so premiums in the first two years of a 25-year policy might consist entirely of commission payments. Of the £17 billion premium income paid to life insurance companies in 1993, £2 billion was paid in commissions (1996b, 206).

8   Callen and Lomax (1990, 507) found that U.K. mortgage rates tracked the three-month London Inter-Bank Offer Rate (LIBOR) more closely in the 1980s than in previous years. The LIBOR fluctuates with international financial pressures and with changes in short-term U.S. interest rates.

The new configuration of mortgage lenders came to rely heavily on the capital market (wholesale funds) instead of the traditional deposit base. While building societies raced to include wholesale funds among their funding sources, centralized lenders issued bonds in these markets in order to raise their loanable funds. Beginning in 1987, lenders bundled their floating rate mortgages as securities and sold them off into these markets (Bradt 1991).[9]

The positive side of wholesale markets was the greater flexibility in liquidity management it afforded lenders: when loan demand increased, lenders could access the funds they needed by issuing bonds or shorter-term securities. However, these bonds are unsecured, and the use of shorter-term securities to finance housing assets created maturity mismatches. Also, the mortgage industry's heavier use of these markets added to the increased volatility in market-determined mortgage interest rates, an already mentioned problem for borrowers.

Other aspects of the marketization of lending practices and financial deregulation have added to the life-cycle risks of borrowers by adding to their indebtedness. Instead of requiring 20–25 percent equity for a home purchase, in the 1980s lenders required as little as 10 percent. Additionally, lenders fostered the growth in second mortgages – "home equity" loans – which allowed homeowners to borrow against their built-up equity. These changes combined to increase both indebtedness and homeowners' tenure risk.

These innovations – together with the high, volatile interest rates, high speculative housing prices, and the economic contraction of the early 1990s – created a situation in which

> falling house prices reinforced the downturn. Payment arrears quickly matured into possessions, and by 1994, 250,000 owners had lost their homes and 150,000 households still had arrears exceeding 12 months. Possession sales further fed house price drops, and negative equity affected an estimated 1.5 million owners (Maclennan 1995, 687).[10]

The changes in the foreclosure and arrears rates between 1980 and 1991 indicate graphically that the combined forces of global leveling and financial deregulation have increased the tenure risk of homeowners. In 1980, the foreclosure rate (as a percentage of outstanding mortgages) started at 0.06 percent, the 6-12 months arrears rate stood at 0.25 percent, and the 12+ months rate was 0.08 percent. By 1989, these rates were 0.17 percent, 0.73 percent, and 0.15 percent, respectively. Just two years later in 1991, these rates had climbed to 0.77 percent, 1.87 percent, and 0.93 percent respectively (Whitehead 1993).

9   Mortgage securitization was given a boost in February 1989 when the Bank of England ruled that securitized loans could be treated as off–balance-sheet items. This rule change facilitated commercial banks' use of securitization, since it meant that securitization could be used to improve capital/asset ratios and hence to achieve compliance with Basel Accord standards.

10 Margaret Hughes reported in *The Guardian* (August 1, 1996) that, according to the Council of Mortgage Lenders, 24,100 homes had been repossessed in the first six months of 1996, a decline from the previous year. Further, arrears were down by 10% compared to the second half of last year.

As an aid to distressed owners, Britain has an income-based shelter support policy that pays between 50 percent and 100 percent of the interest on a mortgage when a borrower becomes unemployed (Diamond and Lea 1992b).[11] But as the previous rates indicate, this level of public support is inadequate to counter the new market's increased tenure risk.

Housing policy

By the Thatcher period, Britain's avowed housing policy was the advocacy of owner occupation and the idea that state provision of social housing had failed (Kleinman 1996, 19–28). Promotion of these policies led to the privatization of social housing, reduced construction of new rentable social housing, and reliance upon private housing rentals. In 1980 the Right to Buy policy established the right of tenants in council housing and housing associations to purchase their homes at major discount from market prices with automatic local authority financing. In 1987, after scathing attacks on the public housing providers, a Tory White Paper voiced a new policy of support for the private rental sector (Malpass 1993, 81–2). Then, the passage of the 1988 Housing Act forced housing associations to rely primarily on private finance for new housing construction (Lomax 1995, 853), forcing the rents to more than double in some cases (Kleinman 1996, 40). By the 1990s, the desired result was achieved: Britain has the highest rate of owner-occupation among the OECD nations.

The effect of this privatization policy has been to allow into social housing only those too economically incapacitated or too poor to afford market-provided housing. Social housing has been reduced to the tenure of last resort (Malpass 1993; Maclennan 1995).

These policy changes have meant increased entry and tenure risk for newly formed households, the unemployed, single-head-of-household families, and the elderly. The supply, quality, rent, and availability of rental housing play a determinant role in the level of life-cycle risk for these groups. As data from Boleat (1985) and Whitehead (1993) indicate, the number of public and private rental units had declined by almost 2 million between 1979 and 1990. In addition to fewer available dwellings, the rents had skyrocketed. Local authority rents rose from £401 to £1,237 between 1980 and 1990, while dwelling prices moved from £23,000 to £64,6357, forcing private rental rates up along with them. In this same time period, the proportion of income spent on rents moved from 9 percent to 15 percent; on housing it rose from 12 percent to 19 percent. The combination of increasing rents with fewer, more expensive dwellings meant increased life-cycle risk for Britons.

---

11 John Major's recent budgets cut these housing support benefits, extending the length of the time period of unemployment before housing benefit payments commence and reducing payment levels for qualifying households. These cuts obviously increase households' tenure risks directly.

Housing and housing finance in France

France has a history of heavy state intervention in housing and financial markets. The French government has subsidized low-income housing since 1912, primarily through a system of locally controlled housing organizations, or HLM. The HLM were the descendants of the philanthropic communes established in the 19th century; in the early 20th century, the HLM were funded and taken over by local governments and construction interests.

After World War II, war damage, a disorganized financial system, and population increase created a vast housing shortage. This shortage exerted great upward pressure on the rental prices for usable units, and consequently drove entry, reentry, and tenure risk to politically dangerous levels. To combat tenure risk, the French government endorsed rent controls on existing rental units in the 1948 Rent Act and provided a rental assistance program to some households in unaffordable housing (the Allocation Familiale de Logement, or AL). Participation in AL was categorical – that is, it was available to certain household categories (such as families with children), not universally (Wood 1990). To combat entry and reentry risk, "the greater proportion of state aid to housing has, since the war, been directed toward the construction of dwellings...with little discrimination in allocation of funds between income groups" (Pearsall 1984, 12).

The HLM, whose mandate encompassed low- and moderate-income households, were the principal conduits for the social housing construction surge, although many subsidized private dwellings were also built. By 1970, social housing accounted for 15 percent of French housing stock but 60 percent of all rental units (Boleat 1985). These housing construction initiatives were financed by a 1 percent corporate tax for housing and by government construction subsidies – notably, HLM financed their projects at 2 percent interest repayable over 65 years.

Even in the shadow of World War II, however, the French government began developing its distinctive approach to housing: it continually took steps to encourage housing construction and the revival of market-based housing, while focusing its resources and subsidies either directly or indirectly on households in need of assistance. For example, the 1948 Rent Act that imposed rent controls on existing units decreed that no controls would apply to new units. Further, the French mortgage interest deduction is much less attractive than in Britain and the U.S. – only 25 percent of mortgage interest can be deducted from tax liability, and only for five years – and this tax writeoff was adopted only in 1983 (Wood 1990). While efforts to assure that all segments of the population are well housed has been de facto policy since the war, only in 1989 was a law implementing a right to housing explicitly adopted (Schaefer 1993, 172–6). In effect, the French have historically mitigated life-cycle risk with a combination of imperfectly coordinated categorical and universal guarantees.

French policy concern has always centered on how to create financing mechanisms that could increase the level of market-based housing. While the Bretton Woods system was in place, this preoccupation with finance constraints was necessary because the French capital markets are relatively thin, located as they are between the chronically strong-currency German state and the City of London. Very long-term mortgages could not be supported, so in 1965 the government implemented a program allowing households to put tax-free deposits into savings banks to be used for homes they intended to purchase in the future. All households also have the right to establish tax-protected savings accounts for every individual (including children) and to borrow against these accounts for housing-related purposes up to specified maxima.

The end of the Bretton Woods system heightened financial pressure on the French system, sometimes requiring measures to protect the franc (and French financial markets) from external pressures, even at the expense of making these markets less functional in allocating credit. In 1972 severe pressure on the franc led to credit controls, which remained in effect for 15 years. These controls included a rule that commercial banks could not make loans of more than 10 years' maturity – thus precluding these institutions from participating in financing housing.

Rising personal incomes and public willingness to absorb higher housing costs led the French government to implement reforms in 1977 that further encouraged market-based financing and home ownership (Boleat 1985, 165–6). Housing finance was opened more thoroughly to general intermediaries. Commercial banks were allowed to enter the mortgage market (by relaxing the loan-maturity ceiling mentioned above), and a secondary market facility was established. This law further bolstered homeownership by creating two new categories of loans: the unsubsidized contractual loan·(the *pret conventionne* or PC), provided by private banks, which entitled recipients to participate in the housing allowance program; and a new category of subsidized homeowner loan, the *pret aidé a l'accession a la propriete* (PAP), provided by the publicly owned Crédit Foncier de France. These new loan programs were designed to supplement the older housing-savings system. By 1982, the PC and PAP constituted 15 percent and 19 percent, respectively, of outstanding homeowner loans, with housing savings loans constituting another 19 percent and conventional mortgage loans just 19 percent (Boleat 1985, 165).

The 1977 reforms also signaled a shift away from "bricks and mortar" subsidies (as epitomized by the *sector aidé* loans, which were radically cut). To compensate for the reduced public efforts to supply housing, the government created a supplement for lower-income households, both renters and homeowners, termed the *aidé personnalizee au logement* (APL). While the APL is an income-related housing subsidy, it is units and not households per se that are supported. By 1984, 19 percent of owner-occupants were receiving either APL or the older AP assistance, versus 24 percent of tenants in private rental housing and 41 percent of those in social housing (Wood 1990). Over time, the concentration of APL aid in social housing, combined with the increased ownership opportunities for financially able households, have led to the concentration in social housing of lower-income households, a disproportionate number of whom are ethnic minorities (Harloe 1995).

Diamond and Lea describe France as moving in the 1980s and 1990s "from a heavily segmented, subsidized, regulated system toward a market-driven system" (1992a, 39). Certainly most of the new rent controls imposed by the Socialist government in the early 1980s were relaxed in 1986 (except for selective local controls)

(Gyourko 1990). And certainly the French depository system felt the strain in these years of the same financial-market pressures that had hit the U.S. and the U.K. 10 years earlier: corporations began accessing money and capital markets directly for credit, and mutual funds took deposit funds away from banks. French banks responded to the new competitors by taking risks and lending at low margins – just as the Basel Accords were setting new capital adequacy standards. Subsequently, many French banks have had to take steps to improve their balance sheets. Among these steps are the strategic use of loan securitizations, pursuant to a 1989 law providing for closed-end securitized loan pools.

Marketization in France

But evidence is also plentiful that the French embrace of market allocation was tentative at best. For one thing, 23 percent of 1990 mortgages were funded by explicitly subsidized lending (between PAP and PC loans). And the other 49 percent of mortgages financed by depository institutions are implicitly subsidized because these lenders' deposits pay below-market (or even zero) interest rates. In 1989, 56 percent of commercial banks' liabilities were deposits, of which 78 percent were short-term or regulated accounts (though it should be noted that France lacks deposit insurance).[12] Only about 28 percent of all mortgages were funded in 1990 by securities sold in financial markets; of these, half are finance company placements, while the other half are placements – primarily for subsidized PAP loans – by the Crédit Foncier.[13] For another thing, French markets continue to feel the effect of financing constraints. Competitive mortgages are primarily fixed-rate instruments for 10–20 years with a loan-to-value ratio in the range 60–80 percent; as such, they are insufficient to fully fund most households' home purchases. Thus, households still rely on multiple loans from multiple sources to obtain housing. Some of the supplemental loans are subsidized. The most important of the explicitly below-market, supplemental loans are the *plans d'epargne-logement* (PELs) and the *comptes d'epargne-logement* (CELs); these loans are provided in the wake of contract or household savings plans. PELs and CELs are often considered first mortgages.[14]

Loan securitization has not directly affected French housing finance as it has in the U.S. and U.K. Two factors have prevented securitization of French housing loans. First, the data needed to calculate prepayment risk do not exist; in any case,

12 This system is perched to undergo a transition similar to that in the U.S. French banks have traditionally relied on widespread cross-selling of financial services, with mortgage lending viewed as part of a long-term relationship with customers who save, conduct transactions, and carry out other financial functions at their banks. This pattern is being challenged by the growth of securities markets (Bruneel 1992). Money market mutual funds (*monetaires*) have grown exponentially, until now their amount equals just under 60% of banks' liquid deposit totals. *Monetaires* obviously constitute a longer-term threat to this mortgage-funding channel.

13 The largest residential lender in France is a public agency, the CDC, which finances public housing loans with low-cost deposits collected by savings banks in tax-free passbook accounts.

14 In systems that use multiple mortgages to finance home purchase, the number associated with any one mortgage is an indicator of that creditor's legal status in case of default. The lower the number, the higher the creditor ranks when the foreclosure is complete and its liquified assets are distributed.

French law makes it difficult for any lender to foreclose on a nonperforming housing loan. Second, French mortgages are in many cases offered at below market rates – in part as a reward for households' pooling of savings for housing purchases. The large proportion of below-market-rate loans makes it impossible to fund housing loan pools with funds paying the market rate. And much of the free market lending that has occurred – about 15 percent of all free market loans – has been supported by guarantees known as *cautions*. These guarantees are provided indirectly by Credit Foncier against a mortgage lien in the event of default, and only for the lowest-risk loans. The system closely resembles the Federal National Mortgage Association (FNMA, or Fannie Mae) underwriting in the U.S. (see Stone and Zissu 1992), including the implicit government subsidy that makes the market liquid.

Finally, and perhaps most tellingly, the government's Credit Foncier has operated in another way to soften the verdict of market-based risk bearing. Many households that obtained loans in the 1981–85 period did so at very high (fixed) nominal interest rates, in booming real estate markets. Subsequently, many of these households' loans generated unsustainable tenure risk for low- and middle-income owners. The Credit Foncier stepped in to help these households renegotiate these loans at terms more suited for the subsequent low inflation environment of the late 1980s and 1990s. Further, the "law scrivener" has protected lower-income households against excessive indebtedness. Because of this interference in the markets, and because free entry has kept profit margins low, the mutual, savings, and state-owned banks have had difficulty selling equity shares.

In sum, the French system has both historically and today been characterized by a large amount of public underwriting, guarantees, and other activity – all aimed at keeping households' life-cycle risks and intermediaries' financial risks to a minimum. At the same time, financial risks have grown. Liquidity risk, borne by banks and other lenders, is high due to the undeveloped character of secondary markets; the growth of *monetaires* (money market mutual funds) may heighten banks' financial risks. Intermediaries still bear a large amount of financial risks: they face considerable repayment and interest rate risk, though they face only minimal default risks because of French laws that protect lower-income households against default. Whether protections against life-cycle risk will be maintained for all households, however, is unclear, due to the increasing social divide between homeowners and those in social housing – a divide that some have not been slow to exploit for political gain. The growing association of low-income status with minority ethnicity may challenge the long-standing French commitment to *egalité, liberté, fraternité*.

Housing policy and finance in Germany

After World War II the German government implemented a housing policy aimed at rationing the existing housing stock and stimulating the construction of new rental housing. Throughout the postwar period the government has played a central role in housing the nation. Even when the Conservative-Liberals controlled the government in the 1980s and encouraged more market-based allocation in housing, the active role of government was never questioned.

Housing policy

German housing policy and other social programs start from the widely held premise that its citizens' social welfare should not be left entirely to the market. This philosophy, *soziale Markwirtschaft*, means the market must be socially responsible. In response to the decimated state of available shelter after World War II, the 1950s housing programs strove to increase housing supply and keep rental costs down. As in France, subsidies for new housing construction and rent control on both new and old housing formed the heart of these programs.

Unlike other OECD nations, Germany had a booming economy in the 1970s, and this boom spurred housing construction. In the 1980s the Conservative-Liberals ascended to power. Thinking the housing shortage problem solved, they dismantled rent controls, cut back on construction of social housing, and implemented a housing allowance (Tomann 1990; Kleinman 1996). That is, they acted like the conservatives in power in Britain and the U.S.

By the mid-1980s, the housing situation had changed: a new crisis had emerged. Now there was, again, a need for housing, but demand was met by shortage. In response to increased demand, prices rose, and private investment in housing increased. At the same time, government responded by building more social housing. From its nadir in 1987, when it accounted for only 19 percent of new housing, social housing rebounded to account for on average 30 percent between 1990 and 1992 (Kleinman 1996,108–9). Even though there was a resurgence in social housing construction, it has not played the same role in the 1990s as in earlier times. As in Britain, France, and the U.S., this housing is increasingly being used to house the poor, not a cross-section of the working population. Unlike in these other countries, however, the owner-occupier is not the dominant form of tenure, so the role of private rental housing remains an important one.

Housing finance

The housing finance system in Germany funds both social and private housing, hence both rental and owner-occupied dwellings. This lack of distinction is important, since a majority of German households rents its housing. In 1967, only 32 percent of the population were owner-occupiers, and at the height of owner-occupancy, the 1980s, only 43 percent claimed that tenure. In 1991, owner-occupation fell to 40 percent (EC Mortgage Federation 1990). Of the over 60 percent of the population that rents, 15 percent live in social housing (Ball and Martens 1990).

Housing finance is accomplished through a large set of financial institutions, each of which, historically, has specialized in an aspect of lending. The historically important lenders, savings banks, mortgage banks, and *Bausparkassen*, were joined by the commercial banks in the 1970s in a new form of universal banking, *Allfinanz*. Transformation of the system via mergers and acquisitions resulted not in new financial institutions or instruments, only in heightened competition among the different product lines.

The German mortgage origination process has usually been broken into two components: a first mortgage, historically emitted by a mortgage bank, and a second mortgage, provided by a *Bausparkassen*. A first mortgage is restricted by law to cover only 60 percent of a building's value, while a second mortgage can cover an additional 20 percent. A third mortgage, which has only recently emerged as a necessary part of housing finance, can cover up to 10 percent. With the advent of *Allfinanz*, the institutions and their share of the mortgage market changed. Commercial banks originated almost 7 percent of first mortgages and over 15 percent of second mortgages by 1983, almost a doubling in share in each market compared to 1970. The other lenders all lost in these markets, except for mortgage banks, which gained 1 percent in second mortgages in this same time period (Ball 1990, 171).

In addition to these institutional rearrangements, borrowers were feeling the impact of rising house prices and interest rates in the 1970s. As an adaptation to these rising prices, a third mortgage, which was unsecured, became common. The question now hiding under all these changes is, what effects were these changes having upon the risk within the financial system and the life-cycle risk of the population?

Financial risk

According to Kregel (1993), the German financial depository system, even with its universal banking structure, is governed by a strong "prudential" set of regulations. Financial institutions are supervised closely, so they must adhere to strict rules. Important among them are the requirements for matching maturities of assets and liabilities, limitations on loan sizes and their proportion to deposits, capital adequacy rules, and distributions of risk levels on loans (Kregel 1993, 671–2).

Institutions that also rely on funds from capital markets – such as the mortgage, commercial, and savings banks, which use bank bonds or a collateralized pool of mortgage bonds to fund their loans – are still subject to these same prudential regulations (Ball 1990, 183; Kregel 1993).[15] These markets are especially important for third mortgages, which are unsecured. The unsecured bond market is highly liquid, and the third mortgages that savings and commercial banks originate are both reviewable rate (variable rate) and renegotiable (fixed-rate for one to 10 years, but usually less than five years). So the interest rate risk for the institution is attenuated, but the default risk for the borrower is increased. As for the ever-present innovation in a market system, regulators have been carefully watching market developments and incorporating the new financial instruments into their regulatory requirements (Kregel 1993, 672). Beyond the regulatory net also lies the confidence that the central government would intervene to prevent the failure of a major bank (Ball and Martens 1990).

Another aspect of the German banking system, the ownership structure of financial institutions, also prevents innovations from necessarily increasing the individual or systemic level of risk. The majority of financial institutions are publicly or cooperatively owned. Savings banks are publicly owned and operate only within the

---

15 While the use of mortgage bonds is historically widespread in Europe, these differ significantly from the securitized mortgage bonds now heavily used in the U.S. and Great Britain (Hullender 1991).

jurisdiction of their regional public authority, so these geographical structures limit their competitiveness. Mortgage banks and *Bausparkassen,* also, are at least partially owned by public authorities. This public ownership has led to cooperative relationships rather than competitive ones (Ball and Martens 1990, 177).

Household risk

Have the risks born by households increased with the changes in housing policies and the financial structure? Borrowers in the restructured system bear the same risks they had before – default risk, tenure risk from interest rate volatility in a variable rate mortgage, and entry risk due to high equity requirements. But have the financial and housing policy changes produced higher risk levels? And how have renters been affected?

The push to homeownership found many buyers in default or in foreclosure and arrears in the 1980s. For the private borrower, the risk profile remained the same, but between 1980 and 1985 there was an increase in defaults: from an average of 0.1 percent to 0.5 percent (Diamond and Lea 1992a, 98). Martens estimates that, while troubled borrowers remained a small proportion of outstanding mortgages, defaults and foreclosures doubled between 1980 and 1985. This period in the 1980s indicates an increased degree of turbulence for borrowers, and the increase in defaults produced increased tenure and reentry risk.

Unfortunately, during the 1980s both private and social housing construction declined, so the number of housing units actually decreased in net terms. Thus, the rental housing policies tended to exacerbate the risks experienced by those who defaulted. The government did attempt to respond to the housing market's changes by replacing its "bricks and mortar" policies with the housing allowance, but the shortages persisted.

Overall, life-cycle risk is less prevalent in Germany than in either the U.S. or Great Britain. Entry, tenure, and reentry risks are attenuated by a robust rental sector. However, this statement should not be misconstrued. The social housing sector experienced selloffs in the 1980s and declines in construction that diminished its capacity to provide housing for the population (Harloe 1995). While the 1990s saw a resurgence in social housing construction, new problems of de facto segregation by race, income, and ethnicity have changed the nature of life in social housing (Kleinman 1996). The question of whether the government's investment in housing will continue as German politicians try to reduce their budget so as to be in compliance with European Monetary Union admission criteria also looms unanswered.

Policy discussion and conclusion

Financial internationalization is here, but the era of financial globalization has not yet arrived. Housing finance systems have not become homogenized and standardized in OECD countries. The claim made by many (such as O'Brien 1992) that financial innovations have necessitated the homogenization of housing finance systems is wrong. There is little evidence that capital has moved across borders to purchase mortgages or mortgage-backed securities, in large part because European countries have been unable or unwilling to replicate the characteristics of U.S. mortgage-backed securities.

There has been a widespread move toward market-based allocations of housing resources. However, these shifts have not been uniform; and they have by no means created standardized financial instruments with uniform risk characteristics. The interweaving of market risks with national policies and (national) budgetary commitments makes even instruments that are similar on the surface very different in practice. Consider, for example, the very different procedures that accompany homeowner default in the countries examined here: except in the U.S., homeowners are cushioned – but this cushioning depends on government commitments that are not written in stone. Further, our cross-country comparison has shown that marketizing housing finance does not make housing systems more socially efficient. Indeed, some of the nations faced with the most desperate housing supply and housing affordability gaps are those that have moved most rapidly to market-oriented systems of finance.

The proponents of marketization have predicted that globalization would bring about a homogenization of allocation processes and a convergence of prices. But a unified world market has not emerged, and none is in view. Instead governments have, of necessity, continued to play vital roles in allocating national resources, and market arrangements have continued to reflect the historical, social, and cultural mores of their societies. Decisions on regulation, completeness, and efficiency continue to be based both on economic theory and on cultural perceptions and priorities.

The financial innovation and economic disruption that prompted change in housing policy and finance in the 1970s and 1980s did not produce a uniform international response. Among the nations examined here, there is evidence of a "universal shift away from subsidies to housing suppliers, in favor of subsidies to lower-income households on the demand side of housing markets" (Kemp 1990). But otherwise the experience with these nations' reallocation of risks and rights has been very diverse. The U.S. has reduced intermediation risks while allowing households' lifecycle risks to rise, especially for those with lower incomes. Britain has allowed entry risk to rise for the poorer households who cannot afford private-sector rents and lack the wealth for a downpayment. Germany has reduced its engagement in social housing, but other sectors – especially the private for-profit and nonprofit and the cooperatives – have leaped into the breach. Still, affordable housing is a problem for the very poor. France, with its large social rental base, has made efforts to spread housing subsidies evenly among all the poor; this has kept tenure risks down, but entry and reentry risks are at all-time highs. Meanwhile, the housing performance of the private sector in the U.S. and U.K., the most thoroughly marketized economies, has been mediocre in producing affordable lower-income housing units.

However, certain general themes emerge amidst these diverse reactions to globalization:

(1) government remains an important actor in the housing market;

(2) risk has been shifted from financial institutions to households;

(3) this shift in risk may lead to increased distress for financial institutions and households; and

(4) the social contract for housing has been discarded; a new contract should be negotiated.

In the United States, where the safety net is woefully frayed, housing policy changes have already increased not just the number of households unable to afford the "American dream," but also the number of those who can no longer afford to house themselves. Homeownership rates are declining, the rental stock is declining in both number and quality, and the lack of affordable housing for the poor has reached crisis proportions. Schwartz, Ferlauto, and Hoffman (1988) have estimated that 2 million new housing units are needed annually to meet housing demand, but housing unit growth will be less than 1.5 million. And while deregulation and securitization led to greater housing finance access for some middle- and high-income families, these shifts have, taken together, increased financial risk for low-income families, in many cases leading to the ultimate tenure risk – homelessness.

This situation calls out for the negotiation of a new social contract for housing provision. An appropriate starting point is the Housing Act of 1949, which declares:

> ...the general welfare and security of the Nation and the health and living standards of its people require housing production and related community development sufficient to remedy the serious housing shortage, the elimination of substandard and other inadequate housing through the clearance of slums and blighted areas, and the realization as soon as feasible of the goal of a decent home and a suitable living environment for every American family, thus contributing to the development and redevelopment of communities and to the advancement of growth, wealth, and security of the Nation (81st Congress, 1949, 413).

This law states the rationale and goal of the old social contract – to provide adequate, affordable housing. The law's weakness resides in its failure to concretize the goal with housing unit numbers, budget allocations, and financing arrangements. By incorporating these tangible elements into the already-stated goals, the outline of a new contract starts to emerge.

In constructing the new contract, the changing nature of families and work must be recognized. This recognition is important because the low-income households that have especially felt the problems of affordability and homelessness in the new era of global leveling are disproportionately households without a male wage earner. Minority households and households headed by males without a college degree also fall through the cracks in housing policy. The current restructuring of households into diverse configurations – households headed by single women, households of grandparents raising grandchildren, households of unrelated adults that are both with and without children, and single-person households – means that housing needs too have changed. The changing nature of the family has also resulted in a reduction in the size of households. The size of a dwelling required for these households is smaller than in the past (Apgar et al. 1991; Fronczek and Savage 1991; Levy and Michel 1991; Maclennan 1995).

Along with the new household is a new structure of work. In the post-World War II period the "social compact" struck in numerous countries meant employees were able to rely on stable long-time employment patterns. In middle-income occupations it was the "job for life," with a single employer work scheme that dominated; and in working-class occupations, high-wage unionized jobs dominated. With the globalizing of output and input markets and the breaking of the "compact," wages have fallen and the notion of long-term employment with a single employer has been lost to a "downsizing is rightsizing" view (Glyn et al. 1990). These changes have produced an income distribution that is more skewed and have pushed many employed workers into the category of the working poor. A new contract must acknowledge these changes, so that the emerging housing needs generated by a reorganizing economy can be met.

In a previous paper (Dymski and Isenberg 1995), we delineated various Housing and Urban Development and state-backed programs that arrange forms of housing finance that are nontraditional for the U.S.: lease-purchase mortgage loans, community land trusts, sweat equity downpayments, and below-market interest rates. Also included in our policy analysis was a proposal for using community development banks to finance mortgage lending. These policies are novel in the American context. Looking more broadly at other countries' experiences, one can see a much greater variety of proposals, and, hence, the possibilities for appropriate combinations of policies multiply. With the menu of possibilities thus enriched, a good deal of future research is required before we can tell what combinations would work best in different environments.

Still, the set of proposals described above does give one example of a program that can provide affordable, adequate housing that reduces household life-cycle risk. It is therefore indicative of the possibilities that could emerge if we were successful in implementing a new social contract.

Comment by Jane D'Arista on "Housing finance in the age of globalization: from social housing to life-cycle risk"

The particular contribution of this chapter is that it creates a new context in which to reassess the benefits and drawbacks of the changes in housing finance over the last two decades that have been widely debated in both academic and political arenas. The comparative experiences of the four countries examined here – the United States, the United Kingdom, France, and Germany – underscore the differences in the mechanisms they have used to achieve the goal of providing adequate housing stocks as well as the different ways in which housing finance in each country has been transformed. Nevertheless, the paper finds a strong commonality in the reduction in government support for housing as a social good in all four countries. Moreover, it describes the erosion in households' access to adequate and affordable housing that has already occurred, arguing that a continuation of current finance systems is certain to further reduce access for low-income families and increase financial and life-cycle risks for most families.

While the paper discusses governments' withdrawal from their former role in supplying affordable housing, the primary focus is, as noted, on changes in housing finance, and the commonality in the experience of these four countries is deregulation. The authors provide an especially useful analysis of the ways in which risks have been shifted from financial institutions to households – making the point that risk has only been shifted, not reduced – and that the increased risk for households can only lead to a symmetrical increase in risk for financial institutions. This point, I think, cannot be stressed enough: that there is increased risk in the system as a whole. Thus, the goal of deregulation in reducing government involvement in housing finance (or in many other areas of finance, one might add) has not been met. As clearly shown in the case of each country, governments remain important actors in mortgage markets. But they could become even more involved as increased systemic risk results in more numerous disruptions and even crises that require intervention, following a pattern of ex post socialization of risk that has become a more frequent method of resolving problems in both national and international markets.

The comparison between an efficient markets and a social efficiency approach that the authors offer here is a too-short version of this innovative and highly useful contribution made in an earlier version of the chapter. Their analysis of the life-cycle risks of households contributes an invaluable perspective to the discussion of the pros and cons of changes in housing finance and policies that has tended to focus primarily on financial risks. If one adds "systemic" to the list of financial risks, the need to include life-cycle risks in an evaluation of efficiency becomes even more compelling.

Another contribution of the paper is the very useful distinction it makes between financial internationalization and financial globalization. While I agree with the distinction, I believe the actual role of internationalization in transforming both housing and housing finance markets has been greater than described here. While the authors attribute changes in housing finance to deregulation in national markets, many would argue that deregulation was driven by the growth of unregulated external (Eurocurrency) markets that undermined all efforts to allocate funds that required regulatory support. Administrative regulations involving interest rate levels, reserve or liquidity requirements, or quantity restrictions on (or incentives for) credit flows were viewed by banks in countries of the OECD as costs to be evaded by shifting operations offshore. Thus, many governments bowed to ideological pressures for deregulation reluctantly but as a defensive response. The objective, in part, was to make national markets competitive with external markets; to repatriate funds back to domestic intermediaries in the hope that this would moderate unacceptable changes in the supply and cost of credit to borrowers who could not access the external markets.

The process of deregulation also included the importation of some of the innovations in financing that had been developed in the external markets – in particular, the widespread use of floating rates on loans. Their introduction in the 1970s as a means to shift the risk of recycling petrodollar deposits away from financial institutions to developing countries provides an illustration of the effects of this shift in risk to borrowers in a period before interest rate ceilings were removed in national markets. As the 1982 Third World debt crisis made clear, floating rates made it impossible for 15 countries to continue to service their dollar-denominated external debt as U.S. interest rates rose in the early 1980s. Moreover, the rapid escalation of nonperforming loans that threatened the viability of the international financial system undermined the assumption that floating rates reduce risk for lenders. Again, it is a practice that increases, rather than reduces, risk to both creditors and borrowers by increasing the risk that loans cannot be repaid.

In refuting claims that financial globalization has arrived, the authors make the very valid point that "housing finance systems have not become standardized or homogenized in OECD countries"; that globalization has not "brought about a homogenization of allocation processes and a convergence of prices." I would argue, however, that these may not be the best criteria to use in describing the effects of globalization on housing markets and housing prices. While it is true that "there is little evidence that capital has moved across borders to purchase mortgages or mortgage-backed securities," the substitution effects of capital flows have had very significant effects on both the cost of housing finance and of housing itself in many OECD countries, beginning with the rise in housing prices in Germany in the early 1970s in response to a torrent of capital inflows in anticipation of the realignments in exchange rates that effectively ended the Bretton Woods system.

The German experience was followed by an equally sharp rise in housing prices in the United States as intervention by foreign central banks in support of the dollar greatly expanded the stock of dollar-denominated foreign exchange reserves and greatly increased the share of foreign holdings of U.S. financial assets. Because dollar reserves were invested in the U.S. national market in Treasury bills, the Treasury choked off flows of domestic savings into government securities to accommodate the expansion of foreign holdings, raising the minimum denomination for individual purchases from $1,000 to $10,000. Given interest rate ceilings and the absence of yet-to-be-invented money market mutual funds, savings and loan deposits were the only place for nonaffluent households to put their savings. With so much money funneled into a single set of institutions with limited lending powers in so short a period of time (1971–73), the substitution effects of foreign official inflows resulted in driving up the price of existing housing rather than increasing the stock.

These substitution effects also played a significant role in the runup in housing prices in most OECD countries in the second half of the 1980s and the subsequent steep declines in the early 1990s. These changes in housing prices did not result in a single median price for housing across (or even within) countries, but they were at least as significant as changes in financing costs and, perhaps, more disruptive. Certainly, the policy objectives of national housing finance programs were undermined in all countries. In the U.S., the increase in tax expenditures associated with rising housing prices underscored the regressive shift in the allocative effects of this policy. A larger share of the benefits of the tax deduction for interest on home mortgages went to upscale homeowners, as more families who had previously qualified for mortgages on the basis of income failed to qualify at the higher price level.

In any event, this view of the role of international capital flows strongly supports the conclusions of this paper that deregulation and securitization have increased financial risk for low-income families; that a new social contract is needed; and that, while the goals have not changed, the means to achieve them must be updated to reflect changing characteristics of households and work. The arguments this chapter offers in support of these conclusions are powerful, and the message has grown even more important in the context of a new round of international financial crises that will tend to further undermine the stability of national and international financial markets.

Part IV

Trade, wages, and the environment: north and south

10

Openness and equity: regulating labor market outcomes in a globalized economy

Jim Stanford

Introduction

Advocates of interventionist employment and labor market policies have long recognized that the internationalization of economic relations held the potential to undermine the pursuit of domestic goals such as full employment and wage growth. As the architects of progressive labor market policies struggled to construct the instruments for employment and income regulation at a *national* level (including both macroeconomic demand management policies and more micro-level structures of labor market regulation such as unionization and minimum wages), the emergence of a fundamentally deregulated *international* economy threatened to undermine the effectiveness of these measures.

What has been the effect of globalization on labor markets, and on the institutions and policies that were established in the postwar era to promote more equitable and socially beneficial outcomes in labor markets and in income distribution generally? The answer to this question depends centrally on one's underlying theoretical model of what determines those labor market outcomes in the first place. In mainstream economic theory, where competition and market-clearing determine employment and income distribution in a fashion that is both self-regulating and socially optimal, international economic integration promises a movement of the global economy toward a more efficient general equilibrium position, thus creating the basis for a mutual, Pareto-improving increase in social well-being (across nations and potentially across social classes). In alternative models, demand side constraints become relevant, and labor market outcomes depend on an interaction of socio-institutional and macroeconomic factors; globalization may then have negative effects on both labor market outcomes and on the ability of existing policy instruments to regulate or offset those outcomes.

This chapter is divided into two major parts: a summary of competing theoreti-

The views expressed in this chapter are those of the author and should not be attributed to CAW-Canada. Nonincriminating thanks to Robert Blecker, Robert Pollin, Gerald Epstein, Dean Baker, and two anonymous referees for very helpful comments on earlier drafts. Much of the research contained here was conducted with the assistance and supervision of David M. Gordon, who will be sadly missed.

cal perspectives regarding the impact of openness on labor markets and income distribution, and an empirical application of one of those perspectives to the recent history of international economic integration in North America. We first review the theoretical assumptions underlying mainstream models of labor market equilibrium in an open economy setting, and summarize several recent applied mainstream studies of the importance of globalization in influencing recent labor market trends. We also summarize key insights from non-neo-classical, "heterodox" theoretical traditions, which together cast doubt on mainstream conclusions regarding the efficient and beneficial effects of international economic integration. However, even in heterodox analysis, which admits the *possibility* that a lack of competitiveness could undermine labor market outcomes in a globalized economy, there is disagreement as to the *practical* importance of the links between labor market outcomes, foreign trade and investment, and output. Empirical research is needed to better understand the complex balance of factors that will affect labor in a globalizing economy.

Thus, the second part of the chapter attempts to empirically operationalize an alternative theoretical approach (broadly labeled as "structuralist" – in recognition of the importance placed on structural and institutional, rather than market-clearing, determinants of income distribution, productivity, and competitiveness), using the historical experience of the Canadian economy as a case study of an attempt to regulate labor markets within a highly open international economic context. We find that openness in general has strengthened the mechanisms of profit-led growth in the Canadian economy, and made it more difficult for governments to regulate labor market outcomes directly. Some policy interventions still seem powerful, however, at regulating aggregate demand and hence indirectly strengthening labor markets – most notably efforts to stimulate investment expenditure (through, perhaps, direct public investment).[1] The labor market impacts of specific bilateral trade liberalizations (which have attracted much criticism from advocates of equity-promoting labor market interventions) are found to be potentially negative (unlike the predictions of mainstream models) but nevertheless quite small.[2] In general, the development of policies aimed at regulating effective demand (and investment in particular) in an open economy setting would seem to hold considerable potential for achieving more equitable labor market outcomes despite the constraints posed by globalization.

Contrasting theoretical approaches

The Walrasian tradition: theory and practice
Table 1 summarizes several of the key underlying theoretical assumptions of standard neo-classical economic theory, regarding both the microeconomic operation of labor markets themselves and the implications of globalization for labor market outcomes. The expectation of mutual gains resulting from international economic

1   The papers in this volume by Andrew Glyn and Robert Pollin also highlight the potential benefits of public investment in an open economy setting.
2   See the discussion in Section 3 for cautionary remarks regarding this finding.

Table 1 *Neo-classical and heterodox models of labor market outcomes: key assumptions and policy implications*

	Neo-classical model	Heterodox model
Determination of income distribution	Market-clearing; marginal productivity	Bargaining power; social & institutional structures
Determination of labor intensity	Automatic	Bargaining power; social & institutional structures
Primary employment constraint	Labor supply (supply-side)	Labor demand (demand-side)
Long-run unemployment	"Natural" unemployment is voluntary, and reflects labor market rigidities	Equilibrium unemployment is involuntary and recreated endogenously
Role of investment	Passive outcome of capital market clearing via flexible interest rate	Active, leading role; capital market clears via income effects
Macroeconomic constraint	Short-run "shocks" only; economy settles at full employment	Demand constraint is a normal feature of the aggregate economy
Importance of overall "competitiveness"	Not relevant	Affects demand constraint
Impact of globalization	More efficient factor allocation; win-lose factor price effects	Positive or negative impact on demand constraint and employment

liberalization follows directly from the Walrasian general equilibrium analysis of the functioning of factor markets. Market-clearing pressures, reflected in a flexible wage, "clear" the markets for labor and all other productive inputs. Market-clearing factor prices (including the wage) are determined by the real productivity of each factor. As for demand side factors, which might constrain employment at a level insufficient to absorb labor supply, the neo-classical model admits their relevance primarily in the short run. In the long run, the economy automatically settles at its full employment level of output. This continued belief in the self-adjusting nature of the full employment equilibrium[3] is still key to the mainstream view that international liberalization cannot undermine domestic employment and production.

At the international level, the labor market plays no special analytical role. Labor is simply one productive input among many, and labor costs are no more important than expenses on any other factor. Every trading nation is blessed with an endowment of the various factors of production, which in turn determines that nation's relative competitiveness in the international sale of particular classes of commodities. The problem of an economy's *overall* competitiveness in winning international

3   In modern versions of the assumption, the intervention of the central bank to maintain unemployment at its "natural" level is often invoked.

markets or attracting investment can never arise;[4] thus, any popular "obsession" with the importance of labor costs in determining competitiveness is seen as uninformed and misguided.

From the application of Walrasian value and distribution theory to the international economy, the famous Heckscher-Ohlin trade theorems are derived. Most important for our present purposes is the *factor price equalization (FPE) theorem*, which suggests that factor prices (and therefore commodity prices) will be equalized across trading countries.[5] With full employment and diminishing returns to substitution, as a country specializes in goods that use intensively its relatively abundant factor, the domestic price of that factor will gradually increase until the country's relative factor abundance (and thus its competitive edge in producing the commodity in question) has been eliminated. In a capital-abundant (and hence relatively high-wage) economy, wages will decline as barriers to trade with labor-abundant economies are removed; this, presumably, will be bad for "equity."[6]

Nevertheless, Walrasian analysis implies that welfare gains from trade should be derived by both trading partners. By definition, every economy can produce *something* competitively (by virtue of its *relative* abundance of *some* factor of production), and by specializing in that set of products it will benefit from trade. This result holds even if one country, for some reason, starts with an *absolute* cost disadvantage in the production of *all* traded products.[7] The real economic gains resulting from factor reallocation following liberalization will provide a basis for the compensation of those who may be temporarily displaced by trade-induced restructuring, or who may suffer lower factor incomes as a long-run consequence of FPE. The nation as a whole is left in a Pareto-improved position.

For Walrasians, therefore, the primary labor market policy issues raised by the process of globalization focus on attempting to smooth the process of factor reallocation (through an appropriate system of subsidies, assistance for retraining, etc.), and perhaps – in theory, at least – compensating FPE "losers" via a nondistorting program of transfer payments. There is a long literature in mainstream trade theory regarding the design of these compensating payments – which is ironic given their near-universal absence from real world policy discussions. In practice, the focus of

---

4   Krugman (1994a) takes trade policy writers to task on exactly this point.
5   Complete specialization may prevent full FPE, but the direction of change will be toward equalization.
6   This depends on the distribution of ownership of capital and labor assets, respectively; on the reasonable assumptions that capital is more narrowly owned and that capital-owning households tend to have higher average incomes, a decline in wages and an increase in the profit rate will indeed increase the inequality of income distribution.
7   In fact, in the strict Heckscher-Ohlin version of comparative advantage theory (unlike the Ricardian version), there is no apparent reason why any country should be at an overall disadvantage in the initial position. In a more general Walrasian model (in which technology is allowed to vary between countries), such an overall disadvantage could arise due to one country's overall superiority in productivity in all sectors. In this case, factor price adjustments will be required to reduce product prices in the uncompetitive country until the country's exports are competitive in the more productive economy's markets; free trade will still be welfare enhancing for both countries.

policy makers has been the implementation of modest measures to smooth the adjustment of displaced workers into new industries and to encourage displaced workers to accumulate capital (especially human capital).[8]

Note that in the absence of a compensation scheme, trade liberalization in a Walrasian model cannot be defended as a Pareto-improving policy change. The virtually universal absence even of proposals for such schemes in real world trade policy discussions (let alone support for making trade liberalization *contingent* on compensation) must therefore be seen as somewhat contradictory to the equally universal faith of mainstream economists in the merits of trade liberalization – *if* the strict Paretian position is maintained that only policy changes that do not create "losers" can unambiguously be considered welfare enhancing. Mainstream proponents of free trade regularly gloss over this important distributional issue implied by their own model, sometimes by equating the social good with aggregate economic efficiency, or by appealing to offsetting effects (such as economies of scale) that are held to overwhelm FPE losses for particular groups. But this gap between pure welfare theory and mainstream policy practice is neither surprising nor especially damaging to the advocates of liberalization. Once the Walrasian view is accepted (at least implicitly) that free trade will indeed increase gross domestic product, "national" welfare, and overall efficiency, then the argument that free trade should nevertheless be opposed because of a failure to compensate FPE losers (who represent, in the Walrasian view, an interest group that has profited from efficiency-destroying barriers to trade) will not carry much weight in modern policy debates.

Continued development of mainstream international trade theory has generated a rich range of variations on this underlying Walrasian theme. More complex and indeterminate models incorporating factor-market "distortions," sector-specific factors, economies of scale, and other "imperfections" can – in theory at least – greatly complicate the straightforward policy conclusions generated by the pure Walrasian model. In some cases, welfare *losses* may even result from international economic integration under imperfect market circumstances. Once again, however, the gap between pure theory and applied practice is a large one, and most of these models remain theoretical curiosities with little impact on policy direction. In the case of factor-market distortions, the first-best policy prescription in virtually every case is to attempt to eliminate the offending domestic distortion (by reducing trade union power, eliminating minimum wages, or taking other steps to make factor markets more "competitive"), rather than to interfere with international economic relationships. And in the case of models that incorporate various versions of scale economies, the more elaborate theoretical treatment has if anything tended to *reinforce* the policy bias in favor of international liberalization – by suggesting, for example, that the potential gains from scale economies could offset or even overwhelm FPE losses for adversely affected sectors.[9]

---

8   See Baily et al. (1993) for a typically mainstream set of policy prescriptions emphasizing trade liberalization combined with incentives for education and mobility.

9   In many cases, the theoretical attention given to increasing returns issues is far out of line with any conceivable real world applicability; Blecker (1996) makes this point in relation to

Growing public controversy regarding the impact of globalization on labor markets and income distribution in recent years has spurred some of the leading lights of mainstream international economics to undertake new applied empirical research into the relationship between economic openness and labor markets.[10] The bulk of this research has been dedicated to discounting, with the help of a variety of empirical evidence, public concerns that persistent unemployment and the stagnation of real wages (especially in Canada and the U.S.) have any significant connection to globalization. Any alleged deterioration in the economic prospects of workers is generally ascribed not to international trade, but rather to a skill intensive bias in technical change that has led to a negative structural shift in the demand for "pure" labor. Once again, the appropriate policy response, true to Walrasian tradition, is not to interfere with labor market outcomes and certainly not with international economic relations, but rather to encourage individuals to accumulate more of the skills that are in demand in the modern economy.

Interestingly, not all mainstream theorists accept the view that international economic integration has had benign implications for labor markets (at least in North America). A debate is raging between the preceding "pragmatists" and several writers who adhere more "purely" to the conclusions of Heckscher-Ohlin theory – despite the explosive political-economic implications of this analysis within a presumed labor-scarce economy such as that of the U.S.[11] Some research in this tradition has concluded that FPE effects have indeed played some (usually small) role in explaining the growing polarization of U.S. labor market outcomes. Once again, however, the focus of these studies is often placed on income differentials between "skilled" and "unskilled" workers (with the latter typically defined as a narrow minority of the labor force), rather than on the more broadly based decline in real incomes that has affected most categories of labor in North America; the approach also ignores the potential effects of international liberalization on demand side equilibrium and on institutional processes in labor markets (since, true to the Walrasian tradition, aggregate demand is not an issue, and factor prices are determined by market-clearing, not by institutions). Thus, the dominant policy prescription still fits nicely into the mainstream consensus: do not interfere with market processes in either labor markets or in international trade, but rather encourage workers to acquire more "skills" so that they, too, can benefit from the supply side efficiency gains of international liberalization. From a heterodox perspective, neither camp in this great "debate" has convincingly answered our key question – namely, has globalization undermined progressive employment and income distribution policies by diverting net export and investment demand toward less egalitarian low-cost re-

the NAFTA debate. In general, mainstream trade models have incorporated returns to scale in a very selective and one-sided fashion, with the effect of eliminating or minimizing the potential for one-sided trading relationships and uneven development that was highlighted by earlier, often heterodox writers (such as Sraffa, Graham, and Kaldor).

10 Notable contributions include Krugman and Lawrence (1993) and Lawrence and Slaughter (1993). Deardorff and Hakura (1994) and Belman and Lee (1996) provide surveys of this growing literature.

11 An important example of this latter approach is Leamer (1993).

gions? – since neither camp even admits this outcome as a possibility in the supply-constrained, market-driven model that they both accept.

The experience of European economic integration has provided another opportunity for applied research on the effects of liberalization on labor markets and institutional structures. Here the evidence is mixed, although there is certainly no indication of a dominant convergence in wages and labor costs.[12] Some studies have found a *mild* tendency toward wage convergence, while others have noted a marked *divergence* of wage levels and even of unit labor costs (especially since the 1980s). These results suggest the continued importance of factors (perhaps including geography, industrial mix, or institutional factors) that are diffusing pressure for labor market harmonization, even within a unified European market.

Heterodox building blocks: micro and macro

Standard mainstream conclusions regarding the benign impact of international economic integration on labor market outcomes and social policy can be challenged with the help of insights gleaned from theoretical traditions broadly characterized as non-neo-classical, or "heterodox." Key assumptions and conclusions typical of this alternative approach are summarized in the right column of Table 1. It should be noted that these alternative perspectives do not always reach conclusions regarding the impact of overall labor cost competitiveness on aggregate trade and macroeconomic performance that contradict those of the traditional approach. But together they do cast doubt on several links in the overall chain of neo-classical analysis, and suggest several directions for an alternative model that – while not being unduly alarmist about the labor market implications of globalization – will at least lay the groundwork for a more balanced consideration of the issue.

Mainstream support for globalization derives clearly from the foundations of Walrasian general equilibrium analysis: factor-market clearing at the microeconomic level, and a consequent faith in self-adjusting full employment at the macroeconomic level. An alternative approach to understanding the effects of international economic integration can best be rooted, therefore, in a refutation of these micro and macro starting points.

Of course, a rejection of market clearing is a defining feature of heterodox theories of wage determination and income distribution. For the classical economists, wages were determined by the conditions of subsistence; for Marx, the definition of "subsistence" was socially constructed, dependent in part on the relative political-economic power of the conflicting classes. For Keynes and his stricter post-Keynesian adherents, wages are a "conventional" variable. Structuralist models in the Kaleckian tradition revive the Marxian emphasis on the "state of the class struggle" to explain wage determination, now also influenced by the state of aggregate demand.[13] Labor-intensity models emphasize the variability of labor effort, relating wages not only to the state of the socioeconomic institutions governing the labor market but

---

12 Recent works include Flanagan (1993), Collins (1994, Chapter 4), and Erickson and Kuruvilla (1994).

13 See, for example, Skott (1989).

also to the nature of technology.[14] In none of these cases does the labor market "clear," and no automatic link exists between wages and productivity (as is true of the Walrasian system). While productivity growth opens up the *possibility* of paying higher wages, with less impact on the competitiveness of a product or the profitability of investment, no objective, automatic mechanism links the two variables. The extent to which productivity growth is reflected in wages depends on the concrete determinants of bargaining power and income distribution. Unit labor costs (and hence the cost competitiveness of production) will vary over time and space, driven in part by variation in the socioeconomic regimes that govern the wage-setting and labor processes.

The heterodox rejection of the market-clearing analysis of price determination and income distribution also carries far-reaching consequences at the macroeconomic level. Positive unemployment is a normal feature of the capitalist economy, which (in most heterodox models) is typically demand constrained – such that changes in the intensity of demand will lead to changes in employment. This demand constraint is of tremendous importance in analyzing the impacts of international economic integration. Since globalization may now affect (positively or negatively) the employment of productive inputs, and not just the relative efficiency of a given amount of employment, demand side effects are crucial to the analysis of the final impacts of any policy change; the *overall* competitiveness of an economy (not just *relative* costs) becomes relevant to its open economy performance. Nor are these demand side effects transitory or short run in nature. In heterodox models, unemployment is not a short-run result of temporary rigidities or imperfections: it is the normal state of affairs. Moreover, since factor incomes are influenced by both institutional factors and aggregate demand conditions, factor endowments will no longer be a reliable guide to the direction of specialization in a liberalized environment.

Investment plays a uniquely important role in most heterodox macroeconomic models, and this importance is magnified in an open economy setting. Investment is no longer a passive outcome of the clearing of the market for capital – one that operates like any other, cleared by a flexible price (the interest rate) that ensures that all available factor supply (autonomous savings) are utilized efficiently in production. Instead, investment expenditure is granted a behavioral independence, carrying asymmetric importance as the demand injection that sets the capitalist productive process in motion. Factors affecting the volume and timing – and, in an open economy context, the spatial location – of investment will be highly relevant to the determination of macroeconomic equilibrium and hence employment.

Another common feature of the heterodox approach is that the distribution of income itself affects the demand side processes determining macroeconomic equilibrium. By disaggregating savings behavior across households, the strength of demand multipliers will tend (in a "Cambridge savings model") to increase with a redistribution of income toward labor. This introduces an element of indeterminacy

14 See especially Bowles (1985).

that has sparked a growing literature regarding the compatibility or incompatibility of "growth" and "equity." On the one hand, demand conditions will depend *negatively* on wages, through the impact of profitability on investment. On the other hand, demand conditions may depend *positively* on wages through the consumption function. If the latter effect predominates, the economy is wage led (or "stagnationist"); if the former predominates, it is profit led (or "exhilirationist"). Several recent writings have attempted to identify and define the conditions in which one effect or the other will predominate, with resulting consequences for demand, distribution, and growth. Of particular interest here, Blecker (1989) and Bhaduri and Marglin (1990) consider the implications of economic openness for a structuralist macroeconomic equilibrium; both find that profit-led mechanisms are likely to be significantly stronger in an open economy setting, due to the sensitivity of net exports to the cost competitiveness of the domestic economy and the effect of import penetration in reducing the domestic consumption multiplier.[15]

Heterodox analyses of globalization

What are the implications of these heterodox conceptions of microeconomic and macroeconomic processes for understanding the impact of globalization on labor markets and employment policy? Several heterodox contributions are worth reviewing in this regard. Brewer (1985) illustrates the potentially dramatic effects of international economic integration on output and employment in a non-market-clearing model when capital is permitted to be internationally mobile. Brewer shows that with fixed wages[16] and mobile capital, production location is determined by absolute labor cost advantage. When *either* capital is immobile *or* wages are flexible (in the market-clearing, full employment sense), trade reverts to a comparative advantage process. Brewer's model illustrates the dramatic consequences for the traditional model when factor-clearing assumptions are dropped and when capital is mobile. Similarly, Stanford (1995a) finds that it is international capital mobility, and not international trade in commodities, which opens up the possibility of adverse international shifts in the location of production motivated by labor cost savings alone. Without capital mobility, sustainable international differences in profit rates will tend to offset differentials in labor costs, so that high labor costs alone will not cause an economy to be generally uncompetitive in international trade. The possibility certainly exists (especially under capital mobility) that domestic labor market outcomes will be adversely impacted by economic integration with lower-cost jurisdictions.

But not all writers in the heterodox tradition then conclude that absolute labor costs (or at least absolute *wage* costs) are indeed crucial to trade and investment

---

15 Neither of these models considers the additional impact of net foreign investment flows, influenced by relative domestic profitability, on the wage-demand tradeoff; this would further strengthen the view that an open economy is more likely to be profit led. The econometric simulations reported below attempt to integrate this mechanism.

16 This assumption is *not* essential to his model, as long as wages are not determined by market clearing.

performance. Low wages alone are no guarantee of success in attracting investment and penetrating export markets. Rather, successful accumulation will depend
on the existence of a more complete and well-rounded set of socioeconomic conditions, including a stable and supportive institutional environment and a virtuous,
sustainable linkage of rising wages with enhanced productivity. For example, Gordon (1988b) finds low wages to be an inadequate explanation of successful open
economy development, both in developed and in newly industrializing economies;
he stresses instead the dynamic benefits of simultaneous accumulation, productivity growth, and wage growth in the achievement of competitiveness. The structuralist development literature has similarly stressed the importance of institution-
building and virtuous circles of productivity growth to the achievement of
international competitiveness.

Another set of heterodox models that is skeptical of the importance of labor costs
in international trade and investment places emphasis on the *nonprice* determinants
of international competitiveness. These include dynamic investment models originating with Kaldor,[17] which emphasize the benefits accruing to producers experiencing faster rates of capital accumulation and economic growth. Being more competitive on both cost and noncost bases, the faster-growing economy experiences greater
demand for its products and thus even faster growth: "growth breeds growth." A
dynamic investment climate, not lower wages, is required to enable an economy to
compete more successfully. Koechlin (1990) supports a similar view with his finding that investment in major countries of the OECD (Organization for Economic
Cooperation and Development) has been more responsive to purely domestic macroeconomic variables (such as growth in GDP) than to wage differentials and other
determinants of international variations in profitability. Fagerberg (1988) identifies
three distinct types of competitiveness in international trade: price competitiveness,
technological competitiveness (in the tradition of Schumpeter and Kaldor), and "capacity" competitiveness (that is, the ability to supply a product when competitors
may be supply constrained). Fagerberg finds the latter to be a particularly important
explanation for the poor trade performance of the U.K. and the U.S., where capacity
had grown (until recently, at least) more slowly than in other OECD countries. Subsequent work in neo-technology models of international trade has further developed
this view that static labor costs are relatively unimportant in determining international competitiveness and hence trade flows.[18] Of particular interest here, Johnson
and Stafford (1993) develop a model of technological convergence to suggest that a
deterioration in U.S. labor market conditions has resulted from the *loss* of technological leadership and the quasi rents which that leadership formerly earned. Com-

---

17 Indeed, in his original empirical work on this subject (1978b), Kaldor found that the fastest-
growing countries (measured with respect to both GDP and exports) tended to be those with
the *fastest*-growing relative unit labor costs (measured as unit labor costs expressed in a
common currency, weighted according to the relative importance of a country's trading partners). This has since come to be known as "Kaldor's Paradox" (Fagerberg 1988, 355). Kaldor's
models sparked a large literature on "deindustrialization"; see Stafford (1989) for a survey,
and Rowthorn and Wells (1987) for a critique from a structuralist perspective.

18 For recent examples, see Dosi et al. (1990) and Amendola et al. (1993).

petitiveness matters, but it is not labor cost competitiveness that is key. Also in a North American context, Milberg (1991), applying a Pasinetti-type model of dynamic process innovation to a sectoral analysis of Canadian foreign trade, finds that dynamic rates of innovation are at least as important as static productivity and hence unit cost comparisons in explaining relative export success.

However, regardless of what are considered to be the most important determinants of international competitiveness (wage or nonwage, cost or noncost), heterodox models agree that the demand side implications of the presence or absence of *competitiveness* are crucial to understanding the final economic impacts of international economic integration. This differs fundamentally from the mainstream model, in which national competitiveness is not an issue. Obviously, in a demand-constrained system, if a decline in competitiveness results in a loss of investment expenditure and the reallocation of demand (in both home and foreign markets) from home-produced to foreign-produced commodities, the immediate implication will be a tightening of the demand constraint on domestic output and hence employment.[19]

Conclusion: optimists, pessimists, and agnostics

In summary, the heterodox literature has not reached a consensus regarding the relative importance of labor costs in the determination of trade and investment patterns and hence the ultimate impact of globalization on labor markets. Clearly, when the assumptions of the traditional Walrasian approach regarding the market-clearing determination of factor prices and the supply-constrained nature of general equilibrium are relaxed, the *potential* is created that labor cost differentials will have important and possibly damaging implications for aggregate open economy economic performance. Heterodox models disagree, however, regarding the extent to which labor costs on their own are important in explaining the actual historical development of world trade and capital accumulation, as compared to alternative factors such as technological competitiveness or non-trade-related determinants of domestic investment rates. They also disagree on the extent to which poor trade performance explains adverse trends in labor markets, as compared to other equally plausible heterodox explanations of the same observed trends (such as the erosion of progressive labor market regulation or the restrictive stance of macroeconomic policy).

These differences in emphasis among contrasting heterodox perspectives are summarized in Table 2. Heterodox "pessimists" would view labor cost competitiveness as crucial to economic performance in an open economy setting, and expect that wages are the key determinant of cost competitiveness. Institutions have a direct and inflexible impact on income distribution (and hence on costs); indirect effects (such as the impact of aggregate demand on wages) are less important. Institutionally determined cost differences are not likely to be offset by other factors (such as exchange rate fluctuations), and hence the "race to the bottom" will continue until

---

19   And contrary to common practice, this loss of demand cannot be identified merely with a trade deficit. Thirlwall (1979) showed that demand conditions throughout an economy may endogenously tighten to eliminate a nascent trade deficit through negative income effects.

Table 2 *"Pessimists, agnostics, and optimists":*
heterodox perspectives on globalization and labor markets

	"Pessimists"	"Agnostics"	"Optimists"
Importance of cost to overall competitiveness	Key	Significant	Secondary
Importance of wage levels to cost competitiveness	Key	Significant	Secondary
Importance of productivity levels to cost competitiveness	Secondary	Significant	Key
Importance of institutions to income distribution	Key	Significant	Secondary
Importance of equilibrating mechanisms (exchange rates, income effects)	Secondary	Significant	Key
Sustainability of differences in socioeconomic regimes	Poor	Undermined	Still possible

institutional differences are eventually eliminated. The bleak conclusion is that globalization has severely undermined the potential for implementing progressive economic and social policies at a national level. This view is typical of many of the arguments made by labor advocates against recent economic integration initiatives in North America.

A more "optimistic" approach, on the other hand, would view wage levels as being of secondary importance to open economy performance, emphasizing instead the crucial role of nonprice competition in international trade and the importance of productivity and technological change in determining cost competitiveness. Indirect influences (such as aggregate demand pressure) on income distribution, along with other equilibrating factors,[20] will further serve to offset and stabilize imbalances in competitiveness that may be caused by international variation in labor market and social policies. The conclusion is happier: international differences in socio-

---

20 For example, the profit squeeze equilibrium described by structuralist macroeconomic models could itself serve an important equilibrating function: a loss of net export demand, by creating slack in domestic labor markets and hence falling labor costs, would be partly offset by a rebound of domestic investment. The opposite would occur in a competitive foreign economy, limiting its growth and success. Income effects on trade flows add further stability and balance to the model, as does the sensitivity of labor costs to aggregate demand conditions. Domestic fiscal and monetary policy might adjust to changes in international competitiveness, in ways quite different from those suggested by mainstream theorists. For example, the monetary authority might *tighten* in an uncompetitive country – both to increase unemployment and thus discipline labor costs, and to attract incoming foreign capital to help finance any trade deficit that is encountered in the interim. Fluctuations in exchange rates may also play an important, albeit poorly understood, equilibrating role.

economic regimes may be quite sustainable under globalization, and room continues to exist to press for progressive policies at the national level.

"Agnostics" might fall somewhere in between these two camps: labor cost competitiveness matters, but how much does it matter? Indeed, there are not clear *theoretical* distinctions between these various heterodox perspectives; they all agree that cost competitiveness can be important in determining the outcomes of international economic relations, and that neo-classical market clearing provides no guarantee that these relationships need be mutually beneficial. Rather, the appropriate degree of pessimism or optimism depends on the balance of cost and noncost, direct and indirect factors influencing labor market outcomes and competitiveness. In other words, the issue becomes an *empirical* one – in which case further concrete case studies are needed of the determinants of competitiveness and the relative importance of international competitiveness within the context of the overall determination of employment and income distribution. We now turn to one such empirical investigation.

Labor markets and competitiveness in the Canadian economy

Recent Canadian experience
Recent developments affecting Canada's domestic and international economic performance constitute a useful case study of the impacts of globalization on labor markets and economic policy. In the first place, Canada's economy is very open, and it has become markedly more so in recent years. Exports and imports now each constitute over 40 percent of Canadian GDP, compared to about 15 percent during the early 1960s.[21] Especially rapid growth in both exports and import penetration over the past five years, in the wake of the Canada–U.S. Free Trade Agreement (implemented at the beginning of 1989), has been unprecedented.

At the same time, however, Canada (until recently, at least) has attempted to pursue a somewhat different strategy of labor and social policy from that of its trading partners – different in particular from the U.S., which accounts for over 80 percent of Canada's foreign trade and a similar share of bilateral foreign investment. Labor market institutions and social policies have evolved in markedly different directions in the two countries over the past two decades, with consequences for wage determination and income distribution. For example, private sector trade union penetration is close to three times higher in Canada, real minimum wage protection has not been eroded, and social policy has been more forcefully interventionist in its efforts to modify the private pattern of income distribution. The consequence has been a growing gap between unit labor costs in the two economies – a gap that is even larger when the lower level and lower rate of growth of labor productivity in Canada is considered. Figure 1 illustrates the comparative trends in real unit wage costs (in national currency terms) in the two countries. Unit costs have fallen in both

21 It should be kept in mind, however, that these are gross flows, which double count the value of two-way trade in intermediate inputs. Far less than 40 percent of value-added or of final Canadian demand is internationally traded.

countries (reflecting both the generally weakened state of labor markets and the growing importance of nonwage labor costs), but the decline started sooner and has been much steeper in the U.S.[22]

What are the labor market and macroeconomic implications of this loss of labor cost competitiveness for Canada's economy, relative to an increasingly important "world" economy (which, for Canada's purposes, consists almost entirely of the U.S.)? The heterodox "pessimists" surveyed above would expect a severe loss of investment, production, and employment to occur in Canada as a result of the institutional divergence between Canada and the U.S. Consequently they would also expect, in the longer run, strong political-economic forces to emerge pressing for the harmonization of labor market institutions and social policies between the two economies. In one immediately visible manner, however, this deterioration in labor cost competitiveness has been offset (as a heterodox "optimist" might predict) by compensating changes elsewhere in the economy – in particular by a significant long-run depreciation in the real exchange rate.[23] Figure 2 indicates, indeed, that this depreciation has followed the changes in labor cost competitiveness relatively closely, with the result that in *common currency* terms the deterioration of the cost competitiveness of Canadian production has been much less severe. Indeed, by the mid-1990s a lower Canadian dollar had created a significant labor cost advantage for Canadian industry, which began to notably increase its share of total North American manufacturing investment and output.

Nevertheless, Canada's overall labor market performance during the recent period of heightened openness has not been particularly impressive. Unemployment has been chronically high: compared to an unemployment rate virtually equal to that of the U.S. in the early 1980s, Canada's unemployment rate has been almost twice as high through most of the 1990s. At the same time, real wages have declined (although not as quickly as in the U.S.), and wage polarization has grown markedly (as in other countries). Most ominously, a strong political tendency in favor of the dismantling of many of Canada's labor market and social policy innovations has emerged in recent years. The champions of this tendency sing approvingly from the same hymn book as did former Canadian opponents of the FTA: namely, that in an integrated global economy, no independent options for labor market and employment policy exist. The apparent *correlation* between the enhanced openness of Canada's economy and the regressive direction of both labor market outcomes and labor market policy would certainly seem to support the view of the heterodox "pessimists" reviewed above.

22   No comparable data on unit *total* compensation costs (as opposed to unit wage costs) is available on an economy-wide basis for the two economies. Unit cost calculations are further complicated by well-known difficulties in measuring hourly productivity (including measuring the working hours of salaried employees, adjusting for quality innovations in computers and other products, etc.); these difficulties are likely to affect Canadian and U.S. data similarly, so that the trend in relative costs is still approximately as indicated in Figure 1.

23   This long-run trend was interrupted by a strong but temporary appreciation beginning in the late 1980s, corresponding with the negotiation of the FTA and the adoption of much higher real interest rates by the Bank of Canada. By 1992 the Canadian dollar began to depreciate again. See Stanford (1995b) for a more detailed asset-market theory of exchange rate determination that is consistent with this competitiveness-equilibrating behavior of the Canadian exchange rate.

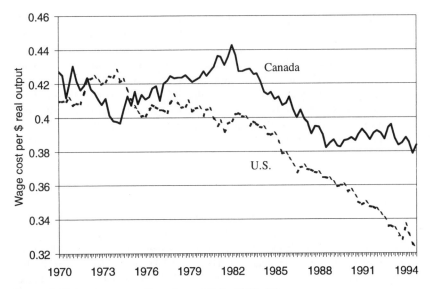

Figure 1 *Unit wage costs, Canada and U.S., 1970–94*

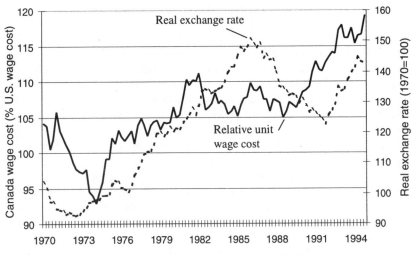

Figure 2 *Wage costs and the exchange rate, Canada, 1970–94*

Clearly there is a range of interacting and counteracting forces at work in explaining the strengths and weaknesses of Canada's economy and labor market under globalization. And so the following empirical exercise will attempt to incorporate the various factors affecting the relationships between labor markets, social institutions, competitiveness, and macroeconomic performance – including the *direct* impact of institutions on labor costs, the *indirect* influence of aggregate demand and productivity trends on labor market outcomes, and the *offsetting* or *stabilizing* impact of variables such as the exchange rate and monetary policy. Perhaps this approach can shed light on the extent to which globalization is to blame for the weakening of labor markets in Canada, and the extent to which it might still be possible for that country to pursue a relatively independent socioeconomic regime.

The model

The empirical simulations that follow are conducted with the use of an open economy macroeconometric model of the Canadian economy, corresponding broadly to a structuralist theoretical perspective. The model simulates production, employment, investment, aggregate trade balances, and key financial market outcomes for Canada, on the basis of quarterly data from 1960 to 1992.[24] The model contains some 45 endogenous variables, of which 20 are econometrically estimated stochastic equations. Modeled variables include standard macroeconomic aggregates, including private net investment, household consumption, inventory accumulation, depreciation, and the components of the current account.[25] Given our particular focus on the impact of labor cost differentials on the course of economic integration, the model also contains more labor market detail – including the determination of wages, productivity, employment, and labor supply – than is common in other macroeconometric models of similar size. Monetary policy is portrayed through a central bank reaction function;[26] inflation responds to aggregate demand conditions, monetary policy, and costs. Finally, the model also reflects considerable open economy detail, including a disaggregated determination of commodity trade[27] and the endogenous modeling of exchange rates, debt service payments, and migration; open economy linkages are also included in several of the domestic behavioral equations (including most importantly the determination of investment and interest rates).

The model's equations incorporate most of the usual behavioral mechanisms appearing in any medium-sized mainstream macroeconometric model. But they also include several chains of causation that together impart the model with structuralist properties. The most important of these are reflected within the following behavioral equations:

---

24 The exchange rate equation in the model is estimated from 1970, at the advent of a flexible Canadian exchange rate. Full details of the model are not reported here due to space constraints; see Stanford (1995a) for a full description, which will be sent to interested readers on request.

25 Government consumption is assumed to be exogenous.

26 Asset markets are not explicitly described in the model.

27 Six equations of the model describe bilateral export and import flows between Canada and the U.S., Mexico, and the rest of the world, respectively.

(1) consumption depends not only on disposable income but also on the *distribution* of income – varying negatively with the share of profits in GDP and positively with government transfer payments to (primarily low-income) persons.

(2) net private investment depends independently on profitability (including Canadian profitability relative to profit rates in other countries) and the stability of private property institutions; it also varies positively with the labor cost competitiveness of Canadian production.

(3) real wages are influenced by the range of structural and institutional features governing labor markets (including trade unionization, minimum wages, and income security programs).

(4) productivity is variable, responding to the same range of labor market institutions.

(5) monetary policy responds not just to changes in inflation, but also to changes in profitability and international competitiveness.

(6) inflation reflects distributional conflict via changes in unit labor costs and business markups.

(7) bilateral trade flows reflect absolute competitiveness on a number of grounds: labor costs, technological competitiveness, and "capacity" competitiveness (in the sense described by Fagerberg (1988)).

(8) the exchange rate reflects not only relative inflation rates and interest rates, but also the competitiveness and relative profitability of the domestic economy.

Estimation of the model's behavioral equations was conducted subject to usual statistical tests, and hence these structuralist chains of causation were included only when proven to be statistically relevant. This in itself is testimony to the relevance of socioeconomic institutions and distributional struggles in real world economic processes, and provides some insight into the relative importance of the different behavioral relationships we need to consider. For example, bilateral trade flows are indeed found to depend quite consistently on unit labor cost competitiveness; but Kaldorian "capacity competitiveness" (in which rapid accumulation is key to the penetration of world markets) is found to be an almost equally important determinant of trade success. Similarly, unit labor cost competitiveness and the relative level of foreign profits are significant determinants of domestic net private investment;[28] this supplements standard heterodox mechanisms visible in a closed economy setting (such as profitability). Finally, an additional interesting impact of globalization is captured by the two monetary variables that appear in the model: the interest rate and the exchange rate. The exchange rate (as suggested in Figure 2) clearly depreciates in response to an erosion of labor cost competitiveness; the domestic interest rate also increases with domestic unit labor costs, both to help defend the depreciating currency and perhaps to attempt to reduce domestic labor costs by imposing a tight-money "cold bath" on the macroeconomy.

More interesting than equation-by-equation econometric results, however, is the behavior of the entire model. Complete model simulations can better capture the

---

28 Indeed, as measured by its standardized regression coefficient, unit labor cost competitiveness is the single most important right-hand-side variable appearing in the investment function.

feedback and indirect links of causation that are so important to the simultaneous determination of costs, trade, output, and employment. In the following simulation experiments, a full base-case solution of the model is used as a benchmark. The estimated effects of policy shocks are then calculated by resimulating the model after incorporating the relevant exogenous shifts.

Simulated effects of trade liberalization

The Canada–U.S. FTA and the subsequent North American Free Trade Agreement with Mexico have received much criticism from the advocates of interventionist labor market and social policy in Canada for allegedly undermining the extent to which an independent Canadian direction in these policies can be sustained. We utilize model simulations to attempt to estimate the labor market effects of these two agreements.

Three different trade liberalization scenarios are simulated. The first simulation estimates the effects of the real world FTA that was implemented starting in 1989, by imposing a gradual reduction in tariffs phased in over a 10-year period starting in that year. This will provide an indication of the actual economic effects of that agreement to date. Since the 1989–91 data included within the model's full sample already reflect the first three years of the FTA, to simulate the effects of the actual FTA a counterfactual dynamic solution of the model must be conducted, on the assumption that tariff rates had stayed constant at the levels that were in place in 1988 (rather than declining gradually as required by the FTA). The estimated effects of the FTA will consist of the difference between this counterfactual simulation and the base-case solution.

The medium-run effects of *complete* North American trade liberalization are then estimated by imposing a full FTA and a full NAFTA, respectively, assumed to have been fully implemented in the first quarter of 1988. The FTA consists solely of the elimination (gradual in the real world case, immediate in the second experiment) of tariffs on bilateral trade between Canada and the U.S. The NAFTA consists of the elimination of tariffs on *all* intra-North American trade, as well as an exogenous 10 percent increase in the reported rate of profit in Mexico.[29] The estimated effects of NAFTA are reported *incrementally*, relative to a counterfactual base-case that already includes the estimated effects of the full FTA.

In addition to these three trade liberalization experiments, the results of three further policy simulations are also reported. A "pro-investment" simulation considers the economic impacts of an exogenous 1 percent increase in domestic investment. A constant exchange rate simulation estimates the likely impacts for the Canadian economy if the post-1989 real appreciation of the Canadian currency that was coincident with the implementation of the FTA had not occurred; it is assumed

---

29 This latter measure is an analog to the assumed reduction in the perceived risk premium on investment in Mexico that is incorporated into many model simulations of the impacts of NAFTA. No risk premium appears in the macroeconometric model, but increasing the Mexican profit rate has exactly similar effects. The increase in Mexican profitability is relevant in the model's investment equation, which considers trade-weighted foreign profitability as a determinant of domestic investment.

Table 3 *Trade liberalization simulations*
(change relative to no-liberalization base case by 1991.4)

	Actual, gradual FTA[1]	Immediate FTA[2]	Immediate NAFTA[3]	1% increase investment	Constant exchange rate[4]	Enhanced foreign comp'ness[5]
Cap. utilization (GSP)[6]	0.00	0.12	-0.02	0.13	10.56	-3.35
Investment[6]	-0.01	-0.05	-0.02	0.10	4.16	-1.88
Current acct. balance[6]	0.01	0.16	0.00	-0.07	4.27	-0.83
Unemployment rate[7]	0.00	-0.12	0.02	-0.06	-8.05	2.49
Exchange rate[8]	0.03	0.74	0.01	-0.04	17.91	2.75
Hourly wage[8]	0.00	-0.09	0.00	0.25	2.88	0.13
Profit rate[8]	0.00	0.78	-0.08	-0.49	33.46	-13.58
Relative ULC[8]	0.48	1.20	0.06	0.29	-11.96	7.04
Exports[8]	0.11	1.03	0.85	0.11	30.97	-4.91
Imports[8]	0.00	0.05	0.00	0.41	4.78	3.42

[1] Actual Canada–U.S. FTA tariff reduction schedule, beginning 1989.1.
[2] Immediate abolition of Canada–U.S. tariffs beginning 1988.1.
[3] Immediate abolition of intra-North American tariffs beginning 1988.1, and 10% reduction in risk premium on investment in Mexico; effects measured relative to full CUFTA.
[4] Real Canadian exchange rate held constant at 1988.1 level throughout simulation period.
[5] Unit labor cost competitiveness of foreign output improved by 10%.
[6] Change as percentage of potential output.
[7] Change in absolute percentage points.
[8] Change in percent.

in this case that the exchange rate had stayed constant at its average 1988 level. Finally, to further contrast the effects of *bilateral* trade liberalization with the effects of *one-sided* shifts in international competitiveness, a simulation is conducted that assumes a 10 percent increase in the unit labor cost competitiveness of foreign production. Each simulation is conducted from the relevant starting point (1989 for the real world gradual FTA, 1988 for the other simulations) and extends to the end of 1991. Simulation results are reported in Table 3.

The gradual real world FTA is seen to have virtually no economic impact on Canada. Modestly higher exports to the U.S. are roughly offset by a decline in domestic investment (resulting from the post-FTA deterioration in the unit labor cost competitiveness of domestic production). The impact of the FTA on overall aggregate demand and on labor markets is not visible. In contrast, a full and immediate FTA is seen to have marginally *positive* net benefits for Canada: lower investment is more than offset by stronger growth in exports, and an accompanying exchange rate depreciation adds strength to the expansion. Relative to a full FTA, NAFTA has very small negative implications for Canada – it produces a small decline in investment (by virtue of the increased attractiveness of Mexico as an investment site), but no offsetting net improvement in the current account (because of the extremely small trade flows between Canada and Mexico).

Note, then, that while the structuralist simulation admits the possibility that multilateral international economic liberalization could indeed undermine domestic labor market conditions (as NAFTA was simulated to do), the expected size of these effects is very small. This immediately casts some doubt on the contention that trade policy per se has played a major role in recent adverse labor market or social policy developments.[30] Note also, however, that the model is definitely not capturing the full extent of the competitive pressure and industrial restructuring that has been unleashed by North American trade liberalization. The simulated increase in exports after the real world FTA is only a fraction of a percentage point, and the increase in imports barely discernible; these small estimated effects result from the very small size and gradual pace of the FTA tariff removal and from the very small *apparent* price elasticity of demand included in the estimated export and import equations. In fact, of course, trade flows have changed hugely in the wake of the FTA (although not solely *because of* the FTA): Canada's exports and imports have actually grown by over 50 percent each since the implementation of the FTA. This is testimony to the inability of this type of model – estimating changes in trade flows as a product of a change in tariff-adjusted prices and a price elasticity of demand – to capture the structural effects of trade liberalization.[31]

The apparently secondary importance of mutual trade liberalization in explaining changes in Canadian economic performance is reinforced by the results of the other policy simulations. The pro-investment simulation suggests that just a 1 percent policy-induced increase in investment produces economic benefits for Canada that are substantially larger than the benefits from North American trade liberalization. This suggests strongly that trade liberalization is not the "engine of growth" that its proponents claim; even extremely modest policies aimed at stimulating domestic demand can have significantly larger positive impacts. The counterfactual simulation of a constant exchange rate indicates that the appreciation of the Canadian dollar that occurred after 1989 resulted in massive, negative results for Canada. This suggests that the impact of this appreciation was far more damaging to Canada

30 This is quite different, however, from concluding that *trade* has not had such effects, as is illustrated by simulations (described below) of shifts in exchange rates and foreign competitiveness.

31 If all of the growth in Canada's foreign trade since the FTA were to be ascribed to the FTA, then the *apparent* price elasticity of demand would be in the order of 25 – dozens of times greater than is indicated by the historical data. Clearly there is a deep process of industrial and trade restructuring occurring that is driven by far more than just the tariff reductions. Two factors seem especially important in the Canadian case: the reorientation of Canadian manufacturing facilities (initially established to avoid tariffs and serve the Canadian market) toward the continental market, and a coincident trend toward vertical disintegration (or "outsourcing") by manufacturers, with much of the resulting new trade in intermediate inputs naturally crossing the Canada–U.S. border. How to capture these structural shifts in corporate strategy within a macroeconometric model remains a difficult, unanswered question. One is naturally suspicious that if the model is not capturing most of the trade effects of the liberalization, it is probably not capturing the full labor market effects of the liberalization, either – although the direction of the labor market effects of these types of restructuring is not at all clear. The small estimated effects of the FTA and NAFTA are not contingent on any similarity of factor prices between Canada and the U.S. (its dominant trading partner); a similar result would be obtained in a similarly structured U.S.–Mexico trade liberalization simulation. Given an initial equilibrium, modest bilateral tariff reduction cannot lead to large changes in labor market outcomes regardless of how different those outcomes initially were.

than was the FTA itself. Similarly, a 10 percent increase in foreign unit labor cost competitiveness (through higher productivity and/or lower wages) has strong negative simulated effects on the Canadian economy. In this case, unlike the bilateral reduction of tariffs, the competitiveness of Canadian production is asymmetrically undermined; in a demand-constrained system, the consequences are severe.[32] The exchange rate and foreign competitiveness simulations suggest that asymmetric foreign trade and investment shifts can indeed undermine domestic labor markets, even if specific bilateral trade agreements do not have such marked negative impacts.

This begs an interesting question. Specific bilateral or multilateral trade liberalization initiatives, because of their essentially mutual nature, do not seem to significantly harm labor markets relative to an initial, preliberalization equilibrium. But more one-sided shifts in international competitiveness, *under conditions of openness*, can be harmful. Therefore, is not the *cumulative effect* of the incremental liberalizations that culminate in that *state of openness* more negative than suggested by simulations of the step-by-step liberalizations themselves? One might argue that these shifts in international competitiveness would not be so harmful if economies were closed; on the other hand, it is still the shifting international competitiveness, and not openness per se, that is harmful. This distinction would seem important for policy conclusions, and deserves further study.

At any rate, the structuralist simulations are clearly not supportive of the more exaggerated claims of free trade opponents regarding the negative impacts of recent continental trade liberalization initiatives for Canadian workers and labor market policies. The effects of the FTA and NAFTA on demand, employment, and wages in Canada may indeed be negative, contrary to the expectations of mainstream trade theory. But those effects – at least as captured by this model – are almost certainly small, and without doubt far less significant than the negative impacts of other contemporary economic phenomena (such as weak investment rates or unbalanced exchange rates).

Other policy simulations

The relative effectiveness of various economic policy tools within an open economy context can be further investigated with the assistance of the macroeconometric model. The properties of the model are tested by implementing two types of exogenous shocks. Five different types of "competitiveness shocks" are imposed by exogenously altering key domestic price or cost variables that are important to overall macroeconomic behavior: the exchange rate, the interest rate, the inflation rate, wages, and productivity. In the case of the competitiveness shocks, the simulated shock consists of a *procompetitive* exogenous shift (i.e., one that makes Canadian-made products *more* internationally competitive) in the relevant variable of 10 percent (in wages, productivity, and the exchange rate) or one percentage point (for the interest and inflation rates). Three different types of "demand shocks" are also im-

---

32 This result highlights the stark difference between the present model and a supply-constrained Walrasian system, in which increased foreign productivity can have no negative impact on the domestic economy (apart from possible but minor terms-of-trade effects).

posed, by applying exogenous increases in consumption, investment, and exports.[33] Each simulated shock consists of an exogenous increase in the relevant demand category equal to 1 percent of potential output. By comparing and contrasting the response of the model to these shocks, insight can be gained into the relative importance of the various factors influencing Canadian competitiveness and economic performance.

The dynamic simulation begins in the first quarter of 1987, when the exogenous shock is applied. The induced changes in relevant variables are then measured at the end of a five-year simulation period, relative to the closing values of the base-case model. To investigate the extent to which globalization has undermined the effectiveness of various policy tools, similar simulations are performed for a closed economy version of the macroeconometric model. This closed economy model is constructed by exogenizing the key open economy links of the model,[34] and then re-estimating the equations for the remaining endogenous variables while excluding any open economy chains of influence that may have been included in the equations of the full model.[35]

The results of these shock simulations are reported in Table 4. Of particular interest to the present discussion is the model's response to the two labor market shocks: reduced wages and increased productivity. The differences between the responses of the open economy and closed economy models to these same labor market shocks are striking. Recall the widespread conclusion that wage-led growth mechanisms are likely to be weaker in an open economy setting, in which the positive impact of higher wages on aggregate demand is offset not only by the standard decline in domestic investment, but now also by potential declines in net incoming foreign investment and in trade competitiveness. The model simulations provide a dramatic verification of this hypothesis.

The labor market shocks indicate that the closed economy model is mildly wage-led, since both lower wages and higher productivity lead to small net declines in aggregate demand and employment. The open economy model, on the other hand, is clearly profit led, since the same shocks have the opposite effect: higher aggregate demand and (in the case of lower wages) higher employment. Consumption is negatively affected by procompetitive labor market shocks in both versions of the model. But in the open economy case, the offsetting positive effects are stronger: domestic investment is *more* sensitive to the higher profitability that accompanies lower unit labor costs (due to the international competitiveness terms that appear in the open economy investment function), and there is also an incremental demand boost provided through higher net exports.

33 By virtue of the high degree of aggregation in the model, an exogenous increase in private consumption would have exactly the same macroeconomic repercussions as an increase in government (or public) consumption.

34 The bilateral trade, debt service, migration, and exchange rate equations are fully exogenized for the closed economy simulations; in addition, the influence of open economy factors on the investment and interest rate equations is also excluded.

35 Two of the shock simulations – export demand and the exchange rate – are not relevant in the closed economy case and hence are performed only with the open model.

Table 4 *Shock response simulations (change in outcome variables after five years)*

Outcome variable	GDP[1]	Con-sum.[1]	Investment[1]	Curr. acct.[1]	UE rate[2]	Exch rate[3]	Hrly. wage[3]	Int. rate[2]	Price level[4]	Rtv. ULC[3]
COMPETITIVENESS SHOCKS										
10% wage reduction										
Open model	2.08	-1.84	1.78	0.96	-1.35	-4.27	-11.45	-1.44	0.12	-6.58
Closed model	-0.63	-2.12	0.91	n.a.	0.73	n.a.	-11.22	-1.52	-2.57	n.a.
10% productivity increase										
Open model	2.59	-2.77	2.83	0.84	5.31	-8.57	-10.72	-5.25	-6.00	-11.78
Closed model	-0.83	-3.36	1.63	n.a.	7.99	n.a.	-10.79	-4.60	-8.98	n.a.
1 point decrease in real interest rate										
Open model	0.78	0.09	0.41	0.16	-0.48	1.19	-0.18	-0.59	2.55	-1.30
Closed model	0.63	0.06	0.38	n.a.	-0.29	n.a.	-0.23	-0.80	1.92	n.a.
1 point decrease in the annual inflation rate										
Open model	0.04	0.16	-0.00	-0.22	0.17	-0.22	0.71	-0.73	-4.64	0.78
Closed model	0.41	0.19	0.12	n.a.	-0.07	n.a.	0.65	-0.64	-4.60	n.a.
10% depreciation (increase) in the exchange rate[5]										
Open model	5.47	1.63	1.92	1.74	-3.55	6.42	3.83	0.94	4.35	-2.09
DEMAND SHOCKS										
Increase investment by 1% of potential output										
Open model	1.12	1.01	0.90	-0.79	-0.24	0.47	4.29	1.48	2.64	3.60
Closed model	2.59	0.57	1.90	n.a.	-1.55	n.a.	1.35	0.18	2.22	n.a.
Increase consumption by 1% of potential output										
Open model	0.69	0.28	0.14	-0.75	-0.36	-0.08	0.85	0.24	0.88	0.90
Closed model	2.36	0.65	0.62	n.a.	-1.36	n.a.	1.65	0.29	2.13	n.a.
Increase exports by 1% of potential output[5]										
Open model	1.48	0.53	0.34	0.55	-0.80	-0.27	1.54	0.41	1.77	1.78

[1] Change in aggregate demand variables as share of potential output.
[2] Change in absolute percentage points.
[3] Change in percent.
[4] Difference in change in cumulative price level, in percentage points.
[5] These simulations are not applicable to the closed model.

This leads to a somewhat pessimistic conclusion. In an open economy setting, it would seem that measures aimed directly at increasing wages will indeed be undermined by the adverse impact of these measures on international competitiveness and hence on the demand constraint. On the other hand, lower wages may enhance competitiveness and marginally reduce unemployment, but at the social cost of reduced living standards for most citizens. Even a supposedly more "humane" approach to achieving labor cost competitiveness – through higher productivity rather than lower wages – has questionable social impacts: higher unemployment,[36] and an equally large decline in real wages.

Other policy tools at the disposal of government, however, may – on their own or in conjunction with progressive labor market initiatives – help to attain both rising wages and vibrant growth in an open economy setting. For example, a one percentage point decline in interest rates has a strongly positive effect – one that is actually *stronger* in the open economy model. The resulting demand stimulus is heavily weighted toward investment. A slight decline in real wages resulting from a mild acceleration of inflation restrains the growth in consumption spending. The depreciation of the exchange rate resulting from lower interest rates also stimulates both investment and net exports.[37] In contrast, a reduction of the annual inflation rate by one percentage point has virtually no effect in the open economy model, in contrast to its relatively strong response in the closed economy system. An appreciation of the real exchange rate (resulting in part from a modest overshooting of nominal exchange rates to changes in relative rates of inflation) and an increase in real wages (resulting from a deceleration of inflation) both serve to undermine open economy competitiveness, thus offsetting the gains that would otherwise result from the lower interest rates that accompany lower inflation. A depreciation of the exchange rate has the expected strongly beneficial effect in the open economy model, with the demand stimulus weighted more toward investment and less toward consumption.

As expected, the multiplier impacts of all of the demand side shocks are much smaller in the open economy model than in the closed economy version. But the final demand multiplier resulting from the increase in investment is still significant, and exceeds unity even in the open economy model. The positive effect of new investment on export competitiveness (by increasing both productivity and "capacity competitiveness"), and the other demand side spinoffs from new investment, result in strong macroeconomic conditions and a very strong positive impact on wages.

In contrast, increasing consumption is notably less effective in an open economy setting. The deterioration in the trade balance is almost as great as in the case of

36 The unemployment rate increases even though total output grows, because the boost to aggregate demand provided by enhanced competitiveness is insufficient to absorb all of the workers displaced by the productivity shift.
37 The positive effects of the decline in interest rates are enhanced in the whole model simulation by the expansionary boost provided by exchange rate depreciation and by the beneficial effects of investment on export competitiveness. Because of these simultaneous effects, the ultimate sensitivity of investment to interest rates is three times as great in the whole model simulation as is implied by the investment equation alone (in which interest rate effects are relatively weak — with an implied elasticity, evaluated at the 1987–91 sample means, of less than 0.1).

investment stimulus, even though the final demand growth resulting from the expansion is barely one-half as large; this is because, unlike a pure fiscal stimulus, the expansion of investment simultaneously enhances (through productivity growth and new technology) the competitiveness of domestic production, and this reduces the leakage on imports that otherwise accompanies domestic income growth.

Finally, by relaxing the balance-of-payments constraint on the macroeconomy, a direct increase in exports (resulting, perhaps, from some unilateral trade policy or an exogenous shift in international demand patterns) has an especially strong final demand impact, dissipated modestly through rising wages and exchange rate appreciation. This simulation suggests that export-led growth is, indeed, a powerful strategy for expanding output, investment, and employment. Of course, only some economies can expand in this fashion;[38] the beggar-thy-neighbor consequences of the export-led strategy are borne by those economies that experience offsetting declines in net exports.

Conclusion

Heterodox economic theory rejects many of the underlying precepts that inform mainstream free trade prescriptions, and as a consequence suggests a fundamentally different analysis of the consequences of globalization for labor markets. Costs are in part institutionally determined, and there is no guarantee that an economy need only discover its "comparative advantage" to participate successfully in global commerce. Hence, the overall competitiveness of an economy (both with respect to the salability of its products and its attractiveness as a host for mobile investment expenditure) is not automatic, and matters intensely in a non-Walrasian, demand-constrained system. International economic relationships can be one-sided, unbalanced, and harmful to labor market outcomes in an uncompetitive economy. However, heterodox theorists continue to disagree about the relative importance that should be ascribed to the effect of institutionally determined labor cost differentials on output, employment, and wages – as compared to numerous other determinants of economic performance that retain their relevance even in a globalized setting.

Our empirical experiments in the Canadian context suggest that bilateral trade liberalization initiatives, in particular, may have been incorrectly targeted for primary criticism by advocates of continued labor market interventionism. The small impact of tariff reductions on overall relative cost structures, and the inherent *mutuality* of the measures enacted (whereby both sides are exposed to greater international competition), mean that the agreements themselves cannot be blamed for much of the deterioration in labor market outcomes. This general conclusion must be tempered by an awareness that existing simulation models are clearly not capturing the full effect of these bilateral agreements on the structure of investment and production.

---

38 Just as only some economies can expand through exchange rate depreciation, which had similarly positive effects.

At the same time, the policy shock simulations suggest that the growth of openness in general may indeed have undermined the effectiveness of those equity-enhancing policies that have been aimed *directly* at labor markets (such as measures to directly increase wages). These policies are undermined to an increasing degree by cost-based international competition for product market shares and scarce investment capital.

This suggests, on the one hand, a modestly pessimistic policy conclusion: measures aimed at directly increasing wages in an open economy are likely to be stymied by the resulting negative effects of reduced cost competitiveness on investment and exports. This poses a challenge to traditional social-democratic policy prescriptions, which emphasize the potential complementarity of rising wages with strong economic growth – led especially by consumer spending, and perhaps also by the growth of the public sector. While this virtuous circle of causation may have operated during the postwar "golden age" of the mixed economy, it no longer seems to be in force in the Canadian setting.

Economic growth, at the present juncture, is led by profit-seeking investment and by exports into fiercely competitive world markets; at one level, both of these are incompatible with egalitarian labor market and social policies. The current investment- and export-led recovery in Canada, together with the radical redesign of social programs (weakening wage regulation and other institutional supports for labor), suggest that the Canadian economy is structurally and institutionally evolving in response to this profit-led (or "exhilirationist") imperative.

But on the other hand, our results also suggest that there are other, perhaps more fundamental policy tools that may help to resuscitate hopes of successfully combining equity with participation in the global economy. In particular, public intervention would seem to hold out particular promise in the area of stimulating real investment (either directly through private or public investment policy, or indirectly through measures such as the reduction of real interest rates). By directly injecting investment expenditure into the system *independently* of the profit-led dynamic that would otherwise be required to ensure capital accumulation, this approach bypasses to some extent the profit constraint otherwise limiting employment and wage growth. The macroeconomic spinoffs from investment spending are much greater in an open economy context than consumption (whether private or public), thanks to the procompetitive benefits of new investment. Indeed, our simulated direct investment stimulus produced a much stronger positive but *indirect* impact on wages than would be possible from attempting to increase wages *directly* through institutional measures.

It goes without saying, of course, that globalization has also affected the ability of governments to attempt to manage the investment process. The problems likely to be encountered in trying to reduce interest rates or directly regulate accumulation are not addressed here; we simply suggest that this will be the more fruitful direction to which policy makers concerned about trying to promote equity and wage growth in a globalized environment should turn their attention.

Comment by Jaime Ros on "Openness and equity: regulating labor market outcomes in a globalized economy"

This paper draws an important distinction between two types of effects of openness on equity: those of international economic integration on income distribution, and those on the effectiveness of domestic redistributive policies. Since the last ones ultimately affect also income distribution (and thus the first effects, broadly understood, include the second), and given that the chapter deals mostly with international trade effects, it will be useful to reformulate the paper's questions as follows: What are the effects of more open trade policies on income distribution, given an otherwise intact policy regime? What are the effects on income distribution operating through induced changes in the policy regime? Thus formulated, the two questions are clearly different: a more open trade regime may have little direct effect on wages and employment while, at the same time, by enhancing the negative effects of, say, an exogenous increase in wages on employment, it reduces the effectiveness of labor market policies. This outcome may then lead to their abandonment (institutional convergence at the bottom) with potentially adverse effects on income distribution within a large number of countries that go well beyond the initial effects of greater openness.

In his review of theoretical approaches, Stanford complains that the second question has not been answered in the mainstream literature on the effects of international economic integration. I agree and would add that it has not been asked. The focus there has been on the direct effects. The heterodox literature has done better: Marglin and Bhaduri's writing on wage-led and profit-led regimes deals with the effectiveness of distributive policies and, to the extent that wage- and profit-led mechanisms operate differently in more or less open economies, this provides a useful approach to the second question. This is the approach, as I see it, that motivates Stanford's empirical work in the last and central section of his paper.

In this last section, Stanford presents the results of two sets of simulations using a macroeconomic model of the Canadian economy. In one set of simulations, Stanford evaluates the effects of the Canada–U.S. FTA and NAFTA. These show no impacts or very small effects. The results are not much different from other simulations on the effects of NAFTA on the U.S. economy (or even on the Mexican economy). All this suggests that the direct effects of trade opening can hardly account for the poor labor market performance of Canada in recent years.

In another set of simulations, Stanford compares the effectiveness of wage policy on aggregate demand and output under two policy regimes. In one, the economy is "closed" in the sense that "the key open economy links of the model" are made exogenous. He then compares the effects of labor market shocks in this regime to those in the actual open economy regime. This comparison clearly suggests that the counterfactual "closed economy" is mildly wage led while the actual open economy is profit led.

This part of the chapter is most original and ingenious, and it is a pity that Stanford has not done more to lead the reader through his assumptions and explain in much more detail the results and their implications. Consider the assumptions. It is unclear to me how the wage change was modeled. It should be a nominal change (not a real change, which will be the outcome of interactions between the goods and labor markets), and, if this is the case, then it is possible to argue that a more open trade policy by enhancing competition in the goods market increases the capacity of wage policy to increase the real wage. It may do so at the cost of higher unemployment (through adverse competitiveness effects), but the fact that this cost is absent (or lower) in a closed economy is simply the counterpart of the inability of wage policy to affect the real wage. The ideal world for the operation of wage policy is one in which prices behave as in a profit-led economy (nominal wages increase real wages and reduce profits), but employment behaves as in a wage-led economy, so that the increase in real wages raises aggregate demand and employment. Unfortunately, we cannot have both, and the paper does not address the resulting tradeoffs.

Similarly, consider the implications. The confirmation that wage-led mechanisms are weakened and profit-led mechanisms strengthened in the open economy as compared to the "closed economy" informs us very little about how much the FTA or NAFTA have done to undermine or strengthen these mechanisms. Unless the Canadian economy was on a wage-led regime before these trade policy changes happened, their impact on the effectiveness of wage policy may still be very small. Then, reversing these changes may do very little to restore the effectiveness of labor market policies.

11

Integration and income distribution under the North American Free Trade Agreement: the experience of Mexico

Mehrene Larudee

Introduction

When a developing country liberalizes trade and investment, what is the effect on growth, income distribution, and the possibilities for achieving a more equitable society? And to what extent does liberalization accelerate technical progress and thereby enhance national economic independence? Drawing on the experience of Mexico under the North American Free Trade Agreement (NAFTA), the evidence suggests that, for developing countries, the benefits of liberalization are smaller and the costs higher than is generally claimed. A major reason why standard theory and many predictions have overstated these benefits in the case of NAFTA is that they overlook technology differences between developing countries and their richer trading partners. The consequences of technology differences, this chapter will argue, are that the benefits of liberalization fall less to wages and more to profits than is generally predicted. The consequences of liberalization for technical progress are mixed, and the influence of foreign capital tends to grow. And, by committing a nation to a competitive battle for foreign investment, liberalization also tends to undermine labor rights and working conditions, as well as many social programs and environmental protections.

Before embarking on this analysis, though, a few words on globalization are in order. Globalization is often talked about as if it were inexorable, and as if the only choice we faced were how to respond to it. In fact, however, globalization has two main components. One is the market component, driven by the independent decisions of different firms seeking to best one another in competition. This effort consists in the search for low-cost production sites and the contest for market share, and is a force that is, in a certain sense, inexorable. The other component is political: decisions by countries, unilaterally or multilaterally, to remove barriers to trade and investment and to offer subsidies to foreign investors. The political component is not at all inexorable: the decision is sometimes made to liberalize trade and investment, sometimes not. The consequences of such political decisions are the main focus of this chapter.

Debate continues over the benefits and costs of trade and investment liberalization. Based in part on the experience of the East Asian newly industrializing countries (NICs), a number of authors have argued that selectively protectionist policies in the context of a coherent industrial policy exercised by a strong state can contribute materially to economic growth (Amsden 1989; Pack and Westphal 1986; Shapiro and Taylor 1990). These authors would dispute the interpretation in, for example, the World Bank's 1993 study, *The East Asian Miracle*, that it was the degree to which East Asian government policies mimicked or gave play to market interactions that explain their success. Taylor (1996) provides a concise summary of the main issues in assessing the role of the state and the problems that can result from liberalization under the wrong circumstances. Edwards (1993) surveys a number of studies of the effect of trade liberalization on growth, including major multicountry studies, and concludes that a definitive causal link between trade liberalization and acceleration in growth has yet to be established. Agosin and Ffrench-Davis (1995) note that economies should be opened up in a way that does not indiscriminately destroy installed capacity; they also note that deregulating capital markets leads to appreciation of exchange rates and high real interest rates, discouraging the kind of productive investment in restructuring industry that is needed to make trade liberalization successful. The analysis by Ros (1994a) casts doubt on the benefits of trade liberalization for Mexico. With respect to the consequences of trade liberalization for income distribution, Bourguignon and Morrisson (1989) analyze these consequences in six countries, concluding that the effect of trade liberalization varies depending on the particular conditions present in each country. Wood (1994) argues that the skill levels possessed by the labor forces of trading partners are the key determinants of how trade affects income distribution. Empirical evidence on the effects of trade and investment liberalization on both growth and income distribution, then, does not strongly confirm any theoretical model, and remains open to various interpretations.

Benefits and costs of liberalization

It is typically claimed that, for a developing country, trade and investment liberalization with a more developed country brings the following benefits:

(1)   an increase in output;
(2)   higher real wages;
(3)   a lessening of wage inequality based on skill;
(4)   greater foreign capital inflow;
(5)   gains in productive efficiency; and
(6)   technology transfer.

While there certainly are forces that bring the first three benefits – higher output, higher real wages, and a narrowing of the skill-based wage differential – these forces are sometimes weak. And if the two countries start out at different technological levels, the process by which the less-developed country (LDC) catches up technologically will likely generate layoffs and undermine the growth of real wages. The result may often be productivity increases whose benefits are not widely shared among the population. This has so far been the case in recent years in Mexico. We now consider in detail these potential benefits.

Increase in output

Free trade is advocated, in general, on the ground that it increases total output with existing resources by allocating them more efficiently. By removing barriers, it opens up options for production and trade that were not available before. Some of these options are bound to offer a more efficient use of resources, resulting in higher output. Freeing capital flows is advocated on the same ground: it opens up options that were previously shut off, and some of these will more efficiently use existing resources, raising total output.

Increasing total output is certainly desirable, in that, at least potentially, it can lead to a widespread increase in living standards. It is important to note that the comparative advantage argument for liberalization does not say that there will be an increase in the *growth rate* of output, but rather that there will be a *one-time* increase in output. There is also nothing in theory that guarantees that this one-time increase will be large. In fact, the evidence that trade and investment liberalization lead in general to more rapid growth is weak at best, despite several major empirical studies attempting to establish this relationship (Edwards 1993). One difficulty in establishing such a relationship is that an adequate measure of the degree of trade liberalization is hard to define, and another is the difficulty in disentangling macroeconomic fluctuations from the long-term effect of liberalization.

In the case of NAFTA, studies predicting its effects (e.g., Lustig et al. 1992) generally found that Mexico would enjoy the biggest gains in output as a percentage of gross domestic product, but that most of these gains would come not from countries reallocating existing resources to exploit comparative advantage, but rather from new foreign investment from outside North America. The pure "gains from trade," per se, were expected to be quite small. This was in part because much of the trade between the U.S. and Mexico was already duty free under several different laws and programs. One of these is the U.S. tariff code provision (HTS 9802[1]) that allows U.S. firms to send U.S.-made components abroad for assembly and then to reimport the finished products, paying tariff only on the value-added. During 1990–93, 44–49 percent of the value of U.S. imports from Mexico fell under this provision, mostly trade with Mexico's maquiladora sector. And of this, 50–53 percent (or about 25 percent of all U.S. imports from Mexico) was exempt from duty because it represented U.S. components (USITC 1995).

---

1   HTS stands for Harmonized Tariff System; the previous name for the same provision was TSUS (Tariff System of the U.S.) 806.30 and 807.00; the current provisions are HTS 9802.00.60 and HTS 9802.00.80 (USITC 1995).

Certain other goods were completely exempt from duty under the Generalized System of Preferences (GSP); for example, in 1989, 9 percent of U.S. imports from Mexico were duty free for this reason (USITC 1991). In addition, U.S. firms with assembly operations in Mexico's maquiladora sector could import both capital and intermediate goods into their maquiladora plants exempt from Mexican tariffs. Initially, all inputs had to be imported and all outputs exported, but later changes relaxed these restrictions. Under NAFTA the program is to be phased out by the year 2001 (USITC 1994). Apart from these exemptions, Mexico's average trade-weighted tariff was only 10 percent in 1989, much lower than the 25 percent level that prevailed in 1985, before Mexico's major unilateral trade liberalization (USITC 1991). With these substantial dutyfree segments of U.S.-Mexico trade, it is not surprising that rather small gains from trade liberalization alone were expected after NAFTA.

Gains in output were expected to come instead mainly from increased investment in Mexico, particularly from outside North America. In the first three years of NAFTA's existence, 1994–96, however, the average growth rate of output turned out to be substantially below its pre-NAFTA three-year average. In fact, due to the peso devaluation of 1994–95 and the ensuing crisis, Mexico experienced a negative growth rate of GDP, and a sharply negative growth rate of GDP per capita, during 1994–96 (see Table 1). Of course, the annual growth rate was expected to recover, and the possibility remained that several years of sustained rapid growth would raise the post-NAFTA average growth rate above the pre-NAFTA growth rate. However, at this writing the claim that NAFTA succeeded in raising the average growth rate in Mexico could not be supported by the data. As Table 1 shows, the average growth rate from 1951 to 1982 under protectionist policies of import substitution industrialization was far higher than since 1982.

Because the 1994 peso devaluation played such a crucial role in interrupting growth, it deserves detailed discussion. This, however, will be deferred to a later section.

Higher wages

The textbook Heckscher-Ohlin trade model interprets a country's comparative advantage as flowing from the factors of production it possesses. If these are defined as capital and labor, then a country's trade pattern is supposed to be determined by the average amount of capital that each worker in the country has to work with relative to its trading partners. Prior to the opening of trade, the country (say, the U.S.) with a high ratio of capital to labor will have a higher wage than the country (say, Mexico) with less capital per worker. Under certain assumptions,[2] when trade opens up between the two countries, the real wage is expected to rise in the low-wage country due to an increase in the aggregate demand for labor there. This happens because the

---

2   These assumptions are: both countries produce each of two goods, using capital and labor; the supply of capital and of labor in each country is fixed; capital and labor are perfectly mobile between sectors within a country, and perfectly immobile between countries; production functions are identical across countries and exhibit constant returns to scale; preferences are identical and homothetic; perfect competition prevails, without trade barriers or other market imperfections; and there are no factor intensity reversals.

Table 1 *Growth rate of GDP in Mexico, 1951–96*

Year	Growth rate of GDP (%)	Year	Growth rate of GDP (%)	Year	Growth rate of GDP (%)
1951	7.7	1967	6.3	1982	-0.6
1952	3.9	1968	8.1	1983	-5.3
1953	0.3	1969	6.3	1984	3.7
1954	10.0	1970	6.9	1985	2.8
1955	8.5	1971	4.2	1986	-3.5
1956	6.9	1972	8.5	1987	1.7
1957	7.6	1973	8.4	1988	1.3
1958	5.3	1974	6.1	1989	3.1
1959	3.0	1975	5.6	1990	4.4
1960	8.1	1976	4.2	1991	3.6
1961	4.9	1977	3.5	1992	2.8
1962	4.7	1978	8.3	1993	0.7
1963	8.0	1979	9.2	1994	3.5
1964	11.7	1980	8.3	1995	-6.2
1965	6.5	1981	8.0	1996	5.1
1966	6.9				

Sources: For 1951–91, Pedro Aspe, *Economic Transformation the Mexican Way* (1993), pp. 69–70, Table 2.1; for 1992–96, Economist Intelligence Unit, *Country Report, Mexico* (1997, 4th qtr.). Figures for 1995–96 are based on 1993 prices, while figures for preceding years are based on 1980 prices.

relatively labor-abundant country (Mexico) has a cost advantage in shifting its resources to producing goods that use much labor but relatively little capital in production (say, clothing), and importing from the other country (the U.S.) goods that use more capital and relatively less labor in production (say, machine tools).

The increased demand for labor is supposed to produce benefit (2) for the developing country, that is, an increase in the real wage. In fact, since the higher-wage country is supposed to shift to less labor-intensive goods, there should also be a tendency for the real wage to fall there, and hence from both directions wages in the two trading partners should tend to equalize.

Empirical studies of the effect of trade liberalization on income distribution have not found definitively that, when a lower-wage country liberalizes trade with a higher-wage country or countries, it raises the wage in the lower-wage country. There is some evidence of wage convergence among countries in the OECD (Organization for Economic Cooperation and Development) that were becoming gradually more economically integrated during the last several decades (Leamer 1993). However, to date, Mexico – again, affected powerfully by the 1994–95 peso devaluation – shows no evidence of convergence with U.S. wages following NAFTA. The Mexican average real wage fell sharply during the peso crisis, as nominal wages lagged far behind inflation. While inflation was fairly quickly brought down from its peak of over 50 percent, the damage to real wages had already been done, with a decline of 15 percent in 1995 and 8 percent in 1996 (IADB 1997, 285). The pattern established in the 1980s seemed destined to be repeated – a rapid decline in the real wage during the inflation that followed devaluation (the 1982–83 devaluation that accompanied the debt crisis), and then, over many years, stagnation or only very partial recovery of the real wage toward its previous level. Table 2 shows the evolution of the real wage in Mexico. Even the recovery of the real wage after the 1986 trade liberalization occurred primarily among higher-paid white-collar workers, while production workers' wages were stagnant (OECD 1997, 91; Rendón and Salas 1993).

Among the central assumptions of the Heckscher-Ohlin trade model, there are two whose violation may have a major influence on the distributional impact of trade liberalization. These are (1) the assumption that both countries have the same technology before trade opens up, and (2) the assumption that there are no factor intensity reversals (explained below). Violation of either of these assumptions is capable of offsetting or even reversing the standard result that a country like Mexico with a low capital-labor ratio should experience a real wage increase when trade opens up.

The same-technology assumption. The assumption that both countries have access to the same technology means that both have full access to the same knowledge about what different techniques (combinations of capital and labor) can be used to produce a unit of a given good. It means they not only know what all the possible techniques are, but are also already familiar with how to operate them. It means too that there are no industrial secrets or special skills possessed by employees of a firm and unavailable (or unknown) to other firms in other countries. It further implies that each country produces with perfect efficiency: resources are employed without waste or misallocation, using the best-known practice.

That both countries have access to the same technology does not mean, however, that both actually use the same technique – the same combination of capital and labor – to produce the same good. Instead, firms choose a technique based on how expensive labor is relative to capital. Where labor is cheaper, if firms can use it to replace part of capital in the production process, they will. Where labor is more expensive, capital will tend to be used in place of labor.

Now, the same-technology assumption is surely violated. We know this for several reasons. First, one strong argument that countries like Mexico should liberalize trade has long been that their production was inefficient and backward under protectionist policies. Liberalization would force formerly sheltered firms to shape up, to achieve the best-practice technique and organization, or be bested by competitors. While this process has the benefit (listed above as benefit (5)) of increasing productivity, it also reduces the total demand for labor, as firms rationalize production and lay off redundant workers. Thus, rationalization and modernization – excluded from the standard trade models – undermine the assumption, and along with it, the conclusion, that increased trade will increase the demand for labor, at least in the short to medium run. Even though a country like Mexico may shift to producing more labor-intensive goods, the increase in labor demand generated may be partly or wholly offset by the reduction in labor demand from rationalization of produc-

Table 2 *Real wages, total compensation, and maquila employment, Mexico, 1980–96*

Year	Real compensation index, manufacturing	Real compensation index, all maquila workers	Real wage index, maquila production workers	Total maquila employment
1980	100	100	100	119,546
1981	103	99	99	130,973
1982	100	108	104	127,048
1983	77	86	81	150,867
1984	72	84	78	199,684
1985	73	84	76	211,968
1986	67	82	71	249,833
1987	66	83	70	305,253
1988	66	80	66	369,489
1989	72	85	66	429,725
1990	71	86	64	446,436
1991	74	84	63	467,352
1992	77	86	62	505,698
1993	78	86	62	542,074
1994	81	90	66	583,044
1995	69	83	59	643,502
1996	64	79	54	754,858

Sources: Real compensation index in manufacturing (wages, salaries, and benefits) for 1980–94 was calculated from *OECD Economic Surveys, Mexico* (1992, 1997), and for 1995–96 using IADB, *Economic and Social Progress in Latin America* (1997), p. 285. Figures from 1989 on are based on 1993 prices. Maquila employment is from INEGI, *Industria Maquiladora de Exportación*, Estadísticas Económicas, February 1997, Personal Ocupado; maquila wage indices are calculated from the same source, the table Sueldos, Salarios y Prestaciones Reales por Persona Ocupada, and are based on data in 1994 pesos.

tion. While productivity rises, real wages may rise little or not at all for a considerable period after liberalization.

In Mexico, despite trade liberalization in 1986, investment liberalization in 1989, and NAFTA's implementation in 1994, aggregate manufacturing employment has not grown even though manufacturing output has risen steadily. But growth in employment in the maquiladora manufacturing sector (see Table 2), mostly foreign-owned and producing for export using imported inputs, has been paralleled by a decline in employment in the non-maquila manufacturing sector. Perhaps it is not surprising that manufacturing employment has not grown with output, since much the same has happened in many developed countries, including the U.S. Increases in productivity have implied little change in employment as output has grown.

In fact, Mexican manufacturing employment actually fell slightly from 1980 to 1993, by 126,000 jobs (Márquez 1995), even as both output and exports grew. Before 1980, the output elasticity of employment averaged 0.5 in the manufacturing sector, so that a 1 percent increase in output could on average be expected to produce a 0.5 percent increase in employment. However, for 1986–93, following trade liberalization, this elasticity was far lower. Even for those sectors in which both output and productivity grew (labeled as having undergone "modernization"), and even in the subgroup of these modernizing sectors for which employment actually grew, the output elasticity of employment ranged only between 0.21 and 0.78. For all other sectors, even modernizing sectors where output and productivity both grew, employment either was stagnant or declined. In addition, some sectors failed to experience growth in output, and of course suffered even worse declines in employment (Márquez 1995).

If export growth led to higher real wages, we would hope to see significant wage growth, for example, in the very rapidly growing maquila sector. Gambrill (1993, 1995) reviews the performance of wages in the maquila sector relative to the rest of manufacturing. From 1977 to 1992 the purchasing power of the average maquila wage fell by 45 percent, and the decline was uninterrupted except during 1981 and 1982, despite the rapid growth of maquila output and employment during the 1980s and 1990s. The real wage in the rest of manufacturing also showed the same pattern, except that from 1988 to 1994 it increased steadily, though remaining well below its 1977 level. Among the three categories of workers – white-collar salaried workers (*empleados*), technicians (*técnicos*), and blue-collar hourly production workers (*obreros*), only *empleados* experienced rising salaries during the 1980s (with real salaries in 1993 approximating those in 1977), while real wages of both *técnicos* and *obreros* declined (Gambrill 1995). Real wages in the maquila and non-maquila manufacturing sectors never regained their 1980 level, and again fell sharply after the peso crisis (see Table 2).

The no-factor-intensity-reversal assumption. In Mexico, apart from technology differences in manufacturing, there is another important reason for labor demand to decline as a result of trade liberalization. In the Heckscher-Ohlin model, it is assumed that one good (such as tools) can be designated relatively capital intensive and the other (such as food) labor intensive regardless of the different factor prices (wage, price of capital) that prevail in the two countries that open up trade. This assumption means that, if at one factor price ratio (wage divided by price of capital) tools use a higher capital–labor ratio in their production than does food, then at *all* factor price ratios tool production uses a higher capital–labor ratio. In other words, we may accurately call tool production "capital intensive" and food production "labor intensive," regardless of factor prices. The technical term for this assumption is that there is no "factor intensity reversal."

Before NAFTA's passage, a situation that might be described as a violation of this assumption prevailed between Mexico and the U.S. Maize production in the U.S. is highly capital intensive, more so even than manufactured goods, while maize production in Mexico is more labor intensive than manufactured goods in Mexico (Burfisher et al. 1992; Larudee 1995). Thus, a factor intensity reversal exists, if both countries are using the same technology. At pre-NAFTA prices, this created the possibility that labor demand would actually decline in both the U.S. and Mexico following liberalization. Mexico would import cheap U.S. maize, driving maize farmers off the land and thereby cutting deeply into labor demand and lowering the real wage. In the U.S. a small shift of labor into maize production would cause an infinitesimal decline in U.S. wages, because so little labor is used in growing maize. But several studies (Levy and van Wijnbergen 1994; Hinojosa-Ojeda and Robinson 1991; Robinson et al. 1991) estimated that in Mexico about 700,000 to 800,000 members of the labor force would be displaced from maize farming after NAFTA and would migrate to cities, depressing urban wages.

One could reasonably argue, of course, that the different factor usage in maize production in the U.S. from that in Mexico is a result of differences in technology, in the sense of differences in climate (in the U.S., days are longer during the key growing season), differences in terrain (much Mexican land is hilly and less conducive to use of tractors), economies of scale in U.S. farming, or other factors. However, it does not matter; all that matters is that – for whatever reason – opening up trade causes Mexico to import cheap U.S. maize and displace hundreds of thousands of maize growers, depressing labor demand in Mexico. Of course, variation in the peso/dollar exchange rate as well as in the world price of corn could change this situation. But the danger is clear, and a very slow 15-year process of liberalization of maize trade was written into NAFTA evidently to avoid any such catastrophic consequences.

Narrowing the skill-based wage differential

A different version of the Heckscher-Ohlin model is used to draw the conclusion that when a less-developed country liberalizes trade with a more-developed country, the wage differential between skilled and unskilled labor in the LDC should narrow. The argument is parallel in structure to the capital/labor case, but the two factors each country possesses in different ratios are assumed to be, not capital and labor, but skilled labor and unskilled labor. (Capital is absent in this version of the model; one rationale is that if capital is free to move between countries then it cannot define a country's comparative advantage; see Wood (1994).) Opening up trade causes the country with a higher ratio of skilled to unskilled labor (say, the U.S.) to produce mainly goods that require mostly skilled labor (say, machine tools), while the country with mainly unskilled labor (say, Mexico) shifts to producing mainly goods that require mostly unskilled labor (say, clothing). As a result, in the relatively unskilled country, the demand for unskilled labor rises. This lifts unskilled wages, shrinking the wage differential between skilled and unskilled workers.

Unfortunately, as Hanson and Harrison (1995) have observed, skill-based wage inequality in Mexico did not narrow after the trade and investment liberalization of the 1980s – in fact, it grew; the trend continued during the 1990s, as the ratio of production workers' wages to white-collar wages fell steadily (OECD 1997, 91). It is not hard to see why this might occur. Probably the traded goods sector employs a higher proportion of skilled professional and technical personnel than the proportion it employs of all unskilled workers. This is because there is a large nontraded goods sector (including most of the informal sector) that employs a vast number of unskilled or low-skilled workers. Hence, an increase in the demand for skilled labor by the traded goods sector may increase the wage level of skilled workers more than does an increase in the demand for unskilled labor by the traded goods sector. The simplest Heckscher-Ohlin model omits nontraded goods and so arrives at a different conclusion.

Attracting foreign investment

Mexico has always offered a convenient low-wage site from which to produce for the huge U.S. market, with low transport costs for finished goods, relative to other low-wage sites. For much of the postwar period, however, majority foreign ownership of enterprises in Mexico was not generally permitted. A major exception was the maquiladora program, which after 1965 allowed foreign ownership of firms that imported intermediate and capital goods and exported all their product; initially such firms had to be located close to the U.S. border, but this restriction was later removed.

It was only in 1989 that Mexico liberalized its investment rules to allow 100 percent foreign ownership in a wide range of industries. The privatization of state enterprises, along with the creation in 1990 of a legal framework for franchising arrangements, also added to foreign capital inflow, and in the early 1990s both portfolio and direct foreign investment (DFI) grew (see Table 3).

NAFTA further liberalized investment as well as trade. It also created greater incentives for non-North American firms to produce inside North America because it imposed domestic content requirements while continuing to allow tariffs against goods imported from outside North America. For example, Samsung invested $800 million in constructing five plants in the border region beginning in 1995, reportedly motivated by NAFTA rules of origin and the desire to avoid paying tariffs (McCosh 1997). Ironically, then, gains to Mexico from increased capital inflow from outside North America stemmed from a combination of liberalization and protectionism, that is, from liberalization that was regional only. Of course, Mexico has also attracted increased investment from the U.S.

Foreign investment has undoubtedly increased GDP by increasing productive capacity. At the same time, it is important to weigh the costs and benefits of foreign investment, something that does not seem systematically to have been done. Part of the benefits of increased value-added flow to foreign owners, while a greater presence of foreign capital is likely to increase its influence on economic decisions. Liberalized capital flows also carry the danger of heightened macroeconomic instability, which may reduce the average rate of growth. These issues will be pursued in the section on the 1994 peso devaluation.

Increased productive efficiency

An important goal of liberalization is to increase productivity, in part by exposing formerly sheltered firms to greater competition and forcing them to adopt best-practice production techniques. Productive efficiency should rise for three reasons:

(1) Foreign firms produce an increasing share of output, so that these exceptionally efficient firms increase the average level of productive efficiency;

(2) Existing nationally owned firms increase their productive efficiency because they have more motive to do so and, in some cases, because they also have increased means (for example, they may receive technical assistance as suppliers to foreign firms);

(3) Some existing low-productivity nationally owned firms fail, raising average productivity in the industry.

LDCs like Mexico might prefer that nationally owned firms modernize rather than give way to more productive MNCs, both because the incomes generated are more likely to be recirculated through the economy and because this implies greater economic independence. But Agosin and Ffrench-Davis (1995) have pointed out that, although liberalization strengthens the motivation for firms to modernize, they may lack the means to modernize unless the government provides them with assistance. In Mexico, the rationalization process was accelerated by the 1994 peso devaluation, which pushed many small firms into bankruptcy. The danger is that liberalization, instead of strengthening nationally owned firms, will replace them by MNCs, reduce the fraction of value-added that flows to national income, and increase the influence of foreign capital over national policies.

Technology transfer
An LDC like Mexico seeks technology transfer in order to become more competitive in the goods it now produces and to shift to producing higher-tech products, as ways of achieving faster growth and greater independence. It also may hope, by producing more of the intermediate and capital goods it uses, to reduce its current account deficit and thereby achieve greater macroeconomic stability. The hope is that technology will be transferred not only to nationals who are employees of MNCs, but also to nationally owned firms, perhaps through movement of skilled, trained employees among firms, or perhaps through interaction between MNCs and the national firms that supply their inputs.

Some LDCs have imposed explicit requirements on MNCs that they transfer technology, on the assumption that such transfers would not otherwise occur. Mexico's recent experience has been mixed; there seems to have been substantial hiring and training of nationals by MNCs, but the transfer of technology to nationally owned firms has been more limited. The next section will describe how the 1994 peso devaluation brought about only very limited switching by MNCs to Mexican suppliers, evidently because these would-be suppliers have found it difficult to meet quality standards. Technology transfer is a key element in using trade and investment liberalization as a strategy for growth, but the experience of Mexico suggests that government policy intervention may be needed to ensure that substantial technology transfer occurs.

An important factor in the outcome of liberalization in both the short and medium term is what happens to the exchange rate. We turn now to this issue, and discuss the Mexican peso devaluation of 1994, its causes, its consequences, and its lessons.

The 1994 peso crisis

The 1994 peso devaluation points to additional ways in which the costs of trade and investment liberalization may partly or wholly offset its benefits, worsening average living standards, income distribution, and the growth rate of output, while increasing the influence of foreign capital in the economy and the share it receives of value-added. Moreover, devaluation affects technology transfer in some ways positively and in other ways negatively, in ways described below.

The Mexican devaluation of 1994 was in part a result of the political and economic process leading up to the passage of NAFTA. There was some awareness on the part of informed observers and officials that overvaluation was increasingly becoming a problem by 1993, as the current account deficit was large and growing (see Table 3). Its cause was primarily the massive inflow of portfolio investment into Mexico in the early 1990s, skyrocketing to $29 billion in 1993. Ros (1994b) notes several reasons for the spectacular surge in portfolio investment: (1) privatization of state enterprises including the telecommunications firm Telmex, a number of banks, the television networks, and other large firms; (2) the decline of world interest rates; (3) recession in the international economy; (4) the fall in the country risk premium due in part to Mexico's negotiated debt reduction agreement; (5) the deregulation of foreign investment by the Salinas administration in 1989; and (6) the opening of financial markets. Some of these factors also contributed to a gradual increase in DFI into Mexico, but the increase in portfolio investment was far larger. Another contributing factor was the atmosphere of NAFTA-based euphoria created by a public relations apparatus working overtime to produce a climate of public and legislative opinion in which NAFTA's passage was assured.

A 1993 Congressional Budget Office study of NAFTA emphasized the importance of the Mexican exchange rate in maintaining a positive public attitude toward free trade agreements and their extension to new regions. However, the study erroneously concluded that passage of NAFTA would make a devaluation either orderly or unnecessary:

> [...if NAFTA were not approved...] [c]apital flows into Mexico would probably decline and might well reverse. In that case, a financial crisis in Mexico would be threatened, with the possibility of a collapse of the peso and the associated risk of renewed capital flight or the necessity of painfully high short-term interest rates. If failure to ratify NAFTA had such effects on Mexico, economic and political links between the United States and the rest of Latin America might suffer. The willingness of foreign governments throughout the world to enter into complex trade negotiations with the United States could also be damaged.
>
> Some observers argue that, in the long run, Mexico would recover from the setback of NAFTA's failure because the underlying potential of its economy would remain, and investment and trade would continue, albeit perhaps more slowly than they would under support for the current market-based, outward-oriented approach to their economic policies. But the extent to which financial markets and Mexican domestic politics have built up the significance of NAFTA suggests that a rejection could produce a substantial setback (CBO 1993, 17).

Table 3 *Foreign debt, foreign investment, and current account balance,
Mexico, 1980–96 (billions of current dollars)*

Year	Public & private foreign debt	Direct foreign investment	Portfolio investment	Current account balance
1980		1.6		-10.4
1981		1.7		-16.2
1982		0.6		-5.9
1983		0.7		5.9
1984		1.4		4.2
1985		1.7		0.8
1986		2.4		-1.4
1987	109.5	3.9		4.2
1988	99.2	3.2		-2.4
1989	93.8	2.5		-5.8
1990	104.4	3.7		-7.5
1991	114.1	3.6	12.8	-14.9
1992	112.3	3.6	18.0	-24.4
1993	131.6	4.9	28.9	-23.4
1994	140.0	10.0	8.2	-29.4
1995	165.7	6.7	-10.1	-0.7
1996				-1.9

Sources: For foreign debt, IADB, *Economic and Social Progress in Latin America* (1997), p. 285;
for DFI, INEGI, http://dgcnesyp.inegi.gob.mx/cgi-win/bdi.exe, January 13, 1998; for current account, 1980–95, IMF, *International Financial Statistics Yearbook 1997*, pp. 590–1, Washington,
D.C.: IMF, p. 285; for 1996, Economist Intelligence Unit, *Country Report, Mexico* (1997, 4th qtr.).

The quote is illuminating in its confirmation of the political and ideological role
that NAFTA was seen as playing. NAFTA was not just an agreement to liberalize
trade and investment: it was a symbol and a signal, a drum roll celebrating the entry
of the neo-liberal era. But it was precisely this role for NAFTA that signaled to
investors that failure was not politically permissible, and hence that the risk to them
was less than it might seem based on economic fundamentals alone. In effect, a
bailout was waiting in the wings, because Mexico was too important to the neo-
liberal program to be allowed to fail. Though there was no formal advance commitment to a bailout, there was a strong unspoken commitment to NAFTA's success as
a cornerstone of market-oriented economic reforms in the Western hemisphere. By
reducing the perceived risk to investors, the NAFTA political process accelerated
foreign capital inflow into Mexico, accelerated overvaluation of the peso, and increased the size of the resulting crisis. A similar dynamic has been noted with respect to another historical situation – bank lending to Third World countries in the
1970s leading to the debt crisis. In that era, while no one bank could count on being
rescued from bad loans, a widespread default would constitute such a threat to the
world financial system that a bailout would become an economic and political imperative, and this fact may have reduced banks' caution in lending.

The NAFTA economic/political process also seems to have increased the influence of foreign capital in determining how the overvaluation would be handled in 1994. A June 1994 *Wall Street Journal* story reports that U.S. investment banks and mutual funds played a powerful role in Mexican government policy, though this has been denied by Mexican officials. Soon after the March 23 assassination of presidential candidate Luis Donaldo Colosio, a group of New York financial institutions called the Weston Group made several suggestions to the Mexican government about how to stop the peso's slide; the group then organized a consortium of investors, called the Weston Forum – including such members as Fidelity, Oppenheimer, Soros Fund Management, Salomon Brothers, and others – to pressure the Mexican government to adopt these measures (Torres and Vogel 1994).

One suggestion it made to the government was to issue a large number of long-term *tesobonos*, a government security that paid off in a quantity of pesos indexed to the peso-dollar exchange rate. Thus, the Mexican government assumed all the exchange rate risk except the risk that peso-dollar convertibility might be suspended. The Weston Forum also suggested that Mexican banks be allowed to increase their foreign currency liabilities from 20 percent to 25 percent of their total assets. In the short term this would make possible greater purchases of pesos, although it would also put the banks at greater risk in the event of a major devaluation. A third suggestion was that the small daily devaluations of the peso be slowed, and that the central bank use its reserves to bring the value of the peso back from 3.36 to 3.15 pesos to the dollar. The Weston Forum said that it was willing to invest an additional $17 billion in Mexico during the rest of 1994 if the government implemented reforms. These suggestions were pressed on Mexican officials in two April meetings; the day before the second meeting scheduled for April 20, some forum members and other investors declined to buy enough *cetes* (a treasury certificate whose payoff was not indexed to the exchange rate) to replace those coming due, and short-term interest rates jumped to 18 percent while stock prices fell 5.2 percent. The action was reportedly a signal to the government of the power the Weston Forum was able to exercise (Torres and Vogel 1994).

During the remainder of 1994, the government greatly increased its sales of *tesobonos* and reduced its sales of *cetes*. This meant that the Mexican government – and taxpayers – assumed an enormous level of exchange rate risk, even though there was ultimately no danger the government would fail to meet its peso obligations, since it could always print pesos. The danger to investors, rather, was that peso-dollar convertibility would be suspended, an option that, remarkably, never seems to have been considered.

While delaying the devaluation allowed the ruling PRI party to win the August presidential elections, the method required to do so was a time bomb that blew up in December after the new president, Ernesto Zedillo, took office. Michael Adler, a Columbia University Business School professor and an advisor to the Weston Group, warned in the summer 1994 issue of the *Columbia Journal of World Business* of the precarious peso situation and said that the U.S. would like to avoid a devaluation:

...a case can be made that, at least as far as the United States is concerned, a Mexican devaluation that is unnecessary on fundamental economic grounds would be inimical to U.S. interests.

The reason is that such a devaluation could conceivably produce an unnecessary acceleration in the shift of U.S. jobs to Mexico....Such a devaluation could easily be tagged by the Administration's opponents as a hostile, beggar-thy-neighbor move that was inconsistent with President Clinton's campaign and pre-NAFTA promises....[T]he United States might readily be persuaded to cooperate in averting a devaluation which under present circumstances would be likely to harm both countries (Adler 1994, 90).

The seriousness of the peso crisis was exacerbated by NAFTA's central ideological role that made it "too important to fail." The role of NAFTA as the linchpin of a larger program of economic reforms helped to make capital flows even more volatile than they would otherwise have been. The crisis began in December 1994 with a devaluation that went quickly out of control. As the peso fell rapidly to about half its former value, interest rates skyrocketed, creating a crushing burden on debtors of all kinds and causing purchases of consumer durables, including autos, to fall catastrophically. Inflation, declining consumer demand, rising unemployment, and falling real wages added up to a 6.2 percent decline in GDP for 1995.[3] Bailout funds from the U.S. and the International Monetary Fund (IMF), together with the business cycle upswing in the U.S., Mexico's main trading partner, helped the Mexican economy begin to recover quickly. But for 1994–96 the growth rate of GDP per capita was still negative, putting the average Mexican at a lower standard of living after NAFTA than before.

The devaluation did stimulate exports, while production for the domestic market lagged, causing low capacity utilization and widespread bankruptcies. As for the pace of industrial modernization in Mexico, the crisis had contradictory effects. By reducing the dollar cost of Mexican labor, it sharply accelerated growth in maquiladora output and employment, as increasing numbers of foreign firms chose to use Mexico as an export platform (see Table 2). It also allowed Mexican firms to export more of their product. Firms that used Mexican inputs and sold their products for dollars enjoyed the greatest cost advantages. At the same time, Mexican firms suffered cost increases as a result of the devaluation. The peso cost of importing intermediate and capital goods rose. Firms that had incurred dollar-denominated debt to pay for past imports of intermediate or capital goods also suffered an increasing burden in the peso cost of servicing these debts. High interest rates made matters worse. These factors created contradictory effects of the devaluation on Mexico's technological progress: while a cheap peso increased the price competitiveness of Mexican firms seeking to be suppliers of intermediate goods to multinationals, it reduced their ability to meet quality standards by making it more difficult to buy state-of-the-art capital equipment.

Data on demand for intermediate and capital goods produced in Mexico show

---

3   When measured at 1980 prices, the decline in GDP in 1995 was 6.9 percent; when measured at 1993 prices it was 6.2 percent.

that, at least in 1995, increased price competitiveness of these goods was not a very strong factor in decisions about their purchase. The best that can be said is that, in the context of an overall decline in purchases of intermediate and capital goods, purchases of domestic intermediate and capital goods declined less than purchases of imported intermediate and capital goods. Purchases of domestic intermediate goods rose about 1 percent per year from 1992 through 1995, while in 1995 overall purchases of intermediate goods fell 7 percent. The difference was more pronounced for capital goods. In 1995, purchases of domestic machinery and equipment fell by 11 percent over the previous year, while purchases of imported machinery and equipment fell by 32 percent. Nevertheless, because this was a reversal of a previous trend toward rising imports, in 1995 imported capital equipment was almost exactly the same percentage of total gross fixed capital formation – 22.8 percent – as it had been in 1992 – 23.2 percent (SCNM 1996).

The American Chamber of Commerce in Mexico conducted surveys of its member firms, asking (1) what percentage of the firm's inputs were imported and what percentage were domestic, and (2) whether the company had initiated an "import substitution" policy (after the devaluation) and, if not, why not. Results of the March 1996 survey indicated that the manufacturing enterprises surveyed had reduced the percentage of total inputs that were imported only from 53 percent in 1994 to 51 percent in 1995 after the devaluation; it was estimated that in 1996 that percentage would again be 53 percent. When asked to explain, firms generally said that quality and reliability of supply were the obstacles to switching to Mexican inputs (AmCham 1996, III–12–13).

An LDC that continues to be dependent on importing intermediate and capital goods will tend to have a persistent current account deficit that, if not financed consistently by capital inflows, will create constant pressure for devaluation. Table 3 shows the recent history of Mexico's current account balances. While the 1994 devaluation nearly restored the trade and current account balances, as the peso appreciates in real value the deficit in the current account can once again be expected to rise. The fact that the crisis added to Mexico's total foreign debt (public plus private) – bringing it to $166 billion in 1995, higher than ever before in Mexico's history – will exacerbate the problem with the current account as interest payments are made.

During most of the postwar period, the Mexican government has had at its disposal a variety of policy tools to maintain control over the balance of payments. For example, the 1977 Automotive Decree specified that each auto firm must increase its exports in order to balance its imports and payments abroad by 1982; this impelled GM and Chrysler to establish engine plants and other auto parts production in Mexico by 1981. The 1983 Automotive Decree strictly required a balance-of-payments target for each automaker. NAFTA eliminates all such performance requirements, and few tools will be left to the Mexican government to restore the balance of payments (Berry et al. 1993). One tool Mexico still has is the right to impose trade barriers against non-NAFTA countries, and during the crisis in 1995 it did raise tariffs on apparel, textiles, and leather goods from 20 percent to 35 percent to protect against competition from low-wage Asian countries (*EFI,* September 4–10, 1995).

Progressive economic policy

The problem confronting Mexico is not just that trade and investment liberalization have done little to raise wages or improve the income distribution in Mexico or enhance national control of the economy. In addition, its development strategy that centers on trade and investment liberalization typically entails an implicit commitment to respond to the needs and desires of foreign investors. A strategy focused on exports implies maintaining competitive labor costs. And as MNCs produce an increasing share of value-added, their influence is likely to strengthen political pressure to keep real wages down, for example by allowing the nominal minimum wage to lag behind inflation.

There will be pressure, too, to "flexibilize" labor markets by reducing labor rights and benefits. Mexico's labor law has been remarkably favorable to workers, though enforcement has been lax. But liberalization has brought pressure to weaken the law rather than to enforce it. For example, the law mandates that firms operating in Mexico must annually share 10 percent of their profits with their employees (although this provision is much honored in the breach).

Likewise, permanent workers who are fired or laid off are entitled to a lump-sum amount of severance pay of at least three months' wages (IADB 1996, 190). This amount, if paid, would often be comparable in percentage of income replacement to total unemployment insurance benefits available to a U.S. worker under similar conditions. And the Mexican method of payment in principle actually offers some advantages: the worker need not remain unemployed to collect the severance pay, and the money is supposed to be available all at once, and therefore sooner, than it would be available to a U.S. worker. However, the severance pay provision is also unevenly enforced, and workers often get less than the amount to which they are entitled.

In this paper, I have argued that trade liberalization is likely to have unacceptable effects on income distribution under the conditions in which it often is adopted. In an LDC like Mexico, one of whose motivations for trade liberalization is to rationalize production to achieve competitiveness, and where some very low-productivity labor-intensive sectors exist, the wage increases promised by trade theory may not materialize, at least until after rationalization is complete. Productivity rises in tandem with a reduction in labor demand, and labor shares little in productivity gains. The obvious solution is to incorporate into free trade agreements some guarantee that labor incomes will rise with productivity – for example, by increasing the minimum wage at the same rate as productivity. An increasing minimum wage should be accompanied by unemployment insurance (or an equivalent in severance pay) that provides a high percentage of income replacement.

Another way for labor to be guaranteed a share of productivity increases would be for profit sharing to be legally mandated. As mentioned earlier, in Mexico this is already the case: annually, each firm is required to distribute 10 percent of its pretax profits to its workers (*Business Frontier* 1996). The problem is that this law is not being enforced.

A third method of securing for labor a fair share of productivity increases is an increase in the corporate profits tax, with the revenues designated for social spending, or used to provide tax relief to labor households.

Each of these policy proposals has its limitations. Policies that channel income only to those who are employed in formal sector firms will reach only part of the labor force, and only that part that is already better off, except to the extent that it benefits other households through lending and gift giving within extended families, or through spending by formal sector workers on informal sector products and services. Moreover, any redistributive policy runs the risk of scaring off some foreign investment, a point that is sure to be emphasized by foreign investors. Whatever the difficulties of particular policies, the central principle is clear: with good reasons to doubt that the market will fairly distribute the gains from trade and investment liberalization, some means need to be found to share these gains more widely.

In addition, the problem of highly volatile capital flows needs to be addressed, and the possibility of imposing capital controls should be seriously considered. There is evidence that such controls have played a positive role in economic growth in Japan, South Korea, Brazil, and Chile (Amsden 1989; Nembhard 1996).

There are other important issues with respect to NAFTA that have not been addressed here, including the issues of environmental protection and labor rights. Anderson et al. (1996) discuss NAFTA's record to date on these issues. Of particular importance is the question of NAFTA's restrictions on the ability of local, state, and federal governments to make policy, stemming from the fact that NAFTA allows policies to be challenged before its dispute resolution body on the grounds that they might constitute unfair subsidies to trade or unfair barriers to trade as described in the agreement. Some analysts believe that challenges could be made to such programs as Canada's universal health care system (interpreted as an unfair subsidy to firms producing in Canada, since they do not have to pay employees' health care costs) and to local mandatory recycling, on the grounds that such recycling subsidizes firms buying recycled raw materials.

In short, NAFTA should be repealed and then drastically renegotiated, this time in a much more democratic manner, with extensive popular participation in formulating policy.

Conclusion

Mexico was anticipated to be the big winner from NAFTA, and some of the benefits to the United States were expected to flow from the growth of Mexico's income and therefore the increasing market for U.S. exports. The first year under NAFTA, 1994, produced only moderate growth of output, despite rapid growth of trade, and 1995 was disastrous for output, employment, and wages, though not for exports. While the crisis cannot be entirely attributed to NAFTA, it was linked to the agreement's larger-than-life role in the constellation of economic reforms planned for the Western hemisphere, which led to overselling of NAFTA, excessive inflow of portfolio investment, overvaluation of the peso, and, eventually, crisis.

The evidence from studies of trade liberalization in a number of countries is mixed, and does not show a consistently large positive effect on labor demand. For Mexico, we have discussed several reasons why, even in the absence of the peso devaluation, labor demand and therefore the real wage might not rise as a result of NAFTA. Even if eventually Mexico is able to achieve a higher growth rate of output than would have been possible without NAFTA – an outcome that is still in doubt – there is reason to question whether the market alone will share these benefits with labor in proportion to labor's current share of national income. In the case of the U.S. and Mexico, trade and foreign investment are not taking place between countries with the same technology, as implied by the Heckscher-Ohlin model, but, rather, they are a means of diffusing technology. And if there are many small enterprises – whether maize producers or industrial or commercial businesses – that are driven out of business either by trade or by investment in modern, efficient businesses, aggregate labor demand is likely to fall. While growth in productivity is *potentially* beneficial to all, it is only actually so if its fruits are widely distributed; and if the market does not distribute its benefits through increased labor demand and wages, then other means must be found to accomplish that distribution.

Likewise, attracting foreign investment – whether through devaluation or by other means – contributes to growth of output by increasing the capital stock and by increasing technology transfer. However, at the same time, more foreign investment reduces the domestically owned share of national income and so reduces the likelihood that this additional output will be recycled through the national economy. Devaluation stimulates investment in the export sector. But firms producing mostly for the domestic market (and which continue to do so) are hurt not only by loss of sales revenue but by higher peso costs of debt service, imported intermediate goods, and capital goods. Such firms will then find it harder to purchase the capital equipment they need to modernize and become competitive. Liberalization is typically accompanied by the exhortation to competitiveness, and in such a context flexibilization of labor markets is often urged, through reduction in labor rights to job security, severance pay, and so forth. But while flexibilization may increase employment and output, it does so in part by lowering average wages. If wage elasticity of labor demand is less than 1, average labor incomes will fall.

In light of these observations, free trade agreements should be concluded only if they guarantee a share of productivity increases to labor that equals labor's current share of income. This guarantee could be accomplished, perhaps, through increases in the minimum wage until the average wage reflects productivity increases; or perhaps through a law requiring the implementation and enforcement of profit sharing; or perhaps through taxation of profits and provision of social services. NAFTA should be renegotiated to include such guarantees.

It is truly remarkable that the standard description of Mexico's economic history recounts the evils of import substitution industrialization (ISI) policies and the glories of market-oriented economic reforms, while the numbers tell precisely the opposite story. During the ISI policy regime, Mexico achieved an average annual growth rate of GDP in excess of 6 percent for the three decades from 1951 through 1981.

Since that time its growth rate has been far lower, and from the implementation of NAFTA through the end of 1996 Mexico had experienced a negative growth rate of GDP per capita.

The peso crisis did not have to happen. It must be recognized that volatile capital flows can be destabilizing, and measures must be taken to prevent a recurrence of such a crisis. One way to do this is by implementing capital controls or including an agreement to tax speculative financial and currency transactions. Free trade agreements should in addition refrain from constraining governments to very limited policy options for responding flexibly to economic crisis.

Finally, Mexico still suffers from the same two constraints on growth that it has faced for some time: its large foreign debt and its heavy dependence on intermediate and capital goods imports. Creative ways to reduce the debt may be found, and justice would be served if they included recovering funds from those who benefited from the debt accumulation in the first place by pocketing government funds. Alternatively, some portion of the debt could simply be forgiven. As for the prospects for Mexico in developing its capital goods and intermediate goods industries, more attention should be given to the goals of modernizing and expanding these industries and training and retaining skilled personnel in them. Among alternative policy options, industrial policy should not be ruled out.

On the positive side, economic integration motivates labor unions and citizen groups to join across borders in seeking progressive economic policies at a regional level, including protections for labor rights and the environment. While such efforts have so far been limited, there is hope that they will grow. The experience of Mexico signals the need to shape future economic integration in ways more widely beneficial to the population. It is wise to heed that warning and to find ways to realize the benefits of economic integration without suffering its ills.

Comment by *Thea Lee* on "Integration and income distribution under the North American Free Trade Agreement: the experience of Mexico"

This is an insightful, thorough, well-supported essay on an understudied topic: the impact of trade and investment liberalization on income distribution, growth, and equity in developing countries. Mehrene Larudee cuts through much of the ideology and textbook stereotypes to discuss the case of Mexico under NAFTA. Larudee succeeds in conveying the complexity of the real world events that motivate and accompany economic integration.

The issue of how developing countries fare under trade and investment liberalization is crucial to the political debates currently taking place around trade agreements with Africa and Latin America, as well as the terms of IMF funding. Conventional wisdom holds that trade liberalization provides unmitigated benefits for developing countries, while critics have argued that the rules contained in trade agreements make a difference to the outcomes, especially with respect to distributional effects.

Larudee argues that standard economic theory and the predictions of many NAFTA supporters overstated the likely benefits of NAFTA to Mexico. She provides an excellent analysis of the actual and expected gains from trade and investment liberalization for Mexico, and this chapter will be both absorbing and useful reading for people involved in the NAFTA debate on either side. However, Larudee's analysis of NAFTA's impact occasionally tends to treat liberalization as a yes-or-no choice, rather than a how-to.

The paper reviews six benefits typically claimed to accrue to developing countries as a result of trade and investment liberalization with a more developed country. Larudee provides both theoretical and empirical evidence to refute or undermine each and therefore to explain why the actual economic outcomes in Mexico after NAFTA have been so much more unfavorable than widely predicted.

Larudee devotes the most attention to the impact of trade liberalization on wage growth. She presents strong and consistent evidence that Mexican wages fell (in inflation-adjusted terms) as trade barriers were removed and as exports soared. In particular, wages in maquiladora plants (where export assembly is concentrated) fell dramatically during the period of rapid growth in output, employment, and exports (real wages declined 45 percent from 1977 to 1992). This evidence is directly contrary to the sanguine pronouncements of the NAFTA and free trade boosters, particularly those who claim to be concerned primarily with developing countries and poverty issues.

While Larudee discusses the peso crisis and its relationship to NAFTA elsewhere at length, it would also have been helpful for her to put the wage impacts she describes into context in this section. NAFTA defenders are likely to attribute the entire post-NAFTA wage decline to devaluation rather than to any impact of trade liberalization per se. Larudee avoids the issue somewhat by treating Mexico's liberalization as starting in the 1980s, but she can and should directly address the peso crisis argument here.

One problem with Larudee's analysis in this section is that she recognizes, but does not fully integrate, the distinction and interactions between foreign direct investment and trade liberalization. Some sections, in particular the wage section, focus only on trade liberalization, while others single out investment liberalization. But wages are affected by both the tariff reductions and the investment liberalization. As Larudee points out, most of the expected gains to Mexico from liberalization were predicted to come from increases in foreign direct investment, not reduction of already-low trade barriers. Therefore, it does not necessarily make sense to isolate trade liberalization in this context.

This raises a second, and perhaps more important, issue. Larudee focuses much attention on two "broken assumptions" of the Heckscher-Ohlin model that might explain why Mexico has appeared to experience both falling real wages and growing inequality in the wake of NAFTA, rather than the opposite, as standard theory would predict. These are that Mexico and the United States do not share access to identical technology and that goods produced in Mexico and the United States may be produced with opposite concentrations of factors of production (i.e., there is a "factor intensity reversal"). As Larudee explains, the fact that these assumptions do not hold in the U.S.–Mexico case can help to explain why the predictions of the standard trade model do not hold.

While these are important – and true – points, I fear that Larudee's focus on these two technical assumptions is misleading. This focus gives the impression that the rest of the Heckscher-Ohlin edifice is pretty solid. On the contrary, I would argue that virtually all of the key Heckscher-Ohlin assumptions fail to describe the U.S.–Mexico trade relationship – full employment, balanced trade, perfect competition. The question, of course, is to what degree and with what significance.

Most crucially, what is missing from the standard Heckscher-Ohlin model is any sense of market power in goods markets or bargaining power in the capital-labor relationship. The underlying power relationships are key to understanding economic integration policies like NAFTA and are given insufficient attention in this chapter.

In her conclusion, Larudee states: "Liberalization is typically accompanied by the exhortation to competitiveness, and in such a context flexibilization of labor markets is often urged." But perhaps this has the causality reversed. The exhortation to competitiveness, the ability of businesses to pressure workers to accept wage cuts, and the pressure on governments to ease up on environmental or public health regulations can all be seen as the reasons to pursue policies like NAFTA, not as side effects.

Thus, one wishes Larudee had explored a third reason why trade and investment liberalization resulted in falling wages in Mexico: the growing imbalance in bargaining power between workers and employers as a result of conscious government policy. Far from being an unintended consequence of liberalization or something external to it (like the asymmetrical technology access or the factor intensity reversals), this imbalance of bargaining power was the central point of NAFTA, its *raison d'etre*. This imbalance of power reflects the violation of implicit Heckscher-Ohlin assumptions: that factor markets are competitive and that trade liberalization is a politically neutral process.

Larudee's policy recommendations mention a variety of proposals designed to force a more equitable distribution of the fruits of trade liberalization and to mitigate the destabilizing impact of liberalization. Among them are tying the minimum wage to productivity increases, forced profit sharing, capital controls, industrial policy, and debt relief. Strangely, she mentions only in passing two of the central demands that social movements have raised in the context of NAFTA and fast track authority for new trade agreements: enforceable workers' rights and environmental standards.

Particularly in the Mexican context, the government's ability to impose labor-sweating policies effectively depends on the absence of strong independent unions (at least until recently). President Salinas actually promised to tie the minimum wage to productivity increases the day the NAFTA labor side agreement was concluded. And as Larudee points out, Mexican law contains a profit-sharing requirement. The failure of the government to implement and enforce these policies is connected to the complicity of the government-allied primary Mexican labor federation (the Confederation of Mexican Workers, known as CTM).

Designing trade policy that works is partly about having good ideas, but it is important to recognize that, ultimately, the key to success will lie in supporting the institutions and organizations that can carry out those ideas.

12

Malthus redux? Globalization and the environment

Eban Goodstein

Introduction

High and growing levels of consumption in the developed countries, coupled with high and only slowly declining rates of population growth in less-developed countries, pose a serious threat to the environment and ultimately to human welfare. Local ecological problems faced today are dramatic: overgrazing and overfishing, deforestation, fresh-water shortages, urban air pollution, pesticide poisoning, wetlands loss. Even more challenging are threats to the global environment: global warming, loss of biodiversity, ozone depletion. We need only consider that over the next 50 years world population will likely at least double, and world gross domestic product triple (World Bank 1992, 26), to see the potential for a Malthusian (or "neo-Malthusian") day of reckoning on the horizon.[1]

Given these grim trends, one can nevertheless still sketch out an approach to achieving a sustainable global future – sustainable in the economic sense of nondeclining welfare for the average person (Pezzey 1992). Following the Bruntland Commission (World Commission on Environment and Development 1987), it is taken here as a given that balanced economic growth in developing countries is vital to insure sustainability. For our purposes, balanced growth means a growth process that significantly raises living standards for the bottom half of the income distribution.

Such growth will be necessary to boost per capita health, sanitation, education, and social insurance expenses to deal with the needs of rapidly growing populations. Provision of these necessities to poor families, in turn, will lay the foundation

---

1   This paper employs a somewhat simple-minded reduction of the Malthusian debate to a race between resource limits and technology. Malthus, of course, did not see it that way, in part because he did not recognize the technological potential to escape resource limits, and in part because the policy issue he was addressing was poor relief, not resource depletion. However, Malthus clearly laid the foundation for the "neo-Malthusian" debate, currently raging between neo-classical and ecological environmental economists. In particular, it is worth going back to Malthus (1914) to note his attention to both short-run price increases from resource shortages, as well as long-run catastrophic outcomes.

The author wishes to thank Peter Dorman, Robin Broad, Bob Pollin, Jerry Epstein, Marty Hart-Landsberg, and John Wish for helpful suggestions.

for lower population growth rates (Dasgupta 1995). Balanced growth in developing countries, coupled with broad-based clean technology development and transfer from the North to mitigate the impacts, provides two of the three legs of a program needed for avoiding a Malthusian fate on a global scale. (The third leg, redirecting Northern consumption into less resource-intensive channels (Goodland et al. 1992), is equally important, but will not be addressed further in this paper.)

Realizing this vision requires two things. First, the growth process in the South must not come at too high an expense in terms of the resource base. Both environmental sources of inputs into the economy and environmental sinks absorbing waste products from the economy must be maintained on a sustainable basis. If not, future generations will be impoverished, not enriched, by growth.

Second, the development and diffusion of clean technology must be supported at a level well beyond what the unregulated market alone will achieve. This will require first that national governments around the world effectively regulate polluting industries, so that the costs imposed on society are borne by the polluters and reflected in the price of dirty technology. But simply leveling the playing field will not promote rapid enough growth of clean technology to insure sustainability (Duchin and Lange 1992). As will be discussed, technology development and adoption is a path-dependent process; thus, there is a critical need for government investment in clean technology promotion.

What is the relationship between the subject of this book, globalization, and the Bruntland vision of a sustainable future? Globalization, in my view, is rooted in recent, significant improvements in transportation and communication technology. These technological changes have facilitated increased trade, investment, and financial flows, which in turn have promoted corporate flexibility. This flexibility is exercised in production location decisions (including outsourcing) and natural resource access. Flexibility in turn has helped shift economic power away from labor, both organized and unorganized, and toward corporations.

This shift has been reflected in the global revival of a powerful free market ideology. Finally, the policy agenda spawned by the rise in corporate power has been deregulation at the national level and liberalization of trade and investment, increasingly codified in agreements like the North American Free Trade Agreement (NAFTA) and the World Trade Organization (WTO) in the international arena. The term "globalization" refers then to this whole interrelated and mutually reinforcing complex: a material basis in technological change, increased trade, investment and financial flows, enhanced corporate power, an ideological shift in favor of free markets, and the imposition of laissez faire policies.

This chapter explores the impact that globalization is having on the prospects for achieving a Bruntland solution to the Malthusian ecological trap that confronts us. I will explore two areas of conflict. First, Daly (1993) has argued that the simple expansion of global trade is undermining sustainability. It does so by disguising environmental limits in developed countries, thus substantially reducing incentives for clean technology development. At the same time, he argues, trade liberalization accelerates the unsustainable depletion of natural resources in developing countries. From this perspective, it is not the political response to globalization but rather its technical base that inevitably works against sustainability.

By contrast, the second and perhaps more persuasive charge against globalization is a distinctly political one: state power is inadequate to meet the challenge posed by increased corporate flexibility. Clearly, the Bruntland vision requires strong governments in the South to redistribute the benefits of growth and, in both the South and North, to enforce environmental and resource protection and measures and to promote the development and diffusion of clean technologies. While governments in developing countries are struggling to create effective systems of environmental protection – a process aided by globalized information access – it may well be that such efforts are too feeble to offset an unsustainable drawdown of Southern resources in an increasingly liberalized trade environment. At the same time, "competitiveness" concerns act as a strong break on state actions in the North.

Yet, are the policy prescriptions of wide-open liberalization and deregulation inevitable? In the face of increased corporate flexibility, governments might choose to develop new redistributional or regulatory strategies. Instead, many face strong pressures to withdraw from economic intervention of all types.

In both the South and North, this withdrawal is being aided by another feature of globalization: the revival of free market mythology. With respect to developing countries, there is a popular but facile argument that globalization, by expanding trade, insures growth, and that growth alone will somehow solve environmental problems. The link between free trade and growth is of course questionable; but an unregulated growth process undoubtedly depletes resources and exhausts environmental sinks. In many cases, poor countries are drawing down their stock of natural capital to supply international markets, without investing the resource rents that are generated into a stock of created capital upon which to base long-run development. In the absence of a strong state regulatory presence, a resource-based, trade-driven development process will not be sustainable.

In the developed countries, deregulation is propelled by a similar globalization myth – that environmental protection has simply become too costly. Does increased corporate flexibility require a downward leveling of environmental standards, in order for First World industry to remain competitive? The answer is clearly no. Environmental regulatory compliance costs have had little impact on firm location decisions. Yet, even though the "pollution haven" phenomenon is not real, it nevertheless carries great political weight in the United States, if not yet in Europe, and thus poses a substantial threat to a sustainable future.

If the current wave of unfettered liberalization and deregulation threaten to lead us down an unsustainable path, what alternatives exist that are feasible in the face of corporate flexibility? The Bruntland policy prescription is for vigorous environmental and resource protection efforts in the South and for clean technology development and transfer from the North. The good news is that this agenda is not fundamentally challenged by the underlying economics of globalization; indeed, the new technologies that underlie the globalization process can help further the Bruntland goals.

First, many governments in the South have passed good environmental and resource protection legislation and, in remarkably short order, have begun to develop significant environmental expertise. However the *enforcement* capabilities of governments in the South remain weak. Policy should focus on strengthening enforcement efforts via direct aid and in the design of trade agreements. Expanding the idea of "citizen suits" found in NAFTA, in which nongovernmental organizations (NGOs) can bring persistent violations of resource protection laws to the attention of trading authorities, provides one such avenue.

But isn't a system of lax regulations (or enforcement) a prerequisite for attracting investment in a globalized economy? No, since, as evidence suggests, environmental regulations have little impact on firm location decisions. By this same token, environmental and resource protection regulations in the North do not need to be relaxed in response to increased corporate mobility. Here, the threat of job loss has been vastly exaggerated to benefit corporate interests.

This too is good news, since stringent regulations in the developed world are necessary (but not sufficient) to support the second policy leg of the Bruntland agenda: promoting the rapid development of clean technology. Attacking this problem head on, by boosting direct Northern support for the development of clean technologies, is also not precluded by increased corporate flexibility – though it may be challenged by trade agreements. One of the benefits of the technological revolution underlying globalization is that cost-effective environmental technologies now have the potential to spread rapidly around the globe. Relatively small government investments, for example in solar energy, can thus have major global payoffs.

Finally, although fundamental technological changes underlying globalization have changed the nature of state power, the state is by no means powerless. Globalization has shifted some economic power to corporations, but a similar shift in political power, the resurgence of an uncritical free market ideology, and the adoption of a laissez faire environmental policy agenda, need not follow.

Globalization, trade, and the environment

It is useful to begin a discussion of economic activity and the environment with the notion of ecological limits – regional "carrying capacity." When applied to humans, carrying capacity refers to the maximum level of population at a given level of consumption that can be supported by an environmental resource base. Carrying capacity is not an absolute: it can be increased by the development of cleaner, less-polluting, or less resource-intensive technologies. Indeed, this is the gist of the 200-year-old Malthusian debate: the prospect for a sustainable future clearly hinges in large measure on the outcome of a race between technological progress and resource exhaustion.

Regional carrying capacity, though not global carrying capacity, can also be temporarily overcome by importing resources or exporting waste. As Postel (1994) points out, it is rich countries today that are more likely to have exceeded their regional carrying capacities; for example, "to meet its food and timber demands alone, the Netherlands appropriates the production capabilities...[of an area] 10 times its own acreage of cropland, pasture, and forest."

How does globalization fit into this picture? Daly (1993, 57), in making the case against trade liberalization, has argued that increased global economic activity per se undermines sustainability.

> By spatially separating the costs and benefits of environmental exploitation, international trade makes them harder to compare. It thereby increases the tendency for economies to overshoot their optimal scale. Furthermore, it forces countries to face tightening environmental constraints more simultaneously and less sequentially than would otherwise be the case. They have less opportunity to learn from one another's experiences with controlling throughput and [have] less control over their local environment.

Put simply, in the North, trade reduces incentives for the development of cleaner technologies (including lifestyle changes), since it disguises environmental limits. The flip side of this process is an accelerated and unsustainable depletion of natural capital in the South (Daly and Goodland 1994).

Two examples of the first effect can be seen in the petroleum and hazardous waste trades. In the former case, informal restrictions on trade have served the environment well. Because Japan and Europe have been unable to project military power to protect oil trade routes, they have pursued policies of energy independence. The result has been major improvements in energy efficiency; the Japanese and Germans consume about half of the energy per capita that Americans do, and generate comparably low levels of carbon dioxide emissions.

The U.S., by contrast, continues along as an oil glutton, consuming twice as much gas per capita as any other country and contributing 21 percent of the global emission of greenhouse gasses while sheltering only 5 percent of the world's population (Goodstein 1995a, Chapter 18). Daly's point about disguising limits can perhaps best be illustrated by U.S. attitudes toward preservation of Alaska's Arctic National Wildlife Refuge – a place that few of us will ever visit. Americans oppose what would be, by international standards, carefully regulated oil development in the region. At the same time, however, we are perfectly willing to completely despoil Nigerian fisheries, or inflict horrific environmental catastrophes – including war-related damage – in the Persian Gulf. Why should we be willing to pay more to preserve one remote ecosystem than another? Daly's response is "out of sight, out of mind."

The principle that nations should be forced to keep their own waste products clearly in sight has been affirmed in the extension of the Basel Convention in 1993, in which developed countries (with the exception of the United States) agreed to a total ban on the export of hazardous waste to the developing world (*New York Times,* March 26, 1994).

Yet the logic of globalization calls for expanded, not restricted, trade in waste. Indeed, in 1992 Lawrence Summers, former chief economist at the World Bank, advocated such policies in an internal World Bank memorandum (*Economist,* February 8 and 15, 1992). While Summers undoubtedly envisioned a Pareto improve-

ment from toxic trade – poor communities perhaps receiving sewage treatment facilities in exchange for waste storage – in the real world this kind of deal is problematic, to say the least. Less charitably, the Brazilian environment minister characterized the argument as "perfectly logical, but perfectly insane." Restricted trade
keeps the consequences of our actions close to home, where we have both the community of interest and the political tools to manage them. Restricted trade also forces
us to develop the recycling, treatment, and waste reduction technologies needed for
sustainable development.

Let us grant with Daly that the simple expansion in the volume of trade indeed
disguises environmental limits, slowing the pace of technological change in the North
and accelerating resource depletion in the South. Does this mean that all trade should
be restricted to promote sustainable development? Might not trade in general nevertheless promote the economic growth in poor countries that the Bruntland vision demands? And don't poor countries have a right to decide what the correct tradeoff is
between environmental protection and growth in their own countries?

Earlier in this chapter, I accepted the proposition that a sustainable future requires rapid and balanced economic growth in poor countries. Advocates of the
globalization policy agenda of liberalization and deregulation have argued that this
agenda promotes growth. Further, as countries grow richer their population growth
rate declines, and they can afford to clean up and protect their local environment.
Bhagwati (1993, 43) argues: "The fear is widespread among environmentalists that
free trade increases economic growth and that growth harms the environment. That
fear is misplaced." While Bhagwati's view is a bit more nuanced than his wording
suggests, the model he proposes is a bare-bones one: trade promotes growth; growth
generates wealth; wealth produces a cleaner environment. On net, trade and growth
are good for the environment.

This very simple-minded view has diffused widely in a short period of time,
being featured, in a somewhat softened form, in the *1995 Economic Report of the
President* (Council of Economic Advisors 1995, 241–4). Indeed, a large group of
economists and ecologists felt compelled to attack it in a recent article in *Science*
(Arrow et al. 1995).

There is undoubtedly an element of truth to the model, but it is generally
unpersuasive. First, the trade-growth link is controversial. Chichilinsky (1994) provides a theoretical rationale for the underdevelopment of resource-based economies
in poor countries. She argues that property rights are much more poorly defined in
the South than in the North; this leads to the underpricing and overexploitation of
Southern resources.

More generally, in a recent survey article Rodrik (1992, 103) concludes: "A reasonable hypothesis is that trade policy plays a rather asymmetric role in development:
an abysmal trade regime can perhaps drive a country into economic ruin; but good
trade policy cannot make a poor country rich." Moreover, "good trade policy" may not
be thoroughly liberal trade policy (Amsden 1989; Wade 1990). NAFTA, for example,
actually prohibits Mexico from engaging in aggressive industrial export promotion of
the type pursued, for example, by Korea (Grinspun and Cameron 1992).

If liberal trade policy is not the key to growth, uncontrolled growth is clearly a recipe for environmental disaster. How then is the growth–environment link defended? There is little doubt that balanced economic growth in poor countries improves access to clean water and sanitation and reduces exposure to indoor air pollution in the form of smoke from cooking fires. These are by far the two largest environmental health risks facing the citizens of less-developed countries (World Bank 1992). Moreover, urban air quality for some pollutants exhibits an inverted U-shape, with cities in richer countries exhibiting much cleaner air than cities in the newly industrializing world (Grossman and Krueger 1991; World Bank 1992). Finally, and most significantly from an environmental perspective, rising living standards often lead to falling population growth rates.

Yet these observations do not establish the claim that growth alone improves environmental quality, for many reasons. First, for poor countries, growth must be sufficiently balanced so as to raise income levels, and thus access to basic services, for the majority of the population. Moreover, the experience in Eastern Europe demonstrates that growth is insufficient to insure improvements in air and water quality. Absent accountability to local communities – democratic or otherwise – pollution from production units will remain unregulated regardless of national laws and increase with economic growth. O'Connor (1994) illustrates the critical role that increasingly open political climates have played in spurring environmental protection efforts in fast-growing East Asia; Wheeler (1996) finds that education is an important factor, independent of income, in determining the level of environmental enforcement in poor countries.

Second, many facets of environmental quality continue to deteriorate with economic growth, even in rich countries. These include increases in unregulated pollutants such as carbon dioxide; increases in pollutants tied to local production sites such as hazardous, nuclear, or municipal wastes, oil spills, and traffic congestion; and pressure on natural ecosystems and scarce environmental resources such as beaches, wetlands, biodiversity reserves, and wilderness.

Third, local improvements accompanying growth may mask global deterioration in environmental quality. Reductions in ambient levels of sulfur dioxide in urban areas in the U.S. have been bought at the expense of increased acid rain problems, as stacks were built higher, and sulfur sludges, which themselves present a pollution problem. Generally, local improvements in environmental quality may simply reflect the export of environmental problems to other mediums, other regions, or other countries. For example, Sedjo (1994) argues that protection of North American forests is generating increased wood harvesting overseas, in both developing and developed countries.

Finally, suppose that the somewhat restrictive conditions under which liberalized trade does promote growth are indeed met; can we wait for growth alone to resolve environmental problems? Suppose, for example, we grant Mexico a very generous average economic growth rate of 4 percent. It would take the country 25 years to achieve the cutoff of around $4,000 per capita at which urban air quality appears to begin to improve (Grossman and Krueger 1991; Selden and Song 1992).

Until that time, air quality in Mexico City, already the worst in the world, will presumably continue to deteriorate. In addition, given an expanded population and level of economic activity, the nation's overall resource base will continue to be drawn down, well beyond what many would argue are serviceable recovery levels.

Despite these objections, balanced growth must be a component of sustainable development, primarily to provide a foundation for reduced population growth. But increased reliance on natural resource exports will often fail to generate the desired outcome. Growth in GDP arising from exploiting natural capital can be a misleading indicator of true increases in social welfare. First, reductions in subsistence production and consumption from the expansion of export agriculture will not show up in national accounts. For example, the subsistence production of Mexican corn farmers who lose their livelihood as a result of expansion of the cattle industry to serve the North American beef market will not appear as a reduction in GDP. This is not a frivolous example: close to half of Latin America's prime farmland is devoted to beef production, primarily for export (Leonard 1987).

In addition, recent research has indicated that GDP growth based on the exploitation of natural capital can disguise an unsustainable drawdown in resources (Pearce and Atkinson 1993). Cattle grazing on marginal forest lands, for example, will clearly boost GDP over the short term. To the extent that profits generated and taxes raised from these endeavors are used to develop an educated populace, or to invest in human-made capital, intensive grazing might be justified on the basis of sustainable development. But often, companies who exploit natural resources, and governments who tax them, fail to reinvest all of the resource rents generated. Indeed, the government share of resource rents often flows directly back to the developed world in the form of debt repayment. When rents are not invested, the natural resources are not replaced with human-made capital to form the basis for future development, and growth is unsustainable.

In the area of nonfuel minerals, we have seen the recent publication of a book focusing on the "dismal" economic performance of the major developing country mineral exporters over the last 20 years (Tilton 1992). The book was surprising, because among the authors are some leading advocates of rapid mineral development, many of whom had advised these same countries. While still committed to exports, the authors are clearly puzzled by the failure of trade to promote prosperity.

Free trade agreements have already begun to bind the hands of governments that seek to reduce the rate of exploitation of natural capital within their borders. Attempts by Canada's National Energy Board to slow down development of the nation's natural gas deposits have been crippled by lawsuits filed by U.S.-based transnational corporations under the U.S.–Canada Free Trade Agreement. In a similar vein, Canadian requirements to monitor fish catches in depleted areas were disallowed (Shrybman 1992). While there were certainly legitimate trade issues at stake in these cases, the fear is that trade agreements nevertheless undermine politically feasible, if not first-best, environmental protection measures.

The trade–growth link alleged by globalization advocates is a tenuous one. Moreover, even when trade does promote growth, the assumption that growth alone will improve environmental quality is absurd. Active government policy to provide a social safety net, increase access to education, redistribute land, promote corporate and state environmental accountability, regulate polluters, and provide natural resource protection and conservation are essential for reducing population growth and protecting the resources on which future generations will depend.

Growth in the South has indeed brought with it increased attention to environmental problems. World Bank studies show evidence of increasing environmental protection efforts throughout the developing world, with such efforts being strongly correlated with per capita income (Wheeler 1996). However, it is not clear that resource and environmental protection capacities in developing countries have expanded fast enough from a sustainability perspective.

The conventional economic view appears to be that national governments in fact intervene at an "optimal" (Pareto-efficient) level. If governments in poor countries have weak regulations or enforcement capabilities, this reflects an implicit weighing of benefits and costs fully reflecting local tastes and incomes. But as the discussion above of accountability and access to information make clear, this is at best a naive perspective.

Moreover, even if through some invisible political hand intervention is indeed occurring at a Pareto-efficient level, there may well be too little resource and environmental protection from a sustainability perspective (Howarth and Noorgard 1990). This is because there is no market mechanism to prevent current generations in poor countries (or rich countries) from spending more than their intergenerational share of the endowment of natural capital. And, as noted above, there is considerable evidence that resource depletion is indeed occurring at an unsustainable rate in the developing countries.

In this section, I have reviewed Daly's argument that the simple increased volume of trade that accompanies globalization undercuts sustainability. It does so by disguising ecological limits in the North; this both discourages the development of clean technology and promotes overly rapid resource depletion and excessive pollution in the South. However, I would argue that, although the material pressures that Daly identifies are real, it is the political response to globalization that matters more. Trade per se is not the villain, though it is no hero either.

While some progress has been made in controlling environmental degradation in poor countries, in many areas the impact of increased trade is degrading the environment at a rate that is far shy of optimal – if not from an efficiency perspective then certainly from a sustainability one. At the same time, developing country governments face the same kind of political pressures to avoid "excessive" regulation faced in industrialized countries. To the extent that increased corporate flexibility and its attendant free market mythology undermine government powers in the South, growth induced by globalization will not take us in the direction envisioned by the Bruntland Commission. What impacts does globalization have in the North?

Globalization, competitiveness, and the environment

Globalized production might impact environmental quality in wealthy countries through one of two interrelated channels. On the one hand, Northern countries might protect their local environment by satisfying their consumption of dirty products through importation from the South. On the other hand, political pressure to reduce capital flight to such pollution havens might lead to a downward leveling of environmental standards.

We argued above that Northern consumption of timber, minerals, livestock, and agricultural products often comes at the expense of Southern sustainability. In this section, by contrast, we shall see that there is little evidence to support growing Northern imports from pollution-intensive manufacturing. It is therefore ironic that political pressure to promote the "competitiveness" of U.S. industry through downward leveling of standards has been most intense in the manufacturing sector.

Consider one example. In 1990, the United States Business Roundtable published a study predicting the impact on employment of the Clean Air Act amendments, which were passed later that year (Hahn and Steger 1990, ES.15). Their conclusion left "little doubt that a minimum of two hundred thousand (plus) jobs will quickly be lost, with plants closing in dozens of states. This number could easily exceed one million jobs – and even two million jobs – at the more extreme assumption about residual risk." In part because of concerns about widespread job loss, the act authorized retraining funds of $50 million per year for displaced workers.

Four years later, a grand total of 2,363 workers had applied for aid because they felt their jobs were affected by the Clean Air Act (U.S. Department of Labor 1994). While this number does not tell the whole job loss story, it does suggest a yawning gulf between rhetoric and reality.

In the United States, a belief in a major tradeoff between jobs and the environment, fueled by these kinds of wildly inflated numbers, is deeply embedded in public discourse. A 1990 poll revealed that one-third of the respondents felt that their own job was likely or somewhat likely to be threatened by environmental protection measures.[2]

These fears, easy to understand in the context of increased economic insecurity and deindustrialization, are nevertheless without much foundation. Stringent national environmental standards were first imposed in the countries of the OECD (Organization for Economic Cooperation and Development) beginning in the early 1970s. Over the ensuing 25 years, a substantial body of research has developed assessing the impacts of environmental regulation on employment. There is a surprising degree of consensus among economists on three main points:

(1) At the economy-wide level, there is simply no tradeoff between environmental protection and employment.

2   "Americans Are Willing to Sacrifice to Reduce Pollution, They Say," *Wall Street Journal*, April 20, 1990.

(2) The number of manufacturing workers laid off due primarily to environmental regulations has been quite small – on the order of 1,000 to 3,000 per year in the U.S.

(3) Few firms relocate to poor countries primarily to take advantage of lax environmental regulations.

These issues are explored in detail in Goodstein (1994) and Jaffe et al. (1995) and will not be rehashed here. The basic point is that industrial competitiveness and aggregate job growth in manufacturing is essentially independent of the level of environmental regulation. This is primarily because regulatory compliance costs remain a small portion of total business costs. This is not to downplay the need for worker adjustment and retraining programs – economic insecurity is on the rise. Rather, it is only to state that the need for these programs has little to do with environmental regulation at its current level.

There is, however, one body of evidence that appears to work against this consensus viewpoint, and in favor of the pollution haven hypothesis. Several studies have found that the world share of pollution-intensive, or "dirty," industrial production has been rising in the South and declining in the OECD countries since the early 1970s.

Lucas, Wheeler, and Hettige (1992) found that in the 1960s "toxic intensity [in manufacturing] grew most quickly in the high-income economies. During the 1970s and 1980s, after the advent of strict OECD environmental regulation, this pattern was sharply reversed." ("Toxic intensity" is a measure of the share of manufacturing output claimed by high-pollution industries.)

Low and Yeats (1992) report that the North American share of dirty output declined by one-third from 1965 to 1988, while the share originating in Southeast Asia doubled. At the same time, the total share of dirty output in world trade fell from 19 percent to 16 percent.

These findings might be interpreted as suggesting that multinationals substantially reduced "dirty" investment in rich countries and increased it in developing countries. However, Hettige et al. find that "paradoxically...outward-oriented, high-growth LDCs have slow-growing or even declining toxic intensity, while toxic intensity increases more rapidly in inward-oriented economies." It is presumably these outward-oriented, high-growth LDCs that should be attracting manufacturing capital from the developed world under the pollution haven hypothesis.

In a more detailed paper, Lucas, Wheeler, and Hettige (1992) suggest that the results may be explained by "a shift towards a different global distribution [of production]" without direct investment. In other words, closed economies may have fostered the domestic growth of polluting industries such as chemicals and oil, mineral, and paper refining as part of a resource-based industrialization strategy.

Commenting on the Low and Yeats' results, Jaffe et al. (1995, 145) suggest that the share shift may be due, among other factors, "simply to increased demand within the latter (developing countries) for the products of pollution-intensive industries." Moreover, they argue that natural resource endowments probably play a large role in determining production locations for relatively dirty industry. Raw material dependent industries are indeed often relatively pollution intensive.

If the relationship is very tight, then heavily regulated industries may be less footloose than other sectors. This means that raw-material-dependent industries would be less likely to shrink in the face of import competition. The impact on the relative competitiveness of export industries should be similar: "ceteris paribus," raw material dependence should reflect a genuine comparative advantage, leading to better-than-average export growth.

Earlier studies of changes in the pollution content of developed country imports have proven inconclusive. Kalt (1988), working at the two-digit level, found that manufacturing industries with high abatement costs had a significantly worse net export performance over the period 1967–77. Oddly, however, the relationship was much stronger when heavily regulated chemicals were excluded. Robison (1988) found that the abatement content of two-digit U.S. imports, including manufacturing and nonmanufacturing industries, rose relative to U.S. exports, primarily over the period 1977–82. However, this finding may result from his peak-to-trough comparison. Tobey (1990), using a qualitative measure of international stringency of regulation, found no impact on net exports in five pollution-intensive industries.

Grossman and Krueger (1991) looked at the impact of abatement costs on U.S. imports from Mexico at the three-digit standard industrial classification (SIC) level, U.S. imports from Mexico entering under offshore assembly provisions (also at the three-digit level), and the two-digit sectoral pattern of value-added in the maquiladora region. Only in one case – offshore assembly imports – was the relationship significant. However, it worked in the opposite direction than expected. Imports appeared to be higher in industries with lower pollution abatement costs. Finally, Repetto (1995) summarizes World Bank data showing that, on net, heavily regulated U.S. industries exhibited significantly superior export performance than average over the period 1970–90.

To further the assessment of whether or not the U.S. economy is becoming increasingly dependent on "dirty" imports, I assembled a dataset covering 412 four-digit SIC industries. Employing a richer dataset than other researchers, I examined the growth of U.S. imports and exports over the business cycle peak years 1973–78 and from 1978–85 (the import-export data were not available for subsequent years). I regressed real import (and export) growth against a measure of pollution intensity, controlling for labor skill levels and, bearing in mind the Jaffe et al. hypotheses, the rate of market growth and the industry's dependence upon raw materials.

Pollution intensity was measured by the average share of pollution abatement control expenditure in total domestic output for each industry over the business cycle. The conventional wisdom is that higher environmental costs should compromise competitiveness. The wage variable used here reflects the share of unskilled labor in total output; higher wages should encourage import growth and discourage export growth. Following Grossman and Krueger (1991), we also include a human capital variable, which is value-added minus the unskilled wage bill, over total output. "Ceteris paribus," more human capital should reduce imports and increase exports.

Market growth is the change in the real value of total shipments (including exports), plus imports, and should be positively related to both dependent variables.

Table 1 *Mean and standard error for each variable*

	1973–78	1978–85
Percent change in imports	0.346 (0.629)	0.606 (0.662)
Percent change in exports	0.406 (0.654)	-0.093 (0.580)
Environmental cost share	0.003 (0.006)	0.005 (0.008)
Raw materials share	0.052 (0.124)	——
Market growth	0.097 (0.259)	0.051 (0.359)
Unskilled wage share	0.214 (0.084)	0.208 (0.080)
Human capital share	0.113 (0.054)	0.114 (0.055)

Finally, the raw materials share was calculated using the 1972 input–output tables. A higher raw materials share should reflect a comparative advantage for the industry, slowing import penetration, and boosting exports. For more details, please see the data appendix.

Table 1 provides the means and standard errors for the variables. On average, import shares grew in real terms 35 percent over the period 1973–78, accelerating to 61 percent from 1978 to 1985. Export shares grew on average 41 percent over the earlier period but declined 9 percent over the latter. Environmental operating costs were quite small, averaging 0.3 percent of total sales, and rising very slightly in the latter period. For heavily regulated industries, this figure rose to a maximum of 7 percent (for primary zinc) in this sample.

Table 2 provides the ordinary least squares (OLS) regression results.[3] For 1973–78 the relationship between the environmental compliance cost share and import growth is positive, but it is small and statistically insignificant. However, consistent with Kalt's results, export industries facing heavy regulation did suffer in the early period: an increase in the environmental cost share from 0.01 to 0.02, "ceteris paribus," led to a reduction in exports of 21 percent.

However, from 1978 to 1985, the impact of environmental regulation reverses

3   Since writing this chapter I have extended the econometric work reported here. A new dataset allowed a separate examination of developing and developed country imports, using the change (not the percentage change) in the import share as the dependent variable. I obtained comparable results to those reported here for imports from developed countries; I found no statistically significant impact for developing country imports. The export work remains to be completed. See Goodstein 1997.

Table 2 *OLS regression results (t-statistics in parentheses)*

Dependent variable	Percent change in real imports		Percent change in real exports	
	1973–78	1978–85	1973–78	1978–85
Environmental cost share	3.493	-8.833[a]	-21.119[a]	6.614[c]
	(0.683)	(-2.257)	(-4.146)	(1.719)
Raw materials share	-0.784[a]	-0.393	-0.256	-0.621[a]
	(-2.712)	(-1.493)	(-0.949)	(2.577)
Market growth	0.980[a]	1.053[a]	0.816[a]	0.588[a]
	(7.655)	(11.836)	(6.365)	(6.686)
Unskilled wage share	0.445	-0.189	1.191[a]	-0.273
	(0.996)	(-0.426)	(2.614)	(-0.623)
Human capital share	-0.013	-0.029	0.220	0.020
	(-0.559)	(-1.302)	(0.919)	(0.918)
Constant	0.196[a]	0.661[a]	0.225[a]	-0.143[b]
	(2.373)	(8.859)	(2.721)	(-1.955)
Adjusted R^2	0.167	0.334	0.178	0.148
N	337	336	337	335

[a] Significant at the 1% level.
[b] Significant at the 5% level.
[c] Significant at the 10% level.

itself. Consistent with Grossman and Krueger's (1991) finding, industries with a higher regulatory burden both faced lower import penetration and exhibited better export performance than did other sectors. Based on the point estimates, an increase in the environmental cost share from 0.01 to 0.02 would have led to a decrease in imports of 9 percent and an increase in exports of 7 percent. The results are statistically significant, highly so in the import case and at the 10 percent level in the export case.

In the earlier period, the raw materials share variable has the expected sign and is significant for imports; it is wrong-signed but insignificant for exports. Over the latter period, the raw material coefficient estimates have the expected signs, and the estimate in the export equation is significant.

Market growth performs as expected in all the regressions. Over both periods, the human capital and wage share variables add little to the explanatory value of the equation; the one significant exception, on the wage variable in the 1973–78 export equation, has an unexpected positive sign.

Overall, the results provide no support for the hypothesis that the U.S. is satisfying an increasing proportion of its consumer needs through dirty imports of manufactured goods. If anything, heavily regulated industries fared better in terms of import penetration. There is some evidence for a negative impact on the export performance of U.S. industry in the early years of regulation; however, in the later period, there was a positive correlation between regulation and export growth. On net, between 1973 and 1985 these results do suggest a depressing effect on exports, but Repetto argues that, by 1990, the overall export performance of firms facing stiff regulation was better than average.

The reason for the better-than-expected performance of highly regulated industries over the period 1978–85 is not clear. The result does not appear to be driven by a relative decline in demand for pollution-intensive products, since the regression controls for market growth. Nor can the relative decline in import shares of pollution-intensive industries be accounted for by their raw material intensity. The regression also controls for this effect, which was found to be significant in the two cases. The result may be due to pollution-intensive industries being relatively skilled. This effect was captured only imperfectly through the unskilled labor and human capital variables.[4]

Another possible explanation for this result is the so-called "Porter hypothesis" (Porter 1991; Porter and van der Linde 1995) that environmental regulation, while imposing short-run costs on firms, actually enhances their long-run competitiveness. Jaffe et al. (1995) provide a clear, if skeptical, overview of the ways in which this might happen: from favoring forward-looking firms that develop products in future demand; to reducing inefficiencies in production, in particular through speeding investment in modern processes; to promoting "outside-the-box" thinking; to forcing an expansion in research and development spending.

To sum up: these results indicate first that the export performance of U.S. industry was first hurt, then aided, by environmental regulation. Moreover, there is a substantial, currently unexplained relative reduction in the share of imports entering the U.S. from pollution-intensive industry from 1978 to 1985. This reduction is consistent with the Porter hypothesis. It also, in turn, suggests that the growth in the South's share of the world's dirty industries documented by Hemmala et al. and Low and Yeats is feeding primarily Southern demand. As with the vast majority of research in this area, I find no support for the pollution haven hypothesis, broadly defined.

Nevertheless, and in spite of accumulated evidence to the contrary, the pollution haven hypothesis has generated widespread concern about job loss in the United States. Such fears have been both fanned and exploited by conservative Republicans, who as part of their Contract with America in 1995 began a widespread assault on domestic environmental and natural resource regulation. Republicans that year advanced serious proposals to weaken most major environmental regulations, and attempted to cut funding at the Environmental Protection Agency by one-third. In 1992, then-President Bush used this argument, for example, to both weaken the global warming treaty and spurn the biodiversity treaty at the Rio summit.

---

4   Three potential problems: the wage variable as defined will miss any union premium, which might encourage relocation. The human capital variable as defined might also be picking up x-inefficiency, or a union wage premium. Finally, since the bulk of trade is intra-OECD trade, relative wage shares may not matter much.

The "jobs-versus-the-environment" debate is less prominent in Europe than in the United States, providing some additional evidence that the pollution haven phenomenon is more a political creation than an economic reality. Nevertheless, and in spite of solid economic evidence to the contrary, the frightening perception of global competition for dirty industry has induced very real downward leveling pressures on environmental protection regulation.

Corporate flexibility, sustainability, and policy

Downward leveling of standards is just one example of a policy race to the bottom: national, state, and provincial governments competing with one another – by lowering taxes, social controls, and wages – to attract footloose foreign direct investment. To the extent that globalization induces this kind of behavior, it clearly undercuts attempts to realize the Bruntland vision of a sustainable future. Governments in the South sacrifice the ability to make the social investments needed to stabilize population growth and to conserve their natural resource and environmental base. Governments in the North weaken environmental regulation in a futile effort to promote competitiveness. At the same time, globalization helps convert regional ecological problems into global ones, as citizens in developed countries fail to recognize the environmental limits that are being pressed by their high levels of consumption.

Are there alternative policy responses to globalization, more consistent with a vision of sustainable development? One point of this paper has been that, at least vis-a-vis environmental regulations, the race to the bottom is not only counterproductive but unnecessary: firm location decisions are not affected, and national competitiveness is not undermined, by stringent regulations. Indeed, the previous section presented some evidence to support the opposite view, known as the Porter hypothesis, that environmental regulation can actually improve competitiveness. Clearly, "economic reality" does not dictate environmental deregulation.

Keeping this point in mind, the remainder of the chapter will consider policies that serve the twin environmental goals laid out by the Bruntland Commission: environmental and resource protection in the South, and clean technology promotion in the North.

Enforcement in the South
If balanced growth is to be successful in raising average living standards in the South, it must be accompanied by increasingly tough environmental and resource protection measures. And as we have seen, economic research suggests that developing countries have little to lose in terms of discouraging foreign investment from imposing relatively stringent environmental regulations. This is good news.

But the problem today is not so much the level of regulation as the level of enforcement. Most developing countries, recognizing the importance of environmental resources, have passed significant environmental legislation. Mexico, for example, has environmental laws approaching those of the United States in terms of stringency. But spending by Mexico's regulatory authority is less than a hundredth that of its northern neighbor (Friedman 1992).

Even in a country with a relatively efficient bureaucracy such as Costa Rica, by 1985 landless farmers had already cleared one-quarter of the total forest reserves that the government had set aside for protection (Carriere 1991). Central American environmental aspirations are thus proving unachievable. Lax enforcement has invalidated national goals.

All countries have two problems enforcing the laws that they pass: limited resources, and the opportunities for political influence and corruption in the enforcement process. These problems are often acute in developing countries.

The promotion of enforcement efforts in poor countries should follow a dual track. First, a global environmental compliance fund should be established, supported by a uniform 1 percent tax on imports.[5] This money should then be distributed back to developing countries to support compliance with environmental and natural resource protection laws, including efforts to promote sustainable development in resource-dependent communities. Second, trading authorities should establish a process for bringing last-resort "citizen suits" against firms that persistently violate domestic environmental laws.

A 1 percent tax on merchandise imports would raise about $40 billion, less than one-third of what U.S. firms and consumers currently spend to comply with environmental laws and regulations but about the same as total OECD development aid to low-income countries.

Why a trade tax? If implemented as part of a multilateral "Green GATT" (i.e., an environment-friendly version of the General Agreement on Tariffs and Trade), it would provide a reliable and visible source of income to support sustainable development efforts. And it may be politically viable – developing nations might support it since they would be its direct beneficiaries. (For this to be true, trade-dependent countries would of course have to receive higher levels of aid.) Political support in the North would come from those who view globalization as undermining the viability of their communities, if not their material standard of living. Such an across-the-board tax might even appeal to free traders, if it were to preempt more vigorous or targeted "protectionist" measures.

Contrary to much free trade rhetoric, the trading system is not a fragile creature. Bhagwati (1988) reports that average tariff levels from 1953 to 1963 were over twice as high as from 1973 to 1983; growth in global income over the latter period was substantially slower (4.3 percent vs. 2.5 percent). Clearly the lower tariffs did not cause the growth slowdown. Yet, it is equally clear that global income growth has been higher, with much higher levels of protection than we now see. An across-the-board tax would recognize that it is stability and nondiscrimination in the trad-

---

5   Esty (1994) makes an extended case for such a fund; he argues for a much smaller tax (1/100th of a percent) levied on both trade and currency flows. The latter is dwarfed by the former, so that his proposed tax would raise from $10 billion to $20 billion per year. He cites EC-GATT Commissioner Tran Van Thinh's call for a 0.25 percent import tax on all except the least-developed countries to support a similar proposal.

ing system that promotes economic development through trade, not the level of tariffs per se.

In addition to promoting sustainability directly, an import tax to support environmental compliance would probably be justified on static efficiency grounds. International trade accounts for around one-eighth of world oil consumption; fossil fuels are associated with a variety of (currently uninternalized) environmental problems, ranging from oil spills to urban air pollution, acid rain, and global warming (Daly 1991; Gabel 1994). In addition, energy production is heavily subsidized, to the tune of $28 billion per year in the U.S., not including military expenditures to protect Persian Gulf oil fields and shipping lanes (Koplow 1993). Developing countries, too, engage in massive energy subsidies, with electricity prices averaging half of those in the OECD (Daly 1993). A 1 percent import tax would help offset these energy subsidies, as well as the direct environmental costs associated with trade.

Failure to enforce environmental and resource protection laws is in part a function of lack of economic resources, which an enforcement fund should help remedy. But domestic political considerations are also significant. In the United States, we have had our own problems with lax enforcement, arising from the political influence of business. One solution has been to allow so-called "citizen suits": citizens, typically environmental NGOs, can sue a corporation that violates an environmental law (Goodstein 1995a, Chapter 13).

I propose that companies that fail to comply with the environmental regulations in effect in the country in which they are operating could be subject to a similar procedure – in which the punishment would be the imposition of import duties or fines.[6] On the one hand, this would encourage the growth of environmental NGOs in developing countries, which could monitor compliance with national laws and seek recourse in an international setting, if domestic enforcement proves infeasible. On the other hand, it also shifts much of the cost of enforcement, both political and economic, away from poor countries to rich countries. But it does not impinge on national sovereignty: this is not eco-imperialism, but rather eco-support.

Citizen suits are already built into a couple of international agreements. Recently, Friends of the Earth successfully sued the U.K. government in the European Court of Justice over illegal levels of nitrates in drinking water. The NAFTA side accords also include a weak citizen suit provision that, while ineffective, does provide the outline of how such a procedure might work. The side accord sets up an international Commission on Environmental Cooperation, which has the authority to investigate "persistent" noncompliance. Given a negative ruling, an "action plan" for compliance is set up; if that fails, the country itself must pay a fine; if that fails, trade sanctions can be invoked (Houseman 1994).

This process is so hemmed in by bureaucratic restrictions – put in place to protect the free trade agreement – that it will not serve as an effective enforcement mechanism. Yet expanding this idea along the lines suggested above would allow trade to serve as a dynamic instrument in support of long-run sustainable development.

6   Wheeler (1996) offers a similar proposal, to address issues of environmental justice in the South.

Clean technology promotion

The second policy leg of the Bruntland agenda involves the rapid development and diffusion of "clean technologies" (Goodstein 1995a) – technologies that are both environmentally superior and cost competitive with existing technologies. Clean technologies – from solar energy, to energy-efficient houses, to agricultural and manufacturing techniques – must be able to compete on a price basis with existing technologies if they are to diffuse rapidly throughout the economy. Over the last 20 years, tremendous progress has in fact been made in these areas, and this progress has been driven almost exclusively by increasingly stringent government regulation. This regulation has been costly; it has often been bureaucratic, cumbersome, and at times even counterproductive – yet the overall payoff in terms of cleaner, and sometimes cheaper, technologies has been impressive (Goodstein 1995a, Chapters 17 and 18).

This vital progress is clearly threatened by a race-to-the-bottom response to globalization. Especially in the United States, transnational corporations are opposing domestic regulations, with increasing success, on the grounds of "competitiveness." Competitiveness arguments also lie behind the U.S. failure to support the Basel Convention and the Rio biodiversity agreement, as well as U.S. efforts to weaken the Rio greenhouse agreement.

In fact, as noted above, the so-called "pollution haven" hypothesis is essentially a myth. Yet the facts are unlikely to influence this debate. The pollution haven hypothesis is so plausible, and has such influential political support, that it will remain a powerful force restraining environmental regulation in the North, and perhaps the South.

In this climate, internalizing environmental externalities through more stringent regulation has become increasingly difficult. While in the United States, it may be possible to hold off an assault on existing environmental regulations, widespread tightening of regulations seems unlikely over the near term of a decade or so (barring unexpected evidence of an environmental catastrophe). This resistance to tighter regulation reflects not only the political pressures of globalization but also the increasing marginal difficulty of achieving environmental goals through so-called "end-of-the-pipe" regulation. This in turn means that the past strategy of promoting clean technology by "leveling the playing field" is unlikely to continue to bear fruit.

However an alternative strategy – direct promotion of clean technology – is quite attractive. Elsewhere, I have argued that, in addition to viewing pollution as an externality, we should also recognize it as a consequence of past technology choices in a path-dependent environment (Goodstein 1995b). Briefly, path dependence posits the existence of significant positive feedback loops in the process of technological development and diffusion – focused R&D efforts, economies of scale in production and marketing, learning by doing. If these exist, there is some bad news and some good news. The bad news is that the dirty technologies with which we are endowed have been "locked in" by early adoption; market R&D will tend to focus on marginal improvements in these technologies.

The good news is that relatively small initial investments by the government in new technologies can throw the economy onto a different and, in this case, cleaner path. If, due to positive feedback mechanisms, costs for new technologies fall rapidly, then clean alternatives can be competitive over the medium term. It is this medium-term outlook, as well as the presence of tremendous positive externalities, that mandates government investment. Shepherding these technologies through their infant phase will be achieved by the market only over the long run.

But what about the problem of the government "picking winners"? The other attractive feature of the path dependence view is that it provides a mechanism to avoid boondoggles. If the cost of the new technologies does not decline rapidly toward market levels, then they do not exhibit a path-dependent development process, and the rationale for government support disappears. The policy solution to the picking-winners problem is thus to condition subsidies on rapid cost declines.

Evidence that this approach can work is found by looking at the development of wind and solar electric energy. In both cases, cost reductions have been dramatic for relatively small initial investments by the government. In a span of 15 to 20 years, wind energy has become a competitive option for utilities; solar thermal and photovoltaics are close to the threshold. In both cases, initially generous but declining subsidy levels put pressure on subsidy recipients to cut costs, and winnowed out unpromising technologies (Goodstein 1995b).

Enhanced corporate flexibility provides three political obstacles to the success of a government-sponsored clean technology promotion effort. First, as we have discussed, globalization has often induced a general weakening of government legitimacy. Second, in a global economy, national corporations and, indeed, the citizens of a nation, will benefit less from state investment in technology, as rival corporations in other nations quickly adopt the advances (Nelson and Wright 1992). Corporations and citizens will thus have less to gain from government technology policy, except in the defensive sense of protecting a share of leading-edge jobs.

The flip side of this point, of course, is that the external benefits of clean technology development are huge. This is precisely because the communication and transportation technologies underlying globalization can facilitate their rapid adoption worldwide.

The third obstacle emerges in the design of trade agreements; to the extent that agreements prohibit favoring national firms, they place restrictions on the technology policy toolbox. Esty (1994, 17) argues that market-based environmental regulations (pollution taxes and tradable permits) mesh well with trade agreements; but when governments rely on "second-best policy tools...they will continue to run head on into the demands for an open economy advanced by free traders." Government procurement policies, technology-forcing regulations, or direct subsidies all face potential challenges under trade agreements.

In summary, what impacts is globalization having on the prospects for the development and diffusion of clean technology? The pollution haven story, even if more imagined than real, will serve as a powerful check on tightening regulations in the North. However, given positive feedback in clean technology development, globalization greatly strengthens the case for government investment, since the benefits will be rapidly disseminated. This kind of rapid technological diffusion is in fact critical for the success of a Bruntland-type strategy. Finally, however, globalization reduces the political base for a national technology policy, both through the anti-state ideology it encourages, since rival corporations in other nations will more quickly adopt new technological breakthroughs, and through limitations on government technology policy built into trade agreements.

Conclusion

The title of this chapter resurrects the name of the Reverend Malthus; this is not done lightly.[7] Global limits – in water, fisheries, forests, agricultural land, protective ozone shields, carbon absorption capacities – have already been challenged by human consumption and population growth. Global population is likely to at least double over the next half century; consumption will triple. Alternatives to the Bruntland vision are easily imagined: elites in the North and South getting richer (at least for a time) and the poor, especially in impoverished countries, barely getting by, all of us in an increasingly unproductive, unforgiving, and inhospitable natural world.

But there is a way to bury Malthus yet again. Growth leading to sustainability in developing countries requires high and enforceable environmental standards in both the South and the North. These standards are both achievable – they will not discourage investment – and essential. They are essential to protect the environment today, but more significantly to drive vital business investment in the clean technologies we must have tomorrow to accommodate a world with twice as many people and three times the level of output. However, high standards alone will not be sufficient. Governments in the developed world must also directly support the rapid development of clean technologies.

I have defined globalization as a technologically driven process that has generated increasing flows of trade and investment; these new technologies have provided corporations with greater flexibility in their choice of input markets. This increased flexibility has in turn increased corporate power, which, finally, has fed renewed faith in laissez faire policies, both at the national and international levels.

Globalization intersects with sustainability on two fronts: first, it has an impact on living standards in the South, and, second, it has an impact on the development of clean technology. Daly (1993) has argued that the increased volume of trade, per se, undermines both environmental standards and incentives for investing in clean technology. Furthermore, because the stock of natural capital in poor countries is depleted through trade, living standards decline. In contrast, Bhagwati (1993) has argued that trade is "good for environmentalism" since it promotes growth. But this kind of economic reductionism, perhaps fostered by political debates over trade agreements, is not helpful. Arrow et al. (1995, 521) seem to have it right:

7   Or perhaps even correctly; see footnote 1.

Economic growth is not a panacea for environmental quality; indeed it is not even the main issue. What matters is the content of growth – the composition of inputs (including environmental resources) and outputs (including waste products). This content is determined by, among other things, the economic institutions within which human activities are conducted.

Rather than focus on trade and the environment, we need to evaluate the political responses to the trade induced by globalization. What kind of institutions are we crafting? From a Bruntland perspective, not only is the environmental content of growth critical, but so also is the distribution of the benefits of growth. If poor people are not well served by economic growth in developing countries, population pressures will continue to mount.

If we do focus on the institutional response to globalization, we can see that poor countries are not protecting their resources adequately, that rich countries are unduly fearful of capital flight to pollution havens, and that rich countries are underinvesting in clean technology. While these political responses are understandable, and in part reflect shifts in the balance of political and ideological power flowing from the globalization process, none of them is preordained by fundamental economic forces. Indeed, the improvements in communication and transportation technology that underlie globalization have already allowed poor countries to quickly capitalize on environmental expertise developed elsewhere and, more broadly, are laying the foundation for rapid worldwide adoption of clean technologies. Our challenge is to see this promise through.

Data Appendix

The dataset was assembled as follows. Shipment, employee, export, and import figures at the four-digit SIC levels were obtained from the National Bureau of Economic Research (NBER) file TRADJMA.DTA, available on the NBER web site, *nber.harvard.edu*. These data are described in Abowd (1991). These data were then matched with four-digit information on operating costs for compliance with environmental regulations, as measured in the PACE survey. (These data were provided on disk courtesy of Professor Wayne Gray, Clark University and the NBER). Four-digit output price deflators were obtained from the NBER file ASM2, also at the NBER web site.

Raw material shares were calculated using data from *The Detailed Input-Output Structure of the U.S. Economy: 1972* (U.S. Department of Commerce, Washington, D.C.). Raw materials were defined as commodities 1.0100–10.0000 (livestock, agricultural, forest and fishery products and services, and mining) and 20.0100 (logging camps and contractors). Raw material shares were available only for 375 industries.

The unskilled wage share variable was defined as the total number of employees in the industry times the average manufacturing wage, obtained from the *Economic Report of the President*, all divided by total shipments. This follows the conceptual approach to defining an unskilled labor share in Grossman and Krueger (1991).

Comment by Peter Dorman on
"Malthus redux? Globalization and the environment"

In "Malthus Redux?" Eban Goodstein makes it clear that sustainability and globalization are false opposites. While it is true that the process of globalization we are passing through today is in conflict with ecological imperatives, achieving sustainability requires globalization of a different sort. In broad strokes, Goodstein contrasts these two globalizations, the actual and the necessary, and offers guidance in how to make the transition.

The two goals Goodstein sets before us are balanced, sustainable growth in the South and the development of environmentally benign technologies, initially in the North but to be quickly disseminated worldwide. These are being obstructed by pressures emanating from "actually existing globalization": the international trading system places trade considerations above ecological ones, and the greater muscle of multinational capital has created a poor political climate for public action. The solutions he proposes are a global fund to finance the enforcement of environmental regulations in the developing world, international arbitration of complaints by non-governmental organizations (NGOs) that national laws are not being enforced, and aggressive government investment in clean technologies. It is his view that the obstacles to this program are not economic in an objective sense but political. We need only the will to see them through. I agree with the general direction Goodstein has taken; it reflects a happy blend of expertise and good sense. I differ on some of the details of his analysis, however, and the rest of these comments will focus on these differences. First I will make a few remarks on the relationship between economic growth and sustainability, and then explain why I think the barriers to achieving an eco-globalization are more severe than Goodstein suggests.

Goodstein's discussion of the role that balanced economic growth can play in promoting sustainability is a welcome change from the simplistic rejection of all growth that one sometimes hears in environmental circles. Nevertheless, I think it relies on a too-mechanistic interpretation of the demographic transition, according to which improvements in a society's material standard of living bring birth rates down, thereby restoring the balance between fertility and mortality originally upset by advances in public health. As the evidence cited in Cohen (1995) indicates, however, fertility does not passively reflect prosperity. Other social factors, such as gender equity and education, can trigger declines in birth rates; in fact, most fertility transitions predate their purported economic cause. This indicates that, on environmental grounds, it is vital to redefine "development" to stress human development in its fullest sense. This does not mean that improvements in the material quality of life are unimportant, just that quantitative economic growth should not be overstressed. A different qualification to the growth imperative arises from the concept

319

of sustainability itself. Goodstein employs the criterion of "equal capital": any reduction in natural capital should be offset by a corresponding increase in human-made capital if an economy is to be judged sustainable. I think this position is too one-sided, since it implies perfect substitutability between the two sorts of capital. Of course, the opposite position, that natural capital should not be drawn down at all, is also too extreme, since it implies no substitutability whatsoever. Our knowledge in these matters is not well developed, so it is difficult to say just how much substitution should be allowed. No doubt the degree of substitutability differs across resources. The point is that the dutiful reinvestment of resource royalties does not establish sustainability in either the developing or the industrialized world, although it is a necessary first step. In certain critical resources, such as arable land, it is arguable that strict preservation should be begun today, even if it means slower economic growth.

Setting aside these modest differences over objectives, the biggest questions concern how to achieve them. What obstacles does the current political-economic order present to ecological reform? How can these obstacles be overcome? I will look at three critical obstacles and then briefly sketch a set of responses.

(1) Financial markets and institutions play a crucial role in promoting unsustainable development. There are two reasons for this. First, the aftermath of the global debt crisis of the early 1980s, which is sadly still with us, places pressures on countries that would protect their natural resources. Continuing high levels of debt service not only retard development in much of the South; they also impel countries to adopt the desperate strategy of bartering irreplaceable resources for temporary financial relief. Worse, the International Monetary Fund, its influence leveraged by debt dependency, and its mission enlarged by ideological militancy, has imposed economic "reforms" throughout the developing world that are deeply inimical to environmental responsibility. Second, the wave of financial liberalization that has swept through the world economy has greatly reduced the scope for public policy and has increased the weight given to profitability relative to other economic criteria. It is difficult to envision an agenda such as Goodstein's making much progress in a world subject to the excessive influence of finance.

(2) The current process of trade liberalization is in conflict with environmental goals. Goodstein questions this on the basis of regression evidence, his and others'. This is not the place to examine matters of technique, but it is important to consider the larger methodological issue at stake in this literature. Regression analysis is a powerful tool – providing we have quantitative measures of the relevant variables, these measures are accurate, and we have an appropriate estimation model. This is seldom the case in economics, however, and it is certainly not the case in this particular area of research. I would be the last to advocate abstention from econometrics, but a reasonable strategy would be to supplement regression methods with case studies for which the relevant information is more complete and qualitatively richer. Thus, how can we make sense of the trade regulation regression results *and* case studies such as those provided by Chapman (1985, 1987)? A first step might be to

take a close look at the residuals in regression models and see if they are consistent with what we know about industry cases. This is an important task, despite the relatively low share of costs attributable to environmental regulation. At stake is the likely effect of *future* regulation, which, if it is going to be responsive to the hard constraints of sustainability, will have to be much more costly than past regulation.

(3) The political economy of contemporary globalization is openly hostile to ecological reform. Global corporations have become too powerful relative to the public institutions that regulate them, and they use this power to resist interference with their control over products, production methods, and location decisions. At the same time the political left, which carries the banner for regulating capital, has been thrown on the defensive, hardly able to maintain past gains, much less conquer new ground. These are global developments and cannot be explained by the particular historical or political circumstances of individual countries. As long as they remain in place, programs as eminently reasonable as Goodstein's have no hope of enactment.

It would be nice to close with a brief paragraph containing all the answers. I can't do this, not even in a Joycean paragraph of thousands of words, but I can offer a few general suggestions. First, radical debt relief that restores an appropriate flow of capital from North to South is essential. Without this nothing else appears possible. Second, global finance should be tamed. This is easier said than done, but elsewhere in this volume there are good ideas. My point in this context is that financial reform is a precondition of sustainable development. Third, trade needs to be regulated at both the micro and macro levels. Social standards should have a place in the trading system, and coordinated management of capital flows (which are reciprocally trade flows) is needed to dampen the mercantilist export pressures that put natural capital at risk. Finally, the left must somehow awaken from its slumber and place the socialization of capital – inserting public interests within corporate decision making – at the heart of its program. The goal is not only to instill ecological and humane values in production, but also to transform the most powerful political opponent of social progress into its willing instrument.

Part V

Migration of people in a global economy

13

Freedom to move in the age of globalization

Bob Sutcliffe

Immigration and globalization

Globalization is seen as the growing (and in some versions the unprecedented) international integration of economic life, involving a major rise in trade and foreign direct investment relative to production, an enormous surge in international financial transactions, and the growth of global economic institutions such as the multinational corporation and international organizations such as the European Union, the World Bank, the International Monetary Fund (IMF), the Bank of International Settlements, the Group of Seven, and so on. Many believe that this process is diminishing the economic power of the national state; others emphasize the tendencies toward the globalization of culture – McDonald's, karaoke machines, and satellite dishes. Some of these trends are indeed strong, but most accounts of globalization are probably exaggerated. The globalization of trade and direct investment is not unprecedented;[1] the increases in overall trade and investment are actually highly concentrated in a few countries and leave many poor countries completely out of the process; very few firms seem to be global in a qualitatively "new" sense;[2] I doubt that the national state has lost as much power as many of our rulers would like us to believe.

The impression is widespread that the global movement of people is part and parcel of the broader process of economic and cultural globalization. Labor and other markets are seen as increasingly globalized through the international movement of both workers and capital. Some observers see this as an "age of migration."[3] But this impression is even more exaggerated than other aspects of globalization. An often quoted figure is that roughly 100 million people (around 1.6 percent of the world's population) live outside their country of citizenship, possibly the highest

---

1 See Andrew Glyn and Bob Sutcliffe, "Global but Leaderless? The New Capitalist Order," in Ralph Miliband and Leo Panitch, eds, *Socialist Register 1992*, London: Merlin Press, 1992; and Bob Sutcliffe and Andrew Glyn, "Still Underwhelmed: Indicators of Globalization and Their Misinterpretation," 1998, forthcoming article.
2 See Winifred Ruigrok and Rob van Tulder, *The Logic of International Restructuring,* London: Routledge, 1995
3 See, for instance, Stephen Castles and Mark J. Miller, *The Age of Migration: International Population Movements in the Modern World,* London: Macmillan, 1993.

percentage ever since the concept "country of citizenship" came to have any meaning (some time in the 19th century). But the majority of these emigrants are involuntary refugees from political strife in one developing country living in a neighboring one. While the line between forced and unforced migration is difficult to draw, the number of intentional, if sometimes not exactly willing, migrants can be put at about 50 million, or about 0.8 percent of the world's population. Given that migrants have a higher concentration of people of working age than the population in general as well as a high work-activity rate, they may represent up to 1 percent of the economically active population worldwide.

At the same time, the 40,000 or so multinational companies, as defined by UNCTAD (the United Nations Conference on Trade and Development), employ in total about 12 million workers outside their countries of origin. This figure is well under 1 percent of the world's economically active population and probably a little over 1 percent of the employed population.[4]

As a comparison, about 18 percent of the world's output is exported from its country of production, and approximately 5 percent of the world's capital stock is foreign owned.[5] So there is a (very loose) statistical sense in which employment and residence are quantitatively less globalized than production or investment.

In another sense, the voluntary movement of people is a clearer exception to globalization. While in the last two decades production and investment have become more globalized with the encouragement of governments and international organizations, the same authorities, politicians, and the media have become increasingly hostile to the international movement of people. Of the three major receiving areas of recent years – Western Europe, the Persian Gulf oil-producing states, and the U.S. – the first two have taken major steps to curtail immigration and the third appears to be moving in the same direction, although the outcome is more in question. In short, globalization at the policy level does not include the movement of labor. In the case of the migration of people, in many respects what is going on is counter-globalization: while market, political, and cultural forces all make for increased migration, there is an unprecedented effort by governments to limit the movement of people.

Actually existing globalization is characterized by very different levels of global mobility, according to which element of the economy is being referred to. And there is a tendency for mobility to be greater the more abstract and less human is the potential mover: finance is the most global part of the world economy, while workers, especially unskilled workers, are the least.

---

4   These figures are very roughly calculated by the author based on the data in UNCTAD, *World Investment Report 1995* and *1996*.
5   Another of the author's very rough calculations based on dividing UNCTAD's estimate of the value of direct investment by the World Bank's estimate of global gross national product multiplied by a guestimated capital-output ratio of 2. See Sutcliffe and Glyn 1998 (fn. 1) for more details.

Views on migration

If we knew the views of an economist on nine subjects we could probably predict with great accuracy his or her opinion on almost any 10th. Almost – because the exception would be immigration. No group, as distinguished by economic ideology, seems to have an agreed view on the question of immigration. That doyen of liberal economists, Henry Simons, wrote half a century ago that "[w]holly free immigration...is neither attainable nor desirable. To insist that a free trade program is logically or practically incomplete without free migration is either disingenuous or stupid. Free trade may and should raise living standards everywhere....Free immigration would level standards, perhaps without raising them anywhere." Few of his disciples have deviated far from this point of view. Gary Becker, comparing early 20th century U.S. immigration to that of today, argues that "the world is now a very different place. Because of the expanded welfare state, immigration is no longer a practical policy. These days open immigration would merely induce people in poorer countries to emigrate to the United States and other developed countries to collect generous transfer payments." Most textbooks on international economics seem to have taken the advice attributed to Milton Friedman: "about immigration the less said the better."[6] Perhaps the silence is a discreet one, since the question of immigration reveals deep and presumably embarrassing differences within the category of free-market fetishists and neo-liberal economists. While the *Wall Street Journal* was at least consistent in 1988 in advocating a Constitutional amendment saying "There shall be open borders," many economists who think that the principles of the free market should apply to virtually all aspects of human life, even to what occurs in the kitchen and the bedroom, nonetheless sometimes blanch before the idea of applying them to human beings crossing national frontiers. Even Julian Simon, a supporter of more liberal immigration policies, stops short of recommending open frontiers, finding another solution consistent with free market principles: fixing quotas and setting up a market in U.S. immigration permits. Among other advocates of the universal free market, it is not uncommon to find total opposition to immigration, justified sometimes by a crude nationalist version of free market economics ("immigration will level downwards"), sometimes by the argument that immigration is bad for the least privileged (especially African Americans), and sometimes supported by more "sophisticated" arguments in which zero immigration becomes an optimal solution because potential host communities have objective functions that may include "preferences for cultural, ethnic, and religious purity." On this kind of argument ethnic cleansing could be seen as an equilibrium position.

For progressive economists to accuse free market fetishists of inconsistency and contradiction on this issue, however, would be a case of the pot calling the kettle black. Progressive and left opinion is equally without an agreed position on immi-

---

6   The quotes from Simon, Becker, and Friedman are all taken from Vernon M. Briggs Jr., "International Migration and Labour Mobility: The Receiving Countries," in Julien van den Broeck, ed., *The Economics of Labour Migration*, Cheltenham, Glos: Edward Elgar, 1996.

gration. But there is a frequently encountered approach that has grown with the debate on globalization and which probably tends to create a general prejudice against immigration.

The mean progressive or left opinion about globalization as a whole seems to be negative, though the standard deviation is rather large. Opposition is sometimes based on detailed argument but is often rather instinctively based on the idea that, since globalization is encouraged by the ideological and economic potentates of world capitalism, progressives ought to be against it.

In the context of general progressive hostility toward and suspicion of globalization, immigration tends to be seen as basically demand determined, resulting from capitalists' demand for greater quantities of labor power in a particular place. It is, therefore, regarded as an instrument of capital to divide and weaken the working class. Many progressive writings on modern immigration contextualize it as a new stage in a long history that began with slavery and continued with indentured labor. The fear exists that for the left to advocate freer movement of labor is to connive in a capitalist-supported measure designed to reduce wages and worsen conditions. While progressives have discussed many issues regarding immigration, progressive economists in particular have largely discussed the issue as part of the labor market and its history. This is what one would expect from more orthodox economists. Not only is such a limited approach methodologically incomplete, it also carries the danger of disguising anti-immigrant opinions behind anticapitalist ones.

Not that the effects on the labor market can be ignored. Most empirical studies suggest that the effects of immigration on wage rates and employment levels in host countries are small, even negligible.[7] Sometimes this research has been seized upon by opponents of immigration control in support of their positions. I think this is unwise, partly because the methodology may be suspect[8] but more fundamentally because the argument for freer immigration is of a different kind, not one rooted in its contingent economic effects. I do not think that the progressive position on immigration should be different if the empirical evidence about labor market effects were to show something different. What would possibly be different are the other policies necessary to compensate for any negative effects of immigration.

A progressive viewpoint on immigration should, in my view, not start at all from economic consequences but from rights and freedoms. Freer, and ideally completely free, movement of people is desirable in itself because it would represent an immense expansion of freedom of people to be, live, and work where they choose. Migration can be an important way in which human beings expand their experiences and live fulfilling lives. And the free movement of people internationally should

---

7   There is a useful summary of this empirical work in Georges Tapinos and Ana de Rugy, "The Macroeconomic Impact of Immigration: Review of the Literature Since the Mid-1970s," in SOPEMI, *Trends in European Migration 1993 Report*, SOPEMI/OECD, Paris, 1994, and in the chapter by Gregory DeFreitas in this volume.

8   See, for instance, Barry Chiswick's reviews of George J. Borjas, "Migrants and Strangers," in *Journal of Economic Literature*, Vol. 29, June 1991, and of George J. Borjas and Richard B. Freeman, eds., "Immigration and the Work Force," in *Journal of Economic Literature*, Vol. 31, June 1993.

be seen as an important element in individual human rights, just as it is nationally. In this sense, we should start to discuss this question by looking not at what migration has been in the past but at what it could become in the future: to see it not as a continuation of the story of slave trade but as something that can be an expression of greater freedom of choice.

In view of this, I only partly agree with those who argue that immigration should be seen as part of the overall issue of globalization and that our position on immigration should spring from a coherent attitude toward globalization as a whole. In many of its aspects it is not a separate issue; but in one central way it is, because, unlike the movement of goods and capital, it directly involves human rights. So while I have a usually positive view of both globalization and freer immigration, I think it would be logical even for those who have a more negative view of globalization to hold a positive view of freer immigration.

In any case, neither globalization nor migration policy are a zero-sum game between capital and labor. While aspects of actually existing globalization are biased in favor of capital or certain sections of it, some ideal of globalization in itself should surely remain one that progressives can embrace as progressives generally did in the 19th century. Globalization poses new tasks in finding ways in which rights and gains can be defended in a more global context and in which the inequities of the process can be redressed. One of the benefits of the freer movement of labor in this context is that it can in principle facilitate a more internationally integrated labor and progressive movement.

In spite of the horrors of recent, particularly European and African, history, I work with the completely unprovable hypothesis that there is more hope for peace and social progress in a *mestizo* world.

Recent migration policy in Europe: a warning

Counter-globalization in migration policy has in recent years been most evident in Western Europe. And this experience can produce important warnings. Around 1973, nearly all European countries cut back legal migration of non-asylum-seeking first migrants (those often referred to as "economic" migrants) to virtually zero. This was partly justified by politicians on the grounds that the economic crisis had profoundly changed the European labor market and that Europe was, economically speaking, full. This argument has been backed up by the development of an ideological campaign to denigrate ("demonize" is the very apposite word used by Tahar Ben Jelloun) the economic migrant as self-seeking, greedy, and undeserving. The success of this campaign would have been greater if at the same time the same politicians had not been trying to inculcate exactly the same characteristics in the domestic population as it denigrated in foreigners: enterprise, flexibility, seeking one's own economic advantage by moving if necessary. In a famous remark, one of Margaret Thatcher's leading henchpersons, Norman Tebbit, said that the answer to unemployment was for the jobless to do what their fathers had done in the 1930s:

get on their bikes and look for work. To repeat a comment made elsewhere: "On your bike, as Norman Tebbit said, and you are a saint shining with neo-liberal virtues. On your ferry, and you are a demon against whom great European democracies change their constitutions in panic."[9]

After 1973 limited family-reunion migration remained legal and all countries in principle admitted those seeking political asylum. Some of them, like Germany, had a very liberal policy toward migrants of this kind. Since the demand for non-asylum-seeking migration did not abate, there was an altogether unsurprising rise in the number of migrants trying to enter through the remaining legally open doors. The demonization has come to take the form of denouncing those who are seen as thus abusing the asylum or family rules as "bogus asylum seekers." While the need for asylum in principle is still generally accepted, there is now a large section of the media and the political class in Europe that in effect denounces *all* immigrants as bogus. This insinuation is used to impose humiliating conditions on immigration applicants. And it has been used as a justification for the universal hardening of immigration laws that has taken place in Europe since the fall of the Berlin Wall. Two major countries, France and Germany, have made emergency alterations to their constitutions to bring about this tightening, and immigration law has been tightened in all the others. The *Moscow News* observed with irony in 1993 that "Russia and the West have swapped parts. An Iron Curtain has dropped before the majority of those wanting to enter Europe."[10] While Germany's move to remove refugee status from all those arriving in the country by land (by defining all its neighbors as incapable of producing political refugees) was directed largely against arrivals from Eastern Europe, it is justified increasingly in racist terms, something that is even more commonplace in the rest of Europe.[11]

All European states now tighten their immigration laws and worsen their treatment of immigrants more or less continuously in a process of competitive dissuasion rather akin to competitive devaluation. All wish to avoid the perception among potential asylum seekers that their regime is "softer" than that of any other country. At the same time, while the European states are increasingly coming together to plan joint anti-immigration strategies, they are still using ad hoc, temporary institutional formats that bypass the institutions of the European Community and so avoid any kind of scrutiny by the press, the public, or the European Parliament. In order to

9 Bob Sutcliffe, "Immigration: Rights and Illogic," *Index on Censorship*, No. 3, 1994.
10 Quoted in Arye L. Hillman (Bar-Ilan University, Israel), "The Political Economy of Migration Policy," in Horst Siebert, ed., *Migration: A Challenge to Europe: Symposium 1993*, J.C.B. Mohr (Paul Siebeck) Tübingen, 1994, p. 272.
11 This is an example of modern European scholarly thought on immigration policy: "I would like to argue that immigration has to be limited, especially in times of high unemployment and economic distress. It also has to be more limited for potential immigrants who are perceived as being very different because of their culture, ideology, and religion. If their religion makes it difficult for them to be assimilated or contains supreme values that conflict strongly with the values of the native population, then they can only be allowed to immigrate in limited numbers." Peter Bernholz (University of Basel), "Comment on Arye L.Hillman, "The Political Economy of Migration Policy" (see footnote 10).

implement the tighter external frontiers, there are now more police, and suggestions are being heard that the military should increasingly take part in the administration of immigration control. In a belated move to implement the Schengen agreement, France recently "abolished" its frontier with Spain. Immigration officials, however, have now been routinely replaced by soldiers in jungle camouflage uniforms carrying automatic weapons. And the routine stopping of foreign vehicles inside France and the checking of identities against computer records are increasingly frequent. The frontier has not been knocked down like the Berlin Wall let alone vaporized. The frontier is no longer a wall nor a fence; it has been melted and spread across the country. Human rights are at their weakest in the vicinity of frontiers, and if the contemporary frontier is no longer to be a barrier but a thin layer of control spread across countries, then we should all take fright.

The countries of the European Union now have a policy that on paper permits immigration exclusively on humanitarian grounds. But, by closing all other routes to legal migration, governments have ensured that the humanitarian route cannot function. The result is that the distinction made between the "deserving" refugee and the demon economic migrant has ended by prejudicing the position of all potential migrants, including the most needy political refugees. The lesson is surely that a more humanitarian migration policy will exist only when other avenues for migration remain open and other migrants are not demonized.[12]

Migration and development

The great growth area of migration studies in Europe and the U.S. is about how to control, reduce, and eliminate immigration in developed countries. There is also a smaller but significant growth of literature about the causes and effects of migration in the developing countries. A part of this, however, dovetails very well with anti-immigration arguments in the North, as suggested by Patnaik and Chandrasekhar's paper on migration in this volume: this literature argues that emigration is detrimental to development in the developing countries, and hence it gives some respectability to immigration control in the developed ones. The same obsession with controlling immigration has led to an increasingly heard opinion that developed countries must support human rights in developing ones in order to reduce the number of refugee-creating situations, as well as arguments that aid policies to developing countries should be reoriented with a view to stemming immigration. In a recent French parliamentary election, Jean-Marie Le Pen of the fascist National Front advocated aid to developing countries, but as a reward for curbing emigration to the North.

Despite the frequency of these arguments, there is no more orthodoxy on the question of migration as applied to development than there is in any other area of

---

12   For more details of this process, see Bob Sutcliffe, "Immigrants and Refugees: Policies and Rights," *Contemporary Sociology*, Vol. 25, No. 5 September 1996, and the books reviewed in that essay.

debate concerning migration. Four quite different arguments can be found in the literature: (1) migration hampers development, (2) development hampers migration, (3) migration encourages development, and (4) development encourages migration. In category (1) are the "brain drain" arguments originally devised for European countries, especially Britain, in relation to the U.S. and later applied to developing countries. The evidence for such arguments has been a little difficult to find in view of widespread failure to employ qualified people who do not emigrate. As a result, there has recently been a tendency to hear a "brain overflow" argument, which blames the failures of underdevelopment for emigration of skilled people rather than the other way round. Argument (2) represents the implicit hope of many who want to stem immigration by improving the prospects for prospective migrants in their own countries. The argument that more development in the country of origin of immigrants will increase jobs and reduce migration seems about as obvious as the argument that more immigrants in the receiving countries will adversely affect labor. And it seems just about as difficult to substantiate with facts. In fact, a limited consensus seems to be emerging in official circles that the short- to medium-term effect of development is the opposite: that by increasing contacts with the international economy and raising incomes, development accelerates emigration because people have more money to finance migration and more knowledge of and contacts with potential receiving countries.[13] Argument (3) has several elements, which have been supported by an increasing number of empirical studies stressing the positive effects of returning migrants, the positive effects of the absence of migrants on opportunities for the remaining members of families, and the positive effects of migrants' remittances. During the last 20 years the total quantity of migrants' remittances to developing countries (taking into account under- and overestimating aspects of the statistics) has almost certainly been greater than the volume of "development aid," infinitely more than the volume of aid that genuinely benefits growth or welfare, and more than the volume of foreign private investment. And yet these latter two subjects receive immensely more discussion than migrants' remittances. International macroeconomic studies of remittances tend to be very skeptical of their positive effects; these studies argue frequently that remittances are mostly spent on consumption rather than investment and tend to increase imports. But these criticisms seem beside the point because, even if true, they do not undo the fact that remittances mean more income for migrants' families and that, since they are in foreign exchange, they pay for the imports they generate. It is not as if the alternative would be for the country to have the same quantity of foreign exchange in another form. As already mentioned, a consensus is developing around the idea that development will not stem migration but may even increase it (argument 4). This is in turn fueling a political reaction against aid and toward ever-more restrictive anti-immigration policies in developed countries. Thus, the development and migration debate is increasingly fueling the immigration control debate.

13 See, for instance, United Nations Population Fund, *The State of World Population Report 1993*, New York: United Nations, 1993.

Migration and progressive policy

At the risk of seeming simplistic, I would like to argue that to be progressive is to believe in progress. But to recognize progress we have to have some idea of the objective. In other words, we need to define utopias as a necessary part of designing practical policies for today.

What would be the utopia, as applied to the question of migration? I maintain that it would be (1) the reduction to the minimum possible of the obligation to move from one's place of residence in order to survive and prosper, and (2) the right of complete global freedom of movement and residence. In other words, in my utopia all would have the right to voluntary migration. This is no more than the extension of rights that are taken for granted within the borders of national states. Disagreement over these constituents of utopia seems to me a fundamental disagreement over political values. Disagreement over whether, in a world with considerably greater freedom of movement, there would be a large amount of or only a little migration is a simple disagreement of prediction, impossible to settle and of no fundamental importance. Disagreements of what to advocate and fight for (or even do) before the utopia is reached are the difficult ones and will shift frequently as political circumstances change.

I believe that this utopia is not just a pious hope but suggests several clear do's and don'ts of progressive policy on migration:

(1) Oppose the general restrictive tendency of government immigration policy in the major developed receiving countries. We should be in favor of greater and not less ease of immigration.

(2) Avoid the dangerous practice of making opportunistic use of the anti-immigration climate to argue for other progressive objectives. It is not as uncommon as it should be to hear arguments for more development aid or for more support for human rights in developing countries on the grounds that such policies would reduce immigration.[14] Such arguments amount to moral complicity with anti-immigration sentiments.

(3) Recognize that, aside from the question of the overall immigrant numbers, there is an enormous catalog of abuses of human rights and dignity surrounding immigration policies and practices. Injustices gather like vultures around frontiers. Almost all bases on which human beings suffer injustice and discrimination are used as grounds for special discrimination in relation to immigration rights. Thus, women in general migrate on different terms from men; it is more difficult for them to be independent migrants, and migration law frequently intensifies their dependent

---

14 For instance: "sustainable supra-national political action should be taken to force the governments of emigration countries to respect basic human, political and democratic rights *in order to prevent the emigration of political refugees.*" (emphasis added), Thomas Straubhaar and Peter A. Fischer, "Economic and Social Aspects of Immigration Into Switzerland," in Heinz Fassmann and Rainer Münz, eds., *European Migration in the Late Twentieth Century*, Aldershot: Edward Elgar, p.146.

position with regard to the men of their families. Women who separate from their husbands often lose their residence rights. Gay men and lesbians also suffer discrimination in immigration law; many countries, including the United States, restrict immigration according to sexual preference. Disabled people have fewer rights to immigration because they are seen as a potential burden on social services. Illness is also used by many countries as grounds for denial of immigration rights, even when no public health hazard is involved. AIDS is particularly important here: many countries, including the United States, discriminate against HIV-positive people and people with AIDS. Spain has recently started to insist on an HIV status test for all refugees and immediately expels anyone who is positive. Perhaps most of all, immigration policies discriminate on the grounds of race. Here it should be noted that, during the last two decades, U.S. immigration policy has become less structurally racist (after the ending of the pre-1965 quotas), while European immigration policy has become increasingly so. Thus, a part of progressive policy on immigration should be to oppose all these and other examples of social discrimination and injustice in immigration policy.

(4) Recognize that the burden of hosting ever-larger quantities of forced international migrants who are obliged to become refugees must be equitably shared. Today, this burden is largely undertaken by poor countries.

(5) Eliminate discriminatory policies against noncitizens. Even when immigrants are legal, they seldom enjoy the same democratic rights in their host countries as do natives and citizens. Progressive policy should fight to end this discrimination by supporting the easy acquisition of all rights by noncitizens – in a sense, creating a more transnational form of citizenship – and the liberalization of naturalization procedures.[15] This question is in the center of the political struggle over immigration in the U.S. today. Undocumented immigrants in particular need to be able to acquire secure rights, since their status is not only extremely dangerous for themselves but also weakens the bargaining power of labor as a whole by preserving a specially underprivileged class of workers who can easily be super-exploited. The least-studied question in migration studies is the effect of illegality as opposed to the effects of the presence of immigrants. Migrants of almost any degree of legality have to spend a great deal of time and emotional energy in a Kafkaesque game with the national bureaucracy in order to maintain their current rights: they must keep their papers in order, get replacements when necessary, register and re-register with the police, and so on – all of this erodes their bargaining power in the labor market. If immigrant workers and their inferior legal status really do worsen the bargaining power of workers in general, then the obvious policy is to attempt to incorporate immigrant workers as fully and rapidly as possible in the trade unions and other institutions that compensate for the market weakness of labor, and to fight for full immigrant access to all the rights that national workers possess.

Some recent writers on migration, recognizing that more control has led to more illegal immigrants, hypothesize that this is in fact part of the plan, since it enables

15 For an excellent discussion of this, see Rainer Bauböck, *Transnational Citizenship: Membership and Rights in International Migration*, Aldershot, England: Edward Elgar, 1994.

governments to please several conflicting constituencies at the same time and to produce scapegoats for its economic failure. It also provides a source of internal conflict within the working class.[16]

These policies all seem to me steps toward the aim of bringing about, as soon as and as completely as possible, the right of all human beings to move about their planet with at least as much freedom as their most abstract creation, money. Today people move across frontiers most easily when they are disguised as commodities or as capital: people with lots of money, people with marketable scarce skills, temporary low-paid laborers, slaves (in the form of indentured domestic workers and workers in the sexual pleasure industry), and illegal migrants who are profitably smuggled across borders like contraband goods. There will be progress when they can move because they have begun to gain the human right to do so.

I am aware of the existence of a long and complex debate within theories of human rights about which if any rights are absolute and unconditional. The consensus of this debate is that few rights can be regarded as such, since the exercise of any particular right by one person or group might in certain circumstances conflict with the exercise of other rights by others. For some this argument is enough to invalidate the concept of human rights altogether. For braver souls such contradictions stimulate the search for a more complex and sophisticated concept of human rights and their practical implementation. The right of one person or group to move across frontiers could, in certain arguments, interfere with the ability of others to exercise other rights. So where does that leave an argument such as this one, which recommends resting the argument about immigration on the base of human rights?

First, there is no space to deal with the question of contradictions between the right to move around the planet and other recognized rights. I acknowledge that such conflicts can appear, but I deny that they appear in any specially extreme sense when it comes to crossing international borders. It is a problem, therefore, though not in my view an insuperable one, in the case of all discussions based on rights. When rights of any kind in a community conflict, policies have to be sought that reconcile them. With immigration and its effects there is no difference in principle. To give a hypothetical example: if greater rights for immigration for some threaten the right to earn a living for others, then the route toward the reconciliation of the two should be by way of employment and other economic policies.

Second, nobody to my knowledge uses the argument that rights can conflict to question the established right of people to move freely in their country of citizenship or residence. The right to move without restriction in our "own" country is so established and accepted that a threat to it at this stage would create a universal outcry. Yet the logic or the right to move about "our" planet is similar to the right to move about "our" country. The only difference is established by the existence of a set of, in many ways, accidental and arbitrary lines. Surely they cannot be allowed to affect our rights. It therefore seems illegitimate to regard the question of the

16 Robert Miles and Dietrich Thränhardt, eds., *Migration and European Integration: The Dynamics of Inclusion and Exclusion*, London: Pinter Publishers, and Madison/Teaneck, N.J.: Fairleigh Dickinson University Press, 1995.

conflict of rights as serious in the case of moving from Irún to Hendaye (one centi-meter) but beyond discussion in the case of moving from Maine to Hawaii (more than 10,000 kilometers).

Third, my argument in this short chapter is not that to begin the debate on immi-gration from the starting point of human rights resolves all problems. I simply wish to insist that most other common angles of approach to the subject lead to some bias against immigration, and also that there is an almost complete silence in all interna-tional human rights declarations on the subject of moving across borders. These two facts justify that special emphasis be put on human rights in this debate: they are highly relevant yet they are ostentatiously unmentioned. This stick must be bent a long way before an appropriate progressive perspective on immigration crystallizes.

14

Immigration, inequality, and policy alternatives

Gregory DeFreitas

The mobility of labor seldom if ever matches that of capital, but the end of the Cold War seemed for a time to be the start of a new era of accelerated population movements. Just as foreign investment and trade restrictions were being widely dismantled, so too were many national barriers to intercountry migration. The most dramatic case was, of course, the opening of Eastern Europe's borders to permit massive out-migration. From 1989 to 1992, over 2.1 million applied for asylum in the West. Concurrently, the European Union moved toward relaxation of internal border checks under the Schengen Accord. And in the United States, new 1990 entry criteria raised considerably the official ceiling on legal green card admissions.

However, by the mid-1990s, all Western European countries had moved to sharply curtail in-migration from non-EU nations, and full implementation of Schengen was being delayed by several countries that were worried about weak external border controls in poorer member states. In the U.S., new restrictive legislation was passed in 1996 to strip most immigrants of important legal protections, exclude them from public assistance programs, impose higher income tests on Americans wishing to sponsor them, and limit claims for political asylum.

This sharp reversal of policy, both here and abroad, reflects in part the emergence of highly nationalistic and ethnocentric political forces opposed on principle to sizable foreign-born populations in their midst. But it is also driven by broader public concerns about the perceived economic impacts of immigration. In particular, the view that immigrants displace native workers from many jobs, depress wage levels in certain occupations, worsen earnings inequality, and abuse public assistance benefits has become almost commonplace. Public opinion polls in the U.S. now regularly show that at least three out of five adults favor cuts in immigration.

This paper begins with an overview of recent trends in the volume and composition of immigration to the U.S. It then offers a critical review of the major studies to date on its economic impacts here, drawing some comparisons with European findings. In brief, this research does not support claims that immigration (at least at current levels) significantly harms domestic wages or employment. And immigrants appear to contribute more in federal, state, and local taxes than they use in public assistance and services. There are cost pressures on government budgets in localities where the foreign born are concentrated, but they could be eased by federal fiscal reforms. The final section proposes a new national strategy for immigration.

Although an "open borders" approach would not be a feasible policy, highly restrictive legislation is unnecessary and misguided. Instead, a new progressive approach would reshape the immigration system to promote mainly humanitarian goals while simultaneously helping to improve job prospects here and abroad.

Legal and illegal migration patterns

Public concern about immigration has been fueled by reports that it has jumped to unprecedented levels, much of it illegal. As Figure 1 shows, more were admitted to legal permanent residence status in the 16-year period 1981–96 than in any 20-year span since the turn of the century. Over 7.6 million received green cards in 1990–96 alone, an annual average (1.1 million) double that of the 1980s, which was in turn two-thirds above that of the seventies.

There are four main reasons for these larger inflows. First, in 1965 Congress finally repealed the European-biased national origins quota system in effect since the 1920s.[1] This led to a surge of new migration by Asians and others long excluded, many taking advantage of expanded admissions for family reunification. The effects are evident in the changing national origins mix of Figure 1. In the 1950s, Europeans were two-thirds of all legal immigrants and Asians only 6 percent; by the 1980s, the European share had dropped to 15 percent while Asians represented 45 percent. Second, the end of the Vietnam War in 1975 generated massive refugee flows from Southeast Asia, which have been supplemented since then by smaller but still significant numbers from Cuba and the former Soviet Union. Third, the overall numbers in the 1990s were markedly inflated by the one-time-only amnesty granted some 2.7 million undocumented aliens. This was authorized by the 1986 Immigration Reform and Control Act (IRCA), whose other main component was penalization of employers who knowingly hire illegal immigrants. If the amnesties are excluded, the total admissions in the nineties falls to just under 3 million (or about 747,000 per year). The Immigration Act of 1990 has been the other principal cause of more entrants of late, since it greatly increased the number admitted each year to 675,000. This was to be a "flexible ceiling" that could be exceeded (as it regularly has been) whenever more visas for immediate relatives of U.S. citizens were needed, while still allowing at least 226,000 slots for other family-based claims.

However, even including the special amnesty-inflated numbers, the relative size of the immigrant population is not unprecedented. Its share of the national population today is about 8 percent, well below the 14.6 percent share at the turn of the century.[2] A better measure of immigrant density relevant to the absorptive capacity of the economy is the proportion of the population who are recent entrants. Figure 2 traces the pattern since 1820 in the ratio of immigrants arriving in the previous

1   For a summary of the major recent changes in immigration law, see DeFreitas (1994).
2   The U.S. share is also lower than that of a number of industrialized nations, such as Canada (15.6 percent foreign born), Switzerland (17.1 percent), Australia (22.7 percent), and Luxembourg (28.4 percent). For these and other 1991 estimates see OECD (1994c).

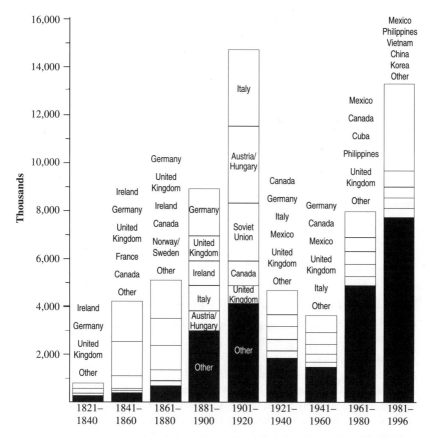

Figure 1 *Immigrants admitted to the U.S. from top 5 source countries, 1821–1996*

Source: U.S. Immigration and Naturalization Service (1994), updated with 1994–96 INS data.

decade to the total population at the end of that decade. It shows clearly that, while the recent migrant share has risen of late, it remains far below the levels successfully absorbed into the 19th and early 20th century economies. In 1990 it was still less than one-third the 1910 level.

Of course, official statistics will be biased downward insofar as they neglect all those who enter the country to stay without legal documents. For many years, the guesstimates of the illegal population most often cited by the media and politicians were in the range of 8 million to 12 million. By 1993, a national poll found that two-thirds of the public believed that most immigrants came into the U.S. illegally (Nelson 1993). But the most careful demographic estimates put the annual inflow of the undocumented at 200,000 to 300,000: that is, only about one-fifth of total (legal plus illegal) immigration. By the mid-1980s, the resident undocumented alien population was estimated at 3–3.5 million – far below the 8–12 million often claimed by

Figure 2 *Immigration flows relative to U.S. population, 1820–1990*

Source: U.S. Immigration and Naturalization Service, *INS Statistical Yearbook,* 1994; and U.S. Census Bureau, S*tatistical Abstract of the United States* 1994.

the media and politicians (Warren and Passel 1987). Since nearly 3 million of these were granted IRCA amnesty and included in the legal immigration data reported above, Figures 1 and 2 probably do not seriously understate the full numbers of immigrants in recent years. But since the data prior to the eighties fail to include the illegal migrants of earlier decades, the difference between past and present are exaggerated.

In addition, the more relevant measure is the *net* increase in population after subtracting emigrants leaving the U.S. Emigration figures are not regularly collected by any government agency, so available estimates are infrequent and imprecise. According to the U.S. Immigration and Naturalization Service (INS), nearly one-fourth of 1980s' immigrants remigrated to their homelands. The Census Bureau (1992) projects that, adjusting for emigration of about 160,000 annually, net immigration will average about 880,000 per year in the near future.

Wage and employment effects

While the population share of immigrants today is not unprecedented, current volumes still represent a marked increase over recent decades. The fact that the 1990s opened with more immigrants entering an economy mired in recession ignited renewed questioning about whether immigration worsened domestic wage and job prospects.

Standard neoclassical economics does not offer a ready answer. Foreign- and native-born labor are typically modeled as separate productive factors that may be either complements or substitutes. If complementary, then increases in immigration will raise the productivity of and the rate of return on both inputs, which may also expand employment opportunities. But if they are substitutes, then immigration threatens native wage and employment levels. In the common textbook presentation, undergraduates are told that more immigration pushes the labor supply curve downward to the right, tracing out lower wage equilibria. The falling wage in turn induces more native workers to either drop out of the labor force or be replaced by immigrants.

The earliest attempts to empirically test immigration's effects on domestic wage levels relied on single-year national cross-sections of 1970 or 1980 census microdata. For a set of cities or metropolitan areas, the wage of local native workers was regressed on the number of or proportion of labor force participants who were immigrants, plus a variety of control variables. A few papers also tested the impact of recent immigration on earlier immigrants' wages and found that it was significantly negative. But most studies found that higher immigration levels were associated with weak or statistically insignificant effects on natives' wages. A summary of these and later selected studies, with reference citations, is contained in Table 1.

These early findings were thought to be subject to several biases. First, since they looked only at aggregate native wages, any negative immigration impact on low-skilled natives may have been offset by positive effects on the high skilled. Likewise, different immigrant cohorts may have different effects, which need to be distinguished empirically. Another possible weakening influence on immigration coefficients may have been the rapid exodus from high-immigration labor markets of those natives whose jobs were most threatened by immigrant labor. In a much-cited paper, Filer (1992) reported that, at least in 1975–80, the number of immigrant arrivals did seem to be offset by comparable native outflows or reduced native inflows to high-immigration regions. A fourth possible problem is the endogeneity of immigration: if immigrants tend to move to high-wage cities, single-equation wage models mistake the direction of causation. Still another consideration is the influence of labor market segmentation. Foreign inflows to secondary jobs in the industrial periphery may have quite different effects than inflows to largely primary jobs in core industries.

In an effort to take into account these potential sources of bias, DeFreitas's 1988 study used 1980 census microdata to estimate the effects of 1975–79 Hispanic immigrants on less-skilled native workers in the 79 largest metro areas. A multi-equation model was tested in which instrumental variables were used as regressors for both immigration and native workers' migration. Separate estimates were made for native non-Hispanic whites, African Americans, and Hispanics (each subdivided by sex), and for core and peripheral labor market sectors. The main results were: recent Hispanic immigration had insignificant wage effects for native white women, black men, and Hispanics, regardless of the sector of employment. The only group experiencing statistically significant (though small) negative effects was black women.

Table 1 *Impacts of the number of immigrants on native-born workers' wages*

Study	Effects of immigration on:	Findings
Grossman (1982)	All natives, 1970	10% increase in immigrants is related to 0.2% lower factor share of native labor
DeFreitas & Marshall (1983)	Manf. workers, 1970–80	10% increase in immigrants' share of manf. workers is related to 0.5% lower wage growth in manufacturing
Borjas (1987)	White, black, Hispanic natives, & Hispanic immigrants, 1980	10% increase in Mexican immigrants is related to 0.03% lower white wages, 0.07% lower black wages, and 10% lower Mexican immigrant wages
Bean et al. (1988)	Black & Mexican natives in Southwest, 1980	10% increase in recent Mexican immigrants is related to 0.4–0.8% higher white and black male wages, and 0.2–1.1% higher female wages
DeFreitas (1988)	Low-skill white, black, & Hispanic natives, 1980	10% increase in recent Hispanic immigrants is related to 4.9% higher white male wages and 0.9% lower black female wages; insignif. effect on others
Altonji & Card (1991)	Low-skill natives 1970–80	10% increase in immigrants' share of population is related to 0.2%–0.9% lower native wages, and 4% lower wages of immigrants
Butcher & Card (1991)	Intercity wage growth, 1979–89	Increase in recent immigrants' share of city population has positive (but insignif.) relation to wage growth of both low- and high-skill workers
Borjas, Freeman, & Katz (1992)	Low-skill workers, 1968–88	Increase in low-skill immigrants' share of labor force may account for one-fourth of the 10% fall in high school dropouts' wages relative to better educated in 1980–88
Enchautegui (1994)	White, black & Hispanic native men, 1980–90	10% increase in recent immigrants' share of labor force is related to 0.5% higher white wages; insignif. effect on blacks and Hispanics. Best native wage growth in high-immigration metro areas
Wial (1994)	White, black, Hispanic, & Asian natives, 1980–90	Increase in immigrants' share of labor force by 1 pctg. point has small positive (less than one one-hundreth of a point) or insignificant effects on inequality indexes

In contrast, low-skill white male natives actually appeared to gain significantly from higher immigration.[3]

As earnings inequality has worsened over the past decade, the continued relevance of such studies based on the 1980 Census has been questioned. Borjas has argued that U.S. immigrants' "quality" has steadily deteriorated, rendering them increasingly substitutable with low-wage natives. Based on a model of international skill sorting, he contends that past declines in education's rate of return here discouraged immigration of the highly skilled, even from low-income nations like Mexico. The less skilled are conversely more attracted by a narrower earnings distribution and better options for welfare and unemployment benefits than in their homeland. This, together with the greater legal access to visas for non-Europeans created by the 1965 reforms, has widened the education gap between natives and recent immigrant cohorts. For example, in 1970, 40 percent of the native born and 48 percent of the foreign born had not attained a high school degree. But by 1990 the gap had widened to 22 percentage points (15 percent of natives, 37 percent of immigrants). The clear implication is that larger numbers of less-educated immigrants may have intensified the competition for jobs and wages with non-college natives and thereby lowered the latter's relative and absolute living standards.

This view has been challenged by a growing number of studies. For example, Lalonde and Topel (1991) show that there have been increases, not declines, in the average years of schooling of most nationalities. The fact that the native-immigrant schooling gap has widened is entirely explained by the post-1965 shift in the national origins mix toward non-European countries. Relative to natives of similar race and ethnicity, recent immigrants' educational background is no weaker than in the past. They conclude: "Immigrants' long-run earnings potential is similar to that of ethnically similar natives. In this sense we think that fears about declining immigrant quality have been exaggerated."

Past generalizations about immigrant quality have missed the important fact that most of the decline in mean years of immigrant education is the fault of illegal entrants: three-fourths of those from the main source countries of the undocumented lack a high school diploma. In contrast, one-third of recent legal entrants hold a college degree, compared with only one-fifth of U.S. natives (Fix and Passel 1994). Moreover, new research suggests that the secular fall in immigrants' average education and wage levels relative to natives appears to have halted, and begun a modest reversal (Funkhauser and Trejo 1995).

Has the alleged growth in low-quality immigration flows exacerbated the widening earnings gap between high school dropouts and better-educated Americans?

---

3   Altonji and Card's (1991) quite different study of less-skilled workers yielded mostly insignificant coefficient estimates for the effect of immigrant population share on natives' weekly wages, whether in 1970 and 1980 cross-sections or in a simple 1970–80 first-difference model. The notable exception was a significant elasticity estimate of -0.086 in an instrumental variables model. However, the instrument they chose for the decadal change in the local immigrant density was the immigrant density in 1970. Given the highly dubious value of this instrument, the resulting elasticity estimate should probably be taken as a questionable upper bound. See also Borjas' (1994, fn. 28) criticism.

Borjas, Freeman, and Katz used 1967–87 Current Population Survey data to study the influences of immigration and trade on the wage gap. Based on simulations from a factor-proportions model, they estimated that, of the 10 percent fall in drop-outs' relative wages in the 1980s, from one-fourth to two-fifths of the total could be associated with immigration. However, since their CPS data combine the native and foreign born without differentiation, this result is highly questionable. As Borjas (1994, fn. 31) himself concedes: "The decline in the relative wage of unskilled workers could be attributable to the fact that the unskilled wage fell because the new immigrants earn even lower wages than the unskilled native population." Friedberg and Hunt (1995) estimate that over half the estimated immigrant contribution to inequality could be due to this composition problem alone. The Borjas, Freeman, and Katz estimates are further overstated by their conflation of the impacts of in-creased supplies of unskilled immigrants and of unskilled natives, since the latter are stronger substitutes for each other.

Moreover, their methodology has been challenged on other grounds, particularly its reliance on the questionable assumption of a tight correspondence between wage and skill levels. As David Gordon (1996, 200) has pointed out: "The translation from labor supply effects to earnings effects is mediated by a simple estimation of the association between skills and earnings without allowing any other factor (ex-cept a linear time trend) to affect earnings, again effectively assuming what ought to be tested."

In fact, more recent studies do not support claims that immigration has worsened earnings inequality. Enchautegui's 1994 paper examined the impacts of recent im-migration on both cross-sectional male wage levels in 1980 and 1990 and on male wage growth over the eighties. She found no significant negative effects on wage levels of native whites, African Americans, or Hispanics. If anything, the results suggested that the ability of the economy to absorb immigrants had improved be-tween 1980 and 1990. Moreover, areas of high immigration (where the immigrant share of the population was at least 10 percent) were the only parts of the country in which natives' real wages grew. Even after regression controls were introduced to take into account the possible endogeneity of immigration to these areas and a host of other factors, higher rates of native wage growth were positively correlated with higher immigrant concentrations. Wial's 1994 study adopted a very different statis-tical approach but likewise concluded that immigration has not played an important role in recent trends in earnings inequality.

Do immigrants worsen the job prospects of the native born? The representative studies cited in Table 2 suggest that – whether measured by the unemployment rate, employment-population rate, or weeks worked per year – employment among the native born does not appear to have been harmed substantially by higher immigra-tion. This is not to say that there may be some negative effects on some groups: for example, in my own work I found that the subset of non-college black men in pe-ripheral, largely unstable low-wage jobs average fewer weeks worked in cities with high immigrant concentrations. Anything harming the prospects of this most vul-nerable group warrants concern, even if the estimated effect is relatively small (10

Table 2 *Impacts of the number of immigrants on native-born workers' employment*

Study	Effects of immigration on:	Findings
Muller & Espenshade (1985)	Black natives, 1980	No significant relation between Hispanic population share in a metro area and black unemployment rate
DeFreitas (1988)	Low-skill white, black, & Hispanic natives, 1980	No significant relation between recent immigration and annual weeks worked of whites, Hispanics, or most blacks. For black men in peripheral industries; a 10% increase in immigration is related to 2.8% fewer weeks worked
Card (1990)	Black natives in Miami, Atlanta, Houston, L.A., & Tampa, 1979–85	No significant relation between arrival of Mariel boatlift Cuban influx in 1980 and changes in black joblessness in Miami relative to other cities
Altonji & Card (1991)	Low-skill white & black natives, 1970–80	10% increase in immigrants' share of population is related to 2.3% higher employment rate; insignif. effect on labor force participation rate
Winegarden & Khor (1991)	Young whites & blacks (16–24), 1980	10% increase in undocumented aliens' share of state population is related to 1.3% higher unemployment rate of young whites; insignif. effects on young blacks
Simon, Moore, & Sullivan (1993)	Urban unemploy. rates, 1960–77	Insignificant association between intercity differences in immigrant population share and unemployment levels, and insignificant association between time-series changes in immigration and changes in unemployment
Enchautegui (1993)	White, black, & Hispanic natives, 1980–90	No significant difference between probabilities of black joblessness in high-immigration metro areas and in other areas; no increase in blacks' relative probability of joblessness in high-immigration areas in 1980s

percent higher immigration associated with 2.8 percent fewer weeks worked).

The lack of sizable adverse employment effects could be (as noted above for wages) simply reflecting a tendency for job displacement to take the form of greater out-migration from high-immigration areas by natives more vulnerable to immigrant competition. But, contrary to Filer's findings for the seventies, Butcher and Card (1991) show that the dominant 1979–89 pattern has been a strong *positive* correlation between in-migration rates of natives and recent immigration to major metropolitan areas. That is, rapidly growing cities in California, Florida, and Texas drew larger numbers of both native- and foreign-born movers.

Of course, the fact that most national studies have not found strong negative effects on native job holding does not mean that individual native workers are never passed over in hiring or displaced from current jobs in favor of immigrants. Some criticize the national studies for operating at too aggregate a level to detect the real consequences of immigration in specific labor markets and industries. A number of case studies of apparel (Waldinger 1996), construction (Grenier et al. 1992), restaurants (Bailey 1987), and other industries have shown how successive waves of immigrants can establish their own niches. They then expand and insulate their jobs from competition with natives through ethnic networks that fill nearly all job openings. New arrivals from abroad are guided by long-settled friends and relatives to work opportunities in immigrant-owned businesses or in other firms with sizable migrant concentrations. Employers, immigrant or not, come to prefer these networks as low-cost recruitment and screening devices, but this effectively excludes native job seekers. In my own 1996 survey of hundreds of New York City employers, I found a high degree of labor market segmentation between native-born and foreign-born youth. Yet employers' weak demand for young native workers is more a function of the city's anemic job growth, employers' low estimation of local school quality, and other factors than immigration.[4]

What then explains the fact that such a large body of national studies show little or no net impact of immigration on natives' wages or employment? First, immigration does not just expand the supply of labor; it also increases demand. Immigrant expenditures on consumer goods, cars, and houses generate multiplier effects rippling through the economy to spur job growth for natives as well. Industry case studies are too narrow to capture these broader effects. Immigrants also average higher self-employment rates, creating their own business demand for related business services and materials, often from nonimmigrant suppliers. While this increases labor market segmentation, immigrant niches absorb workers who might otherwise have to compete with natives for jobs elsewhere. Still another explanation is that many of the most recent immigrants are more complements than substitutes, since they take the harshest, low-status work that even low-wage natives tend to spurn. And the growth of immigrant concentrations in cities like New York, Los Angeles, and Miami draws foreign capital here, as businesses in their homelands seek to become part of these expanding markets.

Roughly comparable findings on immigration impacts have emerged from research in Western Europe. Zimmermann's (1995) review of studies in a variety of countries concludes that the effects of immigration on earnings and unemployment are generally quite small. For example, in Germany, destination of the largest number of migrants, studies of the period 1985–89 by Pischke and Velling (1994) and of 1988–92 by Gieseck et al. (1995) found either insignificant or positive effects of recent immigrant inflows on earnings and employment levels.

However, many of the same studies that have found no adverse wage impacts on natives have still concluded that new immigrants to the U.S. do tend to depress the earnings of one group of workers: earlier immigrants. Recent research surveyed by the National Research Council (1997) estimates that a 10 percent increase in immi-

---

4   See DeFreitas (forthcoming).

gration lowers real wages of the resident foreign-born workforce by amounts ranging from 4 percent to 9 percent. This impact is likely to be stronger the more clustered are different cohorts of migrants in the same industrial niches.

Public sector impacts

Do immigrants drain the public treasury, overusing welfare and social services while
underpaying taxes? This question has drawn national attention since California vot-
ers approved Proposition 187 in November 1994. This barred undocumented aliens
from all public assistance, education, and nonemergency medical care and required
doctors and teachers to report patients or students who lacked legal residency papers. Other states quickly followed suit, though legal challenges have so far blocked
full implementation.

Of course, concern over the possible fiscal burden imposed by immigrants is not
new. In the first wave of laws restricting immigration to the U.S., the 1882 Immigration Act prohibited persons "likely to become public charges." Today's foreign-born
welfare recipients are often contrasted unfavorably with our hard-working immigrant
ancestors who arrived in the days long before government entitlement programs. But
historical research now shows that an enormous number of those arriving at the turn of
the century and before needed public assistance. A national government survey of
large cities in 1909 found that 53 percent of all city charity cases were the foreign born
and their children (U.S. Immigration Commission 1911). In Chicago, immigrant families were three times more likely than natives to be on the dole. Many exhausted their
savings on travel expenses, then arrived to suffer unemployment, low wages, and
work accidents.[5] They had a similarly large impact on public services. Children from
immigrant families accounted for one-half of public school students in the 30 largest
cities. In New York City, the foreign born accounted for over three-fourths of students
and for about half of all hospital expenditures.

Current welfare recipiency
How does the present compare with the past? Research on the 1976 Survey of Income and Education (Blau 1984) and on the 1980 Census (DeFreitas 1991; Tienda
and Jensen 1986) found that, while the poverty rate of immigrants exceeded that of
natives, there was relatively little difference in their incidence of public assistance
recipiency. In 1979, the poverty rate of foreign-born families was about 50 percent
higher than that of natives, but the former's average recipiency rate (10 percent) was
only 25 percent more than native's (8 percent). And the main reasons for the higher
immigrant rate were the larger shares of elderly, minorities, and Indochinese refugees in the immigrant population.

Heavy Indochinese immigration continued into the 1980s and, according to the
1990 Census (U.S. Department of Commerce 1993), nearly one-half of all Cambo-

---

5   See, for example, Katz (1986, 1995).

dian and Laotian immigrant households are recipients of Aid to Families With Dependent Children (AFDC), as are one-fourth of Vietnamese. These very high rates have caused concern that such refugees have become increasingly welfare dependent. Bach and Aguiros (1991) found that, in the first five years after arriving here, these refugees exhibited labor force participation rates approaching those of natives. And they estimated that about two-fifths of refugee households who had received some public assistance were off the rolls within two years; three-fifths were nonrecipients within five years. But they report big interstate differences in welfare exit. Only one in four refugees living in California left the rolls within five years. Whether this reflects the economic difficulties in that state or other factors requires further study. It is clear, however, that one trend of the recent past has likely had a strong harmful effect on refugees' move to self-sufficiency: the substantial resettlement assistance authorized by the 1980 Refugee Act has been steadily scaled back. In fact, annual real dollar appropriations have been cut in half since 1980 (Tienda and Liang 1994). The result has been to shift more and more of the burden of refugee assistance to financially strapped states.

Besides certain refugees, the other group with above-average use of public assistance is elderly 1980s' entrants. While fewer than one in 10 native-born elderly receive welfare benefits, one in four post-1980 elderly immigrants do. Three-fourths of foreign-born elderly receiving Supplemental Security Income (SSI) have no other income source; this is less than half as likely to be true for natives on SSI (Fix and Passel 1994). This seems to reflect the fact that most immigrants now come from countries with few if any government or private pensions, and the elderly among them lack sufficient U.S. work experience to qualify for Social Security.

In contrast, recently arrived Mexicans have been markedly less likely to get public assistance than natives. Jensen (1988) attributes this in part to the large fraction of undocumenteds (as many as two-thirds of the 1975–80 cohort) among them. More recent analysis of a 1988 survey of undocumented Mexicans supports this finding: under 2 percent of them received welfare in the past 12 months, compared with 7.6 percent of all Americans; only 2.1 percent used Medicaid, compared to a 9.5 percent national rate; and Food Stamp, SSI, and Medicare usage was similarly lower for the undocumented (Tienda and Liang 1994, Table 13.4). Illegal entrants are prohibited by law from receiving any public assistance aside from emergency care under Medicaid and benefits under the Women, Infants, and Children (WIC) program. But some gain access to aid, either because their U.S.-born children are eligible for welfare benefits or because they use widely available fraudulent identification papers. Still, it appears that, despite their high poverty rate, the undocumented largely avoid the risks of detection associated with government programs and rely instead on kinship support networks.

Net fiscal effects

The most volatile question in recent controversies is also the most difficult to resolve empirically: how do total costs of providing government assistance and services to immigrants compare to the public revenues derived from them? Data on program usage and on tax payments rarely contain nativity information, so past estimates have proven highly sensitive to researchers' many assumptions.

Two of the most publicized reports on the issue are those of Los Angeles County (1992) and of Rice University economist Donald Huddle (1993). The Los Angeles study concluded that immigrants cost the county $947 million in social services in 1991, but paid county taxes of only $139 million. But subsequent research by Jeffrey Passel and Rebecca Clark revealed that the Los Angeles figures overestimated immigrant social service costs by one-third and underestimated their taxes by nearly one-half.[6] Moreover, the Los Angeles report itself estimated that the total taxes (local, state, and federal) paid by these immigrants exceeded their total social service costs by $1.8 billion.

Huddle extrapolated from the flawed Los Angeles report to claim that, nationally, the foreign born drained the public treasury by $43 billion in 1992. Among his own additional errors, Huddle greatly overestimated the public assistance costs attributable to immigrants by assuming that, for every six new immigrants, one native worker is forced out of his or her job and onto welfare. This was based on his own small-scale Houston study and runs counter to the national findings summarized in our Tables 1 and 2.

The National Research Council, in its own analysis of both short-run and long-run fiscal impacts, identified another bias built into these and most other studies: they typically omit the positive effects of employed native-born children of immigrants who no longer live in their immigrant parents' household. When these effects are included, the council concluded (1997, 7–39):

> Under most scenarios, the long run fiscal impact is strongly positive at the federal level, but substantially negative at the state and local level. The federal impact is shared evenly across the population, but these negative state and local impacts are concentrated in the few states that receive most of the immigrants....The 1996 Personal Responsibility and Work Opportunity Reconciliation Act, by prohibiting new immigrants from receiving means-tested benefits for a period after arrival, will make the long-term fiscal impact per immigrant more positive by about $8000.

Toward a new policy

Immigration seems to be one of that handful of issues capable of creating sharp internal divisions within both the right and the left. Among conservatives, there has always been a strong nativist contingent deeply worried about its perceived threats to American culture and social cohesion. Fused with the tax- and budget-cutting fervor of recent years, this put great momentum behind recent congressional efforts to slash legal immigration and end the eligibility for AFDC benefits of even long-resident legal aliens. But libertarians, confident in the powers of markets to set supposedly optimal migration levels, favor a more "open borders" policy.

6   On Passel's analysis with colleagues of both the Los Angeles and Huddle studies, see Fix and Passel (1994) and the papers cited therein.

Most moderates and liberals kept uncomfortably quiet until recently, in the latest round of debates over immigration. In July 1995, President Clinton sided with the recommendations of the bipartisan U.S. Commission on Immigration Reform. These included: reducing legal admissions to 550,000 per year; cutting refugee admissions in half to 50,000 per year; increasing the legal responsibilities of American sponsors for their immigrant charges; and establishing a national computer registry of all lawful residents to aid employers in screening out undocumented job candidates.

In the fall of 1996, Clinton signed into law the Illegal Immigration Reform and Immigrant Responsibility Act. While lacking provisions for specific numeric cuts in admissions or a national registry, the law was designed to reduce both legal and illegal entry. It authorized a doubling in size of the border patrol and gave sweeping new discretionary powers to officials at ports of entry to summarily exclude refugees fleeing their homelands without proper travel documents. Applicants for immigration status were stripped of important legal protections, like the right to file class action suits against the INS. For the first time, U.S. residents wishing to sponsor family or friends from abroad will from now on be required to show an annual income at least 25 percent above the official poverty level ($19,500 for a family of four in 1996). Some estimates indicate that about 30 percent of current sponsors could not meet such an income test. The law (which went into effect in April 1997) also expands the legal obligations of sponsors to support immigrants and to reimburse the government for any welfare benefits they obtain. Since the 1996 overhaul of welfare policy excludes most legal noncitizen immigrants from receipt of public assistance for at least the first five years after arrival, the combined effects of these dramatic legal changes will be to make legal immigration much more difficult for many low-income families.

On the left, pro-union sympathies have historically led many to back low or no immigration as a means to protect labor organizing efforts and wage levels. At the opposite end of the spectrum, others espouse open borders. This is most often defended as a step toward the traditional progressive goals of income equality and international solidarity. Some, like Bob Sutcliffe, go further, contending that: "A progressive viewpoint on immigration should start from rights and freedoms and not from consequences....The free movement of people internationally should be seen as an important element in individual human rights, just as it is nationally." [7]

The claim that immigration deserves the status of a human right raises a host of difficult ethical issues well beyond the scope of this paper.[8] Neither the United Nations Universal Declaration of Human Rights nor the Helsinki Accords include immigration among their long lists of fundamental rights, though they do assign such status to emigration. For its signatories, recognizing people's freedom to leave their countries did not also imply the right to move to any country they wished nor the

7   Sutcliffe (1998, this volume, pp. 328, 329).
8   In considering these issues, I particularly benefited from the valuable exchanges on the ethical controversies surrounding contemporary immigration in the special spring 1996 issue of the *International Migration Review*, particularly the papers by J.H. Carens and Myron Weiner.

obligation of any one country to accept them. Even if one rejects the current international consensus and accepts immigration as a prima facie right, this does not resolve the problem of reconciling it with many other, potentially conflicting rights. For example, if an open borders policy were to threaten the right to economic security of low-income residents of the receiving country, whose rights take priority: those of the domestic poor or those of the immigrants? Still more extreme consequences could be expected in a world where all nations would be unlikely to open their borders simultaneously; some hostile states might take advantage of those who abandon all immigration controls. A populous, authoritarian nation could transfer millions of its citizens into a smaller neighboring country, overwhelming the latter and robbing its residents of their rights to political freedom and national self-determination. For these and other reasons, modern human rights theory from the 17th century onward was developed largely in the context of a given society or nation.

Any genuinely progressive policy agenda should give high priority to eradicating racial or ethnic biases in immigration, combating nativist impulses, and promoting global economic equality. But open borders seem a highly questionable and probably counterproductive means to these ends. While there is no consistent evidence that immigration to the United States has so far had sizable effects on natives' wages or employment or on public sector budgets, some of the research reviewed above did find negative, though relatively small, immigration impacts on low-wage native workers. This alone should motivate efforts for corrective policies today and instill caution in advocates of greatly expanded immigration. Moreover, it is dangerous to extrapolate from econometric findings based on current immigration levels that the same would be the case with an open borders policy. For example, the Census Bureau (U.S. Department of Commerce 1992) now estimates that even if annual immigration were to rise from the current 1 million (legals plus illegals) to only 1.4 million, by the year 2020 this would drive the U.S. population up to 340 million – nearly 90 million more than today. The foreign born would more than double their share of the national population. History suggests that the more sudden are such large demographic shifts, the more likely they are to fuel economic, political, and racial frictions, and a xenophobic backlash.

Moreover, the weight of the empirical evidence to date does point to some adverse wage impacts on earlier cohorts of migrants already settled in the U.S. A high proportion of recent immigrants already have relatively low incomes, and increased job competition with newcomers concentrated in immigrant niches could carry even more damaging consequences as noncitizens are stripped of the right to obtain public assistance benefits.

While individual immigrants and their families usually do raise their living standards abroad, exporting workers is a very inefficient approach to Third World economic development. Those with the motivation and resources to emigrate are seldom from the neediest segments of the source country population, but rather are more often the skilled and semi-skilled. Their emigration represents a subsidy to the receiving country from the nation that trained them, as well as a loss of valuable talents to their homeland.

Migrants often do send sizable remittances back home, but research suggests that these typically increase income inequality and dependence on consumer imports among migrants' relatives, rather than help to meet the social investment needs of their home countries. Durand and Massey's (1992) review of 37 community studies concluded that they were "remarkably unanimous in condemning international migration as a palliative that improves the material well-being of particular families but does not lead to sustained economic growth within sending communities." If the same amount of money could somehow be bundled in assistance packages from the West to progressive Third World governments, the long-term development impacts could be markedly greater.

Rather than either highly liberalized or highly restrictive policies, it seems to me that an alternative progressive approach would combine a generous and humanitarian admissions system with adequate protections of labor and living standards both here and abroad. At a minimum, this approach should include the following considerations:

First, it must be explicitly recognized that the principal purpose of immigration should be humanitarian, not economic. The United States was founded in part as a haven for those fleeing political and religious persecution. In today's competition for scarce admissions slots, the highest priority should go to those refugees in the greatest danger at home. Surely, few if any human rights can reasonably claim a higher priority than the right not to be tortured and the right to be spared unjust execution for political or religious beliefs. Secondary priority should be assigned to immediate family members of past immigrants. This appeared to be the intent of the 1965 immigration reform. But in practice it gave vastly higher priority to reunification of even distant family members of U.S. residents and admission of skilled workers than to refugees in harm's way, who were left to the whims of ad hoc administrative decisions. The 1980 Refugee Act aimed at a more systematic approach and replaced the Cold War definition of "refugees" (as anyone fleeing Communism) with that approved by the U.N.: "persons with a well-founded fear of persecution based on race, religion, nationality, membership in a social group, or political views."

But the still-strong Cold War bias has continued to favor what are now largely economic migrants from Cuba, Indochina, Eastern Europe, and the former Soviet Union. Recent history has produced no shortage of genuine refugees from political and ethnic violence, and our immigration system needs to reserve an adequate number of places to provide temporary or long-term haven to as many as is feasible. This may at times mean assigning lower priority to the other main humanitarian goal, speedy reunification of immediate family members. Of course, no one country should be expected to accept all who claim to be refugees from anywhere in the world. And even in seemingly obvious refugee crises like that of Haiti in 1994, massive population displacements will require coordination of multinational resettlement efforts.

Second, for individual cities and states to cope with large inflows of refugees or others, the federal government (which alone controls immigration policy) must finally accept the responsibility to fully shoulder the resultant costs. About 60 percent of all new immigrants move to just four states: California, New York, Florida, and Texas. Since the tax revenue generated by immigration flows disproportionately to Washington, adequate funds must be redistributed to localities to provide the additional public benefits, health, schooling, and other services needed to prevent overtaxing existing resources. It is in the nature of sudden flight by refugees that many are ill-prepared for a new country. So the past decade's trend of sharp cuts in federal assistance for resettlement, language, and job training must be reversed and the funds better targeted to promote rapid movement toward work and self-sufficiency.

Third, so long as unlimited immigration between high- and low-income countries remains an unrealistic prospect, some form of border control will be necessary. But the INS is a notoriously inefficient and understaffed organization, with a record marred by corruption and harsh treatment of apprehended illegal entrants (Sontag and Engelberg 1994). It needs thorough reorganization, as well as better screening, training, and supervision of its agents. New staff and resources should be allocated to expedite the lengthy visa application and review processes and to establish a flexible, quick-response capability to deal with future refugee emergencies.

Fourth, occupational skills alone should not be a sufficient basis for admission. Thanks to fierce lobbying by business groups and encouragement from economists claiming immigrants' "quality" had fallen, Congress in 1990 expanded the permanent visa category for people with "needed skills," with very little research evidence about the possible consequences for skilled native workers or on the prospects of the unskilled for occupational mobility. So great was the resultant concern over growing competition with skilled migrants that it sparked at least one strike (Boeing) and led Secretary of Labor Robert Reich to change his department's rules. Starting in early 1995, the length of H1-B stays was cut from a maximum of six years to three, and Labor Department investigations of employer abuses were allowed to be launched even without prior employee complaints.

These modest steps provoked an opposition campaign by the National Association of Manufacturers, the U.S. Chamber of Commerce and Microsoft and other computer companies. They insisted that global firms need large numbers of skilled foreigners to stay competitive and grow, thereby enabling them to expand their U.S. base. But these claims ring hollow. A number of computer firms were increasing their applications for H1-B visa holders in the early 1990s at the same time that they were sharply downsizing their permanent workforce of largely native-born professionals. And many on H1-B temporary visas, after mastering key elements of the work process at U.S. firms, return home to train others to do the same work. This then facilitates the export of jobs abroad by American firms seeking low-cost high-tech labor. Computer programmers, cinematographers, and aircraft machinists appear to be among those most at risk of replacement.[9]

9   See the research findings in DeFreitas (1996) and Smith (1996). It appears that employers increasingly view H1-B visas as an attractive substitute for (as well as a first step toward eligibility for) permanent skilled visas. The application process is much faster and employers need only show that they'll pay the prevailing local wage and post notices of intent to hire foreigners. They are not required to demonstrate that qualified Americans are unavail-

What is needed now are more, not less, limitations on and monitoring of such firms' practices. International exchange of ideas and skills can still be achieved by granting brief visas to foreigners willing to train U.S. workers. And the more than 300,000 student visas now granted each year provide ample opportunity for those from abroad seeking access to training here.

Fifth, instead of exporting more high-wage jobs or importing professionals to meet supposed "skill shortages," business and government must be induced to finally provide first-class schooling, training, and retraining for the vast numbers of low-wage and underemployed Americans. And they must as well help generate enough new good-paying jobs for these workers to fill. This has become all the more necessary in the wake of the strict work requirements and five-year lifetime benefits limits imposed by the 1996 welfare law. It may demand difficult and politically unpopular choices of some mix of new industrial policies and temporary trade barriers to preserve existing high-skill jobs (particularly in manufacturing) and promote the development of new ones.[10]

Intensification of antidiscrimination efforts in employment and housing will also be needed if low-wage minority workers are to benefit from any future job growth. Recent research shows that African American job seekers are at a particular disadvantage in gaining access to suburban job vacancies. The 1992–94 Multicity Study of Urban Inequality found that blacks were far more likely to be the victims of suburban employers' discrimination than Hispanics, who also are less residentially segregated (Holzer 1995). This suggests that Hispanic immigrants are able to work in a wider area of local labor markets than African Americans and to take advantage of the increasing concentration of blue-collar jobs in the suburbs.

Still another set of changes would help decrease U.S. employers' preferences for undocumented immigrants. These would include aggressive enforcement of health, safety, and other workplace labor standards and a sizable hike in the minimum wage. Comprehensive labor law reform is also necessary if workers, native and foreign born, are to ever be able to exercise their democratic right to organize and join unions without undue employer interference.[11] This will diminish the competitive advantage of many firms relying on exploited migrants at the same time that it betters the lot of most workers.

Finally, to reduce the need of so many Third World workers to emigrate, the

able before hiring immigrants. Nor are they required, if training immigrants to meet future skill needs, to also train native workers. In the 1990s, nearly nine out of 10 H1-B applications were approved (U.S. Department of Justice 1994).

10 See the survey of policy options to reduce inequality in Bluestone (1994), including his discussion of immigration reform.

11 Contrary to stereotypes of docile, antiunion immigrants, empirical analysis of national longitudinal data by DeFreitas (1993) has found that young immigrants have higher unionization rates and generally stronger "demand" for unionized jobs than natives. While immigrants have been used to restrain union efforts in some historical periods, the recent positive record of some unions (e.g., the International Ladies' Garment Workers Union (ILGWU, now a part of UNITE) and the Service Employees' International Union) in organizing the foreign born suggests that new union attitudes and organizing methods may be able to tap a large potential source of future membership growth.

United States must end its historic pattern of itself creating large displaced populations through its foreign policies. The most obvious examples are this country's many military and economic interventions on the side of repressive regimes in the Caribbean, Central America, and Indochina.[12] In addition, U.S. support of the extreme privatization measures that the International Monetary Fund demands of borrowers have doubtless aggravated unemployment and induced more emigration in many poor countries. And the North American Free Trade Agreement appears to have begun hurting certain sectors of Mexico's economy enough to generate new pressure for northward migration.

The U.S. needs to begin leading other rich nations in funding projects that foster sustainable development and job growth in poor nations.[13] This could be partially financed by imposing "social tariffs" on the products of multinational companies whose labor and environmental standards are below acceptable levels.[14] As capital becomes ever more mobile, the only way to reduce labor migration is through improving living and working conditions in both sending and receiving countries.

Conclusion

The worrisome trends toward increasing wage inequality and underemployment in recent years have focused renewed attention on the possible role played by immigration. The growing body of empirical research on the economic impacts of immigration has produced many and various findings, but there does not seem to be any consistent evidence of broad net negative effects on wage or employment levels among native born workers. While immigrants may well obtain some jobs sought by or already held by native workers, they generate a roughly comparable volume of new jobs. Nor has a strong case been made that immigrants' use of government benefits and services are unmatched by their tax contributions, at least at the federal level. Among recent nonrefugee immigrants of working age, only 2 percent received welfare benefits in 1989, compared to 3.7 percent of working-age natives. Overall, immigrants appear to be paying more than enough in taxes to cover the public benefits they receive.

Immigration today remains essential to the basic goals of offering a haven for refugees and reuniting families. It also offers a valuable source of cultural diversity and dynamism for this country. Efforts to sharply curtail immigration should be opposed, as should nativist efforts to widen racial and ethnic divisions.

At the same time, more than a million people are now moving (legally or illegally) to this country each year – far more than to any other place in the world. This has caused short-run strains on public resources, like the schooling systems of the

---

12 On the migration-inducing influences of U.S. government policies and of direct foreign investment abroad, see Sassen (1988).

13 See, for example, the papers in Bohning and Schloeter-Pareded (1994).

14 Of course, this and my other policy proposals are highly controversial and require far more careful and lengthy discussion than the space limitations of this chapter permit.

few cities where immigrants have clustered. There is also evidence that new immigration may lead to some adverse impacts on certain workers, particularly earlier immigrant cohorts. And with millions of public assistance recipients being forced by the 1996 welfare reforms to find jobs in coming years, there is growing concern about the possibility of heightened competition in low-wage labor markets.

Those hoping to change the existing system must wrestle with difficult questions about the optimal volume and composition of future migration streams and their possible consequences for future generations resident here. I have outlined a new progressive approach that adopts a competition-reduction strategy between native and migrant workers. This approach minimizes the green cards allocated for highly skilled foreigners as one means of curtailing the "reserve army" aspect of immigration and pressuring business and government to focus more on job creation and training for indigenous low-wage workers. Preference would instead be given to genuine political refugees and immediate family members of U.S. residents. Coupled with more effective resettlement assistance for newcomers and with much-needed reforms in employment and foreign policies, this more humanitarian approach may offer a better means of meeting our international responsibilities in a world of frequent refugee crises, without worsening the economic prospects of U.S. workers.

15

Notes on international migration suggested by the Indian experience

Prabhat Patnaik and C.P. Chandrasekhar

Demand factors in migration

The bulk of international migration from India, whether historically or even today, has been "structured" from the demand side, i.e., the number, the destination, and the exact characteristics of the migrants have been determined by the requirements of the host economies. Central to that structure are a group of formal or informal "agents" who are not independent operators but are dependent on employers from abroad. These agents in turn access groups of workers with appropriate characteristics through a well-established network, often even involving social and kinship connections, resulting in the mass migration of workers from specific locations.

The 19th century migration of Indian workers, from specific locations in Bihar, East U.P., Andhra, and Tamilnadu, to work on plantations in the West Indies, Mauritius, Fiji, and South Africa, was organized through the mechanism of the "indentured" system, where the selected workers were "tied" to a labor contract for a specified period of time through the payment of advances. Much the same kind of a mechanism was used in the post-oil-price-hike period to organize the large migration of workers, this time mainly from Kerala, to West Asia. These workers were drawn predominantly from three districts (Trichur, Malappuram, and Cannanore) with large Muslim populations.

Incidentally, this pattern of migration being structured from the demand side, which entailed a combination of: (1) the number of migrants being "rationed" from the demand side, (2) the migrants being physically selected, and (3) a system of advances to tie them to a labor contract, was seen even in the case of long-distance internal migration to inhospitable terrains like the Assam tea plantations in the 19th century; it was even in vogue for the recruitment of the noncasual (i.e., non-"badli") segment of the workforce in the Calcutta jute mills.

To be sure, not all international migration from India was structured along these lines. Migration to the advanced capitalist countries in the postwar period was not based on the system of agents and advances emanating from the employers. Nonetheless, of course, it was demand determined, though not so elaborately demand structured: the immigration policies of developed-country governments attempted to control both the quantum and the characteristics of migrants at all points of time, based on a formal assessment of local labor requirements.

Why people migrate

Successful migration at the international level is not an act of choice. To be fair, of course, even neo-classical writings and their offshoots like the Todaro model (Todaro and Maruszko 1987) do not claim this; what they do insist upon is the role of individual choice in internal migration. But even at this level the argument is flawed, and it is worth discussing this briefly before we take up its extension to the international level.

The basic problem with the Todaro model is that it explains an ex-post total situation as a mere aggregation of a mass of individual decisions based on an ex-ante calculation of probabilities. Such an explanation necessarily requires the assumption that a person's choice is independent of his precise context and location; i.e., whether he is a potential migrant in the rural area or an actual migrant but unemployed in the urban area, his choice of residence remains unaffected (for otherwise the urban unemployed would migrate back to the rural area). This is violative of the elementary principle that one's ability to take risks is dependent upon one's economic position.

In other words, if a person is in the city without a job, then he cannot still go on making decisions as if the choice was between being in the village and migrating to the city with, say, a 90 percent chance of a job. And the total ex-post situation must depend upon what, given the fact that he is now unemployed, he decides to do with the options available to him. What is more, considerations of these options in the event of not getting employment would also enter into the original choice about migration and not the simple calculus of wage differentials and probabilities. They may even be quite decisive, which explains why, even in situations where there is apparent freedom of migration, there tends to be a concentration of migrants from particular villages from particular castes or kinship groups. This is obviously a means of ensuring a certain minimum level of support in the city. But it simultaneously means that not everybody *qua* an individual is effectively free to migrate even when he may be juridically free.

When we come to the extensions of this model to international migration, this basic flaw is compounded further by the sheer lack of realism of the assumptions. Let us see how.

It acknowledges the fact that international migration is structured through a set of agents who most often are located in urban centers, and then argues that rural migrants maximize their opportunity for foreign employment by moving into the urban informal labor market and being readily available to migrate when required by the agent. Since the expected differential in earnings, even after allowing for the probability of obtaining such employment being less than 1, is extremely high, this structure of the market for internationally mobile labor encourages "excessive" urbanization and high urban unemployment. The costs of such excessive urbanization, both in terms of urban infrastructure and lost rural output because of labor shortages, is seen to more than outweigh the benefits of international migration.

The lack of realism of the assumptions is palpable. It is taken for granted that the organization of structured recruitment for mass emigration cannot extend its linkages beyond the urban areas. It is presumed that the act of selection and transport of migrant workers by urban agents is too rapid for even the now well-developed channels of communication with rural areas in developing countries to be in a position to contact and mobilize aspirant rural workers. And in any case, the simple evidence that periods of heavy out-migration, such as to West Asia from Kerala in recent years, are not marked by any particular increases in the degree of overcrowding in the cities, which counters the basic conclusions of the model, is completely ignored.

How migration benefits Third World economies

Models such as these, however, play an ideological role. They legitimize restrictions on international migration of workers on spurious economic grounds. If international migration within the developing economies creates problems for these economies owing to urban overcrowding, and if the magnitude of these problems is directly linked to the scale of migration, then it follows that restrictions on such migration serves the interests of the developing world, too. This puts a "human face" on the standard conservative position, namely that there should be *no* restrictions on the freedom of capital flows (i.e., on the penetration by multinational corporations or "financial interests" into the Third World), but labor flows should be strictly controlled.

Structuralist development literature, on the other hand, had always recognized the benefits to the Third World of labor migration from it. First, since withdrawing workers from agriculture does not reduce output, and certainly not by as much as the migrant was consuming, in an immediate sense both the migrant and those who stay behind register an increase in consumption and welfare (presuming that the migrant earns a real wage higher than his premigration consumption level). Secondly, when migration from a specific region tends to be large, in all likelihood real wages or at least the number of days of employment (and hence earnings) of agricultural laborers in the region would tend to rise, with obviously positive welfare implications. A rise in wages in all likelihood would also result in an increase in the share of labor in total agricultural income and a corresponding fall in the share of rents and profits (Griffin 1978). Thirdly, when remittances are large, as they tend to be with international migration, some of these resources would be used for investment in agriculture, resulting in a jump in productivity, with any shortage of agricultural workers being met through internal migration. Thus, output and productivity in agriculture would rise in the wake of emigration. Finally, while prior to emigration there could be structural constraints (typically, fragmented peasant holdings) that result in underemployment of labor and low productivity, the tight labor market resulting immediately from mass migration may necessitate structural changes, such as land consolidation, that have positive productivity implications.

Available evidence from India certainly lends credence to some of these conclusions. While the effect of migration on the wage-rate is more doubtful, the fact that migration increases the earnings from work of those who stay behind seems clear. This is true of internal migration as much as it is of international migration. Two studies of internal migration from Bihar to Punjab give divergent conclusions on wage rates. While Ansari (1990), studying the Muzaffarpur district in Bihar finds an increase in the real wage rate, Jha (1997), for the Purnea district of North Bihar, finds no such increase. Clearly the wage determination in the countryside is a complex affair, and while the magnitude of labor reserves must have an important bearing on it, the relationship is not a simple monotonic one. Both the studies however point to an increase in the employment rate in the countryside as a result of migration. (Even Ansari interestingly finds the employment effects to be much stronger than the wage effects.)

In the case of international migration, for which Kerala is the classic case, this happens to be a high-wage, high-unemployment state. The background to this is provided by the long history of organization of the agricultural and other workers by the Communist movement in the state, which, notwithstanding the high unemployment rate, succeeded in enforcing high wages. Under the circumstances, the large migration to the Gulf did not have any discernible impact upon the wage rate (except possibly in particular pockets), though it certainly restricted the unemployment rate.

Added to these effects, mediated through the local labor market, however, are the effects of remittances upon the living standards of the nonmigrants. Kerala, as is well known, has one of the highest achievements in terms of social indices, e.g., life expectancy, literacy, infant mortality rate, female–male ratio, anywhere in the Third World (much higher than the average for India, higher than China for many indices) and even comparable to the advanced capitalist countries under some. At the same time Kerala's economy had witnessed a near-complete stagnation in terms of the per capita output of the material-commodity-producing sectors during the sixties and seventies. There can be very little doubt that Kerala could maintain its impressive social achievements as well as its high living standards, in the comprehensive sense, largely because of the sustenance provided by the inflow of remittances.

Remittances versus foreign direct investment

The macroeconomic effects of the remittance inflows upon the Indian balance of payments have to be separately considered. Throughout the late seventies and the eighties these inflows were of course a major prop for the Indian balance of payments. What is less well known, however, is the fact that even in the period of "structural adjustment" in the nineties the significance of these flows has far exceeded that of the much-touted items like foreign direct investment (FDI).

"Net private transfers" on the invisibles account of the balance of payments, consisting mainly of remittances from Indians working abroad, averaged $3,113 million per annum during the four financial years 1990/91–1993/94 and stood at

$3,825 million in 1993/94. In 1994/95, however, such transfers are estimated to have risen sharply to $6,200 million. While part of this increase is possibly due to a shift from unofficial to official channels of remittance, the sheer magnitude of these transfers is impressive.

The significance of the magnitudes involved comes through when we note that, as a result of their remarkable rise in 1994/95, private transfers not only exceeded the size of India's trade deficit of $3,946 million but were also much higher than the flow of direct ($1,314 million) and portfolio ($3,581 million) foreign investment, which together totaled $4,895 million. Remarkably, however, despite this overwhelmingly important role of remittances, they are scarcely ever mentioned, let alone celebrated, in the International Monetary Fund–World Bank literature, in government statements, or even in the international and the national press, while figures on foreign investments approved are presented with tedious regularity.

A theoretical argument is often used these days to explain this "discrimination." Investments, it is argued, create capital and the capacity to produce. Remittances are normally directed toward consumption or housing construction, which have less significant long-term consequences.

This argument, however, is fallacious. It is based on a confusion between the micro and the macro levels, between the immediate object of an act and its effect in the overall sense. If the economy is foreign exchange constrained, then remittances, like all kinds of investment inflows, can help the economy by augmenting the supply of foreign exchange. Each of these kinds of flows, however, simultaneously also sets up a demand for foreign exchange but to different extents: investment inflows, by paying for the physical import of equipment; and remittance inflows, by increasing domestic demand for commodities. On balance, then, remittance inflows in such a situation may be more useful for two reasons: first, the foreign exchange content of the commodities demanded owing to remittance inflows would be less than the foreign exchange content of the commodities demanded per unit of investment inflows, leaving more "free" foreign exchange for other uses. Secondly, since the economy *ex hypothesi* is not savings constrained, the government in the case of predominant remittance inflows can use fiscal and other instruments for achieving an appropriate investment rate anyway; if anything it has less freedom to do so in the case of predominant investment inflows, since its ability to use fiscal instruments is restricted by the need to attract such inflows.

On the other hand, if the economy is demand constrained, then remittance inflows can never be harmful for the economy, while FDI inflows, if they are meant for the domestic market and supplant existing domestic producers who usually have lower foreign exchange input (both capital and current) per unit of output, would have a definite contractionary effect on the economy. Such FDI inflows, catering to the domestic market in a demand-constrained system, have an implicit deindustrializing effect upon the economy. The celebration of capital inflows, and the silence over or the running down of remittance inflows, is a part of the so-called ideology of "liberalization" that, in effect, is an endorsement of the conservative argument mentioned earlier.

Migration impacts due to skill-level differences

What is of interest, however, is the fact that Third World governments themselves have internalized this ideology. We mentioned earlier that structuralist development literature had seen the potential benefits of international migration, and this reflected what most Third World governments also felt. There was a resistance on their part to unrestricted capital inflows but a recognition of the benefits of labor outflows. In the era of "globalization," however, the conservative argument too has become "globalized."

Parallel with this has been another shift. Earlier, Third World governments saw the emigration of skilled workers as harmful for the economy, while the emigration of unskilled workers was seen to be a welcome phenomenon. The conservative position in the West, however, was just the opposite: the former was viewed as a natural consequence of interdependence, toward which greater tolerance should be shown, while the latter was considered to be a fallout of developing country backwardness, a disease whose entry should be restricted.

In the wake of "liberalization" in the developing countries, there is a growing tendency for these differences to fade. The return of "nonresident" professionals of local origin, often as employees of transnational firms or new private institutions at huge salaries, has been used to buttress the notion that the migration of domestically trained professionals abroad is not a "drain" but rather a process of accumulation of special skills. These skills are then available for access from an international "brain bank" at an appropriate price, since cultural factors favor the return of these professionals for short or long periods of time. On the other hand, the migration of unskilled workers, as we have seen, is not assessed in anything like such sympathetic terms; instead, it is seen as an unfortunate practice that affects national credibility in the international marketplace.

In fact, however, remittances from skilled migrants are usually negligible. During the years in which remittances have become a significant figure on the current account, most migrants from India were headed for the Gulf. In 1990, for example, laborer outflows to West Asia are estimated at around 144,000, while flows to the three principal developed country destinations – the United States, Canada, and the United Kingdom – were estimated to be in the neighborhood of 45,000 (Nayyar 1994b). This is significant because, among migrants to West Asia, unskilled or low-skilled workers constituted more than 85 percent. Such migrants, unlike those to the developed countries, expect to stay abroad "temporarily," for varying segments of their working lifespans. They therefore not merely support a section of the family that stays home, but they also invest in housing construction and property. The pressure to remit sums of money is higher than in the case of those who migrate to the developed industrial countries, for these are usually skilled migrants with the intention of settling abroad.

A tax on emigration?

Skilled migration amounts, in effect then, to a unilateral transfer of resources, like the "drain" of the colonial period, from the underdeveloped to the developed economies. This "drain" must not be confused with the "brain drain" that is much written about (Bhagwati 1997). Unless authoritarian, and hence repugnant, restrictions are placed on the physical emigration of skilled personnel by underdeveloped countries' governments, an element of "brain drain" is inevitable. Moreover, since the entire program of education and training is often tailored not toward domestic needs but toward the needs of the advanced countries, with a view to creating skills that can operate with, or even innovate in, frontier technologies that are outside the reach of the local economy, much of the emigrant skilled personnel may not even be locally absorbable. No doubt this orientation of education, research, and training programs in underdeveloped countries needs rectification; but until such rectification occurs, and even afterward, though to a lesser extent, there is no harm in viewing such emigration as an export of services, *provided the economy earns sufficient foreign exchange in return* to cover the expenditure socially incurred on the education and training of the emigrants, and something more.

Since the only foreign exchange currently being earned by underdeveloped economies from such emigration is through remittances, and these are paltry for skilled workers, there is in effect a transfer of resources in the form of "unrequited exports" as in colonial times. While physical restrictions on such emigration are not warranted, a tax on emigrants to compensate society for the costs (suitably evaluated) incurred by it on their education and training certainly is.

Some neo-classical economists have taken the position that underdeveloped economies, instead of objecting to free capital movements, should demand a quid pro quo in the form of unrestricted access to their export of services of skilled personnel. For this argument, which is questionable *at best*, to be at all credible, it must be complemented by a tax on emigration. But, ironically, the proponents of the argument do not see the need for it.

Conclusion

The development-underdevelopment dichotomy under capitalism arises because neither labor nor capital-in-production is genuinely freely mobile from one segment to the other, no matter what the juridical situation might be. To this basic paradigm, of course, there are significant modifications: capital moves from the advanced to the backward segment for developing mines and plantations and for recapturing markets it might have lost or never gained; labor is allowed to move from the backward to the advanced segment in case there is a labor scarcity in the latter. In periods of recession, however, the general opposition to labor immigration becomes particularly shrill. It is at such moments that the state in the advanced countries acquiesces in the conservative propaganda that immigrants steal jobs, whether they actually displace domestic workers or not.

All immigrant workers, not just those in the advanced countries, feel particularly vulnerable in such periods. What the ideology of "liberalization" does, moreover, is to deny them even the solace of imagining that there is a "home country" where their role, their contribution, or the money they send are being appreciated and where they would be welcomed back as valued citizens.

Comment by Samir Radwan on "Freedom to move in the age of globalization," "Immigration, inequality, and policy alternatives," *and* "Notes on international migration suggested by the Indian experience"

These three chapters provide three perspectives on migration and attempt to offer policy options as an alternative to those reflected at present in international debate, especially those advocated by the receiving countries.

The chapters start from the same premise, that, despite an increase in migratory flows in recent years, "the voluntary movement of people is a clear...exception to globalization" (Sutcliffe), or, put another way, "the mobility of labor seldom if ever matches that of capital" (DeFreitas).

There is no doubt that the last two decades have witnessed an increase in migratory flows. It has been estimated that roughly 100 million (or 2 percent of the world's population) live outside their country of citizenship. This figure is exaggerated, however, since it covers refugees. According to the International Labor Organization (ILO), migrants in 1993 totaled 30–35 million and their dependents 40–50 million, for a total of 70–85 million.

Despite this magnitude, it is not justified to label the 1990s as the "age of migration," as Sutcliffe does.

The question is: how has the globalization process changed the scene of migration, and what are the policy options to deal with this important aspect?

First, we start with the views of the three chapters. How do they deal with this question?

DeFreitas is mainly concerned with policy reversals both in Europe and the U.S. toward migrants. He concludes that the fear that immigration harms domestic wages or employment are not founded. Moreover, there is no evidence, he says, that migrants are "likely to become public charges" by draining the public treasury, overusing welfare and social services while underpaying taxes. DeFreitas then argues that, because, as he writes, "there is no consistent evidence that immigration to the United States has so far had sizable effects on natives' wages or employment or on public sector budgets," the proposed cuts in admissions are unduly restrictionist. Yet he goes on to say, "it is dangerous to extrapolate from econometric findings based on current immigration levels that the same would be the case with an open borders policy." His preference would be for "a new progressive approach" that limits admission and for "pressuring business and government to focus more on job creation and training for indigenous low-wage workers."

There seems to be an inherent contradiction between the analysis and the policy conclusion that we need to resolve, a point to which we shall come later.

Patnaik and Chandrasekhar use the case of India to demonstrate the benefits from emigration. The case of Kerala shows that remittances by workers in the Gulf have contributed to the maintenance of the high standards of living and reduction of unemployment in Kerala. In fact, the evidence shows that these remittances ($6,200 million in 1994–95) have far exceeded that of "the much-touted items like foreign direct investment" that amounted to $4,895 million during the same year. Their main conclusion is that if the view that emigration is harmful to the poor sending economy is to be meaningful, free labor movement is to be allowed.

Bob Sutcliffe argues that "while market, political, and cultural forces all make for increased migration, there is unprecedented effort of governments to limit the movement of people." He suggests that "a progressive viewpoint on immigration should...not start at all from economic consequences but from rights and freedoms....And the free movement of people internationally should be seen as an important element in individual human rights, just as it is nationally." Sutcliffe suggests a "utopian" solution based on: (a) reduction of causes for migration, and (b) the right to complete global freedom of movement and residence.

Given these three perspectives, what should be the direction for a progressive policy option?

An ideal solution would be to remove the restrictions on the movement of labor, as is the case for capital and commodities. Political opposition, especially in Europe, is not to be underestimated, but this freedom of movement must remain an objective in the long run. In fact, with the increase in foreign investment, one would expect that the pressure for emigration would be reduced in the future as more and more jobs are created in the country of residence of potential emigrants. At present, according to Sutcliffe, the 40,000 multinational companies employ about 12 million workers outside their countries of origin. This will of course assume that foreign investment is job creating and not job destroying.

A second-best agenda for the short- to medium-run would favor the lowering of trade barriers facing developing countries' exports; in other words, increasing the demand for labor in the shape of products. This raises the whole issue of "unfair competition" from countries whose comparative advantage is cheap labor. This issue (popularly known as the social clause) is being debated at the ILO.

Another aspect of the second-best agenda relates to the protection of migrant workers who are actually working outside their country of residence now. The Gulf War has illustrated the vulnerability of these workers in times of conflict. Even in normal times, migrant workers are subject to various forms of ill treatment, discrimination, and harassment. The ILO standards are designed to protect these workers and their families, but the problem is the low level of ratification of these instruments, especially by receiving countries.

In conclusion, the issue of migration is the acid test for globalization. An ideal policy agenda would allow freedom of movement. But, given the political difficulty involved, a second-best solution would be to increase the demand for the products of potential migrants, and to provide them with protection while working abroad. This would require the reconciling of the tradeoffs involved.

Part VI

Globalization and macroeconomic policy

16

The NAIRU: is it a real constraint?

Dean Baker

The economic performance of the countries of the Organization for Economic Co-operation and Development (OECD) has deteriorated by almost every measure from the 1950s and 1960s to the 1980s and 1990s. Growth in gross domestic product has slowed significantly, in many cases to less than half its previous levels. This slow-down has hit the less-affluent segments of society especially hard, since it has been accompanied by an upward redistribution of income, particularly in the United States. It also has coincided with a large increase in unemployment. Countries such as Germany, France, and the U.K., which generally had unemployment rates below 3 percent, and often below 2 percent, during the earlier period, now regularly experience unemployment rates between 8 percent and 10 percent. These high rates of unemployment have placed an enormous strain on public budgets through the demands they place on the social welfare system, in addition to imposing hardships on the people experiencing or fearful of unemployment.

This chapter will examine the causes of this rise in unemployment. Specifically, it will attempt to address the question of whether there has really been a qualitative change in the labor markets of the OECD nations that leads to these higher rates of joblessness. The main method for this analysis will be an examination of the evidence for the existence of a non-accelerating-inflation rate of unemployment (NAIRU) in the various OECD countries.

The existence of a high and rising NAIRU would be important for an analysis of the impact of globalization, because it would suggest that the recent rise in unemployment has been primarily due to internal labor market conditions in each country, rather than restrictive macroeconomic policy necessitated by increased globalization. If rising NAIRUs are responsible for the higher unemployment rates across the OECD, then globalization could have only been an indirect, and presumably less important, factor through its effect on domestic labor markets. If the evidence does not support the existence of a NAIRU near current levels of unemployment, that does not imply that the limits globalization imposes on macroeconomic policy are therefore responsible for high unemployment. But it does leave open this possibility.

Robert Eisner, Andrew Glyn, and the other participants at the Economic Policy Institute Conference on Globalization and Progressive Economic Policy gave helpful comments on an earlier draft of this paper. Jorlie Cruz provided valuable research assistance.

The basic meaning of the NAIRU is straightforward. If an economy is operating at a rate of unemployment below its NAIRU, then inflation will rise, as long as the unemployment rate remains below the NAIRU. Therefore, a country that allows its rate of unemployment to fall and remain below the NAIRU will be subject to an ever-increasing rate of inflation. The choice such a country would ultimately face is to raise its rate of unemployment above the NAIRU, or accept hyperinflation and the collapse of the monetary economy. In this sense, the existence of the NAIRU places a very real check on the extent to which unemployment can be reduced through normal monetary or fiscal policy, and in fact requires that macroeconomic policy be used to prevent the unemployment rate from falling below the NAIRU for significant periods of time.

The conventional view of the increase in unemployment over this period is that it is attributable to changes in the labor market that have led to a secular rise in the NAIRU.[1] From this perspective, the only way in which unemployment can move back toward its earlier levels is to radically restructure the labor market. The conservative approach toward such restructuring emphasizes the reduction in income support and public benefits for the unemployed. The more liberal approach emphasizes education, training, and various forms of wage subsidies to employ the unemployed. However, both perspectives accept the point of view that the problem is not fundamentally one of macroeconomic policy.

This chapter calls that assumption into question. By running standard Phillips curve regressions, in which the change in the inflation rate is structured as being dependent on the rate of unemployment, the chapter tests whether there is clear evidence for the existence of a NAIRU in the various OECD countries. After testing to find the expected negative relationship (i.e., higher unemployment is associated with decreasing inflation rates and lower unemployment with increasing inflation rates), the chapter examines whether the relationship is symmetrical around the NAIRU. Following Eisner's (1995) examination of the relationship between inflation and unemployment in the U.S. economy, the samples are broken up into periods where the economy is above and below accepted measures of the NAIRU.

Eisner's work showed in the case of the U.S. economy that the negative relationship between inflation and unemployment was driven by the periods where the economy operated with rates of unemployment above the NAIRU. This means that high unemployment has the effect of lowering the inflation rate, but there was little or no evidence that low unemployment raised the inflation rate. The implication of this work is that restrictive macroeconomic policy, rather than anything intrinsic to the labor market or labor market institutions, has placed a floor on the unemployment rate in recent years. This chapter examines whether the evidence implies the same about macroeconomic policy in other OECD countries.

The chapter is divided into five parts. The first is a brief discussion of the basic problem, noting the rise in unemployment in various OECD countries and laying out the standard explanation based on changes in labor market institutions. It also

1   Layard, Nickell, and Jackman (1993) provide an excellent account of this view, along with an extensive list of references.

Table 1A *Average unemployment rates*

	1951–59	1960–69	1970–79	1980–89	1990–95
Australia	1.1	2.1	3.8	7.5	9.4
Austria	3.6	1.6	1.3	3.2	5.5
Belgium	4.3	2.3	4.8	10.8	8.3
Canada	3.9	4.7	6.6	9.3	10.1
Denmark	4.1	2.0	3.8	8.9	11.0
Finland	1.4	1.9	3.6	4.9	12.8
France	1.8	1.7	3.8	9.0	10.7
Germany	4.6	0.7	2.3	6.0	6.3
Ireland	5.6	5.0	6.9	14.2	14.4
Italy*	7.0	3.9	4.4	7.0	10.7
Japan	2.2	1.3	1.7	2.5	2.5
Netherlands	2.1	1.2	3.9	9.7	6.6
Norway	2.2	2.0	1.7	2.7	5.5
New Zealand	0.0	0.2	0.6	4.4	8.7
Spain	2.2	2.4	4.3	17.7	19.8
Sweden	1.9	1.3	1.7	2.1	6.6
Switzerland	0.6	0.1	0.6	1.8	2.9
U.K.	2.1	2.7	4.4	9.9	9.1
U.S.	4.3	4.6	6.1	7.2	6.4
OECD average	2.9	2.2	3.5	7.3	8.8

* Unemployment data for Italy begins in 1953.

Source: Standardized unemployment rates from CEP–OECD dataset (1950–90).

juxtaposes an explanation based on macroeconomic policy, emphasizing how this has become increasingly constrained in a period of growing internationalization. The second section briefly examines the theory of NAIRU and how it has evolved over the years. The third section explains in more detail the tests Eisner constructed for the U.S. economy. The fourth section explains how these tests are applied to other OECD countries and presents the results. The last section summarizes the findings and discusses their implications for the NAIRU theory.

The standard explanation for high unemployment

Every OECD country has seen a significant rise in its unemployment rate in the period since 1973 compared with the 25 years prior. The extent and timing of this increase differs considerably between countries, but the basic pattern is striking. Table 1A gives the average unemployment rates for each of the OECD countries through the four full decades, along with an unweighted average.

The standard explanation for this increase focuses on changes in the labor mar-

Table 1B *Average equilibrium rates*

	1960–68	1969–79	1980–88
Australia	2.35	4.01	6.10
Austria	0.94	0.48	2.95
Belgium	3.77	4.82	7.04
Canada	5.46	7.01	8.14
Denmark	1.76	3.88	7.81
Finland	1.40	2.61	4.65
France	1.76	3.88	7.81
Germany	0.47	1.87	4.04
Ireland	6.08	9.13	13.09
Italy	4.31	4.94	5.42
Japan	1.59	1.82	2.14
Netherlands	1.52	4.28	7.27
Norway	2.13	2.22	2.50
New Zealand	0.43	1.96	3.91
Spain	4.55	9.73	14.95
Sweden	1.64	1.93	2.36
Switzerland	0.09	0.83	1.44
U.K.	2.55	5.15	7.92
U.S.	5.01	5.97	6.36
OECD average	2.53	4.03	6.10

Source: Layard, Nickell, and Jackman (1993, p. 436).

ket through this period.[2] The most important such change is the increased availability of income support for unemployed workers. The conventional argument is that, by increasing the generosity and availability of various types of unemployment benefits, governments have both increased the incentive not to work and increased the ability of workers to push up their wages.[3] This requires a higher rate of unemployment, and therefore a greater risk of job loss, to effectively moderate wage demands.

In this view there are no demand-side remedies to high unemployment. Any increase in demand, whether from consumption, investment, government, or net exports, must be offset by a reduction in demand elsewhere, otherwise inflation begins to spiral upward. Macroeconomic policy can seek to shift the composition of demand toward areas that promote long-term growth, but it cannot increase the overall level of demand.

Table 1B gives a set of estimates of equilibrium unemployment rates (the NAIRU) by decade for the OECD countries. The decade-by-decade rise in the equilibrium

2   This discussion draws heavily on Layard, Nickell, and Jackman (1993), which is a thorough exposition of this position. Most theoretical and policy-oriented discussion of the current problem of OECD unemployment either explicitly or implicitly assumes a similar framework (see, e.g., Krugman 1994b; OECD 1994a; OECD 1994b).

3   Layard, Nickell, and Jackman also explain part of the increase in unemployment by a one-time increase in worker militancy in the late 1960s that continues to the present.

unemployment rate is attributable to supply factors. From this perspective, demand is a factor in the current high levels of unemployment in the OECD only to the extent that the actual unemployment rates in Table 1A exceed the equilibrium rates in Table 1B. As can be seen from the tables, most of the rise in unemployment rates from the 1960s to the 1980s is explained by the rise in the equilibrium rates in Table 1B, not a divergence between the two tables.

The remedies to high unemployment require directly affecting the relative gains from work and unemployment. For conservatives, this means reducing or eliminating the income supports available to the unemployed population. This would create greater hardships for the unemployed, encouraging them to accept less desirable employment, and force employed workers to moderate their wage demands in response to an increased fear of unemployment. The liberal approach emphasizes increasing the benefits of working, primarily through government wage subsidies and support for worker training. The latter should increase workers' productivity, and therefore their wages on the job.

There are serious problems with both these routes toward reducing unemployment. The conservative approach, which assumes that unemployment is voluntary, is clearly designed to bring about an upward redistribution of income and will inflict severe hardships on large portions of the population. By imposing harsh enough circumstances on the unemployed, it might be possible to move closer toward full employment, but this is a dubious achievement if it is brought about by lowering living standards for a significant portion of the working class.

The liberal approach is clearly more humane, but it faces significant political and economic obstacles. The main political obstacle is that large-scale education and training programs are expensive, at least in the short run. There are few governments for which large increases in public spending seem a feasible option anytime soon. Even if the political obstacles could be overcome, it is not clear how effective increased education and training will be in reducing the unemployment rate. This is partly because of the difficulties inherent in establishing any large-scale government program, but also because it is not obvious what job workers would be trained for. In the U.S., for example, the Bureau of Labor Statistics projects that workers in food preparation and office and sales clerks will account for over 30 percent of the new jobs created between 1992 and 2005 (Silvestri 1993). For the most part, these are not jobs that risk being unfilled because of the lack of trained workers. If these are typical of the sorts of jobs all the OECD economies are generating, then the problem of unemployment is a result of an insufficient number of jobs, not a lack of adequately trained workers.

This problem raises again the issue of macroeconomic constraints. Such constraints could differ between countries, but nonetheless be the effective limits on reducing national unemployment rates. In the case of the U.S., the Federal Reserve Board has repeatedly stated its policy of keeping the unemployment rate no lower than its perceived levels of the NAIRU.[4] The immediate constraint on reducing the

4   For example, Federal Reserve Board Chairman Alan Greenspan explained in testimony before Congress in April 1994 that he had raised interest rates in a deliberate effort to slow the

unemployment rate in the U.S. is therefore this Federal Reserve Board policy, regardless of whether there is any real basis for its perception of NAIRU.[5]

While the central banks in other OECD countries may not all adhere as strictly to a NAIRU target, they generally have less leeway than the Fed. Since trade makes up a much larger share of the economies of the other OECD nations, they each, individually, have much less ability to run an expansionary macroeconomic policy. Doing so alone leads inevitably to a large increase in the trade deficit. If the currency is allowed to float, its value will drop significantly, leading to an increase in the price of imports and a decline in living standards for most of the population. When currencies have been fixed, expansionary policy leads to chronic balance-of-payments deficits, requiring either devaluation or an abandonment of the policy. Both these processes are often accentuated by capital flight from a country pursuing expansionary macroeconomic policy.[6] As a result of this process, no country individually can break free from a situation in which the dominant course is contractionary. This can leave high unemployment and slow growth locked into place indefinitely.

From this perspective, the main obstacle to lower unemployment rates is the growing integration of the OECD countries over the last 20 years. The reduction or elimination of restrictions on trade flows and capital mobility have made it significantly more difficult for any nation individually (with the possible exceptions of the U.S. and Japan) to pursue expansionary macroeconomic policy. Expansion can best be achieved through a coordinated shift in central bank policy, a development that has proved politically impossible up to the present.

Testing for evidence of the existence of NAIRUs in the OECD countries provides a way of distinguishing between an explanation for high unemployment based on changes in national labor markets and an explanation based on macroeconomic policy. If it can be shown that most nations have settled into levels of unemployment that approximate a NAIRU, then there can be little basis for the contention that macroeconomic policy is leading to high unemployment. Alternatively, if little evidence can be found to support the existence of a NAIRU, then there would be little reason to believe that labor market dynamics present the immediate constraint on reducing unemployment.[7]

economy. He explained that he wanted to keep the unemployment rate from falling to a point where inflation would begin to accelerate (Greenspan 1994).

5   Interestingly, there has been little change in the conventionally accepted measures of NAIRU for the U.S. from the 1950s and 1960s to the 1980s and 1990s (CBO 1994; Weiner 1993; Gordon 1982). From the standpoint of the NAIRU view, the issue to be explained for the U.S. is not why unemployment has been high in recent years but rather why it was allowed to remain so far below NAIRU in the previous period.

6   France's experience in the first years of the Mitterrand presidency probably provides the best case study of the difficulties of running an expansionary policy in isolation.

7   Finding evidence in support of the NAIRU view would not rule out internationalization as a factor in increasing rates of unemployment. It is possible that internationalization has increased the NAIRU in various countries by displacing certain types of labor (e.g. non-college educated). In this way internationalization would have led to higher rates of unemployment directly through its effect on the labor market rather than through the constraint placed on macroeconomic policy.

The theory of the NAIRU

The theoretical origins of the concept of the NAIRU go back to Milton Friedman's argument that the long-run Phillips curve is vertical (Friedman 1968). Friedman put forward this view in response to the position prevailing at the time that the Phillips curve offered a menu of tradeoffs between inflation and unemployment, and that policy should be designed to select the socially optimal combination.

Friedman contended that any tradeoff between inflation and unemployment would necessarily be short lived. He reasoned that unemployment could be pushed under the natural rate (Friedman's less-neutral term for the NAIRU) only if workers failed to recognize the true level of inflation in the economy. If they underestimated the level of inflation, then they would overestimate the real value of the wages they were being paid. As a result of this overestimation, workers who otherwise would have preferred leisure end up working for a lower real wage than is actually acceptable to them. However, the period of time in which workers can be deceived in this manner is limited. Workers eventually adapt their expectations of inflation to the actual levels they have been seeing. This means that the original level of inflation will no longer be sufficient to fool them into working for a lower-than-acceptable real wage. In order to maintain an unemployment rate below NAIRU, it is necessary to fool them with a still higher rate of inflation. The outcome of this process is that either inflation spirals upward indefinitely, or that unemployment is allowed to rise back to its natural rate, where the rate of inflation can stabilize. In order to bring inflation back down to its original levels, it is necessary to push the process in reverse. Workers take time to recognize that the rate of inflation is lower than the one that they had come to expect, and therefore underestimate the value of the real wage for a period of time. This leads to an unemployment rate above the NAIRU.

This view of the NAIRU (and its rational expectations variants, e.g., Lucas 1972) implies both that it is impossible to maintain rates of unemployment below the NAIRU and that it is undesirable even to attempt this sort of reduction in the unemployment rate. The latter conclusion follows from the fact that the only way to drive the unemployment rate below the NAIRU is to deceive workers about the value of the real wage. At the NAIRU unemployment is essentially voluntary. There is no clear value in tricking workers into working for a real wage that is unacceptable to them.

While this view provides a clear theoretical underpinning to the concept of NAIRU, it doesn't seem to fit most of the accepted facts about the business cycle. Arthur Okun summarized the basic case in a paper delivered shortly before his death (1980). He noted, for example, that productivity moves in a clear cyclical pattern, the opposite of what would be predicted in the Friedman NAIRU story. Quit rates also move cyclically, again a pattern that is directly opposite to the prediction of the NAIRU theory. In short, Okun pointed out that the Friedman view of NAIRU is at odds with almost everything that is generally thought to be true about the business cycle.

In recent years, there has been an alternative foundation for the NAIRU constructed from various types of New Keynesian efficiency wage microfoundations.[8]

8   See Gordon (1990) and Stiglitz (1986) for surveys of the efficiency wage literature as New Keynesian microfoundations.

Although there are significant theoretical differences between various efficiency wage models, they all differ from the classical view of the labor market by setting out microfoundations where the labor market does not generally clear. In other words, in these models, the labor market reaches an equilibrium in which there are unemployed workers who would prefer to work at the prevailing wage.

This theoretical outcome gives a very different meaning to the notion of the NAIRU. In the classical view, at the NAIRU unemployment is essentially voluntary. As noted before, unemployment can fall below the NAIRU only as a result of workers being deceived about the true value of the real wage. This requires ever-higher rates of inflation as workers adjust their expectations to rates observed in the recent past. However, since there is involuntary unemployment at the NAIRU in efficiency wage models, it is not necessary to deceive workers about the value of the real wage to drive the unemployment rate below the NAIRU. In efficiency wage models the chain of causation is reversed. Increasing inflation is an outcome of increased wage pressure resulting from lower unemployment, rather than lower unemployment being the result of increased inflation.[9]

This reverse chain of causation weakens the necessary link between an unemployment rate below NAIRU and an increase in inflation. The increase in the rate of inflation depends on workers both recognizing their improved bargaining position as a result of lower unemployment rates and using their power to press demands for higher real wages. It also assumes that wage increases are not offset by either lower profit margins or more rapid productivity growth, and that real wage increases for some groups of workers cannot be offset by lower real wages or lower real wage growth for other groups. Furthermore, the assumption that inflation will continue to increase as long as unemployment remains below NAIRU requires that workers persist in demanding real wage growth that is in excess of productivity growth.[10]

---

9   The discussion in Layard, Nickell, and Jackman (1993, 12–21) presents this view clearly.
10 It is important to distinguish between two different ways in which inflation might respond to a reduction in unemployment. It is possible to imagine a one-time rise in the rate of inflation as workers either quit or received higher wages in the lowest-paying jobs (e.g., restaurant work). This could lead to some change in relative wages and perhaps a reduction in profits in some sectors. It would not necessarily lead to continually increasing inflation. Alternatively, if workers throughout the economy had fairly rigid real wage demands then, if any group of workers received higher real wages, it would necessarily lead to continually increasing inflation, unless offset by lower profit margins or more rapid productivity growth. If the economy experiences only very short periods in which unemployment is allowed to go below the NAIRU, it would be very difficult to distinguish between these two situations.
It is also worth noting in this respect that the increase in the inflation rate predicted in the standard model as a result of the unemployment rate falling below the NAIRU is actually very modest. Fair (1996), running a simulation using a standard Phillips curve model, found that, after three years of the economy operating a full percentage point below the NAIRU, the inflation rate was only 3.02 percentage points higher. Eisner found an even more modest impact in his simulations with the standard model. The finding of a modest effect means both that it is difficult to test the NAIRU view against various counterfactuals, and that the inflationary consequences resulting from prolonged periods of below-NAIRU levels of unemployment are actually quite small.

While this is not impossible, it requires far stronger assumptions about workers' behavior than in the classical NAIRU model.

The reversal of the chain of causation is also very important for the question directly addressed in this paper – the symmetry of the response to changes in the unemployment rate around NAIRU. In the classical view, where movements in the unemployment rate are motivated by the speed with which expectations adjust, it is reasonable to expect that the adjustment process would be symmetrical. In other words, there is no reason to believe that workers would be slower to adjust their expectations of inflation upward, when the inflation rate is higher than had been expected, than they would be to adjust them downward when the inflation rate is lower than expected. However, when changes in the bargaining power of workers are viewed as the driving force for changes in the rate of inflation, there is absolutely no reason to believe that the effect would necessarily be symmetrical at levels of unemployment above and below NAIRU.

It is entirely plausible that the upward impetus to the inflation rate resulting from a 1 percentage point decrease in unemployment below the NAIRU is less than the downward impetus to the inflation rate resulting from a 1 percentage point increase in the unemployment rate above the NAIRU. The size and speed of each response would depend on a wide variety of factors that cannot be assumed to be symmetrical with respect to the NAIRU.

If the response of inflation to changes in the unemployment rate is not symmetrical with respect to the NAIRU, then the NAIRU does not necessarily place a lower bound to the unemployment rate than can be achieved through macroeconomic policy. For example, if the inflation rate falls by twice as much (or twice as quickly) in response to a 1 percentage point increase in unemployment above the NAIRU than it rises in response to a 1 percentage point decline in the unemployment rate below the NAIRU, then trading off periods above and below the NAIRU could provide opportunities for enormous social gains. It would be possible to have much higher levels of output, and much lower average rates of unemployment, without any increase in the average rate of inflation.

The view of the NAIRU based on efficiency wage models provides absolutely no theoretical reason to assume that the response of inflation to changes in the unemployment rate is symmetrical around the NAIRU. The factors that are generally thought to affect the bargaining position of workers, such as layoff rates and help-wanted advertising, neither change in a symmetrical manner with respect to NAIRU nor exhibit patterns that are stable through time. In addition, productivity growth varies inversely with changes in the rate of unemployment, raising the possibility that more rapid real wage increases can often be absorbed by rising productivity growth in periods of declining unemployment, rather than being passed on in higher prices. Many other reasons could be cited for suspecting the relationship between changes in the inflation rate and unemployment is not symmetrical with respect to the NAIRU. In spite of the importance of the assumption of symmetry to the theory of the NAIRU, it seems to have gone largely untested, until recently.

Testing for symmetry: the U.S. case

In testing whether the effect was symmetrical in the U.S., Eisner (1995) used quarterly data in standard Phillips curve regressions, where inflation is a function of lagged inflation, current and past unemployment rates, food and energy inflation, deviations from trend productivity growth, and dummy variables for the impact of wage-price controls in the early 1980s. This can be written formally as:

$$In_t = C + S\ b_iIN_{t-i} + S\ b_jU_{t-j} + b_fFAE_{t-1} + b_pPRD_t + b_cNIXON_t + b_oNIXOFF_t + e_t \quad (1)$$

where:

In_t = inflation at time t,

C is a constant,

$S\ b_i$ = the sum of the coefficients on lagged inflation, with the number of lags varying from 12 to 20,

Sb_j = the sum of the coefficients on current and lagged unemployment rates, with the lags going back four quarters,

b_f = the coefficient of the difference in the previous quarter between food and energy inflation, and the general rate of increase of consumer prices,

b_p = the coefficient for the gap between productivity growth in the current period and the trend rate of productivity growth,

b_c = the coefficient for a dummy variable for the period where wage-price controls were in effect in the early 1970s,

b_o = the coefficient for a dummy variable associated with the period immediately after the removal of wage-price controls in 1974, and

e_t is an error term.

This is exactly the model the Congressional Budget Office (CBO) used in recent estimates of the NAIRU (1994), and is similar to other standard formulations (e.g. Gordon 1982 or Weiner 1993).[11]

After replicating CBO's results with this model, Eisner divided the sample based on whether unemployment was above or below the CBO measure of NAIRU, substituting a high unemployment term (UNH) and a low unemployment term (UNL) depending on whether the economy was above or below NAIRU for the quarter.[12]

---

11 Eisner also included separate constant terms for periods of above- and below-NAIRU levels of unemployment in some of his single equation specifications. This allowed for alternative estimates of NAIRU to be generated from each subsample.

12 The value of UNH is normalized so that it is the difference between the unemployment rate for the quarter and the mean unemployment rate for the above-NAIRU sample for the quarters where the economy is above NAIRU; otherwise it is 0. The value of UNL is normalized so that it is the difference between the unemployment rate for the quarter and the mean unemployment rate for the above-NAIRU sample for the quarters where the economy is below NAIRU; otherwise, its value is 0.

Using a variety of different measures of inflation and the unemployment rate and different lag structures, Eisner consistently found that the standard NAIRU relationship between inflation and unemployment was quite strong for the periods in which the economy was operating with rates of unemployment above the NAIRU. The sum of the coefficient of the lagged unemployment variables was always negative and significant. In addition, the coefficients of the lagged inflation variables summed to greater than 1 when they were not restricted.[13] This indicates that any increase (or decrease) in the inflation rate would persist, unless other factors intervened.

However, Eisner consistently found that the expected relationships between inflation and unemployment did not hold for the periods in which the economy was operating at unemployment rates below the NAIRU. In many specifications, the sum of the coefficients of the unemployment variables was actually positive (although statistically insignificant). In only one specification, using a married male unemployment rate, was the sum of the coefficients negative and significant for the periods where the economy was operating at unemployment rates below the NAIRU. Furthermore, when the periods of high and low unemployment were run in separate regressions, the sum of the coefficients on the lagged inflation variables was consistently less than 1 in the periods of low unemployment, when it had not been constrained to be equal to 1. These results held regardless of the measure of inflation (PCE, CPI-U, benchmark year-weighted PCE, or implicit price deflator), the measure of the unemployment rate (married male or overall unemployment), or the lag structure or duration.

The implication of Eisner's results is that the statistical support for the NAIRU theory is driven entirely by the periods in which the unemployment rate is above the NAIRU. In periods of high unemployment, raising the unemployment rate further will have the effect of lowering the inflation rate. However, in the periods where the unemployment rate is below the NAIRU, there is little or no evidence that inflation will necessarily accelerate. Furthermore, since the sum of the coefficients on the lagged inflation variables was always less than 1, any increase in the inflation rate that does occur may dissipate through time. This would mean that there is little basis for concern that lower rates of unemployment will propel the economy toward hyperinflation.

These empirical findings take on special importance, since there is no widely accepted coherent theoretical foundation for the NAIRU at this point. While it is possible, as noted earlier, to piece together New Keynesian microfoundations for the NAIRU, these are clearly ad hoc formulations designed to explain what is thought to be a statistical regularity. If it turns out that the statistical regularity is entirely driven by the periods when the economy is operating at high levels of unemployment, then the concept of the NAIRU stands without either statistical support or theoretical foundation.

---

13   In regressions where the periods of high and low unemployment were used in separate samples, the sum of the lags on the inflation variable was less than 1.

Testing for symmetry: the OECD

This paper applies the test for the symmetry of the relationship between inflation and unemployment that Eisner used for the U.S. to the several other OECD nations for the period 1970–95. In addition to the U.S., 11 other OECD nations were examined. The nations were selected based on the availability of data and also on the possibility of splitting the sample into periods of unemployment on both sides of the NAIRU. The general specification is somewhat simplified, owing to the more limited availability of data for the rest of the OECD. The basic form of the regression was:

$$In_t = C + S\, b_i IN_{t\text{-}i} + S\, b_j(U_{t\text{-}j} - Ue_{t\text{-}j}) + b_c imp_{t\text{-}1} + b_d\, food_{t\text{-}1} + b_e oil_{t\text{-}1} + e_t \quad (2)$$

where:

In_t = inflation at time t,

C is a constant,

$S\, b_i$ = the sum of the coefficients on lagged inflation,

Sb_j = the sum of the coefficients on the gap between the current and lagged unemployment rates and the equilibrium unemployment rate,

b_c = the coefficient of the difference between the rate of increase in import prices and the overall inflation rate, lagged one quarter,

b_d = the coefficient of the difference between the rate of increase in food prices and the overall inflation rate, lagged one quarter,

b_e = the coefficient of the difference between the rate of increase in oil prices and the overall inflation rate, lagged one quarter, and

e_t is an error term.

All the regressions were originally run with a lagged term for import price inflation, food price inflation, and oil price inflation. When the coefficients were significant, the term was included in future regressions. If it was insignificant it was dropped. A third-degree polynomial distributed lag covering 16 quarters was used to estimate the lagged inflation term.[14] The regressions included the current quarter's unemployment rate and eight lagged quarters. For each country, the regression was first run without restricting the sum of the lags to 1, then it was run with this restriction. The value for the equilibrium unemployment rate or NAIRU is taken from Layard, Nickell, and Jackman (1993, 436). This gap between the actual unemployment rate and the NAIRU appears with a current value and a four-quarter lag.[15]

14 I also experimented with lags as short as eight quarters and as long as 20, and with an unrestricted lag structure. Changing the specification in these ways did not significantly alter the results in any of the countries where I tried it. Therefore, I used the same lag structure in all cases.

15 In the U.S. case, since the NAIRU is usually estimated without a structural break, I entered

After running this regression both without constraining the lagged inflation terms to sum to 1 and with this constraint, I then divided the samples into periods in which the unemployment rate was above and below NAIRU – UNH_t and UNL_t. Each subsample was normalized so that the mean was zero for periods of both high and low unemployment. I also replaced the constant term with a dummy reflecting whether the unemployment rate was above (C_h) or below (C_l) the NAIRU for the quarter. The full form of this regression was:

$$In_t = C_h + C_l + S\ b_i IN_{t-i} + S\ b_j(UNH_{t-j} - Ue_{t-j}) + S\ b_k(UNL_{t-k} - Ue_{t-k})$$
$$+ b_c imp_{t-1} + b_d food_{t-1} + b_e oil_{t-1} + e_t \tag{3}$$

Tables 2A and 2B give the results of the individual country regressions with the undivided sample. Perhaps the most striking aspect of Table 2A is the low value of the sum of the lagged inflation terms in the unrestricted regressions. The U.S. is the only one of the 12 nations where the value exceeds 0.9., with France, Belgium, and Canada being the only others with a coefficient above 0.8. At the low end, the coefficient on the lagged inflation term was 0.51 for Australia and just 0.43 for Germany. Clearly these regressions do not lend support to the belief that any change in the inflation rate will necessarily persist through time. The coefficient of the unemployment gap term was negative in all 12 cases, and it was significant at a 10 percent confidence level in nine of the 12 countries.

The results in Table 2B provide somewhat weaker support for the NAIRU. Imposing the restriction that the lagged inflation terms sum to 1 reduces the number of countries with significant negative coefficients on the unemployment gap term to five – Australia, Canada, the Netherlands, the United Kingdom, and the United States. The coefficient of the unemployment gap term was still negative in 11 of the 12 countries, with France being the sole exception. However, in most of these countries the coefficient is not close to being significant even at a 10 percent level. Therefore, they do not provide strong support for the NAIRU.

Tables 3A and 3B give the results of the individual country regressions with the divided sample. Unfortunately, the division of the sample into periods of above- and below-NAIRU levels of unemployment offers limited insight into the question of symmetry, since there are so few quarters of low unemployment in the sample. Only Ireland has anywhere close to an even divide (44 periods of low unemployment and 41 of high unemployment). For the other 11 nations the periods of high unemployment vastly outnumbered the periods of low unemployment, making it almost impossible to obtain a statistically meaningful sample from the latter. In addition, for most countries the quarters of below-NAIRU levels of unemployment came in the early 1970s, just after the first round of oil price increases by OPEC (the Organization of Petroleum Exporting Countries). These oil price hikes had a significant

the unemployment rate directly, instead of using the gap between the actual unemployment rate and the estimated value of NAIRU. A NAIRU of 6% was used to divide the sample into periods of high and low unemployment.

Table 2A *Phillips curve regressions, unconstrained inflation lags*

Country	Constant	Inflation	Ugap	Food	Imports	Oil	DW	R	N
Australia	6.25	0.51	-1.26	0.20			2.11	0.50	85
	3.14***	2.86***	-3.19***	2.87***					
Belgium	0.94	0.83	-0.11				1.92	0.65	85
	1.43	8.32***	-0.71						
Canada	1.61	0.82	-0.72	0.09		0.04	1.84	0.78	85
	2.56**	9.81***	-3.13***	2.56**		3.91***			
Denmark	1.86	0.73	-0.32		0.18		1.77	0.76	85
	2.34**	8.39***	-1.84*		8.41***				
France	0.88	0.89	-0.21		0.05		1.60	0.85	85
	0.87	9.67***	-0.71		3.20***				
Germany	2.73	0.43	-0.49	0.05	0.05		1.70	0.54	85
	3.69***	2.92***	-2.35**	1.73*	2.42**				
Ireland	1.61	0.78	-0.57		0.09		2.12	0.52	85
	1.05	4.97***	-1.56		1.60				
Italy	5.04	0.61	-1.82			0.18	1.65	0.65	85
	2.26**	4.12***	-2.29**			6.65***			
Netherlands	1.73	0.70	-0.47		0.07		1.83	0.69	85
	3.34***	8.10***	-2.75***		3.99***				
Spain	4.52	0.62	-0.50				2.03	0.59	85
	2.61**	4.39***	-2.95***						
U.K.	4.10	0.71	-1.10	0.36			2.05	0.58	85
	2.65***	5.18***	-2.61**	4.67***					
U.S.	6.20	0.97	-0.87	0.07			2.08	0.43	85
	2.26**	5.58***	-1.92*	2.21**					

T-statistics underneath coefficients
*   significant at 10% level
**   significant at 5% level
***   significant at 1% level

effect on inflation everywhere, but the oil inflation variable was significant only in the cases of Canada and Italy. This raises the possibility that part of the impact of the oil price increases is included in the coefficient of the lagged UNL terms.

Whatever the limitations of the data, these results provide no support for the existence of an asymmetric relationship between inflation and unemployment around the NAIRU. In the regressions run without restricting the value of the lagged inflation term, the coefficient of UNH was negative in 10 of the 12 cases and significant in three. The coefficient of UNL was also negative in 10 of the countries (not the same 10) and significant in five. When the sum of the coefficients of the lagged inflation term was restricted to 1, the coefficient of UNH was negative in eight of the 12 cases and significant in only two (Canada and the Netherlands). The coefficient of UNL was also negative in eight cases and significant in five (Belgium, Canada, France, Ireland, and Spain.) It was positive and significant in the case of Denmark.

These results do little to demonstrate the asymmetry of the NAIRU relationship. However, it is hard to find too much support for the traditional view of the NAIRU in these results either, since most countries did not have a significant negative coef-

Table 2B *Phillips curve regressions, constrained inflation lags*

Country	Constant	Inflation	Ugap	Food	Imports	Oil	DW	R	N
Australia	1.02	1.00	-0.55	0.20			2.14	0.45	85
	1.50		-1.75*	2.74***					
Belgium	0.11	1.00	-0.13				2.34	0.74	85
	0.28		-0.99						
Canada	0.39	1.00	-0.63	0.09		0.04	1.80	0.77	85
	1.35		-2.74***	2.51**		3.41***			
Denmark	-0.40	1.00	-0.03		0.18		1.67	0.73	85
	-1.09		-0.16		8.02***				
France	-0.31	1.00	0.09		0.05		1.61	0.85	85
	-1.07		0.49		3.37***				
Germany	0.18	1.00	-0.14	0.06	0.02		1.71	0.46	85
	0.49		-0.68	1.84*	1.00				
Ireland	-0.32	1.00	-0.25		0.11		2.03	0.46	85
	-0.49		-0.82		1.98*				
Italy	-0.40	1.00	-0.27			0.19	1.65	0.65	85
	-0.54		-0.52			6.96***			
Netherlands	0.31	1.00	-0.34		0.06		2.05	0.65	85
	0.96		1.94*		2.83***				
Spain	0.04	1.00	-0.17				2.02	0.56	85
	0.08		-1.38						
U.K.	1.01	1.00	-0.74	0.39			1.84	0.57	85
	1.52		-1.89*	4.84***					
U.S.	6.00	1.00	-0.87	0.07			2.13	0.47	85
	2.29**		-2.27**	2.21**					

T-statistics underneath coefficients
*   significant at 10% level
**   significant at 5% level
***   significant at 1% level

ficient on the unemployment variable in the regressions with the constraint imposed on the lagged inflation term. Clearly questions can be raised about the quality of the data; many of the series did not include complete data on food, energy, and import prices. Four of the five countries that did have complete data in these categories (Australia, Canada, the U.K., and the U.S.) did have a significant negative coefficient. (Germany was the exception.) Still, if the NAIRU relationship were sufficiently robust, stronger results might have been anticipated, even with flawed data. It is perhaps worth noting here some other recent research that raises questions about the statistical support for the NAIRU. Ray Fair (1996) ran a series of price level equations for 30 countries and tested whether the inclusion of the lagged variables needed for the Phillips curve form of a price equation could be rejected. In 13 of the 14 countries for which he had quarterly data, and in nine of the 16 countries for which he had annual data, it was possible to reject the inclusion of the lagged variables. In another recent study, Staiger, Stock, and Watson (1996) constructed confidence intervals around estimates of NAIRU. They found that in several specifications a 95 percent confidence interval included unemployment rates under 4 percent and over 8 percent. A range of this magnitude can provide relatively little

Table 3A *Phillips curve regressions – divided sample, unconstrained inflation lags*

Country	H	L	Inflation	UNH	UNL	Food	Imports	Oil	DW	R	#H	#L	N
Australia	1.34	5.60	0.76	-0.63	-4.06	0.15			2.20	0.53	74	11	85
	0.81	2.77***	3.89***	-1.05	-1.93*	2.14**							
Belgium	1.09	4.18	0.73	0.02	-5.00				2.18	0.73	79	6	85
	2.02*	2.20**	7.60***	0.10	-2.57**								
Canada	0.31	1.42	0.87	-1.01	-2.81	0.08		0.04	2.12	0.78	63	22	85
	0.53	2.13**	11.31***	-3.05***	-2.00*	2.08**		3.11***					
Denmark	1.16	-0.62	0.77	-0.44	1.38		0.18		2.31	0.73	77	8	85
	1.68*	-0.36	7.86***	1.61	1.33		6.94***						
France	0.52	1.95	0.85	-0.32	-4.28		0.04		1.60	0.86	74	11	85
	0.95	1.45	9.83***	-1.11	-1.71		2.56**						
Germany	1.30	1.57	0.60	-0.50	-0.72	0.06	0.02		1.84	0.44	74	11	85
	2.55**	1.83*	4.62***	-1.69*	-0.36	1.91*	0.96						
Ireland	0.72	4.55	0.66	0.05	-2.91		0.08		1.84	0.51	41	44	85
	0.51	2.43**	4.93***	0.06	-2.92***		1.49						
Italy	2.95	4.42	0.61	-3.06	-3.20			0.19	1.70	0.65	65	20	85
	1.53	1.63	3.19***	-1.55	-0.87			6.78***					
Netherlands	0.78	2.09	0.72	-0.48	-0.73		0.08		2.09	0.62	72	13	85
	1.60	2.47**	7.68***	-2.24**	-0.42		3.36***						
Spain	0.73	4.89	0.78	-0.09	-1.58				1.99	0.60	55	30	85
	0.46	1.71*	4.54***	-0.35	-2.70**								
U.K.	-0.32	7.53	0.79	-0.01	-2.50	0.37			2.12	0.62	62	23	85
	-0.21	4.78***	6.03***	-0.01	-1.08	4.78***							
U.S.	-1.18	0.67	1.10	-0.78	1.79	0.07			2.07	0.42	63	22	85
	-1.10	0.63	7.13***	-1.29	0.55	2.30**							

T-statistics underneath coefficients
* significant at 10% level
** significant at 5% level
*** significant at 1% level

Table 3B *Phillips curve regressions – divided sample, constrained inflation lags*

Country	H	L	Inflation	UNH	UNL	Food	Imports	Oil	DW	R	#H	#L	N
Australia	-0.60	3.83	1.00	-0.08	-3.65	0.14			2.19	0.53	74	11	85
	-1.43	2.74**		-0.21	-1.75	2.11**							
Belgium	-0.23	1.18	1.00	-0.16	-5.21				2.22	0.70	79	6	85
	-0.91	0.73		-0.96	-2.57**								
Canada	-0.54	0.66	1.00	-0.95	-2.82				2.01	0.77	63	22	85
	-1.96*	1.35		-2.85***	-1.98*								
Denmark	-0.36	-2.06	1.00	-0.09	1.93		0.18		2.26	0.71	77	8	85
	-1.25	-1.23		-0.38	1.86*		6.56***						
France	-0.33	-0.03	1.00	0.04	-5.64		0.04		1.63	0.86	74	11	85
	-1.51	-0.04		0.19	-2.35**		2.69***						
Germany	-0.12	-0.03	1.00	-0.33	0.00	0.06	0.01		1.80	0.37	74	11	85
	-0.48	-0.04		-1.09	0.00	1.67*	0.50						
Ireland	-1.34	0.48	1.00	0.16	-2.10		0.10		1.88	0.47	41	44	85
	-1.10	0.47		0.21	-2.14**		1.78*						
Italy	-0.83	-0.32	1.00	0.26	-2.94			0.19	1.68	0.64	65	20	85
	-1.26	-0.21		0.22	-0.78			6.80***					
Netherlands	-0.40	0.75	1.00	-0.40	0.40		0.07		2.09	0.58	72	13	85
	-1.34	0.99		-1.74*	0.23		2.96***						
Spain	-1.20	1.29	1.00	-0.05	-1.91				1.98	0.60	55	30	85
	-1.95*	1.53		-0.20	-3.60								
U.K.	-2.47	6.12	1.00	0.49	-1.93	0.38			2.12	0.61	62	23	85
	-3.33***	4.60***		0.91	-.83	4.86***							
U.S.	-0.57	1.14	1.00	-0.60	2.16	0.07			2.06	0.43	63	22	85
	-1.33	1.52		-1.13	0.68	2.34**							

T-statistics underneath coefficients

*   significant at 10% level
**   significant at 5% level
***   significant at 1% level

guidance to the conduct of monetary policy. This was the same conclusion of an earlier study examining the stability of NAIRU estimates for Canada (Setterfield, Gordon, and Osberg 1992).

Unfortunately, the fact that the OECD countries have generally had unemployment rates well in excess of standard measures of their NAIRUs over the last 20 years makes it impossible to construct a meaningful test for the symmetry of the NAIRU relationship in the countries where there is strong evidence for its existence. Eisner's results are remarkably robust in the case of the U.S. It would be worth knowing if the same relationship existed elsewhere.

Implications and conclusion

The results presented above provide ambiguous evidence concerning the existence of the NAIRU. If the NAIRU relationship does not really exist, then the conventional view – that the OECD countries have experienced slow growth and high unemployment in recent years because of the structures of their labor markets – is difficult to support. Instead, the main obstacle to more rapid growth would appear to be the lack of sufficient demand. Public policy should then focus primarily on the means to generate more internal demand rather than try to restructure the labor market.

The evidence that insufficient demand is the immediate constraint on growth for most of the European nations is overwhelming. The difficulty in testing for the asymmetry of the NAIRU relationship stems from the fact that most countries have not been below estimated values of their NAIRU for 20 years and generally are not even close to it now. The average gap between the actual unemployment rates and the estimated NAIRUs for the countries listed in Tables 1A and 1B is 1.2 percentage points for the decade from 1980 to 1989. In many countries it is considerably higher (3.6 percentage points for Belgium, 2.7 for Spain, 2.5 for the Netherlands). It is important to remember that these gaps are decade-long averages, not measures at cyclical troughs.

It is worth noting that, for most European countries, the unemployment rates have been even higher in the 1990s than in the 1980s. However much labor market rigidities might have contributed to increases in unemployment, it simply is not plausible that they have increased this rapidly, particularly at a time when the welfare state has been contracting in most of Europe. If there is a NAIRU-type constraint on output, Europe, and much of the rest of the OECD, is so far from it at present that it need not be cause for concern.

It is important to carry through further work that can better identify the supply side constraints that do exist, particularly in countries such as the U.S., which are at or below estimated values of NAIRU. This chapter does not provide much insight into the extent to which the NAIRU imposes a constraint on lowering the unemployment rate in these cases. Better data or other methodologies may provide more insight into this issue.

Appendix

The data used for these regressions were derived from data in *International Financial Statistics* (International Monetary Fund) and *Economic Outlook* (Organization for Economic Cooperation and Development). Most of the data were entered as quarterly data, but there were some series that were not available for the whole period (1970 to 1995, second quarter). In the case of France, only annual data for unemployment were available for the years from 1970 to 1984. This was also true for Spain in the years from 1970 to 1974. In both cases, the annual rate was entered for each quarter of the year. The following countries were missing all or part of the listed series for import prices:

Australia – Oil
Belgium – Oil
Denmark – Food, Oil
France – Oil
Ireland – Food, Oil
Italy – Food
Netherlands – Food
Spain – Oil, Import prices

Incomplete series were not included in the regressions.

Comments by Robert Eisner on
"The NAIRU: is it a real constraint?"

Karl Marx indicated that capitalism required a "reserve army" of unemployed. Without it, workers would force wages up to the point that there would be no profits and the system would collapse. Much of the financial community and its outpost in the Federal Reserve, aided and abetted by a disturbing proportion of the economics profession, seem to accept this Marxian doctrine.

In its modern form it is known as the NAIRU, the "non-accelerating-inflation rate of unemployment." Adherence to this dismal dogma may not destroy the system, but it robs it of much of its potential for growth while dooming millions of workers unnecessarily to the disaster of joblessness.

Simply enough, the theory, going back some 30 years now to Milton Friedman and E.S. Phelps, tells us that there is nothing to do to get unemployment below its "natural rate." Efforts to do so by fiscal stimulus or monetary easing might at best bring a very temporary increase in jobs but at the cost of not just more inflation but continuously accelerating inflation. When the attempts to keep unemployment lower are finally abandoned, inflation will settle at its new higher rate, and the only way to get it back where it was is to suffer equal periods and magnitudes of unemployment above the natural rate. What is worse, the dogma tells us, if somehow unemployment slips below its natural rate, the genie of accelerating inflation will be out of the bottle, with all its baleful consequences. Hence, our guardians in the Fed and elsewhere must take prompt, even anticipatory action to prevent this from happening.

Conservatives and liberals alike have accepted these notions and their policy prescriptions. Their differences are largely epitomized by the views of Martin Feldstein, chairman of the Council of Economic Advisors under President Reagan, who has put the NAIRU at 6.5 to 7 percent, while Alan Blinder, formerly of President Clinton's CEA and then vice chairman of the Federal Reserve Board, places it between 5.5 and 6 percent. The working figure for the Fed, until recently, has been 6 percent, as put forth by the Congressional Budget Office and my colleague, Robert Gordon, a most prominent estimator of these things. The CBO's current estimate is 5.83 percent, and Gordon has worked his down to 5.65 percent.

With either number, though, we are now at a danger point: any further fall of unemployment, which has been below 6 percent for almost four years and well below 5 percent as of this writing, will open the way to disaster. And since growth faster than some 2.3 percent is taken to bring reductions in unemployment, such more rapid growth must be prevented. This view explains the Fed actions in raising interest rates numerous times in the mid-1990s and the current fears that it may act to raise interest rates again.

An increasing number of economists have finally come to express skepticism or reject outright the whole concept of the NAIRU. (Critics include Nobel laureates Robert Solow of the Massachusetts Institute of Technology (MIT) and James Tobin of Yale, Ray Fair, also of Yale, Mark Watson at Princeton, James Galbraith at Texas in Austin, M.A. Setterfield dealing with Canadian data, Olivier Blanchard of France and MIT, and Frank Hahn and Rod Cross in England.) It is indeed hard to defend, with double-digit unemployment rates in much of Europe and the "natural rate" apparently varying elsewhere down to 2–3 percent in Japan. Dean Baker's work is a welcome contribution to this critical genre.

The essential requirements of the NAIRU theory are that inflation must generate expectations of future inflation such that, left to itself, the existing rate of inflation is self-perpetuating, and that higher unemployment reduces inflation and lower unemployment raises inflation. Baker takes the basic equations that I have taken from the CBO, in turn, largely following Robert Gordon's work, and reestimates the model, for both the United States and 11 other OECD countries. He also tests the asymmetric model that I have offered, which separates observations for periods with unemployment above the NAIRU and observations with unemployment below the NAIRU.

What I had found is that regression results with 160 quarterly observations, from 1956:1 to 1995:4, appear to confirm the conventional model. The sum of coefficients of current and past unemployment is indeed substantially negative, and the sum of coefficients of past inflation does indeed come to unity or above. This would indicate the existence of a NAIRU, since inflation at some particular rate of unemployment would then be self-perpetuating, and higher unemployment would bring continuously decelerating inflation while lower unemployment would generate awful, continuously accelerating inflation. I also found, however, that forecasts or simulations based on the conventional model regressions brought only slow and modest acceleration of inflation, of a few percentage points or less, for varying periods of unemployment that was a percentage point below a calculated NAIRU of 5.7 percent. No necessary disaster here!

When I estimated my asymmetrical model, the results were strikingly different. The sums of past inflation coefficients summed to less than unity, and/or, for low unemployment, the sums of unemployment coefficients were close to zero; for regressions with the consumer price index (CPI-U), they were even slightly positive. This indicated, as simulations and forecasts illustrated, that, at worst, unemployment below the hypothesized NAIRU would generate a slightly higher equilibrium, but not accelerating, inflation, and that it might even lower inflation. We seemed to have something of an old-style Phillips curve with a twist: estimates of a cubic equation of inflation as a function of unemployment generated curves showing lower inflation for unemployment above 8.7 or 8.8 percent but also lower inflation as unemployment went below those rates, reaching minima in the 4 to 5 percent range. It was only as unemployment got below 4 percent that there was any significant indication of higher inflation.

Baker has confirmed my results with his regressions for the United States. His extensions to the 11 other OECD nations bring somewhat enigmatic findings but add to the indications that the NAIRU does not stand up with any consistency to empirical testing. First, he offers the critical result that, when the inflation coefficient sum is not constrained to be unity, in all cases other than the United States the conventional model yields sums well below 1. There is no NAIRU! There are only old-style Phillips curves; we can have lower unemployment with higher, but not accelerating, inflation. Further, where the past inflation coefficients, contradicting the data, are constrained to equal unity, perusal of Baker's Table 2B indicates that sums of unemployment coefficients are modest in absolute values. In a number of instances they are close to zero and in one country (France) slightly positive. There is little comfort to supporters of the conventional model in any of Baker's findings for the countries other than the United States.

When Baker turns to my asymmetric model, he again confirms my results for the United States. In particular, he gets the required negative unemployment coefficients for high-unemployment observations but (hugely) positive coefficients for low unemployment. His results for the other countries also confirm the rejection of the NAIRU with sums of inflation coefficients less than unity. Baker's unemployment coefficients, though, bounce all over with no consistent pattern. In a number of cases the high-unemployment coefficients are close to zero and even positive, while the low-unemployment coefficients are less than the high-unemployment coefficients and sometimes highly negative. When Baker constrained his inflation coefficients to sum to unity, the high-unemployment coefficients were frequently close to zero and in four of the 11 cases actually positive. This result is consistent with the casual empirical observation that, despite persistent high unemployment in most of Europe, there has been no evidence of the continuously *de*celerating inflation that the NAIRU doctrine would imply.

As Baker indicates, data for the countries other than the United States are of uncertain and varying quality and include fewer observations (only 85) than I was able to use. Further, the estimates of the NAIRU he took for the various countries were such that the number of low-unemployment observations were very few, in all cases except Ireland (44) and Spain (30) ranging between six and 23. Standard errors, particularly for the low-unemployment coefficients, were high.

There are a few things that Baker might try in an effort to sharpen his results. One would be to take different breakpoints for high-unemployment and low-unemployment observations so that he can have roughly equal numbers of observations in each set. (In my work with the U.S. data I actually had slightly more than half of my 160 observations with unemployment below the NAIRU.) Second, Baker might estimate entirely separate regressions for low-unemployment and high-unemployment observations. This would, in particular, permit the sums of the inflation coefficients to differ for the two sets of observations.

Third, Baker might pool his time series for all observations and for all observations other than the United States. This might iron out the individual country variations and possibly show clearer results with lower standard errors.

Overall, Baker has added significantly to the evidence that the NAIRU does not stand up to empirical testing, in the rest of the world as well as the United States. The sooner policy makers take note, the better off we will all be.

17

Internal and external constraints on egalitarian policies

Andrew Glyn

Within Europe the most pressing economic problems from an egalitarian point of view are:

(1) high rates of unemployment and labor market withdrawal, especially among the least-qualified sections of the labor force;

(2) pressures to deregulate the labor market and allow a widening dispersion of pay and increasing numbers of insecure jobs with very low wages;

(3) pressures to reduce budget deficits and finance tax cuts by reducing the provision of public welfare services and levels of income support.

These trends have been at their most acute within the U.K., where, between the late 1970s and the early 1990s:

(1) the nonemployment rate among the least-educated men of working age tripled to reach one-third;

(2) the pay of the worst-paid 10th of wage earners fell by 28 percent as compared to the best paid;

(3) the level of state pensions fell by more than one-quarter as compared to average earnings.

Such trends have generated an astounding rise in inequality; by the end of the 1980s the ratio of the incomes of the top 10 percent to the bottom 10 percent had practically doubled, and the U.K. was challenging the U.S. for the title of most unequal of the advanced countries (Atkinson et al. 1985).

Even Sweden, which epitomized the egalitarian model, has not escaped. The rise in unemployment there since 1990, together with a widening of the previously compressed pay distribution and some cuts in the generous welfare programs, have highlighted the strains to which that model has been subjected.[1]

In the 1960s in particular, access to jobs, income distribution, employment rights,

---

1 OECD-wide trends in employment and pay are analyzed by OECD (1994) and recent issues of OECD's *Employment Outlook*.

I would like to thank Sam Bowles, Wendy Carlin, Bob Pollin, and participants at the Washington conferences and the September Group for most helpful comments.

and welfare provisions were on a seemingly inexorable progressive trend. An egalitarian economic program had to sustain those trends and extend them to excluded groups. Now the tasks are to reverse, or avoid, disastrous increases in inequality.[2] The details of such a program would obviously depend on the particular circumstances of the country concerned. But it seems reasonable to propose the following core package as being generally applicable in Europe:

(1) a substantial increase in aggregate demand to generate additional jobs;
(2) policies to stem and reverse the deteriorating opportunities for, and conditions of, employment at the low-pay end of the labor market;
(3) maintenance of standards of the welfare services.

The first section of this paper outlines briefly some doubts about the viability of such policies. The second section looks at the domestic constraints on their implementation, abstracting entirely from interactions with the rest of the world. The trends toward greater internationalization are then outlined and an evaluation is made, in the fourth section, of the additional constraints that this imposes on policy choices for European countries.

Are expansions still egalitarian?

It is sometimes suggested that expanding output will no longer generate many additional jobs due to the bias of technical progress. If this were the case, even a successful expansion of aggregate demand would have little impact on the labor market. In fact, the notion that technological progress has speeded up is blatantly contradicted by the slowdown in labor productivity growth since 1973. Such a slowdown may perhaps be exaggerated, but could not be explained, by increasing problems of incorporating quality improvements in the output statistics.

Most relevant for policies to reduce unemployment, rapid expansions in output still lead to faster job creation. In the U.K., for example, the period 1985–88 saw output rising by 4.7 percent per year and employment growing by 2.0 percent per year; from 1990 to 1992 output fell 1.4 percent per year and employment declined 3 percent. In the western part of Germany employment increased by 1.5 million between 1989 and 1991 (3 percent per year, or nearly four times the trend growth rate), in response to 5 percent per year growth during the "unification boom." Output growth was 5.3 percent per year higher in a sample of booms during the 1980s than in recessions, and this was practically matched by employment growing 4.3 percent faster (Boltho and Glyn 1995, Table 1). The impact of output on jobs applies in the medium term as well. A cross-section analysis of the (trough-to-trough) period 1982–93 found that, for every 1 percent per year that a country increased its output growth (as compared to the previous cycle), there was a nearly 1 percent per year boost to employment growth

2   The contradiction between the growing need for egalitarian policies and the tendency to argue
    that they are somehow made irrelevant by globalization is discussed in Vandenbroucke (1997).

Table 1 *Unemployment changes by educational level, 1980s*

Change in unemployment rate 1983–86 to 1987–90	Most qualified	Least qualified
Germany	-0.1	-1.2
Netherlands	-1.0	-8.1
Spain	-2.2	-3.7
U.K.	-0.7	-4.7
U.S.	-0.6	-3.0
Finland	-0.4	-2.9
Sweden	-0.1	-1.7

Source: Nickell and Bell 1995, Table 2A. Definitions of educational categories (and precise dating) differ across countries as indicated in notes in original source.

(Boltho and Glyn 1995, Table 3). With labor productivity typically rising in countries of the OECD (Organization for Economic Cooperation and Development) in the range 1.5–2.5 percent per year in sustained expansions, maintaining a 4 percent per year growth for several years provides jobs at a rate of around 1.5–2.5 percent per year.

A more subtle version of the notion that expansion will not boost employment is that it would have a relatively small effect at the bottom end of the labor market. Underlying trends, arising from the bias of technological progress, from trade with low-wage countries and from a weakening of unions (see Wood 1994) are surely reducing demand for the least-qualified section of the labor force. But this does not mean that changes in the general state of the labor market leave those at the bottom end unaffected. On the contrary, their position seems to be disproportionately dependent on the overall demand for labor; Table 1 shows that, in countries where unemployment fell substantially in the later 1980s, the unemployment rate of the least qualified fell much more (in absolute terms) than that of the most qualified.[3]

Particular attention has been focused in Europe on the long-term unemployed. But the fear that their prospects for work will be relatively impervious to demand expansion seems exaggerated. In the recovery of unemployment in the U.K. in the later 1980s, long-term joblessness declined as fast as short-term unemployment, even setting aside the impact of special government programs directed toward reducing long-term unemployment (Robinson 1994).

There are various factors that make the employment prospects of the least qualified sensitive to general labor market conditions. It may be that they are disproportionately employed in the most cyclically sensitive industries, such as construction. It is very likely that within industries unskilled labor is less prone to being hoarded in downturns. There may also be more general processes of "bumping down" in recessions with the educationally more qualified taking the less-skilled jobs. Thus,

3 The larger fall in the absolute unemployment rate of the least qualified means an increase in their relative chances of work even if their relative unemployment rate was unchanged (see Glyn 1995a).

rapid expansions in demand, far from being irrelevant, will have marked effects on the employment prospects of the least qualified.

Even so a generalized demand expansion may not sufficiently reverse the deteriorating position of the least qualified. Expansions can be twisted, through public sector programs, toward sectors that use less-qualified workers and toward areas where deindustrialization has led to the most severe concentrations of joblessness of the unskilled. The orthodox policy is greater relative wage flexibility "to foster the creation of low-productivity jobs, especially in the nontradeable sector, in order to absorb significant numbers of low-skilled unemployed workers" (OECD 1994b, 33). One response is to go with the flow of wage flexibility but seek to offset its consequences for income distribution by in-work benefits or tax rebates for the low paid. A recent study of European unemployment (CEPR 1995) postulated reductions in the relative earnings of the bottom 20 percent of employees of more than 40 percent if their employment prospects were to be brought up to the average. It is hard to imagine that the tax and benefit system would offset changes of this magnitude. So an egalitarian approach should include deliberate policies to twist the pattern of demand toward jobs for the less qualified.

Internal constraints

Expanding demand can have a major effect on the job market, but this does not make it straightforward to achieve. This section outlines the problems faced by attempts to achieve such an expansion, focusing on the constraints that are of domestic origin. The further complications generated by international economic integration are considered in the next section.

Sluggish private capital accumulation
A classic Keynesian expansion is engineered by increases in government spending and/or reductions in taxation. The direct impact on demand for private sector output, as a result of government purchases and/or taxpayers' increasing consumption, would be amplified by multiplier increases in income and consumption. This increase in demand, it is hoped, will generate rising investment, especially if monetary policy is accommodating and interest rates are prevented from rising or are even reduced. If the investment response is strong enough, the budget deficit will be eliminated as incomes and tax revenue are driven up, and then the rise of public spending can be scaled back. In such an expansion the government deficit performs a temporary, "pump-priming" role, and nobody is required to "pay for" full employment. Those previously unemployed gain because their take-home pay is greater than the level of state unemployment benefits. Other workers gain since less tax is required to finance the dole. Employers gain as sales and aggregate profits rise.[4]

4   Such harmony would be disrupted if productivity declined at the margin as employment rose, requiring a fall in real wages, but the evidence is not consistent with this (Blanchflower and Oswald 1994).

If private investment responds only sluggishly to an expansion, then the situation is more difficult. If private investment is less, at high employment, than private savings, then one way to sustain demand is by running a persistent budget deficit. Nobody is obliged immediately to pay for the expansion, but the state is piling up debt, with the implied obligation to raise taxes in the future to cover interest payments. Alternatively, the surplus of private savings can be eliminated if the government undertakes a parallel expansion of government spending and taxation of a sufficient magnitude. This "balanced budget multiplier" expansion relies on redistributing consumption from the employed to the unemployed finding jobs, while the rise in employment and output is confined to the government sector. In this case one section of society has to pay for full employment, in terms of reduced (growth rate of) consumption, though receiving benefits from the improvement in public services.

Such a cost is only postponed by running a sustained deficit; rising investment is required to avoid it altogether. If expanding demand could be relied on to bring the desired response from investment, then other policies, specifically directed at stimulating investment, would be unnecessary. Investment rose rapidly in Europe in the boom of the 1980s, but was noticeably concentrated in the service sectors in most countries (Glyn 1995c). It often took on a strongly speculative character (office development, etc), to the neglect of investment in the traded goods sector. The OECD noted (in the June 1995 *Economic Outlook,* p. 30) that for continental Europe "[b]usiness investment was generally weak during the early 1990s, and it has been slower to respond to improving conditions than in previous upswings." In the U.K. as well it made virtually no contribution to recovery. While investment incentives may play some role in stimulating investment, they are expensive (Bond et al. 1991) and have a rather unreliable impact. It would be risky to bank on investment playing a strongly expansionary role, especially given the likely evaluation by employers of the difficulties in sustaining expansion resulting from other constraints considered below.

Conflicting claims

As described above, expansionary programs, by generating extra resources, have the potential for making all groups in society better off. But, even if this potential is realized and all groups gain, conflicts over income shares may still intensify as a tightening labor market enhances the bargaining position of workers.

Unless the expansion left the unemployment rate above the pre-existing non-accelerating-inflation rate of unemployment (NAIRU) or was accompanied by measures to reduce the NAIRU, accelerating inflation would develop. As the experience of the 1960s and 1970s suggests, rising inflation could well be associated with severe profit squeezes. This period also confirmed the prediction of Kalecki that prolonged full employment would threaten the position of capital, since it generated a range of demands from labor for limiting the managerial prerogatives over the organization of work and allocation of investment (restrictions on dismissals, industrial democracy, planning agreements, nationalizations, etc.). Manifestly, capitalism failed to "adjust to full employment" by "developing new social and political institutions which will reflect the increased power of the working class" (Kalecki 1990, 356) in a way that maintained the rhythm of accumulation.[5]

After the turbulence of the decade or so from the mid-1960s, the subsequent period of mass unemployment delivered low inflation, a striking recovery of profitability, a dramatic reduction of industrial conflict, and the virtual disappearance of the threatening challenges to capital's freedom of maneuver (Glyn 1995c). Does this mean that the NAIRU is much lower now? Jackman, Layard, and Nickell's analysis (1996, Table 2) of OECD unemployment shows relatively little movement between the middle 1980s and the early 1990s in the labor market institutions and policies that they believe determine the NAIRU. On the other hand, the Bank of England, writing about the U.K. labor market, which has undergone the most dramatic changes, suggests that:

> In all probability, the natural rate has fallen over the last decade. Institutional changes have reduced rigidities, and the changing nature of employment has reduced the willingness of workers to push for higher wages at a given level of unemployment. The weakness of earnings growth during the recent recovery is consistent with unemployment being above its natural rate. (Bank of England 1996, 37)

Beliefs about the impact of expansion on inflation can have important effects, regardless of the precise location of the NAIRU. If employers believe that the expansion is unsustainable because of the conflicts that will be generated, they are less likely to respond to the higher demand with increased investment. This in turn weakens the growth of productivity, which could otherwise have moderated the conflict over real incomes by increasing further the size of the cake (see Rowthorn 1995). Focusing expansion on the less qualified, minimizing skill shortages helps to moderate inflationary pressure, but at some point those pressures will build up unless contained within the wage bargaining system. The central problem is to devise a convincing institutional framework within which to resolve the conflicts generated by high employment. Discussion of this issue has practically ceased (with Dore et al. 1994 an important exception), despite episodic resort to policies for coordinating wage increases centrally (in crisis situations in Sweden and Finland and on a more sustained basis in Ireland).

It is sometimes imagined that labor market deregulation, depriving groups previously in a strong bargaining position of the power to pursue their claims, is more effective than incomes policy, which relies on groups forgoing use of their market power. However, if deregulation did succeed in generating large numbers of jobs, it would inevitably restore labor's bargaining strength and lead to demands for reregulation. Reconsideration of systems of bargaining over wages and broader issues seems an absolute priority for the construction of egalitarian programs.

Government deficits

In the simplest case considered above, the effect of an expansionary program on the government deficit is short lived, representing temporary "pump priming" that disappears when private investment expands sufficiently to drive up incomes and

5   Glyn (1995b) provides an interpretation of social democratic experience along these lines.

tax revenues. But if the private sector response is not strong enough, then there is a persistent increase in the budget deficit. Why is this problematic?

The rise in the ratio of government debt to gross domestic product (if the deficit exceeds that which would stabilize the debt burden) heightens the potential for distributional struggle, as the extra interest payments increase claims on output. The likelihood of inflation is increased; for example, workers may attempt to offset taxes raised to pay the interest. The temptation for governments to accommodate such inflation is strong, since the real value of its outstanding liabilities is thereby reduced. Accordingly, at any given rate of unemployment, the higher the deficit (at least beyond certain rather ill-defined limits – see Buiter et al. 1993) the greater the likelihood of faster inflation in the future. This is the rational basis for the adverse response of financial markets.

Financial markets

The response of financial markets to impending difficulties is likely to bring matters to a head earlier than would otherwise be the case. Anticipation of faster inflation in the future will tend to push up market interest rates as investors attempt to avoid the implied future real capital losses on their financial assets. Even if expected real interest rates are not affected, the capital losses and higher nominal rates will tend to inhibit spending and stifle the expansion. The crucial role of financial markets is to anticipate future developments, and these very anticipations have real effects. This would occur in any developed financial market and is not dependent on international financial integration.

Controls over the financial system, such as requiring financial institutions to hold specified proportions of government debt, might prevent market anticipations from being expressed. But in the circumstances just described, this restriction would amount to suppressing the warning symptoms of a problem rather than lead to a solution. If an expansion is going to collapse into faster inflation and a profit squeeze, then preventing the financial markets from registering these prospects can only postpone the destabilizing pressures.

Taxation and the costs of expansion

Even weak private sector investment does not inevitably imply budget deficits at full employment. An alternative policy to maintaining demand by deficit financing is to increase government spending even further, while simultaneously increasing taxation to cover the net costs to the treasury. While there are general benefits from the improvements in the public services or infrastructure, there is no longer a "free lunch" in the literal sense. The additional consumption by those who find jobs (which will be quite limited if unemployment benefits are generous), will have to be paid for by the reduced consumption of taxpayers.

Such an expansion, with all the extra demand emanating from the public sector, is an extreme case. But more generally, it may be necessary to focus expansion on the public sector if private sector spending is weak. This has desirable consequences given the generally egalitarian distribution of benefits from improvements in the public services. Such an expanded role for the public sector would imply rising public sector debt ratios with consequent dangers of financial instability, unless the financing comes from higher tax rates.

Who will pay such higher tax rates? An egalitarian program would naturally impose tax increases in a progressive manner (especially in countries like the U.K., where the tax system has been shifted in a highly regressive direction). Whatever the possibilities for widely supported increases in the progressiveness of the tax system, political circumstances may dictate that tax increases extend beneath "top incomes" and involve some rise in the tax burden on middle incomes. It is a fundamental political problem to gain support for such increases in taxation, even where rather tangible benefits accrue in the form of improvements in health and education services, for example, to say nothing of the less-tangible benefits from reducing social exclusion. Political support for the tax increases has first to be gained, but the institutions regulating wage bargaining also have to be strong enough to prevent the tax increases accepted at the ballot box from being pushed aside through compensating wage increases.

Internationalization: interpreting the indicators

The discussion in the second section identified a set of closely related domestic constraints on the construction and implementation of egalitarian programs. If the private sector is very dynamic, a mere nudge may push the economy toward high employment. There will be a need neither for sustained budget deficits nor for the public sector to maintain the leading role in demand generation. But weak private investment requires an enhanced role for the public sector and support for raising the taxes to finance it. Most fundamentally, institutions have to regulate effectively the distributional conflict that higher levels of demand and employment would inevitably bring. Financial markets, by anticipating all these problems, can bring immediate confrontation with their effects. Before looking at how international economic relations may further constrain expansionary programs, some discussion of trends in internationalization is warranted.

Overseas trade in goods and services
In his latest overview of historical trends, Maddison (1995, 37–8) measures the degree of trade integration by the ratio of exports to GDP at constant prices. This gives dramatic results for Europe in particular – the export ratio declines from 16 percent in 1913 to 9 percent in 1950 before rising to 21 percent in 1973 and 30 percent in 1992. It appears that the importance of trade has tripled since 1950 and now far exceeds the weight in the economy it reached at the end of the classical free trade period.

A rising share of constant price exports implies that the volume of exports has grown faster than the volume of production overall, a comparison frequently made to demonstrate the growing importance of trade (e.g., exports grew by 5.7 percent per year for the European Union 15 countries over the period 1960–94 against the

3.2 percent per year growth rate for GDP; *OECD Historical Statistics,* Tables 3.1 and 4.8). These constant price comparisons do not, however, adequately reflect the changing weight of exports in the domestic economy. This is because the prices of exports rise systematically more slowly than do prices for output as a whole. For EU 15 over the period 1960–94 the deflator for exports rose 4.3 percent per year, while the GDP deflator rose by 6.0 percent per year. So over this period, around two-thirds of the discrepancy between export and GDP volume growth was offset by a slower growth of export prices. The relative fall in export prices reflects the faster-than-average growth of labor productivity in the export sector compared to the economy as a whole. For example, over the period 1960–94 labor productivity in EU manufacturing, where exports are concentrated, grew at 4.1 percent per year, while GDP per person employed increased by only 2.7 percent per year. This relatively rapid productivity growth in the export sector means that the share of employment devoted to exports grew systematically more slowly than the share of exports in output at constant prices. It is the share of export at current prices that most closely reflects the share of labor devoted to exporting activity, and this measure shows a much less dramatic picture than the constant price figures.

In 1994 the shares of exports in GDP did not much exceed the levels of 1913 (Table 2). This is true for the OECD countries in total and for the U.S., Europe, and Japan taken separately. While such a historical perspective is interesting, its relevance to discussions about constraints on post-1945 systems of national economic management may seem limited. More significant is the relatively modest increase over the past two decades. Trade shares lurched up in the early 1970s as OECD countries exported more to pay for the higher cost of oil, and this was repeated in the early 1980s. Since then, however, only in the U.S. has the export share continued to rise. In Europe it stabilized, and for Japan it fell sharply.[6]

The export share shows the proportion of economic activity that has to compete internationally on world markets. If imports consist of raw materials, food, and fuel that are complementary to domestic production, they have to be paid for but they do not threaten domestic industry. But imported manufactures represent an additional competitive pressure. Table 3 shows that the classic division of labor has been unwinding for OECD countries as the share of imported food and materials slipped down; over the past decade falling oil prices have even reduced the share of imported energy to below that of 1964. At the same time, the share of manufactures in total OECD imports has increased dramatically, from 53 percent to 77 percent between 1964 and 1993.

The impact of international competition within domestic economies is most clearly displayed in the degree of import penetration of the domestic market for manufactures (Table 4).

Increasing import competition was noticeable even in the 1950s, and, with the

6   Exports include an import content so that their value exceeds the value-added contributed to them by the domestic economy. Thus, before comparing exports to GDP, the import content should really be subtracted. A very crude adjustment suggests that some 22 percent of European GDP was devoted to export production in 1994 rather than the 28 percent share shown in Table 2.

Table 2 *Exports as percent of GDP, 1913–94*

Current prices	1913	1950	1960	1973	1984	1994
U.S.	(7)	4.6	5.2	6.9	7.9	10.6
Europe	(23)	16.7	19.7	24.2	29.8	28.0
Japan	(20)	11.8	10.2	10.0	15.0	9.5
OECD	(16)	10.5	12.7	15.3	19.0	18.4

Source: OECD *Historical Statistics* for 1960 and later years linked to *OECD National Accounts of Member Countries* for 1950; figures for 1913 assume that the differences as compared to 1950 are equal to those estimated by Maddison for merchandise exports only (1991, Table F7).

important exception of Japan, it has continued unabated with import market shares nearly doubling between 1971 and 1993. Most of this competition comes from other OECD countries. Although the share of so-called "emerging economies" has doubled since the late 1960s, they still take only 20 percent of the market for imported manufactures in Europe and the U.S. and one-third in Japan. Perhaps one reason that import competition is so visible is that import penetration is typically twice the level for high-technology products than it is for low-technology ones (OECD 1996b). The basis for the general impression of increasing international integration through trade surely lies in this growing penetration by imports of domestic manufacturing markets. But manufacturing constituted only 18 percent of OECD employment in 1994 (ranging from 16 percent in the U.S., to 26 percent in Germany), a decline of one-third as compared to 1974. Does internationalization amount, therefore, to increasingly fierce competition about a diminishing and relatively small sector?

The significance of manufacturing is underplayed by its share of employment, since other sectors contribute substantially to manufactured commodities. So part of the output of agriculture, mining, energy, construction, transport, and finance and business services is dependent on the success of domestic manufacturing. Bits of these sectors are, at one remove, subject to the international competition within manufacturing markets. To indicate the orders of magnitude involved, in 1994 other sectors contributed some £70 billion to U.K. manufacturing output (with finance and business services the biggest supplier), as compared to value-added within manufacturing itself of £124 billion. In this sense the importance of manufacturing is at least 50 percent greater than appears from looking at its contribution to value-added or employment. If we extended the calculation to include the value of agricultural and mining output (which is extensively if far from freely traded internationally), it would seem that around 30 percent of the U.K. economy is directly or indirectly contributing to the production of internationally traded goods.

Of course some services are traded directly as well. In 1994 OECD exports of commercial services were about 25 percent of exports of goods; for the U.S. the figure was 35 percent. But these are concentrated in a narrow range of specialized services (international transport, international finance, consulting, and so forth) and are irrelevant for the mass of domestic service producers (tourism is one exception,

Table 3 *Product composition of OECD imports*

	Food	Materials	Energy	Manufactures
1964	18	16	11	53
1975	12	9	22	56
1985	9	7	20	65
1993	9	5	9	77

Source: OECD *Historical Statistics,* Tables 12.1 to 12.6.

Table 4 *Import penetration of domestic markets for manufactures (percent), 1913–93*

	1913	1950	1963	1971	1980	1993
U.S.	3	2	3	8	9	16
Japan	34	3	4	5	5	6
4 large European countries	13	6	11	17	21	29
3 small European countries	24	20	26	33	45	57

Note: Imports as percent of apparent consumption (production plus imports less exports).

Source: 1913–71 Batchelor et al. 1980, Table 3.3; 1980/1993 from OECD 1996b, Table 5.1. There are breaks in the series after 1950 and after 1971.

since it is in competition with a broad range of domestic services). There is no obvious way of quantifying what part of services is seriously internationalized, but any plausible estimate would leave a majority of employment in OECD countries, possibly a substantial and probably a growing majority, largely untouched by international competition. Outside agriculture, mining, and manufacturing only a small proportion of workers are subject to international competition directly or indirectly through services provided to traded goods producers. Wholesale and retail trade, community, personal and social services, utilities, and construction together employ some 60 percent of OECD workers (a little more in the U.S.). They are almost wholly insulated from international competition, even though many of these workers handle (in transport, retailing, repair, and so forth) imported goods.

The impact of internationalization through trade is quite complicated, therefore. For one section of the economy – manufacturing production and its suppliers, together with some specialized enclaves in the services sector – it has intensified considerably.[7]

---

7   Despite increasing competition, the variation across countries in manufacturing profitability has remained stable, apart from the decline in Japanese profitability from its exceptional heights in the 1960s (Glyn 1997, Tables 1 and 3).

Table 5 *Foreign direct investment, 1984–94*

Percent of gross domestic investment	OECD	U.S.	Japan	Europe
Inward	3.8	5.0	0.1	5.1
Outward	5.0	3.4	3.1	7.8

Source: UNCTAD *World Investment Report 1996,* Annex Table 5.

In the U.S. this rise in internationalization has been from a very low initial level, and in Japan it has been much weaker. For the rest of the economy, covering probably a growing majority of those in employment, international competition is of little direct relevance, though these sectors are not immune from the macroeconomic consequences of trends in the traded goods sectors.

Foreign direct investment

The 1980s saw a substantial increase in foreign direct investment (FDI). The *World Investment Report* shows the inward stock of FDI in developed countries rising from 4.8 percent of GDP in 1980 to 8.6 percent in 1994 (for outward FDI the figures are 6.5 percent and 11.2 percent). Although the increase seems impressive, comparing a stock of FDI to GDP does not directly measure its significance. A less problematic measure is the ratio of the flow of FDI to the corresponding flow of domestic investment. This is not subject to the accounting biases, and it shows what the share of the capital stock represented by FDI would be if the flow continued at that rate. As shown in Table 5, the proportions of capital expenditure represented by FDI are still really rather small. Nor does all FDI represent the construction of new production facilities by overseas companies. Typically well over half of FDI inflows into OECD countries represents cross-border mergers and acquisitions. While some of this represents international intrusion into the competitive structure of the industry, many acquisitions are closer to portfolio investments, involving a change in ownership but with relatively little impact on industry behavior.

The sectoral composition of FDI is less biased toward manufacturing than foreign trade. In the early 1990s around one-half of outward FDI from major home countries was in the services sector (the proportion was two-thirds in Japan). Obviously FDI can reach into parts of the service sector immune from direct competition from imports (e.g., McDonald's), and this represents some qualification to the remarks above about their insulation. As yet, however, the impact on services overall is still rather small.

Financial capital

The indicators of the internationalization of financial capital are virtually unanimous in showing spectacular growth. The only difficulty is the now-familiar one of judging whether the particular aspect of internationalization has yet become "large" in relation to its domestic counterparts. As a ratio to world GDP, the stock of cross-border bank lending has grown from 6 percent in 1972 to 37 percent in 1991. Cross border transactions in bonds and equities have grown from less than 10 percent of GDP in 1980 to 80 percent of GDP for Japan, 160 percent for the U.S. and 200 percent for Germany (BIS 1997). The daily turnover of the foreign exchange market of more than $1,500 billion is six times the total gross central bank intervention during the 1992 exchange rate mechanism (ERM) crisis (Eichengreen and Wyplosz 1993). Such explosive growth of international financial transactions renders exchange rates wholly dependent on shifts in market expectations.

Such data on transactions convey little information, however, about the degree of internationalization of ownership of financial assets, since so many transactions refer to shifts in existing portfolios rather than flows of "new money." The U.K. case is interesting, since it is a medium-sized country with highly developed and internationally integrated capital markets. In 1979 6.1 percent of U.K. company securities were owned abroad; by 1995 the overseas share was 23.8 percent, worth around double the total of direct investment in the U.K.[8] Of liabilities of the U.K. public sector, 7.3 percent are held overseas (a very similar proportion to 1979). The U.K. household (or "personal") sector still owned negligible amounts of overseas assets directly in 1995. But life assurance and pension funds, which comprise about half the financial assets of the household/personal sector, hold 19.8 percent of their assets overseas, up from 1.9 percent in 1979. Foreign ownership rising fourfold or even 10-fold in 16 years represents spectacular growth. Leaving aside the banking system, however, it still leaves the vast majority of U.K. portfolios invested in financial assets emanating from the domestic economy and the vast majority of U.K. liabilities held by domestic residents. It is possible to envisage a situation where ownership of financial capital is so internationalized and portfolios so diversified that clearly identifiable national blocs of capital will cease to be very significant. But that is clearly not the situation at present. Thus, domestic capital has not yet "exited" *en masse,* leaving the domestic economy mainly owned by overseas residents. The problem is rather that the international freedom of movement for financial capital adds powerfully to the domestic exit options already available.

Internationalization and egalitarian expansion

This section outlines how the trends toward internationalization summarized in the previous section have interacted with the domestic constraints on expansion summarized in the second section.

Investment
There are a number of ways in which internationalization may have contributed to the weakness of European investment identified in the second section. International financial integration has made it nearly impossible for individual countries to avoid

8   United Kingdom National Accounts 1996 and earlier editions, Tables 12.1–12.12

the worldwide increase in real interest rates that occurred in the 1980s. In the period 1990–93 real long-term rates in European countries lay in the range 4–8 percent, compared with rates of around 2 percent in the 1960s and frequently negative rates in the inflationary 1970s (OECD *Historical Statistics* 1960–93, Table 10.10). But this factor can be overemphasized. On the one hand interest costs have to be set against profitability, which in manufacturing recovered quite spectacularly in most European countries in the 1980s (see Glyn 1995c). Secondly, empirical studies of investment almost generally find that interest costs are of secondary importance.

Since part of any demand stimulus leaks abroad, it can only be sustained if the initial balance of payments is strong enough, or if exchange rate depreciation is feasible as a route for maintaining the current account balance. Fears about the balance of payments can add to other anxieties about whether expansionary programs can be maintained. Uncertainty over exchange rates, at least with countries outside the EU, but also with fellow members after the collapse of the ERM in 1992, has increased the unpredictability of returns, particularly for manufacturing and related sectors. Although still a small proportion of the European market, new sources of supply have added a further element of fragility to market shares.

Conflicting claims

The leaking of demand abroad during an expansion represents an easing of distributional struggles; as long as a current account deficit can be sustained, consumption exceeds production. But deficits have to be reined in and, with integrated capital markets, sooner rather than later. Provided it is not ruled out by adherence to a fixed exchange rate, there is a perfectly straightforward remedy: allow the exchange rate to depreciate sufficiently to generate the extra exports required.

The problem is that depreciation imposes real costs on the economy in terms of the higher real cost of imports. This would reduce the additional resources available for moderating distributional conflict; in particular, workers' real wages would have to decline (relative to the trend in productivity) if the gain in competitiveness were to be maintained. The old notion, that additional employment could only be obtained at the cost of lower real wages for those already in work, reappears in a new guise. Even where additional employment would otherwise have been profitable on the existing capital stock without real wage cuts, the deterioration in the terms of trade may make wage reductions necessary.

So distributional struggles will definitely be heightened by the terms-of-trade effects of maintaining the current account balance. But the relatively modest *increases* in overall trade shares as have occurred could hardly constitute an independent explanation for deflationary bias. If European countries had no reason to hold back from Keynesian policies other than the effects on their payments balances, then it is hard to see why coordinated macroeconomic expansion at the European level, for example, would not happen. Domestic constraints to expansion, for the reasons discussed in the second section, however, make the failure to engineer coordinated expansion easily explicable in terms of fears of renewed distributional conflict. It is hard to believe that the *additional* restraint to the growth of real wages, implied by modest increases in trade shares and thus terms-of-trade costs of expansionary policies, has been a decisive factor constraining expansion.

The impact of internationalization on NAIRUs in Europe is complex. Greater flows of FDI represent greater flexibility for employers to relocate production, and the threat of this may give employers greater bargaining strength over wages and other conditions of work. Less wage pressure would allow a lower unemployment rate. On the other hand, the pressure, via the financial markets, to conform to very low inflation rates in Europe can itself require a higher rate of unemployment in the long term because of the strains imposed on complex bargaining systems, like that of Sweden, by limited room for money wage increases (Calmfors 1993) or because of resistance to money wage cuts by groups whose relative wages would otherwise fall (Akerlof et al. 1996).

Internationalization clearly has a mass of complex and even contradictory effects on struggles over income shares. These complicate the task of devising institutional solutions. But internationalization is not the fundamental factor behind such conflict.

Budget deficits

Where real interest rates exceed trend growth rates, a primary surplus on the budget is necessary to prevent government debt from rising faster than GDP. Whatever the cause of the high real interest rates of the 1980s and 1990s, international financial integration makes it difficult for individual governments to shake them off. Between 1979 and 1995 government (net) interest payments increased from 1.9 percent of Europe's GDP to 4.8 percent (OECD *Economic Outlook,* December 1995). This provided much of the impetus toward cutting deficits, enshrined in the Maastricht targets. Otherwise, only an unexpected burst of inflation can reduce the real burden of interest payments, and this would be very hard to engineer without the position sliding out of control.

Financial markets

In general the best support for an expansion would be as low interest rates as possible combined with a steady fall in the real exchange rate. But under conditions of free capital mobility an expansionary program is liable to lead to a much larger fall in the exchange rate to include:

(1) all of the expected fall in the long-term real exchange rate implied by the expansionary program;

(2) the future nominal appreciation implied by the lower level of interest rates compared to world levels;

(3) all the anticipated impacts of the expansionary program on the inflation rate (which implies a correspondingly lower nominal exchange rate in the future).

Very large depreciations could result.[9] Moreover, they would not occur smoothly over the life of the program, as and when real depreciation became necessary or higher inflation occurred. Rather, they would tend to happen in a rush, simply on

9   A fall in the real exchange rate of 20 percent over four years, say, might be required to sustain the balance of payments position; interest rates at 2.5 percent below the world level

the anticipation of such developments. As discussed earlier in relation to domestic finance, these markets have no interest in giving expansionary policies the benefit of the doubt, if historical experience suggests a substantial inflationary impact. On the contrary, they are geared to anticipating *possible* future problems, and portfolios are shifted to avoid the consequences. Such anticipations will tend to "front load" the impact on real wages of an expansionary program by generating large initial depreciations. The task of holding the line on distributional conflict must be made more difficult by the likely response of foreign exchange markets.

The fact that financial markets can force the abandonment of a politically unrealistic deflationary policy, as in the case of the U.K. in the autumn of 1992, has not suddenly made them the workers' friend! Whatever policy stance is regarded as unsustainable and thus not credible can be tested out by the markets. There is thus every reason to explore all the possibilities for limiting the destructive power of the financial markets, including Tobin taxes, deposit requirements on foreign exchange transactions, and dual exchange rates (see Eichengreen et al. 1995). But while such restrictions could hopefully limit the power of the markets to destroy an egalitarian package that had a fighting chance of success, they could never preserve in place a package that was unviable, for the fundamental internal reasons discussed in the second section.

Taxation

Egalitarian programs will tend to be slanted toward an expansion of public spending on welfare because of its redistributive effect. As argued in earlier sections, where the response of the private sector to expansion is sluggish, a sustained growth of the public sector may actually be necessary to secure high employment. With substantial debt burdens in many European countries, high real interest rates, and sensitive financial markets, the possibility for more than modest and temporary increases in government deficits is remote. This leaves tax financing of public spending as an important component of egalitarian programs, at least in countries like the U.K. with relatively low shares of taxation.

As noted earlier, this raises a host of fundamental political problems – gaining support for tax increases and maintaining discipline over wage bargaining. What additional constraints in the design of taxation packages are caused by internationalization? In most dramatic form it is suggested that taxes on corporate profits and withholding taxes on interest income would be driven toward zero as countries competed to obtain direct investment and to retain portfolio funds. This would leave only resident-based taxes on profit incomes, which could only function if all European, and probably other, governments provided the relevant information about

persisting for the same period would require an immediate further depreciation of 10 percent to bring the rate down so that sufficient real appreciation was anticipated to make the currency worth holding. If the markets expected that the inflationary impact of the program would amount to 2.5 percent per year, an additional decline of 10 percent would be required to offset the resulting nominal depreciation. It is easy, therefore, to see how large immediate falls in the exchange rate could result from expansionary packages even without politically motivated speculation.

cross-border interest and dividend payments. The EU's Expert Committee (Commission 1992) found a general tendency for the variability of tax systems across member countries to be reduced in the 1980s. Corporation tax rates declined a little, but this was balanced by cuts in the value of investment incentives so that the importance of corporation tax revenue actually increased. Top rates of tax on dividends and interest income fell, but this applied to relatively less mobile labor income as well and was not obviously a response to tax competition. Thus, fears of a headlong collapse of taxation of profits are overstated,[10] though of course coordination at the European level is highly desirable.

European integration

This section has so far examined the impact of growing internationalization on egalitarian policies within individual countries, abstracting from the complexities introduced by European economic integration. The freedom of maneuver for economic policies has been limited, for example, by the operation of the European Monetary System. The prospect of European Monetary Union (EMU) would represent a great leap forward in this process. On the one hand, if economic policy is made increasingly at the European level, then it is less constrained by the openness to the international economy than is the case for an individual European country. Some 70 percent of European Union trade is within the union, so export shares and import penetration for the EU are no higher than for the U.S. or Japan. Similarly some 55 percent of EU outward flows of FDI are to other EU members, and around 60 percent of inward flows are from other EU countries. The fact that a majority of EU trade and FDI takes place with other EU countries would not make the euro exchange rate with the dollar and yen irrelevant, or multinational companies powerless to obtain concessions from workers or national governments by threatening to shift the locus of production. Nevertheless, the European economy as a whole is significantly less internationally vulnerable than an individual country acting on its own, and this underlines the benefits from a coordinated demand management policy and a common approach to the conditions governing investment (tax concessions, regional grants, and so forth).

On the other hand, the EMU is likely to be created with the Maastricht criteria cemented into a "stability pact," severely constraining even the anticyclical use of budget deficits. Moreover, the new European Central Bank is likely to try and establish its credentials as a worthy successor to the Bundesbank by stamping on the least threat of an inflationary expansion. So the starting point within EMU is inauspicious for the egalitarian policies discussed above. But the reason for this is quite instructive. Excessive Euro-caution does not stem from fear of the international impacts of expansionary policies, be it on imports, FDI flows, or financial capital. The explanation is the same as that for the Bundesbank's present stance, namely, fear

10 Rodrik (1997) found that openness to trade was associated with higher taxation of labor and lower taxation of profits in a panel of OECD countries for the period 1965–92. However, his data (Chart 5) show only a very weak tendency for taxes on labor to rise more than taxes on capital.

that expansion would founder on the fundamental domestic constraints, above all distributional conflict.

It might appear that EMU would leave an individual country bereft of fiscal and monetary autonomy and able only to throw its weight behind a campaign for expansion at the European level. This would be too pessimistic, however. Nothing in the Maastricht criteria or the stability pact constrains a country's level of public spending, provided it is balanced by taxation. Tax-financed public spending would still create space for egalitarian outcomes, even within a general macroeconomic environment determined at the European level. EMU removes to the European level the most important policies whereby governments affect the private sector – exchange rates, interest rates, fiscal stance. But it would leave determination of the size of the public sector, a central part of an egalitarian program, in national hands.

Conclusion

This chapter has tried to place the problems posed by internationalization for an egalitarian economic program in the broader context of domestic constraints. Trends toward greater internationalization are often exaggerated, especially in relation to the weight of foreign trade and direct investment. Nevertheless, they have constrained policy in a variety of ways, above all by the internationalization of finance, which has increased the speed at which, the drama with which, and the costs imposed when financial markets bring retribution on governments whose policies are not deemed credible. But it is important not to attribute this to narrow class prejudice. For there are very real domestic problems of constructing sustainable egalitarian packages. The costs of such packages have to be accepted, and the conflict that will tend to be released by a sustained expansion of employment has somehow to be contained and channeled into directions consistent with maintaining the momentum of expansion. Internationalization increases some of the costs to be shouldered in an expansion, and can affect feasible distributions of those costs. There could obviously be cases where these could tip the balance against an otherwise viable program.

If we were really sure that the basic domestic constraints on the construction and implementation of egalitarian policies could successfully be overcome, it would be reasonable to concentrate on the additional problems caused by internationalization. But given the experience of left governments over the past 20 years, we should beware of blaming the narrow scope for egalitarian programs mainly, let alone exclusively, on internationalization.

The move toward economic integration within Europe underlines the fact that internal domestic problems, now being transferred in part to the European level, remain the fundamental ones.

Comment by *Robert A. Blecker on* "Internal and external constraints on egalitarian policies"

In his chapter, Andrew Glyn analyzes whether internal or external constraints have been more important in blocking the adoption of more egalitarian economic policies, especially in the European context. Glyn acknowledges that both internal and external constraints exist, and he also accepts that internal and external constraints sometimes interact with each other. But on the whole, Glyn concludes that "internal domestic problems...remain the fundamental ones."

A first point to note is that the "egalitarian policies" discussed in this chapter are somewhat limited in scope. The main focus of the chapter is on the use of expansionary fiscal policies to promote full employment. Even monetary policy is discussed only tangentially, insofar as it impacts on the effectiveness of fiscal expansion. Complementary micro-level policies to enhance equity are not discussed.

Glyn makes a convincing case that boosting aggregate demand would have a positive impact on job creation for "less-qualified" or lower-paid workers. He does not say whether he thinks higher employment would help to significantly narrow the growing inequality in the distribution of income currently observed in Europe and the United States alike. In the U.S. context, at least, the evidence seems to be that the macroeconomic recovery and close-to-full employment conditions of the mid- to late 1990s have not done much to narrow the growing income gaps that arose in the 1980s. Thus, it appears that expanding aggregate demand and creating full employment are necessary but not sufficient steps for achieving more egalitarian outcomes in the face of structural changes that are making societies more unequal.

With regard to the internal constraints themselves, Glyn paints a reasonable picture of the potential obstacles to a fiscal-induced expansion of demand. Private investment might not respond as desired, especially if crowding-out effects dominate accelerator effects in response to a fiscal stimulus. Conflict-induced inflation[1] could negate expansionary demand effects, especially if it squeezes profits (thus diminishing desired investment) or induces contractionary monetary policies (which exacerbate crowding-out). The financing of expansionary government spending is also a potential problem: deficit finance creates a long-term debt burden for the public sector, while the alternative of tax finance encounters political resistance from the wealthy who ought to bear the burden of progressive taxation. All of these problems

---

[1] Although Glyn's point about conflicting-claims inflation is well taken, his use of the concept of a natural rate of unemployment or NAIRU (non-accelerating-inflation rate of unemployment) is rather surprising. Many progressive economists have questioned whether this concept is meaningful or useful, especially when it is acknowledged that the supposed NAIRU is actually a moving target that closely tracks actual unemployment rates. See, for example, the chapter by Baker in this volume.

can in turn be intensified by the reactions of financial markets, in which anticipations of future economic problems can cause present interest rates and financing costs to rise.

While these are all sensible points, I think Glyn tends to underestimate the degree to which the operation of these internal constraints depends on a country's international trade and financial linkages. For example, in a small economy with open capital markets, interest rates are likely to be determined by world capital market conditions. This implies that a fiscal expansion is less likely to crowd out investment via interest rate increases, since increased investment can be financed by external borrowing without putting upward pressure on domestic interest rates. A fiscal expansion is especially likely to be effective if the exchange rate is held fixed and accelerator effects are strong. On the other hand, if the exchange rate is flexible and capital is highly mobile, a fiscal expansion can "crowd-out" net exports instead of domestic investment via exchange rate appreciation.[2] International trade considerations can also affect the degree to which conflicting-claims inflation is a serious problem, a point Glyn seems to accept when he notes that, "The leaking of demand abroad during an expansion represents an easing of distributional struggles." Indeed, one of the reasons that is generally cited for the low inflation in the United States in the late 1990s, in spite of unemployment rates at their lowest levels since the 1960s, is the fact that the huge U.S. trade deficit subjects U.S. workers and firms to a high degree of import competition, which in turn prevents them from obtaining large wage and price increases. With regard to financial market reactions, Glyn rightly observes that "the international freedom of movement for financial capital adds powerfully to the domestic exit options already available." Even the domestic political power of wealthy interests can be greatly strengthened if they can form alliances with their international counterparts; similarly, conservative ideology about economic policy is more potent when shared among international elites.

While Glyn acknowledges such interactions between internal and external constraints, my own view is that these interactions are so important today as to make it difficult to distinguish what is internal and what is external. This in turn makes the whole exercise of deciding whether internal or external constraints are more binding somewhat artificial. While I agree that globalization is sometimes blamed too much for problems that may be domestic in origin, nevertheless, if those problems are connected to a country's international position, then it is not realistic to think that the domestic problems can easily be overcome in the absence of action on the international front.

2   Glyn suggests that "under conditions of free capital mobility an expansionary program is liable to lead to a much larger fall in the exchange rate [i.e., depreciation]." The Mundell-Fleming theorem implies just the opposite: that with free capital mobility an expansionary fiscal policy induces a rise in the exchange rate (appreciation), at least in the short run, and this seems to have occurred in some cases – especially the U.S. in the early 1980s and Mexico in the early 1990s. However, the Mundell-Fleming result depends heavily on the monetary authority not accommodating the fiscal expansion, as well as on other assumptions such as the absence of exchange risk. More analysis is clearly needed of the exchange rate impact of fiscal expansion.

In fact, Glyn's own arguments concerning the European Monetary Union (EMU) support the notion that the domestic and the international have become deeply intertwined. As Glyn notes, the "internal" constraints in the various European countries are "now being transferred in part to the European level." For countries participating in the EMU, there will be a definite loss of domestic policy autonomy. The EMU as a whole, of course, will have much more potential room for maneuver, as does a large country like the United States today. But the domestic constraints in, say, Germany or France are about to become international ones at least at the European level, requiring a consensus among diverse national interests to change the current conservative bias in European monetary and fiscal policies.

Glyn's response to these concerns seems to be that the degree of internationalization of most economies is still limited, as measured by standard indicators such as exports or imports as shares of national income, or foreign direct investment as a share of domestic investment. For purposes of ascertaining the importance of international constraints, however, such data on average shares of international trade or foreign investment may be misleading. What is more important is what is happening at the margin: how much do goods production, direct investment, and portfolio capital move around the world in response to changes in policies and conditions in individual countries? There can be a considerable degree of international mobility of goods and capital in this sense, even if average shares of merchandise trade and capital flows look small – especially in large countries or regions like the U.S. and the European Union.

In spite of these reservations, I think it is important not to go to the other extreme and conclude that more progressive domestic macro policies are hopelessly blocked by international system constraints. For one thing, one must take country size into account. Either the United States or the European Union as a whole has a greater ability to adopt policies that challenge orthodox views than individual European nations or smaller nations elsewhere in the world. Moreover, politics clearly start at home, and therefore demands for more egalitarian policies (including monetary, social, and structural policies as well as fiscal policies) must originate at the domestic level in a number of countries in order to create pressures for international system reforms (e.g., a Tobin tax to reduce the volatility of short-term capital, or a "new Bretton Woods" agreement to stabilize exchange rates).

It would certainly be paralyzing for progressives to think that they cannot advocate domestic policy changes without waiting for international system reforms to come first. If anything, the political logic suggests the reverse: that the battle over the direction of economic policy must start at home, and that action to address international constraints will have to grow naturally out of domestic demands as the limits of internal policy changes are reached and international constraints become more binding. In the end, I think external constraints will have to be addressed in order to successfully overcome internal constraints, but I agree with Glyn that the place to begin is by pushing on the latter and seeing where that leads.

18

The effects of globalization
on policy formation in South Africa

Laurence Harris and Jonathan Michie

The political transformation of South Africa, a long and continuing process marked by its turning point, the democratic elections of April 1994, has been accompanied by expectations of economic transformation. Under the political regime of apartheid, minority control had generated an economic system that was unsustainable: the extreme inequality of income and wealth, principally along ethnic lines, could not be compatible with social stability; economic growth had been negative for a decade, reflecting the structural weakness of the existing economy; and South Africa's relationship to world markets was fragmented by both protection and sanctions, especially since access to world financial markets was interrupted in 1985. With political transformation, structural economic change was an imperative in all three respects. "Nation building" requires old inequalities to be addressed and a reversal of declining average gross domestic product, while the restoration of normal international relations meant South Africa had to achieve a new role in the world economy, a global system that is itself rapidly changing.

Irrespective of policy initiatives, South Africa's economy would change to a greater or lesser degree in response to shocks, but the question is whether South Africa's new government could construct an economic strategy that delivers structural change appropriate to the new political environment at home and abroad. Since 1994 the government has maintained a policy regime similar to the old one. It has implemented neither a radically "liberal" strategy, comprising rapid deregulation and privatization of the large state sector it inherited and complete liberalization of foreign exchange markets, nor a radically "populist" policy of expanded public expenditure to address housing shortages, education inequalities, and unemployment.

While the political transformation enfranchised constituencies for which "development" is top of the agenda, the government has not attempted to reconstruct the state as a developmental state.[1] Unlike, say, South Korea, Taiwan, and Malaysia in

---

1   The roles of various developmental states are discussed in Chang and Rowthorn, eds., *The Role of the State in Economic Change*, Oxford: Clarendon Press, 1995.

The authors are grateful for comments received from the participants at the 1995 and 1996 conferences of the Economic Policy Institute in Washington D.C., and in particular from Jerry Epstein, Stanley Fischer, and Bob Pollin.

previous decades, or even the Afrikaner government elected in 1948, the African National Congress (ANC)-led government did not construct a development plan with the state promoting sectoral targets in a *dirigiste* manner.

The Reconstruction and Development Programme (RDP), constructed as the basis for the ANC's election platform in 1994, at first appeared to be the "development plan," but it could not fulfill that role partly because it was principally oriented toward problems of redistribution and social welfare policy, largely neglecting industrial strategy and macroeconomic policy.

The RDP appeared to be politically stillborn, especially when the ministry responsible for it was wound up, although it was frequently invoked by all parties.[2] But the Medium Term Budget Framework, published in December 1997, and the March 1998 budget make clear that the RDP is regarded as one of the two cornerstones of government policy. The other is the macroeconomic policy framework known as GEAR (Growth, Employment, and Redistribution), first promulgated in June 1996. Unlike the RDP, which is universally and uncritically accepted as the basis both for achieving equity and carrying out expenditure in areas with high external benefits (such as education), GEAR has been a highly controversial policy; its critics regard it as both undermining the RDP because of its emphasis on reduction of the budget deficit, and as being dictated by oversensitivity to international financial markets. RDP and GEAR, now the two foundations of South Africa's policy for regeneration, are complemented by a range of specific policies, such as restructured labor market laws and export-oriented industrial strategy.

General issues

The main question discussed in this chapter is whether South Africa could put together an economic development strategy, a strategy for structural change, and implement it. Or does globalization, which has affected all economies, mean that the way South Africa's economy changes, for better or worse, is necessarily beyond the influence of the government? As South Africa is reintegrated into the world economy, do global markets so constrain the country's options that government effectively loses its sovereignty over policy? One way to view that question is to ask whether a transformed, competitive manufacturing sector can be developed as the engine of growth and trade.

A similar question focuses on the short-term reactions of international markets. To take an extreme, would the reactions of, say, the foreign exchange market prevent government from adopting a growth strategy based on high levels of public expenditure on education? Or would they constrain the ability of the government to adopt an expansionary demand management policy to counter cyclical unemployment? Or would a monetary policy dictated by domestic stabilization goals generate net capital inflows that would push the exchange rate higher than the government desires?

---

2   With the abolition of the RDP ministry, the separate ministries, individually and jointly, have responsibility for implementing the program.

Any such questions about the effect of globalization on national policy are invariably motivated by an assumption about the desirability of market outcomes. The traditional "social democratic" assumption is that social welfare is increased if a government intervenes in key markets to determine prices and quantities different from those produced by private transactions alone; the traditional "free market" assumption is the converse. Today, few governments could be identified clearly at one end of the spectrum or the other; virtually all governments attempt some market interventions, even if espousing a free market ideology, while those claiming that there are benefits to intervention have largely withdrawn from long-term attempts to intervene directly in such key areas as foreign exchange and capital markets.

Whatever assumptions are made about the desirability of market-determined prices and quantities, other considerations may underlie criticisms of market power if it restricts or overrides government action, for the disequilibrium dynamics of market responses to shocks may be undesirable for several reasons. It may be argued that high volatility around equilibrium values is itself undesirable if volatility has a negative influence on foreign trade or physical investment. Alternatively, in moving toward equilibrium, markets may overshoot, as in the classic example of exchange rate overshooting due to differential adjustment speeds in domestic markets or to nonrational expectations. Similarly, discontinuities in market adjustments – as when a long-overvalued exchange rate is suddenly adjusted downward in one large step, i.e., a currency crash – may be seen as undesirable.

Such concerns are not necessarily supported by analysis or evidence. Studies on the relationship between exchange rate volatility and exports, for example, do not strongly demonstrate a significant negative effect. In the South African context, the crash of the rand in February and April 1996, amounting to a devaluation of 18 percent in a short period and followed by continuing depreciation over the following 12 months, fueled fears that government policy was subordinated to capricious movements of global funds. Those fears were misplaced for two reasons. First, the exchange rate adjustment, although sharp, could be justified in terms of a necessary adjustment of relative costs; the ultimate reason for the sharpness of the fall instead of a gradual adjustment was that the South African Reserve Bank had for too long maintained an overvalued exchange rate by intervening in the market, especially through costly forward purchases of rands. Second, there is some evidence that the spot sales of the rand that provoked its sharp fall were made by local commercial and industrial companies rather than global funds with no more connection to South Africa than to other emerging markets. A similar flight of local funds rather than global funds was responsible for the crash of the Mexican peso and Mexican securities at the end of 1994.

Finally, in order to locate the issue facing South Africa – how to formulate policies for growth and redistribution within a changing world economy – let us consider the meaning of globalization, generally used as a shorthand to describe the idea that modern changes in the world economy mark a distinct, new stage in its development.

The concept refers to the existence of global forces in particular spheres, especially finance and trade. More than simply the opening of a country to capital flows or foreign exchange convertibility, or the growth of its international trade owing to liberalization, globalization means that the external markets that countries engage in through such openness are multilateral and dominated by global forces on which individual countries' transactions have no impact; countries typically match the assumptions of the "small open economy" model. In some writings the mark of globalization is the resulting world division of labor in production as corporations organize their subprocesses across borders and on the basis of worldwide sourcing. For others, the distinguishing feature is the large volume of highly mobile international funds, such as those controlled by "arbitrage funds" or "hedge funds" in the early 1990s.

Globalization in those terms does not correspond to the reality of today's markets. Trade is concentrated in blocs instead of being fully global; trade patterns are clustered around a European bloc, a North American bloc, and an East Asian bloc. In East Asia, for example, half of the region's countries' total trade is with each other rather than North America or Europe. Its largest economy, Japan, sells 40 percent of its exports within the region and buys almost the same proportion of its imports from it; its trade with the rest of East Asia is almost as great as its trade with the U.S. and European Union combined.[3] Financial markets do not establish worldwide price equivalence as full globalization would imply; exchange rates do not satisfy purchasing power parity; and money markets do not produce interest rates satisfying covered and uncovered interest parity rules with respect to world rates. And, despite the growth of international portfolios, securities markets do not systematically set prices in relation to a world price of risk; the portfolio choices of the largest international investor countries (the U.S. and some European countries) demonstrate a well-documented "home country bias." Thus, the international economy today is, at most, characterized by a fractured globalization.

Key developmental issues for South Africa

Although South African debates over development have evolved, a *leitmotif* remains the central position all protagonists give to addressing the problems created by the high level of inequality. The aim may be expressed as a reduction of inequality or as a reduction of poverty – sometimes obscuring the difference – and different meanings are attached to each of those goals. But improving the position of the poor, who are seen as suffering from apartheid's legacy, is given as the justification for policy proposals from all quarters. The government's 1996 macroeconomic strategy document makes that objective the dominant one (together with related objectives of job creation and social provision) as it sets out its long-run vision:

As South Africa moves toward the next century we seek:

---

3   For an enumeration of the developing formal regional trading bloc arrangements in those areas and in Latin America, see de la Torre and Kelly, *Regional Trade Arrangements*, IMF Occasional Paper No. 93, Washington D.C.: IMF, March 1992.

(1) a competitive fast-growing economy which creates sufficient jobs for all workseekers;

(2) a redistribution of income and opportunities in favor of the poor;

(3) a society in which sound health, education, and other services are available to all; and

(4) an environment in which homes are secure and places of work productive.[4]

In this section we consider the relationship between policies to reduce inequality or poverty and South Africa's position within today's "fractured globalization." If global markets were to exercise an influence that forces governments to adopt policies contrary to "desirable national goals," as critics of globalization believe, the goal of reducing inequality or poverty would not itself be contentious. But serious disagreements exist in South Africa over the means to achieve such a goal (as well as the definition of the goal), and global market reactions may well differ according to which policy is adopted, leading to a re-evaluation of policy in the light of them. Indeed, the government's presentation of its new statement of economic strategy in June 1996 as "nonnegotiable" was prompted by the belief that there was a need to restore confidence on international markets following the large depreciation of the rand, and that such a "tough" stance by the ANC government, directed against its alliance partners of the Congress of South African Trade Unions (COSATU) and the South African Communist Party (SACP) would achieve this task.[5]

The reduction of inequality or poverty is predicated upon the creation of new jobs. There is no doubt that unemployment in South Africa is high and has an important effect on inequality and poverty, although the correlation between unemployment and poverty is not perfect. A widely quoted estimate for the mid-1990s puts unemployment at over 40 percent, but it is important to note that such estimates are unreliable and probably exaggerate the figure. A report by the International Labor Organization (ILO) suggests that such estimates mistakenly count self-employed and informal sector employees as unemployed and notes that other estimates, based on household surveys for 1993 and 1994, put unemployment at around 30 percent, while others place it even lower.[6]

In any case, these levels of unemployment have been occurring in a context of a precarious macroeconomic stability; inflation has been stable, GDP volatility has been low (and some positive per capita growth has been experienced), and external debt is sustainable. But that stability has been sustained by restrictive monetary and fiscal policy. In 1996, the fiscal deficit, at 5 percent of GDP and on a reducing trend, was moderate in historical and comparative terms; inflation was in single digits

4   Republic of South Africa, Ministry of Finance, *Growth, Employment, and Redistribution: A Macroeconomic Strategy,* June 14, 1996, p. 1.

5   *Financial Times,* June 15, 1996, p. 4. The publication of the growth strategy was followed by a confidence-boosting tour to Washington, New York, and other financial centers. Although the strategy document was well received officially, the depreciation of the rand continued initially.

6   International Labor Organization, *The South African Challenge: Restructuring the Labour Market,* Geneva: ILO Country Review, 1996, Chapter 4.

and, excluding the impetus from exchange rate depreciation, appeared to be stable; and the current account deficit was less than 3 percent of GDP. Gross private savings were 20 percent of GDP (but at a low level net of depreciation), while only 3 percent of GDP was consumed by public sector dissaving. But job creation at under 100,000 per annum was below the growth of the labor force; real interest rates were high, with short-term rates at 7 percent in real terms; and the combination of conservative fiscal policy and high interest rates was seen as necessary to stabilize capital flows, tempering the outflow of capital that followed the portfolio inflows of 1994 and 1995 (which had exerted upward pressure on the real exchange rate at that time).

Accepting that there is a link between unemployment and poverty, debate in South Africa now lies between two alternative, but not mutually exclusive, views. The first, contained in a more or less Keynesian set of policy papers, has argued that the principal policies for job creation should be public investment in infrastructure, especially in the housing stock and social sector assets; and in that context it is usually envisaged that labor-intensive investment projects are available for the public sector to take up.[7] The institutional background to that view is that the new South Africa has inherited a large state sector from the apartheid era – implying that, in addition to public investment, public purchasing power could shape industrial development. The economic rationale rests on the tentative evidence of a "crowding-in" effect from public investment, although the degree of any such crowding-in could also be increased through policy intervention to assist new business startups and the like.

The alternative pole of debate is the view that the key to job creation is policies to increase labor market flexibility, to be accompanied by a reduction in fiscal deficits and government dissaving. That view has been strongly advanced by the South African Foundation representing, in particular, South Africa's largest corporations.[8] Its view is based on the idea that the labor market can and should be dichotomized into a first tier, formal sector market and a second tier market of informal and small employers that should be relatively free of regulations protecting employee and union rights.

The strategy envisaged in the government's 1996 growth scenario is a combination of both approaches. It envisages regulated flexibility for the labor market, under which regulations, nationally agreed rates, and minimum wage laws would be

7   Macro-Economic Research Group (MERG), *Making Democracy Work: A Framework for Macroeconomic Policy in South Africa*, Cape Town: Oxford University Press, 1993. We say "more or less" Keynesian in that, although this document appreciated the relative importance of a sustained development of demand as being key to achieving an expansion of output and employment – rather than believing that relative factor prices alone drive such outcomes as in a non-Keynesian neo-classical world – MERG also stressed the need for any such development of demand to be matched by an expansion of the supply side of the economy. MERG (1993) is therefore a "supply side" document in the sense that it took the supply side to be important – rather than in the usual (mis)use of the term, which is to refer to deregulatory policies that are supply side in the sense of disregarding the demand side (and also therefore in that they act primarily on the supply side, even if this is with destructive results, such as when increased labor turnover inhibits firms' investment in training).

8   South Africa Foundation, *Growth for All: An Economic Strategy for South Africa*, Johannesburg, 1996.

applied differentially across sectors. And the strategy envisages increased public (and private) sector investment.[9]

The case for pursuing a public-sector-led expansionary approach along the lines set out by the Macro-Economic Research Group (MERG) report has been made recently by Michie and Padayachee (1997), where the alternatives put forward by the South African Foundation and the government's June 1996 *Growth, Employment and Redistribution: A Macroeconomic Strategy* document are also critiqued.[10] Our aim here is to consider the more specific issue of how such policies to reduce inequality or poverty relate to South Africa's position in the world economy. Global markets for labor and goods increase the pressure on countries to keep labor costs competitive, and such a notion underlies the "labor market flexibility" strategy. But globalization does not dictate only one direction for labor rewards. If South Africa chooses a development path based on the production of tradable commodities with low skill content and low rates of productivity growth, labor costs can be reduced only by reductions in real wages. But if growth were based on high-value-added, high-productivity tradable products, competitive labor costs could be achieved with high real wages; indeed, efficiency wage considerations of the relation between wage rates and labor costs may warrant higher wage rates than those that clear labor markets.[11]

International, globalized financial markets are not concerned with the details of job creation policies and are unlikely to react more favorably to one type than another. It is not clear which fundamentals do drive portfolio decisions on the merits of one currency or market rather than another, but it would appear that relatively broad indicators, such as current account deficits or government deficits in relation to a sustainable or some threshold level act as signals. If so, then market confidence is unlikely to be affected by the choice of a minimum wage regime or the framework of collective bargaining.

Would it be affected by a job creation policy based on public investment expenditure? Such a program could have a direct impact on markets through its financing,

---

9 Republic of South Africa, Ministry of Finance, *Growth, Employment and Redistribution: A Macroeconomic Strategy*, June 14, 1996.

10 See Michie and Padayachee, "South Africa's Transition: The Policy Agenda," and "Assessment and Conclusions", Chapters 1 and 11, respectively of Michie and Padayachee, eds., *The Political Economy of South Africa's Transition: Policy Perspectives in the Late 1990s*, London: Dryden Press, 1997.

11 See Michie, "Developing the Institutional Framework: Employment and Labour Market Policies" Chapter 8 of Michie and Padayachee, eds., *The Political Economy of South Africa's Transition: Policy Perspectives in the Late 1990s*, London: Dryden Press, 1997, where the South Africa Foundation policies for labor market deregulation are critiqued, and it is argued that a MERG-type policy approach would be in no way in conflict with an export promotion approach. On the contrary, as far as international competitiveness goes, there is no limit to the potential reduction in unit labor costs achievable via increased productivity – in marked contrast to the limited gains to be had from wage cutting – and the upgrading and diversification of the economy that is required in any case for the development of a successful manufacturing sector would also create the conditions for increased world market shares in these new trade areas. By creating the conditions for sustainable export growth, such a policy approach would reduce the global constraints that, it is said by its opponents, should rule it out as a policy option.

and it could have additional effects on market confidence more broadly, but that does not imply the markets act as a constraint on government action. If such expenditure is financed by taxation, or through a deficit that, funded by bond sales, led to increased real interest rates, confidence on the foreign exchange markets could be sustained. If it were funded by money creation, the nominal exchange rate would be pushed lower, perhaps to a level inconsistent with the government's target, but even in such circumstances there is not a one-for-one relationship; the lower currency level may be a price worth paying. The key would be the extent to which such a program led to increased economic growth and job creation, including successful crowding-in of private activity with new firm formation and increased investment, possibly leading to import substitution as a by-product of the immediate goal of meeting new domestic demands (for electrical goods, say, in areas, such as newly electrified squatter camps). And these broader considerations of the effectiveness or otherwise of policies to reconstruct and develop the economy will also be central to "market confidence" (a term that covers a number of phenomena, not least due to the array of relevant markets). The key to increased investor confidence (whether domestic or inward) will be expectations of future consumer demand, rather than necessarily the fear of fiscal deficits, so that even were such a policy to risk harming certain forms of market confidence, such as that referred to above as requiring increased interest rates by way of compensation, it may at the same time be increasing other forms of market confidence, namely the confidence as to whether there are profits to be had in the South African consumer goods markets over the period of years in which inward investors would be seeking markets and making their calculations.

External and internal constraints

In the years leading up to the democratization of South Africa, an intense and extensive public debate occurred over the country's future economic and social direction; at its heart was the possibility of achieving redistribution of resources, expansion of social expenditure, and reconstruction of the country's production and trade. In that debate the constraints on economic policies and outcomes were given considerable prominence, and they were usually conceived as the constraints represented by national-income-accounting identities. Since those concern ex post quantities, there remains room for considering to what extent underlying, ex ante, behavioral relations can be altered, and that focuses attention on constraints in a different way.[12] It highlights the role of supply constraints, rather than the aggregate demand categories of national income accounting, and it opens the question of the extent to which policies can modify output conditions. The interplay of demand and supply conditions can be examined as the intersection of external and internal constraints.

12 See Harris, "Economic Objectives and Macroeconomic Constraints," Chapter 5 in Michie and Padayachee, eds., *The Political Economy of South Africa's Transition: Policy Perspectives in the Late 1990s*, Dryden Press, 1997.

Table 1 *Planned budget of RDP allocations
(before abolition of RDP Ministry)*

RDP allocations (R million)	1994/95	1995/96	1996/97
Urban infrastructure and development	841	1,722	1,999
Rural infrastructure and development	116	898	1,387
Health services	971	1,887	1,760
Education	100	511	1,000
Protection services	12	284	390
Other	783	285	964
Total allocation	2,823	5,587	7,500
Rollover of unspent allocations	1,947	4,245	4,643

Source: Ministry of Finance, 1996, Appendix 4.

The idea that globalization restricts the ability of a government to choose desirable policies implies an external constraint. At its most extreme, it is based on the notion that governments would have a wide range of policy options from which they could choose a desirable and feasible development path were it not for globalization that imposes an external constraint limiting their choices and preventing the achievement of nationally desirable outcomes. Stating the idea in that extreme form demonstrates its weakness, for it raises one type of constraint on policy above all others. A more useful way to consider the relationship between globalization and policy is to consider external factors as one element in a vector of constraints policy makers face.

In South African debates, it has been recognized that internal supply constraints of many types are severe and are overlooked in policy analyses based on standard, demand-driven macroeconomic models. One internal constraint facing any Keynesian-type public investment program is administrative and institutional capacity; for public expenditure to raise production of housing it is necessary to have public administrative capacity and a private building industry organized in firms with efficient contracting and accounting systems. The fact that the sums budgeted for expenditure under the RDP have had little impact on the provision of low-income housing, domestic water supplies, and other stated targets was largely attributable to the lack of such institutional structures. (The sums budgeted and the annual rollover of unspent funds are shown in Table 1.) Another type of internal constraint is the inelasticity of domestic supply, at least in the short run. The degree to which budgeted public investment expenditure translates into domestic production of houses, schools, or infrastructure depends on the existence of excess capacity in construction and in intermediate industries and, in the long run, on the shape of long-run cost functions. Estimates of excess capacity across South African industry have varied,[13] but there is no doubt that in important sectors excess capacity is low.

13 See, for example, Macro-Economic Research Group (MERG), *Making Democracy Work: A Framework for Macroeconomic Policy in South Africa*, Cape Town: Oxford University Press, 1993; and Ministry of Finance *Normative Economic Model*, 1993.

Domestic supply constraints need not prevent expenditure plans from being realized if the demand can be met from imports. Indeed, an enduring feature of South Africa is the high income elasticity of imports of manufactures and, especially, capital goods, reflecting the continued importance of production and export of minerals, processed minerals, and energy instead of a balanced manufacturing sector.[14] At that point the interaction between domestic and external constraints becomes evident, for if a supply response to an expansion of public investment requires increased imports, its viability depends on the impact it has on the current account of the balance of payments and the ability of international financial markets to finance whatever increase in deficits results. The same argument applies to a Keynesian-inspired policy of more general demand expansion; on best estimates, if a demand-expanding fiscal policy alone increased growth rates above 3 percent per annum, a rising current account deficit would make the growth rate unsustainable.

A third type of internal constraint emanates from the political economy of domestic interests. The trade union movement (COSATU), small business representatives, large internationally oriented business groups, and other constituencies have different perspectives on appropriate types of development strategy and are able to pursue perceived sectional interests with varying degrees of strength. Development strategies pursued elsewhere require a settlement of those competing internal interests before they can be adopted in South Africa, and, if the country's polity does not permit a way forward, the adoption of policies is constrained. An extensive privatization program, for example, had long been an aim of the pre-1994 government, and it has had support within the ANC government, but its implementation has been slow because of the opposition of trade unionists and their supporters in the ANC. On the other hand, constituencies seeking protection or managed trade, at least as a temporary measure in a period of transition, have been weak compared to the pressures the large, international corporations have exerted in favor of rapid reduction of tariffs and other protective measures. (The reduction of tariffs between 1994 and 1995 – reductions offered as part of the General Agreement on Tariffs and Trade – is shown for individual sectors in Table 2.)

The existence of those various internal constraints has two important implications. One is that constraints are not immutable but can be changed by South Africa's own policies. Supply constraints within the country, for example, can in principle be alleviated by sectoral development policies, including changed incentive structures and integrated private and public investment plans. Indeed, one of the key aims of a public-investment-led strategy of development would be not just to create new goods, services, and infrastructure that would not have been forthcoming from the private sector left to itself, but also to create the conditions, by tackling supply constraints, overcoming production bottlenecks, and upgrading the productive infrastructure generally, by which the private sector will increase its level of activity, investment, output, and employment.

The second is that, in judging whether globalization has an impact, the question

14 Fine and Rustomjee, *South Africa's Political Economy: From Minerals-Energy Complex to Industrialisation?* London: Hurst, 1997.

Table 2 *Changes in tariffs, output, and employment, 1994–95 (percent change)*

	Employment	Output	Exports	Imports	Tariff
Food	-1.5	0.0	25.8	26.1	15.4
Beverages	-5.8	5.7	-11.8	22.2	64.3
Leather products	3.6	7.0	15.0	10.2	-78.7
Wood products	-5.1	4.8	-16.2	18.2	-20.0
Paper products	4.8	10.9	71.0	35.7	-40.0
Printing and publishing	2.1	-3.9	12.1	12.5	-81.8
Glass products	-3.9	6.6	-14.5	26.8	-52.9
Other nonmetallic mineral products	-7.1	9.1	29.0	37.8	-50.0
Iron and basic steel	0.8	14.0	22.9	28.6	-72.7
Nonferrous metal	-3.4	17.9	119.3	122.9	-16.7
Metal products	-2.2	5.4	55.1	29.8	-56.3
Machinery	13.1	12.5	66.8	22.5	-77.8
Electrical machinery	-3.0	23.4	58.7	32.3	-58.8
Motor vehicles	9.4	15.8	19.1	41.0	-62.5
Other transport equipment	-4.9	-14.2	—	—	0.0
Other industries	-3.5	-11.7	-6.7	-18.6	-12.5
Tobacco	-6.7	-2.3	69.8	-8.1	110.0
Textiles	-7.6	12.0	16.5	15.8	-7.9
Clothing	9.9	14.1	18.0	-8.7	-4.0
Footwear	7.6	5.7	2.6	40.6	20.0
Furniture	6.3	8.5	39.2	37.6	-40.0
Chemical products	-1.4	6.4	43.7	28.5	-36.4
Rubber products	7.6	8.6	58.3	31.3	-71.0
Plastic products	14.6	10.2	49.7	28.4	-81.0
Total manufacturing	1.1	7.4	33.7	27.5	-5.6

Source: Ministry of Finance, 1996, Appendix 4.

should not be formulated as a simple question concerning external constraints: it should not be based on the notion that governments would have a wide range of policy options were it not for globalization that imposes an external constraint preventing the achievement of nationally desirable outcomes. The choice the government makes autonomously, within all the complex circumstances, may well be the same as the one which, say, globalized financial markets consider desirable; the high real interest rates and fiscal conservatism of the recent past are likely to have been chosen by the South African government even if the country were less integrated into globalized financial markets.

Nevertheless, even if globalization cannot be considered in terms of a simple external constraint, international flows will inevitably have a major influence on the strength and direction of South Africa's development. That is well illustrated by the government's 1996 growth scenario (Table 3). Positive growth in GDP was projected, averaging over 4 percent (implying positive growth per capita) and reaching 6 percent by 2000. Similarly, job creation was projected to rise to nearly 300,000 per annum over the four years. But those targets are based on the assumption that

Table 3 *South African government's growth scenario (integrated scenario projections: 1996–2000)*

Model characteristics	1996	1997	1998	1999	2000	Average
Fiscal deficit (% of GDP) (fiscal year)	5.1	4.0	3.5	3.0	3.0	3.7
Real government consumption (% of GDP)	19.9	19.5	19.0	18.5	18.1	19.0
Average tariff (% of imports)	10.0	8.0	7.0	7.0	6.0	7.6
Average real wage growth, private sector	-0.5	1.0	1.0	1.0	1.0	0.8
Average real wage growth, govt. sector	4.4	0.7	0.4	0.8	0.4	1.3
Real effective exchange rate (% change)	-8.5	-0.3	0.0	0.0	0.0	-1.8
Real bank rate	7.0	5.0	4.0	3.0	3.0	4.4
Real government investment growth	3.4	2.7	5.4	7.5	16.7	7.1
Real parastatal investment growth	3.0	5.0	10.0	10.0	10.0	7.6
Real private sector investment growth	9.3	9.1	9.3	13.9	17.0	11.7
Real nongold export growth	9.1	8.0	7.0	7.8	10.2	8.4
Additional foreign direct inv. (US$m)	155	365	504	716	804	509

Results	1996	1997	1998	1999	2000	Average
GDP growth	3.5	2.9	3.8	4.9	6.1	4.2
Inflation (CPI)	8.0	9.7	8.1	7.7	7.6	8.2
Employment growth (nonagricultural formal)	1.3	3.0	2.7	3.5	4.3	2.9
New jobs per year (000s)	126	252	246	320	409	270
Current account deficit (% of GDP)	2.2	2.0	2.2	2.5	3.1	2.4
Real export growth, manufacturing	10.3	12.2	8.3	10.5	12.8	10.8
Gross private savings (% of GDP)	20.5	21.0	21.2	21.5	21.9	21.2
Government dissavings (% of GDP)	3.1	2.3	1.7	0.7	0.6	1.9

Source: Ministry of Finance, 1996, Appendix 4.

foreign direct investment will rise eightfold compared to the actual levels of 1995–96. If foreign direct investment does not expand – either because its world total fails to rise or because South Africa fails to attract a larger share of the total – the projected growth will not materialize unless higher-than-projected domestic investment compensates. Since, on the basis of surprisingly optimistic assumptions, private domestic investment is itself projected to be high, the dependence of the growth strategy on foreign direct investment is evident.

Experience and prospects

The new South Africa has not achieved an "economic miracle" like those achieved in Europe in the 1950s and 1960s or, more pertinently, like those experienced in East and Southeast Asia until the late 1990s. The most salient indicators of severe economic problems are the behavior of unemployment or, from the point of view of regeneration, the rate of creation of new jobs. The model underlying GEAR assumed formal employment outside agriculture would grow at a rate between 1.3 and 4.0 percent per annum, creating enough new jobs to absorb at least the new entrants to the labor market – which demographic estimates put at 450,000 per year – in contrast to the decline that occurred at an annual average rate of 1 percent between 1989 and 1996. In fact, employment in those sectors fell even more rapidly in 1997. The annualized rates of decline were 3.3 percent in the first quarter, 2.4 percent in the second, and 2.2 percent in the third, and there is no evidence that employment in agriculture and the informal sector is growing by enough to compensate. In other words, since GEAR was initiated, South Africa has experienced worse employment declines than before, and they contrast markedly with the positive job growth projected under GEAR.

How does that experience relate to South Africa's location in the open international economy characterized by fractured globalization? To consider the impact of international markets on macro policy, three powerful instruments or variables demand attention; the fiscal deficit, interest rates, and exchange rates.

The government inherited a high fiscal deficit and made its reduction a central objective that became formalized in GEAR as a reduction from 5.1 percent of GDP in 1996 to 3 percent in 2000. That aim has been rigorously followed, achieving a deficit ratio of 4 percent in 1997–98 and budgeting for a ratio of 3.5 percent in 1998–99. Interest rates have been maintained at high real levels. The central bank discount rate was reduced from 17 percent to 16 percent in October 1997, implying a high average real rate of 8.3 percent for that year. And nominal interest rates have remained high while inflation has fallen; on March 9, 1998 the treasury bill rate was 13.5 percent, while by January 1988 the consumer price inflation rate had fallen to 5.6 percent. The nominal exchange rate fell sharply in 1996 and had not recovered by the end of 1997. The impact on the real economy depends on movements in the real effective exchange rate; despite the nominal depreciation of 9.4 percent from March 1996 to March 1997, there was a 4.6 percent appreciation of the real effective rate from April 1996 to April 1997.

The configuration of fiscal and monetary policy reflected in the fiscal deficit, interest rates, and exchange rates reflects both the impact of international markets and the attention paid to them. But it would be incorrect to interpret them as a case of international markets acting as a constraint that prevents South Africa from adopting policies that it would otherwise choose.

A reduction in fiscal deficits has been a government objective because, apart from its impact on external finance, the government has been concerned that high deficits lead to macroeconomic instability, with consequent depressing effects on private investment plans, and place upward pressure on the government's interest burden. The latter would have unfavorable effects on equity, for the taxes to pay interest may lead to redistribution from low income tax payers to high income interest recipients, or, if taxes were not raised, the interest burden could be at the cost of other budget items, thereby squeezing social expenditure. Looked at from the point of view of growth strategy, which requires a rise in South Africa's net saving rate, the low personal savings rate in South Africa, which has continued a 10-year decline, and low corporate savings net of depreciation have constrained the government to reduce the public sector's dissaving. And the reduction in deficits has been achieved while following Keynesian policies on the expansion of public sector investment: real investment by public authorities was raised to an average growth rate of 15 percent in 1996 and 4 percent in 1997, while private domestic real investment grew by only 6.1 percent and 3.1 percent in those years.

Similarly, high real interest rates have been maintained partly to obtain external stability, and partly to control inflation in order to achieve a stable environment conducive to domestic investment. The policy has succeeded in doing more than stabilize inflation in the face of the shocks caused by transition and foreign exchange volatility: it has substantially reduced inflation. Some judge that the decline has been achieved at too high a cost, because high real interest rates have discouraged domestic investment and prevented expansion; in other words, one view is that as a result of external considerations monetary policy has been too tight. Against that, it should be noted that corporate retained earnings have been high throughout recent years of monetary restriction and have not acted as a constraint on investment.

Large changes in the nominal exchange rate have reflected both foreign and domestic portfolio switches reflecting changing expectations about South Africa's prospects. While the decline in nominal effective rates since GEAR produces adjustment costs for different sectors, it could be expected to provide an export-led growth stimulus. In fact, the real effective exchange rate has not matched that depreciation since the announcement of GEAR, thereby giving an additional rationale for the government's objective of reducing inflation.

Conclusion

It is undoubtedly the case that South Africa's economic policy options are circumscribed by the country's current and prospective positions in the international economy. But it is not valid to conclude that globalization is *the* constraint or even a constraint in any simple and direct manner. One reason is that, if we try to pin down the idea that the world economy is globalized in a meaningful way, it becomes clear that, at best, there is a fractured globalization. To the extent that such fracturing involves regional blocs, with which each country has specific trade and finance patterns, countries face real choices concerning the pattern of trade and development they seek.

The idea that globalization acts as a constraint can be put to the test by considering the effects of policies to reduce inequality or poverty (a theme of this volume). In the South African context there is no reason to believe that the main types of policy aiming at that objective would be prevented by South Africa's place in global markets. The need to compete internationally may cause some types of poverty-reducing programs to have higher priority than others, but that does not necessarily imply a reduced effect.

International markets and global forces should, instead, be seen as one among many of the considerations policy makers have to take into account. The presence of internal "constraints" is equally important, and the interaction between the two is one axis of the political economy of policy. In fact, policies that are pursued by domestic constituencies may be given a spurious justification on the unquantifiable grounds that international confidence would suffer from alternative policies; such arguments may have led the South African government to eschew significant land redistribution measures, although without such a campaign there is little reason to believe that international markets have an inherent abhorrence of land redistribution.

In other words, South Africans may make their own history, but – given the complexity of the world both internationally and at home – not in circumstances of their own choosing.

Comment by Keith Griffin on "The effects of globalization on policy formation in South Africa"

The South African economy prior to 1994 combined the characteristics of a colonial economy with some of the features of a Soviet bloc country. Sanctions imposed a form of autarky on the economy. Much of industry was heavily protected and insulated from global competition. The black population was dispossessed, deprived of its land and excluded from high-wage employment and opportunities to accumulate capital. There were rigorous controls over labor mobility and job allocation. At the end of apartheid, South Africa had a highly deformed economy and faced a daunting task of destroying internal colonialism while reintegrating the country into the global economy.

Compare South Africa with Tunisia, a former French colony at the opposite end of the African continent. Both have a per capita income of about $5,000 (in purchasing power parity terms). Yet male life expectancy in Tunisia is 68 years compared to only 61 years in South Africa. The infant mortality rate in South Africa is 50 per thousand live births, whereas it is only 39 per thousand in Tunisia. Both countries have an unequal distribution of income, but the Gini coefficient in South Africa is an extraordinarily high 58.4 as compared to Tunisia's 40.2. High inequality in South Africa is a cause of a high incidence of poverty. Using the World Bank's poverty threshold of $1 per capita per day, the head count index of poverty in South Africa was 23.7 percent in 1993, whereas in Tunisia in 1990 it was only 3.9 percent. The situation today in South Africa is undoubtedly worse. Thus, South Africa has a long way to go even to attain the modest success enjoyed by Tunisia.

Laurence Harris and Jonathan Michie raise the important question in their chapter whether international market forces prevent the government of South Africa from introducing development policies that otherwise would be feasible and desirable. In other words, does the process of globalization act as a constraint on policies intended to reduce poverty and inequality? They conclude that "there is no reason to believe" that such policies "would be prevented by South Africa's place in global markets." I agree with this assessment. Indeed, I would go further: globalization should be seen in South Africa not as a constraint but as an opportunity.

Economic sanctions imposed on South Africa by the rest of the world caused South Africa to become largely de-linked from the global economy and forced the country to pursue a strategy of autarkic development. That strategy failed to raise average incomes or to reduce inequality. On the contrary, average incomes are lower today than they were in 1980, and poverty and inequality almost certainly have increased. South Africa has much to gain from reintegration into the global economy and little to fear. World trade has grown twice as fast as world output since 1950, and foreign direct investment has grown three times as fast as world output. Yet

South Africa's isolation meant that the country missed the opportunities for development created by rapidly expanding trade and foreign investment.

This does not imply that South Africa can rely on international commerce and foreign capital to become engines of growth. Trade is more likely to be a handmaiden of growth than an engine, and foreign capital inflows are unlikely to become significant until internally generated growth accelerates. In other words, if development occurs it will probably be driven by domestic economic forces, but government policies can help to ensure that domestic economic forces are reinforced by the forces of globalization. Thus, a strong case can be made in favor of an "open" economy – low barriers to trade, a stable real exchange rate, and relatively free movement of capital and labor – but this should be seen as creating an environment in which growth can occur rather than as a set of policies sufficient to generate rapid growth.

Even the infant industry argument for protection or promotion should be viewed with considerable skepticism. South Africa's manufacturing sector has been protected for quite some time: if the infants have not yet reached maturity, they are unlikely ever to do so. Moreover, because the economy is so deformed, the structure of the manufacturing sector created by apartheid policies is ill suited to the needs of the new South Africa. The grotesque inequalities inherited from the past have led to a composition of industrial output heavily skewed toward satisfying the demands of upper-income groups. Hence, further protection would only help to perpetuate inequality without diminishing inefficiency. The poor have suffered long enough; they should not be required to bear the cost of propping up high-cost industries that serve the rich.

An "open" economy would bring an end to autarky, but it would not by itself end internal colonialism. That requires more fundamental change in the ownership and control of natural, human, and physical capital.

A good place to start would be in agriculture. This may seem odd, since agriculture accounts for only 5 percent of GDP and about 14 percent of total employment. But a redistribution of land in favor of the black population would be an act of restitution that is long overdue that simultaneously would increase total factor productivity, increase the output of important wage goods, generate some additional employment, reduce poverty among those most severely affected, and improve the distribution of income and wealth. In addition, higher average incomes of the working poor in agriculture would increase the reservation wage in the urban areas, thereby reducing urban inequality and marginally weakening the incentives encouraging rural-to-urban migration. In South Africa, as in the semi-industrialized countries of Latin America, a strong case can be made for land reform on economic and distributive grounds. In any event, the land issue will not go away, and South Africa should learn from the unhappy experience of Zimbabwe and Kenya and deal with the issue decisively.

Next, massive investment in the human capital of the black population – notably in primary and secondary education – would be desirable both because it would result in a permanent improvement in the distribution of income and because spending on the two lower tiers of the educational pyramid would yield high rates of social return. This could be financed in part by reallocating resources away from university education and in part by introducing means-tested school fees structured in such a way that upper-income parents would be required to pay a high proportion of the costs of educating their children. Public investment in the education of black children would be complementary to private investment in physical capital – an example of the "crowding-in" effect that Harris and Michie emphasize – because more- and better-educated workers would lower costs of production and increase the profitability of private sector investment.

The high priority given by government to public investment in housing is understandable given the poor housing conditions of the black population, but some reduction in emphasis may be desirable. If the incomes of the poor begin to rise in response to growth-accelerating and redistributive policies, it is likely that private investment in housing will increase dramatically, with construction and finance largely provided by the poor themselves. The huge private housing boom in rural China that occurred after economic reforms were introduced in late 1978 is an example of what can happen without the need for government assistance.

Government can facilitate the process by granting the poor titles to land, by removing obstacles to investment (controls, construction standards, safety regulations, zoning laws), and perhaps by encouraging the development of financial institutions that specialize in providing mortgages to low-income people. Demand by the poor for investment in housing is likely to be high not only because such investment provides shelter but also because a house with secure title provides space for directly productive activities with potentially high rates of return, e.g., eating establishments and bars, workshops and repair facilities, food processing, handicrafts, and a wide range of commercial activities. Low-income business people often "live over the shop," and an investment in a house creates a multipurpose asset.

It is for this reason and others that a redistribution of productive assets (land, human capital, housing) can raise savings and investment and accelerate growth. There is no necessary tradeoff between measures to reduce inequality and policies to promote growth. The development strategy must be carefully designed, however, to exploit complementarities between public investment and savings and investment by poor people. One obvious possibility raised by Harris and Michie is labor-intensive investment projects in such things as secondary farm-to-market roads, electrification in areas where the poor are concentrated (in the cities as well as the countryside), and improved communications.

All of these things will help to create employment. This brings us to the issue of the need to increase labor market flexibility and stretch out supply elasticities. Evidently it is important to dismantle the labor controls that were put in place during the period of apartheid. This is part of the process of destroying internal colonialism in South Africa. The advocates of "flexibility," however, have more than this in mind, namely, relying on unhampered market forces to guide the allocation of resources and determine the pace of development.

The difficulty with this approach is that the profound structural change through which South Africa must pass if it is to achieve growth with equity cannot be brought about merely by a change in relative prices. Price flexibility in the absence of a high rate of investment does not result in structural change, i.e., it does not lead to a radical transformation of the composition of output and employment. The reason for this is that nonmarginal reallocations of resources are almost impossible to achieve through a redeployment of the existing stock of assets (physical and human) because many existing assets are specific to particular uses. Swords cannot readily be transformed into plowshares, because the capital equipment and labor skills used to produce armaments cannot be converted into the capital and skills needed to produce agricultural implements. In practice, reallocation occurs through additions to the stock of physical and human capital being channeled into newly profitable activities. In other words, investment in the broadest sense is the vehicle for resource reallocation. Hence, the higher is the rate of investment, the faster will be the pace of structural change.

It is of course important to get the key prices "right" and to have a reasonable degree of market "flexibility" so that the structure of incentives guides investment into socially profitable activities, but the central task for the government in South Africa today is to raise domestic savings and investment. The end of internal colonialism and the creation of a more equitable society should make that task easier, and the end of autarky should increase the range of socially profitable investment opportunities.

19

Can domestic expansionary policy succeed in a globally integrated environment? An examination of alternatives

Robert Pollin

Introduction

For roughly the past 25 years, the advanced economies have experienced a significant decline in their average growth rate relative to that experienced in the first quarter-century after World War II. Output growth in the countries of the OECD (Organization for Economic Cooperation and Development) averaged 4.8 percent from 1959 to 1970, the latter phase of the post-World War II "Golden Age" stretching from 1945 to 1970, while during the more recent "Leaden Age," running from the early 1970s to the present, output growth in the OECD has averaged 2.8 percent (1994 is the last year for which we have full data). This Leaden Age growth experience in the OECD is closely associated with changes in employment conditions. In Western Europe, high average unemployment rates have emerged concurrently with the growth slowdown, while in the United States, slow growth has been associated with a sharp long-term decline in average real wages for nonsupervisory workers.

Employment conditions have also been worsening in developing countries. As Singh and Zammit write:

> The employment situation in the South, particularly in Latin America and Sub-Saharan Africa, is dire. There are not only current high rates of urban, especially youth unemployment, but there is also the necessity of providing productive jobs for a labor force which is growing at approximately 3 percent a year. On the basis of past relationships between economic variables, to create jobs at this rate in order to meet the employment needs of new entrants to the labor force, the economies of these countries need to grow at a rate of about 6 percent per annum (1995, 94).

I am grateful for comments by participants at the two conferences on "Globalization and Progressive Economic Policy" sponsored by the Economic Policy Institute in October 1995 and June 1996, especially those from Robert Blecker, Brad DeLong, Jerry Epstein, Robert Eisner, Jeffrey Frankel, Keith Griffin, and the late David Gordon. I am equally grateful to seminar participants at the Metropolitan Autonomous University, Mexico City; the Program in Social Theory and Comparative History, UCLA; The Harvey Goldberg Center for Contemporary History, University of Wisconsin-Madison; and the Departments of Economics of the University of California, Riverside and Southern Oregon University.

Until recently, the East Asian "tiger" economies were the outstanding exception to this unfavorable growth and employment picture. This, of course, changed drastically after the devaluation of the Thai baht in July 1997 and the subsequent collapse of the financial markets in Malaysia, Singapore, Indonesia, the Philippines, and South Korea. Since the fall of 1997, unemployment has jumped sharply throughout the region. Indeed, especially in South Korea, the very idea that mass layoffs and sustained unemployment would be experienced is a concept drastically at odds with the experience of the previous 30 years.

The basic premise of this chapter is an old one that has fallen out of favor. It is that, built around carefully designed demand expansion programs, the tools exist for an active public policy to dramatically improve employment opportunities, average incomes, and living standards in all parts of the world within a relatively short period of time. That such policy tools have not been deployed results, for the most part, from a combination of two factors.

The first is the political/ideological hegemony of the neo-liberal policy agenda, which contends that the only viable path to economic prosperity is through opening and deregulating markets, minimizing government influence over the economy, and, in particular, eschewing active macroeconomic policies to promote employment and output growth. The neo-liberal agenda is heavily supported by most mainstream economists, including those at the International Monetary Fund (IMF) and World Bank. More importantly, the neo-liberal agenda coincides exactly with the perceived self-interests of those who control the major multinational corporations and financial firms. It is not surprising, therefore, that such policies have dominated the policy discussions since the onset of the Asian crisis. At the same time, it is notable that, as the crisis deepened into 1998, the U.S. Treasury, in particular, began urging Japan to pursue expansionary demand policies. Such a departure from the standard neo-liberal position demonstrates that the crisis is sufficiently severe that the ascendancy of neo-liberal policies may be starting to erode.[1]

But in addition to the strictly political and ideological opposition to expansionary policies, further constraints – though almost all of them have political as well as technical dimensions – also inhibit the ability of governments to pursue active policies for full employment and an egalitarian growth path. Some of these constraints have clearly been contributing to the Japanese reluctance to pursue such policies amid the 1997–98 crisis. We know that in a purely demand-constrained economy, it is not difficult to induce an economic expansion within one year by deploying standard fiscal and monetary tools. But economies are rarely constrained purely by demand. Depending on the country, an array of additional constraints can limit the expansionary impulse of a demand-centered policy intervention, such that the initial expansion of employment and output will not be sustainable. The most general

1   See, for example, "Japan: US hits at lack of tax cuts in package to lift economy," *Financial Times* (ft.com), February 21, 1998. At the same time, the U.S. Treasury position calls for Japan to deregulate its financial markets concurrent with expanding demand. One major theme to be developed in this paper is that such a combination is likely to only worsen destabilizing speculative financial practices.

such constraints include the effects of expansion on inflation, interest rates, and exchange rates. They also include the dissipation of the force of an expansion through import, saving, and what I will call *speculative* leakages, this being the unproductive trading of existing assets rather than the creation of new productive assets. There is, finally, the potential of any such program degenerating into a miasma of rent seeking and political corruption.

There are also problems associated with particular countries. Harris (1996) contends that expansionary demand policies are inappropriate for most developing economies for two reasons. First, the economies are not sufficiently "articulated" between their productive, financial, and governmental systems such that, for example, the portfolio decisions in the financial sector are taken with respect to the global market rather than the markets for domestic saving and investment. In addition, the governments do not exercise sufficient sovereignty in the contemporary era of globalization, so that they do not have the power to carry out ambitious policies to raise output and employment.

While Harris addresses these points to developing economies only, the concerns he raises have a more general relevance. Specifically, it appears that the integration of global trade and finance has tightened the constraints on expansionary policy throughout the world. Balance-of-payments problems are likely to emerge more quickly, and the channels have enlarged through which import and speculative leakages can flow. Moreover, even the sovereignty of advanced countries is diminished due to the veto power of global capital markets over any policy that threatens inflation and thereby the value of nominally fixed financial assets.

The aim of this chapter is to discuss in specific terms a range of strategies for overcoming the constraints on an egalitarian growth agenda. The paper recognizes that globalization has made such constraints more imposing. At the same time, not enough attention has been given to designing expansionary policies with the explicit aim of taking the measure of these problems and targeting policies as much as possible toward overcoming them. Among other things, it is important to show how an expansionary program need not be contrary to a country concurrently seeking to expand its exports. Counterposing internal market demand-led policies and an export-oriented agenda as incompatible or mutually exclusive alternatives has always been misleading. Indeed, as I will try to show, when short-run expansionary policies are intelligently integrated into a long-term growth agenda, such a program is consistent with raising productivity and export competitiveness as well as internal demand.

The next section of the paper considers the importance of international cooperation to support sustainable full employment policies. There is no doubt that cooperation would be highly desirable. However, it is difficult to see how any such agreements would occur without pressure first coming from political movements seeking to implement an expansionary program. We are thus left with the initial problem of advancing policies that can be implemented successfully at the level of the domestic economy.

Recognizing this problem, the chapter then considers in Section 3 the familiar issue of how inflation and the non-accelerating-inflation rate of unemployment

(NAIRU) will constrain a full employment program. Because I argue that distribution rather than growth is the primary problem associated with inflation, this section briefly discusses two ways of reducing the distributional effects of inflation: through an incomes policy and the indexation of financial assets.

In the next four sections, the chapter then considers various specific techniques for implementing a short-term expansionary program that will be sustainable over the longer term. In Section 4, I consider the output composition of expansion. An expansion of domestic demand can be led by private consumption, private investment, public consumption, or public investment. The relative weights given to these potential growth nodes is important, since the ability to minimize various constraints will depend on which sectors expand more rapidly. I make the case here for the merits of a public investment-led expansion, both because it should strengthen the impact of a given expansionary impulse and because it will support longer-term productivity gains. Such productivity gains in turn will be supportive of enhancing export performance as one node of a broader long-term growth program.

Section 5 considers various ways of financing an expansion. I consider three broad possibilities: a balanced-budget multiplier, deficit spending, and monetary expansion, and more detailed variations within these broad approaches. For example, within the category of monetary expansion, I distinguish between traditional monetary policy unlinked to concerns over composition and the possibilities for government debt monetization, in which output composition can be directly targeted. Here as well the impact of a given expansionary impulse should vary considerably depending on the relative mix of these financing options.

In Section 6, I pose the question: assuming that virtually any expansionary initiative, even one financed by a balanced-budget multiplier, is likely to induce some significant exchange rate adjustments, how then should a government respond? Significant appreciations or depreciations in the exchange rate of a domestic currency can produce serious problems through their impact on the domestic price level and interest rates. These effects could then induce deflationary pressures and distributional changes that would counter the purpose of the expansion. Nevertheless, there are short-term safeguards, including various types of capital controls or dual exchange rate policies that can be taken to cushion the impact of most such situations. It is notable in the aftermath of the 1994 Mexican financial crisis, and especially amid the 1997–98 Asian crisis, that the IMF itself has begun to see increasing merit in capital controls and similar financial regulatory policies.

This then raises the final issue in pursuing a sustainable expansionary policy, addressed in Section 7: how to construct domestic financial regulations that can create "circuit breakers" against the effects of speculative attacks against the currency. The immediate aim of such policies would be to reduce the longer-term need for capital controls and similar initiatives. However, if properly designed, financial regulations can also be effectively used to channel credit toward activities that promote the broader employment and egalitarian growth agenda. The Asian experience has clearly underscored the centrality of well-designed financial regulations as a factor for sustainable growth policies.

What becomes clear from this exercise is that there are a variety of ways through which an expansionary program may be implemented, but that not all of them will be equally effective at overcoming the constraints on policy, either those operating only at the level of the domestic economy or those that have significant global dimensions. Throughout this discussion I will give attention to the political as well as the more technical economic dimensions of the various proposals, since much of the success of any such public policy initiative depends on the effectiveness and credibility of the policy makers.

Is this policy agenda supposed to be applicable to all countries? That would seem outlandish on the face of it. Of course there are huge structural differences between countries, even those at similar levels of development.[2] There is, therefore, no reason that the specifics that will be relevant to one country under a given situation can be generalized beyond that place and time. However, some basic propositions as to the most efficient ways to raise employment and sustain an egalitarian growth path do have broad applicability. Note that such an assertion is far less sweeping than the neo-liberals' notion that their policy agenda can be applied essentially without variation in any country at any time.

Having said that, there are two sets of special cases that should be noted at the outset. Given that the United States is the largest economy in the world with the most important currency, unique positive spillover effects would result were it to pursue an expansionary agenda. It would increase world demand to a significant extent, and have a favorable effect on investors' expectations worldwide. Moreover, the resources required to sustain a stable dollar amid an expansionary program would be significantly less than those needed for any other economy. A U.S.-led expansion would thus open new possibilities for international cooperation around a full employment and egalitarian growth agenda.[3]

The other set of special cases is the developing countries that, as Harris noted, may well not have sufficient sovereignty at present to carry out an expansionary policy. To the extent this is true, the question should be how to begin constructing the institutions through which sovereign economic policies can be implemented. Some version of the proposals considered here may well be the instrument for defining and then asserting a new phase of sovereignty.

It is finally important to keep in mind the political environment within which this discussion takes place. Progressive political parties campaigning on programs of full employment and an egalitarian growth path do frequently win elections, al-

---

2   The statement of FitzGerald and Vos as to the importance of understanding the specifics of an economy's structure before evaluating the viability of various policy options is apt: "Our conceptual approach implies that no general conclusion can be drawn as to the effectiveness of different macropolicy instruments, or as to the suitability of one organizational form or another. This is not merely an epistemological statement about translating theory into practice: rather, it reflects the proposition that the very heterogeneity of real economies and their multisectoral structure means that only when the logic of each of its components is properly elucidated, can the workings of the whole be understood" (1989, 11).

3   Reflecting its unique features, Elizabeth Zahrt and I (1997) have written a companion paper to this one focusing on the U.S. alone.

most always because of rising concern among working people over jobs and living standards. But because progressive parties have not had either the will or capacity to effectively address these problems, they rapidly dissipate the credibility they bring with them after achieving an electoral victory. As a result, progressive governments are soon overwhelmed by the very forces they were elected to oppose, and often revert to embracing little more than somewhat paler versions of a standard neo-liberal agenda.[4] This scenario has had a devastating impact on the political viability of the left throughout the world. To break free of this syndrome, it is crucial that progressive governments be able to show significant positive achievements within a relatively brief time period, say, within one to two years of taking office. It is thus clearly urgent to formulate a viable short-term strategy – a program that generates positive effects on employment, wages, and output within one to two years – that will also create the basis for long-term growth.

The prospects for international cooperation

As noted, the most general constraints on an expansionary policy initiative are its effects on inflation, interest rates, and exchange rates; the import, saving, and specu-lative leakages; and the various opportunities for rent-seeking and other types of government failure.

Some of these forces, such as the saving leakage or the problems of inflation, can be understood strictly within the framework of a closed economy. But all of them also have an international dimension, and it is that dimension which, generally speaking, creates the most severe difficulties. The classic problem is that of a single country creating an unsustainable current account deficit because its trading part-ners have not expanded along with it. Similar pressures are channeled through the exchange rate, when financial market investors, fearing the inflationary consequences of expansion, would destabilize a country's currency, usually through selling the currency en masse, thereby inducing a depreciation.

The rising degree of trade and financial integration over the past 25 years has

---

4   One classic recent case of this is the Clinton Administration in the U.S., which was elected in 1992 on a platform of "putting people first" – that is, job growth, higher wages, and more public investment – but which abandoned this program immediately after the election in favor of a "putting deficit reduction first" set of tax and expenditure initiatives. See Baker and Schafer (1993) on the economic consequences of this decision and Woodward (1994) on the backroom machinations that led Clinton to reverse his policy direction even before tak-ing office. Given this recent history, there is considerable irony in the proposals of the Clinton Treasury that the Japanese pursue expansionary policies amid the 1998 Asian crisis. An even more important example of the same phenomenon was the Socialist victory in France in 1981 (described well in Halmi, Michie, and Milne 1994) in which the new Mitterand gov-ernment decided to defend financial orthodoxy with respect to the exchange rate immedi-ately after winning office, and thereby effectively foreclosed the prospects for a successful full employment program. Similar patterns have been recently followed in, among other places, New Zealand, Australia, Venezuela, and several European countries, as surveyed in Anderson and Camiller (1994), where social democratic governments held power.

made these problems more formidable, but they are by no means new concerns. As is well known, the initial purpose of the Bretton Woods system of fixed exchange rates as defined by John Maynard Keynes and Harry Dexter White was to allow national governments to pursue expansionary policies without having to experience balance-of-payments deficits and destabilizing currency fluctuations. Of course, the actual practice of the International Monetary Fund and World Bank, the institutions created out of Bretton Woods, never followed the initial Keynes–White approach. In any case, the system collapsed in 1971 after operating for 25 years, and nothing has been created as an alternative.[5]

The problem of global constraints has worsened since the collapse of Bretton Woods. Even before its demise, financial market participants in many countries had been developing and profiting from innovative financial practices through which they circumvented existing financial regulations. A worldwide wave of financial deregulation then rose alongside the movement to circumvent the existing laws. From a global perspective, the result was increasing freedom of short-term capital to flow throughout the world. This enabled financial market speculators to exert significant pressure against governments that pursue policies contrary to their perceived interests. Anything resembling an expansionary/full employment strategy is frequently regarded as suspect because of its anticipated negative effects on the real incomes of nonfinancial and especially financial capitalists, the return on whose assets are fixed in nominal terms.[6]

This is how the external constraint has come to assume overriding importance over the past 20 years. The severity of the external constraint has suggested to many observers that the only way for an expansionary program to be successful is if there is first a sufficient degree of international cooperation to create a supportive environment for such policies. Thus, for example, Eatwell writes:

> The Golden Age of full employment was a product of a particular combination of international relationships – a combination that collapsed in the early 1970s. Much of the rise in G7 unemployment since then can be attributed to that collapse. If this argument is correct, then the pursuit of a full employment policy must involve either withdrawing from the international pressures which create unemployment (the war or siege economy solution) or the creation of an international environment which replicates the expansionary framework of Bretton Woods. Simply to pose the issue indicates the scale of the task. However, there is no intrinsic reason why the G7 should not be able to create a new international regime which would underwrite national full employment policies (1994, 280).

International cooperation would undoubtedly create a far more supportive environment for expansionary policies. On the other hand, the difficulties in creating a viable framework for international cooperation are formidable. To begin with, in the best of circumstances, creating such a framework would take a long time. It took

5 This frequently told history is presented succinctly in Panic (1995).
6 Various aspects of the worldwide trend toward financial innovation and deregulation, and its effects on expansionary macro policy, are presented in De Cecco (1987), Podolsky (1986), Swary and Topf (1992), and Banuri and Schor (1992). The specific sequence of financial deregulations prior to the 1997–98 crisis in South Korea is presented in Chang (1998).

four years to establish the North American Free Trade Agreement (NAFTA) from the time the idea was first formally broached, and seven years to renovate the General Agreement on Tariffs and Trade (GATT) after the Uruguay Round began in 1987. These cooperative policy projects, moreover, were pushed forward by the strong political backing of most sectors of international capital, and they are completely in concert with the ascendant neo-liberal policy consensus. There is nothing close to a comparable international political force promoting economic expansion and egalitarian growth.

Indeed, the only conditions under which these types of cooperative relationships could form would be through progressive national governments that are attempting to implement egalitarian growth policies within their domestic economies. But such governments are not likely to form if they require an environment of global cooperation as a precondition to attempting a domestic growth agenda. Rather, such governments will need to demonstrate some success with their domestic policy agendas before they acquire the credibility to push for international cooperation. In other words, domestic growth is the prerequisite needed to transform any proposals for an international egalitarian agenda into a realistic possibility. A successful expansionary program in a major OECD country, especially the United States, would be most important in this regard, both because of the rise in world demand that would ensue and the positive model from which other countries could draw.

It is also true, as I will discuss further below, that whether a structure of international cooperation can be successful will depend on the capacity of domestic policies to create "circuit breakers" that reduce the burden that international policies need to carry in behalf of an egalitarian growth agenda. Thus, for example, if domestic regulatory structures inhibit speculative financial practices, this will reduce the demands on any designated international institution to accomplish the same task via, say, exchange rate controls.

In short, the initial impetus for building a new institutional framework that can support full employment and egalitarian policies will have to begin within domestic settings. But here we face a Catch-22: if the governments mandated to advance an egalitarian growth agenda are doomed to failure because of international constraints, then it is also certain that the cooperative international policy framework itself will never get formed.

This brings us to our next task: to advance a set of domestic policies that can limit the force of existing external constraints and thereby also create the conditions in which desirable forms of international cooperation become possible.

Inflation and NAIRU

The voluminous literature on the Phillips curve and NAIRU is the obvious place to begin in considering the incompatibility between short- and long-run policy goals. Probably the most widely held view within this literature is that expansionary policy can lower unemployment and increase growth, but only at the cost of accelerating inflation. Moreover, these short-term gains in employment and real growth will be temporary when the unemployment rate falls below the NAIRU rate. Efforts to lower unemployment below NAIRU will thus only succeed in raising inflation, with no sustainable benefits in terms of growth or unemployment.

This is not the place to address in depth the literature on NAIRU.[7] For our purposes here, it will be sufficient to make a few basic points. First, following the substantial critical literature on NAIRU, it is at least evident that any "natural rate" or "non-accelerating-inflation rate" of unemployment is entirely dependent on the broader institutional setting in which expansionary policies are pursued. Otherwise, there would be no explanation for the widely disparate experiences with unemployment across countries or in a given country over time (see Rowthorn and Glyn 1990).

Second, it does not follow that, if such supportive institutional structures are established, we can then expect to have eliminated the likelihood of inflationary pressures resulting from expansionary policy. Inflation will normally rise when unemployment falls as a consequence of increased growth.[8] The real issue here is how much inflation will accelerate and what are the costs of such increased inflationary pressures. The preponderance of evidence shows that, as long as inflation remains moderate, the costs of such inflation are negligible. The most recent research supporting this finding is that of Bruno and colleagues at the World Bank (1995). In a study of the relationship between inflation and economic growth for 127 countries between 1960 and 1992, Bruno and colleagues found that average growth rates fell only slightly as inflation rates move up to 20–25 percent. Of particular importance for our concerns here, Bruno found that during 1960–72, economic growth on average *increased* as inflation rose from negative or low rates to the 15–20 percent range. This is because, as Bruno explains, "in the 1950s and 1960s, low-to-moderate inflation went hand in hand with very rapid growth because of investment demand pressures in an expanding economy" (1995, 35). Thus, inflation that results directly from economic expansion does not, according to Bruno's data, create any significant barriers to expansion.[9]

Beyond this, the problem of inflationary pressure resulting from expansionary policies needs to be understood in terms of its distributional effects. As is well known, the reason full employment induces inflation is that it increases workers' bargaining power in labor markets and thus tends to bid up wages and to shift the distribution of income in favor of wages. This then creates an incentive for capitalists to support the return to unemployment as a means of disciplining labor and regaining a higher share of national income.

7   Cross's edited collection (1995) presents a range of perspectives. Additional critical perspectives include Blanchard and Summers (1988), Gordon (1988b), Omerod (1994), Eisner (1995), Sawyer (1997), and Baker (1998 this volume).

8   Unemployment may alternatively fall through downward labor market flexibility, in which case upward wage and price pressure will not ensue. But I do not consider this "low road" to reducing unemployment as desirable or as a path that a progressive government would want to pursue. See Singh's (1996) discussion on this point.

9   More generally, Michl (1995) provides an outstanding critical survey of the literature, demonstrating that the costs of inflation are low, especially relative to the costs of unemployment.

On the other hand, everything else equal, capitalists will benefit from full employment in as much as capacity utilization rises, and productivity may rise as well insofar as rising output encourages productivity gains (i.e., the "Verdoorn effect"). It therefore follows that at least certain sectors of capital should favor full employment and even accept the shift in relative shares, as long as, in absolute terms, profits are growing along with the rate of capacity utilization.[10] This point is crucial in that it suggests that a progressive government may well be able to find supporters among the capitalist class for an expansionary program.

At the same time, inflation is an instrument of redistribution from creditors to debtors to the extent that the financial assets are unindexed to inflation and thus fixed in nominal terms. As such, in an unindexed financial market, bondholders will be adamantly opposed to an expansionary policy that generates accelerating inflation, since their income will not rise with the rate of capacity utilization but will fall with inflation.

The most widely deployed policy instrument for addressing the distributional conflicts surrounding inflation is of course an incomes or pay-bargaining policy. These were used with significant success in some countries, notably the Nordic Social Democracies, while other OECD economies suffered high unemployment in the 1970s and 1980s. However, even these countries seem to have yielded more recently to the pressures of global competition and the external constraint, as these pressures have intensified.[11]

Should a progressive government embrace a system of incomes policy as a component of its expansionary policy? The fundamental problem with such a policy is that it forces labor to limit its wage claims at precisely the point of its maximum bargaining power. Whether labor should be willing to do so should depend first, of course, on the level at which capital will agree to an administered division of national income. In the United States, for example, average wages for nonsupervisory workers in 1997 were 14 percent below their 1973 level in real terms even while productivity rose by 34 percent between 1973 and 1997. This means that a program in which wages rose at the rate of aggregate productivity growth would be a substantial advance. More generally, though, the attractiveness of any such program will depend on the commitment capital is willing to make to policies that support full employment and egalitarian growth over the long term. The critical concerns

10   Indeed, it is clearly not necessarily the case that full employment should engender a shift in shares of national income in favor of wages relative to profits, if utilization and productivity rise faster than wages. However, evidence for OECD countries in the 1960s and early 1970s, the last period of tight labor markets in most countries, shows that this shift in relative shares did occur. See, for example, Glyn, Hughes, Lipietz, and Singh (1990), Weisskopf (1992), and Sherman (1991). However, for the United States since 1993, falling unemployment produced neither accelerating inflation nor a rise in the wage share of national income. The primary reason for this, as shown for example in Lown and Rich (1997), is that upward wage pressure in the most recent U.S. expansion has been far weaker than in previous business cycles.

11   See Pontusson (1994) and Marshall (1995) for discussions of the decline of the Swedish model.

here would be issues around the organization of the workplace and labor markets and those involving financial institutions and credit allocation.[12] However, it may also be the case that obtaining such social contracts from corporations may be increasingly difficult if the mobility of firms increases as globalization proceeds (see Crotty, Epstein, and Kelly in this volume).

Especially given these concerns, a less elaborate approach to overcoming especially the bondholders' opposition to expansion is to establish a workable system of indexing bonds to the inflation rate. Over the post-World War period, bond indexation has generally worked successfully in a number of countries in that it has contributed to reducing arbitrary income redistributions resulting from inflation. This includes countries experiencing hyperinflation such as Brazil in the 1960s, as well as countries in which inflation was relatively modest, such as the U.K., Sweden, Australia, and Canada.

Several problems would nevertheless emerge in trying to implement bond indexation policies in the contemporary environment. The most serious is that such policies would freeze the real interest rate at the historically high levels that have prevailed through the 1990s. This high level of real interest rates, both in absolute terms and relative to growth rates of gross domestic product for most national economies, would not be an acceptable starting point for implementing an indexation policy.[13] We would assume, therefore, that one feature of a successful expansionary policy would be to lower the rates to something approximating their historical averages before indexation could be viable.

Other concerns would also emerge through indexation policies. One is that, to the extent bond indexation weakens the bondholders' opposition to inflation, some approximation of price stability will erode as a public policy goal, which in turn will embed inflation as an inertial force in the economy. A final, more narrow, weakness of an indexing policy is that it can be applied only to newly issued debt; outstanding bonds will still be equally vulnerable to inflation. But a policy of indexing government bonds also has collateral strengths. In particular, it should raise the government's credibility in pursuing an expansionary program that does not encourage excessive inflation, since the burden of the newly issued government debt will no longer fall with inflation.[14] Given the range of strengths and weaknesses of both an incomes policy and bond indexation, the most viable approach is that both instruments serve as compliments to each other.

12 See Nolan (1994), Gordon (1996), and Appelbaum and Berg (1996) for treatments of the relationship between work organization and employment, and Pollin (1995) for a discussion of the role of financial system organization.

13 The figures for real interest rates since 1959 are presented in Felix's (1998) contribution to this volume.

14 A range of assessments of the viability of bond indexing include Tobin (1971), Friedman (1974), Steinherr (1978), Fischer (1978, 1983), Munnell and Grolnic (1986), Weiner (1983), Shen (1995), and several essays in Dornbusch and Simonsen (1983). Taylor (1988, 61 and passim) is a particularly useful discussion based on a review of the experiences of a range of less-developed economies. It is notable that the U.S. Treasury announced in May 1996 that it would issue index bonds for the first time beginning later in the year. The Treasury cited

Composition of expansion

Expansionary policy initiatives can be divided according to whether they are consumption- or investment-led and according to whether they are centered on the public or private sectors. The simplest approach is to directly target private consumption spending through a tax cut. The stimulus from the tax cut results through the immediate rise in consumption spending undertaken by liquidity-constrained households.[15] This was the idea underlying the famous 1964 Kennedy/Johnson tax cut in the United States. Its effects were felt almost immediately after passage of the law, because withholding rates on paychecks were reduced immediately. The multiplier effects of such a consumption-led expansion are then intended to increase investment through the multiplier.

However, there are serious problems with a private consumption-led expansion. The first is that in most countries it is likely to have a significant import content. The domestic multiplier and accelerator effects are therefore weakened, and the balance of payments and exchange rate are disturbed. For many less-developed economies, expanding consumption may also face an agricultural constraint, such that demand expansion may simply increase the price of agricultural goods when the supply of such goods is limited by institutional barriers. Sustaining the consumption-led expansion would therefore require reducing the barriers to increasing the food supply.[16] More generally, a private consumption-led expansion will not necessarily promote longer-term growth of industrial capacity or productivity. It will do so only if the investment accelerator emanating from the consumption expansion is strong.

A private investment-led expansion has the merit that it is directly targeting the economy's productive capacity for growth, and therefore raises the likelihood that long-term productivity will rise along with short-term expansion. The policy tools that directly encourage private long-term investment are, however, weaker than those targeted directly at consumption, and only indirectly at investment via the accelerator. Central banks can reduce short-term interest rates, but it is highly uncertain what such a change would have on long-term rates, as demonstrated by the volatility of yield curves in recent years. It is further unclear that a fall in long-term rates will by itself significantly boost investment, given the long-running evidence on the relative weakness of the interest elasticity of investment relative to other determinants of investment growth.[17]

Using tax policy to promote private investment is, under most circumstances, an

the standard argument that this will provide bond purchasers with another inflation hedge. At least publicly, it did not consider the possibility that this may also soften the resistance of the financial market investors to an expansionary program.

15 Evidence supporting the idea that a substantial majority of households in OECD countries are liquidity constrained is presented in Carroll and Summers (1991). The relative proportion of liquidity-constrained households would be at least as high in less-developed countries.

16 Dutt (1996) provides a good overview discussion of this problem.

17 In the U.S., for example, Koepke's recent comprehensive econometric "horse race" (summarized in Berndt 1991, Chapter 6) on the relative factors determining investment finds that accelerator and profit/cash flow effects are significantly more powerful than cost-of-capital/

even weaker tool. For example, Karier (1994), working with U.S. data, finds that tax credits to stimulate private investment are highly inefficient – only 12 percent of the credits are actually spent on new investment, while the other 88 percent are used to pay higher dividends, buy stocks or bonds, or otherwise reduce reliance on external sources of funds.[18] The case for a capital gains tax cut to spur private investment is still weaker. Such a tax cut is not even targeted to reward new investment per se, but rather any increase in asset prices. Such asset price increases may result from an increase in long-term profitability of firms. But they are more likely to reflect short-term financial market trends that are only marginally connected to the long-term productive viability of firms, as was the case with the surge of inward portfolio investments in Latin America and East Asia in the 1990s.[19]

This brings us to public consumption and investment as foci for expansionary policy. A strong initial advantage of both public spending targets is that the import leakage of the expansion can be minimized, which then strengthens the domestic multiplier and accelerator effects of the expansion.

Getting more specific, what is the difference between a public consumption- versus investment-led expansion? Are military spending and health care, for example, consumption or investment goods? To avoid unnecessary controversy, we will simply distinguish these categories according to whether the spending can be assumed to promote productivity growth. This allows us to then argue that, of the two options, a public investment-led program will have the advantage of also forging a strong link between short-term expansion and long-term productivity and sustainability.

The benefits on the supply as well as the demand sides of a viable public investment expansionary program are quite broad ranging. In the context of less-developed or semi-industrialized economies, targeting an infrastructure program on the agricultural sector – on irrigation systems, rural road building, and improving production and marketing techniques – can play a major role in relaxing the agricultural constraint on an expansionary initiative (Dutt 1996; Rao 1993). By focusing on rural development, such a program would also reduce pressures for urban migration. This approach to employment expansion has been advanced, for example, by

interest rate changes. This same finding has been supported by Fazzari's (1993, 1994) innovative microlevel research on the determinants of investment. We also see roughly similar results in studies of the Indian economy. Pandit (1995, 205) summarizes the literature as follows: "There is some evidence in favor of the accelerator hypothesis but this is not sufficiently robust. However, either the level of output or change in it turns out to be an important determinant of private corporate investment in almost all studies." Pandit also says that several studies find the quantity of commercial bank credit to be an important determinant of investment, writing that "this is consistent with the fact that credit is rationed and the interest rate fails to reflect fully the extent of excess demand in the organized capital markets."

18 This finding is consistent with earlier studies, such as Eisner (1973) and Chirinko and Eisner (1982).

19 See Ffrench-Davis and Griffith-Jones (1995) on the Latin American experience, and International Monetary Fund (1997), especially Chapter 6 of background material, on Asia. More generally, the issue of the informational content of financial market fluctuations is a longstanding concern within various strands of Keynesian literature. See the discussions by De Long et al. (1990) and Crotty and Goldstein (1993) for a range of perspectives on this.

Keith Griffin under the United Nations Development Program auspices in a variety of settings, including Bolivia, Mongolia, Uzbekistan, and Vietnam.[20] More generally, both in industrialized and less-developed economies, a public investment program that succeeds in lowering supply costs will then also have a favorable effect on private sector expectations, promoting private sector investment through this supply side effect as well as through the demand accelerator channel.[21]

The overall point then is that a public investment-led expansion is likely to be most effective both through minimizing import leakages and through meshing short- and long-term goals of policy. This does not mean that public investments won't themselves entail purchasing some imported goods, especially in less-developed economies pursuing large-scale public infrastructure projects. Imports of construction inputs such as steel and cement would likely increase in such situations. It also does not mean that the other targets of expansionary policies should be overlooked completely. Indeed, because each type of expansion path has weaknesses as well as strengths, there are benefits to including both private consumption (its speed of implementation) and public consumption (low import content) as features within an overall package of initiatives whose leading thrust is public investment.

A public investment-led expansionary program can, of course, open widespread opportunities for rent seeking, e.g., the "crony capitalism" in Asia that, after the onset of the crisis, has been so widely denounced. The only way to control the problem is to create broad-based forms of democratic accountability as the expansionary program is established. Thus, public investment should initially concentrate on small-scale, labor-intensive projects, such as expanding educational or health services, or smaller-scale construction. Such projects create the means for substantial local control over the allocation and management of funds. While this hardly guarantees that the funds will be well spent, it does encourage the development of local institutions of accountability. By contrast, large-scale public works projects such as airports or subway systems are not only less labor intensive, but they also create far more openings for large-scale corruption.[22]

20 See Griffin, Geneletti, Pollin, and Thorp (1990), Griffin and Pollin (1990), and Griffin (1995, 1996, 1998).
21 FitzGerald (1996, 150) notes that this supply side approach is consistent with both Keynesianism and modern endogenous growth theory. It is also important to note the implications of this approach in considering the relative mix of public and private sectors in various contexts, including transitional economies. Within this framework, the public sector is not seen as stifling private investment initiative, but rather providing the foundation around which a private sector can more effectively develop (Chang and Rowthorn 1995). Within transitional economies, it would therefore follow that raising the efficiency of public enterprises is a much more viable strategy, even for promoting the private sector, than wholesale privatizations. This has been seen vividly in the experience of China relative to that of the Eastern European economies (Griffin and Khan 1995). In the context of the United States, there is now a wide literature on the effects of public investment on productivity growth. The weight of evidence supports the idea that large productivity gains are attainable through significant increases in public investment (e.g., Munnell 1990, 1992). However, even more skeptical analysts do not deny that positive supply side effects would result (Gramlich 1994).
22 Tanzer (1984) provides a striking account of this problem in the case of the giant-scale mineral extraction and processing industry in Brazil.

Alternative strategies for financing expansion

The viability of any expansionary program will depend to a large degree on how it is financed. It is crucial, of course, that the program be financed in a way that minimizes the balance of payments, inflation, and public debt constraints. But the financing must also be sufficiently strong that it actually achieves an expansion. We consider now the various paths to achieving these ends.

Taxation and the balanced budget multiplier

A purely tax-financed program is capable of increasing employment if increased tax revenues are used to expand employment opportunities. In addition, such a program will not directly create problems with the balance of payments, inflation, or public debt. It is for these reasons that Glyn, in various contexts, has advocated a public expenditure-led full employment program that is tax-financed.[23]

It is questionable, however, whether such a strategy can also promote aggregate expansion and thereby provide discernible benefits for the employed as well as the unemployed. The situation in the United States – where unemployment has been relatively low compared to other OECD countries but, as of 1997, real wages, even after seven years of expansion, were still 14 percent below their level of 25 years earlier – provides a clear case for questioning the merits of a primarily redistributionist strategy. In this case, as well as in all others where average living standards have stagnated or declined, the aim of an employment program should be to provide benefits to the employed wage earners as well as the unemployed. The imperative, in other words, is for a program that promotes aggregate growth as well as redistribution. An employment program that relies primarily on redistribution from employed working people to the unemployed would be, with justification, a politically unviable agenda for a progressive government.

To some extent, such a broadly based expansionary policy may be capable of being financed through taxation, if the taxes are targeted carefully to minimize their contractionary effects – that is, if the tax-generated redistribution creates a positive balanced budget multiplier. The first priority here should be to tax unproductive activities (that is, following Bhagwati's 1982 definition of "directly unproductive profit seeking" as activities that may be privately profitable but do not directly increase the flow of goods and services). One example of this type of tax is a securities transaction excise tax, which would both discourage unproductive speculative finance as well as raise revenue. The level of such a tax could be set according to whether priority is to be given to raising revenue or discouraging speculation. But in countries that have highly active speculative trading, even a low tax rate on such activities would generate substantial revenue. Thus, in the U.S., a transaction tax of 0.5 percent on equity trades that was then scaled down appropriately by maturity for all bonds and derivative instruments would have raised roughly $30 billion in 1992 if total trading had fallen by 50 percent.

---

23 Glyn develops this point in his contribution to this volume, but also in Glyn and Rowthorn (1994) and Glyn (1997).

There are several challenging, but not insurmountable, issues involved in making such a tax neutral and workable, the most important of which is designing it such that domestic taxpayers cannot avoid the tax by moving their trading to alternative domestic markets or offshore.[24]

Beyond this, the obvious limitation of the tax is that it will be relevant only for those countries that have active markets for short-term trading of financial assets. But this is not as small a number as one might assume: as of 1991, 20 countries had some version of a securities tax in place (Campbell and Froot 1993), though, as part of the trend toward deregulation, many have since been reducing or eliminating the tax.

Another way to support an expansionary program through taxation would be through a highly progressive income tax, a wealth tax, or a luxury consumption tax. Unlike a securities transaction tax, these taxes would not be targeted directly at unproductive activity. They would rather be directed at redistributing resources from households with high wealth, income, and levels of luxury consumption toward the unemployed and working people. The marginal propensity to consume should rise as a result, which is to say that the saving leakage of an expansionary impulse diminishes. In addition, the import intensity of consumption should decline, since a higher proportion of demand would be targeted at domestically produced necessities.[25]

Finally, there may well be positive growth and employment effects from changing the composition of taxation even if no additional revenue were raised. The most pertinent case here would be to eliminate payroll taxes, shifting the burden of this revenue source onto other sources, such as the income tax. A payroll tax directly raises the costs of employment and therefore acts as a disincentive to expand employment. The size of this disincentive is disputable, since it depends on the incidence of the tax, assuming that businesses can pass along at least part of the cost in higher prices. Nevertheless, there would be in almost any case a positive employment effect from raising the same revenue though alternative means.

The viability of any such balanced-budget multiplier approach to financing an expansion will, of course, depend on the specific conditions under which new taxes are introduced or shifts in the composition of revenue sources are implemented. But in most instances, it is not likely that this approach in general is likely to produce

24 Clearly, the tax implemented in Sweden in 1984 and lifted in 1990 was not designed adequately for avoiding this problem. The tax was levied only on trades arranged by Swedish brokerage services, and some assets, such as debentures, were exempt completely. This invited market participants to simply arrange their trading through non-Swedish brokers or to trade assets that were either exempt or traded by counterparties rather than brokers. Alternatively, the tax in the U.K. was a tax on the transfer of legal ownership of equity shares in the U.K. With this much broader and more neutral basis, as Campbell and Froot argue (1993), the British tax has operated much more successfully than that in Sweden. Baker, Pollin, and Schaberg (1995) provide a discussion on the most effective ways of designing a neutral and broad-based tax.

25 Wolff (1995) discusses the alternative design of wealth taxes in OECD countries. For less-developed economies, the argument for the heavy taxation of luxury consumption is developed by FitzGerald (1993), working within a Kaleckian framework.

sufficient expansionary force to push an economy toward full employment and rising mass living standards. It is therefore important to consider two other financing options, namely, deficit spending and monetary expansion.

Deficit spending

Over the past 20 years, intensive worldwide debates on the problem of public deficits have obscured some basic matters of concern. One of the most serious and widespread distortions is the idea that proponents of expansionary policy to promote growth and full employment support deficit spending as a matter of principle. In fact, deficit spending is only a policy tool that has both positive and negative attributes. Its viability as a tool depends on how those various attributes stack up in any given situation. Let us then briefly consider what are widely regarded as the two major constraints on such policies, namely "crowding out" and the burden of the debt.

Crowding out.[26] Two possibilities concerning the effects of public deficits – "crowding out" and "crowding in" – are often juxtaposed. But in fact they are not strictly comparable issues, since whether a government expansion "crowds in" more investment through a multiplier/accelerator process depends on questions surrounding *expenditures*, that is, whether the government can succeed in increasing aggregate expenditures in a demand-constrained economy and what the composition of new expenditures will be in terms of their effects on the import, saving, and speculative leakages.

By contrast, crowding out is more focused on deficit spending per se as a means of financing expansion. More precisely, the issue is whether government borrowing will absorb national saving to the extent that it makes credit for private investors unavailable or prohibitively expensive. Everything else equal, we can accept the first premise here that an increase in government borrowing will exert some upward pressure on long-term interest rates. But what will be the outcome of this upward pressure? This will depend on the forces determining the supply and demand curves in credit markets. On the supply side of the market, the crucial influence will be the nature of the system of financial intermediation in place and that system's capacity to innovate. A more innovative financial structure implies that, even with a given supply of national saving and no monetary accommodation, the credit supply curve can either flatten or shift outward in response to an increase in credit demand. This would mean that the upward interest rate pressure from an increase in government borrowing is more moderate than in the case when a financial structure is less flexible.

The net effects of the increase in government borrowing will also depend on the demand for funds by potential alternative users. That is, the effects on interest rates of an outward shift in the government credit demand curve will depend on the level of demand coming from other sectors. For example, the equilibrium level of interest rates following an increase in government borrowing will be lower if the government borrowing increase is accompanied by a reduction in private credit demand to finance speculative asset transfers. Thus, in some circumstances, a securities trans-

26　This discussion follows that in Pollin (1997).

action tax that discourages borrowing to finance speculative asset transfers might also then reduce any possible crowding-out constraint on government borrowing.

Finally, the full effects of any increase in interest rates due to government borrowing must be evaluated in terms of how much such an interest rate increase will affect productive investment decisions relative to other factors influencing investment decisions, such as the rate of profitability or the accelerator. Here, in evaluating their impact on investment, is where the relative effects of an expenditure-led crowding-in process versus a borrowing-led crowding-out effect can be evaluated in the same terms. As noted earlier (see footnote 17), survey studies by Koepke for the United States and Pandit for India find that accelerator and profit/cash flow effects are significantly stronger than the cost of capital/interest rate changes.

Overall, then, the extent to which an increase in government borrowing exerts upward pressure on interest rates available to private investors, and whether such an effect will then crowd out private investment, are both highly contingent. Moreover, the factors influencing both outcomes – e.g., the composition of the increase in aggregate expenditures or the speculative demand for private credit – can be influenced by policy initiatives. Finally, any upward interest rate pressure generated by increased government borrowing can also be countered through monetary expansion, an issue we raise below.

Is the public debt self-financing? Fiscal deficits can be self-financing in a purely demand-constrained economy, since deficits will induce income expansion that in turn will cover the increased debt burden. In such a case, the deficit will induce income expansion, which in turn will cover the increased debt burden. Thus, the debt will become burdensome only if interest obligations rise faster than GDP, and this should not occur as long as the deficit spending is increasing demand by raising the utilization rate of existing capacity.

There are, however, two problems with this formula. The first, as already emphasized, is that all economies frequently face constraints other than insufficient demand. But we have seen that various types of supply constraints, such as those on agriculture or infrastructure, can be addressed through an expansionary program as long as that program carefully targets the sectors for spending growth. The benefits here of a public investment-led expansion are especially notable.

Secondly, even strictly on the demand side, an expansion may fail to sufficiently induce rising incomes if the import, saving, and speculative leakages are strong. In this case, weak multiplier and accelerator effects will mean that the government debt was not utilized efficiently, and that the interest on the debt is more likely to grow relative to national income. But here again, as we have discussed earlier, the point is that the composition of the expenditure expansion must be targeted carefully to minimize the import, saving, and speculative leakages.

Redistribution through public debts. Early proponents of public deficits as a policy tool argued that the accompanying expansion of public debt would not be burdensome since the debt was "owed to ourselves." That is, revenues from taxpayers were simply transferred to the government bondholders, with no net change in national income. But the idea that "we owe it to ourselves" could only be meant metaphorically, since not everyone in a country will purchase government securities, nor will the purchasers represent a balanced cross section of society. Rather, a government's creditors are overwhelmingly wealthy individuals and domestic institutional and foreign investors. Thus, a high debt burden can have significant redistributive effects, from nonwealthy taxpayers to the wealthy individuals and disproportionately wealthy shareholders of domestic and foreign financial institutions and other institutional investors. How serious these effects will be depends on the interest rate at which the funds were purchased. Clearly, in a low interest rate environment, the problem will be minimized. But even when rates are higher, the redistributive effects can be compensated for through countermeasures within budgetary policy. However, establishing a means of compensation does then add an additional target to any policy initiative.

Monetary expansion

Money growth unlinked to composition of expansion

This policy tool, of course, operates through two channels, the exchange rate and the domestic interest rate. Operating through the exchange rate, monetary expansion can rapidly improve a country's trade competitiveness. We will consider the desirability of such an effect in the next section.

Considering for now the domestic effects of monetary expansion, the first point that needs to be made is that its impact will vary dramatically depending on the nature of a country's financial system. Across countries, it is therefore difficult to make positive generalizations about the impact of monetary policy. Nevertheless, one can formulate across countries some negative generalizations about the viability of monetary policy, based on the inherent limitations of the instrument.[27]

The most robust channel through which monetary policy is supposed to affect domestic activity is through lowering short-term interest rates. The fall in short-term rates is then supposed to lower the long-term rates set by the market at which businesses borrow for investment and households borrow to finance home, automobile, and durable good purchases. It is generally true that the market-set long-term rates will fall along with the short-term rates controlled by the central bank. However, this effect is highly variable, not only across countries but also within countries over time, as is demonstrated by the instability of yield curves in recent years in OECD countries.[28]

However, even if long-term rates do fall commensurately with short-term rates, that is unlikely to have a significant effect on productive investment. This is due to the weak interest elasticity of investment noted earlier. The stronger interest elastic-

27 The importance of examining monetary policy under the specific conditions operating in a country is discussed in depth by FitzGerald and Vos (1989). Epstein and Schor (1990), Grabel (1997), and Pollin (1995) address the issue in terms of the broad organizational features of countries' financial systems, in particular whether systems, following Zysman (1983), are bank- or capital-market based.

28 The relationship between short- and long-term rates for the U.S. economy is considered in Pollin (1991).

ity influence is rather on the household sector's purchases of homes, cars, and durables. But this factor is relevant only for the small number of countries for which these types of consumption goods constitute a significant share of GDP and for which these goods are purchased on credit. The United States clearly represents the prototypical case here, and only a few other OECD countries fit relatively well within this mold. However, even accepting that monetary expansion can induce a consumption-led expansion, the purchases of cars and durables, though not houses, are likely to have a high import content, thereby weakening the multiplier and accelerator effects of the expansionary impulse.

Monetary expansion, finally, encourages speculative leakages. More specifically, in countries with an active market for short-term financial asset trading and without adequate financial regulations, monetary expansion is likely to encourage destabilizing speculation. This was certainly the case in Mexico in 1994 (see DeLong's comment on this chapter).

Overall, then, given the emphasis we have placed on the composition of expansion in terms of boosting aggregate demand and achieving full employment, traditional monetary policy is a weak tool because, by design, it does not directly attempt to influence the composition of the expansion. It can also be a dangerous tool when deployed in the context of a highly speculative, poorly regulated, financial market.

Monetizing government debt

In this case, the country's monetary authority itself purchases the government bonds associated with an expansionary program, such as a public investment program. Though some debt monetization now occurs on a routine basis, this is not usually regarded as a viable financing approach for an expansionary policy.[29] Nevertheless, monetizing an increase in government spending has several distinct advantages. It will not create distributional problems nor will it increase the debt burden. It also provides the link between monetary expansion and control over the composition of expansion.

At the same time, it could create inflationary and exchange rate problems, which may in turn generate distributional effects. These would occur first to the extent that monetary expansion exceeds the growth rate of output. Such a mismatch in growth rates becomes more likely the greater are the import, saving, and speculative leakages from a demand stimulus. But this then means that all of these influences are minimized, at least in the first round of spending, when the monetary expansion is being used to finance explicit public investment expenditures.

The more likely channel through which such policies can engender negative inflationary and exchange rate outcomes is through their effect on expectations. The

---

29 This was not always the case. Indeed, the related concept of a "real bills doctrine" was the guiding idea behind the U.S. Federal Reserve's policy at its inception. It is true that this approach – in which bank notes are lent in exchange for "real bills," i.e., titles to real value or value in the process of creation – proved itself to be impractical in a strong form (Green 1987). At the same time, the core idea of the doctrine – that central banks should seek to issue reserves in close concern with the nonfinancial sector's explicit needs for productive financing – remains valid.

idea that government spending is being financed through monetary expansion will raise inflationary expectations, and thus strong opposition among rentiers, even if the government spending is well targeted and the country has a creditable record with similar such efforts.

In general, then, though financing through monetization offers clear advantages, it is almost certainly too dangerous as a financing technique unless it is used as a subsidiary measure within a broader set of financing methods. Even then, to minimize the negative expectations resulting from such an action would first require that financial markets have been brought under some significant degree of regulatory control.

How to respond to an exchange rate crisis?

Even if the types of measures considered above are taken to minimize the external constraint on expansionary policy, it is nevertheless unlikely that such external pressures can be avoided altogether. The exact nature of the external pressures will vary, depending on how the expansion is financed, the conditions in financial markets at the time the government launches its initiative, and, of course, the country. What are some likely possibilities?

In the case of a pure fiscal expansion, the initial impact will be to raise domestic interest rates. This will attract foreign capital, producing, in turn, an appreciation of the domestic currency. However, as discussed above in our consideration of crowding out, the extent of this effect will depend on the forces determining the slopes of the credit supply and demand curves. In fact, the slopes of these curves will vary widely across countries. For example, in advanced economies with well-developed domestic financial markets, the supply of credit is likely to be less interest sensitive (i.e., the credit supply curve will be upward sloping, but more horizontal-tending) than in economies with less well-developed systems of intermediation.

In any case, a more likely scenario is that the expansion would not be completely financed through deficit spending but rather, at least in part, through some form of monetary expansion as well. In this case, the expansion will create pressures toward an exchange rate depreciation. These pressures toward depreciation will be reinforced by the unfavorable view that financial market investors would have of any egalitarian policy initiative. In this situation, some inflationary pressures are likely to emerge quickly. The severity of these pressures will depend on the level of import penetration in the domestic economy as well as the J-curve. The inflationary pressures should then encourage a rise in domestic nominal interest rates as well. Note that here, the rise in nominal interest rates will not result from crowding out, but rather in response to the emergent inflationary pressures. If such inflationary pressures are strong, the upward interest rate tendency will emerge independently of whether policy makers might also deliberately seek to raise real rates as a mechanism to defend the currency.

Such forces acting on the exchange rate will be ameliorated insofar as the expansionary program is tax financed, since a tax-financed program will have no direct effect on either the public sector borrowing requirement or any need for monetary expansion. Nevertheless, even a purely tax-financed program is likely to destabilize the exchange rate – most likely encouraging a selloff and consequent depreciation – to the extent that both domestic and foreign rentiers would suffer through tax-based redistributions. In other words, the only type of progressive program that would not create exchange rate problems would be one that strictly redistributes from working people to the unemployed and very poor. But this program will also carry no expansionary impulse, nor is it likely to be supported by the constituents of a progressive government, especially in countries where the employed working class has experienced real wage stagnation or decline. It is therefore reasonable to expect pressures toward a depreciating exchange rate to accompany any egalitarian policy agenda. The pertinent question is therefore how to manage under these circumstances.

Here, of course, the answer first depends on the country being considered. For the United States, the situation would be unique because of the role of the dollar as a key international currency.[30] On the one hand, there will inevitably be less destabilization of the dollar due to the vested interest other countries have in maintaining a stable dollar. This is due first to the fact that the U.S. import market is so large that other countries will want to maintain the dollar high enough so that their U.S.-bound exports remain competitive. Holders of dollar-denominated financial assets similarly will want to at least maintain the value of the dollar. By the same token, foreign exporters are also eager to remain competitive within the U.S. market, which limits the extent to which policy makers would, alternatively, encourage a dollar depreciation. These factors will engender policy initiatives by central bankers throughout the world to counteract large, rapid fluctuations of the dollar. Finally, the foreign demand for physical and financial assets of the U.S. is likely to remain strong in the foreseeable future, especially given that the closest substitutes, German and, especially, Japanese assets, have significant problems of their own. Indeed, given the importance of the dollar and U.S. assets for business, it is quite plausible that an expansionary program initiated within the U.S. would provide the basis to initiate international cooperation to pursue expansionary programs elsewhere. This, of course, would be the most desirable outcome, and it is one that U.S. policy makers should promote as a piece of their expansionary policy arsenal.

Because of the central role of the U.S., there is, however, the danger that, should there be a real move to dump the dollar and allow it to depreciate, a crisis of great severity would result. This is an unlikely scenario. However, the conditions that are most likely to encourage it would be if domestic inflation were to appear to be out of control.

Other than for the U.S. and, to a lesser extent, Japan and Germany, pressures for a currency depreciation following from an expansionary initiative will almost always have a substantial impact on a country's domestic economy. But it is important to consider some of the details of international finance to be able to specify the nature of these effects.

---

30 The following draws from Epstein (1993) and has benefited from very helpful discussions with Jerry Epstein.

It is first of all critical to recognize the sharply divergent patterns of gross and net capital flows across borders. As Epstein (1995) points out, gross capital flows have expanded enormously over the postwar period, and especially since the collapse of Bretton Woods. However, net capital flows – which measure a country's net foreign investment position – have been much more stable over this same period. This result is supported by, among other evidence, the well known Feldstein-Horioka (1980) paper on the high correlation between domestic saving and investment.[31] The overall effect of this dichotomy between high gross and low net capital flows is that financial market instability will likely exert a strong influence only on a country's exchange rate and the variables directly associated with that – i.e., domestic inflation and interest rates. It should not have nearly as substantial an impact on the country's capacity to obtain long-term financing for domestic investment unless, of course, the short-term adjustments in financial markets cannot be stabilized within a longer period of roughly one year.

How then to respond to the most likely outcome of a short-term expansionary initiative, i.e., an outflow of short-term capital? There are likely to be real effects on the economy from the depreciation operating through the inflation and exchange rates. A case could therefore be made for seeking to support the exchange rate if, over a significant period of time, the costs of sustaining such a policy are not excessive. But the more likely case is that the costs of maintaining the currency's value will be large. In these more likely cases, the first response to the market should be to allow the exchange rate to depreciate. The literature on speculative attacks finds that attacks occur most frequently when countries pursuing a new policy regime attempt to fix their exchange rate during the adjustment period, even though it is unlikely that the existing rate will be sustainable over time (IMF 1995c, 70–9).[32]

While allowing the exchange rate to depreciate will benefit export competitiveness in the short run, there are also likely to be serious negative consequences. Surveying a research project on 18 developing economies, Taylor (1988) writes:

> Intermediate imports comprise a large proportion of prime cost in developing countries, nearly as much as labor on a national basis when domestic intermediaries are netted out. Devaluation increases import costs, which under mark-up rules soon pass into higher prices. The resulting cuts in the real wage and aggregate demand are also frequently mentioned....they make devaluation contractionary. There are additional linkages to the same result. Depreciation when there is an existing trade deficit gives with one hand by increasing export revenues, but takes more with the other in terms of higher import costs. There is an overall national income loss in local currency terms; hence contraction (p. 42–3).

31 Contrary to Feldstein and Horioka's own interpretation of these results, it by no means follows that this correlation between domestic saving and investment means that domestic saving *causes* the rate of domestic investment. See Blecker's (1997) discussion on this, including a lengthy survey of the literature, as well as Epstein (1995) and FitzGerald (1996) for alternative interpretations of this result.

32 This, of course, was the situation in the 1994 Mexican crisis, which is the focus of this IMF discussion.

In summarizing the overall effects of exchange rate depreciation, including fiscal policy effects, Taylor concludes that depreciations cause short-run stagflation in developing economies. This scenario will not be so severe in the more advanced economies where, in particular, intermediate inputs comprise a smaller proportion of total production costs. Nevertheless, the situation described by Taylor has general relevance, especially in allowing us to consider how to counterbalance these effects, after adjusting for their degree of severity in any given situation.

The first counterweight to the contractionary effects of depreciation would be the expansionary program itself. But in addition, allowing the exchange rate to depreciate would mean that other short-term policy tools should be deployed to minimize the negative interest rate and inflationary effects. Viable policy options are available in both cases.

Interest rates. The rise of long-term interest rates associated with the exchange rate depreciation may actually be seen as an opportunity to undertake a desirable set of credit allocation initiatives. Specifically, a higher market interest rate creates space for policy makers to provide significant interest subsidies to preferred borrowers. Such a policy, for example, was at the heart of South Korea's industrial policy subsequent to the liberalization of financial markets in 1965. The rise in market rates accompanying the liberalization allowed the government wide latitude in offering below-market rates to its favored firms, which were those achieving success in penetrating export markets.

Such policies in South Korea, of course, were at the heart of what, since the onset of the 1997 financial crisis, is termed "crony capitalism." But it should not be forgotten that such favoritism – or cronyism – contributed substantially to a remarkably successful growth performance for a more than a quarter-century. The crisis of this model could not therefore be due to favoritism in credit markets per se, but rather to some change in either the conditions under which privileges were granted or some change in the operation and regulation of markets that made the granting of privileges more likely to engender instability.

Chang (1998) argues that Korea's credit allocation policies themselves never actually failed but rather, by the mid-1990s, were largely discarded, in favor of a much more liberal policy environment. According to Chang, of particular importance within Korea's deregulatory transition were the complete opening of the domestic financial market to foreign lenders, who had been largely prevented from operating within South Korea for the previous quarter-century, and, in 1993, the virtual abandonment of the investment coordination policies that had been in place since 1962. In the absence of a clear regulatory structure or public investment goals, it is not surprising that the residue of the South Korean government's authority over financial markets fostered mere cronyism. As such, nothing in the 1997–98 crisis gainsays its earlier achievements, or the general conclusion that governments are capable of selecting criteria for awarding credit subsidies that would be consistent with both the efficient allocation of credit and a broader egalitarian growth program.[33]

33 In-depth discussions on the quarter-century of success with Korea's credit allocation policies are presented in Harris (1988) and Chang (1994). One may acknowledge and learn from

As an instrument of such a policy initiative, perhaps the simplest and least costly would be to establish differential asset reserve requirements on financial intermediaries. Thus, for example, if public policy called for investing 20 percent of the country's resources in housing, each financial institution would be freed from carrying sterile cash reserves as long as 20 percent of its portfolio was in housing. But if it carried no housing loans, it would be forced to hold 20 percent of its assets as cash reserves. At present, a close equivalent to such an asset-weighting policy operates in every OECD country through the international risk-based capital adequacy standards formulated at Basel in 1988. For the OECD countries at least, it would be relatively simple to supplement the Basel asset-weighting system with additional relative weights assigned to various assets.[34]

Inflation. As noted earlier, the costs of the domestic inflation associated with an exchange rate depreciation may not be significant. In terms of growth, we noted earlier Bruno's finding that moderate inflation – even perhaps a rise in inflation of up to 20 percent – is not a significant barrier to growth. If a country's imports are disproportionately composed of luxury goods, the effect of the depreciation-induced inflation may well be favorable in terms of both growth and distribution. The primary concern with a depreciation-induced inflationary environment is its effects on the prices of necessary consumption or investment goods, which will normally constitute a significant share of an economy's total expenditures.[35] In this case, several options are available. For investment goods, one is to use the credit subsidies described above as a way to maintain support for favored sectors. Similarly, with respect to necessary consumption goods, the government could simply subsidize them, especially insofar as domestic substitutes are available for imports. The merits of such a policy would obviously have to be weighed according to its costs and benefits.

If the costs of direct subsidies for necessities are high, the next move would be for the government to pursue some version of a dual exchange rate policy, that is, separate rates for trade and capital transactions, and perhaps also for necessary and luxury goods and for goods in which domestic industries compete. The government would then defend one rate, such as that for trade transactions, but allow the rate used for capital transactions to float. As Crotty and Epstein (1996b) report, such a policy has been widely used, particularly in developing countries. Even as recently as 1990, 34 developing countries were pursuing some form of a dual exchange rate policy.

The problem with a dual exchange rate policy is that it can be exploited by speculators, who purchase foreign currency at the controlled rate, then purchase foreign assets abroad. In the event that such evasion problems are serious, the next

these successes while still recognizing the obviously crucial point that such a planning approach always opens the possibility for large-scale rent-seeking activities. How to deal with this problem is discussed briefly in the next section and at length in Pollin (1995).

34   The details of this and similar policy tools is discussed in more depth in Pollin (1993).

35   Taylor (1988, 42) estimates that intermediate import costs constitute around 20–40 percent of GDP in a small, open, developing economy.

step would be for the government to impose quantitative restrictions on capital out-flows. Despite the past 15 years of financial deregulation, many countries have maintained quantitative control measures in place. Crotty and Epstein report that, as of 1990, various forms of quantitative controls were in place in 11 industrial coun-tries and 109 developing countries (Crotty and Epstein 1996b).

It is true that these controls are not regularly enforced. But there have been re-cent cases in which these controls were put to use over a short period of time. One set of experiences occurred during the Exchange Rate Mechanism crisis in the fall of 1992. At this time, Ireland and Portugal enforced existing controls with some success. Spain successfully imposed new controls over this same period.

It is important to recognize, however, that in none of these recent cases were the controls maintained for more than three months. An IMF report on these experiences is actually fairly even handed in assessing their effectiveness over the period under which they were enforced. At the same time, this IMF report argues that quantitative controls "are never effective in the long run and may in fact make things worse" (1995, 108). Amid the 1997–98 Asian crisis, the first deputy managing director of the IMF, Stanley Fischer, provided some support for an even longer-term commitment to capital controls, at least with respect to inward credit surges, stating that "capital controls could be acceptable to the IMF for a transitional phase until the financial system of a country is sufficiently strong to deal with surges in short-term loans from abroad" (*New York Times*, nytimes.com, February 3, 1998). The broader issue then is what type of long-term, comprehensive regulatory policies should countries pursue that would be consistent with both financial stabilization and egalitarian growth.

Creating domestic circuit breakers

Anticipating that a dual exchange rate policy or quantitative capital controls are likely to be effective only over a limited period of time, the next crucial step in implementing a sustainable expansionary policy should therefore be to use the breath-ing space provided by capital controls to create a permanent framework for regulat-ing financial markets.

Two appropriate instruments of such a policy agenda that we have already dis-cussed are securities transaction taxes and differential asset reserve requirements. The point, however, is not to rely on any particular set of instruments, but rather to use whatever instruments are most appropriate within a given set of circumstances to meet the broader policy aims. The basic principles for such a policy framework should be as follows.[36]

First, the regulatory environment should be consistent in the way it affects all financial intermediaries; in other words, following D'Arista and Schlesinger (1993), that policy engender an upward leveling of the regulatory environment. Such an approach minimizes opportunities for rent seeking by exploiting regulatory differ-ences among different types of intermediaries. A consistent regulatory structure is

36 These issues are the subject of Pollin (1995) and Dymski, Epstein, and Pollin (1993).

also easier to design, implement, and enforce. These benefits are especially important in situations such as those we are considering, in which a progressive government has a limited time period in which to implement its program.

The second principle on which to design the financial regulatory environment is the promotion of financial market activities in which social rates of return exceed private rates. Thus, for example, the impact of alternative investments on employment and community development should be a criterion by which lending flows are regulated. This is not to say that such employment or community effects are always readily measurable or that implementing such polices is straightforward. For example, whose employment opportunities or community should be the target when measuring social effects? As Barber and Ghilarducci (1993) show, many such problems have, however, been clarified through experiences in establishing social criteria for pension fund investing, and the ability to handle them has been advanced. Such experiences can form the basis for a progressive government's most general approach to the issue.

One obvious criterion in measuring social rates of return is the benefits accruing through financial stability itself. Thus, any new regulatory environment should seek to limit the immediate sources of instability: herding behavior, the contagion effects of market trends, and the spillover effects from financial market activity to the broader economy. At the most basic accounting level, the longer-term cause of instability is when finance and investment patterns engender a flow of funds in which debt commitments systematically outstrip the cash flows necessary to service them. A regulatory environment that circumscribes speculative finance and promotes social investment criteria should then also serve to reduce the emergence of such gaps between debt commitments and cash flows. Within both a short- and longer-term framework, one specific target of a financial stabilization policy should be to limit capital inflows. These capital inflows – often a result of herd behavior among lenders – encourage financial instability through their effect on the domestic cash reserve multiplier. In addition, an unregulated market for capital inflows will worsen the impact of subsequent outflows once the financial market herd has shifted its direction. As noted above, the IMF itself has become increasingly supportive of inward capital controls as a tool for preventing the destabilizing financial practices experienced in Latin America and Asia in the 1990s.[37]

Overall then, following this approach to domestic financial regulation should provide viable domestic circuit breakers, which in turn will limit the impact of the external constraint on domestic expansionary policy.

Some concluding thoughts

The aim of this chapter has been to consider some alternative ways of pursuing viable short-term expansionary policies that would also be consistent with a sustainable egalitarian growth path over the longer term. Its premise is that the con-

---

37 Fuller discussions of the advantages of such policies are presented in Devlin, Ffrench-Davis, and Griffith-Jones (1995) and Griffith-Jones and Stallings (1996).

straints on such initiatives are real and serious, increasingly so as the integration of the global economy within a neo-liberal policy framework proceeds apace. At the same time, it is futile for progressive governments to await the formation of a reconstituted Bretton Woods or some other supportive international arrangement to relieve the various external constraints before they are willing to pursue an expansionary program. The point of this chapter is rather to show the range of policy initiatives that can be successfully deployed in different national settings even after taking the full measure of the external constraints and other difficulties.

Of course, international cooperation in support of full employment would greatly facilitate any domestic expansionary program. But to create pressure for such forms of cooperation will require that successful domestic political movements throughout the world demand them. Their successes should then create demonstration effects. This is the path through which international cooperation for full employment and egalitarian growth is most likely to become a reality.

Comment by J. Bradford De Long on "Can domestic expansionary policy succeed in a globally integrated environment?"

There used to be a strand of thought that argued that the world economy constrained domestic economic policy in only one way: through fixed exchange rates. Let the exchange rate float, argued economists as far left as John Kenneth Galbraith and as far right as Milton Friedman, and then domestic policy will be free and unconstrained – and can be as stimulative (if the outside world should happen to be deflationary) or as committed to price stability (if the outside world should happen to be inflationary) as domestic politicians wish.

Yet for 25 years floating exchange rates have been the rule rather than the exception. And over these 25 years we have learned that this is not the case.

Let me try to give this point – Robert Pollin's point – some more empirical substance. Let me focus on Mexico in 1994–95, because it shows not only how brutal the limits placed on domestic policy by the integration of the world's financial market can be, but also how to at least mitigate the damage.

In the late 1980s, the authoritarian PRI party ruling Mexico shifted its economic policies in a "neo-liberal" direction. Instead of extremely tight restrictions on imports (even imports of the capital goods that serve as one of the major channels of technology transfer to the Third World), the party adopted policies of freer trade. Instead of the high-inflation, high-deficit, high-spending mix that had characterized Mexico's fiscal and monetary policies in the past, it sought monetary stability and balanced budgets. Instead of expansion of the publicly owned sector, the PRI sought "privatization" at home and capital from abroad.

The hope was that such a shift would pay benefits in a number of directions:

First, privatization might – it was hoped – lead to higher productivity in the formerly publicly owned sector. Firms whose principal goals had been to transfer money to favored clients of the PRI oligarchy would find themselves, instead, with the principal goal of earning profits – and satisfying consumers as a step toward earning profits. Second, the liberalization of domestic financial markets might – it was hoped – shift the allocation of investment. Instead of access to capital being limited to those who knew the right people, it might become open to those who could see how to profitably and productively satisfy a strong consumer demand. Third, the reduction in government deficits might – it was hoped – boost the social rate of investment, and thus boost the rate of productivity and real income growth.

Fourth, freedom to buy imports would raise middle-class standards of living, and might make Mexico's upper-middle class happier with the PRI. Fifth, a shift to "neo-liberal" policies might attract large enough capital inflows to allow Mexican investment to outpace domestic savings, further boosting the rate of productivity

461

and real income growth. Sixth, a shift to "neo-liberal" policies would make high Mexican officials heroes in the world financial governance community – boost their reputations abroad at least.

Seventh, privatization would make the privatizees – those who found an opportunity to snatch up ownership of large chunks of capital at what they hoped was a bargain-basement price – very grateful to the privatizers.

Thus, Mexico's steps toward "neo-liberal" policies were taken for a bunch of reasons: some good, some bad, some naive, some subtle.

I happen to think that the policy shift toward neo-liberalism was not a bad thing, or not the worst thing. Put it this way: it was perhaps the best of a number of bad options, certainly not the worst-bet for a Mexican government to have undertaken in the late 1980s. It appeared likely to have led to somewhat faster aggregate economic growth than many other alternatives. It seemed likely to impose significant social costs as well. For example, Mexico's subsistence agriculture sector seemed likely to wither under the force of competition from Iowa. But the social cost could be kept small with appropriate redistributional programs, and the PRI would have every incentive to keep the social cost small.

Were there preferred alternatives? The East Asian "developmental state" model promises an egalitarian distribution of income, rapid productivity and production growth, rapid transformation to a comparative advantage based on mastery of manufacturing technologies, increasing democratization, and a government able to make the redistributions and carry out the infrastructure investments to diminish the social costs of industrialization. The East Asian model is attractive even given the 1997–98 financial crisis.

But as Lant Pritchett has observed, there are few things worse than state-led development carried out by an antidevelopmental – a parasitic – state. It seems clear that the PRI government in Mexico lacked that relative autonomy and bureaucratic capability found in East Asia.

In 1994 Mexico took a policy step away from neo-liberal orthodoxy. There was the forthcoming "election" – which there is good reason to hope was the last Mexican "election" that has to be enclosed in quotation marks. Second, aggregate economic growth had been disappointing over the previous several years: as Rudi Dornbusch and Alejandro Werner put it, Mexico had wound up with "reform, stabilization, and no growth." In part for these and in part for other reasons, the Mexican government shifted its monetary policies in a strongly expansionary direction in early 1994.

Some saw this step away as dangerous. Others held that Mexico's step away from neo-liberal orthodoxy in economic policy in early 1994 was unlikely to be an event with major consequences. Capital flows into Mexico had created pressure pushing the peso upward, not downward, in 1993: if even a small portion of Mexico's export manufacturing sector could use foreign-financed capital to invest and attain the productivity found in, say, Hermosillo, then Mexico's economic growth future looked very bright. Rapid production growth would provide the best circumstances for Mexican industrial workers to push for real wage increases.

Mexico should have been able to get away with a short, temporary, election-year-driven deviation from monetary orthodoxy in the direction of extra Keynesian stimulation. After all, growth would continue as long as foreign investors continued to have confidence in Mexico as an export platform. Confidence in Mexico might be undermined by large, repeated fiscal deficits funded by money printing. But there was no reason for it to be undermined by the more-or-less standard election-year operation of the political business cycle.

Yet this neo-liberal consensus view was very wrong.

December 1994 saw a devaluation – a small devaluation. It seemed to those who modeled the Mexican economy that this small devaluation of 20–30 percent or so, the size recommended by Dornbusch and Werner, would be sufficient to contain the effects of the monetary expansion and the political instability of 1994. If Mexico had been a profitable export platform at the higher exchange rate, it was an even more profitable export platform at the lower. If foreign investors had been eager to pour capital into Mexico when keen-eyed observers like Dornbusch, Calvo, and their co-authors saw devaluation as likely, they would be even more eager to pour capital into Mexico now that no one was arguing that the peso was overvalued.

Wrong.

A classic liquidity panic followed. Never mind that to an investor interested in Mexico over the long term, Mexico post-1994 (with its lower real exchange rate) would appear a better bet than Mexico pre-1994. In spite of "fundamentals" stronger in 1995 than in 1993, the dominant forces governing financier decision making in early 1995 were (a) let's get out of Mexico so that I no longer have to explain what it's doing in my portfolio, and (b) let's get out of Mexico before everyone else's running for the exit brings on a Great Depression in Mexico.

You could point out that those investors with long enough horizons to avoid the panic selling would avoid much of the losses from the crisis (albeit at the cost of running enormous risk). You could point out that those willing to be "contrarian" and put money into Mexico would (if Mexican politics did not degenerate into near-anarchy) realize very high returns. You could point out that an investor who thought that in terms of long-run fundamentals Mexico was a good deal in 1993 could not think that Mexico was a bad deal in 1995 without violating the canons of consistency and rationality in financial decision making.

So much the worse for consistency and rationality in finance. The most likely explanation is that investors, fund managers, and financiers lack the sophistication that economic theorists believe they ought to possess in assessing the financial effects of macroeconomic policies.

Economists focus on the determinants of the money supply process – not only whether the central bank is allowing the money stock to grow, but why the central bank is allowing the money stock to grow and what the money stock will do in the future. Thus, they make a sharp distinction between temporary increases in money growth (as in, for example, an election year) and permanent increases (as when a central bank trying to keep interest rates low monetizes large persistent government budget deficits): the second should be inflationary; the first should not. Yet financiers and fund managers appear to examine the news with a much less sophisti-

cated, much more knee-jerk model – in which all deviations from financial orthodoxy are equally sinful, no matter whether economists' models classify them as
mortal or as only venial sins.

In some ways this is an old story. Few recall 19th century financier Jay Cooke,
without whose fundraising and bond selling skills Sherman's armies would never
have gotten to Atlanta and Grant's armies would never have gotten to Richmond.
He went spectacularly bankrupt in 1873, having played double-or-nothing with his,
his bank's, and his clients' money one time too many while trying to build the Northern
Pacific Railroad.

After the Jay Cooke bankruptcy, British investors fled the United States. And
perhaps one in 10 nonfarm jobs in the American economy vanished as a result of the
collapse in railroad construction alone. To rely on foreign capital inflows to finance
one's industrialization was an extremely risky development strategy for the U.S. in
the 1870s. It is an extremely risky development strategy in the 1990s as well.

So why run the risks? Why not simply close off all capital flows – except for a
small selection? Because the temptation is enormous: when foreign investors are
willing to finance domestic industrialization, extraordinary gains in productivity –
private and public – are possible at a very low cost. Capital is cheap in the First
World. Capital is expensive in the Third World. There is every temptation for those
searching for means to fund industrialization in the Third World to try to tap the
cheap capital of the first.

So what is to be done? Let me propose two steps:

(1) Recognize that openness to capital inflows in boom times amplifies recessions when international finance turns cautious and panicky. International finance
will turn cautious and panicky: it always has in the past, it always will in the future.
Countries need to have someone – whether the International Monetary Fund, Japan,
the United States, or some other consortium – standing behind them. Someone must
be ready to make large-scale exchange stabilization loans when the wheel turns and
it is their turn to suffer not-very-irrational capital flight.

(2) Accept "cold" and reject "hot" money: try to obtain all of the benefits of capital mobility by allowing long-term investors interested in financing industrialization
to come in, and try to avoid all the costs of expectational volatility by keeping short-
term investors subject to irrational fads and fashions in expectations out. Some obvious steps include: taxes on short-term investments that are liquidated in less than a
year; penalties on banks (and corporations) that borrow abroad in major international
reserve currencies like the dollar, the mark, the yen; and surtaxes on foreign holdings
of domestic financial assets but not on direct investments by foreigners.

Without these steps to try to widen running room, the lesson from East Asia
1997–98, Mexico 1994–95, and the European Monetary System 1992 is clear. If
developing countries want to draw on global capital to finance industrialization,
then they have very little running room in terms of their freedom to tune their macroeconomic policy to domestic conditions. Even with these three steps, the running
room regained is small.

Bibliography

Abowd, John. 1991. "Appendix: The NBER Immigration, Trade and Labor Markets Data Files." In J. Abowd and R. Freeman, eds., *Immigration, Trade and the Labor Market.* University of Chicago Press for the NBER: Chicago.

Adler, Michael. 1994. "Lessons From Mexico's Roller-Coaster Ride in the First Quarter of 1994." *Columbia Journal of World Business* 29(2): 84–91.

Agosin, Manuel R., and Ricardo Ffrench-Davis. 1995. "Trade Liberalization and Growth: Recent Experiences in Latin America." *Journal of Interamerican Studies and World Affairs* 37(3): 9–58.

Ahluwalia, I.J. 1985. *Industrial Growth in India,* Delhi; New York: Oxford University Press.

Aitken, Brian, Ann Harrison, and Robert E. Lipsey. 1995. *Wages and Foreign Ownership: A Comparative Study of Mexico, Venezuela, and the United States.* Working Paper No. 5102. Cambridge, Mass.: National Bureau of Economic Research.

Akerlof, George, William Dickens, and George Perry. 1996. "The Macroeconomics of Low Inflation." *Brookings Papers on Economic Activity 1996.1.* Washington, D.C.: Brookings Institution.

Akhtar, M.A. 1995. "Monetary Policy and Long-Term Interest Rates: A Survey of Empirical Literature." *Contemporary Economic Policy* 13(July): 110–30.

Akyuz, Yilmaz. 1994. *Issues in Financial Policy Reform: Myth and Reality.* Geneva: UNCTAD.

Alexander, William E., Thomas Balino, and Charles Enoch. 1995. *The Adoption of Indirect Instruments of Monetary Policy.* IMF Occasional Paper No. 126. Washington, D.C.: IMF.

Altonji, Joseph, and David Card. 1991. "The Effects of Immigration on the Labor Market Outcomes of Less-Skilled Natives." In J. Abowd and R. Freeman, eds., *Immigration, Trade, and the Labor Market.* Chicago: University of Chicago Press, pp. 201–34.

Amendola, Giovanni, et al. 1993. "The Dynamics of International Competitiveness." *Weltwirtschaftliches Archiv* 129(3): 451–71.

American Chamber of Commerce in Mexico (AmCham). 1996. *Business Planning '96: Analysis of the Mexican Marketplace.*

Amsden, Alice H. 1989. *Asia's Next Giant,* New York, N.Y.: Oxford University Press.

Amsden, Alice H. 1994. "Why Isn't the Whole World Experimenting with the East Asian Model to Develop? A Comment on the World Bank *East Asian Miracle Report.*" *World Development* 22:615–70.

Amsden, Alice H., Jacek Kochanowicz, and Lance Taylor. 1994. *The Market Meets Its Match.* Cambridge, Mass.: Harvard University Press.

Anderson, Perry, and Patrick Camiller, eds. 1994. *Mapping the West European Left.* New York, N.Y.: Verso.

Anderson, Sarah, John Cavanagh, and David Ranney, eds. 1996. *NAFTA's First Two Years: The Myths and the Realities.* Washington, D.C.: Institute for Policy Studies.

Ansari, M.A. 1990. "Migration and Agricultural Development: A Study of the Effects of the Migration of Bihari Labourers." M.Phil dissertation, Jawaharlal Nehru University, New Delhi.

465

Apgar, William, Denise DiPasquale, Jean Cummings, and Nancy McArdle. 1991. *The State of the Nation's Housing*. Cambridge, Mass.: Joint Center for Housing Studies of Harvard University.

Appelbaum, Eileen, and Peter Berg. 1996. "Financial Market Constraints and Business Strategy in the U.S." In J. Michie and J. Grieve Smith, eds., *Restoring Full Employment: Rebuilding Industrial Capacity,* Oxford: Oxford University Press, pp. 192–224.

Archibugi, Daniele, and Jonathan Michie. 1995. "The Globalisation of Technology: A New Taxonomy." *Cambridge Journal of Economics* 19(2).

Arrow, Kenneth, et al. 1995. "Economic Growth, Carrying Capacity and the Environment." *Science,* 268(April 28): 520–1.

Atkinson, A.B., L. Rainwater, and T.M. Smeeding. 1985. *Income Distribution in OECD Countries.* Paris: OECD.

Bach, Robert L., and Rita Aguiros. 1991. "Economic Progress Among Southeast Asian Refugees in the United States." In H. Adelman, ed., *Refugee Policy: Canada and the United States.* Toronto: Centre for Refugee Studies, York University; Staten Island, New York: Center for Migration Studies of New York.

Bagchi, A.K. 1971. "The Theory of Efficient Neo-Colonialism." *Economic and Political Weekly,* Special No. (July).

Bailey, Thomas. 1987. *Immigrant and Native Workers: Contrasts and Competition.* Boulder, Colo.: Westview Press.

Baily, Martin Neil, Gary Burtless, and Robert E. Litan. 1993. *Growth With Equity: Economic Policymaking for the Next Century.* Washington, D.C.: Brookings Institution.

Bairoch, Paul, and Richard Kozul-Wright. 1996. "Globalisation Myths and Realities: Some Historical Reflections on Integration, Industrialisation and Growth in the World Economy." UNCTAD Discussion Paper No. 113. Geneva: UNCTAD.

Baker, Dean, and Todd Schafer. 1993. "Putting Deficit Reduction First?" *Challenge,* May–June, 4–10.

Baker, Dean, Robert Pollin, and Marc Schaberg. 1995. "The Case for a Securities Transaction Tax: Taxing the Big Casino." Department of Economics, University of California-Riverside. Manuscript.

Balakrishnan, P., and N. Pushpangadan. 1994. "Total Factor Productivity Growth in Manufacturing Industry: A Fresh Look." *Economic and Political Weekly,* July 30.

Ball, Michael, and Maartje Martens. 1990. "German Universal Banking and the Mortgage Market." In M. Ball, *Under One Roof.* New York, N.Y.: St. Martin's Press.

Ball, Michael. 1990. *Under One Roof.* New York, N.Y.: St. Martin's Press.

Bank for International Settlements (BIS). 1993a. *Central Bank Survey of Foreign Exchange Market Activity in April 1992.* Basle: BIS.

Bank for International Settlements (BIS). 1993b. *Survey of Foreign Exchange Activity in April 1992.* Basle: BIS.

Bank for International Settlements (BIS). 1996. *Central Bank Survey of Foreign Exchange and Derivatives Market Activity, 1995.* Basle: BIS.

Bank for International Settlements (BIS). 1997. *Annual Report.* Basle: BIS.

Bank of England. 1996. *Inflation Report.* London: Bank of England.

Banuri, Tariq, and Juliet Schor. 1992. *Financial Openness and National Autonomy: Opportunities and Constraints,* Oxford: Oxford University Press.

Barber, Randy, and Teresa Ghilarducci. 1993. "Pension Funds, Capital Markets, and the Economic Future." In G. Dymski, G. Epstein, and R. Pollin, eds., *Transforming the U.S. Financial System: Equity and Efficiency for the 21st Century,* Armonk, N.Y.: M.E. Sharpe, pp. 287–320.

Barnet, Richard J., and John Cavanagh. 1994. *Global Dreams: Imperial Corporations and the New World Order.* New York, N.Y.: Simon and Schuster.

Batchelor, R., R. Major, and A. Morgan. 1980. *Industrialisation and the Basis for Trade.* Cambridge; New York: Cambridge University Press.

Bean, Frank, B. Lindsay Lowell, and Lowell J. Taylor. 1988. "Undocumented Mexican Immigrants and the Earnings of Other Workers in the United States." *Demography* 35(Feb.): 35–52.

Bell, B. 1995. *The CEP–OECD Data Set (1950–1990).* Oxford: Institute of Economics and Statistics, University of Oxford.

Belman, Dale, and Thea Lee. 1996. "International Trade and the Performance of U.S. Labor Markets." In Robert A. Blecker, ed., *U.S. Trade Policy and Global Growth.* Armonk, N.Y.: M.E. Sharpe.

Bernanke, Ben, and Alan Blinder. 1988. "Credit, Money, and Aggregate Demand." *American Economic Review* 78(May): 435–9.

Berndt, Ernst R. 1991. *The Practice of Econometrics: Classic and Contemporary,* Reading, Mass.: Addison-Wesley.

Berry, Steven, Vittorio Grilli, and Florencio Lopez de Silanes. 1993. "The Automobile Industry and the Mexico–U.S. Free Trade Agreement." In Peter M. Garber, ed., *The Mexico–U.S. Free Trade Agreement.* Cambridge, Mass: MIT Press, pp. 219–77.

Bertero, Elisabetta. 1994. "The Banking System, Financial Markets, and Capital Structure: Some New Evidence From France." *Oxford Review of Economic Policy* 10(4): 68–78.

Bettelheim, Charles. 1968. *India Independent.* Translated from the French by W.A. Caswell. London: MacGibbon and Kee.

Bhaduri, Amit, and R. Skarstein. 1996. "Short-Period Macroeconomic Aspects of Foreign Aid." *Cambridge Journal of Economics* 19(March).

Bhaduri, Amit, and Stephen Marglin. 1990. "Unemployment and the Real Wage: The Economic Basis for Contesting Political Ideologies." *Cambridge Journal of Economics* 14(4): 375–93.

Bhaduri, Amit. 1987. "Dependent and Self-Reliant Growth With Foreign Borrowing." *Cambridge Journal of Economics* 11(September): 269–73.

Bhagwati, Jadish 1982. "Directly Unproductive Profit-Seeking Activity." *Journal of Political Economy* 90(5): 998–1002.

Bhagwati, Jadish. 1997. "The Brain Drain: International Resource Flow Accounting, Compensation, Taxation and Related Policy Proposals." In J. Bhagwati, *Writings on International Economics.* Delhi: Oxford University Press.

Bhagwati, Jagdish. 1988. *Protectionism.* Cambridge, Mass.: MIT Press.

Bhagwati, Jagdish. 1993. "The Case for Free-Trade." *Scientific American,* November.

Bhalla, S. 1987. "Trends in Employment in Indian Agriculture, Land and Asset Distribution." *Indian Journal of Agricultural Economics,* October–December.

Blanchard, Oliver, and Lawrence Summers. 1988. "Beyond the Natural Rate Hypothesis." *American Economic Review Papers and Proceedings* 78: 182–7.

Blanchard, Oliver. 1984. "The Lucas Critique and the Volcker Deflation." *American Economic Review,* May: 211–5.

Blanchflower, D., and A. Oswald. 1994. *The Wage Curve.* Cambridge, Mass.: MIT Press.

Blau, Francine. 1984. "The Use of Transfer Payments by Immigrants." *Industrial and Labor Relations Review* 37(January): 222–39.

Blecker, Robert A. 1989. "International Competition, Income Distribution and Economic Growth." *Cambridge Journal of Economics* 13(3): 395–412.

Blecker, Robert A. 1991. "Still a Debtor Nation: Interpreting the New U.S. International Investment Data." Briefing Paper. Washington, D.C.: Economic Policy Institute.

Blecker, Robert A. 1997a. "The New Economic Integration: Structuralist Models of North-South Trade and Investment Liberalization," *Structural Change and Economic Dynamics* 7(3): 321–45.

Blecker, Robert A. 1997b. "Policy Implications of the International Saving-Investment Correlation." In R. Pollin, ed., *The Macroeconomics of Saving, Finance and Investment,* Ann Arbor, Mich.: University of Michigan Press.

Blomstrom, Magnus, and Ari Kokko. 1994. *Home Country Effects of Foreign Direct Investment: Evidence for Sweden.* Working Paper No. 4639. Cambridge, Mass: National Bureau of Economic Research.

Blomstrom, Magnus, Gunnar Fors, and Robert E. Lipsey. 1997. "Foreign Direct Investment and Employment: Home Country Experience in the United States and Sweden." *Economic Journal* 107(November): 1787–97.

Bluestone, Barry, and Bennett Harrison. 1982. *The Deindustrialization of America: Plant Closings, Community Abandonment and the Dismantling of Industry.* New York, N.Y.: Basic Books.

Bluestone, Barry. 1994. "The Inequality Express." *The American Prospect,* Winter: 81–93.

Blundell-Wignall, Adrian and Frank Browne 1991. *Macroeconomic Consequences of Financial Liberalization: A Summary Report.* Working Paper No. 98. Paris: OECD Department of Economics and Statistics.

Blundell-Wignall, Adrian, and Frank Browne. 1991. *Increasing Financial Market Integration, Real Exchange Rates and Macroeconomic Adjustments.* Working Paper No. 96. Paris: OECD Department of Economics and Statistics.

Blundell-Wignall, Adrian, Frank Browne, and Paolo Manasse. 1985. *Monetary Policy in the Wake of Financial Liberalisation.* Working Paper No. 77. Paris: OECD Department of Economics and Statistics.

Bohning, W.R. and M.-L. Schloeter-Paredes, eds. 1994. *Aid in Place of Migration.* Geneva: International Labour Organization.

Boleat, Mark, 1985. *National Housing Finance Systems: A Comparative Study.* Kent: Croom Helm.

Boltho, Althea, and Andrew Glyn. 1995. "Macroeconomic Policies, Public Spending and Employment." *International Labor Review* 134(4-5): 451-470.

Bond, S. et al. 1991. "Investment and the Role of Tax Incentives." In A. Britton, ed., *Industrial Investment as a Policy Objective.* National Institute of Economic and Social Research Report Series No 3. London.

Boratav, Korkut, Oktar Turel, and Erinc Yeldan. 1996. "Dilemmas of Structural Adjustment and Environmental Policies under Instability: Post-1980 Turkey." *World Development* 24: 373–93.

Borjas, George J. 1987. "Immigrants, Minorities, and Labor Market Competition." *Industrial and Labor Relations Review* 40(April): 382–92.

Borjas, George J. 1990. *Friends or Strangers: The Impact of Immigrants on the U.S. Economy.* New York, N.Y.: Basic Books.

Borjas, George J. 1994. "The Economics of Immigration." *Journal of Economic Literature* 32(Dec.): 1667–1717.

Borjas, George J., Richard Freeman, and Lawrence Katz. 1992. "On the Labor Market. Effects of Immigration and Trade." In G. Borjas and R. Freeman, eds., *Immigration and the Work Force: Economic Consequences for the United States and Source Countries.* Chicago: University of Chicago Press, pp. 213–44.

Bosworth, Barry. 1989. "Institutional Change and the Efficacy of Monetary Policy." *Brookings Papers on Economic Activity 1989:1.* Washington, D.C. Brookings Institution, pp. 77–125.

Bourguignon, François, and Christian Morrisson. 1989. *External Trade and Income Distribution.* Paris: OECD Development Centre Studies.

Bowles, Samuel, David Gordon, and Thomas Weisskopf. 1984. *Beyond the Waste Land: A Democratic Alternative to Economic Decline.* Garden City, N.Y.: Anchor.

Bowles, Samuel. 1985. "The Production Process in a Competitive Economy: Walrasian, Hobbesian and Marxian Models." *American Economic Review* 75(1): 16–36.

Boyer, Robert. 1996."The Convergence Hypothesis Revisited: Globalization but Still the Century of Nations?" In S. Berger and R. Dore, eds., *National Diversity and Global Capitalism.* Ithaca, N.Y.: Cornell University Press, pp. 29–59.

Bradt, Kenneth W. 1991. "Securitization in Europe." In C. Stone, A. Zissu, and J. Lederman, eds., *Asset Securitization: Theory and Practice in Europe.* London: Euromoney Books, pp. 1–24.

Breman, J. 1995. *Of Peasants, Migrants and Paupers.* Delhi; New York: Oxford University Press.

Brewer, Anthony. 1985. "Trade With Fixed Real Wages and Mobile Capital." *Journal of International Economics* 18(2): 177–86.

Brittan, L. 1995. "Investment Liberalisation: The Next Great Boost to the World Economy." *Transnational Corporations* 4(1).

Bronfenbrenner, Kate. 1996. "The Effects of Plant Closing or Threat of Plant Closing on the Right of Workers to Organize." Report to Department of Labor, September.

Bruneel, Didier. 1992. "The Reform of the French Financial System." In H. Cavanna, ed., *Financial Innovation.* London: Routledge, pp. 135–76.

Bruno, Michael. 1995. "Does Inflation Really Lower Growth?" *Finance and Development* (September).

Buiter, W., G. Corsetti, and N. Roubini. 1993. "Excessive Deficits: Sense and Nonsense in the Treaty of Maastricht." *Economic Policy* (16): 58–100.

Burchell, Robert W. and David Listokin. 1995. "Influences on United States Housing Policy." *Housing Policy Debate* 6(3): 559–618.

Burfisher, Mary, Karen Thierfelder, and Kenneth Hanson. 1992. *Data Base for a Computable General Equilibrium Model of the Agricultural Sectors of the United States and Mexico and Their Interactions.* Staff Report No. AGES 9225. Washington, D.C.: U.S. Department of Agriculture, Economic Research Service, Agriculture and Trade Analysis Division.

Burke, James. 1997. *The Effects of Foreign Direct Investment on Investment, Employment and Wages in the United States.* Amherst, Mass.: University of Massachusetts-Amherst.

Business Frontier. 1996. "Mandatory Employee Benefits in Mexico." *Federal Reserve Bank of Dallas Business Frontier.* Issue 1.

Butcher, Kristin, and David Card. 1991. "Immigration and Wages: Evidence From the 1980s." *American Economic Review* 81(May): 292–96.

Byres, T.J., ed. 1998. "The Indian Economy: Major Debates Since Independence." Delhi; New York: Oxford University Press.

Cable, V. 1995. "The Diminished Nation-State: A Study in the Loss of Economic Power." *Daedalus* 124(2).

Calder, Kent. 1997. "Assault on the Bankers' Kingdom: Politics, Markets, and the Liberalization of Japanese Industrial Finance." In Loriaux et al., eds., *Capital Ungoverned: Liberalizing Finance in Interventionist States.* Ithaca, N.Y.: Cornell University Press.

Callen, T.S., and J.W. Lomax. 1990. "The Development of the Building Societies Sector in the 1980s." *Bank of England Quarterly Bulletin* (November): 503–10.

Calmfors, L. 1993. "Lessons From the Macroeconomic Experience of Sweden." *European Journal of Political Economy* 9: 25–72.

Camdessus, Michel. 1995. "The IMF in the Globalized World Economy." *IMF Survey,* June 19.

Campbell, John, and Kenneth A. Froot. 1993. "Securities Transaction Taxes: Lessons From International Experience." Working Paper No. 4587. Cambridge, Mass.: National Bureau of Economic Research.

Campbell, John, and Robert J. Shiller. 1991. "Yield Spreads and Interest Rate Movements: A Bird's Eye View." *Review of Economic Studies*, 495–514.

Card, David. 1990. "The Impact of the Mariel Boatlift on the Miami Labor Market." *Industrial and Labor Relations Review* 43(January): 245–57.

Carriere, Jean. 1991. "The Crisis in Costa Rica: An Ecological Perspective." In D. Goodman and M. Redclift, eds., *Environment and Development in Latin America.* New York, N.Y.: Manchester University Press.

Carroll, Christopher D., and Lawrence H. Summers. 1991. "Consumption Growth Parallels Income Growth: Some New Evidence." in B.D. Bernheim and J.B. Shoven, eds., *National Saving and Economic Performance.* Chicago: University of Chicago Press, pp. 305–43.

Cavanagh, John, et al. 1996. "South-North: Citizen Strategies to Transform a Divided World." San Francisco: International Forum on Globalization.

Caves, Richard E. 1996. *Multinational Enterprise and Economic Analysis.* 2nd edition. Cambridge: Cambridge University Press.

Centre for Economic Policy Research (CEPR). 1995. *Unemployment: Choices for Europe.* London: CEPR.

Cerny, Philip G. 1994. "The Dynamics of Financial Globalization: Technology, Market Structure, and Policy Response." *Policy Sciences* 27: 319–42.

Chakravarty, S. 1987. *Development Planning: The Indian Experience.* Delhi: Oxford; New York; Toronto and Melbourne: Oxford University Press, Clarendon Press.

Chakravarty, S. 1993. *Selected Economic Writings.* Delhi; Oxford; New York and Toronto: Oxford University Press.

Chandrasekhar, C.P. 1995. "The Macroeconomics of Imbalance and Adjustment." In P. Patnaik, ed., *Macroeconomics. Oxford in India Readings: Themes in Economics Series.* Delhi; Oxford and New York: Oxford University Press.

Chang, Ha-Joon, and Ajit Singh. 1993. "Public Enterprises in Developing Countries and Economic Efficiency." *UNCTAD Review* (4): 45–82.

Chang, Ha-Joon, and Bob Rowthorn, eds., 1995. *The Role of the State in Economic Change.* Oxford: Oxford University Press.

Chang, Ha-Joon, and Bob Rowthorn. 1995. "The Role of the State in Economic Change: Entrepreneurship and Conflict Management." In H-J. Chang and B. Rowthorn, eds., *The Role of the State in Economic Change.* Oxford: Oxford University Press.

Chang, Ha-Joon. 1993. "The Political Economy of Industrial Policy in Korea." *Cambridge Journal of Economics* (17): 131–57.

Chang, Ha-Joon. 1994. *The Political Economy of Industrial Policy.* London and Basingstoke, Macmillan.

Chang, Ha-Joon. 1997. "Perspective on Korea: A Crisis From Underregulation." *Los Angeles Times,* December 31.

Chang, Ha-Joon. 1998. "Korea: The Misunderstood Crisis." Faculty of Economics and Politics, University of Cambridge. Manuscript.

Chapman, Duane. 1985. "Global Pollution and International Trade." Staff Paper No. 85–24. Ithaca, N.Y.: Cornell Agricultural Economics.

Chapman, Duane. 1987. "The Economic Significance of Pollution Control and Worker Safety Costs for World Copper Trade." Staff Paper No. 87–25. Ithaca, N.Y.: Cornell Agricultural Economics.

Chichilinsky, Graciella. 1994. "North-South Trade and the Global Environment." *American Economic Review* 84(4): 851–74.

Chin, Menzie, and Michael Dooley. 1995. "Asia-Pacific Capital Markets: Integration and Implications for Economic Activity" Working Paper No. 5280. Cambridge, Mass.: National Bureau of Economic Research.

Chirinko, Robert S., and Robert Eisner. 1982. "The Effects of Tax Parameters in the Investment Equations in Macroeconometric Models." In M. Blume, J. Crockett, and P. Taubman, eds., *Economic Activity and Finance.* Cambridge, Mass.: Ballinger, pp. 25–84.

Chisari, Omar O., Jose Maria Fanelli, and Roberto Frenkel. 1996. "Argentina: Growth Resumption, Sustainability, and Environment." *World Development* 24: 227–40.

Chitrakar, Ramesh, and John Weiss. 1995. "Foreign Investment in Nepal in the 1980s: A Cost Benefit Evaluation." *Journal of Development Studies* 31(3): 451-66.

Christiano, Lawrence, and Martin Eichenbaum. 1991. *Identification and the Liquidity Effect of a Monetary Policy Shock.* Working Paper No. 3920. Cambridge, Mass.: National Bureau of Economic Research.

Chudnovsky, D., ed. 1993. *Transnational Corporations and Industrialisation.* London: Routledge.

Cohen, Gerald D., and John Wenninger. 1994. *Changing Relationship Between the Spread and the Funds Rate.* Working Paper No. 9408. New York, N.Y.: Federal Reserve Bank of New York.

Cohen, Joel. 1995. *How Many People Can the Earth Support?* New York, N.Y.: Norton.

Collins, Susan M. 1994. *Distributive Issues: A Constraint on Global Integration?* Washington, D.C.: Brookings Institution.

Commission of the European Communities. 1992. *Report of the Committee of Independent Experts on Company Tax.* Brussels: CEC.

Congressional Budget Office (CBO). 1993. *A Budgetary and Economic Analysis of the North American Free Trade Agreement*. Washington, D.C.: U.S. Government Printing Office.

Congressional Budget Office (CBO). 1994. *The Economic and Budget Outlook: An Update*. Washington, D.C.: Congressional Budget Office.

Cook, Timothy, and Hahn, Thomas. 1989. "The Effects of Changes in the Federal Funds Rate Target on Market Interest Rates in the 1970s." *Journal of Monetary Economics* (November): 331–5.

Council of Economic Advisors. 1995. *Economic Report of the President*. Washington, D.C.: U.S. Government Printing Office.

Cross, Rod, ed. 1995. *The Natural Rate of Unemployment: Reflections on 25 Years of the Hypothesis*. Cambridge: Cambridge University Press.

Crotty, James, and Don Goldstein. 1993. "Do U.S. Financial Markets Allocate Credit Efficiently? The Case of Corporate Restructuring in the 1980s." In G. Dymski, G. Epstein, and R. Pollin eds., *Transforming the U.S. Financial System: Equity and Efficiency for the 21st Century*. Armonk, N.Y.: M.E. Sharpe, pp. 253–86.

Crotty, James, and Gerald Epstein. 1996. "Capital Controls for a New Social Contract." *Socialist Register*.

Crotty, James, and Gerald Epstein. 1996. "In Defense of Capital Controls." *Socialist Register*, 118–49.

Crotty, James, Gerald Epstein, and Patricia Kelly. 1997. "Multinational Corporations, Capital Mobility and the Neo-Liberal Regime: Effects on Northern Workers and on Growth Prospects in the Developing World." *Seoul Journal of Economics* 11(4): 297-340.

Crotty, James. 1993. "Rethinking Marxian Investment Theory: Keynes-Minsky Instability, Competitive Regime Shifts and Coerced Investment." *Review of Radical Political Economics* 25: 1–26.

Cullenberg, Stephen, and George DeMartino. 1995. "Economic Integration in an Uneven World: An Internationalist Perspective." *International Review of Applied Economics* 9(1).

Cumby, R.E., and F.S. Mishkin. 1986. "The International Linkage of Real Interest Rates: The European–US Connection." *Journal of International Money and Finance* 5(March): 5–23.

Cumby, R.E., and M. Obstfeld. 1984. "International Interest Rate and Price Level Linkages Under Flexible Exchange Rates." In J.F. Bilson, and R.C. Marston, eds., *Exchange Rate Theory and Practice*. Chicago: University of Chicago Press.

D'Arista, Jane, and Tom Schlesinger. 1993. "The Parallel Banking System." In G. Dymski, G. Epstein, and R. Pollin, eds., *Transforming the U.S. Financial System: Equity and Efficiency for the 21st Century*, Armonk, N.Y.: M.E. Sharpe, pp. 157–200.

Daly, Herman, and Robert Goodland. 1994. "An Ecological-Economic Assessment of Deregulation of International Commerce Under GATT." *Ecological Economics* 9: 13–22.

Daly, Herman. 1991. "The Perils of Free Trade." *Scientific American* (November).

Dasgupta, Partha. 1995. "The Population Problem: Theory and Evidence." *Journal of Economic Literature* 33(4): 1879–1902.

Davis, L.A. 1993. "U.S. Trade in Merchandise and Services by Foreign-Owned U.S. Firms." In *Foreign Direct Investment in the United States: An Update*. Washington, D.C.: Office of the Chief Economist, U.S. Department of Commerce.

De Cecco, Marcello, ed. 1987. *Changing Money: Financial Innovation in Developed Countries*. New York, N.Y.: Basil Blackwell.

Deardorff, Alan V., and Dalia S. Hakura. 1994. "Trade and Wages: What Are the Questions?" In J. Bhagwati and M. H. Kosters, eds., *Trade and Wages: Leveling Wages Down?* Washington, D.C.: American Enterprise Institute.

DeFreitas, Gregory, and Adriana Marshall. 1983. "Immigration and Wage Growth in U.S. Manufacturing in the 1970s." *Industrial Relations Research Association Proceedings* 36(December):148–56.

DeFreitas, Gregory. 1988. "Hispanic Immigration and Labor Market Segmentation." *Industrial Relations* 27(Spring): 195–214.

DeFreitas, Gregory. 1991. *Inequality at Work: Hispanics in the U.S. Labor Force*. New York, N.Y.: Oxford University Press.

DeFreitas, Gregory. 1993. "Unionization Among Racial and Ethnic Minorities." *Industrial and Labor Relations Review* 46(January): 284–301.

DeFreitas, Gregory. 1994. "Fear of Foreigners: Immigrants as Scapegoats for Domestic Woes." *Dollars and Sense* (January–February).

DeFreitas, Gregory. 1996. "Nonimmigrant Visa Programs: Problems and Policy Reforms." In L. Lowell, ed., *Temporary Migrants in the U.S.* Washington, D.C.: U.S. Commission on Immigration Reform, pp. 189–98.

DeFreitas, Gregory. Forthcoming. *Futures at Risk: Youth in the New York Economy.*

DeLong, J. Bradford, Andrei Shleifer, Lawrence H. Summers, and Robert J. Waldmann. 1990. "Noise Trader Risk in Financial Markets." *Journal of Political Economy*, 703–38.

Devlin, Robert, Ricardo Ffrench-Davis, and Stephany Griffith Jones. 1995. "Surges in Capital Flows and Development: An Overview of Policy Issues." In R. Ffrench-Davis and S. Griffith-Jones, eds., *Coping With Capital Surges: The Return of Finance to Latin America*. Boulder, Colo.: Lynne Rienner, pp. 225–60.

Devlin, Robert. 1989. *Debt and Crisis in Latin America: The Supply Side of the Story*. Princeton, N.J.: Princeton University Press.

Diamond, Douglas B., and Michael J. Lea. 1992a. "Housing Finance in Developed Countries: An International Comparison of Efficiency." *Journal of Housing Research* 3(1): 1–271.

Diamond, Douglas B., and Michael J. Lea. 1992b. "The Decline of Special Circuits in Developed Country Housing Finance." *Housing Policy Debate* 3(3): 747–77.

Diaz-Alejandro, Carlos. 1985. "Goodby Financial Repression: Hello Financial Crash." *Journal of Development Economics* 19.

Dicken, P. 1992. *The Global Shift*. New York: Guildford Press.

Dixit, Avinash. 1992. "Investment and Hysterisis." *Journal of Economic Perspectives* 6(Winter).

Dore R., R. Boyer, and Z. Mars. 1994. *The Return to Incomes Policy*. London: Pinter.

Dorman, Peter. 1998. "Actually Existing Globalization." In M. Schechter, ed., *Actually Existing Globalization*. New York, N.Y.: St. Martin's Press, forthcoming.

Dornbusch, Rudiger, and Alberto Giovannini. 1990. "Monetary Policy in the Open Economy." In B. Friedman and F. Hahn, eds., *Handbook of Monetary Economics, Vol. II*. Amsterdam: Elsevier Science, pp. 1231–1303.

Dornbusch, Rudiger, and Mario Henrique Simonsen, eds. 1983. *Inflation, Debt, and Indexation.* Cambridge, Mass.: MIT Press.

Dosi, Giovanni, Keith Pavitt, and Luc Soete. 1990. *The Economics of Technical Change and International Trade.* New York, N.Y.: NYU Press.

Duchin, Faye, and Glenn-Marie Lange. 1992. *Strategies for Environmentally Sound Economic Development.* New York, N.Y.: Institute for Economic Analysis.

Duguay, Pierre. 1994. "Empirical Evidence on the Strength of the Monetary Transmission Mechanism in Canada." *Journal of Monetary Economics* 33: 39–61.

Dunning, J.H. 1983. "Changes in the Level and Structure of International Production: The Last One Hundred Years." In M. Casson, ed., *The Growth of international Business.* London: Allen and Unwin, pp. 84–139.

Durand, Jorge, and D.S. Massey. 1992. "Mexican Migration to the U.S.: A Critical Review." *Latin American Research Review* 23: 3–43.

Dutt, Amitava Krishna. 1996. "The Role of Keynesian Policies in Semi-Industrialized Countries: Theory and Evidence From India." *International Review of Applied Economics* 10(1): 127–40.

Dymski, Gary, and Dorene Isenberg. 1995. *Second Thoughts on the Revolution in Housing Finance.* Drew University and University of California, Riverside.

Dymski, Gary, and Dorene Isenberg. 1996. "Social Efficiency and the 'Market Revolution' in U.S. Housing Finance." In proceedings of an international conference, "Evolving Roles of Government in Japan and the United States," edited by Shinya Imura, Takashi Nakahama, and Hiroshi Shibuya; in Japanese translation.

Dymski, Gary, and John Veitch. 1992. *It's Not a Wonderful Life: Housing Affordability in Los Angeles.* University of California, Riverside.

Dymski, Gary, and Robert Pollin, eds. 1994. *New Perspectives in Monetary Macroeconomics: Explorations in the Tradition of Hyman P. Minsky.* Ann Arbor, Mich: University of Michigan Press.

Dymski, Gary, Gerald Epstein, and Robert Pollin, eds. 1993. *Transforming the U.S. Financial System: Equity and Efficiency for the 21st Century,* Armonk, N.Y.: M.E. Sharpe.

Eatwell, John. 1994. "The Coordination of Macroeconomic Policy in the European Community." In J. Michie and J. Grieve Smith, eds., *Unemployment in Europe,* London: Academic Press, pp. 209–19.

Eatwell, John. 1996. *International Financial Liberalization: The Impact on World Development.* Discussion Paper Series. New York, N.Y.: United Nations Development Programme, Office of Development Studies.

Economic Planning Board (EPB). 1981. *Oegoogin Tooja Baeksuh* (White Paper on Foreign Investment). Seoul: Government of Korea; in Korean.

Economist Intelligence Unit (EIU). 1997. *Country Report. Mexico.* 4th Quarter. London: Economist Intelligence Unit.

Edey, Malcolm, and Ketil Hviding. 1995. "An Assessment of Financial Reform in OECD Countries." Economic Studies No. 25. Paris: OECD.

Edwards, Sebastian. 1993. "Openness, Trade Liberalization, and Growth in Developing Countries." *Journal of Economic Literature* 31(3): 1358–93.

Eichenbaum, Martin, and Evans, Charles. 1993. "Some Empirical Evidence on the Effects of Monetary Policy Shocks on Exchange Rates" Working Paper No. 4271. Cambridge, Mass.: National Bureau of Economic Research.

Eichengreen, B., J. Tobin, and C. Wyplosz. 1995. "Two Cases for Sand in the Wheels of International Finance." *Economic Journal* 105(January): 162–72.

Eichengreen, Barry, and Charles Wyplosz. 1993. "The Unstable EMS." *Brookings Papers on Economic Activity, 1993.1*. Washington, D.C.: Brookings Institution.

Eisner, Robert, and Paul J. Pieper. 1990. "The World's Greatest Debtor Nation?" *North American Review of Economics and Finance* 1(1).

Eisner, Robert. 1973. "Tax Incentives for Investment." *National Tax Journal* (September): 397–401.

Eisner, Robert. 1995. "A New View of the NAIRU." Department of Economics, Northwestern University. Manuscript.

Eisner, Robert. 1997. "A New View of the Nairu." In P. Davidson and J. Kregel, eds., *Improving the Global Economy: Keynesianism and the Growth in Output and Employment*. Brookfield, Vt: Edward Elgar.

El Financiero International (EFI). Various dates. Weekly newspaper. Mexico, D.F.

Enchautegui, Maria E. 1993. *The Effects of Immigration on the Wages and Employment of Black Males*. Washington, D.C.: Urban Institute.

Enchautegui, Maria E. 1994. *Can the United States Continue to Absorb Immigrants? The 1980–90 Wage Experience*. Washington, D.C.: Urban Institute.

Epstein, Gerald, and Herbert Gintis. 1992. "International Capital Markets and the Limits of National Economic Policy." In T. Banuri and J. Schor, eds., *Financial Openness and National Autonomy,* Oxford: Clarendon Press, pp. 167–197.

Epstein, Gerald, and Juliet Schor. 1990. "Macropolicy in the Rise and Fall of the Golden Age." In S. Marglin and J. Schor, eds., *The Golden Age of Capitalism: Reinterpreting the Postwar Experience*. New York, N.Y.: Oxford University Press, pp. 126–52.

Epstein, Gerald. 1993. "Monetary Policy in the 1990s: Overcoming the Barriers to Equity and Growth." In G. Dymski, G. Epstein, and R. Pollin, eds., *Transforming the U.S. Financial System: Equity and Efficiency for the 21st Century*. Armonk, N.Y.: M.E. Sharpe, pp. 65–100.

Epstein, Gerald. 1993. "The United States as a Debtor Country." In G. Epstein, J. Graham, and J. Nembhard, eds., *Creating a New World Economy*. Philadelphia, Pa.: Temple University Press, pp. 199–22.

Epstein, Gerald. 1995. "International Financial Integration and Full Employment Monetary Policy." *Review of Political Economy.* 7(2): 164–85.

Epstein, Gerald. 1996. "International Capital Mobility and the Scope for National Economic Management." In R. Boyer and D. Drache, eds., *States Against Markets: The Limits of Globalization,* New York, N.Y.: Routledge, pp. 211–26.

Epstein, Gerald. 1996. "International Profit Rate Equalization and Investment: An Empirical Analysis of Integration, Instability and Enforcement." In Epstein and Gintis, eds., *Macroeconomic Policy After the Conservative Era*. Cambridge: Cambridge University Press, pp. 308–31.

Erickson, Christopher L., and Sarosh Kuruvilla. 1994. "Labor Costs and the Social Dumping Debate in the European Union." *Industrial and Labor Relations Review* 48(1): 28–47.

Estrella, Arturo, and Gikas Hardouvelis. 1990. "Possible Roles of the Yield Curve in Monetary Policy." In Federal Reserve Bank of New York, *Intermediate Targets and Indicators for Monetary Policy: A Critical Survey.* New York, N.Y.: Federal Reserve Bank of New York, pp. 339–62.

Esty, Daniel C. 1994. *Greening the GATT.* Washington, D.C.: Institute for International Economics.

European Commission (EC). 1995. "A Level Playing Field for Direct Investment World-Wide." Brussels: the EC.

European Community Mortgage Federation. 1990. *Mortgage Credit in the European Community.* Brussels: European Community Mortgage Federation.

Evans, Peter. 1987. "Class, State, and Dependence in East Asia: Lessons for Latin Americanists." In F. Deyo, ed., *The Political Economy of the New Asian Industrialism.* Ithaca, N.Y.: Cornell University Press.

Evans, Peter. 1995. *Embedded Autonomy.* Princeton N.J.: Princeton University Press.

Evans, Peter. 1998. "TNCs and Third World States: From the Old Internationalisation to the New." In R. Kozul-Wright and R. Rowthorn, eds., *Transnational Corporations and the World Economy.* London and Basingstoke: Macmillan Press, forthcoming.

Fagerberg, J. 1988. "International Competitiveness." *Economic Journal* 98(2): 355–74.

Fair, Ray. 1996. "Testing the Standard View of the Long-Run Unemployment-Inflation Relationship." Yale University. Manuscript.

Fama, Eugene. 1984. "Forward and Spot Exchange Rates." *Journal of Monetary Economics* 14: 319–38.

Fatouros, A.A. 1996. "Towards an International Agreement on Foreign Direct Investment?" In OECD, *Towards Multilateral Investment Rules; OECD Documents.* Paris: OECD, pp. 47–67.

Fazzari, Steven. 1993. "Monetary Policy, Financial Structure and Investment." In G. Dymski, G. Epstein, and R. Pollin, eds., *Transforming the U.S. Financial System: Equity and Efficiency for the 21st Century.* Armonk, N.Y.: M.E. Sharpe.

Fazzari, Steven. 1994. "Why Doubt the Effectiveness of Keynesian Fiscal Policy?" *Journal of Post Keynesian Economics* 17(2): 231–48.

Federal Reserve Bank of Minneapolis. 1994. "Congress Should End the Economic War Among the States." *Annual Report.* Minneapolis, Minn.: Federal Reserve Bank of Minneapolis.

Federal Reserve Bank of New York. 1992. *Summary of Results of the U.S. Foreign Exchange Market Turnover Conducted in April 1992.* New York, N.Y.: Federal Reserve Bank of New York.

Feenstra, Robert C., and Gordon H. Hanson. 1996a. "Globalization, Outsourcing and Wage Inequality," *American Economics Review* (May): 240–45.

Feenstra, Robert C., and Gordon H. Hanson. 1996b. "Foreign Investment, Outsourcing and Relative Wages." In R. Feenstra, G. Grossman, and D. Irwin, eds., *Political Economy of Trade Policy: Essays in Honor of Jagdish Bhagwati.* Cambridge, Mass.: MIT Press, pp. 89–127.

Feenstra, Robert C., and Gordon H. Hanson. 1997. "Productivity Measurement and the Impact of Trade and Technology on Wages: Estimates for the U.S., 1972–1990." Working Paper 6052. Cambridge, Mass.: National Bureau of Economic Research.

Feldman, Marsh, and Richard Florida. 1990. "Economic Restructuring and the Changing Role of the State in US Housing." In W. van Vliet and J. van Weesep, eds., *Government and Housing: Developments in Seven Countries.* Vol. 36 of *Urban Affairs Annual Reviews.* Newbury Park: N.Y.: Sage, pp. 31–46.

Feldstein, Martin, and Charles Horioka. 1980. "Domestic Saving and International Capital Flows." *Economic Journal* 90: 314–29.

Feldstein, Martin. 1994. "Tax Policy and International Capital Flows." *Weltwirtschaftliches Archiv* No. 130.

Felix, David, and Ranjit Sau. 1996. "On the Revenue Potential and Phasing in of the Tobin Tax." In M. Ul Haq, I. Kaul, and I. Grunberg, eds., *The Tobin Tax: Coping With Financial Volatility.* New York, N.Y.: Oxford University Press.

Felix, David. 1993. "Developing Countries and Joint Action to Curb International Financial Volatility." *UNCTAD Bulletin* 21(1): 7–9.

Felix, David. 1994. "Debt Crisis Adjustment in Latin America: Have the Hardships Been Necessary?" In G. Dymski and R. Pollin, *New Perspectives in Monetary Macroeconomics: Explorations in the Tradition of Hyman P. Minsky.* Ann Arbor, Mich: University of Michigan Press.

Felix, David. 1996a. "Statistical Appendix." In M. Ul Haq, I. Kaul, and I. Grunberg, eds., *The Tobin Tax: Coping With Financial Volatility.* New York, N.Y.: Oxford University Press.

Felix, David. 1996b. "Financial Globalization vs. Free Trade: The Case for the Tobin Tax." *UNCTAD Review.* New York, N.Y.: United Nations.

Ffrench-Davis, Ricardo, and Stephany Griffith-Jones, eds. 1995. *Coping With Capital Surges: The Return of Finance to Latin America.* Boulder, Colo.: Lynne Rienner.

Filer, Randall. 1992. "The Effect of Immigrant Arrivals on Migratory Patterns of Native Workers." In G. Borjas and R. Freeman, eds., *Immigration and the Work Force: Economic Consequences for the United States and Source Countries.* Chicago: University of Chicago Press, pp. 245–69.

Fischer, Stanley. 1978. "The Demand for Indexed Bonds." In M. Sarnat, ed., *Inflation and Capital Markets,* Cambridge, Mass.: Ballinger, pp. 213–42.

Fischer, Stanley. 1983. "Welfare Aspects of Government Issue of Indexed Bonds." In R. Dornbusch and M. Simonsen, eds., *Inflation, Debt, and Indexation,* Cambridge, Mass.: MIT Press, pp. 223–46.

Fischer, Stanley. 1998. "The Asian Crisis: A View From the IMF." Speech before Midwinter Conference of the Bankers' Association for Foreign Trade, Washington, D.C. Speech available through IMF Website.

Fishlow, Albert. 1985. "Lessons From the Past: Capital Markets During the 19th Century and Inter-War Period." *International Organization* 39(3).

FitzGerald, Valpy, and Rob Vos. 1989. "Introduction." In E. FitzGerald and R. Vos, eds., *Financing Economic Development: A Structural Approach to Monetary Policy.* Brookfield, Vt.: Gower, pp. 1–17.

FitzGerald, Valpy. 1993. *The Macroeconomics of Development Finance: A Kaleckian Approach.* London: Macmillan.

FitzGerald, Valpy. 1996. "International Markets and Open Economy Macroeconomics: A Keynesian View. *International Review of Applied Economics* 10(1): 141–56.

Fix, Michael, and Jeffrey S. Passel. 1994. *Immigration and Immigrants: Setting the Record Straight.* Washington, D.C.: Urban Institute.

Flanagan, Robert J. 1993. "European Wage Equalization Since the Treaty of Rome." In L. Ulman et al., eds., *Labor and an Integrated Europe.* Washington, D.C.: Brookings.

Follain, James R., David C. Ling, and Gary A. McGill. 1993. "The Preferential Income Tax Treatment of Owner-Occupied Housing: Who Really Benefits?" *Housing Policy Debate* 4(1): 1–23.

Fortin, Nicole M., and Thomas Lemieux. 1997. "Institutional Changes and Rising Wage Inequality: Is There a Linkage?" *Journal of Economic Perspectives* 11(2): 75–96.

Franke, R.W., and Chassin, B.H. 1989. *Kerala: Radical Reforms as Development in an Indian State.* San Francisco; Institute for Food and Development Policy.

Frankel, Jeffrey A. 1991. "Quantifying International Capital Mobility in the 1980s." In B. and J. Shoven, eds., *National Saving and Economic Performance.* Chicago: University of Chicago Press.

Frankel, Jeffrey A. 1992. "Measuring International Capital Mobility: A Review." *American Economic Review* 82(2): 197–202.

Frankel, Jeffrey A. 1993. "International Financial Integration: Relations Between Interest Rates and Exchange Rates." In D. Das, ed., *International Finance: Contemporary Issues.* London: Routledge.

Frankel, Jeffrey A., and Froot, K. 1990. "Exchange Rate Forecasting Techniques, Survey Data, and Implications for the Foreign Exchange Market. Working paper No. 3470. Cambridge, Mass.: National Bureau of Economic Research.

Frankel, Jeffrey. 1990. "International Financial Integration, Relations Among Interest Rates and Exchange Rates, and Monetary Indicators." In C. Pigott, ed., *International Financial Integration and US Monetary Policy,* New York, N.Y.: Federal Reserve Bank of New York.

Fransman, M. 1986. *Technology and Economic Development.* London: Frank Cass.

Fransman, M. 1994. "Is National Technology Policy Obsolete in a Globalised World?: The Japanese Response." Institute for Japanese-European Technology Studies, University of Edinburgh, Edinburgh, UK. Mimeo.

Fransman, M., and K. King, eds. 1984. *Technological Capability in the Third World.* London and Basingstoke: Macmillan.

Frenkel, Jacob, and Richard Levich. 1975. "Covered Interest Arbitrage: Unexploited Profits?" *Journal of Political Economy* 83(2): 325–38.

Friedberg, Rachel M., and Jennifer Hunt. 1995. "The Impact of Immigrants on Host Country Wages, Employment, and Growth." *Journal of Economic Perspectives* 9(Spring): 23–44.

Friedman, Benjamin. 1988. "Lessons of Monetary Policy From the 1980s." *Journal of Economic Perspectives* 2(3): 51–72.

Friedman, Benjamin. 1989. "Changing Effects of Monetary Policy on Real Economic Activity." In *Monetary Policy Issues in the 1990s.* Kansas City, Mo.: Federal Reserve Bank of Kansas City.

Friedman, Benjamin. 1996. *The Rise and Fall of Money Growth Targets as Guidelines for U.S. Monetary Policy.* Working Paper No. 5465. Cambridge, Mass.: National Bureau of Economic Research.

Friedman, Milton. 1953. "The Case for Flexible Exchange Rates." In *Essays in Positive Economics.* Chicago, Ill.: University of Chicago Press.

Friedman, Milton. 1968. "The Role of Monetary Policy." *American Economic Review* (March): 1–17.

Friedman, Milton. 1974. "Monetary Correction." In *Essays in Inflation and Indexation.* Washington, D.C.: American Enterprise Institute.

Friedman, Sheldon. 1992. "NAFTA as Social Dumping." *Challenge* (September–October).

Fronczek, Peter J, and Howard A. Savage. 1991. "Who Can Afford to Buy a House?" Series H121/91–1. Washington, D.C.: U.S. Bureau of the Census.

Froot, Kenneth A., and Jeffrey A. Frankel. 1989. "Forward Discount Bias: Is it an Exchange Rate Premium?" *Quarterly Journal of Economics* 104: 139–61.

Froot, Kenneth A., Michael Kim, and Kenneth Rogoff. 1995. "The Law of One Price Over 700 Years." Working Paper No. 5132. Cambridge, Mass.: National Bureau of Economic Research.

Fukao, Mitsuhiro, and Masaharu Hanazaki. 1987. "Internationalization of Financial Markets and the Allocation of Capital." *OECD Economic Studies* 8: 36–92.

Funkhouser, Edward, and Stephen Trejo. 1995. "The Labor Market Skills of Recent Male Immigrants: Evidence From the Current Population Survey." *Industrial and Labor Relations Review* 48(July): 792–811.

Gabel, H. Landis. 1994. "The Environmental Effects of Trade in the Transport Sector." In *The Environmental Effects of Trade.* Paris: OECD.

Gallob, Joel. 1991. "Birth of the North American Transboundary Plaintiff." *Harvard International Law Review* 15: 85.

Gambrill, Mónica C. 1993. "On Changing Our Position Towards *Maquiladoras.*" In R. Fernández de Castro, M. Campuos, and S. Weintraub, eds., *Sectoral Labor Effects of North American Free Trade.* Austin, Texas: University of Texas at Austin, Lyndon B. Johnson School of Public Affairs.

Gambrill, Mónica C. 1995. "La Política Salarial de las Maquiladoras: Mejoras Posibles Bajo el TLC." *Comercio Exterior* 45(7): 543–49.

Gertler, Mark, and R.G. Hubbard. 1988. "Financial Factors in Business Fluctuations." In *Financial Market Volatility: Causes, Consequences, and Policy Recommendations.* Kansas City, Mo.: Federal Reserve Bank of Kansas City.

Gertler, Mark, and Simon Gilchrist. 1994. "Monetary Policy, Business Cycles and the Behavior of Small Manufacturing Firms." *Quarterly Journal of Economics* 109: 309–40.

Gieseck, Arne, Ulrich Heilemann, and Hans Dietrich von Loeffelholz. 1995. "Economic Implications of Migration Into the Federal Republic of Germany, 1988–92." *International Migration Review* 29(Fall): 693–709.

Glyn, Andrew, Alan Hughes, Alain Lipietz, and Ajit Singh. 1990. "The Rise and Fall of the Golden Age." In S. Marglin and J. Schor, eds., *The Golden Age of Capitalism: Reinterpreting the Postwar Experience,* New York, N.Y.: Oxford University Press, pp. 39–125.

Glyn, Andrew, and Bob Rowthorn. 1994. "European Employment Policies." In J. Michie and J. Grieve Smith, eds., *Unemployment in Europe.* London: Academic Press, pp. 188–98.

Glyn, Andrew. 1995a. "The Assessment: Unemployment and Inequality." *Oxford Review of Economic Policy* 11(1).

Glyn, Andrew. 1995b. "Social Democracy and Full Employment." *New Left Review* 211: 33–55.

Glyn, Andrew. 1995c. "Stability, Egalitarianism and Dynamism: An Overview of the Advanced Capitalist Countries in the 1980s." In G. Epstein and H. Gintis, eds., *Macroeconomic Policy After the Conservative Era.* Cambridge: Cambridge University Press.

Glyn, Andrew. 1997. "Does Aggregate Profitability *Really* Matter?" *Cambridge Journal of Economics* 21(5).

Glyn, Andrew. 1997. "Paying for Job Creation." In J. Michie and J. Grieve Smith, eds., *Employment and Economic Performance: Jobs, Inflation and Growth.* New York, N.Y.: Oxford University Press.

Goldsmith, William W., and Edward J. Blakeley. 1992. *Separate Societies: Poverty and Inequality in US Cities.* Philadelphia, Pa.: Temple University Press.

Goldstein, Don. 1995. "Financial Structure and Corporate Behavior in Japan and the U.S.: Insulation vs. Integration with Speculative Pressures." Working Paper. Allegheny College.

Goodfriend, Marvin. 1991. "Interest Rates and the Conduct of Monetary Policy." In A. Meltzer and C.I. Plosser, eds., *Carnegie-Rochester Conference Series on Public Policy 34*, Spring, pp. 7–30.

Goodland, Robert, Herman Daly, and Salah El Sarafy. 1992. *Population, Technology and Lifestyle.* Washington, D.C.: Island Press.

Goodman, John B. 1992. *Monetary Sovereignty: The Politics of Central Banking in Western Europe.* Ithaca, N.Y.: Cornell University Press.

Goodstein, Eban. 1994. *Jobs and the Environment: The Myth of a National Tradeoff.* Washington, D.C.: Economic Policy Institute.

Goodstein, Eban. 1995a. *Economics and the Environment.* Englewood Cliffs, N.J.: Prentice Hall.

Goodstein, Eban. 1995b. "Property Rights or Path Dependence? The Economic Roots of Environmental Decline." *Journal of Economic Issues* XXIX(4).

Goodstein, Eban. 1997. *A New Look at Environmental Regulation and Competitiveness* Washington, D.C.: Economic Policy Institute.

Gordon, David M. 1988a. "The Global Economy: New Edifice or Crumbling Foundations." *New Left Review* 168: 24–65.

Gordon, David M. 1988b. "The Un-Natural Rate of Unemployment: An Econometric Critique of the NAIRU Hypothesis." *American Economic Review Papers and Proceeding,* 78: 117–123.

Gordon, David M. 1996. *Fat and Mean: The Corporate Squeeze of Working Americans and the Myth of Managerial "Downsizing."* New York, N.Y.: Free Press.

Gordon, Robert J. 1982. "Inflation, Flexible Exchange Rates, and the Natural Rate of Unemployment." In M.N. Baily, ed., *Workers, Jobs, and Inflation.* Washington, D.C.: Brookings Institution.

Gordon, Robert J. 1990. "What Is New-Keynesian Economics?" *Journal of Economic Literature* (September): 1115–71.

Grabel, Ilene 1997. "Saving and the Financing of Productive Investment: The Importance of National Financial Complexes." In R. Pollin, ed., *The Macroeconomics of Finance, Saving and Investment.* Ann Arbor: University of Michigan Press, pp. 251–98.

Grabel, Ilene. 1996a. "Financial Markets, the State, and Economic Development: Controversies Within Theory and Policy." *International Papers in Political Economy* 3(1): 1–42.

Grabel, Ilene. 1996b. "Marketing the Third World: The Contradictions of Portfolio Investment in the Global Economy" *World Development* 24(11): 1761–76.

Gramlich, Edward M. 1994. "Infrastructure Investment: A Review Essay." *Journal of Economic Literature* 32(3): 1176–96.

Green, Roy. 1987. "The Real Bills Doctrine" In J. Eatwell, M. Milgate, and P. Neuman, eds., *The New Palgrave,* pp. 101–2. London: MacMillan; New York: Stockton Press.

Greenspan, Alan. 1994. "Testimony by Alan Greenspan, Chairman of the Board of Governors of Federal Reserve System, Before the Subcommittee on Economic Growth and Credit Formation of the Committee on Banking, Finance and Urban Affairs," U.S. House of Representatives, Washington, D.C.

Greenwald, Bruce, and Joseph Stiglitz. 1991. "Towards a Reformulation of Monetary Theory: Competitive Banking." *Economic and Social Review* 23(1): 1–34.

Greider, William. 1997. *One World, Ready or Not; The Manic Logic of Global Capitalism.* New York, N.Y.: Simon and Schuster.

Grenier, Guillermo J., et al. 1992. On Machines and Bureaucracy: Controlling Ethnic Interaction in Miami's Construction and Apparel Industries. In L. Lamphere, ed. *Structuring Diversity: Ethnographic Perspectives on the New Immigration.* Chicago, Ill.: University of Chicago Press.

Griffin, Keith, and Azizur Khan. 1995. "The Transition to Market-Guided Economies: Lessons for Russia and Eastern Europe From the Chinese Experience." In B. Magnus and S. Cullenberg, eds., *Whither Marxism? Global Crises in International Perspective.* New York, N.Y.: Routledge.

Griffin, Keith, and Robert Pollin. 1990. "Labor Power, Investment and Development: Proposals for a National Strategy to be Launched in Oruro and Potosi." Report to United Nations Development Program in Bolivia.

Griffin, Keith, Carlo Geneletti, Robert Pollin, and Rosemary Thorp. 1990. "Labor Intensive Capital Formation in Bolivia." Report to United Nations Development Program in Bolivia.

Griffin, Keith, ed. 1995. *Poverty and the Transition to a Market Economy in Mongolia,* New York, N.Y.: St. Martins Press.

Griffin, Keith, ed. 1998. *Economic Reform in Vietnam,* London: Macmillan.

Griffin, Keith. 1978. "On the Emigration of the Peasantry." In *International Inequality and National Poverty.* New York: Holmes and Meier Publishers.

Griffin, Keith. 1996. "The Macroeconomic Framework and Development Strategy in Uzbekistan." Issues in Development Discussion Paper No. 13, Development and Technical Cooperation Department. Geneva: International Labour Office.

Griffith-Jones, Stephany, and Barbara Stallings. 1996. "International Capital Flows: Policy Recommendations for the 1990s." Institute for Development Studies, University of Sussex. Manuscript.

Grinspun, Ricardo, and Maxwell Cameron. 1992. "Mexico: The Wages of Trade." *NACLA Report on the Americas* 26(4): 36.

Grossman, Gene M., and Alan B. Krueger. 1991. "Environmental Impacts of a North American Free Trade Agreement." Working Paper No. 3914. Cambridge, Mass.: National Bureau of Economic Research.

Grossman, Jean B. 1982. "The Substitutability of Natives and Immigrants in Production. *Review of Economics and Statistics* 64(Nov.): 596–603.

Grubert, Harry, and Joel Slemrod. 1994. "The Effect of Taxes on Investment and Income Shifting to Puerto Rico." Working Paper No. 4869. Cambridge, Mass.: National Bureau of Economic Research.

Gyourko, Joseph. 1990. "Controlling and Assisting Privately Rented Housing," *Urban Studies* 27(6): 785–93.

Hahn, Robert, and Wilbur Steger. 1990. *An Analysis of Jobs at Risk and Job Losses From the Proposed Clean Air Act Amendments.* Pittsburgh, Pa.: CONSAD Research Corporation.

Halmi, Serge, Jonathan Michie, and Seumas Milne. 1994. "The Mitterand Experience." In J. Michie and J. G. Smith, eds., *Unemployment in Europe,* London: Academic Press, pp. 97–115.

Hanson, Gordon H., and Ann Harrison. 1995. "Trade, Technology, and Wage Inequality. Working Paper No. 5110. Cambridge, Mass.: National Bureau of Economic Research.

Hardouvelis, Gikas A. 1994. "The Term Structure Spread and Future Changes in Long and Short Rates in the G-7 Countries: Is There a Puzzle?" *Journal of Monetary Economics* (April): 255–83.

Harloe, Michael. 1995. *The People's Home? Social Rented Housing in Europe and America.* Cambridge: Blackwell.

Harrigan, J. 1995. "The Volume of Trade in Differentiated Intermediate Goods : Theory and Evidence." *Review of Economics and Statistics* 77(May): pp. 283–92.

Harris, Laurence. 1988. "Financial Reform and Economic Growth: A New Interpretation of South Korea's Experience." In L. Harris, J. Coakley, M. Croasdale, and T. Evans, eds., *New Perspectives on the Financial System.* London: Croom Helm.

Harris, Laurence. 1996. "Keynesian Policy in Disarticulated Economies." *International Review of Applied Economics* 10(1): 157–61.

Helleiner, Eric. 1994. *States and the Re-emergence of Global Finance: From Bretton Woods to the 1990s.* Ithaca, N.Y.: Cornell University Press.

Helleiner, Gerald K. 1989. "Transnational Corporations and Direct Foreign Investment." In H. Chenery and T.N. Srinivasan, eds., *Handbook of Development Economics.* Vol. 2. Amsterdam: Elsevier Science Publishers.

Helleiner, Gerald K. 1995. *Trade, Trade Policy, and Industrialization Reconsidered.* Helsinki: World Institute for Development Economics Research.

Herring, Richard, and Robert Litan. 1995. *Financial Regulation in the Global Economy.* Washington, D.C.: Brookings Institution.

Hines, James R. Jr. 1996. *Tax Policy and the Activities of Multinational Corporations.* Working Paper No. 5589. Cambridge, Mass.: National Bureau of Economic Research.

Hinojosa-Ojeda, Raúl, and Sherman Robinson. 1991. *Alternative Scenarios of U.S.-Mexico Integration: A Computable General Equilibrium Approach.* Working Paper No. 609. Berkeley, Calif.: University of California, Berkeley, Department of Agriculture and Resource Economics.

Hirst, Paul, and Grahame Thompson. 1992. "The Problem of 'Globalisation': International Economic Relations, National Economic Management and the Formation of Trading Blocs." *Economy and Society* 21(4).

Hirst, Paul, and Grahame Thompson. 1996. *Globalisation in Question,* Cambridge: Polity Press.

Hirtle, Beverley, and Jeanette Kelleher. 1990. "Financial Market Evolution and the Interest Sensitivity of Output." *Federal Reserve Bank of New York Quarterly Review* (Summer).

Hobsbawm, Eric. 1994. *The Age of Extremes: A History of the World, 1914–1991,* New York, N.Y.: Pantheon Books.

Holmes, Thomas J. 1995. "Analyzing a Proposal to Ban State Tax Breaks to Businesses." *Federal Reserve Bank of Minneapolis Quarterly Review,* pp. 29–39.

Holzer, Harry. 1995. *What Employers Want: Job Prospects for Less-Educated Workers.* New York, N.Y.: Russell Sage Foundation.

Houseman, Robert. 1994. *Reconciling Trade and the Environment: Lessons From the NAFTA*. New York, N.Y.: United Nations Environment Program.

Howarth, Richard B., and Richard B. Noorgard. 1990. "Intergenerational Resource Rights, Efficiency and Social Optimality." *Land Economics* 66(1): 1–11.

Howell, David R. 1994. "The Collapse of Low-Skill Male Earnings in the 1990s: Skill Mismatch or Declining Wage Norms?" Mimeo. New School for Social Research.

Huddle, Donald. 1993. *The Cost of Immigration*. Washington D.C.: Carrying Capacity Network.

Hufbauer, G., D. Lakdawalla, and A. Malani. 1994. "Determinants of Direct Foreign Investment and Its Connection to Trade." *UNCTAD Review*. New York, N.Y.: United Nations.

Hullender, Leonard. 1991. "The European Mortgage Market: Its Participants, Their Financial Techniques and Securitization." In C. Stone, A. Zissu, and J. Lederman, eds., *Asset Securitization: Theory and Practice in Europe*. London: Euromoney Books, pp. 1–24.

Hutton, Will. 1995a. "Myth That Sets the World to Right." *The Guardian*, June 12, 1995.

Hutton, Will. 1995b. *The State We're In*. London: Vintage.

Icard, A. 1994. "The Transmission of Monetary Policy in France." *Journal of Monetary Economics* 33(1): 87–103.

Inoue, Yutaka. 1989. "Globalization of Business Finance." *Japanese Economic Studies* 17(4): 41–91.

Instituto Nacional de Estadística, Geografía e Informatica (INEGI). http://www.inegi.gob.mx.

Inter-American Development Bank (IADB). 1996. *Economic and Social Progress in Latin America*. Washington, D.C.: IADB.

Inter-American Development Bank (IADB). 1997. *Economic and Social Progress in Latin America*. Washington, D.C.: IADB.

International Monetary Fund. 1995a. *Annual Report on Exchange Restrictions*. Washington, D.C.: IMF.

International Monetary Fund. 1995b. *Capital Account Convertibility: Review of Experience and Implications for IMF Policies*. Washington, D.C.: IMF.

International Monetary Fund. 1995c. *International Capital Markets: Developments, Prospects, and Policy Issues, 1995 Edition*. Washington, D.C.: IMF.

International Monetary Fund. 1997. *International Capital Markets: Developments, Prospects, and Key Policy Issues, 1997 Edition*. Washington, D.C.: IMF.

International Monetary Fund. Various years. *International Financial Statistics*. Washington, D.C.: IMF.

Jackman, Richard, Richard Layard, and Stephen Nickell. 1996. "Unemployment in OECD Countries." London School of Economics mimeo.

Jaffe, Adam B., Steven Peterson, Paul R. Portney, and Robert N. Stavins. 1995. "Environmental Regulation and the Competitiveness of U.S. Manufacturing: What Does the Evidence Tell Us?" *Journal of Economic Literature* 33(1): 132–61.

Jamal, Vali. 1993. "Surplus Extraction and the African Agrarian Crisis in a Historical Perspective." In A. Singh and H. Tabatabai, eds., *Economic Crisis and Third World Agriculture*. Cambridge: Cambridge University Press.

Jensen, Leif. 1988. "Patterns of Immigration and Public Assistance Utilization, 1970–80." *International Migration Review* 22(Spring): 51–83.

Jha, P.K. 1997. *Agricultural Labour in India.* New Delhi: Vikas Publishing House.

Johnson, George E., and Frank P. Stafford. 1993. "International Competition and Real Wages." *American Economic Review* 83(2): 127–30.

Johnson, George E., and Frank P. Stafford. 1993. "International Competition and Real Wages." *American Economic Review Papers and Proceedings* 83(2): 127–30.

Jones, R.W., and H. Klerskowski. 1980. "The Role of Services in Production and International Trade: A Theoretical Framework." In Jones and Krueger, eds., *The Political Economy of International Trade* Oxford: Basil Blackwell.

Julius, D. 1990. *Global Companies and Public Policy.* London: Pinter.

Julius, D. 1994. "International Direct Investment: Strengthening the Policy Regime." In George Kenen, ed., *Managing the World Economy.* Washington, D.C.: Institute for International Economics.

Kahn, George A. 1989. "The Changing Interest Sensitivity of the U.S. Economy." *Federal Reserve Bank of Kansas City Economic Review* (November): 13–33.

Kaldor, Nicholas. 1978a. "The Case for Regional Policy." In *Further Essays on Economic Theory.* New York: Holmes and Meier Publishers.

Kaldor, Nicholas. 1978b. "The Effect of Devaluations on Trade in Manufactures." In N. Kaldor, ed., *Further Essays on Applied Economics.* London: Duckworth.

Kalecki, Michal. 1972. *Selected Essays on the Economic Growth of Socialist and Mixed Economies.* Cambridge. Cambridge University Press.

Kalecki, Michal. 1990. "Political Aspects of Full Employment." In J.Osiatynski, ed., *Collected Works of Michal Kalecki.* Vol 1. Oxford: Oxford University Press.

Kalt, Joseph. 1988. "The Impact of Domestic Regulatory Policies on U.S. International Competitiveness." In A. M. Spence and H. Hazard, eds., *International Competitiveness.* Cambridge, Mass.: Harper and Row.

Kaminsky, Graciela L., and Carmen M. Reinhart. 1996. *The Twin Crises: The Causes of Payment Crises.* International Finance Discussion Paper No. 544. Washington, D.C.: Board of Governors of the Federal Reserve System.

Karier, Thomas. 1994. *Investment Tax Credit Reconsidered: Business Tax Incentives and Investments.* Public Policy Brief No. 13. Jerome Levy Economics Institute of Bard College. Annandale-on-Hudosn, New York.

Kashyap, Anil, Owen Lamont, and Jeremy Stein, 1994. "Credit Conditions and the Cyclical Behavior of Inventories." *Quarterly Journal of Economics* (August): 565–92.

Kasman, Bruce, and Anthony Rodrigues. 1991. "Financial Liberalization and Monetary Control in Japan." *Federal Reserve Bank of New York Quarterly Review* (Autumn): 28–45.

Kasman, Bruce. 1992. "A Comparison of Monetary Policy Operating Procedures in Six Industrial Coutries." *Federal Reserve Bank of New York Quarterly Review* (Summer): 5–24.

Katz, Michael B. 1986. *In the Shadow of the Poorhouse: A Social History of Welfare in America.* New York, N.Y.: Basic Books.

Katz, Michael B. 1989. *The Undeserving Poor: From the War on Poverty to the War on Welfare.* New York, N.Y.: Pantheon.

Katz, Michael B. 1995. *Improving Poor People.* Princeton: Princeton University Press.

Kelly, Patricia. 1998. "Ability and Willingness to Pay in the Age of Pax Britannica." *Explorations in Economic History* 35(1): 31-58.

Kemp, Peter. 1990. "Income-Related Assistance With Housing Costs: A Cross-National Comparison." *Urban Studies* 27(6): 795–808.

Keynes, J.M. 1936. *The General Theory of Employment, Interest and Money.* London: Macmillan (Quoted from Harbinger Edition, New York, 1964).

Killick, Tony. 1993. "Enhancing the Cost-Effectiveness of Africa's Negotiations With Its Creditors." *International Monetary and Financial Issues for the 1990s.* Vol. II. New York, N.Y.: United Nations Conference on Trade and Development.

Kindleberger, Charles P. 1985. "Historical Perspective on Today's Third-World Debt Program." In *Keynesians vs. Monetarists and Other Essays in Financial History,* London: George Allen and Unwin.

Kingson, Charles I. 1981. "The Coherence of International Taxation." *Columbia Law Review* 81(October).

Kleinman, Mark. 1996. *Housing, Welfare and the State in Europe.* Cheltenham: Edward Elgar.

Knight, Robert. 1977. "Comparative Burdens of Federal Reserve Member and Non-member Banks." *Federal Reserve Bank of Kansas City Monthly Review* (March): 13–37.

Koechlin, Timothy. 1990. "The Responsiveness of Domestic Investment to Foreign Economic Conditions." Skidmore College. Mimeo.

Koechlin, Timothy. 1992. "The Responsiveness of Domestic Investment to Foreign Economic Conditions." *Journal of Post Keynesian Economics* 15(1): 63–83.

Koechlin, Timothy. 1995. "The Globalization of Investment." *Contemporary Economic Policy* 13(January): 92–100.

Kolaris, James, Arvind Mahajan, and Edward Saunders. 1988. "The Effect of Changes in Reserve Requirements on Bank Stock Prices." *Journal of Banking and Finance* 12: 183–98.

Koo, B. 1993. "Foreign Investment and Economic Performance in Korea." In S. Lall, ed., *Transnational Corporations and Economic Development.* London: Routledge.

Koplow, Douglas. 1993. *Federal Energy Subsidies: Energy, Environmental and Fiscal Impacts.* Washington, D.C.: Alliance to Save Energy.

Kornai, Janos. 1981. *Growth, Shortage, and Efficiency: A Macrodynamic Model of the Socialist Economy.* Oxford: Basil Blackwell.

Kornai, Janos. 1993. "Transformational Recession: A General Phenomenon Examined through the Example of Hungary's Development." *Economie Applique* 46(2): 181–227.

Kozul-Wright, Richard. 1995. "Transnational Corporations and the Nation State." In. J. Michie and J. Grieve Smith, eds., *Managing the Global Economy,* New York, N.Y.: Oxford University Press, pp. 135–71.

Kregel, Jan. A. 1993. "Banks Supervision: The Real Hurdle to European Monetary Union." *Journal of Economic Issues,* 27 (2): 667–76.

Krugman, Paul R. 1994a. "Competitiveness: A Dangerous Obsession." *Foreign Affairs* 73(2): 28–44.

Krugman, Paul R. 1994b. "Past and Present Causes of High Unemployment." Stanford University. Mimeo.

Krugman, Paul R., and Anthony Venables. 1995. "Globalization and the Inequality of Nations." Working Paper No. 5098. Cambridge, Mass.: National Bureau of Economic Research.

Krugman, Paul R., and Robert Z. Lawrence. 1993. "Trade, Jobs, and Wages." Working Paper No. 4478. Cambridge, Mass.: National Bureau of Economic Research.

Krugman, Paul R., and Robert Z. Lawrence. 1994. "Trade, Jobs and Wages." *Scientific American* 270(4): 44–49.

Kurian, K.M., ed. 1975. *India State and Society: A Marxian Approach.* Bombay. Orient Longman.

Kurien, C.T. 1994. *Global Capitalism and the Indian Economy.* London: Sangam Books.

Kuznets, Simon. 1955. "Economic Growth and Income Inequality." *American Economic Review* 45(1).

Lall, S. 1995. "Malaysia: Industrial Success and the Role of the Government." *Journal of International Development* 7(5).

Lall, S., ed. 1993. *Transnational Corporations and Economic Development.* London: Routledge.

Lalonde, Robert, and Robert Topel. 1991. "Immigrants in the American Labor Market: Quality, Assimilation, and Distributional Effects." *American Economic Review* 81(May): 297–302.

Lamphere, Louise, ed. 1992. *Structuring Diversity: Ethnographic Perspectives on the New Immigration.* Chicago, Ill.: University of Chicago Press.

Lange, Oskar. 1970. *Papers on Economics and Sociology 1930-1960.* Oxford: Pergamon.

Larudee, Mehrene. 1995. "Trade Liberalization and Income Distribution: Three Essays with Reference to the Case of Mexico and the North American Free Trade Agreement (NAFTA)." Ph.D. Dissertation, University of Massachusetts, Amherst.

Lawrence, Robert Z., and Matthew J. Slaughter. 1993. "International Trade and American Wages in the 1980s: Giant Sucking Sound or Small Hiccup?" *Brookings Papers on Economic Activity: Microeconomics* 2: 161–211.

Layard, Richard, Stephen Nickell, and Richard Jackman. 1993. *Unemployment: Macroeconomics and the Labor Market.* Oxford: Oxford University Press.

Leamer, Edward. 1993. "Wage Effects of a U.S.–Mexican Free Trade Agreement." In P. M. Garber, ed., *The Mexico–U.S. Free Trade Agreement,* Cambridge, Mass.: MIT Press.

Leather, Philip, and Alan Murie. 1986. "The Decline in Public Expenditure." in P. Malpass, ed., *The Housing Crisis.* London: Routledge.

Leeper, Eric M., and David B. Gordon. 1992. "In Search of the Liquidity Effect." *Journal of Monetary Economics* (June): 341–69.

Lenin, V.I. 1977. *Selected Works.* Vol 1. Moscow. Foreign Languages Publishing House.

Leonard, H. Jeffrey. 1987. *Natural Resources and Economic Development in Central America.* Oxford: Transaction Books.

Levich, R.M. 1985. "Empirical Studies of Exchange Rates: Price Behavior, Rate Determination, and Market Efficiency." In Jones and Kenan, eds., *Handbook of International Economics.* Vol. II. Amsterdam: North-Holland.

Levy, Frank, and Richard C. Michel. 1991. *The Economic Future of American Families.* Washington, D.C.: Urban Institute Press.

Levy, Santiago, and Sweder van Wijnbergen. 1994. "Agriculture in the Mexico–U.S. Free Trade Agreement." In J.F. Francois and C.R. Shiells, eds., *Modeling Trade Policy.* Cambridge: Cambridge University Press.

Lewis, W. Arthur. 1981. "The Rates of Growth of World Trade, 1830–1973." In S. Grassman and E. Lundberg, eds., *The World Economic Order: Past and Prospects.* London: Macmillan.

Lindbeck, Assar. 1997. "The Swedish Experiment." *Journal of Economic Literature* 35(3): 1273–1319.

Lindgren, Carl-Johan, Gillian Garcia, and Mathew Saal. 1996. *Bank Soundness and Macroeconomic Policy.* Washington, D.C.: IMF.

Lipson, Charles, 1986. *Standing Guard.* Berkeley, Calif.: University of California Press.

Lissakers, Karin. 1991. *Banks, Borrowers and the Establishment: A Revisionist Account of the International Debt Crisis.* New York, N.Y.: Basic Books.

Little, I.M.D., T. Scitovsky, and M. Scott. 1970. *Industry and Trade in Some Developing Countries.* Oxford. Oxford University Press.

Locke, Richard, Thomas Kochan, and Michael Piore. 1995. *Employment Relations in a Changing World Economy.* Cambridge, Mass.: MIT Press.

Lomax, Gregory. 1995. "Financing Social Housing in the United Kingdom." *Housing Policy Debate* 6(4): 849–66.

Loriaux, Michael. 1991. *France After Hegemony.* Ithaca, N.Y.: Cornell University Press.

Loriaux, Michael. 1997. "Socialist Monetarism and Financial Liberalization in France." In Loriaux et al., eds., *Capital Ungoverned: Liberalizing Finance in Interventionist States,* Ithaca, N.Y.: Cornell University Press.

Los Angeles County. 1992. *Impacts of Undocumented Persons and Other Immigrants on Costs, Revenues, and Services in Los Angeles County.* Los Angeles: Internal Services Division, Los Angeles County.

Low, Patrick, and Alexander Yeats. 1992. "Do 'Dirty' Industries Migrate?" In *International Trade and the Environment.* Washington, D.C.: World Bank.

Lown, Cara S., and Robert W. Rich. 1997. "Is There an Inflation Puzzle?" *Federal Reserve Bank of New York Review* (December): 51–69.

Lucas, Robert E. 1972. "Expectations and the Neutrality of Money." *Journal of Economic Theory* (April): 103–24.

Lucas, Robert E.B., David Wheeler, and Hemamala Hettige. 1992. *Economic Development, Environmental Regulation, and the International Migration of Toxic Industrial Pollution 1960–1988.* Washington, D.C.: World Bank.

Lustig, Nora, and Jaime Ros. 1993. "Mexico." In L. Taylor, ed., *The Rocky Road to Reform,* Cambridge Mass.: MIT Press.

Lustig, Nora, Barry P. Bosworth, and Robert Z. Lawrence, eds. 1992. *North American Free Trade: Assessing the Impact.* Washington, D.C.: Brookings Institution.

MacDonald, R. 1988. *Floating Exchange Rates: Theories and Evidence.* London: Unwin Hyman.

Maclennan, Duncan. 1995. "Housing to 2001: Can Britain Do Better?" *Housing Policy Debate* 6(3): 655–94.

Maddison, Angus. 1989. *The World Economy in the Twentieth Century.* Paris: OECD Development Centre.

Maddison, Angus. 1995. *Monitoring the World Economy 1820–1992.* Paris: OECD.

Mahalanobis, P.C., P.K. Bose, and M. Mukherjee, eds. 1985. *Papers on Planning.* Calcutta. Statistical Publishing Society.

Mahon, James P. 1996. *Mobile Capital and Latin American Development.* State College, Pa.: Pennsylvania State University Press.

Maisel, Sherman. 1973. "Improving Our System of Credit Allocation." In Federal Reserve Bank of Boston, *Credit Allocation Techniques and Monetary Policy.* Proceedings of a Conference Held at Melving Village, N.H., pp. 15–30.

Malpass, Peter. 1986. "From Complacency to Crisis." In P. Malpass, ed., *The Housing Crisis.* London: Routledge.

Malpass, Peter. 1993. "Housing Tenure and Affordability: The British Disease." In G. Hallett, ed., *The New Housing Shortage.* London: Routledge.

Malthus, Thomas. 1914. *An Essay on Population.* London: J.M. Dent.

Mankiw, N. Gregory. 1986. "The Term Structure of Interest Rates Revisited." *Brookings Papers on Economic Activity 1986.1.* Washington, D.C.: Brookings Institution, pp. 61–96.

Marglin, Stephen A., and Amit Bhaduri. 1990. "Profit Squeeze and Keynesian Theory." In S. A. Marglin and J. Schor, eds., *The Golden Age of Capitalism: Reinterpreting the Postwar Experience.* Oxford: Clarendon Press.

Markusen, James R., and Anthony J. Venables. 1996. "Multinational Production, Skilled Labor and Real Wages." Working Paper No. 5483. Cambridge, Mass.: National Bureau of Economic Research.

Márquez Padilla, Carlos. 1995. "El Sector Manufacturero, Políticas Comercial y Cambiaria y la Cuestión Ocupacional, 1980–1992." *Economía Mexicana, Nueva Época* 4(1): 151–70.

Marshall, Mike. 1995. "Lessons From the Swedish Model." In P. Arestis and M. Marshall, eds., *The Political Economy of Full Employment.* Brookfield, Vt.: Edward Elgar, pp. 202–16.

Marx, Karl, and Frederick Engels. 1972. "The Communist Manifesto." In R. Tucker ed., *The Marx-Engels Reader,* New York, N.Y.: Norton.

Masnick, George S. 1991. "A Critique of Key Assumptions in the Current Housing Affordability Debate: What the Data Tell Us." Presentation Notes Distributed at the Fannie Mae Colloquiam on Domestic Housing Policy, University of Southern California, January 18.

Mauskopf, Eileen. 1990. "The Transmission Channels of Monetary Policy: How Have They Changed?" *Federal Reserve Bulletin* (December).

McCallum, Bennett T. 1994. "A Reconsideration of the Uncovered Interest Parity Relationship." *Journal of Monetary Economics* 33(November): 105–32.

McCauley, Robert N., and Seth Rama. 1992. "Foreign Bank Credit to U.S. Corporations: The Implications of Offshore Loans." *Federal Reserve Bank of New York Quarterly Review* (Spring): 52–65.

McCosh, Dan. 1997. "Assembly Plant Industry Keeps Growing." *El Financiero International Edition,* February 3–9, 1997.

Melitz, Jacques. 1990. "Financial Deregulation in France." *European Economic Review* 34: 394–402.

Michalet, C-A. 1994. "Transnational Corporations and the Changing International Economic System." *Transnational Corporations* 3(1).

Michie, Jonathan, and John Grieve Smith, eds. 1995. *Managing the Global Economy,* Oxford: Oxford University Press.

Michl, Thomas R. 1995. "Assessing the Costs of Inflation and Unemployment." In P. Arestis and M. Marshall, eds., *The Political Economy of Full Employment.* Brookfield, Vt.: Edward Elgar, 54–78.

Milberg, William. 1991. "Structural Change and International Competitiveness in Canada: An Alternative Approach." *International Review of Applied Economics* 5(1): 77–99.

Milberg, William. 1997. "Globalization and International Competitiveness." In P. Davidson and J. Kregel, eds., *Improving the Global Economy*. Cheltenham, U.K.: Edward Elgar, forthcoming.

Milberg, William. 1998. "Globalisation." In R. Kozul-Wright and R. Rowthorn, eds., *Transnational Corporations and the World Economy*. London: Macmillan Press, forthcoming.

Millman, Joel. 1997. "Mexico Plans Multibillion Dollar Rescue of Nation's Privately Run Toll Roads." *Wall Street Journal*, August 25.

Minsky, Hyman P. 1975. *John Maynard Keynes*. New York, N.Y.: Columbia University Press.

Minsky, Hyman P. 1986. *Stabilizing an Unstable Economy*, New Haven, Conn.: Yale University Press.

Mises, Ludwig von. 1935. "Economic Calculation in the Socialist Commonwealth." In Friedrich von Hayek, ed. *Collectivist Economic Planning*. London: Routledge and Kegan Paul.

Mishel, Lawrence, and Jared Bernstein. 1994. "Is the Technology Black Box Empty? An Empirical Examination of the Impact of Technology on Wage Inequality." Economic Policy Institute, Washington, D.C. Mimeo.

Mishel, Lawrence, and Jared Bernstein. 1995. *The State of Working America 1994–95*. Armonk, N.Y.: M.E. Sharpe.

Mishkin, Frederic. 1984. "Are Real Interest Rates Equal Across Countries? An Empirical Investigation of International Parity Conditions." *Journal of Finance* 39: 1345–58.

Mitra, A. 1977. *Terms of Trade and Class Relations*. London. F. Cass.

Modjtahedi, B. 1987. "An Empirical Investigation Into the International Real Interest Rates Linkage." *Canadian Journal of Economics* 20(November).

Mosser, Patricia. 1992. "Changes in Monetary Policy Effectiveness: Evidence From Large Macroeconometric Models." *Federal Reserve Bank of New York Quarterly Review* (Spring): 36–51.

Muller, Thomas, and Thomas Espenshade. 1985. *The Fourth Wave*. Washington, D.C.: Urban Institute Press.

Munnell, Alice, and Joseph B. Grolnic. 1986. "Should the U.S. Government Issue Index Bonds?" *New England Economic Review* (September–October): 3–21.

Munnell, Alice, ed. 1990. *Is There a Shortfall in Public Capital Investment?* Conference Series No. 34. Boston: Federal Reserve Bank of Boston.

Mussa, Michael, and Morris Goldstein. 1993. "The Integration of World Capital Markets." In *Changing Capital Markets: Implications for Monetary Policy*. Proceedings of the August 1993 Jackson Hole Conference. Kansas City, Mo.: Federal Reserve Bank of Kansas City, pp. 245–313.

National Research Council. 1997. *The New Americans: Economic, Demographic, and Fiscal Effects of Immigration*. Washington, D.C.: National Academy Press.

Nayyar D., ed. 1994a. *Industrial Growth and Stagnation*. Bombay; Oxford and New York: Oxford University Press for Sameeksha Trust.

Nayyar D. 1994b. *Migration, Remittances and Capital Flows: The Indian Experience*. Delhi; Oxford and New York: Oxford University Press.

Nayyar, D. 1995. "Globalization: The Past in Our Present." Presidential Address to the Indian Economic Association, Chandigarh.

Nelson, Bruce W. 1993. "Not Quite So Welcome Anymore." *Time* (September Special Issue): 10–11.

Nelson, Richard R., and Gavin Wright. 1992. "The Rise and Fall of American Technological Leadership." *Journal of Economic Literature* 30(4): 1931–64.

Nembhard, Jessica. 1996. *Capital Control, Financial Regulation and Industrial Policy in South Korea and Brazil.* Westport, Conn.: Praeger.

Newman, S., and A. Schnare. 1988. *Integrating Housing and Welfare Assistance.* Working Paper. Cambridge, Mass.: MIT Center for Real Estate Development.

Nickell, Stephen, and B. Bell. 1995. "The Collapse in Demand for the Unskilled and Unemployment Across the OECD." *Oxford Review of Economic Policy* 11(1).

Nolan, Peter. 1994. "Labour Market Institutions, Industrial Restructuring and Unemployment in Europe." In J. Michie and J. Grieve Smith, eds., *Unemployment in Europe.* London: Academic Press, pp. 61–74.

O'Brien, Richard. 1992. *Global Financial Integration: The End of Geography.* London: Pinter.

O'Connor, David. 1994. *Managing the Environment With Rapid Industrialization: Lessons From the East Asian Experience.* Paris: OECD.

Obstfeld, Maurice. 1986. "Rational and Self-Fulfilling Balance of Payments Crises." *American Economic Review* (March).

Ohmae, Kenneth. 1994. *The Borderless World: Power and Strategy in the Interlinked Economy,* London: Collins.

Okita, Saburo, Lal Jayawardena, and Arjun Sengupta. 1986. "The Potential of the Japanese Surplus for World Economic Development." Helsinki: World Institute for Development Economics Research.

Okun, Arthur M. 1980. "Rational-Expectations-With-Misperceptions as a Theory of the Business Cycle." *Journal of Money, Credit, and Banking* (November): 817–25.

Oman, Charles P. 1986. "New Forms of Investment in Developing Countries." In T.H. Moran, ed., *Investing in Development: New Roles for Private Capital?* Washington, D.C.: Overseas Development Council.

Omerod, Paul. 1994. "On Inflation and Unemployment." in J. Michie and J. Grieve Smith, eds., *Unemployment in Europe.* London: Academic Press, pp. 45–60.

Organization for Economic Cooperation and Development (OECD). 1987. *OECD Economic Surveys: France.* Paris: OECD.

Organization for Economic Cooperation and Development (OECD). 1989. *OECD Economic Surveys: Japan.* Paris: OECD.

Organization for Economic Cooperation and Development (OECD). 1992. *OECD Economic Surveys: Mexico, 1991–92.* Paris: OECD.

Organization for Economic Cooperation and Development (OECD). 1994a. *The OECD Jobs Study: Facts, Analysis, Strategies.* Paris: OECD.

Organization for Economic Cooperation and Development (OECD). 1994b. *OECD Jobs Study: Evidence and Explanations.* Paris: OECD.

Organization for Economic Cooperation and Development (OECD). 1994c. *Trends in International Migration.* Paris: OECD.

Organization for Economic Cooperation and Development (OECD). 1996a. *OECD Economic Surveys: Mexico, 1996–97.* Paris: OECD.

Organization for Economic Cooperation and Development (OECD). 1996b. *Technology and Industrial Performance.* Paris: OECD.

Organization for Economic Cooperation and Development (OECD). 1996c. *Towards Multilateral Investment Rules; OECD Documents.* Paris: OECD.

Organization for Economic Cooperation and Development. Various years. *Economic Outlook*. Paris: OECD.

Orr, Adrian, Malcolm Edey, and Ketil Hviding. 1995. "Real Long-Term Interest Rates: The Evidence From Pooled Time-Series." Economic Studies No. 25. Paris: OECD.

Ostry, S. 1990. *Governments and Corporations in a Shrinking World*. New York, N.Y.: Council on Foreign Relations Press.

Ozawa, T. 1995. "The 'Flying-Geese' Paradigm of FDI, Economic Development and Shifts in Competitiveness." Fort Collins, Colo., Colorado State University. Mimeo.

Ozler B., G. Datt, and M. Ravallion. 1996. *A Database on Poverty and Growth in India*. Washington, D.C.: World Bank.

Pack, Howard, and Larry E. Westphal. 1986. "Industrial Strategy and Technological Change: Theory Versus Reality." *Journal of Development Economics* 22: 87–128.

Pandit, V. 1995. "Macroeconomic Character of the Indian Economy: Theories, Facts, and Fancies." In P. Patnaik, ed., *Macroeconomics*. Delhi: Oxford University Press, pp. 187–224.

Panic, Mica. 1995. "The Bretton Woods System: Concept and Practice." In J. Michie and J. Grieve Smith, eds., *Managing the Global Economy*. Oxford: Oxford University Press, pp. 37–54.

Panic, Mica. 1998. "Transnationals, International Interdependence and National Economic Policy." In R. Kozul-Wright and R. Rowthorn, eds., *Transnational Corporations and the World Economy*, London: Macmillan Press, forthcoming.

Patnaik, Prabhat, and C.P. Chandrasekhar. 1995. "The Indian Economy Under Structural Adjustment." *Economic and Political Weekly*, November 25.

Patnaik, Prabhat, and C.P. Chandrasekhar. 1996. "Investment, Exports and Growth: A Cross-Country Analysis." *Economic and Political Weekly*, January 6.

Patnaik, Prabhat, ed. 1986. *Lenin and Imperialism*. London: Sangam Books.

Patnaik, Prabhat, ed. 1995a. *Macroeconomics*. Delhi: Oxford University Press.

Patnaik, Prabhat. 1995b. "The Nation State in the Era of Globalisation." *Economic and Political Weekly* XXX(33), August 19.

Patnaik, Utsa, and M. Dingwaney, eds. 1985. *Chains of Servitude*. Madras: Sangam Books.

Pauly, Louis W. 1994. "National Financial Structure, Capital Mobility, and International Economic Rules: The Normative Consequences of East Asian, European, and American Distinctiveness." *Policy Sciences* 27: 343–60.

Pearce, David, and Giles D. Atkinson. 1993. "Capital Theory and the Measurement of Sustainable Development: An Indicator of 'Weak' Sustainability." *Ecological Economics* 8(2): 103–8.

Pearsall, Jon. 1984. "France." In M. Wynn, ed., *Housing in Europe*. Kent: Croom Helm, pp. 9–53.

Pezzey, John. 1992. "Sustainability: An Interdisciplinary Guide." *Environmental Values* 1(4): 321–62.

Pischke, Jorn-Steffen, and Johannes Velling. 1994. *Wage and Employment Effects of Immigration to Germany: An Analysis Based on Local Markets*. Working Paper. Cambridge, Mass.: MIT.

Podolsky, T.M. 1986. *Financial Innovation and the Money Supply*. New York, N.Y.: Basil Blackwell.

Polak, J.J. 1957. "Monetary Analysis of Income Formation and Payments Problems." *International Monetary Fund Staff Papers* 6: 1–50.

Polanyi, Karl. 1944. *The Great Transformation.* New York, N.Y.: Rinehart.

Pollin, Robert, and Elizabeth Zahrt. 1997. "Expansionary Policy for Full Employment in the United States: Retrospective on the 1960s and Current Period Prospects." In J. Michie and J. Grieve Smith, eds., *Employment and Economic Performance: Jobs, Inflation and Growth.* New York, N.Y.: Oxford University Press.

Pollin, Robert, and Stephanie Luce. 1998. *The Living Wage: Building a Fair Economy.* New York, N.Y.: New Press.

Pollin, Robert. 1990. *Deeper in Debt: The Changing Financial Conditions of U.S. Households,* Washington, D.C.: Economic Policy Institute.

Pollin, Robert. 1991. "Two Theories of Money Supply Endogeneity: Some Empirical Tests." *Journal of Post Keynesian Economics* 13(3): 366–96.

Pollin, Robert. 1993. "Public Credit Allocation Through the Federal Reserve: Why It Is Needed; How It Should Be Done." In G. Dymski, G. Epstein, and R. Pollin, eds., *Transforming the U.S. Financial System: Equity and Efficiency for the 21st Century.* Armonk, N.Y.: M.E. Sharpe, pp. 321–54.

Pollin, Robert. 1995. "Financial Structures and Egalitarian Economic Policy," *New Left Review* (November–December): 26–61.

Pollin, Robert. 1997. "Financial Intermediation and the Variability of the Saving Constraint." In R. Pollin, ed., *The Macroeconomics of Saving, Finance and Investment.* Ann Arbor, Mich: University of Michigan Press, pp. 309–65.

Pontusson, Jonas. 1994. "Sweden: After the Golden Age." In P. Anderson and P. Camiller, eds., *Mapping the West European Left.* New York, N.Y.: Verso, pp. 23–54.

Poole, William. 1991. "Interest Rates and the Conduct of Monetary Policy: A Comment." In A.H. Meltzer and C.I. Plosser, eds., *Carnegie-Rochester Conference Series on Public Policy 34,* Spring 1991, pp. 31–9.

Porter, Michael, and Claas van der Linde. 1995. "Toward a New Conception of the Environment-Competitiveness Relationship." *Journal of Economic Perspectives* 9(4): 97–118.

Porter, Michael. 1991. "America's Green Strategy." *Scientific American* (April): 168.

Postel, Sandra. 1994. "Carrying Capacity: Earth's Bottom Line." *Challenge* (March–April).

Poterba, James. M. 1997. "The Rate of Return to Corporate Capital and Factor Shares: New Estimates Using Revised National Income Accounts and Capital Stock Data." Working Paper No. 6263. Cambridge, Mass.: National Bureau of Economic Research.

Pozen, Robert C. 1996. "Foreign Investors and Corporate Governance: The Japanese Case." *Fidelity Focus* (Fall).

Radecki, Lawrence, and Vincent Reinhart. 1988. "The Globalization of Financial Markets and the Effectiveness of Monetary Policy Instruments." *Federal Reserve Bank of New York Quarterly Review* (Autumn): 18–27.

Radecki, Lawrence, and Vincent Reinhart. 1994. "The Financial Linkages in the Transmission of Monetary Policy in the United States." In Bank for International Settlements, *National Differences in Interest Rate Transmission.* Basle: Bank for International Settlements, pp. 291–337.

Rai, K. 1992. "The Indian Economy in Adversity and Debt." *Social Scientist* (January–February).

Raj, K.N. 1976. "Growth and Stagnation in Indian Industrial Development." *Economic and Political Weekly* (Annual No.).

Rao, J.M. 1993. "Distribution and Growth With an Infrastructure Constraint." *Cambridge Journal of Economics* 17: 369–89.

Raymond, Robert. 1992. "The Effects of Financial Innovation and Deregulation on French Monetary Policy." In S. Frowen and D. Kath, eds., *Monetary Policy and Financial Innovations in Five Industrial Countries.* New York, N.Y.: St. Martin's Press, pp. 82–101.

Reich, Robert. 1992. *The Work of Nations; Preparing Ourselves for 21st Century Capitalism.* New York, N.Y.: Vintage Books.

Rendón, Teresa, and Carlos Salas. 1993. "El Empleo en México en los Ochenta: Tendencias y Cambios." *Comercio Exterior* 43(8): 717–30.

Repetto, Robert. 1995. "Jobs, Competitiveness and Environmental Regulation: What Are the Real Issues?" Washington, D.C.: World Resources Institute.

Reserve Bank of India. 1995. *Annual Report 1994-95.* Bombay: Reserve Bank of India.

Resnick, Bruce G. 1989. "The Globalization of World Financial Markets." *Business Horizons* (November–December).

Reuber, Grant L. 1973. *Private Foreign Investment in Development.* Oxford: Clarendon Press.

Ricardo, David. 1951. *Principles of Political Economy.* Edited by P. Sraffa. Cambridge: Cambridge University Press.

Robinson, Joan. 1956. *The Accumulation of Capital.* Homewood, Ill.: Richard D. Irwin.

Robinson, P. 1994. "The British Labor Market in Historical Perspective." London School of Economics Center for Economic Performance Discussion Paper 202.

Robinson, Sherman, et al. 1991. *Agricultural Policies and Migration in a U.S.–Mexico Free Trade Area: A Computable General Equilibrium Analysis.* Working Paper No. 617. Berkeley, Calif.: University of California, Berkeley, Department of Agriculture and Resource Economics.

Robison, H. David. 1988. "Industrial Pollution Abatement: The Impact on the Balance of Trade." *Canadian Journal of Economics* 21(1): 187–99.

Rodrik, Dani. 1992. "The Limits of Trade Policy Reform in Developing Countries." *Journal of Economic Perspectives* 6(1): 87–105.

Rodrik, Dani. 1996. *Has Internationalization Gone Too Far?* Washington, D.C.: Institute for International Economics.

Rodrik, Dani. 1997. "Trade, Social Insurance and the Limits to Globalisation" Working Paper No. 5905. Cambridge, Mass.: National Bureau of Economic Research.

Ros, Jaime. 1994a. "Mexico's Trade and Industrialization Experience Since 1960: A Reconsideration of Past Policies and Assessment of Current Reforms." In G. K. Helleiner, ed., *Trade Policy and Industrialization in Turbulent Times.* New York, N.Y.: Routledge.

Ros, Jaime. 1994b. "Financial Markets and Capital Flows in Mexico." In J. Ocampo and R. Steiner, eds., *Foreign Capital in Latin America.* Washington, D.C.: Inter-American Development Bank.

Rose, John, and Peter Rose. 1979. "The Burden of Federal Reserve Membership: A Review of the Evidence." *Journal of Banking and Finance* 3(December): 331–45.

Rowthorn, Robert, and Andrew Glyn. 1990. "The Diversity of Unemployment Experience Since 1973." In. S. Marglin and J. Schor, *The Golden Age of Capitalism: Reinterpreting the Postwar Experience.* Oxford: Clarendon Press, pp. 218–66.

Rowthorn, Robert, and J.R. Wells. 1987. *Deindustrialization and Foreign Trade.* Cambridge: Cambridge University Press.

Rowthorn, Robert. 1995. "Capital Formation and Unemployment." *Oxford Review of Economic Policy* 11(1).

Rowthorn, Robert. 1995. "Manufacturing in the National Economy and Related Policy Issues." Paper Presented at the "Future of Manufacturing Forum," Organized by the Australian Manufacturing Council, April.

Rowthorn, Robert. 1996. "Replicating the Experience of the NIEs on a Large Scale." Faculty of Economics and Politics, University of Cambridge. Mimeo.

Sachs, Jeffrey, and Andrew Warner. 1995. "Economic Reform and the Process of Global Integration." *Brookings Papers on Economic Activity 1995.1.* Washington, D.C.: Brookings Institution, pp. 1–118.

Sachs, Jeffrey. 1997. "IMF Is a Power Unto Itself." *Financial Times,* December 11.

Sarver, Eugene. 1990. *The Eurocurrency Market Handbook.* New York, N.Y.: New York Institute of Finance.

Sassen, Saskia. 1988. *The Mobility of Labor and Capital.* New York, N.Y.: Cambridge University Press.

Sawyer, Malcolm. 1997. "The NAIRU: A Critical Appraisal." Working Paper No. 203. Jerome Levy Economics Institute of Bard College. Annandale-on-Hudson, New York.

Schaefer, Jean-Pierre. 1993. "Housing Affordability in France." In G. Hallett, ed., *The New Housing Shortage: Housing Affordability in Europe and the USA.* London: Routledge, pp. 151–78.

Schive, C. 1993. "Foreign Investment and Technology Transfer in Taiwan." In S. Lall, ed., *Transnational Corporations and Economic Development.* London: Routledge.

Schultz, George P., William E. Simon, and Walter B. Wriston. 1998. "Who Needs the IMF?" *Wall Street Journal,* February 3.

Schumpeter, Joseph. 1951. *Imperialism and Social Classes.* Oxford: Basil Blackwell.

Schwartz, David C., Richard Ferlauto, and Daniel Hoffman. 1988. *A New Housing Policy for America.* Philadelphia, Pa.: Temple University Press.

Sedjo, Roger A. 1994. "The Global Environmental Effects of Local Logging Cutbacks." *Resources* 117(Fall): 2–5.

Selden, Thomas M., and Daqing Song. 1992. "Environmental Quality and Development: Is There a Kuznets Curve for Air Pollution?" Paper Presented at the 1993 American Economic Association Meetings.

Sen, A. 1996. "Economic Reforms, Employment and Poverty: Trends and Options." *Economic and Political Weekly* (Special No.).

Sen, A., and Patnaik, U. 1997. *Poverty in India.* CESP Working Paper. Delhi: Jawaharlal Nehru University.

Sen, Sunanda. 1986. "The Financial Oligarchy in Contemporary Capitalism." In P. Patnaik, ed., *Lenin and Imperialism.* London: Sangam Books.

Setterfield, M.A., D.V. Gordon, and L. Osberg. 1992. "Searching for a Will o' the Wisp: An Empirical Study of the Nairu in Canada." *European Economic Review* 119–136.

Shapiro, Helen, and Lance Taylor. 1990. "The State and Industrial Strategy." *World Development* 18(6): 861–78.

Shen, Pu. 1995. "Benefits and Limitations of Inflation Indexed Treasury Bonds." *Federal Reserve Bank of Kansas City Economic Review* 80:3, 41–56.

Sherman, Howard. 1991. *Business Cycles.* Princeton N.J.: Princeton University Press.

Shleifer, Andrei, and Robert Vishny. 1990. "Equilibrium Short Horizons of Investors and Firms." *American Economic Review* 80(May).

Shrybman, Steven. 1992. "Trading Away the Environment." *World Policy Journal* (Winter): 93–110.

Silvestri, G.T. 1993. "Occupational Employment: Wide Variations in Growth." *Monthly Labor Review* (November): 58–86.

Simon, Julian, Stephen Moore, and Richard Sullivan. 1993. "The Effect of Immigration on Aggregate Native Unemployment: An Across-City Estimation." *Journal of Labor Research* 14(Summer): 299–316.

Singh, Ajit, and Ann Zammit. 1995. "Employment and Unemployment, North and South." In J. Michie and J. Grieve Smith, eds., *Managing the Global Economy.* Oxford: Oxford University Press, pp. 93–110.

Singh, Ajit. 1996. "Liberalization and Globalization: An Unhealthy Euphoria." Faculty of Economics, University of Cambridge. Manuscript.

Sistema de Cuentas Nacionales de México (SCNM). 1996. "Oferta y Utilización Trimestral a Precios Constantes de 1980, 1992–1995, Cuarto Trimestre de 1995." Aguacalientes, Mexico.

Skott, Peter. 1989. *Conflict and Effective Demand in Economic Growth.* Cambridge: Cambridge University Press.

Slaughter, Matthew J. 1995. "Multinational Corporations, Outsourcing, and American Wage Divergence." Working Paper No. 5253. Cambridge, Mass.: National Bureau of Economic Research.

Smith, Michael. 1996. "The New High-Tech Braceros?" In L. Lowell, ed. *Temporary Migrants in the U.S.* Washington, D.C.: U.S. Commission on Immigration Reform, pp. 127–62.

Sontag, Deborah, and Stephen Engelberg. 1994. "Chaos at the Gates: A Five-Part Series." *New York Times,* September 11–15.

Stafford, Bernard. 1989. "De-industrialisation in Advanced Economies." *Cambridge Journal of Economics* 13(4): 541–54.

Staiger, D., J.H. Stock, and M.W. Watson. 1996. "How Precise Are Estimates of the Natural Rate of Unemployment?" Working Paper No. 5477. Cambridge, Mass.: National Bureau of Economic Research.

Stanford, James. 1995a. *Social Structures, Labor Costs, and North American Economic Integration: A Comparative Modeling Analysis.* Ph.D. dissertation, New School for Social Research, New York.

Stanford, James. 1995b. "The Impact of Real Competitiveness on Monetary Policy and Exchange Rates in an Open Economy." Canadian Auto Workers, Toronto. Mimeo.

Steinherr, Alfred. 1978. "Indexation of Monetary Assets and Credit Instruments." In M. Sarnat, ed., *Inflation and Capital Markets.* Cambridge, Mass.: Ballinger, pp. 149–78.

Stiglitz, Joseph E. 1992a. "Banks vs. Markets as Mechanisms for Allocating and Coordinating Investment." In J.A. Roumasset and S. Barr, eds., *The Economics of Cooperation: East Asian Development and the Case for Pro-Market Intervention.* Boulder, Colo.: Westview Press, pp. 15–38.

Stiglitz, Joseph E. 1992b. "Capital Markets and Economic Fluctuations in Capitalist Countries." *European Economic Review* 36: 269–306.

Stiglitz, Joseph E. 1993. "The Role of the State in Financial Markets." Department of Economics, Stanford University. Manuscript.

Stiglitz, Joseph. 1986. "Theories of Wage Rigidity." In J.L. Butkiewicz, K.J. Koford, and J.B. Miller, eds., *Keynes Economic Legacy: Contemporary Economic Theories.* New York, N.Y.: Praeger, pp. 153–206.

Stone, Charles Austin, and Anne Zissu. 1992. "*Le pret immobilier cautionne*: An Innovative Substitute for the French Mortgage." *Journal of Housing Research* 3(2): 401–21.

Stopford, J. 1994. "The Growing Interdependence Between Transnational Corporations and Governments." *Transnational Corporations* 3(1).

Stopford, J., and S. Strange. 1991. *Rival States, Rival Firms.* Cambridge: Cambridge University Press.

Straubhaar, Thomas, and Rene Weber. 1994. "On the Economics of Immigration: Some Empirical Evidence for Switzerland." *International Review of Applied Economics* 8: 107–29.

Swary, Itzhak, and Barry Topf. 1992. *Global Financial Deregulation: Commercial Banking at the Crossroads.* Cambridge, Mass.: Blackwell.

Tanzer, Michael. 1984. "Stealing the Third World's Nonrenewable Resources: Lessons From Brazil." *Monthly Review* (April): 26–35.

Tanzi, Vito. 1995. *Taxation in an Integrating World.* Washington, D.C.: Brookings Institution.

Taylor, Alan M., and Jeffrey G. Williamson. 1994. "Convergence in the Age of Mass Migration." Working Paper No. 4711. Cambridge, Mass.: National Bureau of Economic Research.

Taylor, Lance 1988. *Varieties of Stabilization Experience: Towards Sensible Macroeconomics in the Third World.* Oxford: Clarendon Press.

Taylor, Lance, and Ute Pieper. 1996. "Reconciling Economic Reform and Sustainable Development: Social Consequences of Neo-Liberalism." New York, N.Y.: Office of Development Studies, United Nations Development Programme.

Taylor, Lance, ed. 1993. *The Rocky Road to Reform.* Cambridge, Mass.: MIT Press.

Taylor, Lance, ed. 1996. "Sustainable Development: Macroeconomic, Environmental, and Political Dimensions." *World Development* (Special Issue) 24.

Taylor, Lance. 1991. *Income Distribution, Inflation, and Growth,* Cambridge, Mass.: MIT Press.

Taylor, Lance. 1996. "Income Distribution, Trade, and Growth." In R.A. Blecker, ed., *U.S. Trade Policy and Global Growth.* Armonk, N.Y.: M.E. Sharpe.

Thirlwall, Anthony P. 1979. "The Balance of Payments Constraint as an Explanation of International Growth Rate Differences." *Banca Nazionale del Lavoro Quarterly Review* 128: 45–53.

Tienda, Marta, and Leif Jensen. 1986. "Immigration and Social Program Participation: Dispelling the Myth of Dependency." *Social Science Research* 15: 372–400.

Tienda, Marta, and Zai Liang. 1994. "Poverty and Immigration in Policy Perspective." In S.H. Danziger, G. Sandefur, and D. Weinberg, eds., *Confronting Poverty: Prescriptions for Change.* Cambridge, Mass.: Harvard University Press, pp. 330–64.

Tilton, John E., ed. 1992. *Mineral Wealth and Economic Development.* Washington, D.C.: Resources for the Future.

Tobey, James A. 1990. "The Effects of Domestic Environmental Policies on Patterns of World Trade: An Empirical Test." *Kyklos* 43(2): 191–209.

Tobin, James, and William Brainard. 1963. "Financial Intermediaries and the Effectiveness of Monetary Control." *American Economic Review* 53(3): 383–400.

Tobin, James. 1971. "An Essay on the Principles of Debt Management." In *Essays in Economics, Volume 1: Macroeconomics.* Chicago, Ill.: Markham, pp. 378–455.

Tobin, James. 1978. "A Proposal for International Monetary Reform." *Eastern Economic Journal* 4: 153–9.

Todaro, Michael P., and L. Maruszko. 1987. "International Migration." In J. Eatwell, M. Millgate, and P. Newman, eds., *The New Palgrave: A Dictionary of Economics*. Vol 2. London. MacMillan; New York: Stockton Press.

Tomann, Horst. 1990. "The Housing Market, Housing Finance and Housing Policy in West Germany: Prospects for the 1990s." *Urban Studies* 27(6): 919–30.

Torres, Craig, and Thomas T. Vogel Jr. 1994. "Market Forces: Some Mutual Funds Wield Growing Clout in Developing Nations." *Wall Street Journal* June 14, 1994.

Tucker, R., ed. 1972. *The Marx-Engels Reader*. New York, N.Y.: Norton.

Twentieth Century Fund. 1992. *Report on Market Speculation and Corporate Governance*. New York, N.Y.: Twentieth Century Fund.

Uchitelle, Louis. 1998. "IMF May Be Closer to Lending Curb Idea." *New York Times,* February 3.

Ul Haq, Mahbub, Inge Kaul, and Isabelle Grunberg, eds. 1996. *The Tobin Tax: Coping With Financial Volatility*. New York, N.Y.: Oxford University Press.

United Nations Centre on Transnational Corporations (UNCTC). 1991. *Government Policies and Foreign Direct Investment*. ST/CTC/SER.A. 17. New York, N.Y.: United Nations.

United Nations Centre on Transnational Corporations (UNCTC). 1992a. *The Determinants of Foreign Direct Investment, A Survey of the Evidence*. ST/CTC/12. New York, N.Y.: United Nations.

United Nations Centre on Transnational Corporations (UNCTC). 1992b. *World Investment Report*. New York, N.Y.: United Nations.

United Nations Centre on Transnational Corporations (UNCTC). 1993. *Explaining and Forecasting Regional Flows of Foreign Direct Investment*. ST/CTC/Ser. A. 26. New York, N.Y.: United Nations.

United Nations Conference on Trade and Development (UNCTAD). 1994a. *International Monetary and Financial Issues for the 1990s,* Vol. IV, New York, N.Y.: United Nations.

United Nations Conference on Trade and Development (UNCTAD). 1994b. *World Investment Report*. Geneva: United Nations.

United Nations Conference on Trade and Development (UNCTAD). Division on Transnational Corporations and Investment. 1992a. *World Investment Report, 1992; Transnational Corporations as Engines of Growth*. New York, N.Y.: United Nations.

United Nations Conference on Trade and Development (UNCTAD). Division on Transnational Corporations and Investment. 1992b. *World Investment Report 1992, Volume I, Asia and the Pacific*. New York, N.Y.: United Nations.

United Nations Conference on Trade and Development (UNCTAD). Division on Transnational Corporations and Investment. 1994a. *World Investment Report, 1994; Transnational Corporations, Employment and the Workplace*. New York, N.Y.: United Nations.

United Nations Conference on Trade and Development (UNCTAD). Division on Transnational Corporations and Investment. 1994b. *World Investment Report, 1994, Volume IV, Latin America and the Caribbean*. New York, N.Y.: United Nations.

United Nations Conference on Trade and Development (UNCTAD). Division on Transnational Corporations and Investment. 1995. *World Investment Report, 1995; Transnational Corporations and Competitiveness*. New York, N.Y.: United Nations.

United Nations Conference on Trade and Development (UNCTAD). Division on Transnational Corporations and Investment. 1997. *World Investment Report, 1997; Transnational Corporations, Market Structure and Competition Policy.* New York, N.Y.: United Nations.

United Nations Conference on Trade and Development (UNCTAD). Various years. *World Investment Report*, New York, N.Y., and Geneva: United Nations.

U.S. Department of Commerce. Bureau of the Census. 1992. *Population Projections by Age, Sex, Race, and Hispanic Origin: 1992–2050.* Washington, D.C.: U.S. Government Printing Office.

U.S. Department of Commerce. 1993. *1990 Census of Population: Foreign-Born Population of the United States.* Washington, D.C.: U.S. Government Printing Office.

U.S. Department of Commerce. Bureau of the Census. 1994. *Statistical Abstract of the United States.* Washington, D.C.: U.S. Government Printing Office.

U.S. Department of Justice. Immigration and Naturalization Service. 1994. *Statistical Yearbook of the Immigration and Naturalization Service, 1994.* Washington, D.C.: U.S. Government Printing Office.

U.S. Department of Labor. 1994. "Clean Air Employment Transition Assistance Grants as of June 30, 1994." Washington, D.C.: Employment and Training Administration.

U.S. General Accounting Office. 1996. "Mexico's Financial Crisis: Origin, Awareness, Assistance and Initial Efforts to Recover." Report to the Chairman, Committee on Banking and Financial Services, House of Representatives.

U.S. Immigration Commission. 1911. *Reports of the U.S. Immigration Commission.* Washington, D.C.: U.S. Senate, 61st Congress of the United States.

U.S. International Trade Commission (USITC). 1991. *The Likely Impact on the United States of a Free Trade Agreement with Mexico.* Publication 2353. Washington, D.C.: USITC.

U.S. International Trade Commission (USITC). 1994. *Production Sharing: U.S. Imports Under Harmonized Tariff Schedule Provisions 9802.00.60 and 9802.00.80, 1989–1992.* Publication 2729. Washington, D.C.: USITC.

U.S. International Trade Commission (USITC). 1995. *Production Sharing: Use of U.S. Components and Materials in Foreign Assembly Operations, 1990–1993.* Publication 2886. Washington, D.C.: USITC.

Vandenbroucke, F. 1997. "Globalisation, Inequality, Social Democracy." St. Edmund Hall, Oxford. Mimeo.

Wachter, Susan. 1990. "The Limits of the Housing Finance System." *Journal of Housing Research* 1(1): 163–85.

Wade, Robert. 1990. *Governing the Market.* Princeton, N.J.: Princeton University Press.

Wade, Robert. 1995. "The East Asian Miracle: Why the Controversy Continues." In United Nations Conference on Trade and Development, *International Monetary and Financial Issues for the 1990s,* Vol. V. New York, N.Y.: United Nations.

Wade, Robert. 1996. "Globalization and Its Limits: Reports of the Death of the National Economy Are Greatly Exaggerated." In S. Berger and R. Dore, eds., *National Diversity and Global Capitalism.* Ithaca, N.Y.: Cornell University Press, pp. 60–88.

Waldinger, Roger. 1996. *Still the Promised City? African-Americans and New Immigrants in Post-Industrial New York.* Cambridge, Mass.: Harvard University Press.

Warren, Robert, and Jeffrey Passel. 1987. "A Count of the Uncountable: Estimates of Undocumented Aliens Counted in the 1980 U.S. Census." *Demography* 24(Aug.): 375–93.

Weiner, Stuart E. 1993. "New Estimates of the Natural Rate of Unemployment." *Federal Reserve Bank of Kansas City Economic Review,* fourth quarter, pp 53–69.

Weiner, Stuart. 1983. "Why Are So Few Financial Assets Indexed to Inflation?" *Federal Reserve Bank of Kansas City Economic Review,* May 3–18.

Weiss, Linda. 1997. "Globalization and the Myth of the Powerless State." *New Left Review* 225(September/October): 3–27.

Weisskopf, Thomas E. 1992. "A Comparative Analysis of Profitability Trends in the Advanced Capitalist Economies." In F. Moseley and E. Wolff , eds., *International Perspectives on Profitability and Accumulation,* Brookfield, Vt.: Edward Elgar, pp. 13–41.

Wessel, David, Paul Carroll, and Thomas Vogel. 1995. "How Mexico's Crisis Ambushed Top Minds in Officialdom and Finance." *Wall Street Journal,* July 14.

Wessel, David. 1998. "Approval of IMF Funding Is Urged by Greenspan, Two Cabinet Secretaries." *Wall Street Journal,* February 2.

Wheeler, David. 1996. "My Brother's Keeper: New Evidence on Pollution Havens and Environmental Injustice." Paper presented at the 1996 American Economic Association Meetings, San Francisco, Calif.

Whitehead, Christine M.E. 1993. "Privatizing Housing: An assessment of UK Experience." *Housing Policy Debate* 4(1): 101–40.

Wial, Howard. 1994. *Immigration and the Distribution of Earnings.* Working Paper. Washington, D.C.: U.S. Department of Labor.

Williamson, John. 1989. "What Washington Means by Policy Reform." In John Williamson, ed., *Latin American Adjustment: How Much Has Happened?* Washington D.C.: Institute for International Economics.

Wilson, Franklin D. 1979. *Residential Consumption, Economic Opportunity, and Race.* New York, N.Y.: Academic Press.

Winegarden, C.R., and Lay Boon Khor. 1991. "Undocumented Immigration and Unemployment of U.S. Youth and Minority Workers: Econometric Evidence." *Review of Economics and Statistics* 73(Feb.): 105–112.

Wolff, Edward. 1995. *Top Heavy: A Study of the Increasing Inequality of Wealth in America,* New York, N.Y.: Twentieth Century Fund.

Wood, Adrian. 1994. *North-South Trade, Employment and Inequality: Changing Fortunes in a Skill-Driven World.* Oxford: Clarendon Press.

Wood, Adrian. 1995. "How Trade Hurt Unskilled Workers." *Journal of Economic Perspectives* 9(3): 57–80.

Wood, Gavin A. 1990. "The Tax Treatment of Housing: Economic Issues and Reform Measures." *Urban Studies* 27(6): 809–30.

Woodward, Bob. 1994. *The Agenda,* New York, N.Y.: Simon and Schuster.

World Bank. 1985. *World Development Report 1985.* New York, N.Y.: Oxford University Press.

World Bank. 1992. *World Development Report.* Oxford: Oxford University Press.

World Bank. 1993. *The East Asian Miracle: Economic Growth and Public Policy.* Washington D.C.: World Bank.

World Bank. 1994. *World Debt Tables: External Finance for Developing Countries 1994-95.* Washington D.C.: World Bank.

World Bank. 1997. *Private Capital Flows to Developing Countries: The Road to Financial Integration.* Policy Research Report. Washington D.C.: World Bank.

World Commission on Environment and Development. 1987. *Our Common Future.* New York, N.Y.: Oxford University Press.

Zevin, Robert B. 1992. "Are World Financial Markets More Open? If So, Why, and With What Effects?" In T. Banuri and J Schor, eds., *Financial Openness and National Autonomy,* New York, N.Y.: Oxford University Press.

Zimmermann, Klaus F. 1995. "Tackling the European Migration Problem." *Journal of Economic Perspectives* 9(Spring): 45–62.

Zysman, John. 1983. *Government, Markets and Growth: Financial Systems and the Politics of Industrial Change.* Ithaca, N.Y.: Cornell University Press.

Index